Praise for the Third Edition

The new edition of Stephen Medvic's *Campaigns and Elections* carries the reader through the 2016 election up to the 2018 midterm. In clear and comprehensive writing, the book draws important distinctions between elections and campaigns, notes the complexity of covering the subject in which the process varies so much from state to state and from one level of government to the next, and draws the reader in by examining the roles of all the players – candidates, interest groups, parties, the media, and voters. Medvic skillfully explains how 2016 was unique but still understandable in terms of the process, and sagely speculates on what it tells us for the campaigns and elections to come.

L. Sandy Maisel, *Colby College*

Stephen Medvic's textbook is quite an achievement: It is both exhaustively comprehensive and accessible for a college-age audience…. This is an excellent and highly recommended text that provides clarity to the confounding issues of campaigns and elections in the US.

Mark Major, *Pennsylvania State University*

Campaigns and Elections provides a complete picture of campaigns, with great insight into both how campaigns work and what impact they have on election outcomes. Students benefit from the way Medvic clearly and accessibly brings together the broad forces of the political environment: the rules that create constraints and opportunities, the impact of candidates and campaign organizations, and voter behavior. The third edition is updated to reflect social and technological developments, and the ways these have altered the practice of modern campaigns.

Christopher B. Mann, *Skidmore College; Former congressional campaign manager, policy/political consultant, and party executive*

This text is a very impressive study of campaigns and elections in the United States, and a needed contribution to the field. Medvic has done a great job of describing the contemporary situation, while also identifying important questions raised by the electoral process.

Candice Nelson, *American University*

This is by far the most thorough and nuanced text on this subject: Its comprehensive, yet relatively concise, examination balances coverage of institutions and behavior. My students find the book to be clear and exciting; instructors will appreciate the careful reflection on current events both within the unique US electoral system and in historical context. The third edition tackles the complexity of the 2016 elections and demystifies its outcome, with analysis that is a model for student writing – evidence-based and rich with data but never overbearing or unduly complicated. In short, this book accomplishes what it usually takes two books to cover.

Stephen Maynard Caliendo, *North Central College*

Detailing the legal and competitive aspects of elections as well as the contending interests of different political actors, the new edition of *Campaigns and Elections: Players and Processes* is unafraid to ask the thorny normative questions facing American elections and campaigns. "Free and fair elections" rolls off the tongue easily, but freedom and fairness, as Medvic masterfully details, are contending values that our laws, politicians, and voters struggle to bring into balance. Students will walk away from this book with a systematic, historically driven, and theoretically solid information base to understand our strange system of elections as both scholars and citizens.

Michael Wolf, *Indiana University–Purdue University Fort Wayne*

Campaigns and Elections

Stephen K. Medvic's *Campaigns and Elections* is a comprehensive yet compact core text that addresses two distinct but related aspects of American electoral democracy: the processes that constitute c ampaigns and elections, and the players who are involved. In addition to balanced coverage of process and actors, it gives equal billing to both campaigns and elections, and covers contests for legislative and executive positions at the national and state and local levels, including issue-oriented campaigns of note.

The book opens by providing students with the conceptual distinctions between what happens in an election and the campaigning that precedes it. Significant attention is devoted to setting up the context for these campaigns and elections by covering the rules of the game in the American electoral system as well as aspects of election administration and the funding of elections. Then the book systematically covers the actors at every level—candidates and their organizations, parties, interest groups, the media, and voters—and the macro level aspects of campaigns such as campaign strategy and determinants of election outcomes. The book concludes with a big picture assessment of campaign ethics and implications of the "permanent campaign."

New to the Third edition:

- Fully updated through the 2016 elections, looking ahead to the 2018 midterms.
- Examines the "Party Decides" theory of the nomination process in light of the Trump Republican candidacy.
- Covers campaign finance regulation in the wake of *Citizens United* and *McCutcheon*.
- Reviews recent changes to voting laws, including various restrictions on voting (e.g., voter identification requirements) and newly adopted automatic voter registration procedures in several states.
- Expands coverage of media influence in campaigns, including the impact of social media.
- Draws upon recent research on new campaign technologies and of the science of campaigning.
- Adds chapter conclusions throughout the text.
- Fully updates the resources listed at the end of each chapter.

Stephen K. Medvic is the Honorable & Mrs. John C. Kunkel Professor of Government at Franklin & Marshall College. His books include *Political Consultants in US Congressional Elections*; *Shades of Gray: Perspectives on Campaign Ethics*; *New Directions in Campaigns and Elections*; and *In Defense of Politicians*.

Campaigns and Elections

Players and Processes
Third edition

Stephen K. Medvic

Routledge
Taylor & Francis Group

NEW YORK AND LONDON

Published 2018
by Routledge
711 Third Avenue, New York, NY 10017

and by Routledge
2 Park Square, Milton Park, Abingdon, Oxon, OX14 4RN

Routledge is an imprint of the Taylor & Francis Group, an informa business

First edition published by Routledge 2009
Second edition published by Routledge 2014

Library of Congress Cataloging-in-Publication Data
Names: Medvic, Stephen K., author.
Title: Campaigns and elections : players and processes / Stephen K. Medvic.
Description: Third Edition. | New York : Routledge, 2018. |
    "First edition published by Routledge 2009"— T.p. verso. |
    "Second edition published by Routledge 2014"— T.p. verso.
Identifiers: LCCN 2017028737 | ISBN 9781138058439 (hardback) |
    ISBN 9781138058453 (paperback) | ISBN 9781315164274 (ebook)
Subjects: LCSH: Political campaigns—United States. | Political
    campaigns—Law and legislation—United States. | Elections—
    United States.
Classification: LCC JK2281 .M383 2018 | DDC 324.60973—dc23
LC record available at https://lccn.loc.gov/2017028737

ISBN: 978-1-138-05843-9 (hbk)
ISBN: 978-1-138-05845-3 (pbk)
ISBN: 978-1-315-16427-4 (ebk)

Typeset in Minion Pro
by Apex CoVantage, LLC

Contents

Illustrations

Tables

Boxes

Preface

The 2016 presidential campaign was, or at least seemed to be, extraordinary. The historic and unprecedented nature of so much that happened that year—including the nomination of the first female presidential candidate of a major party and the candidacy, and eventual presidency, of a businessman-celebrity with no prior political experience—was certainly unique. As a result, the election generated a significant amount of interest and excitement within the electorate. However, much of what happened that year was not especially extraordinary and can be explained by factors that normally influence election outcomes (and that are identified in this book). Furthermore, campaigns and elections are often exciting, particularly in an era of intense partisan polarization. When elections are competitive, which admittedly is not always, they have all the drama of a championship sporting event, with results that are far more consequential.

I wrote this book, in part, to share my passion for the study of campaigns and elections, which together are, arguably, the most important element of American democracy, but I also wrote it because there are no existing textbooks in this field that address the subject as I do in my campaigns and elections course. Many books focus on the nuts and bolts of campaigns or the operation of elections, but not both. I try—in my class and in this book—to balance coverage of campaigns with an examination of elections. Furthermore, I organize my course around the actors involved in campaigns and elections, including full treatment of candidates, political parties, interest groups, the media, and voters. Some books bury the actors under a focus on processes; others place just one of the actors (often parties) at the center of the discussion.

Campaigns and elections are extremely complicated events. The tangle of laws and regulations governing them, the behavior of the various actors, and the myriad processes involved in choosing our leaders and representatives can seem overwhelming. My hope is that, by providing a comprehensive but accessible treatment of the subject, this book helps students make sense of campaigns and elections. Perhaps, in addition, students will come away with a deeper appreciation for elections and the campaigns that precede them. I find them truly fascinating, and I hope that shows in the pages that follow.

▶ *Themes*

There are two primary themes that can be found throughout the book. The first is the remarkable variety in the laws and regulations that govern campaigns and elections in the United States. These laws and regulations are quite dissimilar, both between the federal and state levels and among the states. The differences in the operation of federal and state elections are readily apparent. The most obvious is the system for choosing presidents; nothing like an electoral college for governors exists. However, there are other distinctions, including the regulation of fund-raising and campaign spending and the media's coverage of campaigns. Among the states, however, there is even greater variation in the operation of campaigns and elections. There are numerous ways of handling campaign finance and redistricting, voter registration, primaries, and election administration. States also differ markedly in their use of initiatives and referenda, the strength of political parties, and levels of electoral competition. This book attempts to capture these and many other differences.

The second theme is that no system of campaigns and elections is perfect; every aspect of a given system has advantages and disadvantages. Furthermore, though we often say that democracy requires free and fair elections, creating a system that is both free and fair is quite difficult. Indeed, efforts to reform particular aspects of campaigns and elections often require choosing among competing values. Typically, the values at stake are freedom and equality. Campaign finance reform, for example, faces a tension between giving individuals the freedom to spend as much as they would like in support of (or opposition to) a candidate and, conversely, providing candidates with roughly equal resources with which to compete. There are trade-offs as well in the choice of an electoral system for legislative elections. Single-member plurality systems tend to produce absolute majorities, which fosters decisive governance, while proportional representation tends toward consensus and coalition building, which enhances the representative function of government. The tensions and trade-offs inherent in the American system of campaigns and elections appear at various points throughout this text.

▶ Approach

Though there are a number of good textbooks for use in campaigns and elections courses, most focus nearly exclusively on either the operation of campaigns or the factors that influence elections, but not both. Furthermore, virtually all of them approach the subject from just one institutional perspective (for example, presidential elections rather than congressional elections) or one level (for example, national versus state and local). This book covers both campaigns and elections for executive and legislative races at both the national and, where possible given space limitations, subnational levels. I have tried to be as comprehensive as possible in this approach while recognizing that some details would have to be left to books with a more specific focus. Nevertheless, my hope is that there is value in providing—in a single, relatively short volume—a comprehensive examination of the essential elements of campaigns and elections in the United States.

The other unique feature of this book is the emphasis placed on the various actors involved in campaigns and elections. Though institutions and laws certainly shape behavior (and are given proper attention in this text), groups and individuals are at the heart of the electoral process. Thus, the text is organized around the major actors. The core chapters are devoted to candidates and their campaign organizations, political parties, interest groups, the media, and voters. This allows sufficient space to explain how these actors function within campaigns and elections. Any laws or regulations that govern the actors' behavior and any processes not covered by a discussion of the actors' place in the system are addressed in separate chapters at the beginning and end of the book.

Finally, normative considerations are included either explicitly or implicitly in every chapter. Reform alternatives are a common part of these considerations, but students are also asked to examine their expectations for the behavior of the various actors covered in the book. Just how informed, for example, must citizens be if democracy is to function properly? Do we demand too much of candidates? There are ample opportunities to compare the ideal functioning of campaigns and elections with the reality of their operation. One goal, of course, is to sharpen students' critical capacities, but I also hope that students will develop reasonable standards by which to evaluate campaigns and elections and the performance of those who participate in them.

▶ Pedagogy

To reinforce the importance of actors in the political process and to introduce active learning, each chapter contains role-play scenarios in which students are asked to imagine themselves as particular actors in a situation related to campaigns and elections and then respond in one way or another to the scenario. This feature can easily be used (or adapted for use) as a source for course assignments. In addition to the role-plays, the chapters include discussion questions, online resources, and suggested readings.

▶ Content

The first three chapters of this book establish the theoretical and legal foundations of campaigns and elections. Chapter 1 explores the role of campaigns and elections in democratic theory, including an examination of the requirements for free and fair elections. The chapter also distinguishes between the functions of campaigns and those of elections. Chapter 2 is the first part of a discussion of the "rules and regulations" governing campaigns and elections. It begins with an examination of the US Constitution and identifies the provisions that pertain to elections. The bulk of the chapter, however, is devoted to voting rights and the electoral systems in use in the United States. Chapter 3 covers the second half of the rules and regulations, which include election administration (voter registration, voting equipment, and the like) and the campaign finance system.

Chapters 4 through 8 are devoted to the major actors involved in campaigns and elections.

- Candidates and their campaign organizations are the focus of Chapter 4. Special attention is paid to the question of who runs for office and why, and political consultants are highlighted as integral elements of the campaign organization.
- Political parties are examined in Chapter 5, which discusses the two-party system, including a brief history of that system; parties as organizations; the nomination process, which is described as a vital piece of party business; and the parties' general election activities.
- Chapter 6 explains what interest groups are, charts their growth over time, and examines their role in campaigns and elections.
- Chapter 7 describes the current media environment and the way campaign news is reported. Particular attention is given to what has been called the "game schema" in use by campaign media. Election Night coverage is also discussed in some detail.
- Voters are the topic of Chapter 8, which begins with explanations of voter turnout at both the aggregate and individual levels. The second half of the chapter examines vote choice and the various influences on voting behavior.

Chapters 9 and 10 cover those aspects of campaigns and elections respectively, that were not dealt with in the previous eight chapters. In Chapter 9, campaigns are described as dynamic processes that require sound planning, strategic thinking, and tactical maneuvering. Chapter 10 explores the uniqueness of presidential elections, examines the realignments literature, and identifies the factors that influence the outcomes of presidential and congressional elections. The chapter ends with discussions of whether campaigns matter—that is, whether they have an impact on election outcomes—and the extent to which elections affect governance.

Chapter 11, the final chapter of the book, begins by taking a step back to paint a broad picture of campaigns and elections in the United States. It then introduces campaign ethics and examines two standards by which campaign behavior can be judged. The chapter concludes with a description of the "permanent campaign" and considers the consequences of this relatively new phenomenon in American politics.

▶ New to the Third Edition

This edition of the book includes results through the 2016 elections. The outcome of the presidential election of that year was surprising to many, if not all, observers. Nevertheless, many aspects of the election unfolded as elections often do. This edition highlights ways in which 2016 challenged conventional political science thinking—particularly with respect to how presidential nominations operate—and the ways in which it was perfectly ordinary.

The new edition pays special attention to recent changes in election law, including developments in campaign finance regulation since *Citizens United* and the passage of new voting restrictions in the wake of the Supreme Court's decision invalidating a key part of the Voting Rights Act. The increasing importance of social media is now covered in chapters on the media and on campaigns; the latest research on data-driven campaigning has been included; and a review of the "Party Decides" theory of nominations appears in the chapter on election determinants (Chapter 10). Finally, I've added a conclusion to each chapter (with the exception of Chapter 11). The conclusions remind readers of the various topics covered in the chapter at hand and provide a "big picture" perspective on the subject under consideration.

Acknowledgments

Like all authors, I am indebted to many individuals for their support and assistance while I wrote this book and revised it for a third edition. James McCann, of Purdue University, gave the original publisher my name as a potential author for a campaigns and elections textbook. I'm forever grateful for his having done so and for the confidence he had in me. Without the help of Michael Kerns, formerly at Routledge, this book would have disappeared after a single edition. That would have been almost too painful for its author to bear. So Michael is due as much thanks as anyone. He not only prolonged the life of the book, he improved it in countless ways with his keen insights.

The guidance and sage advice of Jennifer Knerr, my current editor at Routledge, have been invaluable as I revised the book for this new edition. Her insights have undoubtedly made the book better. I'm especially grateful for her patience as I took far longer than expected to complete the revisions. Thanks also to Ze'ev Sudry and Emma Harder at Taylor & Francis for their excellent production help and to Liz Hudson for her incredibly thorough copy-editing.

At various times, and for various editions of the book, I relied on the assistance of other experts and scholars for specific pieces of information or for access to work that either hasn't yet been published or was not available to me at the time of writing. For their rapid responses to my queries, I thank Richard Winger (Ballot Access News), Anthony Corrado (Colby College), Brian L. Fife (Indiana University-Purdue University Fort Wayne), Anthony G. Fowler (University of Chicago), Anne Hildreth (University at Albany), Matthew Jarvis (California State University-Fullerton), Robin Kolodny (Temple University), Jennifer Lawless (American University), Sandy Maisel (Colby College), Mark Major (Pennsylvania State University), Christopher Mann (Skidmore College), Michael McDonald (University of Florida), Gary Moncrief (Boise State University), and Stephen Farnsworth (University of Mary Washington).

I have had the good fortune to have worked with, and learned from, a number of wonderful political scientists over the years, and they have each had an impact on some part of this book. First among these is the late Barbara Hinckley, who served as my dissertation chair at Purdue University and who still serves as my role model as a political scientist. Others include, in alphabetical order, Stephen Caliendo (North Central College), David Dulio (Oakland University), David Farrell (University College Dublin), Paul Herrnson (University of Connecticut), David Jones (James Madison University), Quentin Kidd (Christopher Newport University), Robin Kolodny (Temple University), Silvo Lenart (Zanthus Corp. and Portland State University), David Magleby (Brigham

Young University), James McCann (Purdue University), Candice Nelson (American University), Kelly Patterson (Brigham Young University), William Shafer (Purdue University), Dan Shea (Colby College), and James Thurber (American University).

I am reminded every day of how fortunate I am to teach at an institution such as Franklin & Marshall College (F&M). The students at F&M are fantastic, and those who have taken my campaigns and elections course have shaped this book in countless ways, without even knowing it. Several of my students served as research assistants as I revised the book for the second and third editions, and they were extraordinarily helpful. Caitlin Krutsick, Anne Hazlett, and Kirsty Richard are among the best students I have ever taught, and they have very bright futures ahead of them.

Thanks also are due to my colleagues in the Government Department at F&M. It is an absolute delight to work in the Harris Center, where I can drop in on any one of my colleagues to get advice or test a new idea. They are, to a person, kind, generous, intelligent, and hard working. A special word of thanks goes to Bob Friedrich and Matt Schousen. They were always willing to serve as sounding boards, and this book benefited significantly from the many conversations I had with them while writing it. Bob and Matt are not only valued colleagues but dear friends. Thanks, too, to Dave Ciuk for feedback on a particular passage of the book for which he has special expertise. Jessica Bortz, our department coordinator, has an uncanny sense of what needs to be done and often seems to finish tasks before she's even asked for assistance. She's integral to the work of the department and we're fortunate to have her as a colleague.

Two dear friends also have my deep gratitude. Keith Shimko (Purdue University) offered useful advice about the textbook-writing process as I first embarked on this project. He has always provided wise counsel, and he remains a trusted adviser. And, for an international relations scholar, he's a pretty good election analyst! When I have a question about some aspect of campaign ethics or political philosophy or when I really want to put an argument to the test, I turn to Dale Miller (Old Dominion University). More important, it's Dale I call for a learned assessment of the latest performance by our beloved Pittsburgh Steelers.

My greatest debt is to my family. This book was written in memory of my father, Steve Medvic, and is dedicated to my mother, Nancy Medvic. My parents' sacrifices made it possible for me to become a professor, and my mom's influence on me is immeasurable. I am tremendously grateful for her unflagging support throughout my life. My sister, Allison, is a phenomenal elementary-school teacher, an even better person, and a continual source of inspiration to me. My stepsons, George and Ross, are smart, funny, and very active young men. My amazing wife, Laura, is a model of patience, strength, and kindness. She never complains about spending every two years as an "election widow," and she single-handedly keeps our household intact when I neglect my household responsibilities to fulfill writing, teaching, and administrative obligations. I hope she knows how much I appreciate all she did to allow me to finish this book and its revisions—and how much I love her. Finally, no father could be prouder of his children than I am of Colin and Abigail. They are talented, thoughtful, and intellectually curious, and they're lots of fun. No matter how stressful or frustrating my work can sometimes be, Colin and Abigail brighten my mood by their presence alone. I hope they forgive me for spending too much time in my study, but I also hope they understand that they are never out of my thoughts, that I cherish our time together, and that I love them more than anything in the world.

1 Campaigns and Elections in American Democracy

Elections can occur without democracy, but democracy cannot endure without elections.

—Dennis Thompson, *Just Elections*[1]

I'T'S HARD NOT TO CONCLUDE that the 2016 presidential election was unprecedented in the history of American politics. Whether the nomination of the first female presidential candidate of a major party, the nearly constant stream of controversial statements (many shared via Twitter) from a candidate who was known to many voters as a reality TV celebrity, or Russian interference in the campaign, the election of 2016 certainly appears to have been unique. Rhetoric on the campaign trail challenged prevailing standards of candidate truthfulness and decorum and, at times, came dangerously close to fearmongering and incitement to violence. Adding to the sense that the election was extraordinary was the fact that the outcome was unexpected; observers and pundits were confident of a Clinton victory, some even projecting her chances of winning at close to 100 percent.

Nevertheless, much of what happened in 2016 was not particularly exceptional and can be explained by examining the factors that typically influence election outcomes. To give just one example, most voters relied heavily on their partisanship to decide how to cast their ballots, despite the fact that many found their party's candidate to be flawed in important ways. Furthermore, though the outcome of the election caused many to question the democratic nature of American elections, it's difficult to point to an aspect of the election that unequivocally violated the requirements for free and fair elections. There are certainly elements of the 2016 race that deserve close scrutiny, including the vilification of the media, the potential for voter suppression in some states, and the oddity of the candidate with the most votes losing the election. However, before we can conclude that the 2016 election—or any election, for that matter—fell short of our democratic ideals, we need a solid understanding of exactly what is required to consider an election democratic. This chapter helps the reader develop such an understanding.

Elections are among the most interesting and important political events in the life of a country. Even non-democratic governments reinforce the value of elections by routinely using them to justify a regime's existence. The 1936 constitution of the Soviet Union guaranteed "all Soviets of Working People's Deputies, from rural and city Soviets of Working People's Deputies to the Supreme Soviet of the USSR, inclusive, are elected by the citizens by direct vote." Furthermore, elections were to take place "on the basis of universal ... and equal suffrage by secret ballot."[2] In practice, of course, the Communist Party controlled nominations, and candidates ran largely unopposed. More recently, North Korea's supreme leader, Kim Jong-Un, garnered 100 percent of the vote in his 2014 bid for the Supreme People's Assembly.[3] In terms of raw numbers, nearly as many elections were held in dictatorships from 1946 to 2000 as in democracies. However, there were also significantly more dictatorships than democracies throughout the world between 1960 and 1990. When this disparity is controlled for, elections are found to have been held almost twice as often in democracies as in dictatorships.[4] Nevertheless, that so many dictatorships have held elections will likely come as a surprise to many readers.

Though elections under totalitarian regimes and dictatorships may serve as propaganda, they are the *sine qua non* of democracy; without them, there can be no democracy. Indeed, one could argue that the degree to which a political system is democratic can be measured by the meaningfulness of its elections, although this point is debatable for a number of reasons. One such reason is that some scholars of democratization prefer to treat the concept of democracy as a dichotomous variable (that is, a country either is or is not a democracy) rather than a continuous one (whereby a country is more or less democratic).[5] According to this view, there can be no *degree to which* a political system is democratic: Either it is, or it isn't. Even so, a political system would never be considered democratic if it didn't hold elections.

Of course, elections, even in democracies, are no guarantee of democratic results. A majority may, for example, vote to curtail the rights of minorities. Or the majority may support a candidate or a party that doesn't fully embrace democracy and all of the checks on power it entails. The rise of right-wing populist parties in Europe, though so far mostly unsuccessful in taking control of government, suggests that democratic elections can very easily produce undemocratic outcomes. Recep Tayyip Erdogan's consolidation of power in Turkey suggests the same. And, regardless of whether or not he holds authoritarian tendencies, the election of Donald Trump in the United States also calls into question the ability of elections to safeguard democratic norms.

Clearly, then, democracy requires more than elections. Among the additional requirements are free expression, the right to association and the freedom to create political organizations, unfettered access to information, and an array of other citizenship rights. Determining which of these is *most* essential for democracy is, of course, futile. Nevertheless, elections certainly can claim historical primacy over other democratic practices. Robert Dahl—a preeminent democratic theorist—has noted that in the common pattern of development in the world's "older" democracies, elections to legislatures arrived early in the creation of political institutions. "The practice of electing higher lawmaking officials," writes Dahl, "was followed by a gradual expansion of the rights of citizens to express themselves on political matters and to seek out and exchange information."[6] That is, elections came first and political rights—rights necessary to contest elections—came later.[7]

If a country is to have meaningful elections, it must also encourage competitive campaigns. When the laws of a country allow only one party to field candidates, for instance, we deem the country's election outcomes illegitimate. If the media are not allowed to freely report on the records of the candidates or parties or if the voters are not allowed to openly discuss their preferences and the reasons for those preferences, we consider the level of democracy to be low or nonexistent.

However, even democracies face obstacles to hosting competitive campaigns. It is possible, for example, that two or more parties will be permitted to field candidates, but only one will do so. This effectively gives voters no choice at all. In other cases, voter turnout is quite low, which raises questions about the representativeness of election results. Campaign finance patterns, norms of media behavior, voter engagement, and various election laws may diminish the competitiveness of campaigns in otherwise democratic electoral systems.

Of course, no electoral system is perfectly democratic. Indeed, it is not entirely clear what it means to say that an electoral system is "democratic" because there are a number of competing models of democracy.[8] Furthermore, democratic principles often come into conflict in designing the rules for campaigns and elections. Freedom and equality, for example, are in tension with respect to campaign finance regulations. According to some, candidates should be free to raise and spend as much as they would like to further their campaign efforts. Yet vast inequalities in campaign spending often give one candidate a distinct advantage over opponents. Thus, some have suggested that in the interest of fairness and equality, limits on campaign spending should be enacted, while others (including the United States Supreme Court) believe that such limits would violate candidates' First Amendment rights to express themselves freely.

This chapter will explore the expectations we have for democratic campaigns and elections. It begins with conceptual clarifications of the terms *campaigns* and *elections* and identifies differences between particular types of campaigns and elections. The chapter then discusses the theoretical role of campaigns and elections in democracy and ends with a look at some ethical considerations.

▶ *What Are Campaigns and Elections?*

People often use the term "election" as a catch-all to refer not just to the casting and counting of ballots but to the campaign leading up to the election as well. You might, for example, hear someone say, "That election was the nastiest in recent memory." What the person means, of course, is that the *campaign*, not the election, was nasty. Unless voters fought with one another at the polling place, the election was probably quite civil. This point may seem like hair-splitting but, as will be clear throughout this book, it is useful to distinguish between the campaign leading up to an election and the election itself.

An election is a mechanism for making collective decisions. It provides a means of expressing individual preferences through the "vote." However, "taking a vote" is not the same as "holding an election." In using the term *election*, we typically assume that a relatively extended campaign will be conducted to try to influence the outcome of the election. Thus, when a local parent teacher organization votes on which fund-raiser to use this year, they are not really holding an election (even if arguments for each alternative were entertained).

Usually, elections choose individuals to perform certain duties. For instance, boards of directors for corporations and nonprofit organizations hold elections to determine their leadership. Viewers choose the winner of *The Voice* by voting in what amounts to a nationwide election for a celebrity. Nevertheless, elections can also be held to determine a course of action for a group of people. For example, the National Labor Relations Board is empowered "to conduct secret-ballot elections so employees may exercise a free choice [as to] whether a union should represent them for bargaining purposes."[9]

As noted earlier, elections are typically preceded by campaigns. A *campaign* is simply a concerted effort to win votes in an election. William Safire explains that the term is taken from military jargon, "where it was first used to denote the amount of time an army was kept in the field, and later a particular military operation." It began to be used in a political context in England as early as the seventeenth century, and "the idea that politics is a form of combat remains."[10]

The vast majority of campaign activity involves communication of one kind or another, and most of it is persuasive in nature. Candidates or groups need votes, so they make arguments that they hope will convince voters to support their cause. As we will see, they also contact voters to encourage them to participate in the election. Some organizations, however, may play the role of a disinterested third party that simply wants to inform voters so that they make a more educated decision at election time.

In this book, we will be concerned only with campaigns and elections that influence government in one manner or another. Most of our focus will be on candidate elections, or those that select representatives to governmental office. However, we will occasionally address noncandidate (or "issue") elections such as initiatives, whereby citizens may propose laws to the legislature, and referenda, in which citizens are asked to approve or reject legislation. An additional set of elections—including both recall and judicial retention elections—allow voters to decide whether an elected official should remain in office. A recall asks voters whether they wish to remove the official before their term expires and may or may not simultaneously allow voters to choose a successor in the event that the official is recalled from office; judicial retention elections ask voters to decide whether to give a judge an additional term when their current term ends.

▶ Further Distinctions: Campaigns and Elections for Different Offices and Levels of Government

Beyond the distinction between campaigns and elections, we will identify differences between executive and legislative races. In a presidential system, like that of the United States and most Latin American countries including Mexico, the executive branch is independent of the legislature, and the chief executive (that is, the president) and legislators are elected separately. In parliamentary systems, which combine the executive and legislative functions as they do in the United Kingdom, Sweden, and Canada, the majority party (or ruling coalition) selects the chief executive (that is, the prime minister) from among the members of parliament. There are, as you might guess, hybrid systems. France's system is designed for a strong presidency but includes a prime minister nominated by the president. Germany's system provides for a chancellor (which is not unlike a prime minister) selected by the parliament and a weak president who is elected indirectly by legislators and plays a largely ceremonial role.

One obvious difference between executive offices (for example, president or governor) and legislative offices (for example, member of Congress or state legislator) is that only one person is elected to executive branch offices, whereas many representatives are chosen to serve in legislatures. This will be a relevant point in our discussion of alternative electoral systems in Chapter 2. Furthermore, the executive and legislative branches have unique responsibilities. Among other things, this means that the criteria by which candidates are judged may differ depending on the office sought. For example, voters may seek leadership skills in executive-branch candidates but want legislators to possess the ability to deliver tangible benefits, like a submarine contract that will provide jobs at a local shipyard.

In addition, executive branch races—whether for president, governor, or mayor—always garner more attention from the media and voters than do legislative contests—whether for Congress, state legislature, or city council; they also are always more expensive affairs. One indicator of the greater attention paid to executive branch campaigns is relative turnout in executive and legislative elections. More people vote in elections for president or governor than vote in congressional or state legislative races in any given year. For example, in Missouri in 2016, nearly 6,000 more voters cast a ballot for president than for US senator, even though the Senate race was one of the most hotly contested in the country, whereas the presidential race was not at all competitive in that state.[11]

The typical pattern of greater attention to executive races than to legislative ones is complicated by another important distinction: that among the various levels of government—federal, state, and local. This book will focus most of its attention on the national level, in part because subnational campaigns and elections take so many forms that covering them adequately would become prohibitively complex. The emphasis on national campaigns and elections is not, however, meant to detract from the importance of state and local ones.

Generally, races for federal office have a higher profile than races for the same branch of government at the state level, which in turn attract more attention than races for the same branch at the local level. Thus, more people voted for president (2,734,958) in the state of Indiana in 2016 than voted for governor (2,719,968), even though the state went comfortably for Donald Trump whereas the gubernatorial race was quite close.[12] Similarly, turnout (not to mention media coverage) will normally be greater for US House races within a state legislative district than for that district's state legislative race.

Examining the various offices and levels of elections simultaneously gives us a better understanding of the relative significance of elections. US Senate and gubernatorial races, for example, are roughly similar in intensity. Both are state-wide offices and, though Senate races attract the attention due to federal elections, gubernatorial races have the high profile expected for the top executive post in a state. In 2016, nine states held both US Senate and gubernatorial elections. In five of those states the senatorial race had higher turnout; in three the gubernatorial race produced higher turnout; and in one the same number of votes was cast in both races.[13] This suggests that races for states' top executive post are comparable in terms of their significance to voters to those for the highest federal legislative office. (Unlike at the federal level, many state executive branch offices, in addition to the post of chief executive, are elected. Depending on the state, examples might be lieutenant governor—which in many states is elected independent of the gubernatorial candidate—and attorney general, secretary of state, state treasurer, and a variety of commissioners such as insurance, agriculture, or railroad. Usually interest in these races falls behind that for governor and the US Senate.)

Ultimately, then, presidential races sit alone atop the hierarchy of campaigns and elections in the United States, followed by gubernatorial and US Senate races on the second rung (and mayoral contests in large cities of national stature such as New York or Los Angeles). On the third rung are US House races and statewide races for executive branch offices other than governor (and mayoral posts in medium to large cities having high stature at the state level). Next in line are elections to state legislative and countywide offices, followed finally by local elections.

It is a curiosity of modern elections that those farthest removed from the daily lives of the average voter are the ones that command the most attention. This is undoubtedly because high-level races are conducted mainly on television. Not only are the national and state media more interested in national and statewide races, but those campaigns find it more efficient to reach voters via the airwaves than face to face. Thus, large amounts of money and considerable media resources are devoted to bringing large-scale campaigns into the homes of the voters. Sadly, this is not the case for lower-level races, which have to scramble for even the slightest coverage. The result is a public that is more active in, and more informed about, elections for which the consequences are relatively less immediate and in which each voter's odds of influencing the outcome are minimal.

▶ Campaigns and Elections in Democratic Theory

This last consideration raises questions about the role of campaigns and elections in democracy. How can we ensure that elections are meaningful and serve democratic purposes? At its 154th session in Paris in 1994, the Governing Council of the Inter-parliamentary Union issued the Declaration on Criteria for Free and Fair Elections. In it, the council maintained, "In any State the authority of the government can only derive from the will of the people as expressed in genuine, free and fair elections held at regular intervals on the basis of universal, equal and secret suffrage."[14] This statement nicely sums up the widely accepted claim of modern democrats, but it tells us little about a host of practical questions with respect to democratic elections. For instance, how often should elections be held and for what offices? Which candidates or parties should have access to the ballot? Who should be allowed to vote? How should voter choice be structured? What are acceptable regulations for campaigns? Many of these questions will be addressed in later chapters. Here, we begin with the basics: that is, what requirements are necessary for a free and fair election? And what is the relationship between elections and democracy? Considering these questions will make clear that electoral systems reflect competing conceptions of democracy.

▶ Free and Fair Elections

Robert Dahl argues that free elections are those in which "citizens can go to the polls without fear of reprisal";[15] elsewhere, he notes that in free elections "coercion is comparatively uncommon."[16] Fair elections, conversely, are those in which "all votes must be counted as equal." To these criteria, Dahl adds that elections must be held frequently. "[W]ithout frequent elections," he writes, "citizens would lose a substantial degree of control over their elected officials."[17]

While Dahl's definitions help clarify the meaning of the phrase "free and fair elections," it remains rather abstract. Election management and administration, however, are very practical endeavors. Indeed, a number of international organizations have been created to assist countries in holding elections.[18] International election observers also monitor elections in countries throughout the world, including the United States. On the invitation of the US government, the Organization for Security and Co-operation in Europe's Office for Democratic Institutions and Human Rights has sent a team of election observers to monitor US elections since 2002.[19] Given the increased demand for these observers, it has become necessary to develop a set of international election standards. Box 1.1 highlights the most common criteria for free and fair elections.

BOX 1.1 *What Constitutes a Free and Fair Election?*

A "free" electoral process is one where fundamental human rights and freedoms are respected, including:

- freedom of speech and expression by electors, parties, candidates, and the media;
- freedom of association; that is, freedom to form organizations such as political parties and NGOs (non-governmental organizations);
- freedom of assembly, to hold political rallies, and to campaign;
- freedom of access to and by electors to transmit and receive political and electoral information messages;
- freedom to register as an elector, a party, or a candidate;
- freedom from violence, intimidation, or coercion;
- freedom of access to the polls by electors, party agents, and accredited observers;
- freedom to exercise the franchise in secret; and
- freedom to question, challenge, and register complaints or objections without negative repercussions.

A "fair" electoral process is one where the "playing field" is reasonably level and accessible to all electors, parties, and candidates, and includes:

- an independent, nonpartisan electoral organization to administer the process;
- guaranteed rights and protection through the constitution and electoral legislation and regulations;
- equitable representation of electors provided through the legislation;
- clearly defined universal suffrage and secrecy of the vote;
- equitable and balanced reporting by the media;
- equitable access to financial and material resources for party and candidate campaigning;
- equitable opportunities for the electorate to receive political and voter information;
- accessible polling places;
- equitable treatment of electors, candidates, and parties by elections officials, the government, the police, the military, and the judiciary;
- an open and transparent ballot counting process; and
- election process not disrupted by violence, intimidations, or coercion.

Source: CommonBorders (n.d.) www.commonborders.org/free_and_fair.htm (accessed May 7, 2013); see also Inter-Parliamentary Union (1994) "Declaration on Criteria for Free and Fair Elections," www.ipu.org/cnl-e/154-free.htm (accessed May 7, 2013).

Notice that the United States meets all of the criteria for free elections. Candidates, voters, party and interest group actors, and the media are able to speak, associate, and assemble without resistance. Information is abundant and access to it unrestricted. Anyone can register as a candidate or a voter (subject to minimal regulation). No violence accompanies elections, and polling places are open for observation. Virtually all adults can cast a ballot and do so in secret. Finally, everyone may criticize the electoral process or its outcomes without fear of reprisal. To be sure, elections in the United States are not perfectly free. Some argue, for example, that voter registration restrictions and/or voter identification requirements in some states are unduly burdensome. By and large, however, elections in the United States are among the freest in the world.

But how fair are elections in the United States? Several aspects of the American system may be cause for concern. For instance, election administration is typically a partisan affair, handled by those with partisan interests rather than by neutral officials. The chief elections officer in Ohio in 2004, for example, was a Republican who himself was an elected official and who was also President Bush's campaign chairman in that state. Furthermore, there is no constitutional guarantee of the right to vote (a surprising fact that will be explained in Chapter 2). The Electoral College and the process of legislative redistricting (or redrawing district boundaries) raise questions about the equitable representation of voters. Suffrage is nearly universal but, in most states, convicted felons lose their right to vote at least temporarily. Many question the media's balance in reporting on campaigns. Candidate and party resources are anything but equitable, with a pronounced discrepancy between incumbent and challenger campaign funds. Finally, the ballot-counting process—how tallies on a machine translate into countable votes—is something of a mystery, and new technology may be increasing the mysteriousness.

Many critics of the American electoral system find these matters troubling and believe they reveal a lack of fairness that should not be tolerated. Others, while perhaps acknowledging some inequality in the system, argue that trade-offs are part of any political system and that these particular shortcomings are justified by other political values, such as freedom or order, which are particularly relevant to the debate over campaign finance and felon disenfranchisement, respectively. Nevertheless, most of the criticism of American elections today— and, indeed, most of the reform efforts—address threats to electoral equality and, thus, fairness.

▶ Elections and Popular Sovereignty

Part of the difficulty in evaluating the democratic nature of elections is that the definition of democracy itself is problematic. At an elementary level, democracy means "rule by the people," but this does not get us far because we need to know who counts as "the people" and what it means for them to "rule." In the United States today, there is general consensus that all adult citizens constitute "the people." There is far less agreement, however, upon how much of a role the people should have in governing. The idealized model of a direct democracy is ancient Athens, where citizens met in the assembly to make the laws. As such an arrangement is impossible in modern, mass societies, the question becomes; how much of a voice should the people have? That is, within a representative form of democracy, how much direct democracy is desirable?

Some argue that the legitimacy of government derives from the will of the people and, therefore, that a measure of that will should be taken at every opportunity. Those holding this view believe that active involvement by the citizenry in the policy-making process is vital to the health of democracy. This theory of democracy is often referred to as *participatory democracy*.[20] Elections, therefore, are opportunities not only to choose representatives but to influence the direction of government; thus, initiatives and referenda—ballot measures that give citizens some say in passing or rejecting legislation—and perhaps even judicial elections, are desirable. Those who hold this view would like to lower barriers to participation and lament low turnout and disparities in candidate resources. They also dislike the Electoral College and other institutions or processes, such as legislative redistricting, that may limit citizens' voices in governing. Needless to say, people on this side of the spectrum find the current electoral system in the United States to be deficient and the status quo unacceptable.

Others argue that there should be checks on the will of the people—that prevailing opinion should be filtered through representatives. From this perspective, the people should have minimal influence over the day-to-day operation of governing, and the lion's share of the responsibility for policy-making should be left to elected and appointed officials.[21] Elections as instruments for holding those officials accountable are important, but their use can be limited to periodically choosing representatives. Those who tend toward this view, therefore, oppose measures that give voters a role in the policy-making process (that is, initiatives and referenda). Compared with those favoring participatory democracy, they are, generally speaking, less concerned about barriers to political participation (as long as a basic level of access is maintained). Consequently, they worry less about low levels of voter turnout or disparities in campaign funding. Finally, they tend not to be troubled by institutions such as the Electoral College, given that the electors are essentially representatives. For these individuals, the American electoral system is satisfactory and the status quo acceptable.

▶ Two Visions of Democracy

Intuitively, one might conclude that the participatory view is the more democratic, but a sophisticated understanding of democracy requires us to recognize that there are advantages and disadvantages in the various models of democratic elections. As a result, evaluating electoral systems as more or less democratic fails to fully acknowledge the strengths and weaknesses of the systems and overlooks the trade-offs between them.

In his study of elections as instruments of democracy, G. Bingham Powell identifies two basic approaches to the relationship between elections and democracy: majoritarian and proportional. The majoritarian vision of democracy prefers "concentrated policy-making power," which requires absolute governing majorities.[22] As such, there are clear winners and losers in both elections and the policy-making process. The proportional approach favors a dispersion of power and the representation of as many viewpoints as possible. Bargaining and compromise are, therefore, necessary to accommodate multiple interests in the policy-making process. According to Powell,

> The concentrated, majoritarian approach views elections as mechanisms for tight control, with election outcomes determining directly the makeup of the policymakers who will make all policies between elections. The dispersed [proportional] influence counterpart emphasizes the representation of all points of view brought into an arena of shifting policy coalitions.[23]

These visions of democracy can be distinguished by a variety of institutional arrangements within a government. Arend Lijphart identified ten such arrangements, according to which democracies can be classified. These include whether executive power rests with a single party or is shared by a coalition of parties; whether the executive branch is dominant or power is balanced between the executive and the legislature; whether a system has two parties or multiple parties; whether there is a unitary and centralized or federal and decentralized government; and whether legislative power resides in a unicameral legislature or in two equally (but differently) powerful legislative chambers.[24] The most relevant institutional arrangement, for our purposes, is a country's electoral system, which can produce a majority party or can award seats in a legislature in proportion to the votes parties receive. (Chapter 2 offers a detailed explanation of electoral systems.) For each of these institutional arrangements, one characteristic reflects the majoritarian model of democracy and the other reflects the proportional vision. So, for example, two-party systems are majoritarian whereas systems that consist of multiple parties are proportional. Unitary governments are majoritarian, whereas federal systems encourage consensus and thus reflect the proportional ideal.

No country has a purely majoritarian or proportional system, but many tend toward one model or the other. The United Kingdom is the prototypical majoritarian system, deviating from that model only slightly on a few of Lijphart's criteria. Majoritarian elements of the UK system include its two major parties (notwithstanding third parties that have, at times, played an influential role in British politics); the fact that the majority party, by forming a cabinet that dominates Parliament, controls the government, which is unitary and (notwithstanding the recent devolution of power to Scotland and Wales) centralized; and the lack of judicial review of Parliament's decisions. The best example of the proportional, or what Lijphart calls the consensus model, is Switzerland, which incorporates consensus principles in nine of ten categories (the exception being that it does not have judicial review).[25] It has, for example, multiple parties, none of which has a majority of the seats in the parliament, which means that the cabinet is formed by a coalition of parties; the legislative branch is roughly as powerful as the executive; and the government is federal and decentralized. The United States is balanced between the majoritarian and consensus models. On six of Lijphart's criteria (including a balance of power between the executive and legislative branches, a federal and decentralized government, and the use of judicial review), the United States follows the consensus approach; on four, including its electoral system, it is decidedly majoritarian.

The point of this discussion of competing visions of democracy is, first, to note that there are different ways to conceive of democracy. More important, it is to suggest that the institutional arrangements of a country's government reflect a particular conception of democracy. This is particularly true of a country's electoral system. Indeed, as one noted scholar claims, "The choice of an electoral system is, in effect, a choice among competing definitions of democracy itself."[26] Or, as Powell puts it,

> Those political systems that have perfected most fully one of the major processes through which citizens seem to use elections for influence do so at the expense of one of the other processes. This trade-off is not only a matter of flaws in constitutional design or human imagination … It is built into the tension between concentrated and dispersed power for policy making and the desirable consequences of each. Students of elections and democracy will always have something to complain about because no set of election arrangements can satisfy conditions for all the desirable electoral roles.[27]

▶ The Role of Campaigns and Elections

We have yet, however, to identify what, precisely, is the role of campaigns and elections in democracy. In other words, what functions do they play in a democratic political system?[28] There may, of course, be overlap between the functions of elections and those of campaigns. Accountability, for example, is achieved not just through elections but by forcing public officials to justify their actions in public during a campaign. Overlap aside, distinct functions of campaigns and elections deserve attention. As campaigns presuppose an electoral event, we will begin with elections.

The Functions of Elections

Elections serve at least four functions in a democracy—choosing public officials, ensuring accountability, influencing the direction of policy, and granting legitimacy to the government.[29] First and foremost, elections are a mechanism for determining who will hold public office. Most often, those who will represent the citizenry are chosen directly by voters. That is, votes are cast for candidates contending for an office, and the winner (or winners in multimember districts) are chosen based on a predetermined formula. In the US electoral system, the formula is simple—the candidate with the most votes wins. In the case of the Electoral College, voters choose others to elect a leader on their behalf, although today these electors almost always behave as if the plurality of voters in their states directly chose a presidential candidate.

A related function of elections is to allow voters to choose the candidates who will run for various offices. Party nominees in general elections are often chosen in primary elections (or primaries), which vary significantly in terms of who may participate but offer some level of input into party business by rank and-file members. It should also be noted that elections can be used to remove an individual from public office before the end of their term. Eighteen states allow these recall elections for state officials, and thirty-six allow recalls at the local level.[30] Perhaps the best-known example of a recall election was held in California in 2003 when sitting Governor Gray Davis was removed from office and replaced by movie star Arnold Schwarzenegger. More recently, the recall of Wisconsin Governor Scott Walker in the summer of 2012 attracted considerable media attention, thousands of activists on both sides from around the country, and tens of millions of dollars in campaign spending.

Second, elections can be used to hold elected officials accountable for their actions in office. Whether one believes that representatives should act "on behalf of" their constituents (often called the trustee model of representation) or "in place of" them (the delegate model), everyone agrees that representatives must periodically answer to those they represent.[31] Of course, representatives may not always act exactly as their constituents would like them to. Usually, voters give elected officials some leeway, but it is a foundational principle of democracy that voters have the opportunity to remove their representative from office when they are particularly put out by something the representative has done—including their personal behavior. Presidents, of course, can be held accountable indirectly during midterm elections, when some voters may punish the president by voting against their party's candidates in races for the House and Senate. The 2018 midterm elections may well serve as a referendum on Donald Trump's first two years in office, just as the 2010 midterms were widely seen as a referendum on the first half of Barack Obama's first term.

Of course, citizens may not all vote retrospectively; that is, they may not look back to an incumbent's or a party's record in previous terms in office as they make their choice. Instead, they may vote prospectively, by listening to candidate and party promises and choosing based on which one they believe offers the best plan for the future. Voters may be particularly apt to apply prospective evaluations to nonincumbents.[32]

The third function of elections, therefore, is to give the people some say over the policy direction of the country (or state, city, and so on). This function takes two basic forms, one weak and one strong. In its weak form, the policy-directing role for elections is accomplished by encouraging elected officials to be responsive to the public. With an election looming (or having just occurred), representatives are keen to show how they are responding to citizens' wishes. In this way, voters are able to influence the actions of elected officials. For example, in 2003, a Republican Congress passed, and President Bush signed, a bill that reformed Medicare to include prescription drug coverage for seniors. In part because such reform ran counter to Republican ideology, the passage of the Medicare bill appeared to be a response to general voter concern about the issue.

The strong version of this function gives voters some degree of control, rather than mere influence, over the policy-making process. When elections play this role, voters control government policy by electing leaders who will act on the agenda they proposed and that the voters, by choosing them, endorsed. This is what the victors mean when they claim a "mandate" from an election. Thus, in 1994, Republicans claimed that their "Contract with America," a set of ten legislative proposals publicized during the campaign, should be enacted because the public elected Republicans to control Congress. Of course, the extent to which elections actually produce mandates, or to which the public is able to control policy, is debatable. (Chapter 10 discusses this matter in more detail.)[33]

There is one other way in which elections can foster public control over policy; we might call this the strongest version of the policy-directing function. Initiatives and referenda, as noted previously, give citizens a direct role in policy-making. With initiatives, citizens propose legislation that either goes directly to the voters for their consideration (the direct initiative) or is sent to the legislature and on to the voters if the legislature fails to act or rejects the legislation (the indirect initiative). According to the National Conference of State Legislatures, twenty-one states provide for the initiative process.[34] A referendum is a vote on a measure placed on the ballot either by the legislature (the legislative referendum) or by citizens in response to a law that passed the legislature but which those citizens oppose (the popular referendum). All fifty states provide for legislative referenda, while twenty-three states allow popular referenda.[35]

BOX 1.2 *Oregon Voters Allow Doctor-Assisted Suicide*

The initiative is a mechanism for citizens to propose (or initiate) legislation. Often, initiatives are used by a group of citizens when the legislature refuses to consider legislation they support. The first state to place a statewide initiative on the ballot was Oregon in 1904. Ninety years later, Oregonians considered one of the most controversial initiatives in American history.

In November 1994, voters in Oregon faced eighteen ballot measures. Among them was an initiative that would allow terminally ill adults to obtain a prescription for lethal drugs to end their own lives. After a contentious campaign, the initiative passed with 51.3 percent of the vote. Opponents immediately obtained a legal injunction, but the courts cleared the way for the law's implementation in 1997. In November of that same year, however, the Oregon legislature referred a bill repealing the Death with Dignity Act to the voters. In this legislative referendum, Oregon voters, by a margin of 60 percent to 40 percent, retained the law, and Oregon became the only state in the nation to allow doctor-assisted suicide.

Beginning in 2001, the Bush administration tried to prohibit doctors in Oregon from prescribing lethal doses of medication, arguing that such prescriptions violated the federal Controlled Substances Act. In 2006, the Supreme Court upheld the state's law in *Gonzales* v. *Oregon*. Through 2015, 991 patients had taken advantage of their right to end their own lives, a right obtained through the initiative process.

Source: Oregon Health Authority (2016) "Oregon's Death with Dignity Act: 2015 Data Summary," http://public.health.oregon.gov/ProviderPartnerResources/EvaluationResearch/Deathwith-DignityAct/Documents/year18.pdf (accessed May 26, 2016).

A fourth function of elections is to grant legitimacy to the government. As long as an election is thought to be free from corruption, the winner is viewed as being the rightful occupant of the office at stake. In this way, elections help support the rule of law, at least in developed countries; even those voters whose candidate has lost are expected to acknowledge the authority of the winner.[36] That they do and that politicians themselves would concede power to their opponents without taking up arms is a testament to the moral force of elections in modern democracies. And it is an exceedingly rare political phenomenon in the history of humankind.

In the United States and other developed countries, this function of elections is extremely robust. When the 2000 presidential election resulted in a protracted recount in the state of Florida, many Democrats seemed poised to reject the legitimacy of Republican George W. Bush. During the partisan dispute over how to recount the vote in Florida, a Pew Center for the People and the Press survey revealed that 51 percent of Democrats thought that Bush would not have won legitimately if, in fact, he was declared the winner.[37] Even years later (in March of 2004), according to a National Annenberg Election Survey, 69 percent of Democrats believed that "Al Gore really won the 2000 presidential election but was somehow cheated out of the presidency."[38] Yet there were no violent protests caused by this sense of injustice, and Democrats accepted the presidential authority of George Bush. This demonstrates the powerful ability of elections to bestow legitimacy on governments, and this function serves to foster stability in democratic systems.

A variation of this function is the role elections play as a means for the peaceful expression of dissent. Ballots are extremely blunt instruments for communicating a message, and it is difficult, if not impossible, to glean any intention on behalf of the voter from their ballot. However, when voters cast blank ballots or opt for a third-party candidate, they may be sending a message that they are dissatisfied with the status quo.[39] Indeed, not participating in an election at all is often said to be a statement of dissatisfaction (although, in reality, it is more likely to indicate alienation, a lack of efficacy or, simply, apathy). To the extent that elections provide unhappy citizens with a way to express their displeasure, they may help to reduce the potential for political violence. Admittedly, the 2016 election seemed, at times, to do the opposite. Indeed, Donald Trump often stoked voter anger and even appeared to occasionally encourage violence against protesters at some of his rallies. Still, the actual number of violent incidents during the campaign was quite small and the violence itself was not particularly severe.

The Functions of Campaigns

Campaigns, too, serve at least four distinct functions. Perhaps their most obvious role is to help citizens formulate their preferences and, ultimately, decide for whom to vote on Election Day. In the United States, though, those preferences may be set for many people even before the campaign begins. A long line of research into the voting behavior of Americans concluded that the party identification of most voters determines whom they will vote for regardless of what they hear from the candidates.[40] In fact, some research has found that much of what a voter hears is filtered through a partisan lens that all but ensures the voter will look favorably on their party's nominee.[41]

Recent research suggests, however, that scholars have overlooked the many ways campaigns affect voter decision making.[42] Of course, campaign effects vary by context and depend on circumstances. For instance, events such as party conventions and debates may influence voters' choices, but the impact is most evident among those without strong party identification, who are undecided, or who are "cross-pressured," that is, those pulled in different partisan directions based on conflicting characteristics such as having low income (pro-Democratic) but being an evangelical Christian (pro-Republican).[43] Thus, campaigns help at least some voters make up their minds at election time.

Beyond influencing vote choice, campaigns serve a second function as a forum for debate, discussion, and deliberation.[44] A campaign, after all, is a communication event wherein voters, candidates, parties and interest groups, and the media engage in "crosstalk" as the event unfolds.[45] The discourse that takes place during a campaign produces its own set of effects. One of the most important is political learning within the electorate. Voters clearly learn something about the candidates as they follow a campaign.[46]

A third function of campaigns is to promote citizen participation. At the individual level, campaigns have been shown to have a positive impact on a person's intention to vote.[47] Collectively, campaigns encourage voting by their self-interested pursuit of more voters for their particular sides. As evidence for this, scholars have found that the competitiveness of an election campaign tends to produce higher turnout than races that are not as close; when both sides are working hard to mobilize their voters, turnout increases measurably.[48]

Campaigns foster other kinds of participation as well. They seek, for example, financial support and volunteer efforts. And campaigns foster democratic deliberation. When people discuss the campaign around the water-cooler with co-workers or over dinner with family members, they are participating in politics.

Some candidates' campaigns inspire new activists to enter politics. Many politically active baby-boomers point to the presidential campaigns of Republican Barry Goldwater in 1964 or Democrat Robert F. Kennedy in 1968 as having pulled them into the process. The 1980 presidential campaign of Ronald Reagan also produced a large number of committed activists. More recently, Barack Obama's 2008 presidential bid drew so many young people into politics that the campaign's youth outreach program was dubbed "Generation Obama," and countless millennials were inspired by the 2016 candidacy of a seventy-five-year-old democratic socialist named Bernie Sanders. To the extent that campaigns are successful at getting individuals to participate, they are helping to cultivate the skills and, indeed, the habits of democratic citizenship.[49]

Fourth, campaigns allow "outsiders" an opportunity to voice their opinions. In fact, campaigns serve this function better than elections since, as noted earlier, a vote is ambiguous with respect to the voter's intention. During a campaign, candidates and citizens explicitly express their views in a variety of forums, including debates, newspaper columns and letters, and the Internet. In 2016, Donald Trump ran as the quintessential outsider and, as his promise to "drain the swamp" in Washington, DC suggests, designed his campaign to appeal to those who were frustrated with politics as usual. Indeed, Trump attracted a number of people who felt alienated from mainstream politics (including some who came from the unsavory fringes of political thought in the United States).

Occasionally, a third-party candidacy emerges to represent a viewpoint that is not widely accepted in the country but that, in a democracy, certainly deserves to be heard. This was true of the Socialist candidacies of Eugene Debs and Norman Thomas in the early part of the twentieth century, the states' rights American Independent campaign of George Wallace in 1968, and the candidacies of Ralph Nader in 1996, 2000, and 2004. Ross Perot's 1992 campaign, though not outside mainstream opinion, can be seen as speaking for disaffected voters.[50]

BOX 1.3 *A Socialist for President*

Third-party candidates often come from outside the mainstream of American politics. Nevertheless, they sometimes champion issues that later get adopted by one of the major parties. Such was the case for Eugene Debs, a five-time candidate for president in the early twentieth century.

Debs first gained national notoriety when, as leader of the American Railway Union, he was jailed for his part in the Pullman Strike of 1894. Though he refused the nomination of the People's Party in 1896, Debs did run for president as the Social Democratic Party's candidate in 1900. Having thrown his hat in the ring again in 1904, this time under the Socialist Party's banner, he garnered over 400,000 votes. He did no better in 1908, but four years later he received over 900,000 votes. Debs campaigned unsuccessfully for a congressional seat from Indiana in 1916 but made one more run for the presidency in 1920. This time, however, he did so from a prison cell. Debs and the Socialists opposed US entry into World War I. When, in 1918, he gave an anti-war speech in Canton, Ohio, he was arrested for violating the Espionage Act and was sentenced to ten years in prison. As "Convict No. 9653" (as some of his campaign materials identified him; see Figure 1.1), Debs once again received over 900,000 votes.

FIGURE 1.1   *Eugene V. Debs campaign pin. Source: Stephen K. Medvic.*

The Socialist Party would never again do as well at the polls as it had done under Debs' leadership. But many ideas proposed by Socialists—including women's suffrage, the prohibition of child labor, standards for workplace safety, and the right of workers to organize and strike—would eventually gain widespread support, and become law, in the United States. Third-party candidates rarely win elections, but they can significantly influence the direction of public policy in the country. Eugene Debs certainly did.

Source: Ray Ginger (1962) *Eugene V. Debs: The Making of an American Radical*, New York: Collier Books.

Third-party campaigns are not just vehicles to air unpopular views or vent voter anger. The agenda of a third-party candidate who garners significant support is often co-opted by one of the major parties. Many believe that Perot, for example, put the budget deficit on the table as a key issue in 1992. Cutting the deficit was something Bill Clinton would embrace and, eventually, accomplish as president. So campaigns can also act as a mechanism for influencing policy from outside the dominant political institutions.

The sum total of these campaign functions may be tantamount to the preservation of democracy. As the authors of an important study of campaign communication, *Crosstalk*, put it, "The interactions of the campaign, as well as who wins or loses, have important consequences for governance and for the robustness of the democratic process."[51] Roderick Hart agrees. He was once rather critical of the way campaigns take place in the United States, but his systematic study of "campaign talk" convinced him that the conversations that are our campaigns serve to bolster democracy.[52]

▶ *Normative Considerations*

Most of the material covered in this chapter is normative in nature. That is, it deals with questions of how campaigns and elections ought to operate and the standards by which we should judge that operation. Much of the rest of the book will consist of empirical descriptions; in other words, it will examine how campaigns and elections actually do operate, regardless of how they ought to. Nevertheless, every chapter will address normative considerations because all of the material in this book has implications for how we should organize our political system or how the major players in campaigns and elections ought to behave.

Indeed, when we ask whether campaigns and elections serve our nation's democratic aims, we are asking, in part, whether the participants in those events are properly fulfilling their roles. The structure of campaigns and elections (including the rules and regulations that govern them, the focus of the next two chapters) dictate how they function to a large extent, but it is the players—candidates, political parties, interest groups, the media, voters—who in the end determine whether campaigns and elections are healthy or are not. The last chapter of this book will provide alternative frameworks for judging the players' behavior.

In this chapter, the normative questions all deal with various visions of democracy. By now, it should be clear that there is no single checklist that can be applied to a country to determine whether its political system is or is not democratic. Instead, there are competing visions of democracy. The result is that all countries face trade-offs in fashioning a system of campaigns and elections. Is the freedom of the major players paramount, or is it more important that they play on a level field? Should the system encourage participatory democracy, or should it rely more heavily on representative democracy? Is the proportional (or consensus) model of governing desirable, or is majoritarianism more attractive?

In determining what one values in a political system, it helps to think of these trade-offs as if they were mutually exclusive. That is, if forced to choose, which of the two options would you prefer? Two of the discussion questions at the end of this chapter force you to think in just those terms. The empirical world around us, however, is a bit messier than that. In reality, there are no pure examples of one vision or the other. All countries find themselves on a spectrum between extremes for each of the trade-offs. Thus, both the freedom and the equality of actors are important, and the question becomes where, precisely, to draw the line. Direct democracy, where full participation is required, is impossible in a modern mass society. Thus, within the framework of a representative democracy, the question becomes how much participation to encourage. And as the political system of the United States illustrates, consensus and majoritarian forms of governing are not entirely incompatible. The United States has adopted elements of both.

▶ *Conclusion*

Elections are the cornerstone of democracy. This chapter has tried to explain why that is the case. In addition to drawing a distinction between campaigns and elections, we have explored the role of elections in democratic theory. For elections to fulfill their role as vital instruments of democracy, they must be free and fair. Upon close inspection of the criteria for free and fair elections, we found that elections in the United States are quite free, but that there are numerous ways in which they could be more fair. Ultimately, though, the precise role of elections in democracy depends upon the vision of democracy one embraces. The purpose and design of majoritarian elections differ significantly from those in proportional (or consensus) systems.

This chapter also identified the functions of campaigns and elections. Elections are a mechanism for choosing public officials, obviously, but they also ensure accountability, influence the direction of public policy, and grant legitimacy to the government. Campaigns help citizens formulate their voting preferences, serve as a forum for debate and deliberation, promote citizen participation in politics, and give marginalized groups an opportunity to voice their opinions.

The theoretical groundwork for the role of campaigns and elections in a democracy was laid in this chapter. The next two chapters establish the framework, including the legal and regulatory structure, within which campaigns and elections take place. Chapters 4 through 8 will then examine the activity of the major players in campaigns and elections, and Chapters 9 and 10 explore the processes that result from that activity. Finally, Chapter 11 places the structure, players, and processes of campaigns and elections in a broader context and addresses the health of these vital events.

Elections are often extremely exciting, but they can be frustrating too. The operation of campaigns and elections is often complex and making changes to the way they work entails trade-offs. Fixing one aspect of an electoral system may create new problems. In the chapters that follow, we will examine the various elements of campaigns and elections. The goal is to better understand those elements so that we may engage in a critical assessment of their operation.

▶ *Pedagogical Tools*

Role-Play Scenario

You are the head of a team of international election observers being sent to monitor the first election in a country that has recently transitioned to democracy. The country has had an acting president since the dictator who used to rule the country was overthrown eighteen months ago at the end of a prolonged civil war. Little or no violence has followed since the dictator was ousted, but tensions are running high because of the election. The interim president is on the ballot and is opposed by a former adviser to the deposed dictator. Of the country's three major regions, one shows overwhelming support for the interim president, another is a stronghold of the former dictator's party, and the third is evenly split. Write a short report for your team identifying the factors you will look for to determine whether the election was legitimate. How will you know whether the criteria for a free and fair election were met?

Discussion Questions

1. For democracy to take hold in a country, do you think it is more important to first hold elections or first establish political rights and liberties? Why?
2. Discuss the pros and cons of the participatory and representative approaches to democracy. Which do you think is preferable?
3. Which vision of democratic governance do you find more compelling, the majoritarian or proportional vision? Explain your answer.

Online Resources

ACE Electoral Knowledge Network, aceproject.org.
International Institute for Democracy and Electoral Assistance, www.idea.int.
International Foundation for Election Systems, www.ifes.org.

Suggested Reading

Richard Katz (1997) *Democracy and Elections*, Oxford: Oxford University Press.
G. Bingham Powell, Jr. (2000) *Elections as Instruments of Democracy: Majoritarian and Proportional Visions*, New Haven, CT: Yale University Press.
Matthew J. Streb (2016) *Rethinking American Electoral Democracy*, 3rd edn, London and New York: Routledge.
Dennis F. Thompson (2002) *Just Elections: Creating a Fair Electoral Process in the United States*, Chicago, IL: University of Chicago Press.

▶ *Notes*

1 Dennis F. Thompson (2002) *Just Elections: Creating a Fair Electoral Process in the United States*, Chicago, IL: University of Chicago Press, p. 1.
2 1936 Constitution of the USSR, Chapter XI, Articles 139, 134, www.departments. bucknell. edu/russian/const/36cons04.html#chap11 (accessed June 21, 2016).
3 Terrence McCoy (2014) "Not One Vote Cast Against Kim Jong Un in His First Election," *Washington Post*, March 10, www.washingtonpost.com/news/morning-mix/

wp/2014/03/10/not-one-vote-cast-against-kim-jong-un-in-his-first-election/?utm_ term=.130ef2a4241e (accessed December 30, 2016).

4 Matt Golder (2005) "Democratic Electoral Systems Around the World, 1946–2000," *Electoral Studies*, 24: 103–121, at p. 106.

5 See Robert A. Dahl (1998) *On Democracy*, New Haven, CT: Yale University Press, Chapter 8. For a review of the debate over how to measure "democracy," see David Collier and Robert Adcock (1999) "Democracy and Dichotomies: A Pragmatic Approach to Choices about Concepts," *Annual Review of Political Science*, 2: 537–565.

6 Dahl, *On Democracy*, p. 87.

7 Not all observers hold this view. For instance, in his review of the history of democracy, Fareed Zakaria has argued that if liberal democracy is to take root in a country, constitutionally protected liberties such as freedom of speech must be in place before elections can be held. See Fareed Zakaria (2004) *The Future of Freedom: Illiberal Democracy at Home and Abroad*, Cambridge: Cambridge University Press.

8 See David Held (1987) *Models of Democracy*, Stanford, CA: Stanford University Press; and Frank Cunningham (2002) *Theories of Democracy: A Critical Introduction*, London and New York: Routledge.

9 National Labor Relations Board (1997) *The National Labor Relations Board and YOU*, Washington, DC: National Labor Relations Board, http://nlrb.lettercarriernetwork.info/ NLRB5.PDF (accessed June 21, 2016).

10 William Safire (1993) *Safire's New Political Dictionary*, New York: Random House, p. 98.

11 Missouri results obtained from The Green Papers, www.thegreenpapers.com/G16/MO (accessed December 30, 2016).

12 Indiana results obtained from The Green Papers, www.thegreenpapers.com/G16/IN (accessed December 30, 2016).

13 See results for individual states—Indiana, Montana, North Carolina, North Dakota, New Hampshire, Oregon, Utah, Vermont, and Washington—at The Green Papers, www. thegreenpapers.com/G16 (accessed December 30, 2016).

14 Inter-Parliamentary Union (1994) "Declaration on Criteria for Free and Fair Elections," Geneva, Switzerland: Inter-Parliamentary Council, www.ipu.org/cnl-e/154-free.htm (accessed June 21, 2016).

15 Dahl, *On Democracy*, p. 95.

16 Robert Dahl (1989) *Democracy and Its Critics*, New Haven, CT: Yale University Press, p. 221.

17 Dahl, *On Democracy*, pp. 95 and 96.

18 These include the International Institute for Democracy and Electoral Assistance, or IDEA (www.idea.int), the United Nations Electoral Assistance Division (of the Department of Public Affairs, (www.un.org/wcm/content/site/undpa/main/issues/elections), and the International Foundation for Election Systems, or IFES (www.ifes.org).

19 See Office for Democratic Institutions and Human Rights, "Elections in the United States of America," Organization for Security and Co-operation, www.osce.org/odihr/elections/ usa (accessed December 30, 2016).

20 See Carole Pateman (1970) *Participation and Democratic Theory*, Cambridge: Cambridge University Press; and C. B. Macpherson (1977) *The Life and Time of Liberal Democracy*, Oxford: Oxford University Press.

21 The classic formulation of this view is Joseph Schumpeter's *Capitalism, Socialism and Democracy*, London: Allen & Unwin, 1976; first published 1942.

22 G. Bingham Powell, Jr. (2000) *Elections as Instruments of Democracy: Majoritarian and Proportional Visions*, New Haven, CT: Yale University Press, pp. 4–6.

23 Powell, *Elections as Instruments of Democracy*, p. 6.

24 Arend Lijphart (1999) *Patterns of Democracy: Government Forms and Performance in Thirty-Six Countries*, New Haven, CT: Yale University Press, pp. 3–4.

25 Lijphart, *Patterns of Democracy*, pp. 10–21 and 34–41.

26 Richard Katz (1997) *Democracy and Elections*, Oxford: Oxford University Press, p. 9.

27 Powell, *Elections as Instruments of Democracy*, p. 19.
28 It is possible that elections play a different set of functions for individuals and political systems, though the functions may be analogous. See Richard Rose and Harve Mossawir (1967) "Voting and Elections: A Functional Analysis," *Political Studies*, 15: 173–201. In this chapter, I am primarily interested in the systemic functions of elections.
29 Among the many authors who explore the various functions of elections are Rose and Mossawir, "Voting and Elections"; and Katz, *Democracy and Elections*, Chapter 7.
30 See National Conference of State Legislatures (2012) "Recall of State Officials," June 6, www.ncsl.org/legislatures-elections/elections/recall-of-state-officials.aspx (accessed June 21, 2016). Recall elections cannot be held for federal officeholders.
31 See Hannah F. Pitkin (1967) *The Concept of Representation*, Berkeley, CA: University of California Press, for the classic study of different conceptions of representation.
32 Arthur H. Miller and Martin P. Wattenberg (1985) "'Throwing the Rascals Out': Policy and Performance Evaluation of Presidential Candidates, 1952–1980," *American Political Science Review*, 79: 359–372.
33 Those who are skeptical that election results could produce mandates include Gerald Pomper (1968) *Elections in America: Control and Influence in Democratic Politics*, New York: Dodd, Mead, & Company; and Robert A. Dahl (1990) "Myth of the Presidential Mandate," *Political Science Quarterly*, 105: 355–372. Others are more sanguine; see Patricia Heidotting Conley (2001) *Presidential Mandates: How Elections Shape the National Agenda*, Chicago, IL: University of Chicago Press. On the public's control over policy—or lack thereof—see Lawrence R. Jacobs and Robert Y. Shapiro (2000) *Politicians Don't Pander: Political Manipulation and the Loss of Democratic Responsiveness*, Chicago, IL: University of Chicago Press.
34 See National Conference of State Legislatures (2015) "Initiative and Referendum States," www.ncsl.org/research/elections-and-campaigns/chart-of-the-initiative-states.aspx (accessed December 30, 2016).
35 National Conference of State Legislatures, "Initiative and Referendum States."
36 Interestingly, elections may undermine the rule of law in some countries. Chaturvedi and Mukherji have found that elections tend to incite violent crime in less developed countries (though there is no link between elections and violence in developed countries). See Ashish Chaturvedi and Arnab Mukherji (2004) "Do Elections Incite Violent Crime?" Department of Economics, University of California, Irvine and RAND Graduate School. Unpublished manuscript.
37 Pew Research Center for the People and the Press (2000) "Voters Side with Bush for Now," November 14, www.people-press.org/reports/display.php3?ReportID=24 (accessed June 21, 2016).
38 Annenberg Public Policy Center of the University of Pennsylvania (2004) "Large Majority of Democrats Still Bitter Over 2000, National Annenberg Election Survey Shows," March 19, www.annenbergpublicpolicycenter.org/large-majority-of-democrats-still-bitter-over-2000 (accessed June 21, 2016).
39 Geoff Peterson and Mark Wrighton (1998) "Expressions of Distrust: Third-Party Voting and Cynicism in Government," *Political Behavior*, 20: 17–34.
40 This literature is too large to cite here, but the classics in the field date to the 1940s, 1950s and 1960s; see Paul Lazarsfeld, Bernard Berelson, and Hazel Guadet (1944) *The People's Choice*, New York: Columbia University Press; Bernard Berelson, Paul Lazarsfeld, and William H. McPhee (1954) *Voting: A Study of Opinion Formation in a Presidential Campaign*, Chicago, IL: University of Chicago Press; and Angus Campbell, Philip E. Converse, Warren E. Miller, and Donald E. Stokes (1960) *The American Voter*, New York: John Wiley & Sons.
41 Gerber and Green have raised questions about the prevalence of this phenomenon, known as "selective perception"; Alan Gerber and Donald Green (1999) "Misperceptions about Perceptual Bias," *Annual Review of Political Science*, 2: 189–210. See also Berelson et al., *Voting*; Campbell et al., *The American Voter*; and John R. Zaller (1992) *The Nature and Origins of Mass Opinion*, Cambridge: Cambridge University Press.

42 Shanto Iyengar and Adam F. Simon (2000) "New Perspectives and Evidence on Political Communication and Campaign Effects," *Annual Review of Psychology*, 51: 149–169.

43 Sunshine D. Hillygus and Simon Jackman (2003) "Voter Decision Making in Election 2000: Campaign Effects, Partisan Activation, and the Clinton Legacy," *American Journal of Political Science*, 47: 583–596. See also Daron R. Shaw (1999) "A Study of Presidential Campaign Event Effects from 1952 to 1992," *The Journal of Politics*, 61: 387–422.

44 Stanley Kelley, Jr. (1960) *Political Campaigning: Problems in Creating an Informed Electorate*, Washington, DC: The Brookings Institution.

45 Marion R. Just, Ann N. Crigler, Dean E. Alger, Timothy E. Cook, Montague Kern, and Darrell M. West (1996) *Crosstalk: Citizens, Candidates, and the Media in a Presidential Campaign*, Chicago, IL: The University of Chicago Press.

46 R. Michael Alvarez and Garrett Glasgow (1997) "Do Voters Learn from Presidential Election Campaigns?" California Institute of Technology, unpublished manuscript; and Randolph R. Stevenson and Lynn Vavreck (2000) "Does Campaign Length Matter? Testing for Cross-National Effects," *British Journal of Political Science*, 30: 217–235.

47 Sunshine D. Hillygus (2005) "Campaign Effects and the Dynamics of Turnout Intention in Election 2000," *The Journal of Politics*, 67: 50–68.

48 Gary W. Cox and Michael C. Munger (1989. "Closeness, Expenditures, and Turnout in the 1982 US House Elections," *American Political Science Review*, 83: 217–231. Some research suggests that other aspects of campaigns, like negative advertising, depress turnout; see Stephen Ansolabehere and Shanto Iyengar (1995) *Going Negative: How Political Advertisements Shrink and Polarize the Electorate*, New York: The Free Press. However, this conclusion is in dispute; see Martin P. Wattenberg and Craig Leonard Brians (1999) "Negative Campaign Advertising: Demobilizer or Mobilizer?" *American Political Science Review*, 93: 891–899.

49 Alan S. Gerber, Donald P. Green, and Ron Shachar (2003) "Voting May Be Habit-Forming: Evidence from a Randomized Field Experiment," *American Journal of Political Science*, 47: 540–550.

50 James A. McCann, Ronald B. Rapoport, and Walter J. Stone (1999) "Heeding the Call: An Assessment of Mobilization into H. Ross Perot's 1992 Presidential Campaign," *American Journal of Political Science*, 43: 1–28; and Mari Boor Tonn and Valerie A. Endress (2001) "Looking Under the Hood and Tinkering with Voter Cynicism: Ross Perot and 'Perspective Incongruity,'" *Rhetoric and Public Affairs*, 4: 281–308.

51 Just et al., *Crosstalk*, p. 233.

52 Roderick P. Hart (1994) *Seducing America: How Television Charms the Modern Voter*, Oxford: Oxford University Press; Roderick P. Hart (2000) *Campaign Talk: Why Elections Are Good for Us*, Princeton, NJ: Princeton University Press.

Rules and Regulations I

Voting Rights and the U.S. Electoral System

T HE LEGAL CONTEXT in which campaigns and elections take place in the United States is a complex web of rules and regulations established at the local, state, and national levels. As the National Commission on Federal Election Reform's Task Force on Constitutional and Federal Election Law put it, "The American electoral system falls at the intersection of many different regulatory regimes—some federal, some state; some constitutional, some statutory; some general, some specific; and some mandatory and some prohibitory." [1] Though election regulations may be enacted at various levels of government, there is an accepted "hierarchy of authority," namely, "federal constitutional law trumps federal statutory law, which trumps state constitutional law, which in turn trumps state statutory law, not to mention state administrative regulation."[2] Nevertheless, the administration of elections is the responsibility of local authorities.[3] By one estimate, there are roughly 13,000 electoral jurisdictions in the United States.[4]

The complexity created by the various statutes and administrative bodies that deal with elections and the dramatic increase in the number of election-related cases heard by the Supreme Court since 1960 have given rise to a new specialty in the practice of law: election law.[5] Increasingly, law schools offer courses in election law, and there are now textbooks devoted to the subject.[6] One of these textbooks grew in size by 50 percent in the three years between publication of the first and second editions.[7] There are also at least two election law blogs devoted to covering developments in this area on a day-to-day basis.[8]

Any attempt to summarize the laws governing campaigns and elections in a chapter or two would be futile. Nevertheless, Chapters 2 and 3 cover the major issues with respect to the legal and administrative framework within which campaigns and elections take place. They look at "ballots, bucks, and maps" (as the Georgetown Law School course on election law is subtitled)—that is, suffrage, campaign finance, and redistricting—and the design of our electoral system and the administration of elections. This chapter will explore voting rights and the US electoral system at the congressional and presidential levels and redistricting for legislative seats. Chapter 3 will examine election administration and campaign finance.

Though each chapter will address some unique approaches to running elections in the states, for a number of reasons the primary focus of this book is on federal elections. First, many of the disputes in election law are constitutional matters and, as noted earlier, the federal Constitution is paramount on these questions. This is particularly true for voting rights, the subject of much of this chapter. Second, though states are permitted leeway in regulating many aspects of campaigns and elections, the federal government can—and does—step in when problems arise that generate national attention. The crisis produced by the 2000 presidential election is a case in point. Finally, on topics such as campaign finance, the variety of state laws is so great that it would be difficult to give adequate treatment to them all.

► *Campaigns and Elections in the Constitution*

We begin this chapter where all discussions of the law in the United States begin—with the US Constitution. The original Constitution—as written in 1787, before being amended—devotes fewer than one in five words to elections (and says nothing about campaigns).[9] However, this is a considerable portion of a document that was also designing an entire system of governance, including three branches of government, the roles and responsibilities of those branches, and the relationship between the national and state governments. Furthermore, the Framers expected elections to be largely the purview of the states, thus reducing the need for detail in the Constitution. As a result, the Framers laid out only the essentials regarding elections; the amendments to the Constitution—chiefly those that are not part of the Bill of Rights—address elections to a far greater extent than the original Constitution does. This is particularly true with respect to voting, which receives very little attention in the original.

The Appendix lists the provisions in the Constitution that are directly related to, or that pertain predominantly to, elections. Typically, the Constitution gives state governments the ability to determine how elections will be held within their borders. Yet Congress is also granted the ability to regulate federal elections.[10] For example, in what is perhaps the most famous clause in the Constitution with respect to elections (the aptly named "Elections Clause," Article I, section 4, clause 1), the "Times, Places and Manner of holding Elections for Senators and Representatives, shall be prescribed in each State by the Legislature thereof." However, this clause also allows Congress to alter these regulations as it sees fit.[11]

Other parts of the Constitution deal with the qualifications to vote or to hold office, the latter affecting who can be a candidate for federal offices. For instance, Article I, section 2, clause 1 (also know as the "Qualifications Clause") provides for the election of members of the House of Representatives, but it leaves to the states the specific qualifications for voters in House races by requiring only that they have the "Qualifications requisite for Electors of the most numerous Branch of the State Legislature." Article I, section 2, clause 2 says that a representative must be twenty-five years old, must have been a citizen for seven years, and must live in the state from which he/she is elected; a senator must be thirty years old, have been a citizen for nine years, and must live in the state from which he/she is elected (Article I, section 3, clause 3); and only natural-born citizens who are at least thirty-five years old and have been a resident within the United States for fourteen years can be president, according to Article II, section 1, clause 5. The Electoral College, which is not so named in the Constitution, is described in Article II, section 1, clauses 2, 3, and 4. (Notice that it is up to the states to determine how the electors are chosen.)

► Election-Related Protections Afforded by Constitutional Amendments

As noted, a significant portion of the amendments to the Constitution address elections—roughly 28 percent of the words therein. This is particularly true of the seventeen amendments beyond the Bill of Rights—fully 33.3 percent of the words therein. Eight of these seventeen amendments deal directly with elections or voting. The Twelfth Amendment, proposed as a result of the election of 1800 and ratified in 1804, alters the workings of the Electoral College (as discussed more fully later in this chapter); the Twenty-Second Amendment limits the president to two terms in office; and the Twenty-Third Amendment gives the District of Columbia three presidential electors. The popular election of US senators is provided for in the Seventeenth Amendment. The Fifteenth, Nineteenth, Twenty-Sixth Amendments prohibit the denial of the right to vote based on race, sex, and age (for those eighteen years old and older), respectively. Finally, the Twenty-Fourth Amendment bars the use of the poll tax.

Of course, many other parts of the Constitution have implications for elections. The two most important are the Equal Protection Clause of the Fourteenth Amendment and the First Amendment's protection of free speech and the right of association. The Equal Protection Clause ensures that election laws will treat all voters similarly (unless a law "can be shown to bear a necessary relationship or be narrowly tailored to a compelling state interest"[12]). This clause serves as the basis of the "one person, one vote" principle that emerged from a series of Supreme Court decisions in the 1960s. Equal protection also played a prominent role in *Bush* v. *Gore*, the Supreme Court decision that effectively ended the 2000 presidential recount in Florida (introduced in Chapter 1).

The First Amendment is obviously critical to the democratic functions of campaigns and elections. Not only should campaign actors be permitted to speak freely in the course of a campaign, but the media have a right to cover campaigns and elections free from government control. This has relevance for debates over campaign finance reform and regulation of media coverage of elections (for instance, with respect to early calls on Election Night). The First Amendment also protects the right of political parties and interest groups to freely associate.

As with all laws in the United States, the Constitution serves as the foundation for election law. It provides the basic framework for election administration but leaves many of the details to federal and state statute. Much of the rest of this chapter covers an array of statutes dealing with a variety of election-related issues. We will begin by looking at the most fundamental of these issues—the right to vote.

▶ The Right to Vote

Though it sounds like an urban legend, it is in fact the case that the right to vote is not provided for in the US Constitution.[13] The United States is one of only eleven countries of the 119 electoral democracies not to have a constitutional guarantee of the right to vote.[14] This seems puzzling, as a number of amendments to the Constitution refer to the "right to vote." However, the Fifteenth, Nineteenth, and Twenty-Sixth Amendments say only that one's vote cannot be denied on the basis of race, sex, or age, and the Twenty-Fourth Amendment states the same with respect to failure to pay a poll tax (or any other tax). In theory, therefore, the franchise could be taken from individuals as long as it was taken away from everyone (or denied for reasons not based on those prohibited in the aforementioned amendments).

In practice, this hardly seems possible in a country with deep democratic roots. Yet this very issue was raised by the Florida recount in the 2000 presidential election. According to Article II, section 1, clause 2 of the Constitution, the method for choosing presidential electors is up to the state legislatures. Having given the right to vote for president to the people, the state legislatures can also take it back. In Florida in 2000, various court challenges were delaying the final count in the presidential race, thereby threatening to cost the state its vote in the Electoral College.[15] The majority opinion in *Bush* v. *Gore* made it quite clear, however, that the Florida legislature could, at any time, reclaim the power to appoint Florida's electors.[16] Though select committees of both chambers of the legislature voted along party lines to hold a special session for this purpose, the legislature ultimately stayed out of the process. Nevertheless, this incident suggests that, at least under extraordinary circumstances, the right to vote can be taken away from US citizens.

Clearing the Hurdles of Race and Gender

Historically speaking, universal suffrage—or more accurately, near universal suffrage, as discussed later in the chapter—has been achieved only relatively recently in the United States. Though the laws varied from state to state, basically only White adult men who owned property could vote at the founding of the republic.[17] In the first third of the nineteenth century, virtually all White men had been granted the right to vote by the states. Though the Fifteenth Amendment, ratified in 1870, removed race as a barrier to voting in theory, in practice African-American men (and later African-American women) were still systematically disenfranchised by various practices until the mid twentieth century. Native Americans gained US citizenship in 1924, but they remained unable to vote in most states for years afterward. Along with African Americans and Hispanics, Native Americans often faced obstacles to voting even after they had been granted the right to vote.

Prior to the twentieth century, women were denied the vote in all but four states.[18] Wyoming was the first to fully enfranchise women, doing so initially as a territory in 1869 and then upon admittance to the union as a state in 1890. Early in the twentieth century, the women's suffrage movement became successful in state after state, so that fifteen states allowed women to vote for all offices (and in a number of additional states, they could vote in some local elections or for president only, or both). Still, from a constitutional perspective, well more than half the nation's population could not claim the right to vote until ratification of the Nineteenth Amendment, which guaranteed women that right in 1920, 132 years after the first elections under the Constitution of the United States.

Restricting the Right to Vote

A number of methods, both formal and informal, were used to keep minority voters from registering or casting ballots. Many of these were invented during the "disenfranchisement movement" in the South from 1890 to 1908.[19] One approach was to require that people seeking to register to vote prove their literacy by passing a test given by the (White) voter registrar. Since many Blacks were literate and some Whites were not, in practice the literacy tests were unfairly administered; Whites were rarely given the tests and Blacks who took them were rarely judged objectively.[20] Nevertheless, to further ensure discrimination, White legislators in the South enacted a number of alternatives to the literacy requirement to enable illiterate Whites to skirt the system. One such alternative was an "understanding clause," by which registrars required illiterate individuals to orally interpret a passage read to them from the Constitution. Other alternatives included "good character clauses," also invoked at the registrar's discretion, and property requirements. Some states also used "grandfather clauses," whereby those who had been registered prior to a certain date or who were descended from a registered voter could register without passing a literacy test. Few African Americans would have had ancestors who were registered voters since most were descendants of slaves. Thus, grandfather clauses were written to include nearly all Whites in the voting process while excluding as many Blacks as possible.

Of all forms of voter disenfranchisement, the "White primary" was probably the most effective. According to V. O. Key, Jr.., disenfranchisement via literacy tests and poll taxes (discussed next) "had to be accomplished by methods appearing to comply with the Federal Constitution. The color line could not be drawn outright; other lines that might happen to coincide with it had to be the basis for discrimination." Party business, however, was theoretically outside the purview of the Constitution, which meant that the Democratic Party could "discriminate on whatever line it chose."[21] What it chose throughout the South was to prohibit Blacks from voting in its primaries. Since the South was a one-party region controlled by the Democrats at that time, whoever won the Democratic nomination was assured of victory in the general election. Thus, to be barred from the Democratic primaries was essentially to be denied participation in choosing representatives.

The poll tax, which was also adopted during the disenfranchisement movement, was more widely used than the literacy test (Figure 2.1). Unlike most taxes, the poll tax was not really intended to be a source of government revenue; it was, as Key pointed out, simply "a condition for exercise of the suffrage."[22] That condition applied to Whites as well as Blacks, though, as with other methods of disenfranchisement, it was not evenly enforced.[23] Indeed, during the time of the White primary, the poll tax probably had a more pronounced effect on poor Whites than on African Americans. The combination of literacy tests and the White primary so thoroughly excluded Blacks from the polls that the poll tax had a comparatively limited effect on Black voting rights.

Dismantling Obstacles and Extending the Right to Vote

Grandfather clauses were found to be unconstitutional in 1939 and, in 1944, the Supreme Court ruled that primaries were not, in fact, private activities but a "state function."[24] As such, the Fourteenth and Fifteenth Amendments applied to—and forbade—the use of White primaries. After the abolition of the White primary, the poll tax "remained as a legitimate way to keep the ballot box closed," as did

FIGURE 2.1 *1935 Poll Tax Receipt from Texas*

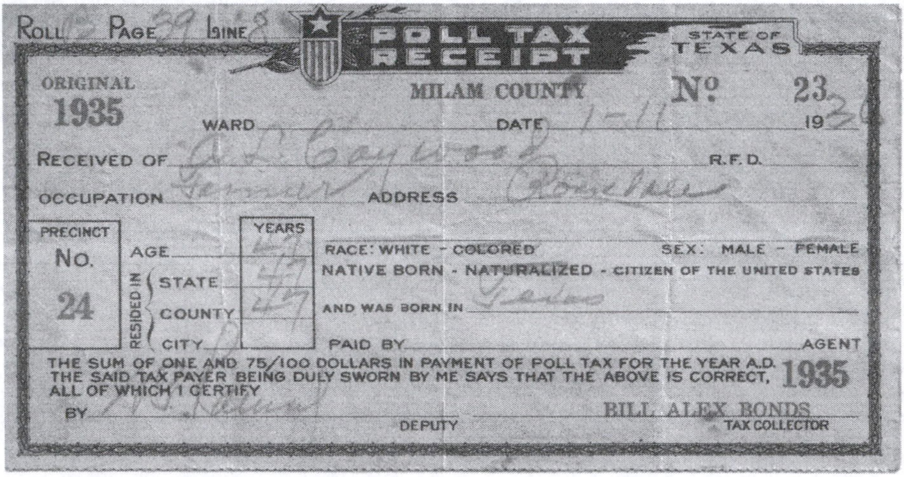
ROLL PAGE 39 LINE 8

POLL TAX RECEIPT

STATE OF TEXAS

ORIGINAL 1935

MILAM COUNTY

No. 23

WARD DATE 1-11 193

RECEIVED OF

R.F.D.

OCCUPATION Farmer ADDRESS

PRECINCT No. 24

AGE / RESIDED IN STATE / COUNTY / CITY — YEARS

RACE: WHITE - COLORED SEX: MALE - FEMALE

NATIVE BORN - NATURALIZED - CITIZEN OF THE UNITED STATES

AND WAS BORN IN Texas

PAID BY AGENT

THE SUM OF ONE AND 75/100 DOLLARS IN PAYMENT OF POLL TAX FOR THE YEAR A.D. 1935

THE SAID TAX PAYER BEING DULY SWORN BY ME SAYS THAT THE ABOVE IS CORRECT,

ALL OF WHICH I CERTIFY

BY DEPUTY

BILL ALEX BONDS

TAX COLLECTOR

"In Texas, the receipt must be presented at the polls or an affidavit made in writing that it has been lost" (Key 1949: 588). Source: Jerry Caywood.

the literacy test.[25] Nevertheless, the abolition of White primaries had angered many Southern Whites, leaving some of them to find illegitimate ways to keep Blacks from voting. A local newspaper in Georgia warned in 1946 that "some hooded and secret order such as the Ku Klux Klan will ride again, and all power acquired by the ballot will be lost by terrorism" if Blacks exercised their right to vote in Democratic primaries.[26] Indeed, intimidation and physical violence were often used to keep African Americans from registering and voting.

BOX 2.1   *The Use of Terror to Disenfranchise African Americans*

Many harrowing accounts document violence against volunteers, both Black and White, who registered African Americans to vote in the South prior to the Voting Rights Act of 1965. The following is taken from Laughlin McDonald's *A Voting Rights Odyssey: Black Enfranchisement in Georgia* (Cambridge: Cambridge University Press, 2003).

> Black voter registration efforts met the stiffest, and frequently the most openly violent, resistance in counties with substantial black populations where black political power, from the white point of view, was most threatening. One of them was Terrell County in southwest Georgia, north of Albany, dubbed "Terrible Terrell" by civil rights activists ....
>
> Carolyn Daniels, a black beautician in Dawson, was ... active in the registration campaign in Terrell County and put up several SNCC [Student Nonviolent Coordinating Committee] workers in her home. One evening in August 1962, as the group was preparing a midnight snack after returning from a trip to Albany, several shotgun blasts ripped through the house. John Chatfield, a twenty-year-old white college student from Vermont, was struck twice.[1] Several months later, Daniels's home was bombed causing extensive damage. The home of a neighbor, Willie Westin was sprayed with more than fifty rounds of submachine gun fire.[2]
>
> Voter registration meetings had also been held in nearby Lee County at the Shady Grove Baptist Church. Agnew James, a forty-three-year-old black man living in Leesburg who had first registered in March 1962, was one of the leaders of the local registration movement. One evening in July, he drove over to the church with his wife and sixteen-year-old daughter to attend a voters' meeting, but found the entrance to the churchyard blocked by policemen. "A man who seemed to be wearing state patrol clothes waved his flashlight at me," recalled James, "and I stopped. He threw his light right in my face, so I turned my head away; I seen three white men standing in the back of my car. One of them called out the number of my license plate."[3]
>
> The man in the patrol clothes then began questioning James. "Nigger, you know what kind of meeting they're having? Whose plantation do you live on?" When James told him that he lived on land owned by a black, "that is when he got to cursing," says James's wife, Odethia, who was sitting in the seat beside him. "I guess every other word he said after that was cursing. He said, 'Nigger you can go in that church and we will beat damn hell out of you or you can turn around and go back the way you came from.'"[4]
>
> Agnew James looked at his wife and daughter, briefly considered his options, and concluded that it would be too dangerous to go into the church.

"My wife kept pulling at my sleeve," he recalls, "saying 'let's go.' I never did cut my motor off. I backed out and went down the road."[5]

The next month, arsonists burned the Shady Grove church to the ground.[6] Two more black churches were burned several weeks later, the Mount Olive Church at Sasser and the Mount Mary Church at Chickasawhatchee in Terrell County.[7]

The Dawson paper speculated that blacks themselves had burned the churches and shot into the Daniels's home. After all, the paper asked,"[w]ho had the most to profit—to gain—from the shooting into the negro house and the burning of the churches. Certainly it was not the good white people of Terrell County."[8]

As it turned out, the white people of Terrell County did have a hand in the church burnings. Three local white men eventually confessed to burning one of the churches.[9] In October 1962, two white men from Lee County were charged with burning the Shady Grove Baptist Church.[10]

---

1   *Dawson News*, August 16, 1962; Atlanta Constitution, April 29, 1963.
2   *Dawson News*, Dec. 12, 1963.
3   *United States* v. *Zeke T. Mathews*, affidavit of Agnew James, August 8, 1962.
4   *United States* v. *Zeke T. Mathews*, affidavit of Odethia James, August 8, 1962.
5   *United States* v. *Zeke T. Mathews*, affidavit of Agnew James, August 8, 1962.
6   *Dawson News*, August 16, 1962.
7   *Dawson News*, Sept. 13, 1962. Another black church, the High Hope Baptist Church near Dawson had been torched the preceding year. *Macon Telegraph*, Oct. 5, 1962.
8   *Dawson News*, Sept. 13, 1962.
9   *Dawson News*, Sept. 20, 1962.
10   *Dawson News*, Oct. 11, 1962.

Despite the use of terror, Black registration increased dramatically between the late 1940s and the end of the 1960s. James Alt reports that the estimated average percentage of voting-age African Americans who were registered in the South in 1947 was 12 percent; by 1968, that number had risen to 62 percent.[27] A substantial part of this increase was due to the persistent efforts of civil-rights activists who risked their lives—and sometimes lost them—attempting to register Black voters, but federal action also had an influence. The Twenty-Fourth Amendment to the Constitution, ratified in 1964, prohibited the use of poll taxes in federal elections, and the Supreme Court extended this to state elections in 1966.[28]

The Voting Rights Act (VRA) of 1965 suspended the literacy test and its alternatives in states with a history of discrimination against African-American voters; that suspension was extended to the entire nation in 1970 and made permanent in 1975. Furthermore, as Alt notes, "Under section 6 [of the VRA], the Attorney General could send federal examiners directly to various counties to facilitate registration of blacks."[29] The use of these examiners had a significant influence on Black registration rates between 1965 and 1968. It is not an exaggeration to say, as the editors of a book on the impact of the VRA do, that the VRA spurred a "quiet revolution in the South."[30]

The VRA and its later amendments contain a number of important provisions, including the aforementioned ban on the use of literacy tests as a requirement for voting and the provision of federal examiners or election monitors, or both, to oversee voter registration and voting in areas with a history of discrimination. Notwithstanding these vital provisions, some scholars point to two particularly significant aspects of the law.[31] Section 2 of the Act, which protects minority voting rights, declares: "No voting qualification or prerequisite to voting, or standard, practice, or procedure shall be imposed or applied by any State or political subdivision to deny or abridge the right of any citizen of the United States to vote on account of race or color."[32] Initially, this merely reiterated the protections of the Fifteenth Amendment to the Constitution, but Section 2 was amended in 1982 to broaden the conditions under which the Act would be considered violated. Specifically, attempts to dilute minority voting strength (for example, by the use of at-large voting districts, which increase the number of people voting in a given area and put minority voters at a disadvantage) have come under scrutiny as a result of the 1982 amendments.

The other significant provision of the VRA is found in Section 5. Originally, the VRA applied (per Section 4 of the Act) to "states or localities that in 1964 used a literacy or other test as a condition for registering or voting and in which less than half the voting age population voted in the 1964 presidential election." At the time of its passage, six southern states, plus many localities in North Carolina, were "covered" by the law. Later amendments added other states and localities, including Alaska, Arizona, Texas, and parts of New York and California. Section 5 of the Voting Rights Act of 1965, which applied to the covered states and localities, requires "preclearance" by the US attorney general (or US District Court for the District of Columbia) before any changes to voting procedures can take effect.[33] Section 5 was renewed for twenty-five years in 1982 and was set to expire in 2007. Despite initial objection to another renewal of the preclearance requirement from some southern members of Congress, Section 5 was renewed by overwhelming majorities in both chambers (including a vote of ninety-eight to zero in the Senate) in the summer of 2006.

The chorus of Section 5 critics grew louder in the years following the VRA's renewal in 2006. Those critics argued that the provision was outdated and unfair given that it covered only some states. Indeed, Shelby County, Alabama challenged the constitutionality of Section 5 in 2013 in the Supreme Court case *Shelby County* v. *Holder*. The county's argument was that the formula used to determine which states and localities are to be covered had not been updated since 1975 and that circumstances in Alabama and elsewhere had changed since the VRA was enacted. More fundamentally, Shelby County argued that Congress does not have the constitutional authority to impose Section 5 on the states, particularly as only some states and localities are subject to its rules.

Defenders of Section 5 maintained that discriminatory practices are still widespread and that this is especially true in the parts of the country covered by Section 5. Furthermore, the Fifteenth Amendment, which says that the right to vote cannot be denied on the basis of race, gives Congress the power to "enforce this article by appropriate legislation." If Congress isn't capable of determining how to enforce the Fifteenth Amendment, who is?

In its decision in the Shelby County case, the Supreme Court effectively gutted Section 5 of the VRA. They did so not by striking down Section 5, but by finding Section 4 of the Act unconstitutional. Section 4 provided the formula for determining which jurisdictions would be required to get preclearance for changes to voting procedures. In the majority opinion, Chief Justice John Roberts argued that Section 4's formula was out of date. "Our country has changed," wrote Chief Justice Roberts, "and while any racial discrimination in voting is too much, Congress must ensure that the legislation it passes to remedy that problem speaks to current conditions."[34] Thus, the Court did not question Congress's authority to require some states to get federal preclearance for changes to their voting laws; instead it questioned Congress's method for identifying states that would be covered by such a requirement.

It is difficult not to conclude that the Supreme Court's decision has had significant consequences. According to the Brennan Center for Justice, in the fifteen years prior to *Shelby*, eighty-six laws were blocked by Section 5.[35] In the wake of the decision, several states that had previously been covered by Section 5 rushed to alter voting laws. Within hours of the announcement of the Supreme Court's decision, for example, Texas moved to implement a strict photo ID requirement for voting that had been prevented by Section 5. North Carolina not only imposed a photo ID requirement, but scaled back its early voting period and narrowed the time allowed for voter registration.[36]

These new restrictions on voting rights have, of course, been challenged in the courts. In 2016, laws in several states, including Texas and North Carolina, were found to be discriminatory and, consequently, were struck down.[37] Cases like these must now be brought under Section 2 of the VRA, which can still be used to sue states and localities that pass laws infringing on minorities' voting rights. However, some legal experts argue that Section 2 lawsuits can only address the most egregious violations of voting rights. Furthermore, Section 2 of the VRA may itself be the target of a constitutional challenge in the near future.[38] Thus, many voting rights advocates worry that we have entered an era of voting rights retrenchment.[39]

At roughly the same time as the movement for full minority voting rights was gaining ground, eighteen-to-twenty-year-olds were agitating for the right to vote. In his excellent history of the right to vote, Alexander Keyssar points out that a voting age of twenty-one "had been a remarkable constant in state laws governing the franchise" since the nation's founding. During and after World War II, however, the movement to lower the voting age gained momentum. Elected officials began to give weight to the argument that, as President Eisenhower himself put it, "If a man is old enough to fight he is old enough to vote."[40] It was the Vietnam War, however, that really gave the issue urgency. Men as young as eighteen years old were fighting and dying in a war that had become quite unpopular.

That they were not permitted a voice in their own country's elections became impossible to justify. In 1971, within a few years of the height of antiwar protests—and perhaps, in part, because of them—Congress passed the Twenty-Sixth Amendment—and the states ratified it—giving eighteen-, nineteen-, and twenty-year-olds the right to vote. (In fact, the Twenty-Sixth Amendment was ratified faster than any other amendment to the US Constitution.[41])

Contemporary Restrictions on the Right to Vote

Today, we have *nearly* universal adult suffrage. However, some people in the United States remain disenfranchised. Perhaps most obviously, noncitizen residents (that is, legal immigrants) are unable to vote in most elections. Few people would argue that they should be allowed to do so in state or federal elections, though noncitizen resident suffrage at the state level has a history in the United States.[42] Indeed, from the early nineteenth century until the 1920s, legal aliens were able to vote for president in many parts of the country.[43] Nearly a century later, though, the question is whether noncitizen residents should be given the right to vote at the local level.[44] Some municipalities, including Chicago, already allow legal aliens to vote for school boards and a few, such as those in Cambridge, MA, and Takoma Park, MD, allow them to vote in all local elections,[45] but in the vast majority of locales in the United States, noncitizens are not permitted to vote.

In fact, many *citizens* of the United States are effectively disenfranchised because they have no representation in the national government and no right to cast a ballot in presidential elections. Residents of the District of Columbia, while full tax-paying citizens, do not have a voting representative in Congress. The District of Columbia does, however, enjoy representation in the Electoral College as a result of the Twenty-Third Amendment. US citizens in the federal territories of Puerto Rico, Guam, American Samoa, and the US Virgin Islands not only do not have voting representation in Congress, they have no voice in presidential general elections. The argument many make to justify this exclusion is that citizens in US territories do not pay federal taxes. However, they are expected to fulfill all the other responsibilities of citizenship, including service in the military; they are, for instance, subject to the draft.[46]

Another group of citizens who are often prohibited from voting by law are those with intellectual and developmental disabilities. In most states, citizens who have been deemed "mentally incompetent" by a court or who are under legal guardianship lose their right to vote.[47] Disability advocates argue that among people with such disabilities, levels of impairment vary significantly from person to person, and some persons with cognitive disabilities may nonetheless be competent to cast a ballot. Perhaps more important, such exclusion sends a symbolic message to the mentally disabled that they are not full citizens. Still, if one assumes that the capacity to cast an informed, rational vote is a prerequisite to the right to vote—which is why, for example, children are not afforded this right—some provision should be made for excluding those who do not have this capacity. The growing number of US citizens with Alzheimer's disease and other forms of dementia requires serious thought about the standards to be used in making such determinations.[48]

One other group of citizens often find themselves disenfranchised: those convicted of felonies are barred from voting in many states. In all but two states (Maine and Vermont), felons cannot vote while incarcerated.[49] Some democracies consider it unjustifiable to curtail a citizen's right to vote in this way. In Israel, for example, the assassin who killed Prime Minister Yitzhak Rabin in 1995 was permitted to vote from jail in the 1996 elections.[50]

In the United States, the loss of a convict's right to vote extends beyond inmates. In thirty-four states, parolees are not allowed to vote. Those on probation cannot cast ballots in thirty states. Furthermore, in twelve states, at least some individuals who have completed their sentences are still unable to vote for at least some period of time. Several of these states ban certain ex-felons (e.g., those who have committed particular crimes or have been convicted of multiple felonies) from voting for life. Though states have procedures by which voting rights can be restored, the process is usually complicated and discourages ex-felons from completing it.[51]

Over 6 million Americans are estimated to "have currently or permanently lost their voting rights as a result of a felony conviction," including nearly 8 percent of all Black adults. Of those who have become disenfranchised for this reason, 3.1 million are former inmates who have served their time.[52] Some polling has shown that 80 percent of Americans think ex-felons should have their voting rights restored once they are out of jail. When specific crimes are listed, however, support for restoration drops. This issue is certain to remain controversial as civil rights and civil liberties groups push for full restoration of felons' voting rights, while others, particularly victims' rights organizations, oppose it.[53]

Though not an outright prohibition, a recent restriction on the ability of certain Americans to vote is worth mentioning. Voter identification laws require voters to show some form of identification at the polling place. These laws have become popular in recent years, particularly with Republican legislatures, and are now in place in thirty-four states.[54] Some of these laws are relatively benign and permit a variety of forms of identification; others require certain types of photo ID. In Texas, for instance, a license to carry a concealed handgun is among the approved forms of identification, but a student ID card, issued by an accredited college or university in the state, is not. In addition, some states have procedures for voting when an individual does not have the proper identification that are relatively lenient (e.g., signing an affidavit of identity) while other states use procedures that are quite strict, including casting a provisional ballot and taking steps after Election Day in order to have the provisional ballot counted. Seven states have strict photo ID requirements while another three have strict non-photo ID requirements.[55]

Those who support strict voter identification laws argue that they are necessary to prevent voter fraud. They note that identification is needed to do many things in society, including drive a car or board an airplane. If it's reasonable to require identification in those instances, why not for voting? Opponents of these laws point out that voter fraud is extremely rare and the particular kind of fraud that ID laws address—voter impersonation fraud—is nearly nonexistent.[56] Despite the claims made by Donald Trump following the 2016 election that "millions of people" had voted illegally, very few of the over 137 million votes cast were even alleged to have been fraudulent, let alone confirmed to have been so.[57] Furthermore, opponents of strict voter ID laws point out that voting is a right whereas driving and flying are not. Restricting a right ought to be done cautiously and with minimal chance of infringing on that right.

Ultimately, the concern about voter identification laws, especially those that are more restrictive, is that they may disproportionately affect people who are elderly, poor, and from minority communities. The Brennan Center for Justice estimates that 11 percent of eligible voters in the United States, including 25 percent of African Americans and 18 percent of those older than age sixty-five, do not have the kind of photo ID that many of these laws require.[58] In a report issued for a lawsuit against the voter ID law in Texas, political scientist Stephen Ansolabehere found that more than 600,000 registered voters in that state did not have an approved form of identification. In addition, Hispanics were 50 percent, and Blacks 100 percent, more likely than Whites not to have the proper identification.[59] Of course, some number of individuals without approved identification won't vote regardless of whether there are strict voter ID laws in place. However, for those who might be encouraged to vote, the cost—both in dollars and in effort—of obtaining the required identification may be enough of a burden to discourage them from voting. This is why many opponents of strict voter identification laws, including former US Attorney General Eric Holder, argue that they're a modern form of the poll tax.[60]

The exceptions to universal suffrage noted earlier may or may not be justified. In any case, when a polity excludes some of those living under its laws from participating in the making of those laws, a basic tenet of democracy is violated. Therefore, the withdrawal of voting rights ought to be done with great caution and only after earnest deliberation.

▶ *The Legislative Electoral System*

As discussed in Chapter 1, elections are instruments of democracy. The form the instrument takes, and the type of democracy it helps produce, are shaped in part by the electoral system in use in a given country. Representation, in particular, is influenced by the system in place for legislative elections. Among other things, the electoral system determines how votes get translated into party seats in the legislature and whether a district will have only one or more than one representative. In a system like the one in use in the United States, district boundaries also affect the outcomes of elections. Thus, the process of drawing those lines becomes extremely important. This section first discusses the types of legislative electoral systems, then covers issues of legislative redistricting in the United States.

Choosing Legislators: Single-Member Plurality Versus Proportional Representation

Broadly speaking, there are two types of electoral systems for choosing legislators. (In fact, there are a number of "mixed systems" that combine elements of the two systems we are about to discuss.[61]) The oldest system and the one in use for parliamentary elections in Great Britain and many of its former colonies—including the United States—is the single-member plurality (SMP), or "first-past-the-post," system. Under this arrangement, only one person represents each legislative district. The winner in any given district is the person who gets a plurality of the votes; that is, the person who gets the most votes, but not necessarily a majority of votes, wins the election.[62] In the United States, single-member congressional districts are the product of a 1967 federal law and are not a constitutional requirement.[63]

Alternatively, legislative elections could be conducted under some form of proportional representation (PR). PR systems allow for an allocation of legislative seats in proportion to the votes received by the parties contesting an election. Thus, PR requires multimember districts. The varieties of PR systems are too great to detail here.[64] It is important to realize, however, that PR is more widely used in the world's democracies than is SMP. Indeed, twice as many countries use some form of PR as use SMP.[65]

Under PR, the number of seats in the legislature a party receives for a given district corresponds, roughly, to the proportion of the vote it receives. Assume, for example, we have a state with ten representatives and all ten legislative seats are contained in a single, statewide district. If Party A receives 50 percent of the vote, Party B receives 30 percent, and Party C receives 20 percent, those parties would receive five, three, and two seats, respectively.[66] As a point of comparison, let us now assume that our hypothetical state is broken into ten single-member districts, with Party A receiving a plurality in each district, and Parties B and C sharing the rest of the vote in each. Under SMP, Party A would hold all ten seats. In other words, PR would give all parties representation according to the proportion of the vote each received, while SMP would give all representation to one party.

This example points to an argument that advocates of PR often make, namely, that it is fairer than SMP. If a party wins 40 percent of the vote, why should it not win 40 percent of the seats? It is simply wrong, according to this perspective, to allow a significant minority in a state to be deprived of representation of their views. Though examples of extreme disparity of seats to votes are relatively rare, disproportionate outcomes do occur. In Iowa in 1994, for example, Democratic candidates for the House of Representatives received between 38 and 46 percent of the vote (depending on the district) and so lost in each of Iowa's five districts. Therefore, although Democrats made up roughly 42 percent of the Iowa electorate in 1994, they received 0 percent of the seats in the House!

PR advocates also maintain that proportional systems provide for representation of a wider variety of viewpoints in society. Indeed, PR encourages multiparty systems, whereas SMP tends to produce systems with only two parties. The tendency of SMP to produce a two-party system is often referred to as Duverger's Law.[67] Small parties have a hard time getting votes under SMP because most of their potential supporters will view a vote for a "third party" as a wasted vote. As only one candidate in a given district can win, the two largest parties will get the vast majority of votes. Would-be minor-party members are better off supporting the major party closest to their views than making a futile effort to help elect a minor-party candidate. Thus, third parties rarely form under SMP and, when they do, they virtually never win elections.

Because voters are given more choice under PR, advocates of proportional systems also claim that turnout is likely to be higher under PR than under non-proportional systems. In fact, voter turnout does tend to be higher in PR systems than in those using SMP.[68] Though the difference may not be as great as PR's advocates contend, the level of proportionality in an electoral system has a significant positive impact on turnout levels.[69]

Critics of PR contend that it has the potential for instability. If more than two parties win seats in a legislature, it increases the likelihood that no party will control a majority of the seats, meaning a coalition will have to form to run the legislature (or the entire government in parliamentary systems). When minor parties are part of a governing coalition, they might pull out of the coalition if they become unhappy, causing the government to fall and early elections to be called. The most obvious example of this phenomenon is Italy: The Italian electoral system is a form of PR, and the country has had more than fifty governments since World War II. The constant threat of government collapse gives minor parties far more power in a governing coalition than their numbers in the electorate (or seats in the legislature) would dictate.

Regardless of whether they help form the government, the very presence of small parties in a legislature disturbs some critics of PR.[70] Small parties tend to be ideologically cohesive and, as a result, are often more extreme than larger, "big tent" parties. Consequently, politics may become more polarized in countries whose electoral systems welcome minor parties. Furthermore, the presence of so many parties makes it hard to assign responsibility for government performance and can ultimately confuse the voters. Finally, the PR model spreads representatives over a larger geographical area and may disrupt constituency-representative linkages.

In politics, almost every decision requires trade-offs. In the debate over the most preferable electoral system, the trade-off is between fair representation of a variety of viewpoints on the one hand, and stable, accountable government on the other.[71] The choice of an electoral system has real consequences not only in terms of representation and government formation but with regard to policy outcomes. For that reason, it is important to consider the merits of the two broad types of electoral systems (or of a mixed system) even if, as is presently the case, there is little chance that the United States would move to a PR system.

Legislative Redistricting

Because the United States has single-member districts, it is necessary to draw boundary lines between those districts. This process, called *redistricting*, is typically conducted once every ten years following the constitutionally required census that is taken at the beginning of each decade. The census is taken for the purpose of apportionment, which "is the process of dividing the 435 memberships, or seats, in the US House of Representatives among the 50 states."[72] On the basis of the decennial census, the population in some states will be found to have decreased or increased. As a result, those states will lose or gain representation in the House in the process of reapportionment. In 2010, eight states gained a total of twelve seats, including Texas (which gained four seats) and Florida (which gained two). Those twelve seats came at the expense of ten states that lost seats, including New York and Ohio, which each lost two.[73]

Though changes to district lines take place in virtually all states every ten years, such changes are particularly necessary in states where reapportionment has occurred. In most states, the redistricting process is handled by the state legislature. Though the legislature's plan must meet with the governor's approval, the majority party in a state legislature will essentially control the redistricting process. This means that the lines will be "gerrymandered," or drawn so as to give the majority party an advantage in future elections.[74] When the governor is from the minority party, the majority in the legislature is less free to do as it pleases but typically still has the strongest influence over the final map.

Legal requirements govern the redistricting process and limit the amount of gerrymandering that takes place. A series of Supreme Court cases beginning in the 1960s revolutionized the way district boundaries were drawn. In the first of these cases, *Baker v. Carr* (1962), the Court determined that redistricting disputes were justiciable, that is, they could be brought before the courts for resolution. As a result, many such disputes were taken to court. Gary Cox and Jonathan Katz note that "within a year of the decision, all but 14 states were involved in reapportionment suits."[75]

The 1963 *Gray v. Sanders* case established the now well-known principle of "one person, one vote." The case involved Georgia's rather complicated "county unit system" for nominating candidates. In effect, this system gave more weight to the votes of rural Georgians than to those residing in urban areas, because it gave rural counties a disproportionately large number of "units," which were used to determine the Democratic Party's nominations. This posed a problem because, as Justice Douglas wrote in the majority opinion:

> The concept of "we the people" under the Constitution visualizes no preferred class of voters but equality among those who meet the basic qualifications. The idea that every voter is equal to every other voter in his State, when he casts his ballot in favor of one of several competing candidates, underlies many of our decisions.[128]

Furthermore, "there is no indication in the Constitution that homesite or occupation affords a permissible basis for distinguishing between qualified voters within the State." Douglas ended his argument by appealing to some of the sacred texts of American politics and coined the phrase that now governs voting rights: "The conception of political equality from the Declaration of Independence, to Lincoln's Gettysburg Address, to the Fifteenth, Seventeenth, and Nineteenth Amendments can mean only one thing—one person, one vote."[76] That principle was applied, in short order, to state legislative elections (*Reynolds* v. *Sims,* 1964) and to those for the US House of Representatives (*Wesberry* v. *Sanders,* 1964).

By the early 1980s, a new era of redistricting battles emerged. As Bruce Cain and his coauthors note, "If anyone seriously thought that the one-person, one-vote constraint could cabin political mischief, the 1981 redistrictings dispelled that illusion."[77] Concerns began to arise over vote dilution in terms both of race and partisanship. In a 1980 case (*City of Mobile* v. *Bolden*), the Supreme Court had ruled that for minority plaintiffs to claim that their voting strength would be diluted by redistricting plans, they had to show an intention to discriminate on the part of those drawing district lines. In response, Congress amended Section 2 of the VRA in 1982 to require only that the effects of a redistricting plan be discriminatory.[78] That, in turn, led to *Thornburg* v. *Gingles,* a 1986 case in which the Court developed a three-pronged test for vote dilution cases: the minority community must be large and compact and able to constitute a majority in a single-member district; the minority community must be politically cohesive; and its preferred candidates must consistently lose at the polls.[79]

The *Gingles* decision initiated the creation of majority-minority districts in numerous states.[80] These districts, in which a minority group constitutes a majority, quickly spawned lawsuits. The most famous of these cases, North Carolina's Twelfth Congressional District, was challenged and struck down in *Shaw* v. *Reno* (1993). The district involved had an extremely distorted shape so that it would include enough African-American voters to construct a majority (Figure 2.2). One scholar has described the district as "a long, twisting strand of spaghetti that extended 160 miles from Gastonia to Durham."[81] The Supreme Court ruled that the Twelfth had no purpose other than to place voters in a district based on race. In her majority opinion for the Court, Justice Sandra Day O'Connor even suggested that the district bore "an uncomfortable resemblance to political apartheid."[82]

FIGURE 2.2 *North Carolina's Twelfth Congressional District, 1992*

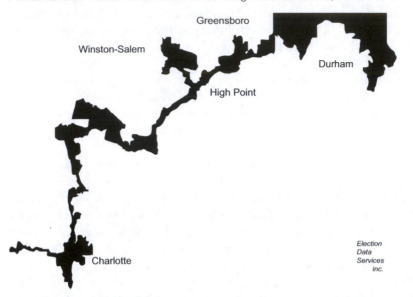

Source: Produced by Election Data Services, Inc. (www.electiondataservices.com.) www.senate. leg.state.mn.us/departments/scr/redist/redsum/NCSUM.

Later cases, such as *Miller* v. *Johnson* (1995), attempted to clarify the Court's standard that race could be taken into consideration but could not be the overriding justification for particular district boundaries. Yet some confusion remained over exactly how to protect minority voting rights. However, in *Georgia* v. *Ashcroft* (2003), states were given options for avoiding the dilution of minority voting strength. They could, for instance, create a small number of districts in each of which a large concentration of minority voters essentially control the selection of a representative; or they could create a larger number of districts, each with a smaller but still significant number of minority voters, who thereby exert influence on the choice of more representatives but cannot solely determine election outcomes.[83]

The Supreme Court first ruled that gerrymanders based on partisanship or "politics" (as opposed to race) are justiciable in *Davis* v. *Bandemer* (1986). In challenging a redistricting map, the Court ruled, a party had to show "evidence of continued frustration of the will of the majority of the voters or effective denial to a minority of voters of a fair chance to influence the political process."[84] Such evidence is exceedingly difficult to find, but the Court has recently reaffirmed the possibility that gerrymandered districts could be so partisan as to violate constitutional protections. In *Vieth* v. *Jubelirer* (2004), the Court upheld a Republican-drawn map in Pennsylvania in a very complicated decision that had four justices arguing for the nonjusticiability of partisan gerrymanders, four justices presenting three separate opinions in which they established new standards to be applied to the redistricting process, and one justice (Kennedy) who "would not foreclose judicial review entirely, nor would he reverse or reaffirm *Davis* v. *Bandemer,* nor would he sign onto any of the standards proposed by the plaintiffs or the other justices," but who sided with those arguing that the Pennsylvania map was acceptable.[85] It remains theoretically possible, therefore, to draw a map that is so egregiously partisan that the Court would strike it down, but what standard one would invoke to win such a ruling is unclear.

In general, then, the guidelines for redistricting are something of a "hodge-podge," given that the Supreme Court has yet to establish a clear standard and that legislative maps are drawn by the states, each of which is governed by its own set of laws. Nevertheless, there are some traditional principles that are widely recognized as worthy of respect. Jason Barabas and Jennifer Jerit identify seven such principles. Though no state uses all seven, three states officially use six of them, and thirty-two others use at least one. According to these principles, districts should be contiguous, meaning they should each be "a single geographic piece"; they should also be as compact as possible; communities of interest, which are "groups of people united by common social, political, economic or ethnic characteristics," should be preserved; political subdivisions, such as cities, towns, or counties, should be respected; and district lines should not change dramatically from one redistricting cycle to the next (that is, the "district core" should be preserved). In addition, though some states expressly prohibit taking this factor into account, many states allow as a matter of principle the protection of incumbents when lines are drawn.[86]

This final consideration raises the question of fairness in the redistricting process. To what extent, as critics of this system maintain, do politicians pick the voters before the voters get to pick the politicians? If lines are drawn to protect incumbents or to give one party an advantage over rivals, the electoral playing field may be uneven.[87] Indeed, there is an alarming lack of competition in American legislative elections.[88] Typically, fewer than forty seats in the US House of Representatives are considered competitive. That is, in more than nine of ten districts in the country, the race for Congress is essentially over before it begins. The same is true for most state legislatures. In Pennsylvania in 2016, for example, 49 percent of 203 General Assembly races were unopposed, and 92 percent were won with 55 percent of the vote or more.[89]

Is redistricting the culprit? Considerable debate about this appears in the academic literature. Some scholars find that partisan redistricting is a significant factor in explaining the lack of competition.[90] Others argue that different factors, rather than redistricting, make most districts safe for one party or the other. They point to recent trends among voters to move into like-minded districts or to change their partisanship to reflect those around them and to the increasing financial advantage of incumbents over challengers.[91] However, there is no debating the conclusion that competition for congressional seats has declined sharply in recent years.[92]

Whether redistricting is to blame for that decline, to many the process appears grossly unfair. Some, therefore, suggest that bipartisan or nonpartisan redistricting commissions be used to draw district boundaries. Though the typical redistricting process is a legislative one, twenty-four states rely on a commission in one way or another during that process.[93] The selection of members of such commissions and the process for adopting redistricting plans vary from state to state. In five states, a commission is used merely as a fallback when the legislature fails to come up with a plan; in thirteen others, a commission is given primary authority to draw state legislative or congressional maps.[94] Whether backups or primary authorities, the composition of most redistricting commissions is partisan. Some states, however, use bipartisan commissions, and one—Iowa—uses nonpartisan legislative staff to draw lines (though the plans must ultimately be approved by the governor and General Assembly). Some questions exists about whether bipartisan commissions actually produce fairer plans than legislatures or partisan commissions, but Michael McDonald found them quite likely to strike bipartisan compromises in drawing maps.[95] As a result, bipartisan redistricting commissions are likely to remain a top priority of election reformers.

▶ Presidential Elections

In countries with parliamentary systems, the only national elections are those for parliament. The majority party in parliament, not the voters, selects the head of government from among its members. In presidential (and semi-presidential) systems, the chief executive is popularly elected. The presidential election system in the United States, however, is unlike any other system in the world for choosing a president.

The Electoral College is not only unique; it is the source of much confusion among Americans. In the aftermath of the 2000 presidential election, Americans learned a great deal about how this arcane institution operates—though, more than anything, they may have learned how much they do not understand about it.[96] This section will explain how the Electoral College operates and will explore the advantages and disadvantages of this institution.

The Electoral College

The Electoral College is made up of 538 electors who cast votes for president on behalf of their respective states. Each state (plus the District of Columbia) is allotted a number of electors equal to the number of members of the House of Representatives and the Senate from that state. For example, Illinois currently has eighteen representatives and, like all states, two senators; therefore, Illinois has twenty electoral votes.

To win the presidency, a presidential candidate must secure a majority of the votes (or 270) in the Electoral College. Originally, state legislatures chose presidential electors. This had changed by 1836, though the legislature in South Carolina continued to choose that state's electors until 1860.[97] Today, electors are chosen by popular vote. In all states but Maine and Nebraska, the plurality winner of the state's popular vote wins all of the state's electors.[98] This so-called "unit rule" makes it possible to win the national popular vote but lose the Electoral College, as Al Gore did in 2000 and Hillary Clinton did in 2016.

The identity of the electors is a mystery to most voters. In only eight states do the names of the presidential electors appear on the ballot; more typical is the "short ballot," which lists the names of the parties' presidential and vice presidential candidates. The electors themselves are party activists and loyalists who are chosen in a variety of ways, the most common being selection at state party conventions.[99]

States also vary as to whether electors are bound to vote for the ticket they are pledged to support. Twenty-four states (and the District of Columbia) formally require that electors cast their votes for their parties' tickets, but only five states have penalties for violating this requirement (the rest are silent as to the faithfulness of electors).[100] Nevertheless, though it is possible for electors to vote for candidates other than those on their respective parties' tickets, it rarely happens.[101] As one can imagine, the political repercussions would be serious for those who voted against their party.

By federal statute, national elections are held on the Tuesday following the first Monday in November in even-numbered years. Every four years, in those years when presidential elections take place, electors meet in their respective state capitols a little more than a month after Election Day, on the Monday after the second Wednesday in December. Prior to the meeting of electors, the governor of each state prepares a Certificate of Ascertainment, which lists the names of the electors who have been chosen (and those who have not) and records the number of popular votes received (see Figure 2.3).

When the electors meet in December, they cast ballots separately for president and vice president. Originally, electors each cast a single ballot with two names on it, one presumably for president and the other for vice president. In 1800, only the second truly competitive election for president in the United States, the inevitable happened. Both Thomas Jefferson and Aaron Burr received the same number of electoral votes. Because of the "tie," the House of Representatives was called upon to determine the winner (who would eventually be Jefferson). The fiasco led to the Twelfth Amendment, which requires electors to cast separate ballots for each office.[102]

After the vote of its electors, each state creates a Certificate of Vote that lists the people receiving electoral votes for president and vice president and the number of votes received. These certificates are then sent to a variety of state and federal officials, the most important being the president of the US Senate, that is, the nation's vice president, who oversees the counting of the electoral votes on January 6th.

FIGURE 2.3 | *2016 Alabama Certificate of Ascertainment*

STATE OF ALABAMA
PROCLAMATION
BY THE GOVERNOR

CERTIFICATE OF ASCERTAINMENT

* * * * *

I, Robert Bentley, Governor of the State of Alabama, hereby certify that, as provided by the laws of the State of Alabama, the Governor and the Secretary of State of the State of Alabama did, on the 29th day of November 2016, canvass the vote in the State of Alabama cast for President and Vice President of the United States in the election held on November 8, 2016, and did ascertain that the vote for electors was as follows:

ALABAMA DEMOCRATIC PARTY
Electors pledged to Hillary Clinton and Tim Kaine:

Valvier Bright	received	729,547	votes
Kathy McShan	received	729,547	votes
Clint Daughtrey	received	729,547	votes
Janet May	received	729,547	votes
Randy Kelley	received	729,547	votes
Unzell Kelley	received	729,547	votes
Joe L. Reed	received	729,547	votes
Darryl Sinkfield	received	729,547	votes
Nancy Worley	received	729,547	votes

ALABAMA REPUBLICAN PARTY
Electors pledged to Donald J. Trump and Michael R. Pence:

Perry O. Hooper, Jr.	received	1,318,255	votes
Grady H. Thornton	received	1,318,255	votes
Frank Burt, Jr.	received	1,318,255	votes
Will Sellers	received	1,318,255	votes
James Eldon Wilson	received	1,318,255	votes
Tim Wadsworth	received	1,318,255	votes
J. Elbert Peters	received	1,318,255	votes
Mary Sue McClurkin	received	1,318,255	votes
Robert A. Cusanelli	received	1,318,255	votes

INDEPENDENT CANDIDATES
Electors pledged to Gary Johnson and William "Bill" Weld:

Aimee Love	received	44,467	votes
Scott Neighbours	received	44,467	votes
Nicole Jordan	received	44,467	votes
Kathy Lachine	received	44,467	votes
Steven Tucker	received	44,467	votes
Lisa P. Albea	received	44,467	votes
Leigh Lachine	received	44,467	votes
Charles Kennedy	received	44,467	votes
James W. Albea, Jr.	received	44,467	votes

FIGURE 2.3 Continued

CERTIFICATE OF ASCERTAINMENT
Page 2

Electors pledged to Dr. Jill Stein and Ajamu Baraka:

M. Tyler Henderson	received	9,391	votes
Albert Terry	received	9,391	votes
Sara Boccardo	received	9,391	votes
Glenn Kennedy	received	9,391	votes
Gene Hunter	received	9,391	votes
Michael Harman	received	9,391	votes
Michael Meares	received	9,391	votes
JJ Berry	received	9,391	votes
Myriah King-Rao	received	9,391	votes

VOTES CAST ON WRITE-INS

Write-ins received 21,712 votes

IN TESTIMONY WHEREOF, I have caused this certificate to be signed and the Great Seal of the State of Alabama to be hereto attached at the State Capitol in the City of Montgomery on this _12_ day of December, 2016.

Robert Bentley
Governor

ATTEST:

John H. Merrill
Secretary of State

Some States Matter More Than Others

Because the national popular vote has no bearing on who wins the presidency, presidential campaigns focus on a handful of "swing," or "battleground," states where either candidate has a realistic chance of winning. In 2016, only eleven states were considered battleground states.[103] These states received virtually all the attention not only of the candidates and parties but of interest groups and the media as well. The candidates traveled almost exclusively to those states, spent the vast majority of their money in those states, and sent nearly all of their volunteers to turn out voters in those states. For voters in the remaining states—including the nation's three largest, California, Texas and New York—there was essentially no presidential campaign in 2016.

Just a little more than 25 percent of the population lives in the eleven swing states from 2016, and this focus on only part of the country and a sliver of the electorate is part of the case against the Electoral College. Those who wish to abolish or at least reform the Electoral College argue that it violates the principle of political equality.[104] That is, it treats voters in different states unequally. To begin with, voters in battleground states get far more attention than voters elsewhere. In addition, one's vote is actually worth more in some states than in others.

To understand why, we can use a thought experiment. Assume that you are the last voter of the day at your polling place—you slide in just as the poll workers are closing the doors. Miraculously, the race for president in your state is a tie as you cast your ballot (though, of course, you wouldn't know that as you voted). Now, if you happen to live in Vermont, your vote will garner three electoral votes for your preferred candidate but, if the same thing were happening simultaneously in California, that voter would be determining who gets fifty-five electoral votes.

To really calculate the "worth" of each vote, however, you have to take into account other factors, like the probability that your vote will actually change the outcome of the election, which will obviously be less likely in big states than in smaller ones. Some years ago, John Banzhaf calculated a "power index" to determine the comparative voting strength of citizens in the various states.[105] An updated calculation of this index, using the 1990 allocation of electoral votes, suggests that a voter in California (whose "power rating" is 3.344) has nearly three times the voting strength of a voter in Vermont (whose rating is 1.192).[106]

Of course, that difference is smaller than what you might expect if you simply compared electoral votes (as my thought experiment above does). In the 1990s, California had eighteen times the number of electoral votes that Vermont had but nearly fifty-three times the population. So doesn't the Electoral College, as its defenders often suggest, help voters in small states? It is true that smaller states are disproportionately represented in the Electoral College given population sizes.[107] It may simply be that—paradoxical as it seems—the Electoral College simultaneously enhances the influence of small *states* while undermining that of individual *voters* in those states.

Recall that only battleground states get attention from presidential candidates. Thus, the states that truly benefit from the Electoral College are the ones that are the most competitive. Among those states, the ones with the most electoral votes benefit the most. Thus, even though New Hampshire has been a battleground state in recent general elections, it receives far less attention than larger swing states such as Florida and Ohio. Lacking battleground status, however, even the two largest states—California and Texas—have been virtually ignored in recent years. Apparently, large and small states can suffer equally under the Electoral College.

Advantages and Disadvantages

Despite the limited playing field for presidential campaigns produced by the Electoral College, proponents of this system maintain that it protects people in small states from having their interests violated. Robert Dahl, describing himself as "baffled" by the claim that people have rights based on geography, quotes James Wilson at the Constitutional Convention asking, "Can we forget for whom we are forming a government? ... Is it for *men*, or for the imaginary beings called *States*?"[108] Defenders of the Electoral College counter that it is important to protect the states in presidential elections because ours is a federal system of government. A federal system is one in which national and subnational governments share power and authority. Contrary to what Electoral College critics argue—namely, that the presidency is a national office and should be elected nationally by a direct vote of all citizens—those who defend the Electoral College believe that the presidency is a federal office. That is, the president should not be viewed (as critics would have it) as a national representative who complements local representatives in the House and those representing states in the Senate. Rather the presidency is a federal office that stands simultaneously for the people and the states and for the nation (in the conduct of foreign policy, for instance).[109]

In their role in our federal system, states oversee important areas of public policy, including education, many aspects of health care, economic development, and security. And states differ from one another in their political cultures, or orientation toward politics, in ways that ought to be preserved.[110] "By tallying votes for the highest office of the land by state," James Stoner concludes, "even giving each state a sort of bonus for being organized as a state, the Electoral College affirms the importance of these self-governing communities and helps secure their interest in self-government."[111]

Thus, the Electoral College is anything but undemocratic according to its defenders. Indeed, two recent books supporting the Electoral College bear the titles *Securing Democracy* and *Enlightened Democracy*.[112] In the debate over how democratic the Electoral College is, defenders give no ground. As Diamond put it,

We already have one man, one vote—*but in the states*. Elections are as freely and democratically contested as elections can be—*but in the states*. Victory always goes democratically to the winner of the raw popular vote—*but in the states*. ... Democracy thus is not the question regarding the electoral college; federalism is. Should our presidential elections remain in part *federally* democratic, or should we make them completely *nationally* democratic?[113]

Supporters of the Electoral College also argue that it produces legitimacy and, as a result, enables presidential leadership. The system confers legitimacy, in large measure, because the Electoral College not only requires a majority winner but exaggerates the margin of victory. In 1980, for example, Ronald Reagan won just 51 percent of the popular vote but 91 percent of the electoral vote.[114] Since World War II, the average disparity between the two votes has been just under 20 percentage points.[115] This inflated margin of victory, it is argued, gives the winner a mandate to govern where none existed in the popular vote. The Electoral College mandate is especially valuable when the winner receives less than a majority in the popular vote (for example, Woodrow Wilson in 1912 and 1916; Richard Nixon in 1968; Bill Clinton in 1992 and 1996; George W. Bush in 2000; and Donald Trump in 2016).

In the end, defenders of the Electoral College simply believe, following the view of the political scientist Herbert Storing, that the output of elections (that is, the officeholders produced) is as important as, if not more important than, the input (the process of voting). The output they have in mind is a leader who is able to govern effectively. As Walter Berns claims, "In all the years I have been engaged with this issue, I have yet to encounter a critic of the Electoral College who argues that a president chosen directly by the people is likely to be a *better* president."[116] Why then, Berns might ask, would we need to change the system of electing presidents?

However, critics maintain that they, too, are concerned with outputs. And two potential outputs bother them in particular. The first is that the popular vote winner can lose the election, as happened most recently in 2016, and at least four times prior to that, in 1824, 1876, 1888, and 2000 (it is likely that it also occurred in 1960).[117] This outcome seems blatantly undemocratic to critics of the Electoral College. In at least five elections (and perhaps six), the person with the most votes did not become president. In other words, in as many as one in ten presidential elections (there have been fifty-eight through 2016), the Electoral College has thwarted the will of the American people.[118]

BOX 2.2   *Did Kennedy Win the Popular Vote in 1960?*

According to conventional counts of the 1960 popular vote, John F. Kennedy received 118,574 more votes than Richard Nixon. Some scholars, however, believe that a more accurate count reveals Nixon to have received more support at the polls, making 1960 another case of the popular-vote winner losing the presidential election. The controversy concerns the allocation of the popular vote in Alabama. In 1960, voters in that state cast ballots for individual electors and not presidential tickets. As a result of the election, six of Alabama's eleven Democratic electors were unpledged to the national ticket of John F. Kennedy and Lyndon Johnson; the other five were pledged to Kennedy and Johnson.

To determine how many popular votes Kennedy received in Alabama, he has traditionally been given the votes for the Democratic elector who received the highest vote total (324,050) on the assumption that this represents the Democratic Party vote. But obviously many Alabama voters purposely chose not to vote for Kennedy since more than half of the Democratic electors were unpledged. Thus, if the votes for the Democratic elector with the most support are divided proportionally between Kennedy and Harry Flood Byrd of Virginia (who received the unpledged electors' votes in the Electoral College), Kennedy would lose 176,755 popular votes. That, in turn, would mean that Nixon won the 1960 nationwide popular vote by 58,181.

Sources: Lawrence D. Longley and Neal R. Peirce (1999) *The Electoral College Primer 2000,* New Haven, CT: Yale University Press, pp. 46–59; and George C. Edwards, III (2004) *Why the Electoral College Is Bad for America*, New Haven, CT: Yale University Press, p. 49, Table 2.3.

The other possible output that disturbs critics is a "contingent election," an election that is thrown into the House of Representatives because neither candidate has won a majority of the Electoral College. This has happened only twice, in 1800 and 1824. The problem with the election of 1800, as mentioned earlier, resulted from a flaw in the original design of the Electoral College. In 1824, in the second contingent election, Andrew Jackson won the popular vote and a plurality but not the necessary majority of the Electoral College vote in a four-candidate race. The Speaker of the House, Henry Clay, supported the runner-up to Jackson, John Quincy Adams and, as a result, the House chose Adams to be president. Though contingent elections have occurred only rarely, George Edwards notes that there have been four near misses since World War II—1948, 1960, 1968, and 1976.[119]

A contingent election is most likely to occur when there is a strong third-party candidate in the race. In 1968, for instance, American Independent candidate (and once and future Alabama governor) George Wallace won 13.5 percent of the popular vote, five southern states, and forty-six electoral votes. If a small number of votes had shifted from Republican Richard Nixon to Democrat Hubert Humphrey in just three states, Nixon would have been deprived of a majority in the Electoral College, throwing the election to the House.[120]

When the House is called upon to decide the outcome of a presidential election, each state delegation is granted one vote; to be chosen president, a candidate must receive a majority of votes (or twenty-six today). Members of each delegation meet to decide how their state's one vote will be cast. This arrangement raises questions about representatives' obligations and the fairness of the process. Would members vote for the winner of their state, regardless of party? Or would members vote for the winner of their own congressional district? In delegations with an even number of members, how would ties be broken? From the standpoint of fairness, a contingent election would, like the distribution of electoral votes, violate the principle of equality because the representatives of, for instance, the one million Rhode Islanders would have the same influence as the representatives of the thirty-seven million Californians. In addition, residents of the District of Columbia would be disenfranchised. Finally, executive independence would be jeopardized. A president chosen by the House, it is argued, would owe their office to that body and, as a result, might have difficulty standing up to its members.

Reform Proposals

Criticism of the Electoral College is as old as the Electoral College itself. According to the Congressional Research Service, "more proposed constitutional amendments have been introduced in Congress regarding electoral college reform than on any other subject." Today, suggestions for change take two forms: reform and abolition.[121]

Most of the reform proposals seek, in one way or another, to avoid the situation wherein the popular vote winner loses the electoral vote. Some do so by addressing the unit rule, or the winner-take-all method of allocating a state's electoral votes. The "district plan" would give one electoral vote to the winner of each congressional district in a state and two to the winner of the statewide vote. Individual states could implement this plan without constitutional amendment, as Maine and Nebraska have already done.[122] One drawback is that it increases the likelihood that no candidate will receive a majority of the electoral votes nationwide, sending the election to the House of Representatives.[123] It has been suggested that Gerald Ford and Jimmy Carter would have tied, 269 to 269, in 1976, had the district plan been in place that year.[124]

A similar plan, the "proportional plan," would allocate a state's electoral votes according to the percentage of votes each candidate received in a state. In a state with ten electoral votes, a candidate receiving 60 percent of the vote would get six electoral votes. Obviously, the possibility of a candidate not receiving a majority in the Electoral College is even greater under the proportional plan than under the district plan. To deal with this, some proposals for a proportional plan would require fewer than a majority of the electoral votes—say, 40 percent—to win.

Another reform idea, and one that has garnered serious consideration, is the "national popular vote," which aims to ensure that the popular vote winner captures the presidency by making the Electoral College essentially a rubber stamp on the popular vote. This plan, developed by law professors (and brothers) Akhil Reed Amar and Vikram David Amar, would have states award their electors to the winner of the nationwide popular vote rather than the winner of their own state. It would take effect once the total number of electoral votes in states adopting the plan added up to an Electoral College majority. In practice, it would amount to a direct popular election of the president and could be implemented without amending the Constitution. To this point, eleven states (including California, Illinois, and New York), with a total of 165 electoral votes, have enacted the national popular vote. In another twelve states, the plan has passed at least one legislative chamber.[125]

Complete abolition of the Electoral College, often referred to as the "direct election plan," is the most radical proposal for changing the presidential election system. Under the direct election plan, the Electoral College would be eliminated, and the winner of the nationwide popular vote would become president. Because the Electoral College is established in the Constitution, this plan would require a constitutional amendment.

One question raised by direct election of the president is whether the winner should be required to obtain a majority of the popular vote. The easiest route would be to simply require a plurality; that is, the candidate with the most votes would win. However, that would likely often produce a president who has not received a majority from those voting, as occurred in four of the last seven presidential elections and is likely in years when a relatively strong third-party candidate is running.[126] For increased legitimacy, many argue that the popular vote winner ought to be required to get a majority of the vote; if the winning candidate came up short of a majority, a runoff election would be held. In a runoff, the top two vote-getters would face one another in a follow-up election held several days or weeks after the first election. Obviously, administration of the runoff election would add to the expense of running elections. Furthermore, turnout tends to decline in the second round of voting.[127]

One clever way to ensure a majority winner but avoid the disadvantages of holding a second round of balloting is a voting procedure called "instant runoff voting" (or IRV).[128] With IRV, voters rank the candidates in order of their preferences. If, after counting the ballots, one candidate has a majority, the election is over and that candidate wins. If no candidate has a majority, the last place candidate is removed and all of the ballots of the voters who ranked that candidate first are recounted using those voters' second-place choices. The process continues until a candidate gets a majority of the vote.

IRV, which incidentally can be used in any election where only one candidate can win (including gubernatorial races and legislative elections such as those for Congress), has benefits besides eliminating the need for second-round runoff elections. Perhaps most important, advocates of IRV point out that it eliminates the "spoiler" roll of third-party candidates. A vote for a third-party candidate cannot cost another candidate the election because the voter's second favorite candidate will receive their vote if a second round of counting is necessary (that is, if no candidate gains a majority in the first count). Furthermore, because a vote for a third-party candidate is not "wasted," such candidacies are encouraged, giving voters more choice.

The presidential election of 2000 brought new urgency to debates over Electoral College reform, and roughly 60 percent of the American public has consistently supported the abolition of the Electoral College.[129] Nevertheless, dramatic change is not very likely, because much of the political establishment believes (correctly or not) that their own interests are protected by the status quo.

For what it's worth, it seems even political scientists would preserve the Electoral College if it were up to them. In a project conceived at the University of Kansas after the 2000 election, thirty-seven political scientists were asked to examine the Electoral College and decide whether it should be retained. Regardless of how votes were counted, the Electoral College as it is currently designed garnered more support than any of the alternatives, but no clear consensus emerged.[130] As a result, one can hardly say that "experts agree." Much disagreement exists as to the best way to elect the president, and debates will continue into the foreseeable future. Nevertheless, nothing is likely to change anytime soon.

▶ *State-Level Elections*

State legislative and executive branch elections are held according to state laws, which makes it difficult to generalize about how they operate. It would be an exaggeration to say the United States is home to fifty unique electoral systems. Nevertheless, there is considerable variation in state election procedures.

Like congressional elections, most state legislative elections operate under the SMP system. However, ten states use multimember districts in at least one of their legislative chambers.[131] Most states that do so allow for only two members per district. Others, however, allow for quite a few more; New Hampshire, for example, has multimember districts of various sizes, including two with thirteen members each. Regardless of the number of representatives, winners in these multimember districts are still determined by plurality vote; that is, the candidates with the most votes win.

Nothing like the Electoral College exists for the election of state chief executives. Gubernatorial elections are generally determined by plurality vote. Once again, however, there are deviations from this practice. In Vermont, for example, if candidates for statewide office fail to get a majority of the vote, the state legislature selects the winner.

Most states provide for the election of statewide executive branch officials beyond governor. Typically, voters will be asked to elect a lieutenant governor, a state treasurer, a state auditor (or comptroller), an attorney general, and a secretary of state. Many states add to this list heads of agencies or departments. In some states, commissioners of agriculture, insurance, and education are elected. Texas elects three railroad commissioners whose jobs consist of regulating energy in the state. Arizona voters choose the state mine inspector.

Terms of office also vary from state to state, but it is typical to elect members of the state's House to two-year terms and the state's Senate to four-year terms. Currently, fifteen states have term limits for state representatives and senators lasting anywhere from six to sixteen years. In nine states, the limits apply to consecutive terms served; in the remaining six, the term limit is a lifetime maximum.[132] In all but two states, governors are elected for four-year terms, and most are limited to two consecutive terms.[133]

Though most states hold their state-level elections in even-numbered years, the vast majority of those hold gubernatorial elections in nonpresidential years. Only eleven states hold gubernatorial elections in presidential years (including New Hampshire and Vermont, which hold such elections every two years).[134] Put another way, most gubernatorial elections are held in midterm election years. A few other states hold "off-year" elections in odd-numbered years; New Jersey and Virginia hold gubernatorial elections in the year immediately following presidential elections, while Kentucky, Louisiana, and Mississippi elect governors in the year just prior to presidential years. One of the most common arguments for off-year elections is that they allow state-level candidates to avoid competing with national candidates for attention. This is also the justification given for holding local elections in either off-years or in off-seasons, such as the spring.

One last difference between national and state elections is a significant one. Most readers know that federal judges are not elected. Generally speaking, it is believed that judges ought to be above politics and that the process of campaigning is so partisan, or at least so political, that judges' images as impartial arbiters would be damaged by running for election.[135] In most states, however, at least some state-level judges must campaign to win a seat on the bench. According to Roy Schotland, "Nationwide, of the almost 1,500 state appellate judges (those sitting on courts with jurisdiction to review lower-court or executive decisions) and over 11,000 state trial judges (general jurisdiction), 87 percent face elections of some type."[136]

To avoid overt partisanship in these races, many judicial elections are officially nonpartisan. In some cases, of course, partisan activists work behind the scenes to recruit, or campaign on behalf of, candidates who are known to be loyal to one of the parties. In other states, judicial elections are openly partisan, with candidates' party labels appearing on the ballot.[137] Nevertheless, many judicial elections are uncompetitive, as incumbent judges often run unopposed.

Finally, some judicial elections are not the kind of elections in which more than one candidate competes for a seat. Instead, they are referenda on sitting judges. These elections, called "retention elections," ask voters whether a judge should be kept (or retained) on the bench. Some of the judges who must run in retention elections initially had to reach the bench by winning a race against other candidates and subsequently faced retention at regular intervals, while others were first appointed to the bench and were then required to stand for retention.

Many other state laws govern party nominations, voter registration, candidate and party ballot access, the use of various voting systems, and campaign finance. Some of these issues will be dealt with in Chapter 3. For now, it is simply worth acknowledging that elections take a variety of forms throughout the United States, apply to a range of offices, and operate according to rules and regulations that, for the most part, are established by the individual states.

▶ Conclusion

The history of the right to vote in the United States is a history of struggle to realize full political equality for all adult citizens. The twentieth century witnessed the the success of the women's suffrage movement with the ratification of the Nineteenth Amendment (1920) and the protection of voting rights for people of color with the passage of the Voting Rights Act (1965). In addition to exploring the history of these efforts, this chapter identified contemporary attempts to restrict voting rights. Those attempts are often justified under the guise of preventing voter fraud. As the chapter notes, however, there is very little voter fraud in the United States and the few instances that do occur will not be curbed by the most popular anti-fraud legislation (i.e. photo ID requirements).

This chapter also provided details of how legislative elections work in the United States. The SMP system used for state legislative and congressional elections has a tendency to produce a two-party system. It also requires the periodic drawing of district boundaries, a process that is vulnerable to gerrymandering. As an alternative to the SMP system, this chapter considered PR. PR would likely make the election of third parties possible and would reduce the incidence of gerrymandering (though nonpartisan or bipartisan redistricting commissions would also address the latter).

Finally, this chapter discussed the operation of the Electoral College. While there are well-known disadvantages to the Electoral College, there are also some advantages. Nonetheless, it is a highly controversial institution made, perhaps, more so by the fact that two of the last five presidential elections ended with the popular vote winner losing the Electoral College vote. Despite many calls for its reform, if not elimination, wholesale change in the Electoral College is highly unlikely.

As noted at the beginning of this chapter, the 2000 election initiated a national discussion of election laws and prompted a federal response to problems with election administration. In addition, the federal government's forays into campaign finance reform have been fodder for considerable debate over the years. In Chapter 3, we turn our attention to election administration and campaign finance with a particular emphasis on the national level and the efforts of the federal government in these areas.

▶ Pedagogical Tools

Role-Play Scenario

Assume you are a state representative and your legislature is considering a bill to enact the "national popular vote" plan. Write a speech in support of, or in opposition to, the bill.

Discussion Questions

1. Should felons automatically have their voting rights restored once they have served their time? Why or why not?
2. Should the United States continue using the SMP system of electing members of Congress, or should it adopt PR? Explain your answer.
3. In what ways is the Electoral College harmful to American democracy? How is it beneficial? On balance, would it be better to abolish the Electoral College or preserve it as it is?

Online Resources

Rich Hasen's Election Law Weblog, www.electionlawblog.org.
FairVote, www.fairvote.org.
US National Archives and Records Administration, US Electoral College Home Page, www.archives.gov/federal-register/electoral-college/index.html.

Suggested Reading

Ari Berman (2015) *Give Us the Ballot: The Modern Struggle for Voting Rights in America*, New York: Farrar, Straus & Giroux.
George C. Edwards (2011) *Why the Electoral College Is Bad for America*, 2nd edn, New Haven, CT: Yale University Press.
David M. Farrell (2011) *Electoral Systems: A Comparative Introduction*, 2nd edn, New York: Palgrave Macmillan.
Anthony J. McGann, Charles Anthony Smith, Michael Latner, and Alex Keena (2016) *Gerrymandering in America: The House of Representatives, the Supreme Court, and the Future of Popular Sovereignty*, Cambridge: Cambridge University Press.
Tara Ross (2012) *Enlightened Democracy: The Case for the Electoral College*, 2nd edn, Dallas: Colonial Press.

► *Notes*

1 Jimmy Carter, Gerald R. Ford, Lloyd N. Cutler, and Robert H. Michel (2002) *To Assure Pride and Confidence in the Electoral Process: Report of the National Commission on Federal Election Reform*, Washington, DC: Brookings Institution Press, p. 220.
2 Carter et al., *To Assure Pride and Confidence*, p. 220.
3 The US Election Assistance Commission was created by the Help America Vote Act following the 2000 election to "serve as a national clearinghouse and resource for the compilation of information and review of procedures with respect to the administration of Federal elections"; Pub.L. 107–252, www.gpo.gov/fdsys/pkg/PLAW-107publ252/pdf/PLAW-107publ252.pdf, 116 STAT. 1673 (accessed June 21, 2016). However, the commission is barely functional, with all four of its commissioner seats vacant during the 2012

presidential campaign. See Amanda Becker (2012) "The Phantom Commission: Agency Formed to Restore Confidence in Elections Is in Disarray," *Roll Call*, November 1, www.rollcall.com/issues/58_33/Agency-Formed-to-Restore-Confidence-in-Elections-Is-in-Disarray-218616-1.html (accessed June 21, 2016).

4 Carter et al. *To Assure Pride and Confidence*, p. 27.

5 See Richard L. Hasen (2003) *The Supreme Court and Election Law: Judging Equality from Baker v. Carr to Bush v. Gore*, New York: New York University Press, pp. 2–3.

6 See Daniel Hays Lowenstein, Richard L. Hasen, and Daniel P. Tokaji (2012) *Election Law: Cases and Materials*, 5th edn, Durham, NC: Carolina Academic Press; and Samuel Issacharoff, Pamela S. Kaplan, and Richard H. Pildes (2012) *The Law of Democracy: Legal Structure of the Political Process*, 4th edn, Westbury, NY: The Foundation Press.

7 Issacharoff et al., *The Law of Democracy*.

8 See *Election Law @ Moritz*, http://moritzlaw.osu.edu/electionlaw (accessed June 21, 2016), and the invaluable Election Law Blog by Professor Rick Hasen, http://electionlawblog.org (accessed June 21, 2016).

9 Specifically, there are (by my count) 817 words pertaining to elections in the original Constitution. That is 18.47 percent of the total word count (which is 4,424, not including signatures; the Constitution consists of 4,543 words when signatures are included).

10 For details, see United States General Accounting Office (2001) "Elections: The Scope of Congressional Authority in Election Administration," Washington, DC: General Accounting Office, www.gao.gov/new.items/d01470.pdf (accessed August 14, 2012).

11 The one exception to Congress's power to change "time, place and manner" regulations was the place where senators would be chosen, which, as Richard Posner notes, "would be the state legislature itself," since originally state legislators were to choose senators. See Richard A. Posner (2001) *Breaking the Deadlock: The 2000 Election, the Constitution, and the Courts*, Princeton, NJ: Princeton University Press, p. 31.

12 Kenneth A. Gross (2002) "Constitutional Restrictions on Federal and State Regulations of the Election Process," in Jimmy Carter, Gerald R. Ford, Lloyd N. Cutler, and Robert H. Michel (eds.), *To Assure Pride and Confidence in the Electoral Process*, Washington, DC: Brookings Institution Press, pp. 222–238, at p. 223.

13 Jamin Raskin (2004) "A Right-to-Vote Amendment for the US Constitution: Confronting America's Structural Democracy Deficit," *Election Law Journal*, 3: 559–573; Alexander Keyssar (2003) "Shoring Up the Right to Vote for President: A Modest Proposal," *Political Science Quarterly*, 118: 181–190.

14 Alexander Kirshner (2003) *The International Status of the Right to Vote*, Washington, DC: Democracy Coalition Project.

15 Jeffrey Toobin (2001) *Too Close to Call: The Thirty-Six Day Battle to Decide the 2000 Election*, New York: Random House.

16 E. J. Dionne and William Kristol (eds.) (2001) *Bush v. Gore: The Court Cases and the Commentary*, Washington, DC: Brookings Institution Press, p. 103.

17 For a masterful and comprehensive account of the history of suffrage in the United States, see Alexander Keyssar (2000) *The Right to Vote: The Contested History of Democracy in the United States*, New York: Basic Books.

18 The history is actually more complex. In some places, women with property were allowed to vote, though typically they were restricted to participating in local elections, especially those for school board (see, e.g., Keyssar, *The Right to Vote*, p. 175).

19 V. O. Key, Jr. (1949) *Southern Politics in the State and Nation*, New York: Alfred A. Knopf, Chapter 25.

20 Key, *Southern Politics in the State and Nation*, p. 576.

21 Key, *Southern Politics in the State and Nation*, p. 619.

22 Key, *Southern Politics in the State and Nation*, pp. 578, 580.

23 See Laughlin McDonald (2003) *A Voting Rights Odyssey: Black Enfranchisement in Georgia*, Cambridge: Cambridge University Press, p. 51.

24 *Lane v. Wilson* (1962) 307 US 268; *Smith v. Allwright* (1944) 321 US 649.

25 Steven F. Lawson (1976) *Black Ballots: Voting Rights in the South, 1944–1969*, New York: Columbia University Press, p. 73.

26 McDonald, *A Voting Rights Odyssey*, p. 53.

27 James E. Alt (1994) "The Impact of the Voting Rights Act on Black and White Voter Registration in the South," in Chandler Davidson and Bernard Grofman (eds.), *Quiet Revolution in the South: The Impact of the Voting Rights Act, 1965–1990*, Princeton, NJ: Princeton University Press, p. 374.

28 *Harper* v. *Virginia State Board of Elections* (1966) 393 US 145.

29 Alt, "The Impact of the Voting Rights Act," p. 367.

30 Chandler Davidson and Bernard Grofman (eds) (1994) *Quiet Revolution in the South: The Impact of the Voting Rights Act, 1965–1990*, Princeton, NJ: Princeton University Press.

31 See David Epstein, Rodolfo O. de la Garza, Sharyn O'Halloran, and Richard H. Pildes (eds.) (2006) *The Future of the Voting Rights Act*, New York: Russell Sage Foundation.

32 The text of the original Voting Rights Act can be found at http://avalon.law.yale.edu/20th_century/voting_rights_1965.asp (accessed June 21, 2016).

33 Lowenstein et al., *Election Law*, pp. 39, 153.

34 *Shelby County* v. *Holder*, WL 3184629 (2013). See opinion at www.supremecourt.gov/opinions/12pdf/12-96_6k47.pdf (accessed June 21, 2016).

35 Tomas Lopez (2014) "'Shelby County': One Year Later," Brennan Center for Justice, June 24, www.brennancenter.org/analysis/shelby-county-one-year-later (accessed December 30, 2016).

36 Lopez (2014) "'Shelby County': One Year Later."

37 Mark Walsh (2016) "Appeals Courts Are Dismantling Stricter Voter ID Laws," *ABA Journal*, November 1, www.abajournal.com/magazine/article/voter_id_laws (accessed December 30, 2016).

38 See Richard L. Hasen (2013) "Is Voting Rights Act Section 2 in Constitutional Danger from the Supreme Court?" *Election Law Blog*, July 17, http://electionlawblog.org/?p=53071 (accessed June 21, 2016).

39 Ari Berman (2016) "Voting Rights in the Age of Trump," *The New York Times*, November 19, www.nytimes.com/2016/11/22/opinion/voting-rights-in-the-age-of-trump.html (accessed December 30, 2016).

40 Keyssar, *The Right to Vote*, pp. 277 and 278.

41 See http://people.delphiforums.com/gjc/amend-howfast.html (accessed June 21, 2016).

42 Ron Hayduk (2006) *Democracy for All: Restoring Immigrant Voting Rights in the United States*, London and New York: Routledge; Jamin B. Raskin (1993) "Legal Aliens, Local Citizens: The Historical, Constitutional, and Theoretical Meanings of Alien Suffrage," *University of Pennsylvania Law Review*, 141: 1391–1470.

43 Leon E. Aylsworth (1931) "The Passing of Alien Suffrage," *American Political Science Review*, 25: 114–116.

44 The debate over this issue is too complex to summarize here. For an online discussion, see the Legal Affairs debate between Jamin Raskin and Matthew Spalding, "Should Non-Citizens Be Permitted to Vote?" http://legalaffairs.org/webexclusive/debateclub_ncv0505.msp (accessed June 21, 2016).

45 For information on alien suffrage, see the Immigrant Voting Project's website, www.immigrantvoting.org (accessed June 21, 2016).

46 Raskin, "A Right-to-Vote Amendment," p. 566.

47 See Bazelon Center for Mental Health Law, "Voting," www.bazelon.org/Where-We-Stand/Self-Determination/Voting.aspx (accessed April 15, 2017).

48 Jason H. Karlawish, Richard J. Bonnie, Paul S. Appelbaum, Constantine Lyketsos, Bryan James, David Knopman, Christopher Patusky, Rosalie Kane, and Pamela S. Karlan (2004) "Addressing the Ethical, Legal, and Social Issues Raised by Voting by Persons with Dementia," *The Journal of the American Medical Association*, 292: 1345–1350. The Competence Assessment Tool for Voting (CAT-V) has been developed to help determine capacity for voting among those with Alzheimer's Disease.

49 Jean Chung (2016) "Felony Disenfranchisement: A Primer," The Sentencing Project, www.sentencingproject.org/publications/felony-disenfranchisement-a-primer (accessed December 30, 2016).

50 Marc Mauer (2004) "Felon Disenfranchisement: A Policy Whose Time Has Passed?" *Human Rights*, 31: 1, www.americanbar.org/publications/human_rights_magazine_home/human_rights_vol31_2004/winter2004/irr_hr_winter04_felon.html (accessed April 15, 2017).

51 Chung, "Felony Disenfranchisement Laws in the United States."

52 Chung, "Felony Disenfranchisement Laws in the United States."

53 Jeff Manza, Clem Brooks, and Christopher Uggen (2004) "Public Attitudes Toward Felon Disenfranchisement in the United States," *Public Opinion Quarterly*, 68: 280–281; and Jeff Manza and Christopher Uggen (2006) *Locked Out: Felon Disenfranchisement and American Democracy*, Oxford: Oxford University Press.

54 National Conference of State Legislatures (2016) "Voter Identification Requirements/Voter ID Laws," www.ncsl.org/research/elections-and-campaigns/voter-id.aspx (accessed December 30, 2016).

55 National Conference of State Legislatures, "Voter Identification Requirements."

56 Francis Wilkinson (2016) "Voter Fraud Myths and Realities: Q&A [with Richard Hasen]," *Bloomberg View*, December 19, www.bloomberg.com/view/articles/2016-12-19/voter-fraud-myths-and-realities-q-a (accessed December 30, 2016).

57 Robert Farley (2016) "Trump Sticks with Bogus Voter Fraud Claims," FactCheck.org, November 28, www.factcheck.org/2016/11/trump-sticks-with-bogus-voter-fraud-claims (accessed December 30, 2016); and Michael Wines (2016) "All This Talk of Voter Fraud? Across US, Officials Found Next to None," *The New York Times*, December 18, www.nytimes.com/2016/12/18/us/voter-fraud.html (accessed December 30, 2016).

58 Keesha Gaskins and Sundeep Iyer (2012) "The Challenge of Obtaining Voter Identification," Brennan Center for Justice. July 18, www.brennancenter.org/publication/challenge-obtaining-voter-identification (accessed June 21, 2016).

59 Stephen D. Ansolabehere (2014) "Declaration of Stephen D. Ansolabehere," *Veasey* v. *Perry*, US District Court for the Southern District of Texas, Corpus Christi Division (No. 2: 13-cv-00193), 2; 42, http://moritzlaw.osu.edu/electionlaw/litigation/documents/Veasey6552.pdf (accessed December 30, 2016).

60 Charlie Savage (2012) "Holder, at NAACP Event, Criticizes Voter ID Laws," The Caucus, *The New York Times*, July 10, https://thecaucus.blogs.nytimes.com/2012/07/10/holder-at-n-a-a-c-p-event-criticizes-voter-id-laws/?_r=0 (accessed June 21, 2016).

61 See David M. Farrell (2011) *Electoral Systems: A Comparative Introduction*, 2nd edn, New York: Palgrave Macmillan, Chapter 5; and Elisabeth Carter and David M. Farrell (2010) "Electoral Systems and Election Management," in Lawrence LeDuc, Richard G. Niemi, and Pippa Norris (eds.), *Comparing Democracies 3: Elections and Voting in the 21st Century,* Thousand Oaks, CA: Sage Publications, p. 31.

62 It is possible, of course, to have single-member majority districts. Under such a system, a candidate would have to get a majority of the vote, or 50 percent plus one, in order to win an election. Because third-party candidates could deprive the top vote-getter of a majority, this system requires provision of a run-off election in the event that no candidate receives a majority after the first round of voting. Perhaps because of the additional cost of a run-off election, very few countries require majority winners in legislative elections (Carter and Farrell, "Electoral Systems and Electoral Management," p. 27, Table 2.1). There is a system of voting, however, that guarantees a majority winner in one round of voting, even if there are more than two candidates on the ballot. "Instant runoff voting" (IRV) asks voters to simply rank candidates in order of preference. Through a process of elimination of last-place candidates and redistribution of votes to the highest ranked candidates still in the running, IRV eventually produces a winner based on a majority vote. See Center for Voting and Democracy, "Ranked Choice Voting/Instant Runoff," www.fairvote.org/rcv#rcvbenefits (accessed June 29, 2016).

63 For the 1967 law, see Title 2 of the United State Code Section 2c (or 2 USC 2c).

64 See Farrell, *Electoral Systems*, for a complete introduction to the variety of electoral systems in use throughout the world.

65 Carter and Farrell, "Electoral Systems and Electoral Management," p. 27, Table 2.1.

66 In reality, the math behind the allocation of seats is rather more complicated; see Farrell, *Electoral Systems*, pp. 67–73, for a discussion of the various electoral formulas used in PR systems.

67 William H. Riker (1982) "The Two-Party System and Duverger's Law: An Essay on the History of Political Science," *American Political Science Review*, 76: 753–766.

68 See Rafael López Pintor and Maria Gratschew (2002) "Voter Turnout since 1945: A Global Report," International Institute for Democracy and Electoral Assistance, www.idea. int/publications/vt/upload/VT_screenopt_2002.pdf, (accessed June 29, 2016).

69 Mark N. Franklin (2002) "The Dynamics of Electoral Participation," in Lawrence LeDuc, Richard G. Niemi, and Pippa Norris (eds.), *Comparing Democracies 2: New Challenges in the Study of Elections and Voting*, Thousand Oaks, CA: Sage, pp. 158–159.

70 To be fair, defenders of PR would suggest setting a relatively high threshold—or a minimum percentage of the vote that must be garnered before a party qualifies for seats—in order to prohibit small parties from winning seats. Typically, the threshold is set between 2 percent and 5 percent, though it can be set at any level (see Farrell, *Electoral Systems*, p. 207). Obviously, the higher the threshold, the harder it is for small parties to qualify for seats.

71 For further elaboration on the debate over electoral systems, see Pippa Norris (2004) *Electoral Engineering: Voting Rules and Political Behavior*, Cambridge: Cambridge University Press, Chapter 3.

72 See Kristin D. Burnett (2011) "Congressional Apportionment," Washington, DC: US Department of Commerce, www.census.gov/prod/cen2010/briefs/c2010br-08.pdf, 1 (accessed June 29, 2016).

73 Burnett, "Congressional Apportionment," p. 4.

74 The term "gerrymander" dates from the early nineteenth century. Massachusetts governor Elbridge Gerry's allies had drawn a district for political advantage in 1812 that resembled a salamander; the press dubbed it a "Gerry-mander." Mark Monmonier (2001) *Bushmanders and Bullwinkles: How Politicians Manipulate Electronic Maps and Census Data to Win Elections*, Chicago, IL: University of Chicago Press, pp. 1–2.

75 Gary W. Cox and Jonathan N. Katz (2002) *Elbridge Gerry's Salamander: The Electoral Consequences of the Reapportionment Revolution*, Cambridge: Cambridge University Press, p. 13.

76 *Gray v. Sanders* (1963) 372 US 368.

77 Bruce E. Cain, Karin MacDonald, and Michael McDonald (2005) "From Equality to Fairness: The Path to Political Reform since Baker v. Carr," in Thomas E. Mann and Bruce E. Cain (eds.), *Party Lines: Competition, Partisanship, and Congressional Redistricting*, Washington, DC: Brookings Institution Press, p. 12.

78 Cain et al., "From Equality to Fairness," pp. 12–13; and Nathaniel Persily (2005) "Forty Years in the Political Thicket: Judicial Review of the Redistricting Process since Reynolds v. Sims," in Thomas E. Mann and Bruce E. Cain (eds.), *Party Lines: Competition, Partisanship, and Congressional Redistricting*, Washington, DC: Brookings Institution Press, pp. 86–87.

79 Persily, "Forty Years," p. 87.

80 Cain et al., "From Equality to Fairness," p. 14.

81 Charles S. Bullock III (2005) "Redistricting: Racial and Partisan Considerations," in Matthew J. Streb (ed.), *Law and Election Politics: The Rules of the Game*, Boulder, CO: Lynne Rienner Publishers, p. 161.

82 *Shaw v. Reno* (1993) 509 US 630.

83 Persily, "Forty Years," p. 85; Bullock, "Redistricting," p. 164.

84 In Cain et al., "From Equality to Fairness," p. 13.

85 Persily, "Forty Years," p. 79.

86 Jason Barabas and Jennifer Jerit (2004) "Redistricting Principles and Racial Representation," *State Politics and Policy Quarterly*, 4, p. 417.

87 It should be noted that drawing safe districts for incumbents will often reduce overall partisan advantages, just as enhancing partisan opportunities will often make incumbent-held districts marginal; see Andrew Gelman and Gary King (1994) "Enhancing Democracy through Legislative Redistricting," *American Political Science Review*, 88: 541–559.

88 Not all scholars view competitive elections as an unqualified good. For an argument that competitive elections may even have harmful effects on democracy, see Thomas L. Brunell (2008) *Redistricting and Representation: Why Competitive Elections Are Bad for America*, London and New York: Routledge.

89 Figures calculated by the author based on election results reported by the Pennsylvania Department of State, www.electionreturns.pa.gov/ENR_New/General/OfficeResults?OfficeID=13&ElectionID=undefined&ElectionType=undefined&IsActive=undefined (accessed December 30, 2016).

90 For example, Cain et al., "From Equality to Fairness"; Michael P. McDonald (2006b) "Redistricting and Competitive Districts," in Michael P. McDonald and John Samples (eds.), *The Marketplace of Democracy: Electoral Competition and American Politics*, Washington, DC: Brookings Institution Press ; and Michael P. McDonald (2006a) "Drawing the Line on District Competition," *PS: Political Science and Politics*, 39: 91–94.

91 For example, Alan Abramowitz, Brad Alexander, and Matthew Gunning (2006) "Don't Blame Redistricting for Uncompetitive Elections," *PS: Political Science and Politics*, 39: 87–90; and Alan Abramowitz, Brad Alexander, and Matthew Gunning (2006) "Incumbency, Redistricting, and the Decline of Competition in US House Elections," *Journal of Politics*, 68: 75–88.

92 Gary C. Jacobson (2006) "Competition in US Congressional Elections," in Michael P. McDonald and John Samples (eds.), *The Marketplace of Democracy: Electoral Competition and American Politics*, Washington, DC: Brookings Institution Press.

93 *See the National Conference of State Legislatures (2015) "Redistricting Commissions: State Legislative Plans," www.ncsl.org/research/redistricting/2009-redistricting-commissions-table.aspx (accessed December 30, 2016).*

94 National Conference of State Legislatures, "Redistricting Commissions." Five other states have advisory redistricting commissions, and Iowa has an entirely unique system, which is described in the text.

95 Michael P. McDonald (2004) "A Comparative Analysis of Redistricting Institutions in the United States, 2001–2002," *State Politics and Policy Quarterly*, 4: 371–395.

96 For extensive explanations of this system, see John C. Fortier (ed.) (2004) *After the People Vote: A Guide to the Electoral College*, 3rd edn, Washington, DC: The AEI Press; and Lawrence D. Longley and Neal R. Peirce (1999) *The Electoral College Primer 2000*, New Haven, CT: Yale University Press. Though his main point is to critique the Electoral College, Edwards offers a nice brief description of its operation in his first chapter. See George C. Edwards III (2004) *Why the Electoral College Is Bad for America*, New Haven, CT: Yale University Press.

97 See William C. Kimberling (n.d.) "The Electoral College," Washington, DC: Federal Election Commission, www.fec.gov/pdf/eleccoll.pdf (accessed June 29, 2016).

98 Maine and Nebraska award two electors to the winner of the statewide popular vote and the rest according to the winner in each congressional district.

99 See Fortier, *After the People Vote*, Appendix C and p. 6.

100 Fortier, *After the People Vote*, p. 7.

101 Prior to 2016, there had only been nine "faithless" electors in the past 100 years. In 2016, seven electors (five Democrats and two Republicans) voted for candidates other than their party's official nominee.

102 For a fascinating history of the election of 1800, see John Ferling (2004) *Adams vs. Jefferson: The Tumultuous Election of 1800*, Oxford: Oxford University Press.

103 Those states were Colorado, Florida, Iowa, Michigan, Nevada, New Hampshire, North Carolina, Ohio, Pennsylvania, Virginia, and Wisconsin. *See Politico (2016) "The Battleground States Project," www.politico.com/2016-election/swing-states (accessed December 30, 2016).*

104 Robert A. Dahl (2001) *How Democratic Is the American Constitution?* New Haven, CT: Yale University Press, Chapter 4; Edwards, *Why the Electoral College Is Bad for America*.

105 John F. Banzhaf III (1968) "One Man, 3,312 Votes: A Mathematical Analysis of the Electoral College," *Villanova Law Review*, 13: 304–346.

106 This calculation was performed by Mark Livingston of the US Naval Research Laboratory. His calculations can be found at www.cs.unc.edu/~livingst/Banzhaf (accessed June 29, 2016).

107 This is the result, of course, of the two electors provided to each state regardless of population size. Just as the Senate treats states equally, the Electoral College tends toward (though, of course, doesn't reach) equality between the states.

108 Dahl, *How Democratic?* p. 52 (emphasis in original).

109 Martin Diamond (1977) *The Electoral College and the American Idea of Democracy*, Washington, DC: American Enterprise Institute.

110 For the classic work on state political cultures, see Daniel J. Elazar (1966) *American Federalism: A View from the States*, New York: Thomas Y. Crowell.

111 James R. Stoner, Jr. (2001) "Federalism, the State, and the Electoral College," in Gary L. Gregg II (ed.), *Securing Democracy: Why We Have an Electoral College*, Wilmington, DE: ISI Books, p. 51.

112 Gary L. Gregg III (ed.) (2001) *Securing Democracy: Why We Have an Electoral College*, Wilmington, DE: ISI Books; Tara Ross (2004) *Enlightened Democracy: The Case for the Electoral College*, Los Angeles, CA: World Ahead Publishing, Inc.

113 Diamond, *The Electoral College*, p. 7 (emphasis in original).

114 Longley and Peirce, *The Electoral College Primer 2000*, p. 194.

115 Author's calculations based on information in Longley and Peirce, *The Electoral College Primer 2000*, Appendix C plus results from 2000 to 2016.

116 Walter Berns (2001) "Outputs: The Electoral College Produces Presidents," in Gary L. Gregg III (ed.), *Securing Democracy: Why We Have an Electoral College*, Wilmington, DE: ISI Books, p. 118.

117 In both 1876 and 1888, the Electoral College winner would likely have won the popular vote as well if there had not been widespread voter suppression of African Americans (and white Republicans) in the South. The 1824 election is unique in that the eventual winner—John Quincy Adams—had fewer popular and Electoral College votes than his next closest competitor (Andrew Jackson) but won when the election was decided in the House of Representatives.

118 Edwards suggests this has happened in 40 percent of the close elections (defined as having been decided by less than 3 percentage points in the popular vote) since 1828 (*Why the Electoral College Is Bad for America*, p. 44). When the 2016 result is added to Edwards' calculation, the percentage of times this has happened in close elections rises to 45 percent.

119 Edwards, *Why the Electoral College Is Bad for America*, pp. 61–73.

120 Edwards, *Why the Electoral College Is Bad for America*, p. 68.

121 Paige L. Whitaker and Thomas H. Neale (2001) *The Electoral College: An Overview and Analysis of Reform Proposals*, Washington, DC: Congressional Research Service, pp. 15, 2.

122 Following the 2012 election, several state legislatures with Republican majorities, in states that awarded their electoral votes to Barack Obama, considered adopting the district plan. As of this writing, none had yet approved such a change.

123 Of course, the process for dealing with a contingent election could also be the subject of reform efforts. In fact, many of the district plan proposals that have been made would also alter the congressional procedures for selecting a president (see Whitaker and Neale, *The Electoral College*, p. 17).

124 Robert L. Dudley and Alan R. Gitelson (2002) *American Elections: The Rules Matter*, New York: Longman, p. 150.

125 See updates at www.nationalpopularvote.com (accessed December 30, 2016).

126 Of course, without the Electoral College, campaign strategies and, consequently, election results might be different. On campaign strategy and the effects of abolishing the Electoral College, see William G. Mayer, Emmett H. Buell, Jr., James E. Campbell, and Mark Joslyn

(2002) "The Electoral College and Campaign Strategy," in Paul D. Schumaker and Burdett A. Loomis (eds.), *Choosing a President: The Electoral College and Beyond*, New York: Chatham House Publishers/Seven Bridges Press. On campaign strategy and the Electoral College in general, see Daron R. Shaw (2006) *The Race to 270: The Electoral College and the Campaign Strategies of 2000 and 2004*, Chicago, IL: University of Chicago Press.

127 See Stephen G. Wright (1989) "Voter Turnout in Runoff Elections," *Journal of Politics*, 51: 385–396; and Charles S. Bullock III, Ronald Keith Gaddie, and Anders Ferrington (2002) "System Structure, Campaign Stimuli, and Voter Falloff in Runoff Primaries," *Journal of Politics*, 64: 1210–1224.

128 For animated illustrations of how IRV works, see www.chrisgates.net/irv (accessed April 15, 2017).

129 See Tables 4–8 in Costas Panagopoulos (2004) "The Polls-Trends: Electoral Reform," *Public Opinion Quarterly*, 68: 623–640.

130 Paul D. Schumaker and Burdett A. Loomis (2002) "Reaching a Collective Judgment," in Paul D. Schumaker and Burdett A. Loomis (eds.), *Choosing a President: The Electoral College and Beyond*, New York: Chatham House Publishers/Seven Bridges Press, p. 181.

131 See Karl Kurtz (2012) "Changes in Legislatures Using Multimember Districts after Redistricting," *The Thicket at State Legislatures*, http://ncsl.typepad.com/the_thicket/2012/09/a-slight-decline-in-legislatures-using-multimember-districts-after-redistricting.html (accessed April 15, 2017).

132 National Conference of State Legislatures (2015) "The Term Limited States," www.ncsl.org/research/about-state-legislatures/chart-of-term-limits-states.aspx (accessed December 30, 2016).

133 Governors in New Hampshire and Vermont are elected to two-year terms with no term limits.

134 For a list of gubernatorial election years, see "All-Up Chart of Governors by Election 'Cycle,'" The Green Papers, www.thegreenpapers.com/G16/GovernorsByElectionCycle.phtml (accessed April 15, 2017).

135 Though see Chris W. Bonneau and Melinda Gann Hall (2009) *In Defense of Judicial Elections*, London and New York: Routledge.

136 Roy A. Schotland (2005) "Judicial Elections," in Paul S. Herrnson (ed.), *Guide to Political Campaigns in America*, Washington, DC: CQ Press, p. 391.

137 Schotland, *"Judicial Elections,"* p. 392.

3 Rules and Regulations II

Election Administration and the Campaign Finance System

C HAPTER 2 MADE CLEAR that elections, and the campaigns that precede them, are extremely complex events governed by an increasingly complicated set of laws and regulations. Administering those regulations requires a Herculean effort on the part of the local, state, and federal officials and the thousands of volunteers who run elections in the United States. The first part of this chapter will explore various aspects of election administration, an area of governmental activity that became prominent following the 2000 presidential election. The aspects to be examined include, among others, voter registration and the equipment and operations that enable voters to cast their ballots.

The remainder of the chapter will address the campaign finance system in the United States. Though not a preoccupation of the average voter, campaign finance and the reform efforts surrounding it constitute quite a controversial topic among political observers, largely because the regulation of campaign fund-raising and spending produces a clash between fundamental values of fairness and freedom. Our discussion will first frame this controversy, then examine the history of the campaign finance system, the current state of the law, and the prospect for future reforms.

► Election Administration

Prior to the 2000 presidential election, very few people paid any attention to the manner in which elections were administered in the United States. In the weeks after that election, however, voter registration rolls, ballot structure, voting systems, and other aspects of election administration were in the spotlight. Complaints had emerged in Florida regarding the removal of otherwise qualified voters from the registration roles, the confusing design of ballots in some counties, and problems voting on the punch-card machines used in some places. The Help America Vote Act (HAVA) of 2002 was intended to address some of these administrative concerns nationally. However, as with so much in our federal system of government, the way in which elections are held in the United States varies from state to state (and often from locality to locality). Thus, it is difficult to craft national measures that adequately address the problems of election administration.

Election administrators around the country are responsible for everything from voter registration and ballot access for parties and candidates to the design of ballots and the selection and maintenance of voting equipment. Of course, they are also responsible for Election Day operations, including the location of polling places, recruitment and training of poll workers and, ultimately, counting the votes. Unlike in most democracies, in America the majority of states elect their own chief election administrator; typically this official is the secretary of state who, like other elected officials, runs on a party ticket. This means, of course, that though election officers have a duty to oversee elections in a neutral manner, they also have clear partisan attachments.[1] In 2000, for instance, the person ultimately in charge of elections in Florida was Republican Secretary of State Katherine Harris, who also happened to be George W. Bush's honorary campaign chairperson for that state. Harris played a critical role during the recount saga in Florida that year but, given her partisan affiliations, many Democrats doubted her ability to oversee the election fairly.

Though ultimate election authority may reside with a state election official or board of elections, the day-to-day administrative responsibilities fall to local election officers. In some states, individuals are responsible for local elections; in others, a board or commission oversees them. Local election officials are elected in many states; they are appointed in others. The point is that election administration is highly decentralized in the United States.

▶ The Help America Vote Act and "Motor Voter"

HAVA, which became law in the aftermath of the 2000 presidential election, was designed to assist states in improving election administration. In so doing, it also established some federal guidelines to govern elections in the states. HAVA aimed to improve elections in three ways: (1) It required and provided funding for states to replace outdated voting equipment and to upgrade other aspects of election administration; (2) it created a federal agency—the US Election Assistance Commission—to serve as a clearinghouse for election-related information; and (3) it established a number of requirements with respect to voter registration and the voting process.[2]

In many democracies, voter registration is state-initiated, meaning that the government is responsible for ensuring that voters register. The extent to which the state fulfills this responsibility ranges from simply encouraging registration and making it widely accessible to contacting eligible registrants or even registering all of its citizens automatically.[3] In the United States, however, voter registration is largely self-initiated; that is, individual citizens are responsible for becoming registered, and they must actively seek the opportunity to do so. While interest groups and parties may conduct voter registration drives to encourage registration, the government is (mostly) a passive participant in the registration process. Its role is simply to process registration forms and maintain voter lists.

However, in recent years, several states have begun to implement automatic voter registration systems. Under such a system, citizens who are eligible to vote are automatically registered to do so when they interact with a government agency (e.g., the state's department of motor vehicles), unless they decline the opportunity. Agencies are then required to transfer voter registration information to election officials. In 2015, Oregon became the first state to implement an automatic voter registration system. Nine other states—California, Vermont, West Virginia, Connecticut, Alaska, Colorado, Georgia, Illinois, and Rhode Island—and the District of Columbia followed soon thereafter. Proposals for automatic voter registration systems are currently under consideration in many other states.[4]

In practice, the United States has had something of a mixed (self- and state-initiated) system of registration since the passage of the National Voter Registration Act (NVRA) of 1993. The NVRA required states to make voter registration available when individuals apply for or renew a driver's license (hence the law's nickname, "Motor Voter"). It also required states to make registration available at all offices where public assistance is provided or where state-funded services are offered to the disabled. Finally, it required the creation of a form that could be used for mail-in registration and limited the ability of states to purge voter rolls of individuals who have not voted regularly.[5] The expressed purpose of the NVRA was to push governments at the federal, state, and local levels to promote the citizen's right to vote by making registration more accessible. In effect, then, it is a state-initiated voter registration program. Its relatively limited scope, however, means that, overall, the voter registration system in the United States is predominantly self-initiated.

The NVRA certainly increased the number of citizens who are registered to vote.[6] Its impact on turnout rates is less clear, though. The assumption was clearly that making registration easier would lower one of the biggest barriers to voting, thereby increasing turnout. Scholarly conclusions have in fact been mixed on whether the NVRA has had a significant impact on turnout.[7] Raymond Wolfinger and Jonathan Hoffman sum up as follows: "Turnout of motor voter registrants was lower than that of other new registrants and of pre-1995 registrants, but greatly exceeded the expectations of scholars who argued that people who registered by this method would not go to the polls."[8]

A handful of states were exempted from the NVRA because they either have no registration requirements (North Dakota) or allow for Election Day registration (EDR) at the polling place. Today, fifteen states and the District of Columbia allow some form of EDR.[9]

States with EDR have significantly higher turnout than those without it, making EDR a popular reform idea among those who would like to increase voter turnout in the United States.[10] In non-EDR states, registration deadlines are set at least one week prior to Election Day (as in Utah) but are most often twenty-one to twenty-eight days out (as in twenty-five states).[11] Though requiring potential voters to register a month before an election is a bit onerous, these deadlines are now much shorter, on average, than in the recent past when some states had registration deadlines of over three months prior to Election Day.[12]

▶ Voting Equipment and Election Day Operations

As noted earlier, HAVA required states to upgrade their voting equipment, and it provided more than $3 billion in federal funding for this purpose. Specifically, states were to replace punch cards, which had been the source of so many voting problems in Florida in 2000, and lever machines. Punch-card machines require voters to use a stylus to poke holes in numbers on the ballot that correspond to the candidates or issue positions they prefer; with lever machines, voters turn small switches (or levers) by the names of the candidates they prefer.[13] Most states had replaced punch-card and lever machines by the 2006 midterm elections. In 2000, about 28 percent of all registered voters lived in counties that used punch-card machines, and another 17 percent lived in counties using lever machines.[14] By 2008, those numbers had fallen to less than 1 percent and just under 7 percent, respectively.[15]

To replace their old equipment, counties increasingly turned to optical-scan and direct-recording electronic (DRE) voting machines. On optical-scan ballots, voters fill in bubbles next to the names of candidates or issue positions they prefer, similar to the way students take Scantron tests. Though numerous versions of DRE machines are in use, they all display the ballot on a screen; voters then make their choices by touching candidates' names on the screen. According to the Pew Research Center, 47 percent of registered voters currently live in jurisdictions that use optical-scan machines exclusively, while 28 percent live in DRE-only areas. Another 19 percent live in counties with that use a mix of optical-scan and DRE machines, and the rest vote by mail or vote on paper ballots that are counted by hand. Almost 56 percent of counties (with more than 56 percent of all registered voters) relied on optical scan machines for voting, whereas 34 percent (with almost 33 percent of registered voters nationally) used DRE.[16]

The widespread use of electronic voting systems raises serious questions about the security of such machines.[17] Much of the concern centers on fears that the voting machines could be tampered with to steal votes. Indeed, Russian attempts to interfere with the presidential election in 2016 have only heightened these fears. According to news reports based, in part, on leaked National Security Agency documents, Russian hackers accessed election systems—including voter and campaign finance databases—in as many as thirty-nine states.[18] Though there is no evidence that voting machines or vote tallies were tampered with, the fact that hackers could enter systems containing sensitive election information is cause for serious concern.

Though less dramatic than an international cyber attack, a 2006 examination of one electronic voting machine by Princeton computer scientists found vulnerabilities that are equally worrisome. The researchers reported that, "an attacker who gets physical access to a machine or its removable memory card for as little as one minute could install malicious code; malicious code on a machine could steal votes undetectably, modifying all records, logs, and counters to be consistent with the fraudulent vote count it creates."[19] They also found that viruses could easily be spread from machine to machine on Election Day. To guard against these problems, the researchers argued for changes to the hardware and software of these machines, but they also suggested election procedures that would ensure accountability.

To this end, a number of voting system reformers have called for "voter-verified paper records" and mandatory audits of voting machines. A voter-verified paper record is a printout of a voter's ballot that allows the voter to check their votes before the ballot is cast. That paper ballot is then kept as a backup in the event that the electronic machines malfunction. It can also be used to conduct random audits of a certain percentage of precincts to ensure that the vote totals recorded by the machines are accurate. Currently, thirty-four states have voter-verified paper records, voter-marked paper ballots (counted either by scanners or by hand), or a combination of the two. Twenty-two states that use voter-verified paper records also have mandatory audits; four others require audits but do not have paper trails.[20]

Beyond voter registration and voting machines, election officials are also responsible for all the pieces of the Election Day puzzle. Most voters give little thought to what goes into carrying out an election, but it is a daunting undertaking. To begin with, ballots have to be created. This has been the responsibility of the government since the adoption of the "Australian ballot" at the end of the nineteenth century. The Australian ballot is a "state prepared and administered ballot that lists all of the candidates on a single ballot."[21] Prior to introduction of the Australian ballot, each party printed a ballot listing only its own candidates. Voters would then choose one of these party "strips" and put it in the ballot box. Because each party's ballot differed in shape and color, voting was not a secret activity.

Election administrators do not simply print ballots; they must also design the ballot, which is a complicated matter.[22] A cumbersome layout can lead to voter error, as the two-page list on the now infamous butterfly ballot in Florida seems to have done in 2000 (see Figure 3.1).[23] Furthermore, the order of candidate names on the ballot can influence who wins. The name listed first is generally thought to have a significant advantage, particularly in elections where voters have little or no information about the candidates, such as nonpartisan, down-ballot (referring to lower-level offices that appear near the bottom of the ballot) or open-seat races (those without an incumbent seeking reelection).[24] As one might guess, each state differs in how it determines name order on a ballot. Perhaps the fairest method, which is used by several states, is to rotate the names on ballots in different jurisdictions so that candidates are listed first on an equal number of ballots. Many states randomly determine the order of candidates on a ballot either across all electoral jurisdictions or at the local level. Others list candidates alphabetically by surname, many list them by party in descending order according to the number of votes the parties received in the most recent gubernatorial (or presidential or congressional) election, and at least one (Massachusetts) always lists incumbents first.[25]

As Election Day nears, election officials must find people to work in each of the polling places in their jurisdictions. As roughly 2 million volunteers are needed nationally, this is obviously a difficult task. In fact, it has been reported that the United States fell short of the number of poll workers it needed by as many as half a million workers in recent elections.[26] It is not hard to understand why. Election Day can be a fifteen-hour day for poll workers in some states, and the monetary compensation is minimal at best. Nevertheless, poll workers are an essential part of the operation of elections.

On Election Day, poll workers are responsible for opening and closing the polling place and for enforcing whatever voting requirements state law dictates. Beyond the registration requirements, some states require voters to show identification at the polls. In 2016, thirty-two states required identification at the polls, and fifteen of those required photo ID.[27] As noted in Chapter 2, voter identification laws, and particularly those requiring photo ID, have sparked considerable controversy because many argue that such requirements are an undue burden on the poor, the elderly, and minority groups. These groups, critics say, are disproportionately likely to not have a driver's license or comparable document. Others argue that without verifying that voters are who they say they are, elections are vulnerable to fraud.[28]

FIGURE 3.1   *The Infamous Butterfly Ballot of 2000.*

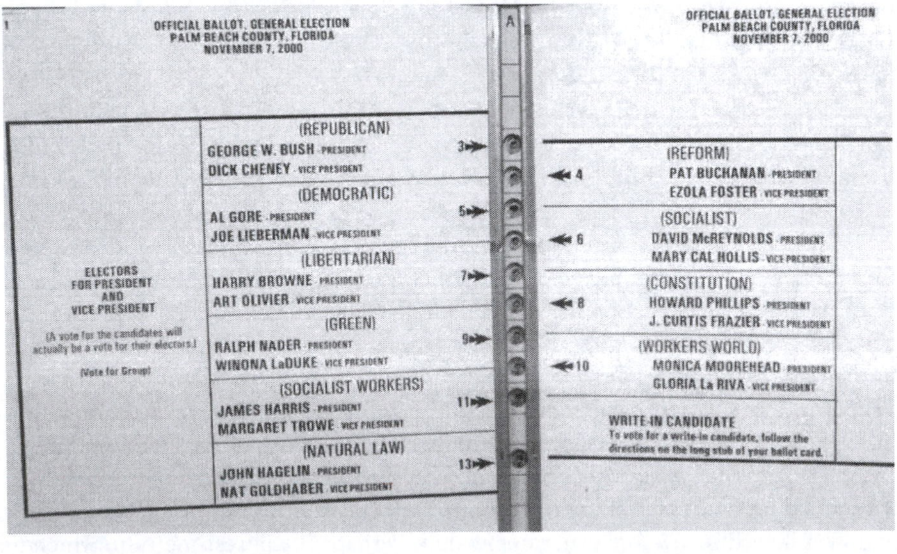

Source: Wikimedia Commons

If voters are not on the registration rolls, HAVA requires poll workers to provide the voter with a provisional ballot, which is cast when a voter's eligibility is in doubt. Many states with identification requirements also offer such ballots to individuals who arrive at the polling place without proper identification. The provisional ballot is marked and held aside until election administrators can determine the voter's eligibility after the election. If the voter is determined to have been otherwise eligible, the provisional ballot will be counted. In 2012, more than 2.7 million provisional ballots were cast, and 72.9 percent of those were counted in whole or in part.[29]

Not all voters who cast ballots in a given election do so on Election Day. All states allow voters to vote absentee if they will not be able to get to their polling places on Election Day. Twenty states require an excuse to vote absentee by mail; the rest allow no-excuse absentee voting by mail.[30] An increasing number of states also allow early voting with no excuse required (sometimes called "no excuse in-person absentee voting"). Early voting allows the voter to cast a ballot in person at a central location, usually the election board offices, typically fifteen days but as much as one month or more before Election Day.[31] (A few states allow voters to cast an in-person absentee ballot as long as they have an excuse.) Currently, thirty-seven states and the District of Columbia allow some form of early voting.[32] In 2016, roughly a third of all votes were cast before Election Day either by absentee ballot or simply as early votes.[33]

Oregon, Washington, and Colorado have no need for early voting or absentee balloting because all ballots in those states are cast through the mail. In Oregon, ballots are sent to voters two to three weeks before the election and must be received (not postmarked) by the appropriate county office by 8 p.m. on election night.[34] Oregon instituted vote-by-mail statewide in 1998, as did Washington in 2011 and Colorado in 2013, based on the argument that the system would increase turnout and decrease the cost of administering elections while preserving the integrity of the vote. The latter is a concern of opponents of the vote-by-mail system, who claim that ballots can be tampered with prior to being cast, but a study of the vote-by-mail system in Oregon found that vote-by-mail is a safe and accurate method of voting. As for the claims about turnout and cost, the study found that though turnout had increased slightly after the implementation of vote-by-mail, there is no evidence that the system saves money.[35] It should also be noted that vote-by-mail, at least in Oregon, has proven to be quite popular with voters, presumably because of its convenience.[36]

One can imagine a time—perhaps in the not so distant future—when elections will be held via the Internet.[37] Indeed, the first Internet election in the United States occurred nearly twenty years ago. In 2000, the Arizona Democratic Party allowed voters to cast ballots online in its presidential primary. Forty-one percent of all Democratic primary voters voted using the Internet from remote locations, another 5 percent used the Internet on-site at polling places on Election Day, 38 percent mailed in their ballots, and 16 percent voted in the traditional manner.[38] Supporters of Internet voting (or "I-voting") are quick to note that turnout in that primary increased dramatically from 1996, though this may very well be attributed to the novelty of I-voting in 2000. There are five states that currently allow some voters (primarily those covered by the Uniformed and Overseas Citizens Absentee Voting Act) to return ballots using a web-based portal.[39]

Like electronic voting machines, I-voting raises serious concerns about ballot security. Owing to such concerns, the Department of Defense in 2004 scrapped a program designed to allow military service members to use the Internet to cast their votes.[40] Currently, the potential problems posed by I-voting outweigh any advantages that might be gained by using it. Nevertheless, plenty of people are working on technological solutions to those problems, and I-voting remains a distinct possibility in the future.

From a theoretical point of view, both vote-by-mail and I-voting raise important questions about the nature of our democracy and "about what kind of experience voting should be."[41] Value seems to lie in what is called place-based voting, or casting a physical ballot at a public polling place. It could be argued that the effort required to show up to a polling place serves as a necessary check against those who do not take voting seriously and, thus, might too easily cast an uninformed vote.[42] In addition, the purely private act of voting online (or mailing in one's ballot, for that matter) threatens the quality of the nation's civic participation in that "it erodes the significance of voting and will hasten the current decline in levels of political engagement."[43]

Supporters, however, argue that vote-by-mail and I-voting make elections accessible to more citizens.[44] I-voting, in particular, may well increase voter turnout as the Internet becomes ubiquitous in American society. Furthermore, proponents of online voting claim that it will improve the efficiency of election administration.[45] If technological advances allow online voting to become secure, it is likely to be used by an increasing number of jurisdictions. It remains to be seen whether the promise of I-voting can be met by I-voting in practice.

Debates over how elections are held in the United States are not likely to abate. As human endeavors, elections and the process of voting will forever be plagued by errors. And as long as there are errors in the system, reformers will seek to correct those errors. Although the mechanics of elections may have been obscure to the average voter before 2000, they are certain to garner widespread attention and discussion for the foreseeable future.

▶ Campaign Finance: Norms and Background

Mark Hanna, the nineteenth-century US senator and Republican Party boss from Ohio, is alleged to have said: "There are two things that are important in politics. The first is money and I can't remember what the second one is." Indeed, money has played a central role in American campaigns from the earliest days of the republic. Attempts to regulate it have met with mixed success at best, and the ability of money to find its way into campaign coffers has led to the widespread use of the "hydraulic metaphor"—"Like water seeking its own level, private money will push its way through the doctrinal exemptions, and around the reform barriers, to swamp the democratic process."[46]

The regulation of campaign finance is one of the most controversial aspects of American elections. Though the campaign finance system in the United States is complex, a certain logic guides it. It is a central goal of this chapter to explain that logic. We begin by discussing the debates that surround campaign finance and providing additional background for the contemporary outcomes discussed in the next section.

Debates Over Campaign Finance Reform: Freedom, Fairness, and Anti-Corruption

In some respects, the central debate over campaign finance reform is a theoretical one. It pits two essential values against one another: equality (or fairness) and freedom (particularly with respect to speech or expression). Though we might like to preserve both values in our political system, they are often in conflict with one another. This conflict can be seen vividly in the realm of campaign finance. To equalize influence in campaigns, we would have to limit the freedom of some to contribute—or spend—as much as they would like, but if we preserve the freedom of such individuals to use their wealth to influence politics, we violate the democratic notion that all citizens should have an equal voice in the system.

Those who argue for equality as the primary principle in campaign finance law make an analogy to the "one person, one vote" dictum for voting.[47] If no voter is to have more influence than another over the outcome of an election, why should some contributors be allowed more influence over campaigns—and, consequently, elections—simply because they have more money? Thus, in the name of equality and the preservation of democracy, limits on campaign contributions are not only permissible but necessary. Because it seeks to prohibit individuals, or small groups of individuals, from distorting election outcomes in favor of their interests, this view is often referred to as the "antidistortion" argument for campaign finance reform.

Most of those who seek a more equitable campaign finance system would also be willing to accept limits on what candidates—and parties, political action committees (PACs), and individuals—can spend in their efforts to win elections. The distinction between contributions and expenditures will be discussed later in this chapter. For now, it need only be said that campaign finance reformers are troubled by what they see as an unfair playing field created by disparities in the amount of money candidates often have and can spend.

Others, however, take such limits to be in violation of an individual's right to free expression.[48] This view applies particularly to limits on expenditures. To get their messages to a wide audience, candidates, citizens, and groups must pay for the medium that will carry those messages. Usually, this medium is broadcast television time, but other avenues are available as well (for example, direct mail, web pages, campaign headquarters, and so on). However, opponents of campaign finance reform believe limits on contributions and on expenditures violate First Amendment rights. According to this view, by contributing to candidates, individuals and groups are simply making statements about which candidates they prefer to see elected.[49] Furthermore, because spending is a form of speech, higher levels of spending mean more speech. Ultimately, as the Supreme Court argued in 1976 in *Buckley* v. *Valeo* (discussed later in this chapter), "the concept that government may restrict the speech of some elements of our society in order to enhance the relative voice of others is wholly foreign to the First Amendment."[50]

Of course, if spending is not considered a form of expression, restricting it for the sake of preserving equality is far more permissible. But even if we assume that spending is speech, many would still maintain that political fairness trumps the right to express oneself through one's checkbook. Similarly, even if those who seek a deregulated campaign finance system recognize the importance of equality, they would argue that freedom should be given more respect. In the end, the debate over campaign finance becomes a theoretical argument about whether equality is more important than freedom in the realm of elections.

In practice, however, the competing sides in the campaign finance reform debate are not those who favor freedom and those who favor equality. Those in favor of stricter campaign finance laws have all but abandoned the antidistortion argument, at least in the legal context.[51] Perhaps that's because the Supreme Court has not, historically, looked favorably on the argument. Only once, in *Austin* v. *Michigan Chamber of Commerce* (1990), has the Court relied upon the antidistortion rationale in its reasoning. Since then, it has failed to embrace, and indeed has rejected, this rationale.

For all intents and purposes, therefore, the debate over campaign finance reform is between those arguing that the preservation of freedom is paramount and those who think it is more important to limit corruption in the political system.[52] Reform proponents believe that especially large contributions, whether to candidates directly or to politically active groups known to support particular candidates, have a corrupting effect on elected officials.[53] Though systematic evidence that money buys the support of elected officials for particular policies is difficult to come by, the Supreme Court has agreed that the potential for corruption—or even the perception that it exists—is enough to justify reform efforts.[54] Thus, the primary goal of many campaign finance reformers is to implement regulations that will reduce corruption or the appearance of corruption.

It does not follow that those who oppose more robust campaign finance laws support corruption. Of course, they do not, but they are likely to define corruption more narrowly (e.g., as actions involving *quid pro quo* exchanges) or to accept different evidence as proof of corruption. They may also believe that reform efforts will be largely ineffective at curbing corruption and that, therefore (or perhaps regardless), those efforts are not worth the cost of constraints upon an individual's freedom of expression.

Thus, debates over campaign finance reform pit competing values against one another. Those values lead different people to pursue different goals. Both proponents and opponents of campaign finance reform seek a more healthy democracy. The disagreement is over how to achieve it.

Early Efforts to Regulate Money in Campaigns

The first attempts to regulate campaign finance in the United States occurred more than 150 years ago. Though George Washington had wined and dined potential supporters without raising eyebrows—it is estimated that he provided a quart-and-a-half of liquor per voter in a 1758 election[55]—the spoils system of the nineteenth century produced the earliest reform efforts. In particular, it was the practice of applying "assessments," or requiring that those who had been given political appointments make contributions to the party, that in 1837 stimulated the first legislative proposal to regulate campaign finance. Though that legislation did not pass, exactly thirty years later a restriction on raising money from government employees at navy yards did become law.[56]

Additional restrictions on assessments became law or were enacted by executive order in the post-Civil War era. In 1883, the adoption of the Pendleton Civil Service Act created a professional civil-service system that established a merit-based process for hiring federal government employees and would eventually end patronage. Furthermore, the Act banned assessments, so that no government employees could be forced to contribute to party coffers. As campaign finance scholar Anthony Corrado explains, "The act reduced the reliance of party organizations on government employee contributions and shifted the burden of party fundraising to corporate interests, especially the industrial giants in oil, railroads, steel, and finance."[57]

The rising cost of campaigns and allegations of corruption in the 1904 presidential election led to the Tillman Act of 1907, a complete ban on corporate political contributions. This was followed in 1910 by a requirement that campaign receipts and expenditures be disclosed and, in 1911, by amendments to the 1910 law that expanded disclosure and set limits on spending in congressional elections.[58] The Supreme Court struck down the latter in 1921 (in *Newberry* v. *United States*), thereby weakening campaign finance regulations, but the Teapot Dome scandal of 1922 produced an enhanced campaign finance law: the Federal Corrupt Practices Act of 1925. This act "recodified many of the earlier reforms, adjusted spending limits for the House and Senate candidates, and placed the onus for disclosing campaign receipts and expenditures on the candidates themselves."[59] However, the new law established no enforcement mechanism and thus was not very effective.[60]

The New Deal era witnessed further campaign regulation. One of the two most significant pieces of legislation from this era is the Hatch Act of 1939, which further prohibited political activity by federal employees and banned solicitation of campaign funds from those in public works programs. Later amendments to the Hatch Act restricted campaign contributions and expenditures. The other important piece of campaign finance law to emerge in the New Deal era was the Taft-Hartley Act of 1947, which made permanent a ban on labor union political contributions that the Smith-Connally Act of 1943 had initiated as a temporary, wartime measure.[61]

Interestingly, the 1943 ban on labor union contributions spurred unions to develop "auxiliary committees" to raise and contribute campaign funds. The Congress of Industrial Organizations (CIO) established the first of these committees, which today we call PACs, immediately after the passage of Smith-Connally. Other unions followed the CIO's lead and, by 1968, there were thirty-seven such labor PACs involved in federal campaigns. Business interests were slow to adopt this strategy, doing so only in the 1960s.[62]

The Federal Election Campaign Act and Public Funding

With the exception of a presidential-election public-funding bill that passed Congress in 1966 only to be repealed in 1967, no further campaign finance legislation was adopted until the Federal Election Campaign Act (FECA) of 1971. That piece of legislation, along with the Revenue Act of 1971, is considered "a major turning point in the history of campaign finance reform."[63] The Revenue Act, which was passed first, established a public funding mechanism for presidential elections. The system works through a voluntary check-off on tax returns that initially allowed $1 (later raised to $3) of a person's taxes to be deposited in the Presidential Election Campaign Fund. The act also created tax credits and deductions for political contributions, but these provisions have since been repealed.

FECA completely supplanted existing campaign finance laws, though it maintained some earlier regulations such as the ban on corporate and union political contributions. The new law also set limits on media spending by candidates; restricted personal contributions by candidates to their own campaigns; and required political committees, such as parties and PACs, and candidates to file periodic fund-raising and spending reports and to disclose pertinent information about contributors who gave more than a certain amount ($100 in 1971).[64]

Though FECA was a significant change to campaign finance law, the 1974 amendments to it were revolutionary. The 1974 FECA amendments passed in the wake of Watergate, a scandal that included illegal campaign contributions and corruption. The amendments had five major provisions.[65] First, the amount of money individuals, PACs, and party committees could contribute per candidate per election was limited to $1,000 for individuals and $5,000 for PACs and parties. Individuals were also limited to total contributions of $25,000 per calendar year. Second, the law replaced limits on media spending with limits on aggregate expenditures by candidates (including limits on personal contributions to one's own candidacy) and by individuals and groups spending

independently on behalf of candidates. Third, the law created the Federal Election Commission (FEC) as the agency in charge of regulating campaign finance.
Fourth, it strengthened reporting requirements for candidates and gave the FEC
administrative responsibility for record-keeping. The final provision of the 1974
amendments was also its most innovative, according to Anthony Corrado. The
law established "the options of full public financing for presidential general election campaigns and public matching subsidies for presidential primary campaigns."[66] In addition, it provided public funds to the parties for their national
nominating conventions.

To qualify for presidential primary matching funds, a candidate would have
to meet certain criteria and agree to abide by predetermined spending limits,
which would be adjusted for inflation.[67] For instance, candidates would have to
raise at least $5,000 in contributions of $250 or less in at least twenty states to
become eligible. Once eligible, candidates would get a dollar-for-dollar match
on the first $250 contributed by individuals for the duration of the primary cam-
paigns. The total amount of matching funds received would be half the spending limit for the nomination phase (which was set at $10 million in 1974).[68] The
entire public funding system would be voluntary, which meant that candidates
could opt not to participate, thereby avoiding spending limits (which applied not
only nationally but in each state as well).

The public funding system also provided national party committees
with money to run their national conventions. In 1974, the amount to be
given to the parties was set at $2 million plus inflation adjustments, though
the base amount was increased in later years. In 2012, each party received
$17.7 million to fund their conventions.[69] Full funding for conventions was
limited to major parties, defined as those whose candidate for president
received 25 percent of the vote or more in the most recent election. Minor
parties could qualify for some smaller amount of funding, provided their
nominee received at least 5 percent of the vote in the most recent presidential
election. Though FEC funding was originally intended to cover the entire
cost of running a convention, the FEC eventually allowed auxiliary committees in host cities to collect goods and services and to raise money to
cover additional convention-related expenses. This supplemental spending
on conventions eventually surpassed the public funds used.[70] In 2014, Congress eliminated public funding for party conventions. As a result, 2016 was
the first presidential election cycle since 1976 in which the conventions were
funded with only private funds.[71]

The final element of the system of publicly funded presidential elections
was the general election campaign. If a candidate opted to take public funding for the general election, they were prohibited from raising or spending
any money beyond the public funds. The amount of those funds was set at
$20 million in 1974 and has been adjusted for inflation since then. Minor-
party nominees would be given an amount in proportion to their party's share
of the vote in the previous election, provided that share was at least 5 percent.

Contributions, Expenditures, and Magic Words

As amended in 1974, FECA was challenged almost immediately in court, and in 1976, the Supreme Court issued its landmark *Buckley* v. *Valeo* decision. All the major provisions of the 1974 law were at issue in *Buckley*, and the Court upheld some of them while throwing out others. Essentially, the Court ruled that spending in campaigns is tantamount to speech, and, therefore, those seeking to regulate campaign spending had to tread lightly given First Amendment concerns. However, spending takes two forms in campaigns: contributions and expenditures. The former is

> money completely given over to another entity, whether to a party, candidate campaign, or political action committee. In other words, the donor retains no control over the use of the money; the entity receiving it decides how it will be spent. An expenditure, on the other hand, represents money controlled and spent directly by the spender. It may be spent on someone else's behalf, of course, and usually is, but the spender makes all the decisions over its use.[72]

In a nutshell, the Supreme Court held that contributions could be limited on a constitutional basis but that expenditures, including independent expenditures (those by groups or individuals who do not coordinate with the candidate), could not. This may seem like splitting hairs, but the Court was trying to strike a balance between avoiding corruption in campaigns and protecting free-speech rights. A contribution, the Court reasoned, "serves as a general expression of support for the candidate and his views, but does not communicate the underlying basis for the support." As a result, a limitation on the amount a person can contribute is "a marginal restriction upon the contributor's ability to engage in free communication."[73] Furthermore, the Court found a compelling state interest in avoiding corruption—or even the appearance of corruption—caused by unlimited contributions to candidates.

Expenditures, however, were thought to be necessary to express one's views and therefore could not be limited. As the Court's decision put it in footnote 18, "Being free to engage in unlimited political expression subject to a ceiling on expenditures is like being free to drive an automobile as far and as often as one desires on a single tank of gasoline."

Campaign spending, of course, has its gray areas. When, for example, is an interest group or a party engaged in communication in support of a candidate, so that contributions to the group can be regulated under FECA, and when is such a group engaged in general attempts to further their policy agenda, for which individuals' contributions to the group would not be covered by FECA? To settle this question, the Court found it necessary to clarify what was meant by "express advocacy" so that the funding of such communication could be subject to regulation. In its now famous footnote 52, the Court defined express advocacy as "communications containing express words of advocacy of election or defeat, such as 'vote for,' 'elect,' 'support,' 'cast your ballot for,' 'Smith for Congress,' 'vote against,' 'defeat,' 'reject.'" These so-called magic words would later play a prominent role in the debate over issue advocacy and the use of "soft money," discussed in the next section.

In response to the *Buckley* decision, Congress passed a series of amendments to FECA in 1976 that actually went beyond what was necessary to bring the law into compliance with the Court's ruling. To begin with, the 1976 amendments changed the method of appointing FEC commissioners, which had been shared by the House, Senate, and president, each appointing two members. The Court ruled that the original method violated the separation of powers, so Congress gave appointment power for all six commissioners to the president.[74]

Next, Congress added new contribution limits, placing caps on how much individuals could give to PACs ($5,000 per PAC, per year) and to a national party committee ($20,000 per year). The 1974 FECA limits of $1,000 on individual contributions to candidates and $25,000 on aggregate individual contributions remained in place. The 1976 amendments also limited PAC contributions to $15,000 a year to national parties and allowed the parties' congressional campaign committees to give Senate candidates up to $17,500 per year. Presidential candidates who accepted public funding were limited to $50,000 in personal contributions to their own campaigns. Finally, Congress made independent expenditures subject to disclosure rules, changed eligibility requirements for presidential primary matching funds, and allowed publicly funded presidential candidates to spend money for general election legal and accounting compliance costs (or "GELAC" funds) beyond the amount of public funds provided for the general election.[75] The contribution limits established by the 1976 FECA amendments, in combination with those from 1974, constituted the heart of campaign finance law until the reforms of 2002.

After the 1976 presidential campaign, Congress found reason to tweak campaign finance regulations. Specifically, the FECA amendments of 1979 eased the process of reporting and disclosing campaign finance activity, raised the base amount of public subsidy for party conventions to $3 million (which would be raised to $4 million again in 1984) plus inflation adjustments, and eliminated a requirement that the FEC conduct random audits of campaign finance reports.[76]

One last provision was the exemption of certain "party-building activities," such as voter registration, get-out-the-vote (GOTV) drives, and volunteer efforts, from party spending limits. As Corrado notes, the 1979 amendments did not create the unregulated (and thus unlimited) fundraising that would come to be called "soft money." Instead, they allowed parties "to use regulated or 'hard' dollar contributions to fund certain narrowly defined activities without having the expenditures count against the limits on a party's contribution to its candidates or against coordinated spending ceilings."[77] Nevertheless, parties would soon find a way to raise soft money for a variety of party activities, including "issue advertisements" (as discussed later in this chapter).

Soft Money, Issue Ads, and 527s

One result of FECA and its amendments was a rapid increase in the number of PACs active in federal campaigns. In 1974, there had been 608 PACs; that number grew to 4,009 by the end of 1984.[78] This growth occurred in large part for two reasons: first, FECA (and at least one FEC advisory opinion) sanctioned the creation of PACs by corporations and unions and allowed them to use their treasuries to pay for organizational overhead. Second, because PACs could contribute more to candidates than could individuals, the former became a significant source of campaign funds.[79] Though PAC growth had leveled off at around 4,000 organizations beginning in the mid-1980s, the number of PACs grew to about 4,500 after the 2008 election and stayed there until 2012, when another dramatic increase occurred (largely as the result of the creation of independent expenditure-only committees, or so-called super-PACs). As of July 2016, there were 6,130 registered PACs.[80]

An even more important development in the years after the passage of FECA and its amendments was the development of "soft money." Much of what national parties do affects state and local parties as well. The dividing line between, for example, federal and state efforts to register voters is not a bright one. In recognition of this fact, the FEC issued a series of advisories in the late 1970s and early 1980s that allowed parties to raise money outside federal limits as long as the money was used for "nonfederal" party activity. This, coupled with the 1979 law allowing national parties to spend unlimited amounts on party-building efforts, led creative party leaders to raise unregulated nonfederal funds, or soft money.[81]

By the late 1980s, raising (and spending) soft money made up a major part of the national parties' campaign activity, but it was the specific uses for soft money that garnered attention—and much criticism—in the 1990s. The parties realized that by avoiding the magic words the Supreme Court had listed in footnote 52 of *Buckley*, they could fund advertising during campaigns with soft money. These commercials, which were called "issue ads" because they mentioned policy positions but were careful not to ask viewers to vote for or against specific candidates, were first used in 1996. As a result of fund-raising for issue advocacy, soft-money receipts grew from $86 million in 1992 to $260 million in 1996 and $495 million in 2000.[82]

Issue ads drew vehement criticism because they usually mentioned elected officials by name and, while avoiding the magic words, were in practice thinly veiled campaign spots. To the average voter, there was little difference between party issue ads and candidate ads. Indeed, in a study of advertising in the 2000 election, the Brennan Center for Justice found that even candidate ads used the magic words only 10 percent of the time. Furthermore, the Brennan Center found that "all ads sponsored by parties, bar none, were perceived as electioneering whether or not they used magic words."[83] The typical format for "sham issue ads," which critics began calling them, would be to raise an issue, attack a candidate from another party for their position on this issue, and end by asking the viewer to call a number provided on the television screen to express support for (or opposition to) the matter at hand.

Just as the parties were discovering issue ads, the Supreme Court heard a 1996 case called *Colorado Republican Federal Campaign Committee v. Federal Election Commission* (also known as *Colorado I* because of a second case involving the same parties). In this case, the Court ruled that political parties could spend unlimited amounts on independent expenditures for their candidates. Prior to the decision in *Colorado I*, it had been assumed by most observers that parties could not be independent of their candidates because the candidate-party link was so intimate; thus, any party spending on behalf of a candidate would, by definition, be limited by the amount parties could legally give candidates. In *Colorado I*, the Court rejected this view.

Party-independent expenditures are often used for express advocacy. Thus, contributions to the parties for these expenditures are limited. Because raising hard dollars was more difficult than raising soft money and because trends in campaign advertising moved away from using overt electioneering language in the first place, *Colorado I* had little practical effect on party spending. However, the court's decision did add to the impression that the system of campaign finance regulation was leaking and huge amounts of money were finding their way through the cracks.

A final development that added to this impression was the appearance of "527 organizations" in the electoral arena. Technically speaking, all groups whose primary purpose is campaign activity, including political parties, are 527 organizations, so named after the section of the Internal Revenue Code that applies to them. Though all such groups must file with the Internal Revenue Service (IRS), only those involved in the express advocacy of a candidate must file with the FEC. That includes political parties and PACs. Thus, the term "527" came to refer to political organizations that engaged in campaign activity but did not report to the FEC. These 527s first became actively involved in campaigns early in the 2000 election cycle, and Congress acted quickly to impose disclosure requirements on these groups.[84] However, nothing stopped them from raising large donations and running ads that supported or attacked candidates under the guise of discussing issues. The 527s would, in short order, become obsolete when other vehicles for campaign spending became available for big donors.

▶ *The Current Campaign Finance System*

The history of campaign finance reform is largely one of political operatives finding loopholes in laws passed by Congress and of reformers trying to close those loopholes. It is also a history of the Supreme Court frustrating the efforts of campaign finance reformers. Events of the past decade illustrate this fact better than any.

Recent developments in campaign finance reform begin with the passage of landmark legislation in 2002. The Supreme Court initially upheld that law in 2003 but, just four years later, the Court would reverse its view of the constitutionality of the law's central provision. Several years after that, in the most significant campaign finance decision since *Buckley* (if not ever), the Court permitted corporations and unions to spend unlimited amounts, directly from their treasuries, to influence elections. By its reasoning, the Court also enabled groups of wealthy individuals to pool their resources and make unlimited independent expenditures. These changes to the campaign finance system are profound, though we have yet to fully understand their ramifications.

The Bipartisan Campaign Reform Act

The many weaknesses in the campaign finance system, but issue ads and soft money in particular, led to renewed efforts to reform the system following the 2000 election. After a few false starts, Congress passed—and President Bush signed—the Bipartisan Campaign Reform Act (BCRA) in 2002.[85] This was the first significant piece of campaign finance legislation in more than twenty years, and it changed the rules rather dramatically.

Perhaps the most sweeping aspect of BCRA, which took effect the day after the 2002 midterm elections, was the complete ban on soft money at the federal level. BCRA prohibited the national party committees, and all federal officeholders and candidates, from raising or spending unregulated, unlimited money.[86] Thus, all money used by parties for federal campaigns must be hard dollars—those raised according to contribution limits.

If BCRA's soft-money ban was the most sweeping change to campaign finance, the regulation of "electioneering communication" was certainly the most controversial. The new law required that if an ad airs within sixty days of a general election and thirty days of a primary and mentions or depicts a candidate for federal office, it must be paid for with hard money. Note that the funding for the ads, not the content of the ads, was being regulated. If a group wanted to run an ad that identified a federal candidate, it would have to use hard dollars to do so; if the group ran a legitimate issue ad—one that does not mention a federal candidate—the group could still use money raised in unlimited amounts.

BCRA also raised some of the contribution limits set by FECA and indexed those limits to inflation. Table 3.1 lists the contribution limits prior to BCRA and the limits in place for the 2016 elections. Finally, the new law allowed candidates facing an opponent who spends large sums of personal wealth to raise money under higher contribution limits. This so-called *millionaire's provision* kicked in when a self-financed candidate exceeded a stipulated threshold of personal spending, taking account of the other candidate's spending, and was offset by any fund-raising advantage that candidate may have had over the self-financed candidate.[87]

TABLE 3.1   *2016 Contribution Limits*

	To a candidate committee (per election)	To any national party comm. (per year)	To any PAC, or state/local party (per year)	Aggregate total and special limits
Individuals can give …				
Pre-BCRA	$1,000	$20,000	$5,000	$25,000 per year
2016	$2,700	$33,400	$5,000 to each PAC; $10,000 to each state or local party	No aggregate limit; up to $100,200 (per account, per year) for special national party committee accounts (e.g., presidential nominating convention accounts)
Multicandidate PACs can give …				
Pre-BCRA	$5,000	$15,000	$5,000	No aggregate limit
2016	Same	Same	Same	Same
National Party Committees can give …				
Pre-BCRA	$5,000	No limit	$5,000	$17,500 to Senate candidate per six-year campaign; otherwise, no limit
2016	Same	Same	Same	$46,800 (combined) to Senate candidate per six-year campaign; otherwise, no limit
State and Local Party Committees can give …				
Pre-BCRA	$5,000 (combined limit)	No limit	$5,000 (combined limit)	No limit
2016	Same	Same	Same	Same

Source: Federal Election Commission, "Contribution Limits for 2015–16 Federal Elections," http://www.fec.gov/info/contriblimitschart1516.pdf (accessed January 2, 2017).

As one might imagine, the new campaign finance system came under immediate attack. On March 27, 2002, the day President Bush signed BCRA, the National Rifle Association (NRA) and Senator Mitch McConnell of Kentucky filed separate lawsuits against the law, challenging its constitutionality.

The Supreme Court heard the case of *McConnell* v. *Federal Election Commission* in 2003 and ruled, at times by a narrow five-to-four margin, that all of BCRA's major provisions were, in fact, constitutional. Only two minor aspects of the law were struck down. Despite that decision—or perhaps because it was so closely divided—a debate continued to rage over whether BCRA violated First Amendment rights.

In 2004, BCRA prohibited an organization called Wisconsin Right to Life (WRTL) from running issue ads (paid for with money raised outside the contribution limits) that mentioned Democratic Senator Russell Feingold, who was up for reelection that year, within the sixty-day window established by the law. After explaining that some US senators were filibustering President Bush's judicial nominees, the ads asked viewers to "contact Senators Feingold and Kohl and tell them to oppose the filibuster." WRTL sued for the ability to run such an ad, and the Supreme Court, with two new justices (Roberts and Alito) having joined the bench since the *McConnell* decision, heard the case in 2007.

The Court's ruling in *Federal Election Commission* v. *Wisconsin Right to Life* reversed its previous decision in *McConnell* and held that BCRA's ban on electioneering communication in the pre-election period was an unconstitutional violation of free speech.[88] Rather than view issue ads that mention candidates as thinly veiled candidate ads, the Supreme Court declared that "a court should find that an ad is the functional equivalent of express advocacy only if the ad is susceptible of no reasonable interpretation other than as an appeal to vote for or against a specific candidate."[89] In other words, only when there is *no other* way to construe an ad but as one for or against a candidate can an ad be treated as express advocacy, but as virtually all ads mention issues to some extent, a reasonable case can always be made that interest group communications are issue ads.

Opponents of BCRA challenged other aspects of the law as well. In the summer of 2008, for example, the Supreme Court struck down the millionaire's provision, finding it to be an "unprecedented penalty" against candidates who wish to spend their own money in running for office.[90] Some scholars argued that though the millionaire's provision was a "relatively tangential" portion of BCRA, the Supreme Court's decision to invalidate it "has much broader implications," such as "laying the groundwork for striking down limits on spending by corporations and unions" and making "public financing plans less effective."[91]

In 2014, in a case called *McCutcheon* v. *Federal Election Commission*, the Supreme Court struck down the aggregate limit on what an individual can contribute to candidates, parties and PACs in a two-year cycle. This limit, which had been established by FECA and amended by BCRA, was $117,000 in 2012. The Court held that aggregate contribution limits restrict an individual's ability to participate in the democratic process while doing nothing to prevent *quid pro quo* corruption (or the appearance of such corruption). The *McCutcheon* decision allowed mega-donors to write checks to more candidates, party committees and PACs than they could previously (or to write extraordinarily large checks to entities called joint fund-raising committees, which are committees made up of a multiple candidate or party committees).

Citizens United, SpeechNow.org, and the Emergence of Super-PACs

The most consequential challenge to campaign finance regulations came just prior to the 2008 Democratic presidential nomination process. An organization called Citizens United had produced and planned to air on cable television a documentary that was critical of Hillary Clinton. However, as a nonprofit corporation, Citizens United was prohibited by BCRA (and earlier Supreme Court decisions) from spending funds from its treasury—though not from its PAC—on "electioneering communications." Furthermore, Citizens United would be subject to disclosure and disclaimer requirements if they were to run the documentary. That is, they would have had to disclose the names of those who had contributed to the organization and would have had to include a brief disclaimer on the screen identifying the person or organization responsible for the broadcast.

Citizens United sued not only for the ability to spend its treasury funds on the documentary but to avoid the disclosure and disclaimer requirements. Having lost their case in the lower courts, they appealed to the Supreme Court in March of 2009. In a surprise move, the Court asked the parties to the case to reargue it, in much broader terms, later that year. In the subsequent oral argument, the Court wanted to consider the constitutionality of limits on corporate spending in campaigns.[92]

In January of 2010, the Supreme Court issued its decision in *Citizens United* v. *Federal Election Commission*. By a five to four majority, the Court ruled that corporations (and, by extension, unions) cannot be prohibited from spending corporate funds to influence election outcomes as long as such spending was done independently (that is, not in coordination with any candidate). The ban on corporate and union direct contributions to candidates was left unaffected, as were BCRA's disclosure and disclaimer provisions.[93]

In granting corporations a First Amendment right to spend unlimited amounts of money in support of, or in opposition to, candidates, the Court rejected the government's argument that large amounts of corporate spending in campaigns could easily lead to corruption or the appearance of corruption. The Court relied on a distinction between independent expenditures on behalf of candidates and direct contributions to candidates. Though the latter could have a corrupting influence and therefore can be regulated, the former could not, so there is no constitutionally acceptable justification for constraining such expenditures. Critics of the *Citizens United* decision point out that the distinction between independent expenditures and direct contributions is not as clear as the Court suggests.[94] They also warned that the decision would open the floodgates to enormous sums of money in elections.

Significant amounts of money did begin to appear in American elections shortly after the *Citizens United* decision but not as a direct result of that ruling. Just two months after the Supreme Court issued its opinion in *Citizens United,* the DC Circuit Court of Appeals relied on the logic of that opinion to rule that individual contributions to organizations that make independent expenditures during campaigns cannot be limited. Prior to this ruling, which was handed down in *SpeechNow.org* v. *Federal Election Commission,* wealthy individuals had three options for contributing campaign funds to noncandidate committees: They could give a limited amount ($5,000 each, with an aggregate limit of $45,600 in 2009–2010) to PACs; give unlimited amounts to 527s but run the risk of violating the law (because the legal status of much 527 activity was uncertain); or spend unlimited amounts by themselves (e.g., by purchasing airtime to run ads that they produced independently). None of these options was particularly appealing, so the prospect of giving large sums of money to organizations with a constitutional right to spend it was quite welcome.

The *SpeechNow.org* decision led to the creation of a new type of PAC called an *independent expenditure-only committee.* These committees, more popularly known as super-PACs, can accept unlimited amounts of money from corporations, unions, other organizations, and individuals and can expressly advocate the election or defeat of candidates. The only stipulations are that they must disclose their donors to the FEC, they cannot contribute directly to candidates, and they must not coordinate their spending with candidates.

In the 2016 election cycle, 2,408 super-PACs reported receipts of nearly $1.8 billion.[95] Super-PACs formed to support every candidate in the two major parties during the presidential nomination process (with the possible exception of Bernie Sanders). Often, the organization's founder was a former staffer or close associate of the candidate, raising questions about the supposed prohibition on coordination. Though it is too early to determine what impact these super-PACs have had, it is clear that some of them, such as American Crossroads (on the right) and the Senate and House Majority PACs (on the left), have become—and will continue to be—major players in American campaigns.

▶ *Campaign Finance Laws in the States*

Before turning our attention to what we can expect on the campaign finance front in coming years, we should briefly examine campaign finance laws in the states. As with so much else in our federal system of government, laws governing campaign fund-raising and spending in state elections differ from state to state. As a result, state laws governing campaign finance can provide insights into how various reforms operate in practice. Furthermore, because the vast majority of elections in the United States are subnational contests, an understanding of the regulations that apply to those elections is valuable in and of itself.

Donald Gross and Robert Goidel argue that, prior to Watergate, state campaign finance regulation consisted of "patchwork responses to scandals and publicity associated with specific campaign practices" and was not comprehensive in any way. To the extent that state laws demonstrated a common theme, it was "that public awareness or publicity (record keeping and public disclosure) is the cornerstone of reform." Watergate reinforced that notion but also suggested the need for contribution limits. Such limits, on individuals but also on corporate, union, and PAC contributors, grew rapidly from the late 1970s to the 1990s.[96]

Today, only twelve states have no limits on individual contributions. In those states with contribution caps, the limits range from a few hundred dollars to more than $10,000 in state legislative races and from several hundred dollars to more than $40,000 (in New York) for gubernatorial candidates. All but thirteen states limit PAC contributions, and all but six limit corporate giving. Of those states that limit contributions by corporations, twenty-one prohibit such contributions completely.[97] One interesting aspect of state campaign finance laws in twenty-nine states is a restriction on giving or receiving campaign contributions, either by lobbyists only or by anyone, during a legislative session.[98] Some have suggested that this restriction be applied at the federal level, but it would not likely be workable given the length of congressional sessions.

Two final elements of state campaign finance regulation are public financing of elections and spending limits. Though the two are different, "in actual practice they are usually closely linked."[99] Thirteen states provide at least partial public funding to at least some candidates for state office, and nine states provide public funds to qualified political parties. Three of these states—Arizona, Connecticut, and Maine—have implemented a reform called "clean elections," whereby the state provides virtually full public funding to all candidates for state office who meet minimum qualifications. Once a candidate accepts public funds, they must not accept any private contributions and must abide by spending limits. Three more states—New Mexico (for Public Regulation Commission and Supreme Court justices), Vermont (for governor and lieutenant governor), and West Virginia (for Supreme Court justices)—have clean elections for some but not all offices.[100] Some have questioned the constitutionality of clean election laws, and the Supreme Court has invalidated certain aspects of these programs.[101] However, clean elections remain a very popular idea among many campaign finance reformers.

Spending limits in the states are usually linked to public financing. Because the Supreme Court's *Buckley* decision prohibited mandatory spending limits, states that would like to have spending limits couple them with voluntary public financing. In those states, if a candidate chooses to accept even partial public funding, they must also accept spending limits.[102] Thus, in addition to purging the system of private dollars, public funds are a mechanism designed to entice candidates to voluntarily limit their expenditures.

▶ *The Future of Campaign Finance Reform*

With the Supreme Court's decision in *Citizens United*, opponents of campaign finance reform may have won the most recent battle over the regulation of money in politics, but there are surely more skirmishes to come. Campaign finance law is currently in flux, and a number of questions remain to be answered. For instance, to what extent is the law regulating express advocacy still in effect? Will contribution limits withstand the inevitable constitutional challenge? Can disclosure requirements be tightened? Beyond these questions, there are various aspects of the current system that many find problematic.

The FEC, for example, is widely believed to be ineffective at enforcing campaign finance regulations. It has been argued that Congress purposely established the FEC as a weak body.[103] Recall that Congress lost the ability to appoint four of the six members of the FEC after the *Buckley* decision. Today, the president appoints all six members of the FEC but does so on the basis of lists approved by leaders of the House and Senate. By tradition, the president also maintains a partisan balance on the FEC. Unfortunately, presidents haven't made the efficient operation of the FEC a priority in recent years. In fact, they've even been reluctant to appoint new commissioners. As of January 2017, five of the six FEC commissioners were serving despite the fact that their terms had expired; in one case, the term had expired on April 30, 2007.

A number of stipulations make it difficult for the FEC to operate effectively. Any action the FEC might wish to take requires four votes, but the party balance on the commission often precludes securing more than three. Indeed, in 2012, the commission deadlocked on nearly one in five votes on enforcement-related questions.[104] The commission is also prohibited from investigating anonymous allegations, has no independent ability to punish violations of the law, and cannot conduct random audits of campaign finance reports. The FEC is also severely underfunded.[105] As a result, reformers would like a complete overhaul of the FEC, which would include strengthening its enforcement responsibilities. Members of Congress, however, worry that an enhanced FEC would too often meddle in campaigns and, though they might not acknowledge this publicly, are afraid of being the focus of investigations. That those same members would have to enact the legislation restructuring the FEC means that significant reform in this area is unlikely.

Super-PACs, perhaps not surprisingly, have attracted considerable attention, and there are several aspects of super-PAC activity that raise concerns. One such concern has to do with the potential for coordination between super-PACs and candidates. Candidates are allowed, for instance, to appear, speak, and be "featured guests" at super-PAC fund-raisers (as long as they don't personally solicit contributions in excess of the legal limit on contributions to regular PACs). Many observers find it hard to believe that there is no coordination occurring when the candidate a super-PAC supports gets top billing at one of the organization's fund-raising events.

Another concern has to do with the level of disclosure super-PACs provide. Though they must report to the FEC their contributors' names and the amounts they gave, political committees do so only periodically. In 2012, for example, the last report political committees had to file before the election was on October 27, covering contributions received between October 1 and October 19.[106] Because super-PACs can receive unlimited contributions, there is no way to know, before the election, whether a contributor gives a particularly large amount in the last three weeks of the campaign.

Furthermore, super-PACs can receive contributions from nonprofit organizations (such as 501[c]4 social-welfare groups). However, contributions to these groups do not have to be disclosed (unless the contributions are earmarked for independent expenditures in specific races). Undisclosed contributions to nonprofit organizations that are used for campaign purposes are referred to as "dark money." A large donor who wished to remain anonymous could contribute to a 501(c)4, which could, in turn, contribute to a super-PAC. It would be very difficult, if not impossible, to trace the original contribution back to the donor. Some political organizations maintain both a super-PAC and a 501(c)4. Former George W. Bush adviser Karl Rove, for example, runs both American Crossroads (a super-PAC) and Crossroads GPS (a 501[c]4 organization). Though Crossroads GPS reported spending more than $50 million on independent expenditures in the fourth quarter of 2012, it had not revealed any of its contributors. Indeed, it refused repeated requests by the FEC to do so.[107]

The activity of tax-exempt nonprofit organizations in campaigns is itself a development that bothers some campaign finance observers. Certain nonprofits are permitted to engage in limited political activity. For example, social-welfare organizations, or 501(c)4s, are allowed to be involved in campaigns as long as such activity is not an organization's primary purpose. However, campaigning appears to be the primary purpose of an increasing number of 501(c)4s. To the extent that this is the case, these organizations are violating tax law and are also circumventing disclosure requirements. However, when the IRS tried to investigate certain groups with tax-exempt status to determine how much political activity they were engaged in, the effort quickly became a scandal. Republicans claimed that the IRS had unfairly targeted conservative organizations.[108]

A final concern among some campaign finance observers is that the system for public financing of presidential elections is, in effect, dead. Prior to the 2000 cycle, only independently wealthy candidates had refused matching funds during the primaries, including Republicans John Connolly in 1980 and Steve Forbes in 1996 (who did so again four years later). However, in 2000, George W. Bush became the first candidate who was not self-funded to opt out of the primary matching fund system. Opting out of that system became a bit more widespread in 2004, when Bush again refused matching funds, as did Democrats Howard Dean and John Kerry. However, the final nail in the coffin may have been struck in 2008 when almost all of the leading presidential contenders—including Democrats Barack Obama and Hillary Clinton and Republicans John McCain, Mitt Romney, and Mike Huckabee—turned down primary matching funds. In addition, Obama became the first major party candidate to forgo general-election public funding. Since then, no major candidate has accepted primary matching funds or public funds for the general election.

The reason candidates have begun to refuse public funding is simple: they believe they can raise far more in private money than they would be allowed to spend under public funding limitations. In 2016, for example, the spending limit for primaries was $48 million, with $24 million provided by the government through matching funds; for the general election, nominees were eligible for $96.14 million in public funds.[109] Of course, both Hillary Clinton and Donald Trump raised significantly more money than that. Indeed, Secretary Clinton raised more than $623 million, and Donald Trump collected more than $329 million.[110] To reformers, the funds raised and spent in recent elections amount to a "wealth primary," in which those candidates without the ability to collect huge quantities of cash are unable to effectively compete.[111] Public financing guards against a wealth primary, but it is effective only if candidates accept the funds it provides. Because so many serious candidates in recent years have financed their campaigns with money raised privately, the public financing system appears to be obsolete. While reformers are actively proposing ways to fix that system, the odds of passing significant reform currently seem long.

Concerns over campaign finance will continue to prompt reform efforts into the foreseeable future, and those efforts, in turn, will provoke opposition. In addition, attempts to improve voting access and ballot integrity, and redistricting and other aspects of the election process, will remain controversial. No electoral system will ever be perfect, and the human element within the process makes any system less so, but inevitable imperfection will not—and should not—stop people from trying to refine the way we choose our leaders and representatives.

▶ Conclusion

Administering elections in the United States is a difficult task. Voter registration lists have to be correct, ballots must be designed in user-friendly ways, voting equipment has to work flawlessly, and final vote tallies must be accurate. In the wake of the 2000 presidential election debacle in Florida, a considerable amount of attention has been paid how our elections are administered. While best practices can be identified, many of the regulations that apply to Election Day procedures are political in nature. As a result, even election administration is now a controversial topic.

Campaign finance regulation has, of course, been controversial for some time. At the most basic level, the debate concerns the trade-off between the freedom to spend money in support of candidates or parties and the fairness of a relatively level playing field for those candidates and parties (though an anti-corruption rationale for campaign finance regulation is more likely to pass judicial muster). Recent deregulatory decisions by the courts have meant that enormous amounts of money can flow into campaigns through a new entity—super-PACs. Furthermore, the political activity of nonprofit organizations, and the "dark money" they raise to fund such activity, have drawn the attention of campaign finance reformers. Whether those reformers can successfully address some of the most pressing problems in the current system remains to be seen, though the prospects are not good.

To this point, we have covered the context within which campaigns and elections take place, providing conceptual distinctions and a theoretical perspective. Chapters 2 and 3 have also examined the rules and regulations that govern campaigns and elections and those who participate in them. It is to those participants that we turn in Chapters 4 through 8, which explore the roles of various actors in campaigns and elections. The goal is to understand how those actors behave, why they behave as they do, and what the consequences are.

▶ *Pedagogical Tools*

Role-Play Scenario

You are a Supreme Court justice when the Court hears a challenge to the limits on individual contributions to candidates. A wealthy donor claims that it violates her right to free speech to cap how much she can give a candidate she supports. The government, in defending contribution limits, argues that eliminating limits will lead to corruption or the appearance of corruption. Opinion on the court is split 4–4; your vote will determine the majority. Do you strike down contribution limits, or do you think they pass constitutional muster? Write a brief opinion explaining how you would rule and why.

▶ *Discussion Questions*

1. Supporters of EDR say it expands access to the polls. Opponents say it increases the potential for voter fraud. Should would-be voters be allowed to register on Election Day? Why or why not?
2. If voting in the future is conducted over the Internet, in what ways would that development be positive and negative for our democracy?
3. Should campaign finance law be guided primarily by the goal of maintaining free elections or that of achieving fair elections? Explain your answer.

Online Resources

United States Election Assistance Commission, www.eac.gov.
National Museum of American History exhibition, *Vote: The Machinery of Democracy*, americanhistory.si.edu/vote/index.html.
Federal Election Commission, www.fec.gov.
Center for Responsive Politics, www.opensecrets.org.

Suggested Reading

Election Administration

R. Michael Alvarez and Bernard Grofman (eds.) (2014) *Election Administration in the United States: The State of Reform after Bush v. Gore*, Cambridge: Cambridge University Press.
Barry C. Burden and Charles Stewart III (eds.) (2014) *The Measure of American Elections*, Cambridge: Cambridge University Press.
Kathleen Hale, Robert Montjoy, and Mitchell Brown (2015) *Administering Elections: How American Elections Work*, New York: Palgrave Macmillan.

Campaign Finance

Richard L. Hasen (2016) *Plutocrats United: Campaign Money, the Supreme Court, and the Distortion of American Elections*, New Haven, CT: Yale University Press.
Raymond J. La Raja and Brian F. Schaffner (2015) *Campaign Finance and Political Polarization: When Purists Prevail*, Ann Arbor, MI: University of Michigan Press.
Robert E. Mutch (2014) *Buying the Vote: A History of Campaign Finance Reform*, Oxford: Oxford University Press.

▶ Notes

1 See the statement by the National Association of Secretaries of State (2005) "Administering Elections in a Nonpartisan Manner," February 6, http://nass.org/index.php?option=com_docman&task=doc_download&gid=89 (accessed June 29, 2016).
2 See Arthur L. Burris and Eric A. Fischer (2016) "The Help America Vote Act and Election Administration: Overview and Selected Issues for the 2016 Election," Congressional Research Service, October 18, https://fas.org/sgp/crs/misc/RS20898.pdf (accessed June 29, 2016).
3 See the entry on "Self-Initiated versus State-Initiated Registration" in the *ACE Encyclopedia of the Administration and Cost of Elections (ACE) Project*, http://aceproject.org/ace-en/topics/vr/vra/vra10 (accessed June 29, 2016).
4 Brennan Center for Justice (2017) "Automatic Voter Registration," August 28, www.brennancenter.org/analysis/automatic-voter-registration (accessed September 15, 2017).
5 See US Department of Justice (n.d.) "About the National Voter Registration Act," www.justice.gov/crt/about/vot/nvra/activ_nvra.php (accessed June 29, 2016).
6 Robert D. Brown and Justin Wedeking (2006) "People Who Have Their Tickets But Do Not Use Them: 'Motor Vehicle,' Registration, and Turnout Revisited," *American Politics Research*, 34, p. 487.
7 Stephen Knack (1999) "Drivers Wanted: Motor Voter and the Election of 1996," *PS: Political Science and Politics*, 32: 237–243; Michael D. Martinez and David Hill (1999) "Did Motor Voter Work?" *American Politics Quarterly*, 27: 296–315; and Brown and Wedeking, "People Who Have Their Tickets."
8 Raymond E. Wolfinger and Jonathan Hoffman (2001) "Registering and Voting with Motor Voter," *PS: Political Science and Politics*, 33, p. 91.
9 *National Conference of State Legislatures (2016) "Same Day Voter Registration," www.ncsl.org/research/elections-and-campaigns/same-day-registration.aspx (accessed January 2, 2017).*

10 Stephen Knack (2001) "Election-Day Registration: The Second Wave," *American Politics Research*, 29: 69–74; Craig Leonard Brians and Bernard Grofman (2001) "Election Day Registration's Effect on US Voter Turnout," *Social Science Quarterly*, 82: 170–183.
11 National Association of Secretaries of States (2016) "2016 General Election: Voter Registration Deadlines and Polling Place Hours," www.nass.org/elections-voting/voter-registration-deadlines-polling-place-hrs-2016-general (accessed January 2, 2017).
12 Benjamin Highton (2004) "Voter Registration and Turnout in the United States," *Perspectives on Politics*, 2, p. 511.
13 Illustrations of punch-card and lever machines can be found at the National Museum of American History's online exhibit *Vote: The Machinery of Democracy*, http://americanhistory.si.edu/vote/index.html (accessed June 29, 2016).
14 See Election Data Services (2004) "New Study Shows 50 Million Voters Will Use Electronic Voting Systems, 32 Million Still with Punch Cards in 2004," February 12, www.sub-dude-site.com/WebPages_Local/RefInfo/GovmtCitizen/VotingMachines/images_ voting/VoteMethodsStudy2004_wMap_andGraph.pdf (accessed June 29, 2016).
15 See Election Data Services (2008) "Nation Sees Drop in Use of Electronic Voting Equipment for 2008 Election—A First," October 17, www.electiondataservices.com/images/File/NR_VoteEquip_Nov-2008wAppendix2.pdf (accessed June 29, 2016).
16 Drew Desilver (2016) "On Election Day, Most Voters Use Electronic or Optical-Scan Ballots," Pew Research Center, November 8, www.pewresearch.org/fact-tank/2016/11/08/on-election-day-most-voters-use-electronic-or-optical-scan-ballots (accessed January 2, 2017).
17 Brennan Center for Justice (2006) "The Machinery of Democracy," October 10, www.brennancenter.org/publication/machinery-democracy (accessed June 29, 2016).
18 Michael Riley and Jordan Robertson (2017) "Russian Cyber Hacks on US Electoral System Far Wider Than Previously Known," Bloomberg.com, June 13, www.bloomberg.com/politics/articles/2017-06-13/russian-breach-of-39-states-threatens-future-u-s-elections (accessed June 13, 2017).
19 Ariel J. Feldman, J. Alex Halderman, and Edward W. Felten (2006) "Security Analysis of the Diebold AccuVote-TS Voting Machine," unpublished manuscript. Center for Information Technology Policy, Princeton University, https://citp.princeton.edu/research/voting (accessed June 29, 2016).
20 See VerifiedVoting.org (2012) "Counting Votes 2012: A State by State Look at Voting Technology Preparedness," www.verifiedvotingfoundation.org/wp-content/uploads/2012/09/CountingVotes2012_Final_August2012.pdf, pp. 24 and 5 (accessed June 29, 2016).
21 Robert L. Dudley and Alan R. Gitelson (2002) *American Elections: The Rules Matter*, New York: Longman, p. 110.
22 Marcia Lausen (2007) *Design for Democracy: Ballot + Election Design*, Chicago, IL: University of Chicago Press.
23 See Jonathan N. Wand, Kenneth W. Shotts, Jasjeet S. Sekhon, Walter R. Mebane, Jr., Michael C. Herron, and Henry E. Brady (2001) "The Butterfly Did It: The Aberrant Vote for Buchanan in Palm Beach County, Florida," *American Political Science Review*, 95: 793–810.
24 See Joanne M. Miller and Jon A. Krosnick (1998) "The Impact of Candidate Name Order on Election Outcomes," *Public Opinion Quarterly*, 62: 291–330.
25 Jon A. Krosnick, Joanne M. Miller, and Michael P. Tichy (2004) "An Unrecognized Need for Ballot Reform: The Effects of Candidate Name Order on Election Outcomes," in Marion R. Just, Edward J. McCaffrey, and Ann N. Craiger (eds.), *Rethinking the Vote: The Politics and Prospects of American Election Reform*, Oxford: Oxford University Press.
26 Federal Commission on Election Reform (2005) *Building Confidence in US Elections*, Washington, DC: American University, p. 54.
27 National Conference of State Legislatures (2016) "Voter Identification Requirements/Voter ID Laws," www.ncsl.org/research/elections-and-campaigns/voter-id.aspx (accessed January 2, 2017).

28 See Edward B. Foley (2005) "Is There a Middle Ground in the Voter ID Debate?" *Election Law @ Moritz*, September 6, http://moritzlaw.osu.edu/electionlaw/comments/2005/050906.php (accessed June 29, 2016).

29 US Election Assistance Commission (2013) "2012 Election Administration and Voting Survey: A Summary of Key Findings," September, www.eac.gov/assets/1/Page/990-050%20EAC%20VoterSurvey_508Compliant.pdf (accessed January 2, 2017).

30 National Conference of State Legislatures (2016) "Absentee and Early Voting," www.ncsl.org/research/elections-and-campaigns/absentee-and-early-voting.aspx (accessed January 2, 2017).

31 For early voting start dates, see the Early Voting Information Center at Reed College, www.reed.edu/earlyvoting/2016_g_calendar.html (accessed January 2, 2017).

32 National Conference of State Legislatures, "Absentee and Early Voting."

33 See Michael McDonald (2016) "2016 November General Election Early Voting," United States Elections Project, www.electproject.org/early_2016 (accessed January 2, 2017).

34 See Oregon Secretary of State (2016) "Voting in Oregon," http://sos.oregon.gov/voting/Pages/voteinor.aspx (accessed January 2, 2017).

35 Paul Gronke (2005) "Ballot Integrity and Voting by Mail: The Oregon Experiment," *A Report for the Commission on Federal Election Reform*, Portland, OR: The Early Voting Information Center at Reed College, http://people.reed.edu/~gronkep/docs/Carter%20Baker%20Report-publicrelease.pdf (accessed June 29, 2016).

36 Priscilla L. Southwell (2005) "Five Years Later: A Re-assessment of Oregon's Vote by Mail Electoral Process," *PS: Political Science and Politics*, 37: 89–93.

37 See US Election Assistance Commission, Voting System Testing and Certification Division (2011) "A Survey of Internet Voting," Washington, DC: Election Assistance Commission, www.eac.gov/assets/1/Documents/SIV-FINAL.pdf (accessed June 29, 2016).

38 Frederic I. Solop (2001) "Digital Democracy Comes of Age: Internet Voting and the 2000 Arizona Democratic Primary Elections," *PS: Political Science and Politics*, 34, p. 290. The 2004 Democratic presidential caucus in Michigan also allowed Internet voting, and a number of other countries, including England, Canada, and Switzerland have experimented with Internet voting. See Keith Axline (2006) "Election '08: Vote by TiVo," Wired.com, November 14, www.wired.com/news/technology/1,72113-0.html (accessed September 6, 2012).

39 National Conference of State Legislatures (2016) "Electronic Transmission of Ballots," www.ncsl.org/research/elections-and-campaigns/internet-voting.aspx (accessed January 2, 2017).

40 Jim Garamone (2004) "Pentagon Decides Against Internet Voting This Year," US Department of Defense, American Forces Press Service, February 6, http://archive.defense.gov/news/newsarticle.aspx?id=27362 (accessed June 29, 2016).

41 Jennifer Stromer-Galley (2003) "Voting and the Public Sphere: Conversations on Internet Voting," *PS: Political Science and Politics*, 36: 731.

42 Stromer-Galley, "Voting and the Public Sphere," pp. 730–731.

43 Rachel Gibson (2001–2002) "Elections Online: Assessing Internet Voting in Light of the Arizona Democratic Primary," *Political Science Quarterly*, 116, p. 570.

44 See Joe Mohen and Julia Glidden (2001) "The Case for Internet Voting," *Communications of the ACM*, 44: 72–85.

45 Gibson, "Elections Online," pp. 572–573.

46 Bruce Ackerman and Ian Ayres (2002) *Voting with Dollars: A New Paradigm for Campaign Finance*, New Haven, CT: Yale University Press, p. 112.

47 Edward B. Foley (1994) "Equal-Dollars-per-Voter: A Constitutional Principle of Campaign Finance," *Columbia Law Review*, 94: 1209–1210.

48 Bradley A. Smith (2001) *Unfree Speech: The Folly of Campaign Finance Reform*, Princeton, NJ: Princeton University Press.

49 John Samples (2006) *The Fallacy of Campaign Finance Reform*, Chicago, IL: University of Chicago Press, pp. 33–40.

50 As quoted in David A. Strauss (1994) "Corruption, Equality, and Campaign Finance Reform," *Columbia Law Review*, 94, p. 1369.

51 Richard L. Hasen (2010) "Citizens United and the Orphaned Antidistortion Rationale," *Georgia State University Law Review*, 27, Article 18, http://readingroom.law.gsu.edu/cgi/viewcontent.cgi?article=2209&context=gsulr (accessed June 29, 2016).

52 Some argue, however, that corruption and inequality are closely linked; see Strauss, "Corruption, Equality, and Campaign Finance Reform." On corruption and campaign finance reform, generally, see Thomas F. Burke (1997) "The Concept of Corruption in Campaign Finance Law," *Constitutional Commentary*, 14: 127–149.

53 Lawrence Lessig (2011) *Republic, Lost: How Money Corrupts Congress—and a Plan to Stop It*, New York: Twelve.

54 Gregory Wawro (2001) "A Panel Probit Analysis of Campaign Contributions and Roll-Call Votes," *American Journal of Political Science*, 45: 563–579; Stephen Ansolabehere, John M. de Figueiredo, and James M. Snyder, Jr. (2003) "Why Is There So Little Money in US Politics?" *Journal of Economic Perspectives*, 17: 105–130; and Thomas Stratmann (2005) "Some Talk: Money in Politics; A (Partial) Review of the Literature," *Public Choice*, 124: 135–156.

55 See Robert K. Goidel, Donald A. Gross, and Todd G. Shields (1999) *Money Matters: Consequences of Campaign Finance Reform in US House Elections*, Lanham, MD: Rowman & Littlefield, p. 17.

56 Anthony Corrado (2005a) "Money and Politics: A History of Federal Campaign Finance Law," in Anthony Corrado, Thomas E. Mann, Daniel Ortiz, and Trevor Potter (eds.), *The New Campaign Finance Sourcebook*, Washington, DC: Brookings Institution Press, p. 8. Much of the rest of this section will rely on Corrado's comprehensive review of the history of campaign finance reform. See also Frank J. Sorauf (1992) *Inside Campaign Finance: Myths and Realities*, New Haven, CT: Yale University Press, Chapter 1; and Goidel et al., *Money Matters*, Chapter 2.

57 Corrado, "Money and Politics," p. 10.

58 Corrado, "Money and Politics," pp. 12–14.

59 Arthur B. Gunlicks (1993) *Campaign and Party Finance in North America and Western Europe*, Boulder, CO: Westview Press, p. 18.

60 Corrado, "Money and Politics," p. 15.

61 Corrado, "Money and Politics," pp. 16–17.

62 Corrado, "Money and Politics," p. 18.

63 Herbert E. Alexander (1984) *Financing Politics: Money, Elections, and Political Reform*, Washington, DC: CQ Press, p. 35.

64 Corrado, "Money and Politics," p. 21; see also Alexander, *Financing Politics*, pp. 35–36.

65 The following discussion of the 1974 amendments to FECA is based on Goidel et al., *Money Matters*, pp. 26–27.

66 Corrado, "Money and Politics," p. 24.

67 For public funding amounts and spending limits in 2012, see Chapter 9.

68 Anthony Corrado (2005b) "Public Funding of Presidential Campaigns," in Anthony Corrado, Thomas E. Mann, Daniel R. Ortiz, and Trevor Potter (eds.), *The New Campaign Finance Sourcebook*, Washington, DC: Brookings Institution Press, p. 185.

69 Federal Election Commission (2011) "Both Major Parties Receive Public Funding for 2012 Conventions," Press Release, November 8. Washington, DC: Federal Election Commission, www.fec.gov/press/20111108convtfunding.shtml (accessed January 2, 2017).

70 Corrado, "Public Funding of Presidential Campaigns," pp. 190–192.

71 R. Sam Garrett and Shawn Reese (2016) "Funding of Presidential Nominating Conventions: An Overview," Congressional Research Service, https://fas.org/sgp/crs/misc/R43976.pdf (accessed January 2, 2017).

72 Daniel R. Ortiz (1997) "The First Amendment at Work: Constitutional Restrictions on Campaign Finance Regulation," in Anthony Corrado, Thomas E. Mann, Daniel R. Ortiz, Trevor Potter, and Frank J. Sorauf (eds.), *Campaign Finance Reform: A Sourcebook*, Washington, DC: Brookings Institution Press, p. 63. On the Buckley decision generally, see E. Joshua Rosenkranz (ed.) (1999) *If Buckley Fell: A First Amendment Blueprint for Regulating Money in Politics*, New York: The Century Foundation Press; and Joel M. Gora (2003) "The Legacy of Buckley v. Valeo," *Election Law Journal*, 2: 55–67.

73 *Buckley* v. *Valeo* (1976) 424 US 1; see the decision at http://caselaw.lp.findlaw.com/scripts/getcase.pl?court=us&vol=424&invol=1#t18 (accessed June 29, 2016).
74 Corrado, "Money and Politics," p. 27.
75 Corrado, "Money and Politics," pp. 27–28. On GELAC funds, see Corrado, "Public Funding of Presidential Campaigns," pp. 195–197.
76 Corrado, "Money and Politics," pp. 29–30.
77 Corrado, "Money and Politics," p. 29.
78 Sorauf, *Inside Campaign Finance*, p. 15.
79 Larry J. Sabato (1985) *PAC Power: Inside the World of Political Action Committees*, New York: Norton, pp. 10–11.
80 Federal Election Commission (2016) PAC Count, 1974–Present, Washington, DC: Federal Election Commission, www.fec.gov/press/resources/paccount.shtml (accessed January 2, 2017).
81 Corrado, "Money and Politics," p. 32; Sorauf, *Inside Campaign Finance*, pp. 146–149.
82 Corrado, "Money and Politics," p. 33.
83 See the Brennan Center for Justice (2001) *Buying Time 2000: Television Advertising in the 2000 Federal Elections*, New York: The Brennan Center for Justice at the New York University School of Law, pp. 29, 30, 31.
84 Corrado, "Money and Politics," p. 34.
85 See Corrado, "Money and Politics," pp. 35–38, for a description of the bill's passage.
86 For a summary of the law, see the Campaign Finance Institute's "Campaign Finance eGuide: Bipartisan Campaign Reform Act," www.cfinst.org/legacy/eguide/shays.html (accessed June 29, 2016), and "eGuide Update Page," www.cfinst.org/legacy/eguide/update/bcra.html (accessed June 29, 2016).
87 Corrado, "Money and Politics," p. 41.
88 *FEC* v. *Wisconsin Right to Life* (2007) 551 US 449.
89 *FEC* v. *Wisconsin Right to Life*, 469–470.
90 *Davis* v. *Federal Election Commission* (2008) 554 US 724.
91 Rick Hasen (2008) "Initial Thoughts on FEC v. Davis: The Court Primes the Pump for Striking Down Corporate and Union Campaign Spending Limits and Blows a Hole in Effective Public Financing Plans," Election Law Blog, June 26, http://electionlawblog.org/archives/011095.html (accessed June 29, 2016).
92 Richard L. Hasen (2011) "Citizens United and the Illusion of Coherence," *Michigan Law Review*, 109: 581–623.
93 *Citizens United* v. *Federal Election Commission* (2010) 558 US 310.
94 Richard Hasen (2012) "Of Super PACs and Corruption," *Politico*, March 22, www.politico.com/news/stories/0312/74336.html (accessed June 29, 2016).
95 Center for Responsive Politics (2017) "Super PACs," January 2, www.opensecrets.org/pacs/superpacs.php (accessed January 2, 2017).
96 Donald A. Gross and Robert K. Goidel (2003) *The States of Campaign Finance Reform*, Columbus, OH: Ohio State University Press, pp. 2, 6, 8. See also David Schultz (ed.) (2002) *Money, Politics, and Campaign Finance Reform Law in the States*, Durham, NC: Carolina Academic Press.
97 National Conference of State Legislatures (2015) "State Limits on Contributions to Candidates, 2015–2016 Election Cycle," www.ncsl.org/Portals/1/documents/legismgt/elect/ContributionLimitstoCandidates2015-2016.pdf (accessed January 2, 2017).
98 National Conference of State Legislatures (2011) "Limits on Campaign Contributions During the Legislative Session," December 6, www.ncsl.org/legislatures-elections/elections/limits-on-contributions-during-session.aspx (accessed June 29, 2016).
99 Gross and Goidel, *The States of Campaign Finance Reform*, p. 10.
100 National Conference of State Legislatures (2015) "State Public Financing Options: 2015–2016 Election Cycle," July 17, www.ncsl.org/Portals/1/documents/legismgt/elect/StatePublicFinancingOptionsChart2015.pdf (accessed January 2, 2017).
101 For example, the Court struck down part of the Arizona Clean Election law in the 2011 case *Arizona Free Enterprise Club's Freedom Club PAC* v. *Bennett*. See Kenneth P. Vogel

(2011) "Supreme Court Issues Limited Campaign Finance Ruling," *Politico*, June 27, www. politico.com/news/stories/0611/57851.html (accessed June 29, 2016).

102 Gross and Goidel, *The States of Campaign Finance Reform*, p. 11.

103 Brooks Jackson (1990) *Broken Promise: Why the Federal Election Commission Failed*, New York: Twentieth Century Fund.

104 Melanie Sloan (2013) "No Vote of Confidence for FEC," *Politico*, April 30, www.politico. com/story/2013/04/no-vote-of-confidence-for-fec-90783.html (accessed June 29, 2016).

105 Thomas E. Mann (2005) "The FEC: Administering and Enforcing Campaign Finance Law," in Anthony Corrado, Thomas E. Mann, Daniel R. Ortiz, and Trevor Potter (eds.), *The New Campaign Finance Sourcebook*, Washington, DC: Brookings Institution Press, pp. 233–234, 238.

106 See 2016 reporting deadlines at Federal Election Commission, "2016 Reporting Dates," www.fec.gov/info/report_dates_2016.shtml (accessed January 2, 2017).

107 Gregory Giroux (2013) "Crossroads GPS to FEC: No Means No," *Bloomberg.com*, April 10, http://go.bloomberg.com/political-capital/2013-04-10/crossroads-gps-to-fec-no-means-no (accessed May 15, 2013).

108 Jackie Calmes (2015) "Senate Report Cites IRS Mismanagement in Targeting of Tea Party Groups," *The New York Times*, August 5, www.nytimes.com/2015/08/06/us/politics/sen-ate-report-cites-irs-mismanagement-in-targeting-of-tea-party-groups.html   (accessed January 2, 2017).

109 Federal Election Commission (2016) "Presidential Election Campaign Fund," www.fec. gov/press/bkgnd/fund.shtml (accessed January 2, 2017); see also Federal Election Com-mission (n.d.) "Presidential Spending Limits for 2016," www.fec.gov/pages/brochures/pubfund_limits_2016.shtml (accessed January 2, 2017).

110 *Washington Post* (2016) "Money Raised as of Nov. 28," www.washingtonpost.com/graph-ics/politics/2016-election/campaign-finance (accessed January 2, 2017).

111 See Jamin B. Raskin and John Bonifaz (1994) "The Wealth Primary: Campaign Fundrais-ing and the Constitution," Washington, DC: Center for Responsive Politics.

4 Candidates and Campaign Organizations

C ANDIDATES OCCUPY an odd place in a democratic political system. Many are not yet (and some will never be) elected officials, but they seem to be something more than ordinary citizens. Most claim not to be politicians, but all of them have committed themselves, at least over the course of the campaign, to the most intensely political process imaginable. Other candidates are already officeholders; some are looking to be reelected to the office they presently hold, but some are seeking to move to a different office.

The strange space within which candidates reside—between government official and citizen—strains the relationship voters have with them. We simultaneously want candidates to be just like us and yet expect them to be of uniquely strong character and unsurpassed experience and capability. We want to know as much about candidates' lives as we need to know to make fully informed decisions but often feel uncomfortable with the amount (and kind) of information we get. On reflection, we are likely to realize how important candidates and their campaigns are in our political system, yet it is all too easy to think of them as nuisances who flood our mailboxes and television screens with self-serving appeals for our votes.

Most Americans take for granted that we will have candidates vying to fill our public offices. Yet to be successful, or to have any hope of being successful, candidates must engage in behavior that nearly everyone else would loathe. Candidates must ask strangers for money, endure withering criticism and personal attacks, and tolerate having their private lives examined by opponents and the media. To be sure, candidates receive praise and support from those who agree with them, but they also face far more condemnation than most of the rest of us will ever encounter, and they do so in full view of the public!

This chapter begins by attempting to identify the types of people who run for office and why they do so. It then explores the process of running for office, including "candidate emergence" and the hardships that candidates face on the campaign trail. Finally, it looks at campaign organizations and the people who make up campaign staffs. Special attention will be paid to professional political consultants, who in recent decades have become essential elements of any serious campaign for office.

▶ *Who Runs for Office?*

Theoretically, any US citizen over a certain age can run for political office. In practice, very few do so, and those who do tend to come from similar social groups. Who are the individuals who agree to put their lives on public display in exchange for an opportunity to represent others in office? As one might imagine, candidates possess a variety of personal attributes and experiences. Nevertheless, the candidate pool for any office in the United States is not nearly as diverse as the population as a whole.

In fact, a political candidate is more likely to be White, male, older, and from the world of law or business than the typical American. Data gathered on 2014 US House candidates indicated that whereas non-Hispanic Whites made up 64 percent of the general population, such individuals constituted roughly 80 percent of all House candidates (including those who ran for their party's nomination). African Americans made up 13 percent of the population and 12 percent of House candidates while Hispanics made up 16 percent of the population, but just 6 percent of those seeking a seat in the House. Men made up 82 percent of all House candidates but only 49 percent of the population. Among those in the public who had reached the age of twenty-five (the eligibility age for the House of Representatives), 70 percent were forty years old or older, whereas 86 percent of all House candidates were forty or older. Finally, while 11 percent of Americans worked in business, banking, or law, 51 percent of all House candidates claimed such occupations.[1]

Recent comparable data for state legislative candidates is unavailable. However, the National Conference of State Legislatures provides demographic information for all states legislators. Only 24 percent of those with seats in state legislatures are female; 9 percent are African American, and 5 percent are Hispanic; the average age of a state legislator is fifty-six (compared to forty-seven for the US adult population); and 43 percent of state legislators are in business or law.[2] While we can't be sure that the candidate pool is equally unrepresentative, it is probably safe to assume that state legislative candidates are about as unlike the general population as are candidates for the US House of Representatives.

Interestingly, although there are fewer minority and women candidates then we would expect if candidates were randomly drawn from the general population, they appear to do as well as their White male counterparts once they run for office. With respect to race, a study of African-American candidates in local elections found that they had an even chance of winning, "once candidate supply is accounted for."[3] And according to political scientists Danny Hayes and Jennifer Lawless, "men and women have performed equally well at the ballot box since the 1980s."[4] In other words, the underrepresentation of minorities and women in office is the result of having fewer women and minority candidates in the first place.

Why do fewer women and minority candidates run for office? The answer is that barriers to entry keep potential candidates from these groups from running or even contemplating running. For instance, Jennifer Lawless and Richard

Fox argue that both traditional family roles, where women continue to be the primary caregiver for children, and the "masculinized ethos" of campaign politics contribute to a "gendered psyche" wherein "politics often exists as a reasonable career possibility for men, but does not even appear on the radar screen for many women."[5] Structural factors, such as the racial makeup of districts and the presence (or absence) of minority elected officials in an area, may deter minority candidacies.[6] Women and minority candidates also face disadvantages in terms of institutional encouragement and support. They are less likely, for example, to be connected to fund-raising networks and may find it difficult to obtain support from party leaders.

It will take time to completely break down the barriers to entry for women and minority candidates. Nevertheless, political opportunities have been expanding in recent years. A record twenty women held seats in the US Senate after the 2012 elections, up considerably from what was then a record six who were in the Senate twenty years ago.[7] As of this writing, there were also six female governors, twelve lieutenant governors, and fifty-seven other statewide elected officials.[8] Hillary Clinton's nomination for the Democratic presidential nomination in 2016 surely opened doors for future female candidates at all levels, though her loss in the general election might reasonably be understood as a setback. Minorities are not as well represented in statewide offices, but Barack Obama's historic victory in the 2008 presidential election, and his reelection in 2012, indicates that a broader electorate is now willing to seriously consider minority candidates.

Though demographic characteristics are socially significant, the most important candidate characteristic from an electoral perspective is incumbency status. A large percentage of candidates on any given ballot will be seeking reelection to the same office they already hold. These incumbents have enormous advantages over most of their challengers. Those advantages, which will be explained in detail in Chapter 10, contribute to the strong likelihood that an incumbent will win reelection. Indeed, 98 percent of those incumbent US House of Representatives members who have sought reelection have won in some recent election years.

Many candidates who challenge incumbents, or who are competing in "open seat" races in which no incumbent is running, may have prior political experience, but some are political novices. Those who have held prior elected office are often referred to as *quality candidates*. Having won elections in the past, these candidates know what to expect from a campaign and understand how to put together a successful effort. They have proven that they can raise money, and they have experienced campaign staffs and volunteers. As a result, these candidates are often more successful than novices are.

Of course, not all novices are the same. Some have previously held appointed office; others may have worked on the staff of an elected official. Though these positions do not provide the kind of campaign experience officeholders enjoy, they can offer access to important political networks. For example, prior to running for the Fifth Congressional District in Texas, Republican Jeb Hensarling served as an aide to Senator Phil Gramm and then served as executive director of the National Republican Senatorial Committee. The contacts Representative Hensarling made in those posts undoubtedly contributed to his later electoral success.

Those in high-profile appointed offices may also have achieved some level of name recognition. Celebrity candidates, too, enjoy name recognition and can trade on it to become serious candidates even without prior political experience. A number of celebrities have won relatively high-profile races without previously having run for office.[9] Arnold Schwarzenegger, a body-builder turned actor whose only prior political experience was serving on appointed California and national physical fitness councils, was elected governor of California in his first bid for office in 2003. Former US Senator Bill Bradley had been a Hall of Fame basketball player before entering the Senate from New Jersey and serving from 1979 to 1997. And, of course, there is Donald Trump, the businessman and reality-television star who reached the pinnacle of American politics in his first bid for office.

Other novices are independently wealthy and can use that wealth to mount serious, or at least high-profile, candidacies. Ross Perot's bid for president in 1992 is perhaps the most obvious example. Perot spent more than $65 million in his entirely self-financed campaign that year and received nearly 19 percent of the vote. In the 2002 Texas gubernatorial race, businessman Tony Sanchez spent $66 million of his own money in a losing effort. These examples suggest that well-heeled novices may not be able to buy their way into office, but plenty of other examples suggest the opposite. Former Goldman Sachs CEO Jon Corzine won his first race for office in 2000, spending more than $60 million of his considerable wealth to become a US senator from New Jersey. And billionaire Michael Bloomberg spent $74 million in his successful bid to become mayor of New York City in 2001.

We have discussed candidate demographic identity, background, and experience, but a question that inevitably intrigues observers is what "kind" of people take the plunge into electoral politics. Candidates who decide on their own to run for office are called *self-starters*. No one from the party recruits self-starters, so it is up to those individuals to first contemplate running and then to actually decide to enter a race. Such decisions require a considerable amount of ambition. The sources of ambition are varied.[10] Perhaps most obvious is a psychological explanation. Some people are simply more driven, whether by a desire for personal recognition or gain or by altruistic considerations. Others have been raised to view public service as an obligation.

The form political ambition takes also varies from person to person. Some, according to Joseph Schlesinger, seek office for only a brief period of time ("discrete ambition"). Republican congressman J. C. Watts of Oklahoma was considered a rising political star when he entered the House of Representatives in 1994. He voluntarily left office, however, after only four terms in the House. Others are content to hold one office as a career ("static ambition"). Representative John Dingell, a Democrat from Michigan, replaced his father as representative of the Fifteenth Congressional District in 1955 and served in that office until 2015. Finally, some hope to climb the political ladder throughout a career that leads to higher and higher offices ("progressive ambition").[11] Richard Nixon, for instance, served two terms in the US House before moving to the US Senate, where he served for only two years before joining the Republican ticket in 1952 as the vice-presidential candidate; after serving as vice president, he ran unsuccessfully for president in 1960 and failed in a bid for governor of California in 1962 before winning the presidency in 1968.

Of course, the decision to become a candidate may suggest not only ambition but a certain level of naivety. Many first-time candidates simply do not know the toll a campaign takes on a candidate and their family. They may also exaggerate their odds of success—or, as in the case of some candidates who seek only to publicize an issue with no hope of actually winning the race, the decision to run may not be based on ambition at all. However, for self-starters who are serious candidates, the decision to run for office is a calculated one, driven by the desire to succeed, that is, to win the office and then enjoy its prestige and responsibilities. In fact, for many of these candidates, the question is not whether to run but when.

▶ Candidate Emergence: Deciding to Run

With some sense of who runs for office, the next question is how potential candidates decide to run. That is, what factors go into their decision to throw their hats into the ring? It is important to note as we think about "candidate emergence" that ours is a candidate-centered electoral system. As opposed to a party-centered system, one that is candidate-centered places most of the burden of running for office on individual candidates. Though a candidate's political party is an important cue for voters and though parties do assist candidates in many ways, ultimately it is the candidate who must take the initiative to run for office, build a campaign team, gather the resources necessary to mount a serious effort, and communicate an agenda that is persuasive to voters.

Potential candidates seek opportunities to run when the time is right.[12] As a result, we can say that ambitious and potentially competitive candidates act rationally and strategically. This means that the context within which they will be running is a significant factor—perhaps the most important factor—in the decision about when to run.[13]

Incumbency and the Decision to Run for Office

A number of elements enter into the context of an election. First and foremost is the office to be sought. For those already holding office, the question will be whether to seek reelection to the same office or, if not, whether to attempt to win another, perhaps higher-level, office. Some incumbents face term limits that force them to seek a new office or to retire from politics altogether. When the incumbent can run for reelection, the decision is often based on the prestige of the office held relative to other potential offices. Typically, the more prestigious the office, the more content an incumbent is to stay in that office, but sometimes candidates seek to move on for reasons other than prestige. For example, a legislator may seek an executive branch office, as Kansas's Sam Brownback did when he left the US Senate after serving more than two terms to run, successfully, for governor in 2010. Or a legislator may choose to move from the state level to the national level. Indeed, many candidates for the US House of Representatives previously served as state legislators.

When an incumbent seeks a new office, the decision to do so is greatly affected by whether the race for that office would be against the incumbent officeholder or for an open seat. Elected officials realize better than anyone how difficult it is to beat incumbents, so they often wait for a desired seat to come open. When a member of the House of Representatives decides to run for a Senate seat, for example, it is typically only when the current senator has announced their retirement. Occasionally, however, an incumbent will give up a secure seat to run against another incumbent. Representative Sherrod Brown of Ohio had served fourteen years in the US House when he decided to challenge sitting US Senator Mike DeWine in 2006. Such a decision is extremely risky (though this particular one happened to pay off for Brown, who defeated the incumbent DeWine). To reduce the danger of ending up out of a job, some elected officials decide to run for another office in the middle of their present term. In the event of a loss, such an official retains the current position. Senator John McCain, for instance, ran for president in 2008 with two years left in his fourth Senate term. After losing his presidential bid, he returned to the Senate, where he faced reelection in 2010.

Nonincumbents with their eyes on a particular office are also influenced by whether an incumbent is seeking reelection. However, the presence of an incumbent may be less relevant for political novices than for quality challengers. Whereas a quality candidate would prefer to run for an open seat, an amateur may realize that the only way to become a candidate in a general election is to run when the primary offers little or no competition. Thus, they may find it more attractive to run when there is an incumbent in place, because that will mean fewer members of their own party seeking nomination. As counterintuitive as it may sound, to the amateur, the odds of winning office seem *better* against an incumbent alone than they do against multiple quality candidates in the primary, followed—in the event of success—by a quality candidate in the open-seat general election.[14]

Sherrod Brown's case illustrates that quality candidates do, occasionally, take on incumbents. This happens most often when an incumbent becomes particularly vulnerable, which can occur in many ways. The incumbent may have cast a particularly controversial vote or may have been in office so long as to seem out of touch with the district. A perfect example of controversial voting took place in Pennsylvania in 2006. State legislators had passed a significant pay raise for themselves (and other government officials) in the middle of the night and without public scrutiny. The resulting voter outrage claimed seventeen incumbents in the 2006 primaries, including the state senate president pro tempore and the senate majority leader. In the general election, a number of additional incumbents lost their bids for reelection.

Even controversial votes or an out-of-touch incumbent will not always produce a strong challenger. What is sure to do so, however, is a scandal involving the incumbent. When an incumbent is found to have done something inappropriate, or worse, challengers will emerge even during primaries. When California Representative Gary Condit admitted to having had an affair with a government intern who disappeared in Washington in 2001 (and whose remains were later found in a Washington, DC park), a member of his own party challenged and defeated him in the 2002 Democratic primary. The challenger, Dennis Cardoza, was a member of the California Assembly and Condit's former chief of staff.

Most incumbents facing a scandal, however, retire rather than defend themselves on the campaign trail. In fact, even in the absence of scandal, incumbents often leave office rather than face a difficult challenger. For instance, as 2008 began to look like a bad year for Republican candidates, by the beginning of spring, twenty-nine Republican members of the House of Representatives had announced their retirement. Many of them faced the prospect of a serious challenge and a tough reelection battle. A considerable number of incumbents also decide to retire in years after congressional redistricting (that is, in years ending in "2"). Faced with the prospect of running in a district that is partially unknown to them, incumbents may opt out of politics.

The Influence of Economic and Political Factors

Whether challenging an incumbent or running in an open-seat race, strong candidates decide to run when the political climate appears beneficial to their candidacy. The mood of the electorate and the economic and political conditions in the nation or in the relevant state or district are significant factors in determining when the time is right to make a bid for office. Gary Jacobson and Samuel Kernell have shown that the state of the economy early in an election year better explains the outcome of midterm congressional elections than the economic or political conditions in the fall. The logic behind such a finding is that strategic politicians have to make decisions about whether to run early in the election cycle, and those decisions—as much as, if not more than the voters' perceptions of the conditions at election time—structure the choices voters are able to make. Jacobson and Kernell also found, though, that the *political* environment in the fall, and specifically the popularity of the sitting president, is a stronger predictor of outcomes than the political situation in the spring.[15] Thus, politicians look to the economy when making their decisions about whether to run—in part because economic conditions are usually less volatile than political conditions—and those decisions, along with political conditions at the time of the vote, influence voters' choices.

Though national conditions can have a significant influence in congressional elections, as they seem to have had in 2010, 2006, 1994, and 1974, local factors operating in the area in which candidates run are typically more important.[16] These include consideration of the strength of individual incumbents and local economic conditions.[17] However, because local economic conditions are influenced by national conditions, which in turn are more likely to affect voters' (and perhaps potential candidates') perceptions of the overall state of the economy, it is hard to isolate the impact of local economic conditions.

With respect to local political factors, the partisan division in a potential candidate's electoral district may be the most critical in their decision-making process.[18] Put simply, serious candidates realize that their party affiliation must fit the district in which they will run. Districts with an overwhelmingly Republican voting history are unlikely to attract many quality Democratic candidates, and vice versa. Indeed, research has found that the "normal vote" in a district, or the average percentage of the vote cast for the parties over some specified period of time, is one of the most robust predictors of candidate quality in congressional elections.[19] The higher the normal vote is for the majority party, the less likely the district is to produce quality candidates of the minority party. This creates a vicious cycle in which good candidates from disadvantaged parties avoid running in districts with long odds, but those odds remain long year after year as the disadvantaged party fails to put up good candidates. It is probably worth noting the opposite effect—in "swing districts," where partisan divisions are fairly even and competition is intense, better-quality candidates emerge on both sides.

Of course, partisanship is not the only relevant aspect of a candidate's compatibility with voters in a particular district. Candidates must also consider whether their ideology matches the ideological composition of the district. No matter how qualified a candidate may be, if they are a conservative in a liberal district, it will be futile to attempt to win a seat in that district. This explains why some local elected officials never run for higher office, despite being popular in their district and having valuable political experience. If a liberal member of the state legislature represents a district consisting of a city, and the city is surrounded by conservative suburbs and rural areas, the liberal representative will see little point in trying to run for office from an area larger than the state legislative district.

As electoral districts become quite a bit larger, however, they usually become more ideologically diverse. So, on one hand, the liberal state representative just mentioned may see better odds in running for governor or the US Senate than for the state senate or the US House of Representatives. On the other hand, the ideological diversity of the larger district may mean that a moderate is more viable than a liberal or a conservative. Again, the potential candidate has to consider ideological fit, and most voters may view a liberal or a conservative as too extreme to represent their relatively moderate constituency. In the end, the liberal state representative is likely to conclude that they are better off staying in an ideologically compatible district.

Practical Considerations

By now, we have a sense of just how complicated the process of deciding to run for office is, but there is plenty more that potential candidates must take into consideration. Foremost on the minds of any potential candidate is the question of how much money will be required to mount a serious effort. In 2014, the average amount spent by challengers who beat sitting US representatives was roughly $2.1 million (including primary spending), and open-seat winners spent almost $1.9 million.[20] If we assume, then, that a candidate will have to spend $2 million to be competitive, they would need to raise approximately $2,740 each day over the two-year election cycle, but as most candidates do not begin raising money until about a year before the election, the more accurate amount required is more than $5,400 a day.

Of course, lower-level races are less expensive. For example, the average amount raised by state house candidates in 2013–2014 was $66,856, and in state senate races, it was $179,876.[21] Averages, however, hide the fact that in many state legislative races, not much spending occurs at all (because, in part, so many of these races are not seriously contested by one party or the other). However, averages also conceal spending on the high end; in California in 2013–2014, for example, the average state assembly candidate raised $563,804 while state senate candidates raised an average of $899,235. One California state senate candidate raised a whopping $3.5 million.[22]

Serious candidates at all levels, therefore, must think long and hard about whether they can raise the necessary funds to run competitive campaigns. Once candidates get their party's nomination, they can expect some help from the party, but how much help the party provides will vary from place to place, race to race, and year to year. The parties' priorities are, generally, to protect vulnerable incumbents and to support challengers and open-seat candidates with a reasonable chance to pick up seats. In years that are *particularly* advantageous for one party, that party's incumbents will mostly be safe and, as a result, the party can put more resources behind challengers and open-seat candidates. The opposite would be true for the party facing strong headwinds. They have to protect their incumbents before anything else. Thus, in 2010, a bad midterm year for Democrats, the Democratic Party allocated 78 percent of its contributions and coordinated expenditures to incumbents who were in jeopardy, whereas the Republican Party gave 80 percent of its financial support to challengers with a reasonable shot at winning.[23]

Potential candidates also take into consideration a number of factors beyond money. How difficult, for instance, is ballot access? That is, what does it take for candidates to get their names on the ballot in the first place? Typically, the nominees of the major parties have easy, often automatic access to the general election ballot. For independent and third-party candidates, however, access to the November ballot is far more difficult. In Pennsylvania, where ballot access laws are among the most restrictive, third-party/

independent candidates were initially supposed to obtain 21,775 signatures to run for statewide office in 2016 before a federal judge lowered the number considerably.[24]

Though getting on the general-election ballot as a major party nominee may be easy, Democratic and Republican hopefuls are on their own to make primary ballots. This may not be particularly onerous; in Pennsylvania, major party candidates need 2,000 signatures to get on a statewide primary ballot, but in a few states, the number of signatures required is rather high. To run for a party's gubernatorial nomination in Massachusetts, for instance, a would-be candidate needs 10,000 signatures.[25] In addition, some states require a considerable filing fee. Primary candidates in Florida pay 6 percent of the annual salary of the office sought; that amounts to $10,440 for a congressional candidate.[26] Finally, some state parties offer "pre-primary endorsements," whereby the party officially gives its approval to one of the candidates competing in the primary. In those states, potential candidates must determine whether they are likely to get their party's endorsement. Though the party's endorsement does not guarantee the nomination, it is a valuable source of support.

Not least among considerations a potential candidate must think about is the impact a bid for office will have on the individual's personal life. Are there private matters that the potential candidate would prefer not be made public? Such matters can extend back into early adulthood. Was the person ever caught plagiarizing or cheating on an exam in college? Have they ever been arrested for drunk driving? Not paid taxes due? Failed to vote in any previous elections? If the answer to any of these questions, and a host of others, is yes, it would likely make the papers and the local evening news during a campaign.

Beyond personal reputation is the question of how a bid for office will affect a potential candidate's nonpolitical career. Will it be possible to take a leave of absence from work during the campaign? How will the candidate make a living while on the campaign trail? Though federal candidates can pay themselves a salary out of campaign funds (subject to some limitations), they rarely do so. That candidates are unpaid helps explain why so many of them come from the legal profession and the business world. These fields allow candidates maximum flexibility and often sources of income while running for office.

Of course, potential candidates must also consult with their families. A decision to enter a race will tremendously affect the candidate's spouse and children. Normal family routines will no doubt be disrupted; in addition, journalists and researchers from the opposing campaign may scrutinize the lives of the candidate's spouse and any adult children, particularly in high-profile races. Indeed, candidates who decline to run for an office as expected will often cite family concerns as the reason, as did former Indiana governor Mitch Daniels when he announced that he would not seek the Republican Party nomination for president in 2012.

BOX 4.1 *Statement from Mitch Daniels Announcing that He Will Not Run for President in 2012*

May 22, 2011

Over the last year and a half, a large and diverse group of people have suggested to me an idea that I never otherwise would have considered, that I run for President. I've asked for time to think it over carefully, but these good people have been very patient and I owe them an answer. The answer is that I will not be a candidate. What could have been a complicated decision was in the end very simple: on matters affecting us all, our family constitution gives a veto to the women's caucus, and there is no override provision. Simply put, I find myself caught between two duties. I love my country; I love my family more.

I am deeply concerned, for the first time in my life, about the future of our Republic. In the next few years Americans will decide two basic sets of questions: Who's in charge here? Should the public sector protect and promote the private sector or dominate and direct it? Does the government work for the people or vice versa?

And, are we Americans still the kind of people who can successfully govern ourselves, discipline ourselves financially, put the future and our children's interests ahead of the present and our own?

I am confident that the answers will reaffirm the liberty and vitality of our nation, and hope to play some small part in proving that view true.

Source: http://tpmdc.talkingpointsmemo.com/2011/05/daniels-not-running-i-love-my-country-i-love-my-family-more.php (accessed May 16, 2013).

Candidate Recruitment

Throughout the decision-making process, a potential candidate may discuss a possible bid for office with party officials or representatives of various interest groups. In fact, party leaders may initiate the discussion. As noted earlier, most candidates in the American electoral system are self-starters. Nevertheless, the parties do attempt, more or less (depending on the sophistication of the party organization), to recruit quality candidates. At the national level, the congressional and senatorial campaign committees for both major parties are active in finding candidates to run in key House and Senate races. As we will see in Chapter 5, state and local party officials are even more involved in identifying candidates with the potential to run competitive campaigns.

Candidate recruitment can take one of two forms. In the standard approach, parties encourage good potential candidates to run for office by offering as much support as they can. Where the parties endorse at the primary stage, party leaders may promise to try to secure such an endorsement. Where preprimary endorsement is not an option, they may offer behind-the-scenes support by talking-up the preferred candidate to party insiders and influential activists and donors. They will also pledge support in the general election. An alternative approach, called *negative recruitment,* discourages less than ideal candidates from running for particular offices.[27] When an ambitious individual indicates an interest in running but party officials think the person is not as viable as another potential nominee, party leaders may step in to try to talk the would-be candidate out of it. They can do so by offering to help the candidate run for a different office or by threatening to withhold support, even in the general election, if the person goes through with a campaign.

Interest groups can also be involved in recruitment, but their level of activity is typically much lower than the parties. Ideological interest groups, however, can be fairly committed to finding candidates who will advance their ideological agenda.[28] Though not an organized interest group, partisan bloggers have also become engaged in recruiting candidates. Even party leaders have recognized the impact of the "netroots"—or online partisan activists—in the recruitment process. In March 2007, the chairman of the Democratic Senatorial Campaign Committee (DSCC), Senator Charles Schumer, posted an entry on the liberal blog Daily Kos inviting readers to suggest people who would make strong candidates for the Senate in twenty-one states where Republicans would be challenged in 2008. "Netroots support is a key metric the DSCC uses to determine the viability of any given candidate," said Schumer. "And the importance of netroots support is often larger in the early stages of an election cycle. Now is the time when the netroots can help find candidates and build the energy they'll need to win."[29]

► *Running for Office*

Once a candidate has pondered all the consequences of a bid for office and has decided to run, months of intense campaigning lie ahead. First, if the nomination is contested, candidates will have to campaign against and defeat other candidates of their own party. To do so, they will have to appear electable, but they will also have to appeal to the "base" of the party. The base consists of party voters who are the most loyal but are usually also the most ideological. Candidates who are in step with the base have a better chance of winning the nomination but may be at a disadvantage with the more moderate general election voters.[30] Thus, candidates face the difficult task of positioning themselves to win the primary without jeopardizing the general election.[31]

Issue Positions and Image

The notion that candidates "position" themselves suggests that they are free to move along the ideological spectrum and willing to do so in ways that make them more electable. This is not entirely accurate. First-time candidates are, of course, blank slates to the voters and the media. Theoretically, they can take optimal positions on the left–right (that is, liberal–conservative) continuum. Candidates with a record, however, are not entirely free to do so. They may claim to have changed positions on some issues, but voters will typically be skeptical of candidates who shift too abruptly or for what appears to be political opportunism. And, in truth, the strongest constraint on candidate positioning, including that of first-time candidates, are the candidate's personal convictions on the issues. Despite the commonly held belief that candidates will say whatever it takes to win, the vast majority of candidates run because they want to influence public policy in ways they believe best for their district or state or for the country.[32] Candidates have positions on most issues before they run and are not likely to take a contrary position merely because it is popular. This fact applies, in particular, to high-profile, controversial, or emotional issues.

Candidates must create an image to go along with their positions on issues. Each contender crafts an advantageous image deliberately, with the help of professional political consultants and based largely on personal traits that the campaign would like to convey. Again, however, the candidate's attributes limit image manipulation. For one thing, personal background may dictate what claims the candidate can plausibly make. Someone who spent considerable time in the military, for example, may be seen as strong or patriotic but not necessarily compassionate; a candidate from an elite profession may appear competent or intelligent but may have difficulty claiming to be in touch with the average voter. A candidate's age may also influence the image voters develop. A younger person may appear energetic whereas an older one may be viewed as experienced.

Women and minority candidates face particular challenges with respect to candidate image. Women are often viewed as empathetic, which may be a benefit when the key issues are health care or education, but that same stereotype suggests to many voters that they are weak, or "soft," on security issues. Some, such as Senator Diane Feinstein of California, who sits on the Senate Select Committee on Intelligence, have successfully overcome that stereotype. Nevertheless, it remains a challenge to female candidates and is a leading explanation for why it has been so difficult for a woman to be taken seriously as a presidential contender. Similarly, racial minorities continue to face often deep-seated prejudices that operate in very complicated ways. Early in the 2008 presidential campaign, Barack Obama was criticized in some quarters for not being "Black enough."[33] And, yet, were he to have been perceived as "too Black" (whatever that may mean), he would have had little chance of winning the Democratic nomination. Though overt racial prejudice is no longer socially acceptable, race subtly influences perceptions of minority candidate images.[34]

Finally, the political parties project their own images, which are likely to affect how their candidates are perceived, particularly those without prior political experience.[35] Democrats are generally viewed as compassionate and empathetic, while Republicans are thought to be strong and moral.[36] Individual candidates may be able to portray themselves as having attributes typically associated with the other party, but doing so successfully takes a great deal of effort and a credible personal narrative.

It is worth noting that image is not wholly distinct from issue positions, and a successful image cannot be devoid of policy content. Indeed, policy preferences signal important information about a candidate's personal characteristics.[37] Just what characteristics are being signaled, however, is open to interpretation by the voters. In 2004, for example, President Bush's critics interpreted his "stay the course" position on the war in Iraq as stubbornness, whereas his supporters saw it as resoluteness. The point is that voters evaluate candidates on the basis of a combination of policy considerations and impressions of the candidates' attributes. Candidates, or at least their campaign staffs, know this and therefore treat image with the same degree of importance as issues when devising campaign strategy.[38]

Under the Microscope

It is clear that in forming an image of a candidate, voters want to know more than the candidate chooses to reveal, and the media are ready to accommodate them. The most difficult sacrifice candidates face is the loss of privacy. As noted previously, any past indiscretion on the part of a candidate is likely to become public knowledge, but the question is just how much of a candidate's personal life voters have a right to know about. The problem is where to draw the line between information that is necessary to evaluate the candidate's potential effectiveness in office and information that is simply titillating. Voters will each draw that line in different places. For some, an extramarital affair is vital information; for others, it's irrelevant. Regardless of where voters draw the line, however, the media will draw their own lines, which for candidates means that most of their life—past and present—is an open book.

Candidates are also in a difficult spot in terms of the expectations voters have of them. Voters expect candidates to be polished but not too slick. They want candidates to have superior qualities without making ordinary citizens feel inferior. Voting patterns seem to suggest that Americans prefer candidates with elected experience, but they do not like "politicians." And voters would like candidates to defend the common good while advocating particular interests. These tensions—which may ultimately be based on the desire for candidates to simultaneously be both leaders and followers—produce a very narrow tightrope that candidates must try to walk.[39]

Grueling Schedules

The candidate who is fortunate enough to win the party's nomination can look forward to additional months of campaigning for the general election—months that will be filled with raising more money and preparing for hundreds of campaign stops, speeches, debates, and television ads. The schedule is a grueling one, even more grueling as a candidate moves up the ballot to higher-level offices, and it gets worse as Election Day approaches. As the schedule below indicates, candidates begin their days on the campaign trail early and end them late at night. At each stop, they have to appear thrilled to be there and must recall names of local dignitaries. Furthermore, they have to be mentally sharp throughout the day so as to avoid an embarrassing gaffe that will make the local evening news or the morning paper. To put yourself in the shoes of a candidate, imagine having to be on guard not to say anything stupid or inappropriate for the next four months!

BOX 4.2   *A Day in the Life of a Candidate*

September 02, 2010
Thursday

4:50 AM—6:00 AM	TRAVEL TIME FROM HOME TO MIDDLETOWN
6:00 AM—7:00 AM	GREET RAIL RIDERS AT MONMOUTH TRANSIT STOP—MIDDLETOWN TRAIN STATION—**Middletown Train Station, Railroad Ave & Church St, Middletown, NJ** **Event Information:** You will be joined by Middletown Council Candidate Mary Mahoney and Freeholder Candidate Janice Venables **Staff:** Sarah and Justin **Contact:** Justin 732-XXX-XXXX
7:00 AM—6:00 AM	TRAVEL TIME FROM MIDDLETOWN TO MONROE
6:00 AM—9:00 AM	TOWNSHIP OF MONROE MAYORS CUP BOCCE BALL TORNAMENT—**Bocce Courts (Newt to Clubhouse) at Clearbrook Monroe, Clearbrook Drive, Monroe, NJ** **Event Information:** Assemblywoman Linda Greenstein is throwing out the first ball and Councilman Gerry Tamburro will be in attendance as well **Staff:** Sarah **Contact:** Sarah 609-XXX-XXXX
9:00 AM—10:00 AM	TRAVEL TIME FROM MONROE TO SOMERSET
10:00 AM—11:25 AM	DOOR TO DOOR CANVASSING IN FRANKLIN TOWNSHIP—**Somerset Run Community, Rose Cliff Ct, Franklin Township, NJ** **Event Information:** Canvassing Somerset Run (Adult Community in Ward 2, District 17) with Councilwoman Roz Sherman. Meet at Roz's House, she will call ahead to gate for entry into Somerset Run **Staff:** Sarah **Contact:** Roz 732-XXX-XXXX
11:25 AM—12:00 PM	TRAVEL TIME FROM SOMERSET TO PRINCETON
12:00 PM—1:30 PM	IBM TOUR AND EMPLOYEE TOWN HALL MEETING—**IBM Building, Aspen Conference Room 111 Campus Drive, Princeton, NJ** Small executive roundtable at Noon, and then expect about 80 employees to join us in the cafeteria at 12:45pm for Q&A/availability
1:30 PM—2:00 PM	QUICK LUNCH ON THE ROAD
1:55 PM—2:00 PM	TRAVEL TIME FROM PRINCETON TO WEST WINDSOR

2:00 PM—2:30 PM	**CAMPAIGN KICK OFF• PRESS CONFERENCE—Princeton Power Systems, 201 Washington Rd, Princeton, NJ** **Event Information (From Media Advisory already released):** ***MEDIA ADVISORY*** REPRESENTATIVE RUSH HOLT TO OFFICIALLY KICK OFF REELECTION CAMPAIGN FOR IMMEDIATE RELEASE: Wednesday, September 1, 2010 On Thursday, September 2nd, Representative Rush Holt will officially kick off his 2010 reelection campaign with a press conference at Princeton Power Systems, Inc. Representative Holt will discuss job creation and economic opportunities in New Jersey's 12th congressional district. This event will begin at 2:00 p.m. Who: Representative Rush Holt What: Representative Holt will officially kick off his 2010 reelection campaign Where: Princeton Power Systems, Inc., 201 Washington Rd, Building 2, Princeton, New Jersey When: 2:00 p.m., Thursday, September 2, 2010 **Advance Team:** Chris D., Terry **Staff:** Sarah
2:30 PM—3:30 PM	**TRAVEL TIME WEST WINDSOR TO FLEMINGTON**
2:30 PM—3:00 PM	**CALL U.S. SECRETARY OF ENERGY DR. STEVEN CHU—FROM CAR** Returning the phone call from earlier in the week from you
3:30 PM—4:30 PM	**HUNTERDON COUNTY DEMOCRAT NEWSPAPER EDITORIAL BOARD MEETING—8 Minneaboning Rd, Flemington, NJ** **Event Information:** Hunterdon County Democrat Newspaper Editorial Board meeting; small group discussion and open Q&A **Staff:** Chris D. **Contact:** Terry Wright, 908-XXX-XXXX
4:30 PM—5:00 PM 5:00 PM—6:00 PM	**TRAVEL TIME FLEMINGTON TO LAMBERTVILLE** **SMALL BUSINESS TOUR IN DOWNTOWN LAMBERTVILLE—Meet at Lambertville Justice Center, 25 South Union St, Lambertville** **Event Information:** Small Business Tour in Downtown Lambertville with Lambertville Council President Steve Stegman. Meet in the parking lot of the Lambertville Justice Center, 25 South Union St, Lambertville (the old Acme) **Staff:** Julie **Contact:** Julie 908-XXX-XXXX
6:00 PM—6:30 PM	**TRAVEL TIME FROM LAMBERTVILLE TO HOME**
6:30 PM—7:00 PM	**BRIEF TIME AT HOME—DINNER**
7:00 PM—8:00 PM	**TRAVEL TIME HOME TO EAST BRUNSWICK**

(continued)

BOX 4.2 A Day in the Life of a Candidate (continued)

September 02, 2010
Thursday

8:00 PM—10:30 PM	JEWISH COMMUNITY ROUNDTABLE—YOUNG ISRAEL EAST BRUNSWICK, 193 DUNHAMS CORNER ROAD EAST BRUNSWICK, NJ 08816–3523 **Event Information:** 25–30 Jewish Community Leaders will be attending. Format will be brief remarks and then Q&A. **Staff:** Chris **CONTACT:** CHRIS 609-XXX-XXXX
10:30 PM—11:30 PM	TRAVEL TIME EAST BRUNSWICK TO HOME

Source: Used by permission of Rush Holt for Congress

▶ *The Structure of Campaign Organizations*

Candidates do not run campaigns alone. To mount a serious bid for office, even at relatively low levels of government, a candidate needs professional advice and many people to carry out the day-to-day logistics of a campaign. They also need high-profile supporters who can assist in raising money and getting votes. The rest of this chapter will examine candidates' campaign organizations, including campaign committees and staffs and professional political consultants.[40]

Campaign Committees

Technically speaking, a candidate's campaign committee *is* the campaign. As the Virginia State Board of Elections defines it, a campaign committee is "the entity responsible for receiving all contributions and making all expenditures on behalf of the candidate."[41] If the campaign is a small one, the campaign committee may consist of no one other than the candidate. However, most serious campaigns, at any level, will have a committee made up of people who are willing to attach their names to the candidate's official campaign body.

With the exception of one member (the treasurer), campaign committees are not active on a day-to-day basis, though the committee may meet regularly to discuss the direction of the campaign. Besides fund-raising, the primary role of a member of the committee is to serve as an informal adviser. Members are kept abreast of campaign decisions and, in turn, offer their own opinions about what the candidate and campaign staff ought to be doing. In this way, the campaign committee functions as a "steering committee."

Members of the committee are relatively high-profile individuals from the community and are usually well connected to opinion leaders and contributors.

They may be asked to serve on the committee because they have a particularly good understanding of politics in the area. Or they may represent an important party constituency. Republican campaign committees, for example, will usually have some social conservatives as members; Democratic committees will certainly have labor representation.

Campaign committees typically have a chairperson, several co-chairs, and a treasurer. The treasurer, who is the only member with significant responsibility, authorizes expenditures, completes and submits campaign finance reports, and maintains financial records for the campaign. In practice, a member of the campaign staff usually fills out the paperwork, including campaign finance reports, and keeps the books, but the treasurer's signature is required on official documents, and it is the treasurer, along with the candidate, who bears ultimate responsibility for the accuracy of those documents.

As the scope of a campaign increases, the structure of the campaign committee gets more complex. In fact, high-level campaigns often have more than one committee. For instance, there may be a separate finance committee consisting of individuals who can spearhead fund-raising efforts. Presidential campaigns have national campaign committees but also state committees. US Senate and gubernatorial campaigns might have committees in key cities and counties in their states.

In addition, campaigns may establish outreach committees that are intended to appeal to certain segments of the voting population. Committees made up of women or of students are popular, so are those consisting of voters from the opposite party, as when a Republican campaign sets up "Democrats for Smith." Often these outreach committees exist in name only (that is, they have no, or very few, members) and are little more than a public-relations ploy, but when the groups are legitimate, they can effectively reinforce an image the campaign wants to express. A now famous example is "Sportsmen for Warner," a group created in 2001 by the campaign of Virginia Democrat Mark Warner when he was a gubernatorial candidate. This group of 1,250 volunteer hunters and anglers knocked on doors throughout the commonwealth for Warner.[42] Sportsmen for Warner are credited with contributing significantly to Warner's victory.

Finally, though it is not an organized committee, every candidate has a "kitchen cabinet." The term originally applied to the confidants who served as informal advisers to presidents. Today, it refers to the friends and family on whose advice a candidate depends. Occasionally, the kitchen cabinet's opinions about how to proceed will conflict with the professional advice of a candidate's campaign staff or consultants. Such a circumstance puts the candidate in the awkward position of listening to close and trusted allies or heeding professionals with more experience (whose advice is rather expensive). Either way, the ultimate authority in a campaign resides with the candidate, not any campaign committee.

Campaign Staff

To run the actual operation of the campaign, a candidate puts together a campaign staff. As one might guess, staff size varies according to the complexity of the campaign. Nevertheless, every campaign, for even the most local offices, has a campaign manager who serves as the chief administrator of the campaign. The manager oversees the daily activity of the campaign and works both in the campaign headquarters and on the road with the candidate. In some small campaigns, the manager will handle everything from scheduling and volunteer coordination to purchasing advertising time and other campaign materials. In a larger campaign, all those details will be delegated to someone else on the campaign staff, and the manager will focus on the implementation of the campaign's strategy. Regardless of the size of the campaign, no one works more closely with the candidate than the manager. For this reason, the manager has to be someone the candidate not only trusts professionally but gets along with personally.

From an organizational perspective, the campaign manager heads the campaign, though paid political consultants may be at the top of the decision-making structure as well. Typically, directors for the financial, political, and communications operations of the campaign, and sometimes a research director, are situated hierarchically below the manager (see Figure 4.1). Presidential campaigns have national directors for each of these functions, along with staff members directing these aspects of the campaign in key states.

By using various directors, campaigns establish a division of labor. Working closely with the campaign's treasurer, the finance director maintains the budget, oversees fund-raising, and ensures that the campaign complies with campaign finance laws. The communications director deals with the media on behalf of the campaign and serves as the official spokesperson when the candidate is unavailable. The communications director also sets up press conferences (including the choice of backdrops) and handles all press releases. The research director gathers information for the campaign on all the opposing candidates and on the campaign's own candidate. Most of this information is in the form of candidate statements, prior positions, or voting records. The research director is also responsible for pulling together policy briefing books for the candidate, which in the case of a presidential campaign can amount to many volumes of information.

The political director oversees the campaign's efforts to reach voters, including the organization of volunteer activities and the management of a coalition of constituency groups (for example, labor, veterans, or farmers). Most important, however, the political director will run the voter contact, or "field," operation. Campaigns contact voters door to door and by phone to build a voter file that tells them who is likely to support their candidate, who will vote against him or her, and who is undecided. This information is then used to target persuadable voters and mobilize supporters on Election Day. Thus, part of the political director's job is oversight of the get-out-the-vote effort. In larger campaigns, the political director will rely on additional staff to assist with many of these tasks.

FIGURE 4.1   *Campaign Organizational Chart*

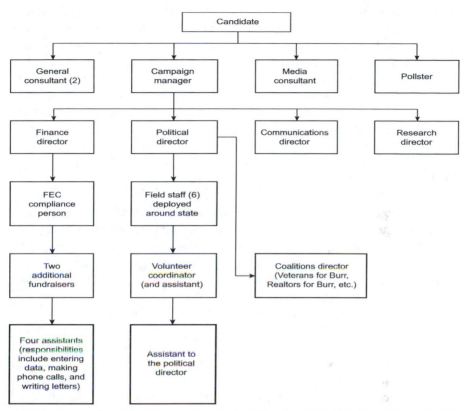

Source: The Richard Burr Committee and the National Republican Senatorial Committee (Medvic 2005: 164).

The political director may, for example, oversee a GOTV coordinator and coordinators for volunteer and coalition operations. If the campaign covers a large geographical area, regional or local field coordinators will be responsible for voter contact in smaller geographical units. Presidential campaigns are likely to have a national field coordinator in addition to field staff at the state level and, in battleground states, at the local level.

Additional staff members are hired to work on other aspects of the campaign. The campaign scheduler, for example, is a vital staff member who works with the candidate and campaign manager and with the political and communications directors to make the best use of the candidate's time and ensure that the candidate's travels are conducted efficiently. "Advance" staffers set up campaign events before the candidate arrives. They identify ideal locations for an event, round up as many supporters as possible to attend the event, get posters up and placards distributed to supporters, and generally ensure that the backdrop to the event is picturesque, which includes eliminating any signs of opposition. One last staff member who has become increasingly important in recent election cycles is the technology coordinator. In small campaigns, maintaining the campaign website may be the responsibility of a volunteer, but larger campaigns will have a paid staffer who is the webmaster and database manager. That person may or may not also direct the campaign's use of other new media (e.g., communication via mobile devices). Depending on the size of the campaign, there may also be a staff member (or members) responsible for outreach to voters via social media (e.g., Facebook). Democrats have generally been at the forefront of technological advances in campaigns, but all campaign organizations make use of the latest technology to achieve their strategic goals.[43]

Political Consultants

The most expensive, and arguably the most valuable, staff members of any serious campaign for office are the professional political consultants. When consultants first emerged as campaign operatives in the 1930s, they were "generalists." Generalists are able to handle every aspect of a campaign, from fund-raising to polling to advertising. In some ways, the early consultants were like sophisticated campaign managers. They usually worked on only one campaign at a time and were responsible for the creation and implementation of the campaign's strategy.

As technology developed and campaigning became more complex, consultants slowly began to introduce a "new style" of politics into campaigns.[44] That style was candidate-centered, poll-tested, and reliant on mass media. By the 1960s, political consulting was "a nation-wide service industry that reached all electoral levels."[45] Consultants began working for multiple campaigns per election cycle and specialized in particular aspects of campaigning. Thus, a campaign would hire different consultants to handle each of the key elements of the campaign. By the 1990s, the use of professional campaign operatives had reached into races even for local offices. According to one estimate, candidates spending as little as $50,000 were routinely employing professional consultants.[46] In small-budget campaigns, consultants may provide a poll or two, develop a strategic blueprint at the beginning of a campaign, or offer occasional advice throughout the campaign.

Though there are still a few general consultants advising campaigns today, most consultants are specialists who handle only one aspect of a campaign. Dennis Johnson argues that there are three tiers of political consulting. The top tier consists of "strategists" who help develop and support the campaign's strategy. Included among them are the pollster and the media and direct mail consultants. "Specialists" occupy the second tier and provide services that are essential to the campaign but are not strategic in nature. This includes fund-raising, research, writing speeches, and buying television and radio time. Finally, "vendors" offer services that tend to be technical, such as printing or website maintenance, and products such as software. Johnson notes that vendors tend to work for candidates of any party, whereas virtually all strategists and specialists work exclusively for one party.[47]

Along with fund-raisers, the strategists are central to any serious campaign for office, and they are the most visible types of consultants. For better or worse, the pollster has become the most essential member of the campaign team. In fact, candidates for high-profile offices such as senator or governor often employ a pollster *before* entering the race. Because pollsters base their strategic conclusions on data (poll results), they have become the chief strategists in most campaigns. Their ascendance is much to the chagrin of generalists and media consultants, who accuse pollsters of taking the heart out of campaigns and replacing it with a cold, scientific approach to campaigning. Pollsters counter by arguing that though emotion is an indispensable element in politics, campaigns should be guided by a rational decision-making process. Polls, they maintain, simply provide the substance for that process.

Fund-raisers, pollsters, and media consultants each play a crucial role in a campaign and produce something of vital importance to the candidate. Fund-raisers get the money needed to run a campaign; pollsters gather information necessary to develop a campaign plan; and media consultants create the messages the campaign will communicate to voters. As noted, candidates pay consultants quite a lot for all this help. So are candidates more successful when they hire consultants than if they do not? The short answer is yes, but consultants, like any other campaign resource, are most useful to candidates who face some sort of disadvantage. Challengers, in particular, benefit significantly by hiring consultants. Consultants are not miracle workers, though; even if they can help a challenger gain an additional ten points against an incumbent, it will not be enough to win in the vast majority of races. Nevertheless, the influence of consultants is demonstrable. Professional campaigns raise more money and receive more votes than nonprofessional ones.[48]

Professional political consultants remain a mystery to most people. Though some consultants such as Democrat James Carville or Republican Karl Rove have become quite well known to the public, most spend their careers in anonymity, toiling behind the scenes. Nevertheless, the industry boasts an elite group of individuals who are even more heavily White (at 97.5 percent) than the candidate pool for which they work and nearly as male (at 82 percent). Consultants are relatively wealthy and are highly educated; 52 percent report household incomes of more than $150,000. Finally, as you might imagine, consultants are more ideological than the typical American. Whereas roughly half of all Americans consider themselves moderate, only 27.5 percent of consultants do.[49]

Though there is no requirement that a consultant have a credential before working on campaigns, an increasing number of programs affiliated with colleges and universities offer programs where future consultants learn everything from the principles of campaign management to polling techniques and fund-raising skills (an example is George Washington University's Graduate School of Political Management). However, most consultants cut their teeth in politics by working for a political party, which makes a very useful training ground. Those hoping to open a consulting firm can gain unique experience and make valuable contacts while working for a party. To the extent that the parties have an "electoral partnership" with consultants, such training can produce benefits for the parties as well.[50]

Increasingly, US–based consultants are also working internationally. James Carville, for instance, has not worked for a domestic candidate since Bill Clinton in 1992 but continues to work in campaigns overseas. A list of some of his previous international clients includes President Nelson Mandela of South Africa, Prime Minister Tony Blair of the United Kingdom, German Chancellor Gerhard Schroeder, and Prime Minister Ehud Barak of Israel. A recent global survey of campaign operatives revealed that 58 percent of those working on Latin American (not including Brazilian) and South African campaigns had cooperated with a US political consultant, as had 40 percent in Eastern Europe, 30 percent in Western Europe, and 23 percent in Russia.[51] This level of activity has led many observers to worry about the "Americanization" of politics in other countries.

Consultant influence abroad is hardly the only concern people have about this industry. Some argue that consultants have driven up the cost of elections. Their often exorbitant fees are expensive enough; but they also utilize expensive technology to produce polls and television ads. Others blame consultants for encouraging overly negative politics and, consequently, for polarizing the nation. Still others believe consultants, by relying heavily on symbolism, have trivialized politics. In fact, the list of alleged consultant offenses is too long to record here in full. Two, however, deserve more detailed explanation not just because they are common and serious but also because they are contradictory.

Some critics claim that consultants are driven by poll results. Consequently, the advice they give is cautious, and the politicians who take that advice campaign so as to offend the least number of voters. Journalist Joe Klein has written that during the 2000 presidential campaign, Al Gore did not talk about the environment—an issue he cares about passionately—because consultants argued that it did not poll well.[52] Critics further claim that candidates who are too reliant on consultants tend to pander to voters in hopes of attracting every possible vote. At its core, then, this line of criticism is about a lack of vision and leadership in politics today, and consultants are thought to be the root cause of the problem.

Whereas the first criticism suggests that consultants encourage candidates to let voters manipulate them, a second criticism is that consultants manipulate voters.[53] Rather than bend to every whim of the voters, consultants enable candidates to twist voter preferences into alignment with their agendas. To do so, candidates frame arguments in ways that appeal to the average voter even when the policy content itself does not. This "spin" is misleading, the argument goes, and amounts to obfuscating at best and dishonesty or outright lying at worst. The central problem here is a lack of democratic responsiveness.

Where one line of criticism accuses consultants of producing politicians who refuse to lead, the other argues that they create politicians who do not follow. Obviously, both cannot be true. As with many such arguments, the reality may be somewhere between—perhaps consultants help candidates determine what voters want and find ways to connect that to where the candidates stand.

More precisely, as we will discover in Chapter 9, consultants may simply identify areas of agreement between voter preferences and candidate agendas and urge candidates to emphasize those areas in their campaign communication.

Ultimately, no matter what consultants encourage candidates to do, it is the candidates who must sign off on what the consultants advise. It is tempting, therefore, to place the blame for the current condition of political campaigns in the United States on the candidates. Of course, it is far more complicated than that. Other actors, and particularly voters, exert tremendous influence over candidate behavior. Perhaps just as Americans get the government they deserve (as has been said), they get the candidates they demand. If candidates do not quite strike the delicate balance of leadership and responsiveness that citizens desire, it may be because the voters—not to mention the media, political parties, and interest groups—make it difficult to do so.

▶ Conclusion

Candidates are not entirely representative of the American public. As we have seen, they are disproportionately White, male, and older and are most likely to make their living in law or business. Most are also equipped with a great deal of ambition—a character trait that ought to be viewed warily in any political system but one that also helps citizens hold politicians accountable (because politicians want to be reelected). At the same time, most candidates are also motivated by a desire to make a positive mark on their communities, states, or the nation.

The decision to run for office is a difficult one. Campaigning requires significant sacrifices and candidates have to seriously consider the toll a bid for office will take on themselves and their families. They also have to be realistic about the likelihood of winning. Most would-be candidates are rational, so they wait to run until the political and economic conditions are optimal.

To help in their efforts, candidates put together organizations made up of individuals who know how campaigns are run. If they can afford to, they will hire professional campaign consultants whose experience will increase the odds of running a successful campaign. Whether those consultants have made candidates too scripted and wooden is a matter of debate. Nevertheless, it is the candidate him or herself who is ultimately responsible for the campaign and for their own behavior.

Whether or not they do it strictly for the sake of democracy, running for office is a relatively noble act and candidates probably deserve more of our gratitude than they currently receive. Indeed, it takes a certain amount of courage to put oneself under a public microscope. Representative democracy needs a large number of individuals who are willing to do that. In the end, we are unlikely to encourage good people to run for office if we don't treat candidates with some level of respect.

► *Pedagogical Tools*

Role-Play Scenario

You are a potential candidate contemplating a run for the state legislature. What questions would you ask yourself before announcing your candidacy? Make a list identifying the pros and cons of running for office.

Discussion Questions

1.   Would it be better to have candidates who possess more impressive qualities (such as intelligence, trustworthiness, and so on) than the average person but who are out of touch with the life experiences of most voters, or to have candidates who can relate to the daily lives of the voters but who are not especially impressive in terms of their personal qualities? Explain your preference.
2.   Political consultants have clearly become influential actors in campaigns. What problems accompany this development? How might one justify the role of political consultants in campaigns?
3.   If the balance between leadership and democratic responsiveness cannot be struck perfectly, would you prefer candidates who lead regardless of where the public wants to go or candidates who respond to the public's desires but do not offer a vision of what the nation needs? Explain your answer.
4.   Do candidates deserve more thanks than they currently receive? Why or why not?

Online Resources

American Association of Political Consultants, www.theaapc.org.
Campaigns and Elections (the trade magazine for the political consulting industry), www.campaignsandelections.com.
Campaign Management Institute, Center for Congressional and Presidential Studies, American University, www.american.edu/spa/ccps/CMI.cfm.
Graduate School of Political Management, George Washington University, https://gspm.gwu.edu/.

Suggested Reading

Danny Hayes and Jennifer L. Lawless (2016) *Women on the Run: Gender, Media, and Political Campaigns in a Polarized Era*, Cambridge: Cambridge University Press.
Dennis W. Johnson (2015) *Political Consultants and American Elections: Hired to Fight, Hired to Win*, 3rd edn, London and New York: Routledge.

Jennifer L. Lawless and Richard L. Fox (2015) *Running from Office: Why Young Americans Are Turned Off to Politics*, Oxford: Oxford University Press.

Stephen K. Medvic (2011) "Campaign Management and Organization: The Use and Impact of Information and Communication Technology," in Stephen K. Medvic (ed.), *New Directions in Campaigns and Elections*, London and New York: Routledge.

▶ *Notes*

1 Population figures are from the 2010 US census. Candidate figures are calculated by the author based on percentages provided in Paul S. Herrnson (2016) *Congressional Elections: Campaigning at Home and in Washington*, Los Angeles, CA: Sage and CQ Press, Tables 2.3 and 2.4.

2 National Conference of States Legislatures (2015) "Legislator Demographics," www.ncsl.org/research/about-state-legislatures/who-we-elect-an-interactive-graphic.aspx# (accessed January 6, 2017).

3 Paru Shah (2014) "It Takes a Black Candidate: A Supply-Side Theory of Minority Representation," *Political Research Quarterly*, 67, p. 275.

4 Danny Hayes and Jennifer L. Lawless (2016) *Women on the Run: Gender, Media, and Political Campaigns in a Polarized Era*, Cambridge: Cambridge University Press, p. 15.

5 Jennifer L. Lawless and Richard L. Fox (2010) *It Still Takes a Candidate: Why Women Don't Run for Office*, rev. edn, Cambridge: Cambridge University Press, pp. 8–14.

6 Richard L. Fox and Jennifer L. Lawless (2005) "Black and White Differences in Nascent Political Ambition: Race and the Decision Dynamics of the Initial Run for Elective Office," Presented at the Annual Meeting of the American Political Science Association, Washington, DC

7 Suzi Parker (2012) "Women Make Historic Gains in the US Senate," *Washington Post*, November 7, www.washingtonpost.com/blogs/she-the-people/wp/2012/11/07/women-make-historic-gains-in-the-u-s-senate (accessed July 11, 2016).

8 Center for American Women and Politics (2016) "Current Numbers," www.cawp.rutgers.edu/current-numbers (accessed January 3, 2017).

9 See David T. Canon (1990) *Actors, Athletes, and Astronauts: Political Amateurs in the United States Congress*, Chicago, IL: University of Chicago Press; and Darrell M. West and John Orman (2003) *Celebrity Politics*, Upper Saddle River, NJ: Prentice Hall.

10 See Linda L. Fowler (1993) *Candidates, Congress, and the American Democracy*, Ann Arbor, MI: University of Michigan Press, Chapter 3.

11 Joseph A. Schlesinger (1966) *Ambition and Politics: Political Careers in the United States*, Chicago, IL: Rand McNally, p. 10.

12 See Linda L. Fowler and Robert D. McClure (1989) *Political Ambition: Who Decides to Run for Congress*, New Haven, CT: Yale University Press; and Schlesinger, *Ambition and Politics*.

13 Thomas A. Kazee (ed.) (1994) *Who Runs for Congress? Ambition, Context, and Candidate Emergence*, Washington, DC: Congressional Quarterly.

14 Jeffrey S. Banks and D. Roderick Kiewiet (1989) "Explaining Patterns of Candidate Competition in Congressional Elections," *American Journal of Political Science*, 33: 997–1015.

15 Gary C. Jacobson and Samuel Kernell (1983) *Strategy and Choice in Congressional Elections*, New Haven, CT: Yale University Press, pp. 68–71.

16 See Jonathan S. Krasno and Donald Philip Green (1988) "Preempting Quality Challengers in House Elections," *Journal of Politics*, 50: 920–936; and Jon R. Bond, Richard Fleisher, and Jeffery C. Talbert (1997) "Partisan Differences in Candidate Quality in Open Seat House Races, 1876–1994," *Political Research Quarterly*, 50: 281–299.

17 William T. Bianco (1984) "Strategic Decisions on Candidacy in US Congressional Districts," *Legislative Studies Quarterly*, 9: 351–364.

18 Jon R. Bond, Cary Covington, and Richard Fleisher (1985) "Explaining Challenger Quality in Congressional Elections," *Journal of Politics*, 47: 510–529.

19 Bond et al., "Explaining Challenger Quality," p. 524.

20 Campaign Finance Institution (n.d.) "House Campaign Expenditures: Incumbents and Challengers, Major Party General Election Candidates by Election Outcome, 1974–2014," www.cfinst.org/pdf/vital/VitalStats_t3.pdf (accessed January 3, 2017); and "House Campaign Expenditures: Open House Seats, Major Party General Election Candidates by Election Outcome, 1984–2014," www.cfinst.org/pdf/vital/VitalStats_t4.pdf (accessed January 3, 2017).

21 J. T. Stepleton (2015) "2014 Candidate Elections Overview," *National Institute on Money in State Politics*, http://followthemoney.org/research/institute-reports/2014-candidate-elections-overview (accessed January 3, 2017).

22 Stepleton, "2014 Candidate Elections Overview."

23 Paul S. Herrnson (2012) *Congressional Elections: Campaigning at Home and in Washington*, 6th edn, Washington, DC: CQ Press, p. 108, Table 4.2.

24 Chris Potter (2016) "Judge Eases Ballot Requirements for Third-Party Candidates," *Pittsburgh Post-Gazette*, July 2, www.post-gazette.com/early-returns/erstate/2016/07/01/Federal-judge-gives-third-parties-a-helping-hand-on-PA-ballot/stories/201607010174 (accessed January 4, 2017).

25 Massachusetts Elections Division (2016) "How to Run for Office in Massachusetts," *Secretary of the Commonwealth of Massachusetts*, www.sec.state.ma.us/ELE/elepdf/Candidates-Guide-generic.pdf (January 4, 2017).

26 Florida Division of Elections (2016) "2016 Qualifying Fees," *Florida Department of State*, http://dos.myflorida.com/media/695241/qualifying-fees.pdf (accessed January 4, 2017).

27 Paul S. Herrnson (1997) "United States," in Pippa Norris (ed.), *Passages to Power: Legislative Recruitment in Advanced Democracies*, Cambridge: Cambridge University Press, p. 192.

28 Herrnson, "United States," p. 193.

29 Chuck Schumer (2007) "2008 Senate Recruiting," *Daily Kos*, March 21, www.dailykos.com/story/2007/3/21/141618/799 (accessed July 11, 2016).

30 Anthony Downs (1957) *An Economic Theory of Democracy*, New York: Harper & Row.

31 Barry C. Burden (2004) "Candidate Positioning in US Congressional Elections," *British Journal of Political Science*, 34: 211–227.

32 Maestas and Rugeley, "The Candidates," p. 145.

33 Ta-Nehisi Paul Coates (2007) "Is Obama Black Enough?" *Time*, February 1, www.time.com/time/nation/article/0,8599,1584736,00.html (accessed July 11, 2016).

34 Nicholas A. Valentino, Vincent L. Hutchings, and Ismail K. White (2002) "Cues that Matter: How Political Ads Prime Racial Attitudes During Campaigns," *American Political Science Review*, 96: 75–90.

35 Wendy M. Rahn (1993) "The Role of Partisan Stereotypes in Information Processing about Political Candidates," *American Journal of Political Science*, 37: 472–496.

36 Danny Hayes (2005) "Candidate Qualities through a Partisan Lens: A Theory of Trait Ownership," *American Journal of Political Science*, 49: 908–923.

37 See Marion R. Just, Ann N. Crigler, Dean E. Alger, Timothy E. Cook, Montague Kern, and Darrell M. West (1996) *Crosstalk: Citizens, Candidates, and the Media in a Presidential Campaign*, Chicago, IL: University of Chicago Press; and Lawrence R. Jacobs and Robert Y. Shapiro (1994) "Issues, Candidate Image, and Priming: The Use of Private Polls in Kennedy's 1960 Presidential Campaign," *American Political Science Review*, 88, p. 529.

38 James N. Druckman, Lawrence R. Jacobs, and Eric Ostermeier (2004) "Candidates' Strategies to Prime Issues and Image," *The Journal of Politics*, 66: 1180–1202.

39 See Stephen K. Medvic (2013) *In Defense of Politicians: The Expectations Trap and Its Threat to Democracy*, London and New York: Routledge.

40 The material in this section follows closely Stephen K. Medvic (2005) "Campaign Organization and Political Consultants," in Paul S. Herrnson (ed.), *Guide to Political Campaigns in America*, Washington, DC: CQ Press.

41 Virginia State Board of Elections (2013) "Candidate Campaign Committees," revised January 1, www.sbe.virginia.gov/Files/CandidatesAndPACs/LawsAndPolicies/Candidates-Summary.pdf, p. 12 (accessed July 11, 2016).

42 Steve Jarding and Dave Saunders (2006) *Foxes in the Henhouse*, New York: Touchstone, p. 102.

43 On the Democrats' early adoption of new media in campaigns, see Daniel Kreiss (2012) *Taking Our Country Back: The Crafting of Networked Politics from Howard Dean to Barack Obama*, Oxford: Oxford University Press.

44 On the development of political consulting, see Stanley Kelley, Jr. (1966) *Professional Public Relations and Political Power*, Baltimore, Md.: The Johns Hopkins University Press; and Larry J. Sabato (1981) *The Rise of Political Consultants: New Ways of Winning Elections*, New York: Basic Books.

45 Dan Nimmo (1970) *The Political Persuaders: The Techniques of Modern Election Campaigns*, Englewood Cliffs, NJ: Prentice Hall, p. 37.

46 Dennis W. Johnson (2001) *No Place for Amateurs: How Political Consultants Are Reshaping American Democracy*, London and New York: Routledge, p. 7.

47 Dennis W. Johnson (2000) "The Business of Political Consulting," in James A. Thurber and Candice J. Nelson (eds.), *Campaign Warriors: Political Consultants in Elections*, Washington, DC: Brookings Institution Press, pp. 39–40.

48 Stephen K. Medvic (2001) *Political Consultants in US Congressional Elections*, Columbus, OH: Ohio State University Press; David A. Dulio (2004) *For Better or Worse: How Political Consultants Are Changing Elections in the United States*, Albany, NY: State University of New York Press.

49 Results are taken from a survey conducted in 1998 for the Improving Campaign Conduct project at American University. See James A. Thurber and Candice J. Nelson (eds.) (2000) *Campaign Warriors: Political Consultants in Elections*, Washington, DC: Brookings Institution Press, Appendix A.

50 Robin Kolodny (2000) "Electoral Partnerships: Political Consultants and Political Parties," in James A. Thurber and Candice J. Nelson (eds.), *Campaign Warriors: Political Consultants in Elections*, Washington, DC: Brookings Institution Press, pp. 110–132.

51 Fritz Plasser with Gunda Plasser (2002) *Global Political Campaigning: A Worldwide Analysis of Campaign Professionals and Their Practices*, Westport, CT: Praeger, p. 27.

52 Joe Klein (2006) *Politics Lost: How American Democracy Was Trivialized by People Who Think You're Stupid*, New York: Doubleday, pp. 20–21 and 151–153.

53 No single source offers this argument in a sustained way, but it shows up in partial form in a variety of places. See, for example, James M. Perry (1968) *The New Politics: The Expanding Technology of Political Manipulation*, New York: Clarkson N. Potter; and Karen S. Johnson-Cartee and Gary A. Copeland (1997) *Manipulation of the American Voter: Political Campaign Commercials*, Westport, CT: Praeger.

Political Parties

AMERICANS HAVE ALWAYS BEEN deeply suspicious of political parties. George Washington warned "in the most solemn manner against the baneful effects of the spirit of party" in his "Farewell Address" in 1796.[1] People blame parties for a variety of sins, including partisan bickering that leads to polarization instead of solutions to problems. And yet most political scientists believe, along with E. E. Schattschneider, that "modern democracy is unthinkable save in terms of political parties."[2] Why are parties so disliked if they are essential to democracy? What makes them essential in the first place? This chapter addresses those questions as it explores the role of political parties in campaigns and elections in the United States.

▶ What Is a Political Party?

Before discussing the history and activity of American parties, it might be a good idea to offer a definition of a *political party*. As one scholar famously defined the term, a political party is "a team seeking to control the governing apparatus by gaining office in a duly constituted election."[3] In other words, it is an organization that seeks to gain power by running candidates for office. A crucial element in the definition of a political party is that parties nominate candidates and provide a banner under which those candidates compete for office. This attribute clearly distinguishes a party from an interest group. Though interest groups may endorse and support candidates, candidates do not stand for them, and the organizations' names do not appear on ballots.

The preceding definition relies heavily on the organizational aspect of political parties, and with good reason: when we think of the term "political party," we probably have an organization in mind. Parties have employees, organizational goals, and internal cultures. And, of course, they are visible actors in elections, with candidates who align with them. But parties are more than that. They are also entities with which most voters (and many nonvoters) identify, and they help structure the operation of government. V. O. Key, Jr. developed this tripartite conceptualization—party organization, party in the electorate, and party in government—in the 1960s, and it is still a useful way to think about parties.[4] Indeed, we will employ it later in this chapter to fully understand parties' relevance to elections.

Before doing so, however, we examine the two-party system in the United States. This will include a review of the historical development of that system and some thoughts about why it includes only two major parties. Then, after a more detailed investigation of Key's framework, we will look closely at party activity during campaigns and elections. This discussion will point to the positive and negative consequences of party activity, as briefly summarized at the end of the chapter.

▶ The Two-Party System

In his classic 1921 study of democracy, the British scholar James Bryce wrote, "Parties are inevitable. ... No one has shown how representative government could be worked without them."[5] The history of political parties in America certainly seems to justify such a conclusion. Washington uttered his warning about the development of parties because they were already emerging within a decade after the Revolution. Philip Klinkner has noted the presence of a "Court-versus-Country" dynamic in American politics that some trace as far back as 1789.[6] These conflicting attitudes, which have their origins in seventeenth-century British politics, can still be seen today. Essentially, Court advocates sought a strong central government, while those of the Country persuasion wanted limited, or at least decentralized, government.[7] One can see how these tendencies formed the Federalist and Anti-Federalist camps during the ratification debates over the Constitution. From there, two distinct parties—the Federalists and the Jeffersonian Republicans—emerged almost immediately in the new government.

The Five "Party Eras"

Party scholar John Aldrich notes, "By the Second Congress (1791–1793), most officeholders could be identified as Federalists or (Jeffersonian) Republicans," and "by the Third Congress, voting patterns can be identified as polarized, broadly along party lines."[8] Those parties were active in the 1796 presidential election and, certainly by 1800, we can safely say that a two-party system had emerged in the United States. This period (the 1790s to the 1820s) launched the first of five "party eras" identified by scholars. A party era is a period of time in which the nature of competition between parties is stable, either because one party dominates throughout the period or because there is rough parity between the parties during that time frame. During the first system, the Federalists contested a few presidential elections and then disappeared rapidly, in large part because of their opposition to the War of

1812. From roughly 1815 to 1825, the country enjoyed the "Era of Good Feelings" as the Jeffersonian Republicans governed with only minimal opposition.

However, factional fighting among the Jeffersonian Republicans came to a head in the election of 1824, marking the start of the second party era (1820s–1850s). John Quincy Adams had become president in 1824, after the election was sent to the House of Representatives when no candidate received a majority of the Electoral College vote. Adams's supporters became the National Republicans; those who backed runner-up Andrew Jackson in 1824 made up the Democratic Republicans (soon to be called Democrats). The National Republicans eventually combined with others opposed to the Democrats in the Whig Party, and the Democrats and the Whigs competed for the rest of this era.

The question of how to respond to the slavery issue divided the Whigs in the 1850s and, by 1856, the party had been replaced by the upstart Republican Party, beginning the third-party era (1850s–1890s). This era, after the Civil War at least, was highly competitive between the two major parties. As Marjorie Randon Hershey points out, "Competition was so intense that this period contained two of the [five] elections in American history where the winner of the popular vote for President lost the vote in the electoral college."[9]

In the fourth party era (1890s–1930s), the Grand Old Party (or "GOP"), as the Republican Party came to be known, dominated national politics. The Democrats' only opportunity to lead during this period arose when Woodrow Wilson won the presidency in 1912 because the Republicans split their vote between William Howard Taft, the incumbent Republican nominee, and Theodore Roosevelt, the former Republican president and nominee of the breakaway Progressive Party. Republicans occupied the White House during this era in all but Wilson's eight years in office; in Congress, Republicans controlled the House for twenty-six years and the Senate for thirty of the thirty-six years in the fourth party era.

Roles reversed as a result of the Great Depression. The fifth party era (1930s–1960s) began when Franklin D. Roosevelt won the election of 1932 and formed a ruling coalition around his New Deal program of public works and social welfare. The New Deal coalition of urban laborers, ethnic minorities, Catholics, Jews, Blacks, and Southerners proved very formidable electorally, and the Democrats won every presidential election between 1932 and 1964, save two (1952 and 1956, when popular former World War II general Dwight D. Eisenhower held the office). They also controlled the House and Senate for thirty-two of the thirty-six years between 1932 and 1968.

The New Deal coalition, though difficult to defeat at the polls, was also difficult to hold together. Strife between Southerners and those in favor of civil rights began to occur as early as the Democratic National Convention of 1948. By the 1960s, a series of events, most notably the rise of the civil-rights movement but also opposition to the war in Vietnam, weakened the New Deal coalition considerably. In fact, some scholars believe 1968 and the victory of Republican Richard Nixon marks the end of the fifth party era. The exact nature of the sixth era, or whether we are even in such an era, is the subject of some debate. Suffice it to say that the Democrats are no longer in the dominant position they found themselves in from 1932 to 1968.

Exceptions to the Two-Party System

The history of political parties in the United States appears to be a tale of two parties battling for power in any given era. However, third parties have, at times, played a significant role in that tale.

The Progressive Party's Role in the 1912 Election

The most impressive third party in terms of votes received in a presidential election was the Progressive Party's second-place finish with 27.40 percent of the vote in 1912—the only time a third party has finished in front of one of the two major parties in a presidential election. The Progressives' success, however, was not based on the appeal of the party but on the party's nominee that year. Having already served as president, Theodore Roosevelt was obviously not a typical third-party candidate. In fact, the third-party candidate with the second highest percentage of the vote was another ex-president: Millard Fillmore received 21.54 percent as the American Party's (also known as the Know-Nothing Party) nominee in 1856. In terms of electoral votes, the Progressive Party again reached the high point with eighty-eight in 1912, but third-party candidates have also received forty-six (the American Independent Party in 1968) and have twice earned thirty-nine electoral votes (the Constitutional Union Party in 1860 and the States' Rights Democratic Party, or "Dixiecrats," in 1948).

Personalities, Issues, and Staying Power

At times, then, third-party candidates have been able to garner respectable levels of support from the voters and have occasionally influenced the outcome of an election (see Table 5.1). As a Progressive, Teddy Roosevelt certainly helped Democrat Wilson defeat sitting Republican president Taft in the 1912 election. Many believe that Ross Perot, running as an independent and not the nominee of a third party, and Ralph Nader, the Green Party's nominee, altered the outcomes of the 1992 and 2000 elections, respectively. The extent to which third parties have had an impact on American politics more generally, or on public policy, is less clear. Some third parties have introduced issues into the public arena that the major parties were not addressing. The Liberty Party and Free Soil Party, for example, were primarily concerned with slavery at a time (the 1840s) when the Democrats and the Whigs would rather have ignored the issue. Some suggest that the Socialist Party, which ran presidential candidates in every election between 1900 and 1956, influenced Franklin Roosevelt's New Deal program.

TABLE 5.1   *Selected Third-Party Performance in US Presidential Elections*

Election	Party (Candidate)	Electoral Vote	Popular Vote
1832	Anti-Masonic (Wirt)	7	7.78%
1848	Free Soil (Van Buren)	0	10.12%
1856	American (Fillmore)	8	21.54%
1860	Constitutional Union (Bell)	39	12.62%
1892	Populist (Weaver)	22	8.51%
1912	Progressive (T. Roosevelt)	88	27.40%
1924	Progressive (LaFollette)	13	16.61%
1948	State's Rights (Thurmond)	39	2.41%
1968	American Independence (Wallace)	46	13.53%
1980	Independent (Anderson)	0	6.61%
1992	Independent (Perot)	0	18.91%
1996	Reform (Perot)	0	8.40%

Note: With the exception of the Independent candidacy of John Anderson in 1980 and the Reform Party in 1996, third parties listed in this table received at least one electoral vote or garnered at least 10 percent of the popular vote.

Source: Dave Leip's Atlas of U.S. Presidential Elections, http://uselectionatlas.org/ (accessed May 17, 2013).

Third parties can introduce controversial issues into the mainstream of public debate because ideologically committed individuals whose main goal is not victory but agenda setting are often the force behind their formation. Once the issue has been addressed by the major parties, the third party's reason for being is gone and it disappears. Alternatively, third parties can arise at the instigation of a strong individual leader, as in Theodore Roosevelt's case or when George Wallace ran for president under the American Independent banner in 1968. Interestingly, Steven Rosenstone, Roy Behr, and Edward Lazarus have noted that *candidate*-centered third-party challenges are a twentieth-century phenomenon, whereas nineteenth-century bids were far more likely to come from "relatively stable minor *parties.*" As they put it, "When prominent politicians abandoned the major parties in the 1800s, they cast their lot primarily with established third parties; men of stature formed their own parties in the twentieth century."[10]

Third parties also sometimes form as splinter groups from within one of the major parties. Typically, they are brought back into the fold after one or two election cycles, as the Dixiecrats were after 1948 (though many supporters never again voted Democratic at the presidential level). The point here is that though third parties can have some bearing on an election or can influence public policy in the short run, they rarely have staying power, and their impact is usually limited.[11]

Nonpartisan Elections and One-Party Rule

Third parties, as Hershey notes, are but one type of exception to the two-party system. Others are nonpartisan elections and one-party monopolies.[12] The Progressive era of the early twentieth century brought about many electoral reforms, including nonpartisan elections in many cities and towns (and one state). Progressives believed that parties were a corrupting force in American politics and sought to remove their influence wherever possible. As a result, party affiliations that followed candidates' names were removed from municipal ballots. Today, roughly three-quarters of all cities, including Los Angeles, Chicago (since 1995), Houston, and Boston, hold nonpartisan local elections; among those with partisan elections are New York City and Philadelphia. Among the states, only Nebraska holds nonpartisan elections for its legislature, though contests for its statewide executive branch offices are partisan. It should be acknowledged, however, that even in supposedly nonpartisan elections, parties are usually active, and candidates' affiliations are known. Chicago and Boston are Democratic cities, regardless of whether their elections are officially nonpartisan.

That many, if not most, big cities can be referred to as "Democratic" points to the other exception to the two-party system, namely one-party monopolies. There was a time when some local party leaders acted as major powerbrokers. These party "bosses" ran local "machines" that could handpick their party's nominees and deliver large blocs of votes to state, federal, and even presidential candidates. Often the party boss was the mayor of a city, such as James Curley of Boston or Richard J. Daley of Chicago. The party machine controlled city or county government and provided jobs and services to supporters in exchange for their loyalty.[13] In their heyday, around the turn of the twentieth century, party machines were quite influential. Their eventual demise had many root causes, not the least of them the Progressive reforms of the early twentieth century (including nonpartisan elections) and the rise of racial politics in cities.

The nation as a whole has experienced one-party rule at various points throughout history. Examples would be Republican dominance from 1896 to 1910 and Democratic control from 1932 to 1946, but national one-party rule has never been as robust as it has at times been at the regional, state, or local levels.[14] The most obvious example of a region where a single party ruled without much (or any) opposition was the South after Reconstruction, where Democrats dominated politics for decades. Similarly, Republicans controlled politics in some parts of New England for more than a century after the Civil War. Recently, however, two-party competition has grown in these regions, and today no state can be considered a "one-party state"; however, many would be classified as "modified one-party states," meaning they support one party over the other much of the time.[15] Nationally, the United States has been in a period of what Samuel Eldersveld and Hanes Walton, Jr. call "balanced two-party competition" for more than half a century.[16]

▶ *Why Only Two Parties?*

We might ask why only two major parties dominate in the United States. Many other countries have political systems in which multiple parties consistently hold positions of power in government. The most common explanation for this variation is that the electoral system in use in a country helps determine the number of parties that win seats. Recall from Chapter 2 the discussion of Duverger's Law. French political scientist Maurice Duverger discovered that where electoral systems determine winners by plurality vote in single-member districts, the systems tend to produce only two parties, but systems using proportional representation in multimember districts produce multiple political parties. Some examples do seem to contradict Duverger's Law. In Britain, for instance, nine minor parties held seats in the House of Commons after the 2015 election, even though Britain has single-member districts with plurality winners.[17] Still, despite exceptions, the tendency is certainly that single-member, plurality electoral systems will produce two-party systems.

It has also been suggested that placing executive power in the hands of a single elected official (for example, a president or a governor) contributes to a two-party system. Without the possibility of holding positions in a coalition cabinet, as can occur in parliamentary systems, third parties are unable to gain a foothold in executive branches within presidential systems.[18] And because the executive branch also garners most of the media's—and therefore the public's—attention, third parties are never given the consideration they might otherwise get. This makes it difficult to create inroads with the electorate. Incidentally, our process for electing the president (the Electoral College) contributes to this particular bias against third parties because it functions as a system of fifty-one single-member plurality districts.[19]

Of course, the two major parties have also placed barriers in the way of third parties. Ballot access laws, as discussed in Chapter 4, hinder third-party candidates by making the requirements for them to get on the ballot more stringent than those for the major parties. Though public funding is no longer accepted by the major party presidential candidates, the system as designed put third-party candidates at a disadvantage by offering public funding only *after* an election and then only if the minor-party candidate received at least 5 percent of the vote. The major parties also tend to co-opt third-party ideas when they appear to catch on with the electorate, and they delegitimize votes for third-party candidates as "wasted," an argument the media help to perpetuate.[20] The plight of third parties is, therefore, a self-fulfilling prophecy. Without easy access to ballots and money, third parties perform poorly at the polls; their poor performance then contributes to the idea that they are inevitable losers, which makes it more difficult to get on ballots and raise money.

▶ *Parties as Organizations*

When most people talk about political parties, they have in mind only a vague notion of organizations that conduct political business, particularly at election time. They are certainly not thinking of the party in the electorate or of the party in government, but they most likely cannot tell you what they mean when they refer to the Democratic Party or the Republican Party.

It is a good bet that the average person understands the Democratic and Republican Parties to be monolithic organizations, yet hundreds of Democratic and Republican organizations exist in the United States at the local, state, and national levels. Indeed, the most important distinguishing characteristic of political parties in the United States is that they are decentralized. No single authority directs the activities of all a party's committees. Though national parties impose some limitations on what their subnational affiliates can do, for the most part state and local parties are autonomous. Their ideologies can vary from one place to the next, and they can organize as they see fit, emphasize the issues they find advantageous, and recruit whichever candidates they choose. Thus, the Republican Party of Georgia will differ in many respects from the Republican Party of Connecticut. At the same time, parties operate as "a set of party organs at all levels loosely held together by a common party name, common symbols of organization, a common history, a sense of identity or loyalty, and to a certain extent, similar beliefs and philosophies."[21] So despite their differences, Republicans from Georgia and Connecticut will have more in common than not.

Organizational Structure

Though the parties are not strictly hierarchical, the national committee for each party holds the most power. The Democratic National Committee (DNC) currently consists of 447 members, while the Republican National Committee (RNC) has 168 members.[22] Membership on the DNC consists of at least one man and one woman from each state and the state party chair and the highest-ranking state party officer of the opposite sex. Additional members are allocated to states based on population, but each state's delegation must be balanced, as far as possible, between men and women. The rest of the membership is made up of representatives from various Democratic constituencies, such as organized labor and civil-rights groups; various Democratic elected officials, including the Democratic leaders in both the House and Senate; and fifty "at-large" members, who are chosen by the DNC chairperson and approved by the DNC. Membership on the RNC is far simpler; one committeeman, one committeewoman, and the chair of the state party represent each state.

The primary function of the national committee is to make policy for the party. By and large, their decisions pertain to the national conventions that each party holds in presidential election years. For example, the national committees decide where their conventions will be held. They also establish rules for the allocation of national convention delegates to the states and for the selection of those delegates by the states. Informally, the national committees also assist state and local parties and candidates in reaching voters. Finally, members of the national committees serve as leading campaigners for their party's nominees, especially the presidential candidate. They are expected to help raise money and to promote the candidate wherever they can. Keep in mind that most members of the national committees are active in state and local politics. Though they are committed to their national parties, most of their efforts are in party building at the subnational level.

Both parties also have officers and an executive committee. Though executive committee members serve on their party's national committee, they have more responsibility for party business than the national committee as a whole. Still, the executive committee's role is somewhat symbolic; party meetings suggest to voters that the parties are active and engaged, but executive committees rarely do much that is newsworthy. The chairperson of the party handles most of the important decisions. Along with their staff, the chair oversees the day-to-day operation of the party.

National Committee Chairs

Members of the national committee elect the chair, though this vote is often just a rubber stamp. Once nominated, presidential candidates are traditionally allowed to pick the person who will chair their party during the campaign. The winning party's chair remains in the position after the election, whereas the losing party typically replaces its chair. The process of electing a party chair usually goes unnoticed but, in 2005, the media paid close attention to the Democratic Party's chair race because the Democrats chose the controversial former Vermont governor and 2004 presidential candidate, Howard Dean.

The position of party chair used to be largely ceremonial, but beginning in the 1970s, activist chairs not only helped rebuild their parties but established the position of party chair as one of considerable power and prestige. The chair's job is both strategic and tactical. They must create a blueprint for party success and then implement it. Of course, implementation requires fund-raising, which is the other critical aspect of the chair's job. Not to be overlooked is the chair's role as the leading party spokesperson. They will be expected to appear in the media and in other public forums to articulate the party line. As an illustration of just how demanding the role of party chair has become, in the span of two weeks in November 2005 (an off-election year), RNC Chair Ken Mehlman "traveled 6,000 miles, stopping in at twenty-five events in five cities; he also participated in seven radio interviews, four television appearances and several dozen chats with local and national newspapers."[23]

Other Party Committees

In a presidential election year, most of the national committees' time will be devoted to the presidential campaign. During midterm elections (those in the middle of a president's term), the national committees will typically assist House, Senate, and gubernatorial campaigns throughout the country. In 2006, however, Howard Dean implemented a plan called the "Fifty State Strategy" that sought to strengthen Democratic state parties in every state, including those that are traditionally Republican strongholds. For example, the DNC gave the North Dakota Democratic Party legal and accounting assistance; in other states, technology or communications directors were hired. In all, 183 state party staffers were paid for by the DNC by the end of 2005. Democratic Party leaders in Congress strongly objected to this plan, insisting that Dean target DNC resources in districts with competitive races. Dean held his ground and appears to have been vindicated when Democrats picked up Senate seats in Republican states such as Montana and Virginia and gained votes in numerous Republican-leaning congressional districts.[24] The argument with congressional leaders illustrates the tension a national party chairperson faces between building the party for the long term and winning elections in the short run.

The main responsibility for assisting House and Senate campaigns regardless of the year lies with the campaign committees both parties have in each chamber of Congress. In recent years, these committees, collectively known as the Hill (for Capitol Hill) committees, have assumed an increasingly important role in House and Senate campaigns, and they have become vital to the success of their candidates.[25] They serve as a source of campaign funds and provide candidates with valuable polling results and strategic advice and with guidance on campaign staffing and assistance with campaign advertising. State and local party committees are also important actors in campaigns at all levels but particularly in races "down ballot" (that is, elections for lower-level offices).

The basic building block of state and local parties is the precinct. The precinct is the geographical unit in which voters are assigned a polling place (see Figure 5.1). Ideally, parties would have a captain for every precinct. In practice, however, many precincts are without a party leader, particularly in areas where a party has little support among the voters. The precinct captain's job is to know the precinct well enough to mobilize sympathetic voters on Election Day. In addition to a number of precincts, if a city or town is large enough, it will be organized into wards, and the parties will have a ward leader for each. Otherwise, the next organizational level for the party is a city or township committee. Building on those committees might be county and congressional district committees, though states differ in terms of their specific organizational levels. Finally, each state party has a central committee to conduct the party's statewide efforts.

Like the national committees, each state party has a chairperson. All state chairs in both parties are members of their party's national committees. However, chairs of state parties that are competitive and professional will have more influence with candidates and national party committees than will those of state parties that are unsuccessful and poorly organized. Whether powerful or not, state party chairs usually toil in the background of electoral politics. Occasionally, however, a state chair commands a great deal of attention. When former

FIGURE 5.1   *Precinct Map, City of Newcastle, Washington*

Source: Department of Elections, King County, Washington, http://your.kingcounty.gov/elections/ gis/maps/cities/2013/newcastle.pdf.

Christian Coalition executive director Ralph Reed became chair of the Georgia Republican Party, the story was widely covered because Reed was considered a significant force in Republican Party politics.

Organizational Activity and Reform

With the parties seemingly central to so much of what is happening in American politics today, it is hard to imagine that less than forty years ago, they were thought to be in steep decline. Political observers in the 1960s began to notice that campaigns were becoming candidate-centered, with candidates as likely to turn to political consultants as to the parties for campaign assistance. At the same time, voters appeared to be increasingly independent at the ballot box. The situation led many to issue warnings about the imminent death, or at least irrelevance, of the parties.[26]

We now know, however, that just as those arguments were being made, the parties were reviving themselves. The Republicans were first to rebuild. Under the leadership of William Brock at the RNC and the chairs of the GOP Hill

committees in the mid-1970s, the Republicans began the process of transforming their party into an organization that could provide its candidates with valuable services.[27] Doing so required money, which the Republican Party was able to
raise in large amounts by taking advantage of developments in direct mail fund-
raising. A sufficiently sized and professional staff was also necessary, and the
Republicans rapidly assembled one. Between 1972 and 1980, the staff of the RNC
grew from thirty individuals to 350, while the staffs of the Republican Hill committees grew from six to forty for the House and four to thirty for the Senate.[28]

The Democrats responded to the times as well, though they did so in two
stages. In the first stage, the Democrats undertook procedural reform. The 1968
contest for the Democratic presidential nomination had been a disaster. The sitting president, Lyndon Johnson, withdrew from the race after a poor showing
in the New Hampshire primary. Opposition to the war in Vietnam was stiff and
becoming fierce. Johnson's vice president, Hubert Humphrey, entered the race
but did not compete in primaries, as he had the backing of much of the Democratic establishment. Senator Eugene McCarthy of Minnesota, who had finished a
strong second behind Johnson in New Hampshire, and Senator Robert Kennedy
of New York, who entered the race after New Hampshire, battled each other for
primary votes. Kennedy was assassinated on the night of the California primary,
leaving McCarthy as the sole antiwar candidate, though Senator George McGovern of South Dakota picked up many of Kennedy's delegates when he entered the
race at the national convention.

The party's internal division over the war was put on display at the national
convention in Chicago. Thousands of antiwar activists protested outside the
amphitheater where the convention took place, and television cameras captured
their brutal treatment by the Chicago police. Inside the amphitheater, Senator
Abraham Ribicoff of Connecticut accused the city of Chicago—and, by implication, Mayor Richard Daley—of using "Gestapo tactics in the streets."[29] The
defeat of a proposed "peace plank" in the party's platform caused antiwar delegates to protest inside the convention. Despite not having run in a single primary, Humphrey received the party's nomination. At the time, primary votes did
not translate directly into convention delegates. The nomination result angered
many Democrats who felt that party leaders were out of touch with the party's
grassroots.

Shortly after the 1968 election, the chair of the DNC responded to the frustration of rank-and-file Democrats by appointing a commission to examine the
party's nomination process. The McGovern-Fraser Commission, as it came to
be known, found a nominating system that was "unduly discretionary, untimely,
closed and discriminatory."[30] The McGovern-Fraser Commission's reform proposal aimed to address each of these deficiencies by opening the process to
minorities, women, and young people and by ensuring that delegate selection
would take place in a reasonable time frame.

The most significant change to the process, however, was that state parties
had to comply with requirements set by the national party. In nominations prior

to 1972, the state parties, not national party rules, determined how delegates to the national convention would be chosen. Party leaders in the states would often handpick delegates. Some of the states that held primaries chose delegates in a secretive manner, with no apparent connection to primary results. The McGovern-Fraser reforms put an end to such activity and removed much of the discretion state party leaders had enjoyed. These changes to the nomination system, which have been revisited by the Democratic Party a number of times since the early 1970s and which ultimately affected the Republican Party as well, "rocked the existing system so fundamentally that the ground has yet to settle."[31]

The second stage of the Democrats' transformation has been called "party renewal." In response to President Jimmy Carter's humiliating loss to Ronald Reagan in the 1980 election, the Democratic Party decided, as Paul Herrnson notes, to "increase its competitiveness by imitating the GOP's party-building and campaign service programs."[32] Though they enhanced their fund-raising capacity, professionalized their staff, and strengthened other aspects of the organization, they remained far behind the Republicans in such efforts. For the next twenty years, the Democrats would play catch-up to the Republicans in party rebuilding.

One of the ways in which both party organizations have reasserted themselves is with candidate recruitment. Though most candidates for Congress and other levels of government remain self-starters (as discussed in Chapter 4), the parties do contact a large number of potential candidates about running for office. In fact, in their study of candidate emergence, Sandy Maisel, Cherie Maestas, and Walter Stone found that party leaders contacted just a little more than 40 percent of the potential candidates the scholars had identified. That number increases to 52 percent in districts that are "marginal" (that is, where the incumbent margin of victory was less than 20 percent in the last election) and 54 percent in open seat races.[33]

The most active party committees in contacting potential candidates were district (or local) parties. District parties contacted 35 percent of all potential candidates, whereas state parties contacted 22 percent and national parties just 17 percent.[34] That ordering of party committees holds across all types of seats and makes sense, given that district party committees have more knowledge of local personalities than will state or national parties. As the vast majority of potential candidates who are contacted by the party hear from the local committee, it is safe to assume that when the state or national party does make contact, it is usually to reinforce the efforts of the local party.

▶ Party in the Electorate and in Government

Parties exist not only as organizations but as psychological attachments in the minds of voters and as coordinating mechanisms for the institutions of government. We will discuss partisanship at the individual level in Chapter 8 on voters. In this section, we examine parties in the electorate as a whole, both in terms of aggregate party identification and attitudes toward parties among the people. Party in government is primarily relevant to the study of institutions (such as Congress), but we will address this aspect of parties insofar as it affects campaigns and elections.

Party Identification

Alongside the historical suspicion of parties discussed earlier, anecdotal evidence suggests that the American people dislike political parties. Voters repeatedly claim to "vote the person, not the party." Despite that assertion, as we will see shortly (and again in Chapter 8), most voters actually vote the party. But something about parties and partisanship seems distasteful to the voters.

It is difficult to get a handle on just what that something is. Most voters do not think about parties in abstract terms. If people say they are unhappy with the parties, it may be because they are simply unsatisfied with the choices they have—that is, the Democrats and Republicans—and not because they dislike parties altogether. Nevertheless, very little empirical work has been done on people's attitudes toward political parties in general.

The best we can do, then, is to extrapolate from what little data exists. As you might guess, the evidence is somewhat mixed. As Eldersveld and Walton point out, the public does tend to agree that parties are necessary for democracy, but a majority also believes that "parties do more to confuse the issues than to provide a clear choice on them."[35] In a 2002 survey conducted for the Improving Campaign Conduct project at American University, fewer people thought the quality of political parties was excellent or good (25.9 percent) than thought the same of candidates (34.8 percent), campaign consultants (31.3 percent), or print and broadcast journalists (35.1 percent and 39.4 percent, respectively).[36]

There has also been a growing reluctance of Americans to identify with a political party. One of the most significant trends in American politics over the last fifty years has been the increase in the number of people who call themselves Independents. When asked about their party identification in 1952, 23 percent of the public claimed not to affiliate with either party; by 2012, that number had risen to 38 percent. Of course, many people will claim to be Independent but, when pressed, will acknowledge that they lean toward one of the two parties. Those who do not are called pure Independents; their ranks rose from 5 percent of the population in 1952 to 14 percent in 2012.[37]

Despite the increase in nominal Independents, the majority of Americans still identify with one of the two parties. In 2016, according to the Pew Research Center for the People and the Press, 48 percent of the public identified as Democrats (or were Democratic "leaners") whereas 44 percent were Republicans.[38] Though these numbers fluctuate based on short-term factors, over the long run, the Democrats have enjoyed a significant advantage in party identification. Even in 1984, when President Reagan was winning a landslide reelection victory, Democrats outnumbered Republicans by 48 percent to 40 percent.[39]

One other way to gauge the level of party affiliation among the voters is to look at voter registration numbers in the states. However, twenty states do not ask voters to register by party. In the thirty states (plus the District of Columbia) that do, 42.8 million people were registered as Democrats as of October 2014, according to the online newsletter Ballot Access News. Republicans numbered 30.9 million, and there were 27.7 million Independents (and at least 2.4 million registered with third parties, though many states keep incomplete numbers on them).[40] These numbers are likely to be exaggerated in the Democrats' favor, however, because many of the states that do not have party registration are states that, given recent voting patterns, would likely have more registered Republicans than Democrats if registration by party were allowed (for example, Montana, North Dakota, and numerous southern states).

As noted at the beginning of this section, voters often claim not to vote according to partisan affiliation. Nevertheless, the best predictor of a person's vote is their party identification. In 2016, despite considerable dissatisfaction with the candidates, exit polls revealed that 89 percent of Democrats (not including leaners) voted for Hillary Clinton whereas 88 percent of Republicans voted for Donald Trump.[41] Interestingly, Independent leaners often vote at higher levels for the nominee of the party they favor than do "weak" party identifiers. In 1992, for example, 71 percent of Independents leaning Democratic voted for Bill Clinton, whereas 69 percent of weak Democrats did so; 62 percent of those leaning Republican cast ballots for George H. W. Bush, whereas 60 percent of weak Republicans did the same.[42] Of course, "strong" party identifiers support candidates of their parties at the highest levels, and they are also far more likely to "straight-ticket vote," or cast all their votes on a ballot for the same party.

Partisan Polarization and Negative Partisanship

Split-ticket voting, the opposite of voting a straight ticket, has been declining in recent years. Whereas 30 percent of voters cast their ballots for candidates of different parties for president and the House of Representatives in 1972, only 14 percent of voters did the same in 2012.[43] This suggests an increased level of partisanship among voters.

While there is some debate over just how polarized the American public is with respect to ideology and policy preferences, there is no doubt that attitudes and feelings toward the other party and its candidates have polarized.[44] Political scientist Lilliana Mason describes this development as "social," as opposed to "issue," polarization. Her conclusion is that "as our political identities fall increasingly into alignment, and our partisanship consequently strengthens, the outcome is a nation that may agree on many things, but is bitterly divided nonetheless."[45] Shanto Iyengar and Sean Westwood have even shown that discriminatory behavior based on partisan biases exceeds that based on racial biases.[46]

Interestingly, feelings about one's own party have remained virtually unchanged since the late 1970s; over those forty years, Democrats and Republicans have consistently rated their warmth of feeling toward their party at around 75 on a "feeling thermometer" scale between 0 and 100 (100 being warmest). Feelings toward the other party, however, have plummeted. Whereas Democrats and Republicans rated their feelings toward the other party at around 45, on average, in the late 1970s, that number is below 30 today.[47] This phenomenon is known as "negative partisanship."[48]

Marc Hetherington and his colleagues have shown that evaluations of presidential candidates' traits—whether the candidates are knowledgeable, moral, strong leaders and caring—have polarized dramatically since 2000. This "trait polarization" has obvious consequences for campaigns and elections, but it also has consequences for governing. As the authors put it, "partisans increasingly perceive the other party's candidate as *personally* flawed." If that candidate were to win, such perceptions might undermine "the legitimacy of a president's leadership and the decisions he or she makes."[49]

Issue Ownership and the Permanent Campaign

Perhaps curiously, given the growth in partisan polarization, the number of people identifying as "strong partisans" has not grown significantly. In 2012, just 35 percent of the public identified themselves as strong Democrats (20 percent) or Republicans (15 percent). This is comparable to the number of strong partisans (37 percent) in 1952.[50] Thus, though party identification remains a significant factor in understanding political behavior, it is also true that a large percentage of voters are not highly partisan. As a result, many voters recognize strengths in each of the parties. Democrats are generally viewed as better at handling issues such as health care, the environment, and education whereas Republicans have an advantage on defense, taxes, and moral values.

The idea that each party "owns" a different set of issues is important for understanding campaign strategy, which we will discuss in Chapter 9.[51] For now, it is worth noting that issue ownership contributes to what Byron Shafer and William Claggett call "the two majorities." Rather than think of a single party as commanding majority support from Americans, it is more accurate to think that either party can build a majority given the right issue context in the electorate. Thus, when the most pressing issues relate to cultural values, civil liberties, or foreign relations (the "cultural/national" dimension), issues about which the public tends to be more conservative and Republicans tend to own, the GOP can build a majority. When the primary concern of voters is social well-being, civil rights, and social insurance (the "economic/welfare" dimension), Democrats have an advantage because the public is more liberal in these areas, and the Democrats own the issues.[52] The concept of issue ownership and the notion that two majorities exist in American politics help to explain how it is that Republicans have been able to win presidential elections in recent decades despite being in the numerical minority. The issue context has simply favored Republicans in many of these races.

Issue ownership is also useful for thinking about the party in government in a way that is relevant to campaigns and elections. Because party strategists on both sides realize that they each own a different set of issues, elected officials often pursue agendas that promote issues their party owns and will naturally give them an advantage in the realm of public opinion. This has led to what has been called the *permanent campaign*. The permanent campaign has two meanings. The first is the notion that elected officials are constantly running for office. It should come as no surprise that politicians want to be reelected.[53] This has been true at least since politics became a career option for ambitious individuals, which occurred in Congress just after World War II and has become true in many state legislatures as well. However, the intensity of reelection campaigns has surely increased in recent years, as nonstop fund-raising and around-the-clock media coverage have become unavoidable elements in contemporary American politics.

A second sense in which a permanent campaign goes on in the United States is the use of campaign techniques by elected officials in the process of governing (see Chapter 11). Because public approval is so vital to the ability to govern effectively, all elected officials, but especially those in executive branches (such as presidents and governors), must maintain popular support. To do so, they turn to the tactics used in campaigns, including polling and advertising. A gubernatorial speech on education is no longer merely an attempt to convince legislators to adopt the governor's policy. It is now a marketing tool, complete with a setting that is picturesque, a backdrop (called "wallpaper") that communicates the central message of the speech, and all the "advance" work that goes into a campaign stop, including the assembly of a supportive audience and press releases suggesting the best interpretation of the event. Not to be outdone, legislators routinely stage public events in support of legislative proposals, and members of Congress have set up campaign-like "war rooms," open to the media, to coordinate the public relations aspects of particularly important votes. Perhaps too often as a result of this permanent campaign, governing becomes a zero-sum game of advancing the short-term fortunes of the party instead of being a search for common ground and compromise.

▶ The Nomination Process

Of course, to engage in the permanent campaign, politicians must first get elected. Before they can do that, however, they usually have to obtain their party's nomination. Though state laws regulate the nomination process and taxpayers' dollars usually pay for primary elections, nominations are actually party business. Party rules govern any number of aspects of the process and, of course, states differ dramatically in how they function in this regard. In addition, state and local candidates are often nominated in ways that differ from how presidential candidates are nominated, even within a given state.

State and Local Direct Primaries

For party leadership, the nomination process is much easier if only one candidate seeks the party's nomination. Thus, as mentioned in Chapter 4, parties occasionally engage in negative recruitment, discouraging individuals who party leaders feel would make less than formidable candidates. However, negative recruitment is tricky and can backfire, so it is used rather sparingly.

When candidates contest a nomination, the party committees usually stay neutral, at least officially. Of course, party leaders may informally endorse a candidate. They can do so by encouraging party activists to support one candidate over others or even, in extreme cases, by offering resources to preferred candidates. In some states, however, the party may formally endorse one candidate. Thirteen states hold preprimary endorsement conventions to anoint a single candidate. In most of those states, this formal endorsement makes it more difficult for non-endorsed candidates to get on the primary ballot.[54] The advantages of being an endorsed candidate are considerable, but endorsement does not always guarantee nomination; the party's primary voters may decide to nominate a candidate other than the party establishment's choice. This happened in the US Senate race in Connecticut in 2006. At the state party's nominating convention, sitting senator Joseph Lieberman received the party's endorsement, but challenger Ned Lamont had enough delegates to force a primary. In the primary, Democratic voters nominated Lamont because of their displeasure with Lieberman's support for the war in Iraq. (Lieberman ultimately ran in the general election as an Independent and won reelection.)

The system for nominating congressional and state-level candidates differs markedly from the presidential nominating system. For nonpresidential nominations, most states use only the direct primary to nominate candidates. In these states, the winner of the party's primary automatically receives the nomination. A few states use some combination of primaries and conventions to nominate their state and congressional candidates.[55]

Primaries can be either "open" or "closed," and the states split roughly evenly in terms of which they use (though there are slightly more open primary states than closed).[56] An open primary is one in which voters of any party affiliation (or none) may vote. Voters do not have to be registered with the party in whose primary they are participating. Obviously, states without party registration use open primaries, but states in which voters register by party may also use them. To vote in an open primary, the voter simply chooses a party's ballot at the polling place. (In some states, the voter must request one party's ballot before entering the voting booth; in others, the voter's choice of ballots is secret and takes place in the booth.)

Washington, California, and Louisiana use what is, essentially, a unique variation on the open primary. Voters are given ballots listing all the candidates; the ballot is officially nonpartisan, though a party affiliation (or, in Washington, a "party preference") is listed by each candidate's name. Voters choose a candidate, of either party, for each office, and the two candidates receiving the most votes, regardless of party, face each other in the general election. In the 2016 US Senate race in California, for example, two Democrats—Kamala Harris and Loretta Sanchez—wound up running against one another.

In 2000, the Supreme Court struck down a slightly different system called the "blanket primary," which had been in use in California (similar systems used in Alaska and Washington were subsequently struck down). The blanket primary allowed voters to vote for a candidate of either party for each office; the top vote-getter from each party would then advance to the general election. The Court ruled that this system violated the parties' First Amendment right to freedom of association.[57] In March 2008, however, the Court ruled the new "top two" primary constitutional.[58]

Louisiana's primary system for state-level offices differs slightly from the "top two" system in California and Washington. In Louisiana, voters choose a candidate of either party for each office and if one candidate receives a majority of the vote in the primary, they are elected to that office (and no general election is held). If no one receives a majority, the two candidates with the most votes, regardless of party, face each other in the general election.

A closed primary is one in which only voters who are registered with a party can participate in that party's primary. Some states use a modified closed primary and allow independents to vote in one of the parties' primaries. States may also make it easy to change one's registration to vote in a given primary— for example, by allowing a change on Election Day—considerably loosening the closed nature of the primary.

As one might imagine, political parties prefer closed primaries, where they are reasonably certain that only those who affiliate with them will help determine who their nominees will be. Open primaries introduce uncertainty and the possibility that those who are not entirely committed to the party will influence its choice of nominees. Conversely, voters are given maximum choice in open primaries, which suits the anti-party sentiment in American political culture.

Presidential Nominations

Direct primaries, then, are central to the nominating process below the presidential level in all the states. The presidential nominating process is an entirely different beast. To begin with, presidential candidates are officially nominated by national conventions consisting of delegates from each of the states and territories. Those delegates are chosen in each of the states by one of two methods: primaries or caucuses. In 2016, the Republican and Democratic parties used primaries to award delegates in thirty-seven and thirty-six states, respectively; the rest used caucuses or state conventions (or some combination thereof).[59]

When they cast ballots in presidential primaries, voters are indicating their preference for a candidate, but (perhaps more important) are also helping to secure delegates to the national convention for their preferred candidate. In most states, the delegates themselves, pledged to the appropriate candidate, are selected at a state convention; however, in a few states, they are chosen directly by the voters in the primary. In the Democratic Party, the number of delegates candidates receive from a state is roughly in proportion to the vote they get in the primary (assuming they surpass a threshold of 15 percent of the vote, per party rules). Traditionally, most Republican delegates were allocated according to some variation on the winner-take-all method. That is, the candidate who received the most votes (either statewide or at the congressional district level) got all the delegates (from that state or district). Changes to Republican Party rules, however, made delegate allocation a bit more proportional in 2012.[60]

A caucus is a meeting of voters at which supporters of the candidates are free to make appeals to convince those attending to cast votes for their preferred candidate. Caucus-goers then vote either by casting secret ballots or by literally forming into groups by candidate choice. Individuals pledged to candidates who have won delegates are then selected to move on to the next level of caucuses, which is typically at the county level, to be held a few days or weeks later. From there, delegates are selected to go to congressional district conventions and then on to the state party convention, which chooses delegates to the national convention. Caucuses may last for several hours, so turnout is usually low, but the commitment by attendees to helping the party is quite high.

Delegates to the national conventions are party loyalists and activists whose primary responsibility is to officially nominate the presidential and vice presidential candidates. Most delegates arrive at the national convention pledged to a candidate, but the Democrats set aside a number of unpledged delegate slots for "PLEOs," or party leaders and elected officials. These so-called "superdelegates" are not bound by the results of primaries or caucuses, but they usually announce their support for one of the candidates before the convention. However, because they are unpledged, they are free to withhold support or even withdraw it once given, as they see fit. In 2007, for example, Representative John Lewis of Georgia, a veteran of the civil rights movement, endorsed Hillary Clinton for president. As Barack Obama became a viable candidate early in 2008, however, Lewis announced that he was switching his support from Clinton to Obama.

Ordinarily, one candidate will have secured a majority of pledged delegates and, thus, the party's nomination prior to the convention. In such instances, the preferences of the superdelegates become largely irrelevant (except for the persuasive power their early endorsements may carry). Early in 2008, however, it appeared possible that the superdelegates would favor a candidate (namely, Clinton) who had fewer pledged delegates than another candidate (Obama). If the leader among pledged delegates had less than a majority in the overall delegate count, the superdelegates could potentially determine the nomination. Critics argued that superdelegates should not overturn the "will of the voters" by tipping the delegate count and, thus, handing the nomination to a candidate who did not win the bulk of the pledged delegates. Others argued that undecided party leaders would ultimately choose on the basis of their assessments of what was in the best interest of the party and should, therefore, be given an independent voice in the process.

Another concern is that superdelegates can create an air of inevitability by endorsing one candidate early in the nomination process. In 2016, supporters of Senator Bernie Sanders objected to overwhelming superdelegate support for Secretary Clinton, which they argued made it appear as though Sanders had no real shot at winning the nomination. In the end, the superdelegates did not determine the outcome of the 2008 or 2016 nominations, but the controversy surrounding their role in the Democratic Party seems unlikely to dissipate as long as they exist. As a result, the Democratic Party's rules committee voted to empower a "unity commission" to meet following the 2016 election and propose changes to the role of superdelegates prior to the 2020 nominating season.[61]

In total, there were 4,763 delegates to the 2016 Democratic National Convention and 2,472 at the GOP convention.[62] To determine how many delegates are allocated to each state, the parties use rather complicated formulas. Factors that are typically part of the formulas include the size of the state, its past electoral performance at the presidential level, and the number of elected officials the party has in that state. In the past, Republicans have also given states an incentive against holding their primaries or caucuses early in the calendar by providing additional delegates for later dates.

The phenomenon known as "front-loading" occurs when multiple states move the date of their primaries and caucuses to a point early in the calendar year. They do so in an attempt to gain influence over the process by garnering the attention of the candidates, not to mention the media. Of course, as more states do so, less attention falls to any given state. In recent years, front-loading has become extreme. In 1976, voters in half of all congressional districts had not voted in primaries until mid-May. That date had inched backward to mid-March by 1988 and to late February or early March by 2004. In 2008, the point at which half of all convention delegates had been selected was February 5, because an unusually large number of states held primaries or caucuses on that date. In 2016, the nomination process reached the halfway point on March 15 for Republicans and March 22 for Democrats.[63]

By tradition, the Iowa caucuses are the first nominating event of the election year and are usually held in January (though in 2016, they were held on February 1). These are followed, a week or so later, by the first-in-the-nation primary in New Hampshire (held on February 9 in 2016). Typically, the parties allow a few more early contests in other states, though these must occur sometime after Iowa and New Hampshire. In 2016, the Democratic Party approved a caucus in Nevada on February 20, and primaries in South Carolina were set by the Republicans and Democrats, respectively, for February 20 and 27. (Republicans held their Nevada caucus on February 23.) In 2008, Florida and Michigan ran afoul of national party rules by holding January primaries without approval. Initially, the DNC stripped Florida and Michigan of its delegates because of this infraction, but the delegations from these states were eventually seated at the convention.

Once the initial contests, particularly Iowa and New Hampshire, have taken place, the most important event on the nominating calendar is "Super Tuesday," the name given to the day on which the greatest number of states schedule their primaries or caucuses. In 2008, February 5 was dubbed "Super-Duper Tuesday" because an unprecedented twenty-four states decided to hold contests on that date. Election observers treated Super-Duper Tuesday essentially as a national primary. Nearly 52 percent of the pledged Democratic delegates and 43 percent of Republican delegates were up for grabs on that one day.[64] In 2016, Super Tuesday was on March 1 as eleven states (and one territory, on the Democratic side) held events.

Presumably, front-loading gives candidates with name recognition and money a considerable advantage over relatively unknown and underfunded candidates. In the past, when the process was spread out over a longer period of time, a candidate could do well in an early, small state such as Iowa or New Hampshire and ride that momentum to later victories. In a compacted calendar, there is little time to take advantage of a good showing in Iowa or New Hampshire before having to compete in dozens of other states spread throughout the country.

Arguments for Reform

Because it places some types of candidates at a disadvantage, many reformers would like to reverse the trend toward front-loading. One suggestion for doing so is the Delaware Plan. It would create four groups of states based on the size of the state. The smallest thirteen states would hold their primaries or caucuses first, say in February or March, to be followed by the next largest thirteen states a month later and so on until the largest twelve states held their elections three or four months after the start of the process. States could hold their primaries or caucuses at any time during their assigned month but not before then.[65]

An alternative plan, based on state size, is called the American Plan. It is more complicated than the Delaware Plan and also provides larger states with the possibility of holding their primaries or caucuses relatively early in the process. The American Plan creates ten intervals, each of which is roughly two weeks in length. In the first interval, primaries or caucuses would be held in randomly selected states with a combined total of just eight congressional districts. Obviously, this would mean that only a handful of small states would be eligible for the first interval. Each interval thereafter would increase by eight total congressional seats, with the order of the later rounds shuffled to allow larger states into the random draw. Thus, the intervals might increase as follows: 8, 16, 24, 56, 32, 64, 40, 72, 48, 80. Under such a scenario, California would be eligible for random selection in the fourth interval.[66]

Another proposal that seeks to counteract front-loading—but does not take state size into consideration—is the Rotating Regional Presidential Primaries Plan put forward by the National Association of Secretaries of State. Under this plan, states would be divided by region. Each of the four regions—the East, the South, the Midwest, and the West (see Figure 5.2)—would be given a month during which states in those regions would hold their primaries or caucuses. The first region, to be determined in the first year of the plan by lottery, would hold elections beginning in March, and the rest of the regions would hold their primaries and caucuses during their assigned month. In the second presidential election year under the plan, the region that had been first would be last, and each of the other regions would move up; this rotation would continue in each presidential election cycle. Under the original proposal, Iowa and New Hampshire would retain their positions as the first caucus and primary, respectively.

Of course, they could also be denied that right and placed within their regions. The status of Iowa and New Hampshire is controversial. Though their small size provides a nice opportunity for voters to meet candidates face to face, they are not particularly representative states. In an analysis of 2006 census data by the Associated Press, Iowa ranked forty-first among the states according to how well it fit the national profile in terms of race, age, income, and other important factors, whereas New Hampshire ranked forty-seventh.[67] The nation was 67.6 percent White according to the census data, whereas Whites made up 91.9 percent of Iowa's population and 94.7 of New Hampshire's.

Some have suggested that we hold a national primary to avoid giving voters in one state more influence over the nomination process than those in other states, but this would simply exacerbate the problems caused by front-loading. Candidates with name recognition and money would have huge advantages in a national primary.

No process for nominating the parties' presidential candidates will be perfect. Indeed, many believe that it is not the calendar but the method used to select delegates (and, thus, nominees) that is flawed. The McGovern-Fraser reforms triggered an increase in the use of primaries. From 1912, when primaries were first widely used, to 1968, an average of just a little more than fifteen states used primaries, selecting an average of 41.43 percent of the delegates to the national conventions. Since 1968, an average of thirty-three states have used primaries in each election cycle to select just under 70 percent of delegates.[68]

This heavy reliance on primaries has had certain consequences. It has certainly opened the process to rank-and-file party members and, to a degree, to the wider electorate, especially in states with open primaries. Yet turnout in primaries is much lower than it is in general elections. Furthermore, if primary voters differ in significant ways from the typical party identifier, the parties' nominees are being chosen by an

FIGURE 5.2   *Map of Regions under the National Association of Secretaries of State's Rotating Regional Presidential Primaries Plan*

Source: National Association of Secretaries of State (2008: 8).

unrepresentative subset of the party's voters. If, for instance, primary voters are more ideologically extreme than the average party identifier, candidates may have to move toward the left or right wing of their party to get the nomination. This, in turn, may add to polarization between the parties. Critics of primaries argue that party leaders are more likely to nominate moderate candidates because electability, not ideological purity, is the central criterion party leaders apply. That, however, is by no means clear. Republicans chose their 1964 nominee, Barry Goldwater, under the old system, and he is still considered one of the most ideologically extreme candidates (at least for his time) ever nominated. And under the new system, Democrats nominated Bill Clinton, a moderate, in 1992. In addition, little evidence suggests that voters in presidential primaries differ dramatically from those who support the parties in the general election.

Those who would prefer that party leaders have a larger role in nominating presidential candidates also claim that primaries have made the process more media-driven and that they have fostered a candidate-centered system. Primaries have undoubtedly contributed to these trends, but those developments were set in motion before 1968 and were likely to have advanced regardless of the nature of the nominating system. Furthermore, political scientist Marty Cohen and his colleagues have offered evidence that party insiders (including "intense policy demanders" who are aligned with the party) have been able to control the nomination by throwing their support behind that candidate early in the process.[69] That is, they were able to do so in 1980s and 1990s. By the turn of the century, party leaders seemed to be having a harder time agreeing on a candidate for the nomination (for reasons we will examine in Chapter 10). Donald Trump's nomination in 2016 certainly suggests that a media-fueled, outsider candidacy can be successful, at least in the absence of a party consensus on a nominee.[70]

One final charge often leveled against the McGovern-Fraser system is that it has made national conventions irrelevant. The primary system has certainly replaced the national convention as the locus of decision making in the nomination process. However, this hardly means that the national convention is irrelevant.

▶ The National Conventions

The parties' national conventions have a long and rich history. The Anti-Masons held the first national convention in 1831, and the Democrats followed suit in 1832. The purpose of the national convention is to nominate the party's presidential and vice presidential candidates. In the heyday of conventions, various party and interest group leaders would attempt to convince (or cajole) delegates to support their preferred candidates. Delegates would vote on the nomination, but the outcome was often uncertain and occasionally contentious. To take an extreme example, the 1924 Democratic National Convention held 103 ballots before nominating John W. Davis. As late as 1952, the Democrats took three ballots to nominate Adlai Stevenson. The last Republican nominee to require more than one ballot was Thomas Dewey in 1948.

Today, the conventions are simply a rubber stamp of what has already been determined by the primaries. That is, by the end of the primary season, one candidate in each party will have secured a majority of the party's delegates, thereby ensuring their nomination. As other candidates drop out of the race, only the presumptive nominee is left, and the national convention becomes merely a coronation. Though each state delegation casts votes for a candidate, the result is a foregone conclusion.

So what purpose do contemporary conventions serve? Perhaps most important, after officially nominating the candidate, the convention approves the party's platform. The platform is a statement of the party's positions on major issues, and its values and vision for the country. A separate committee writes the document prior to the convention and presents it to the convention for approval. It is not uncommon for arguments over certain "planks," or specific parts, of the platform to occur between various wings of the parties. In 2016, supporters of Sen. Bernie Sanders were able to get concessions from the Democratic platform committee on certain key progressive issues, including free college tuition, an expansion of Social Security, and a $15 an hour federal minimum wage. They were unsuccessful, however, in getting their views on trade and health care reflected in the final document.[71]

Very few people actually read the platforms. In fact, the GOP presidential nominee in 1996, Bob Dole, declared publicly that he had not read the document and further asserted that he was not bound by it. Nevertheless, the platform is important to particular constituencies within the party who seek to have their issues addressed in satisfactory ways. As a result, approving a platform that is acceptable to most party activists and that maintains party unity is a critical task for the convention.

In addition to formally nominating the presidential candidate, the convention nominates the vice presidential candidate. The presumptive presidential nominee chooses the running mate, though in the past the convention delegates were sometimes asked to do so. Until recently, the presidential candidate would wait to announce the choice of running mate at the convention. Now presidential nominees announce their pick in advance of the convention, taking the opportunity to make headlines during the slow summer news days between wrapping up the nomination in the primaries and the start of the convention.

The national conventions also perform a symbolic function. They are, in essence, pep rallies for the presidential ticket and the party. The convention is a carefully choreographed launch of the presidential campaign. Each event and every speaker is chosen to help construct an image of the party the presidential campaign wants to convey. In 2000, the Republicans painted a portrait of an inclusive and tolerant party; the official theme was "Renewing America's Purpose. Together." This message was a direct response to the less conciliatory image that had been created during the party's 1992 convention.

Indeed, the 1992 convention is a classic example of the limits of stage management. Presidential candidates who have been defeated for the nomination are usually granted permission to address the delegates, though only after a pledge that they will endorse the party's standard bearer. This often creates an awkward situation for the nominee, particularly if the nomination contest had been contentious. In 1992, Pat Buchanan, who had challenged President George H. W. Bush for the GOP nomination and had even garnered 37 percent of the vote in the New Hampshire primary, was given a prime-time speaking slot on the opening night of the Republican National Convention. Buchanan's speech reflected his socially conservative views and was a salvo in the so-called culture wars. He exhorted delegates to "take back our cities, and take back our culture, and take back our country."[72] Though the speech may have energized some convention delegates, many believed it was too extreme for the American public and that it backfired against the Republicans.

This example may also illustrate that convention delegates are not typical Americans. As party activists, delegates are more involved in and more knowledgeable about politics than either their party's rank-and-file or the average voter.

They are also better educated, wealthier, and more likely to be male. Finally, their views on the issues are out of step with those not attending conventions. For instance, when asked about their opinion on abortion, 33 percent of all voters in 2008 believed that abortion "should be generally available to those who want it," whereas 43 percent of Democratic voters and 20 percent of Republican voters took that position. However, 70 percent of Democratic convention delegates thought abortion should generally be available while just nine percent of Republican delegates held that view. This pattern of Democratic delegates being more liberal than all other voters and Republican delegates being more conservative holds across most issues.[73]

The national conventions culminate with the nominee's acceptance speech. Though the nominee's address has at times been overshadowed by other speeches at the convention, the acceptance speech is the most anticipated and most widely watched event. It was once a way to introduce the nominee to the American people, but as the nominees are now known far in advance of the conventions, the acceptance speech has become an opportunity for the candidate to reintroduce a desired image to the public. In 2000, George W. Bush used his speech to portray himself as a compassionate conservative, and John Kerry used his in 2004 to remind voters of his military record, beginning the address with a salute and adding, "I'm John Kerry, and I'm reporting for duty." Barack Obama sought to bolster the sense that his 2008 presidential bid was historic, perhaps even transformational, when he delivered his acceptance speech at the Democratic National Convention to an estimated 84,000 supporters in Denver's Invesco Field.

▶ General Election Activity

After the national conventions, the general election campaign begins in earnest. In the general election, the parties provide many of their candidates, at all levels, with as much support as they can. This includes strategic advice and services such as polling, advertising, and volunteers. Perhaps most important, it also includes financial assistance. As Election Day nears, the party becomes extremely active in voter mobilization.

Campaign Support

One of the first services the parties provide are campaign-training seminars for candidates and their staffs. The subject matter ranges from fund-raising and campaign finance law to candidate scheduling and campaign uses for social media. Such seminars are intended for novice candidates and staff members, but they highlight the parties' role as clearinghouses of campaign information.

For instance, the parties maintain lists of "approved" political consultants that they share with candidates who are in the market to hire professional campaign operatives.

The parties also offer help in developing campaign strategy. At the presidential level, the nominee's campaign team creates the strategy for the fall campaign, and the national committee follows its lead, with certain limits on how coordinated the effort can be. At all other levels, the parties form the strategies that will guide their own campaign activity. They also provide strategic advice to their candidates, though again there are limits to the level of coordination that can take place. Of course, candidates are always free to ignore the party's advice, but the party may respond by withholding resources and services if they feel a campaign is making strategic mistakes.

Critical to any campaign's efforts is information on issues and voters. Parties provide candidates with reams of background information about pressing public policy matters. The national and state parties also maintain data files on voters (and donors and volunteers) that include dozens of variables such as voting history, address, age, gender, and race. The Republicans got a head start on the Democrats in this area, developing Voter Vault in the mid-1990s. For 2012, Republicans replaced Voter Vault with a new database, GOP Data Center, which reportedly logged 80.5 million voter contacts during the 2012 campaign.[74] In 2016, Republicans released the revamped Data Center 2016, "a powerful query and data management tool that interfaces with the RNC's 300+ terabytes of data and over 20 years of voter contact data."[75] The Democrats began building their files—Demzilla for donors and volunteers, DataMart for voters—a few years after the Republicans. Eventually, they announced the creation of a new voter file interface called VoteBuilder, which recorded 150 million voter contacts in 2012.[76] Both parties' voter files, which are shared with state parties and eventually candidates, enhance voter outreach by allowing parties and candidates to target appeals more effectively.

It is also common for party committees to give candidates access to polling results. The parties employ pollsters to conduct national polls on the general mood of the electorate. This information is useful to candidates but not as valuable as district-specific polling. In competitive races, the parties will do polling of the latter sort and may make the results available to candidates at the reduced rates that they obtain from their pollsters. In addition, the parties have begun to combine voter files and survey data on consumer behavior into models for "microtargeting." Microtargeting is a process of customizing campaign appeals and GOTV efforts for voters who match a certain lifestyle profile. A number of seemingly (or actually) irrelevant correlations uncovered by microtargeters have received much publicity—for example, that people who drink Heineken tend to be Democrats and those who prefer Samuel Adams are more likely to be Republicans.[77] However, findings such as these have raised questions about the value of such an approach to politics.

Fund-Raising

One of the parties' most vital activities is fund-raising, both for themselves and their candidates. Parties help their candidates in a number of ways. First, they assist candidates in finding contributors. They might arrange meetings between candidates and large donors or PACs or help in the development of lists for direct mail solicitation. Party leaders, particularly the chairs of the Hill committees, also have some ability to influence the flow of contributions from wealthy individuals and PACs.

Parties may also make direct contributions to candidates. In state-level races, state law dictates the amount of money parties can give to candidates. In federal races, party committees can give $5,000 per House candidate per election and $46,800 (combined from the national committee and Senate Hill committee) per Senate candidate per cycle.

The parties can also offer "coordinated expenditures," which is money spent on goods and services with the full cooperation of the candidates. These funds cannot be contributed directly to candidates; they must be spent by the parties in coordination with the candidates (unlike party "independent expenditures," to be described shortly). In 2016, party committees were limited to $91,200 in coordinated expenditures per House candidate in states with only one representative and $48,100 in all other states. The formula for coordinated expenditure limits in Senate races is somewhat complicated and is based on each state's voting age population (VAP). The 2016 Senate limits ranged from $96,100 in the smallest states to $2,886,500 in California. Presidential candidates can also receive coordinated expenditures; in 2016, they could get $23.8 million.[78] A party committee can authorize another committee to spend its coordinated funds, a regular occurrence between Hill committees and state party committees. Thus, party coordinated expenditure limits in House and Senate races can effectively be doubled.

Finally, the parties also rely on independent expenditures (or IEs), that is, money spent on behalf of candidates but completely independent of them. Independent expenditures have reached impressive levels in recent years (see Table 5.2). This money is spent on a variety of campaign activities, including phone banks (for voter contact), direct mail, and television and radio advertising. The ads purchased with IEs can be extremely beneficial to candidates. Usually they reinforce the major themes at play in a given race, and they often do the dirty work of the campaign for the candidate. When the party runs a controversial attack ad against their candidate's opponent, the candidate can deny any involvement in the ad. In 2006, the RNC ran an ad in the Tennessee Senate race that some believe played on subtle racial stereotypes.[79] The ad caused something of an uproar, but the Republican candidate was able to steer clear of the criticism because it had been independently produced and paid for by a party committee.

TABLE 5.2   *Party–Independent Expenditures, 1996–2016*

Year	DNC	RNC	DSCC	NRSC	DCCC	NRCC
1996	0	0	1,386,022	9,734,445	0	0
1998	0	0	1,329,000	216,874	0	0
2000	0	0	133,000	267,600	1,933,246	548,800
2002	0	500,000	0	0	1,187,649	1,321,880
2004	120,333,466	18,268,870	18,725,520	19,383,692	36,923,726	47,254,064
2006	0	14,022,675	42,627,470	19,159,901	64,141,248	82,059,161
2008	1,104,115	53,459,388	72,619,305	38,985,273	81,641,432	30,889,551
2010	15,486	0	41,471,801	25,905,909	65,683,837	46,240,571
2012	0	42,394,347	52,556,798	32,344,583	60,545,679	64,653,292
2014	0	0	54,597,217	39,598,830	68,817,280	65,284,544
2016	0	321,531	60,421,908	38,878,722	80,378,630	73,601,651

Source: Federal Election Commission, "Individual Party Details," http://www.fec.gov/disclosure/committeeDetail.do (accessed January 16, 2017).

Note: Data for 2016 is through November 28, 2016.

Conversely, because regulations prohibit coordination with candidates, the content of IE material may not always fit perfectly with the strategy being employed by the candidates themselves. This can cause a great deal of consternation on the part of candidates. In 1998, the Republican House committee employed a $37 million media blitz called "Operation Breakout."[80] Though the early ads touted the accomplishments of the Republican Congress, last-minute ads focused on President Clinton and his affair with White House intern Monica Lewinsky, a scandal that culminated (after the election) in Clinton's impeachment. Many Republican candidates wanted to steer clear of the issue and asked the party to pull the ads, but the party refused to do so.

Getting Out the Vote

One final activity that the parties engage in is voter mobilization, or GOTV efforts. In recent years, GOTV has become one of the key functions of the parties. They spend a great deal of effort during the campaign identifying likely supporters. Then, on Election Day, their goal is to get as many of these voters to the polls as possible.

Though Republicans had an edge on Democrats in many areas of party organization, financing, and services, the Democrats have often had a better GOTV operation. In fact, the Democrats relied heavily on organized labor to mobilize their base, and it was a successful model through the 2000 presidential election. That year, Al Gore received more of the vote than he was expected to get in many battleground states, including Florida. Republicans, led by Karl Rove, examined Democratic success and responded by creating, testing, and implementing their "72-Hour Task Force." For several election cycles during George W. Bush's two terms in the White House, the Republican Party would train volunteers in GOTV techniques and send them into key states and districts to maximize turnout among likely Republican voters (see Chapter 9 for details on mobilization tactics).[81] The 72-Hour Task Force is thought to have contributed to the Republicans' success in the 2002 midterm elections and the 2004 presidential election, but it was unable to stem the Democratic tide in 2006. Though they continue to rely on interest groups to assist with voter mobilization, the Democrats also revamped their GOTV operation after 2004. Both parties have come to realize that massive ad campaigns alone will not motivate voters. Voters must be personally contacted if they are to vote in large numbers.

Typically, both parties' voter mobilization efforts rely heavily on their presidential nominees' campaign organizations. The Obama campaigns in 2008 and 2012 were particularly adept at identifying their supporters and getting them to the polls.[82] In 2016, however, the Trump campaign did very little, if anything, to mobilize voters. Instead, the unorthodox candidate outsourced the entire GOTV operation to the RNC. Fortunately for Trump, the GOP had retooled its voter mobilization efforts in the wake of Romney's 2012 loss.[83]

The Democrats' cooperation with interest groups in their GOTV efforts suggests a new way of thinking about political parties. Scholars have developed a conceptualization of parties that treats them as networks that include "regular party organizations as well as allied organizations, candidates' personal organizations, and individuals working to win elections."[84] Though there is no single guiding entity within these "party networks," the entire unit works toward the same goal: electing its preferred candidates. The various actors can, of course, disagree about strategy or tactics or even over which of the party's candidates should be preferred, but typically the component parts of the network act in unison.

As the notion of party networks should make clear, contemporary political parties are quite adaptable. Though they were once thought to be withering on the vine, the parties have made a comeback. It began with transformations that took place within their own organizations. The rebirth of the parties has continued as they have partnered with other actors such as political consultants and interest groups to change with the shifting electoral and technological landscapes.

Whether this reemergence of the parties is good for democracy is another matter. Some suggest that without parties, American politics would be rudderless, that a purely candidate-centered system would be personality-driven and, therefore, shallow, not to mention confusing to the voters. However, others argue that parties unnecessarily muddy the waters, fighting false battles for political gain rather than working together to solve problems. Regardless of which view is most useful in thinking about them, parties will certainly play a central role in elections for the foreseeable future, if not for the life of the republic itself.

► *Conclusion*

It is difficult, if not impossible, to imagine modern mass democracy without political parties. Indeed, they seem to be an inevitable part of all democratic political systems. While many such systems have multiple parties from which voters can choose, the American system has only two parties with a realistic chance of winning any given election. There are a number of reasons for this, but the primary one is the type of electoral system—"SMP"—used in the United States.

The party organizations are made up of committees at the national, state, and local levels that do the work of the parties. One of the most important responsibilities of the party committees is to recruit candidates to run for office. Often, however, multiple candidates seek the party's nomination and they typically do so (with the exception of presidential candidates) in direct primaries. Presidential nominees are selected by delegates to the parties' national conventions who were allocated to candidates based on the results of primaries (and caucuses) held in the states.

Once candidates are nominated by their parties to run for office, the parties assist them in a number of ways. Two of the most important are fundraising and voter mobilization. The parties raise money to contribute directly to their nominees but also to spend on their nominees' behalf. In recent years, they have also devoted considerable resources for GOTV activities. In close elections, voter mobilization efforts can make the difference between winning and losing, which is why the parties have been so keen to build databases that allow them to identify (as far as possible) the whereabouts of every one of their voters.

Parties also exist within the electorate and in government. Most citizens identify with a political party and have, in recent years, tended to vote loyally for their party. Of course, party affiliation also structures the behavior of elected officials and members of Congress and of states legislatures have become highly polarized in their voting patterns. However, polarization is not solely an elite phenomenon. In addition to the increase in partisan voting among the electorate, citizens have also come to hold particularly negative views of the opposite party. Thus, partisan polarization is now present in all aspects of American political life.

► *Pedagogical Tools*

Role-Play Scenario

You are a political party leader in your state and have responsibility for providing resources (for example, money and staff) to local parties throughout the state. Some in your party want you to provide considerable resources to areas where your party has never been successful. Others want all the resources to go to areas where races have traditionally been competitive. Assume that over the last decade, a fourth of the state has been solidly Republican, another fourth has been safely Democratic, and half the state is competitive. Write a brief memo explaining (and justifying) your decision about how to allocate party resources.

Discussion Questions

1. Which reform of the presidential nomination process—the Delaware Plan, the American Plan, the Rotating Regional Presidential Primaries Plan, or a national primary—do you prefer and why?
2. What do you view as the consequences of the trend toward "microtargeting" and of the renewed emphasis on voter mobilization by political parties?
3. On balance, do you think political parties have a positive or negative influence on democracy? Explain your answer.

Online Resources

Democratic National Committee, www.democrats.org.
Republican National Committee, www.gop.com.
Green Party, www.gp.org.
Libertarian Party www.lp.org.
Party Platforms, 1840–2016 (including all parties receiving electoral votes), www.presidency.ucsb.edu/platforms.php.

Suggested Reading

John H. Aldrich (2011) *Why Parties? A Second Look*, Chicago, IL: University of Chicago Press.

Marty Cohen, David Karol, Hans Noel, and John Zaller (2008) *The Party Decides: Presidential Nominations Before and After Reform*, Chicago, IL: University of Chicago Press.

John C. Green, Daniel J. Coffey, and David B. Cohen (eds.) (2014) *The State of the Parties: The Changing Role of Contemporary American Parties*, 7th edn, Lanham, MD: Rowman & Littlefield.

Seth E. Masket (2016) *The Inevitable Party: Why Attempts to Kill the Party System Fail and How They Weaken Democracy*, Oxford: Oxford University Press.

A. James Reichley (2000) *The Life of the Parties: A History of American Political Parties*, Lanham, MD: Rowman & Littlefield.

► *Notes*

1 See the Avalon Project at Yale Law School, "Washington's Farewell Address, 1796," http://avalon.law.yale.edu/18th_century/washing.asp (accessed October 13, 2016).
2 E. E. Schattschneider (1942) *Party Government*, New York: Rinehart, p. 1.
3 Anthony Downs (1957) *An Economic Theory of Democracy*, New York: Harper & Row, p. 25.
4 V. O. Key, Jr. (1964) *Politics, Parties and Pressure Groups*, 5th edn, New York: Crowell.
5 James Bryce (1921) *Modern Democracies*, vol. I, New York: Macmillan, p. 119.
6 Philip A. Klinkner (1996) "Court and Country in American Politics: The Democratic Party and the 1994 Election," in Philip A. Klinkner (ed.), *Midterm: Election of 1994 in Context*, Boulder, CO: Westview Press; and Stanley Elkins and Eric McKitrick (1993) *The Age of Federalism*, Oxford: Oxford University Press, p. 19.
7 Klinkner, "Court and Country in American Politics," p. 63.
8 John H. Aldrich (1995) *Why Parties? The Origin and Transformation of Political Parties in America*. Chicago, IL: The University of Chicago Press, p. 77.
9 Marjorie Randon Hershey (2013) *Party Politics in America*, 15th edn, Upper Saddle River, NJ: Pearson, p. 129.
10 Steven J. Rosenstone, Roy L. Behr, and Edward H. Lazarus (1996) *Third Parties in America*, 2nd edn, Princeton, NJ: Princeton University Press, pp. 119–120.
11 L. Sandy Maisel (2002) *Parties and Elections in America: The Electoral Process*, 3rd edn, Post-Election Update, Lanham, MD: Rowman & Littlefield, p. 373.
12 Hershey, *Party Politics in America*, pp. 36–38.
13 It should be said that ethnic loyalties may have trumped political support in many cases. See, for example, Michael Johnston (1979) "Patrons and Clients, Jobs and Machines: A Case Study in the Uses of Patronage," *American Political Science Review*, 73: 385–398.
14 Samuel J. Eldersveld and Hanes Walton, Jr. (2000) *Political Parties in American Society*, 2nd edn, Boston, MA: Bedford/St. Martin's, pp. 56–57.
15 Hershey, *Party Politics in America*, p. 30, Figure 2.1.
16 Eldersveld and Walton, *Political Parties in American Society*, Table 3.2, 56.
17 United Kingdom Parliament. "Current State of the Parties," www.parliament.uk/mps-lords-and-offices/mps/current-state-of-the-parties (accessed January 5, 2017).
18 Hershey, *Party Politics in America*, pp. 34–35.
19 Rosenstone et al., *Third Parties in America*, p. 17.
20 Rosenstone et al., *Third Parties in America*, pp. 19–27, 43–45.
21 Eldersveld and Walton, *Political Parties in American Society*, p. 107.
22 P2016.org. "Democratic National Committee—2016," www.p2016.org/parties/dnc16.html; and "Republican National Committee—2016," www.p2016.org/parties/rnc16.html (accessed January 5, 2017).
23 Chris Cillizza (2005) "Party Chairmen Say Yes to Paychecks," *Washington Post*, December 20, www.washingtonpost.com/wp-dyn/content/article/2005/12/19/AR2005121901931.html (accessed October 13, 2016).
24 Elaine C. Kamarck (2006) "Assessing Howard Dean's Fifty State Strategy and the 2006 Midterm Elections," *The Forum*, 4, Article 5.
25 See Robin Kolodny (1998) *Pursuing Majorities: Congressional Campaign Committees in American Politics*, Norman, OK: University of Oklahoma Press.
26 See David S. Broder (1972) *The Party's Over: The Failure of Politics in America*, New York: Harper & Row.
27 Paul S. Herrnson (2002) "National Party Organizations at the Dawn of the Twenty-First Century," in L. Sandy Maisel (ed.), *The Parties Respond: Changes in American Parties and Campaigns*, 4th edn, Boulder, CO: Westview Press, pp. 52–53.
28 Paul S. Herrnson (1988) *Party Campaigning in the 1980s*, Cambridge, MA: Harvard University Press, p. 39.
29 David Farber (1994) *Chicago '68*, Chicago, IL: University of Chicago Press, p. 201.

30 Byron E. Shafer (1983) *Quiet Revolution: The Struggle for the Democratic Party and the Shaping of Post-Reform Politics*, New York: Russell Sage Foundation, p. 232.
31 Maisel, *Parties and Elections in America*, p. 268.
32 Herrnson, "National Party Organizations at the Dawn of the Twenty-First Century," p. 54.
33 L. Sandy Maisel, Cherie Maestas, and Walter J. Stone (2002) "The Party Role in Congressional Competition," in L. Sandy Maisel (ed.), *The Parties Respond: Changes in American Parties and Campaigns*, 4th edn, Boulder, CO: Westview Press, p. 130.
34 Maisel et al., "The Party Role in Congressional Competition," pp. 130–131.
35 Eldersveld and Walton, *Political Parties in American Society*, p. 81.
36 See David A. Dulio and Candice J. Nelson (2006) *Vital Signs: Perspectives on the Health of American Campaigning*, Washington, DC: Brookings Institution Press, Chapter 3.
37 Harold W. Stanley and Richard G. Niemi (eds.) (2015) "Table 3.1: Partisan Identification, American National Election Studies, 1952–2012 (percent)," *Vital Statistics on American Politics 2015–2016*, Washington, DC: CQ Press, http://sk.sagepub.com/cqpress/vital-statistics-on-american-politics-2015-2016/n3.xml (accessed January 5, 2017).
38 Pew Research Center (2016) "Party Identification Trends, 1992–2016," September 13, www.people-press.org/2016/09/13/party-identification-trends-1992-2016 (accessed January 5, 2017).
39 American National Election Study, Cumulative Datafile 1948–2008. Available from Survey Documentation and Analysis, University of California, Berkeley, http://sda.berkeley.edu/cgi-bin/hsda?harcsda+nes2004c (accessed October 13, 2016).
40 Richard Winger (ed.) (2016) *Ballot Access News*, March 1, 31, http://ballot-access.org/2016/03/27/march-2016-ballot-access-news-print-edition (accessed January 5, 2017).
41 "Exit Polls," *CNN*, November 23, 2016, http://edition.cnn.com/election/results/exit-polls/national/president (accessed January 5, 2017).
42 Hershey, *Party Politics in America*, pp. 118 and 119, Figures 6.5 and 6.6.
43 Harold W. Stanley and Richard G. Niemi (eds.) (2015) "Table 3.10 Split Ticket Voting, 1952–2012 (percent)," *Vital Statistics on American Politics 2015–2016*, Washington, DC: CQ Press, http://sk.sagepub.com/cqpress/vital-statistics-on-american-politics-2015-2016/n3.xml (accessed January 5, 2017).
44 Shanto Iyengar, Gaurav Sood, and Yphtach Lelkes (2012) "Affect, Not Ideology: A Social Identity Perspective on Polarization," *Public Opinion Quarterly*, 76: 405–431.
45 Lilliana Mason (2015) "'I Disrespectfully Agree': The Differential Effects of Partisan Sorting on Social and Issue Polarization," *American Journal of Political Science*, 59, p. 142.
46 Shanto Iyengar and Sean J. Westwood (2015) "Fear and Loathing across Party Lines: New Evidence on Group Polarization," *American Journal of Political Science*, 59: 690–707.
47 Marc Hetherington (2015) "Why Polarized Trust Matters," *The Forum*, 13, p. 449.
48 Alan I. Abramowitz and Steven Webster (2016) "The Rise of Negative Partisanship and the Nationalization of US Elections in the 21st Century," *Electoral Studies*, 41: 12–22.
49 Marc J. Hetherington, Meri T. Long, and Thomas J. Rudolph (2016) "Revisiting the Myth: New Evidence of a Polarized Electorate," *Public Opinion Quarterly*, 80, p. 343.
50 Stanley and Niemi, "Table 3.1 Partisan Identification, American National Election Studies, 1952–2012 (percent)."
51 On "issue ownership," see John R. Petrocik (1996) "Issue Ownership in Presidential Elections, with a 1980 Case Study," *American Journal of Political Science*, 40: 825–850; and John R. Petrocik, William L. Benoit, and Glenn J. Hansen (2003–2004) "Issue Ownership and Presidential Campaigning, 1952–2000," *Political Science Quarterly*, 118: 599–626.
52 Byron E. Shafer and William J. M. Claggett (1995) *The Two Majorities: The Issue Context of Modern American Politics*, Baltimore, MD: The Johns Hopkins University Press, especially pp. 23–24.
53 For a classic examination of this tendency, see David R. Mayhew (1974) *Congress: The Electoral Connection*, New Haven, CT: Yale University Press.
54 Marni Ezra (2005) "Nomination Politics: Primary Laws and Party Rules," in Paul S. Herrnson, Colton Campbell, Marni Ezra, and Stephen K. Medvic (eds.), *Guide to Political Campaigns in America*, Washington, DC: CQ Press, pp. 81–82.
55 Hershey, *Party Politics in America*, p. 175.

56 See National Conference of State Legislatures (2016) "State Primary Election Types," www.ncsl.org/research/elections-and-campaigns/primary-types.aspx (accessed January 7, 2017).

57 *California Democratic Party* v. *Jones* (2000) 530 US 567.

58 *Washington State Grange* v. *Washington State Republican Party* (2008) 552 US 442.

59 National Conference of State Legislatures (2016) "2016 Primary Dates," February 9, www.ncsl.org/research/elections-and-campaigns/2016-state-primary-dates.aspx (accessed January 7, 2017).

60 For a discussion of the Republican Party's new rules, see Josh Putnam (2011) "Republican Delegate Allocation Rules: 2012 vs (2008," *FrontloadingHQ*, December 24, http://frontloading.blogspot.com/2011/12/republican-delegate-allocation-rules.html (accessed October 13, 2016).

61 David Weigel (2016) "Democrats Vote to Bind Most Superdelegates to State Primary Results," *Washington Post*, July 23, www.washingtonpost.com/news/post-politics/wp/2016/07/23/democrats-vote-to-bind-most-superdelegates-to-state-primary-results/?utm_term=.8a910033de21 (accessed January 7, 2017).

62 Richard E. Berg-Andersson (n.d.) "Democratic Convention" and "Republican Convention," *The Green Papers*, www.thegreenpapers.com/P16/D and www.thegreenpapers.com/P16/R (accessed January 7, 2017).

63 Richard E. Berg-Andersson (n.d.) "2008 Chronological Cumulative Allocation of Delegates" and "2016 Chronological Cumulative Allocation of Delegates," *The Green Papers*, www.thegreenpapers.com/P16/ccad.phtml and www.thegreenpapers.com/P08/ccad.phtml (accessed January 7, 2017). For prior years, see Thomas Gangale (2004) "The California Plan: A 21st Century Method for Nominating Presidential Candidates," *PS: Political Science and Politics*, 37: 81–87.

64 Author's calculation based on figures provided by Richard Berg-Andersson of The Green Papers (2008) "2008 Chronological Cumulative Allocation of Delegates," April 13, www.thegreenpapers.com/P08/ccad.phtml (accessed October 13, 2016).

65 See the Center for Governmental Studies at the University of Virginia (2001) "The Report of the National Symposium on Presidential Selection," University of Virginia Center for Governmental Studies, www.centerforpolitics.org/downloads/rnsps.pdf, pp. 18–20 (accessed October 13, 2016).

66 See FairVote.org (n.d.) "The American Plan," http://archive.fairvote.org/?page=965 (accessed October 13, 2016).

67 Stephen Ohlemacher (2007) "Census Shows Early Primary States Are Far from 'Average,'" *Boston Globe*, May 17, www.boston.com/news/nation/washington/articles/2007/05/17/census_shows_early_primary_states_are_far_from_average (accessed October 13, 2016).

68 Author's calculation based on figures provided in Harold W. Stanley and Richard G. Niemi (eds.) (2015) "Table 1.23 Presidential Primaries, 1912–2012," *Vital Statistics on American Politics, 2015–2016*, Washington, DC: CQ Press, http://sk.sagepub.com.ezproxy.fandm.edu/cqpress/vital-statistics-on-american-politics-2015-2016/n1.xml (accessed January 7, 2017).

69 Marty Cohen, David Karol, Hans Noel, and John Zaller (2008a) *The Party Decides: Presidential Nominations Before and After Reform*, Chicago, IL: University of Chicago Press.

70 On Trump's media coverage and use and its role in his nomination, see Julia R. Azari (2016) "How the News Media Helped to Nominate Trump," *Political Communication*, 33: 677–680; and Chris Wells, Dhavan V. Shah, Jon C. Pevehouse, JungHwan Yang, Ayellet Pelled, Frederick Boehm, Josephine Lukito, Shreenita Ghosh, and Jessica L. Schmidt (2016) "How Trump Drove Coverage to the Nomination: Hybrid Media Campaigning," *Political Communication*, 33: 669–676.

71 Katrina vanden Heuvel (2016) "The Most Progressive Democratic Platform Ever," *Washington Post*, July 12, www.washingtonpost.com/opinions/the-most-progressive-democratic-platform-ever/2016/07/12/82525ab0-479b-11e6-bdb9-701687974517_story.html?utm_term=.24e197c1387c (accessed January 16, 2017).

72 See Patrick J. Buchanan (1992) "1992 Republican National Convention Speech," August 17, http://buchanan.org/blog/1992-republican-national-convention-speech-148 (accessed October 13, 2016).

73 The New York Times/CBS News Poll (2008) "2008 Republican National Delegate Survey," July 23–August 26, http://graphics8.nytimes.com/packages/pdf/politics/20080901-poll.pdf (accessed October 13, 2016).

74 Nick Judd (2013) "Republican Party's Technology Revival Hopes to Hinge on Data and Data Analysis," *Techpresident.com*, February 7, http://techpresident.com/news/23479/republican-partys-technology-revival-hopes-hinge-more-just-skype (accessed October 13, 2016).

75 Republican National Committee (2016) "RNC Launches Data Center 2016," press release, August 3, www.gop.com/rnc-launches-data-center-2016 (accessed January 16, 2017).

76 Judd, "Republican Party's Technology Revival."

77 Sasha Issenberg (2012a) "Man Microtargets for Food, But Sometimes There Must Be a Beverage," *Slate*, September 28, www.slate.com/blogs/victory_lab/2012/09/28/microtargeting_beer_you_are_not_what_you_drink_.html (accessed October 13, 2016).

78 Federal Election Commission (n.d.) "2016 Coordinated Party Expenditure Limits," www.fec.gov/info/charts_cpe_2016.shtml (accessed January 16, 2017).

79 See Robin Toner (2006) "Ad Seen as Playing to Racial Fears," *The New York Times*, October 26, www.nytimes.com/2006/10/26/us/politics/26tennessee.html?pagewanted=all (accessed October 13, 2016).

80 Anthony Corrado (1999) "On the Issue of Issue Advocacy: A Comment," *Virginia Law Review*, 85: 1805.

81 Mike Allen and James Carney (2006) "Campaign 2006: The Republicans' Secret Weapon," *Time*, October 1, www.time.com/time/printout/0,8816,1541295,00.html (accessed October 13, 2016).

82 See Sasha Issenberg (2012b) "Why Obama Is Better at Getting Out the Vote," *Slate*, November 5, www.slate.com/articles/news_and_politics/victory_lab/2012/11/obama_s_get_out_the_vote_effort_why_it_s_better_than_romney_s.html (accessed October 13, 2016).

83 Don Gonyea (2016) "Here's Why the Republican National Committee Says It Won Tuesday," *National Public Radio*, November 14, www.npr.org/2016/11/14/502045531/heres-why-the-republican-national-committee-says-it-won-tuesday (accessed January 16, 2017).

84 John F. Bibby (1999) "Party Networks: National-State Integration, Allied Groups, and Issue Activists," in John C. Green and Daniel M. Shea (eds.), *The State of the Parties: The Changing Role of Contemporary American Parties*, 3rd edn, Lanham, MD: Rowman & Littlefield, p. 76.

6

Interest Groups

INTEREST GROUPS SHARE a great deal in common with political parties. Like parties, interest groups are organizations that are active in campaigns and elections. Furthermore, the public does not hold them in the highest regard. And as in the case of parties, negative attitudes about interest groups date to the Founding period. In his "Federalist No. 10," James Madison argued that one of the most important benefits of a "well-constructed Union" is "its tendency to break and control the violence of faction." By "faction," Madison was referring to what would later be called a "pressure group" and, later still, an "interest group." Factions, according to Madison, are the root of many of the problems governments face, and the new constitution he was advocating sought to cure their "mischiefs."[1]

Though it could be argued that Madison was right, it could also be said that interest groups are the primary mechanism by which the people have influence over government. Either way, it cannot be denied that they have become influential actors in campaigns and elections. Interest groups engage in nearly all of the campaign activity that parties undertake. They contribute money to candidates and provide them with volunteers; they may officially endorse candidates; they communicate directly with voters through direct mail, email, and commercials; and they mobilize voters, especially their own members and supporters. Furthermore, they are a particularly integral element of the "party networks" described at the end of Chapter 5. The key difference between interest groups and parties is that interest groups do not nominate candidates to run for office under the banner of the interest group.

This chapter discusses interest groups, beginning with what they are and what they do. It includes a brief look at how interest groups came to be so prominent in contemporary US politics and delineates the types of advocacy groups involved. The core of the chapter examines interest group activity in campaigns and elections, ending with a brief discussion of the consequences of interest group involvement in the electoral arena.

▶ *Interest Groups: What They Are and What They Do*

An interest group is an association of people or organizations with shared concerns that attempts to influence public policy. Interest groups play a number of roles. They may represent their constituencies' interests, provide an opportunity for people to participate in politics, educate the public and set the political agenda, and monitor government programs.[2] However, an interest group's ultimate goal is to steer public policy in a direction that accords with its preferences. Virtually all of these functions could be those of political parties as well. As noted, however, the feature that differentiates the two types of political organizations most clearly is that parties nominate candidates for office, and interest groups do not.

Of course, interest groups also differ from parties in the extent to which, and the manner in which, they try to influence government. Interest groups put a great deal of effort into winning the passage of legislation. Though they also attempt to affect the way executive branch regulators carry out the law and the way the judicial branch interprets the law, the primary activity in which most interest groups engage is lobbying elected officials. They do so either directly, by attempting to persuade lawmakers to enact their legislative wish list, or indirectly, by marshaling public opinion to their cause in the hope that public pressure will influence elected officials.

To the extent that interest groups rely on direct lobbying to achieve their goals, access to elected officials becomes of vital importance. To gain access, interest groups need relationships with those in government. One of the most effective ways to build these relationships is to assist office seekers in getting elected (or reelected). Thus, interest groups are keen to participate in campaigns, particularly to help potential allies win office.

The Varied Missions of Interest Groups

To understand the activity of interest groups in campaigns and elections, it is necessary to have an idea of their purposes and characteristics. Why, for instance, do interest groups form in the first place? It was once thought that interests organize as the result of a disturbance in the economy or in society.[3] Political scientists have come to believe, however, that interest group formation is closely linked to the benefits potential members may derive from the group.[4] Generally speaking, there are three types of benefits interest group constituents can enjoy. First are material benefits, which have been defined as "tangible rewards that individuals or companies get in return for their donations."[5] Information, for example, is a benefit that many interest group members rely on, but a desirable change in public policy is probably the most valuable material benefit. Of course, material benefits in the form of favorable policy outcomes will accrue to everyone whose interest a group represents regardless of whether they are members. If labor organizations obtain improvements in workplace safety laws, all workers will benefit from the change, even if they are not union members. The problem of "free riders," or those who receive benefits without paying for them, is a particularly frustrating one for interest groups.

A second type of benefit is a purposive benefit, meaning a sense of contributing to the improvement of the community, state, nation, or world. The goal of a group that provides purposive benefits is not to protect the self-interest of its members. Instead, it aims to address a pressing problem in society, the solution to which may be enjoyed by far more people than merely the group's members. Finally, members of interest groups get solidary, or social, benefits. Many individuals derive pleasure from interacting with others, especially those of like mind. Of course, most organizations offer some combination of these benefits. Without some type of benefit for potential members, an interest group is not likely to last long, if it forms at all.[6]

As the explanation of material and purposive benefits suggests, one way interest groups differ is according to whether they seek private or public goods. Some groups pursue "selective benefits" that go only to their own constituencies. If the National Federation of Independent Business (NFIB) obtains a tax break for small business, only small businesses reap the reward. Of course, the NFIB will claim that small businesses are a vital part of the overall economy and, therefore, what is good for them is good for the entire society. All groups make such claims. Nevertheless, the benefits acquired by some organizations go directly to their own constituents (though, as noted, not necessarily to their members only). Other groups, however, pursue "collective benefits." In seeking clean water or clean air, for example, environmental organizations work for benefits that everyone will enjoy. Of course, the means for achieving desirable outcomes—or even the outcomes themselves—are often opposed by other interest groups. Thus, business interests may fight certain environmental measures because their constituents would be harmed by resulting regulations.

These examples point to substantive differences between interest groups as well. That is, some groups are concerned with economic issues while others focus on social matters. Corporate and labor interests and trade associations are primarily concerned with economic policy. Groups such as the Sierra Club, NARAL Pro-Choice America, the National Rifle Association, and the Christian Coalition have social agendas. Of course, the line between economic and social issues is not always bright. An organization fighting discrimination against a certain group of people may seek to change the social environment, but it is also looking out for the economic interests of the group. The Human Rights Campaign, which advocates civil rights for lesbian, gay, bisexual, and transgendered individuals, is an example of such an organization.

Finally, we can differentiate interest groups on the basis of their organizational structure. Groups can take either a unitary or a federated form. "In a unitary organization," according to Brian Anderson and Burdett Loomis, "members join one central group, which charters, staffs, and funds state offices, and then shape their agenda to provide grassroots pressure on congressional delegations for national level issues." While this form of organization offers centralized control, it also limits organizational flexibility. A federated organization also includes a national group, but it acts only on behalf of subnational affiliates. Though this structure allows more flexibility to operate at different levels of government, the national organization may have less ability to act unilaterally than a national group in a unitary structure. As Anderson and Loomis point out, these structural differences can influence how interest groups make electioneering decisions.[7] Federations, for instance, may face internal disagreement over how much support to give certain candidates.

The Explosion in Organized Interests

The variety of pursuits just described hints at the number and kinds of interest groups active in campaigns and elections. As one scholar has concluded, " 'Explosion' is a completely accurate way to describe the massive number of interest groups that have descended upon Washington, DC, since the 1960s."[8] And as the presence of interest groups in American politics increased dramatically after the 1960s, the form of interest group influence evolved in a particularly significant way. As noted in Chapter 3, labor unions, led by the CIO, had established auxiliary committees to raise and spend money on campaigns after the 1943 ban on union contributions. A number of these committees, also known as *political action committees*, or PACs, had formed between the 1940s and 1960s, but it was not until after the post-Watergate reform of the early 1970s that the growth in the number of PACs, like the growth in interest groups generally, could be said to have exploded. In 1974, the number of PACs stood at 608; that number more than doubled, to 1,360, in just three years. By 1980, the number had nearly doubled again, to 2,551 and, by 1984, just ten years after the passage of the 1974 amendments to FECA, the number of PACs surpassed 4,000. (As of July 2016, there were 6,130 PACs in existence; see Figure 6.1.)[9]

The 1974 FECA amendments stimulated the growth in PACs by limiting contributions from other sources, particularly individuals. Because individuals could give only $1,000 per election to candidates, whereas PACs could give $5,000, the importance of PACs increased tremendously relative to other sources of funds. In addition, the law's public financing provisions for presidential elections enhanced PAC influence in congressional elections. Because they could not contribute to presidential candidates who accepted public funding for the general election, PACs turned their attention to congressional races. Finally, the 1974 amendments also allowed corporations and unions with government contracts to form PACs, something the original FECA prohibited. This paved the way for the widespread formation of corporate PACs, which could solicit funds from shareholders and employees.[10]

FIGURE 6.1   *The Number of PACs, 1974–2016*

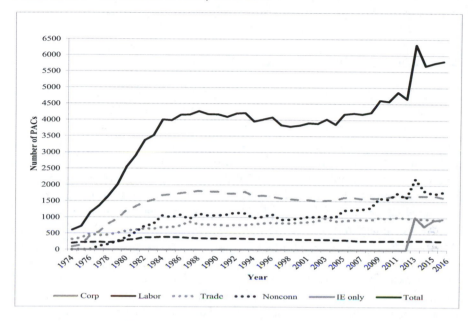

Source: Data taken from Federal Election Commission, "PAC Count, 1974–Present," www.fec. gov/press/resources/paccount.shtml.

Groups of individuals have always been active in American politics. As organizations, however, it has only been recently that interest groups have played a major role in campaigns and elections. Though membership continues to be important to most interest groups, an increasing number of organizations are "bodyless heads," or "advocacy organizations without individual members, groups that represent other organizations, and groups that speak for modest numbers of individual adherents who respond to mass mailings or canvasses by giving money."[11]

However, the Internet has the potential to reverse this trend. The most obvious example of an Internet-based organization that relies heavily on its members is MoveOn.org, a left-wing advocacy group that claims to have an email list of more than 5 million addresses.[12] Technically, MoveOn.org is only a website that disseminates information for two related groups—MoveOn Civic Action, which is an education and advocacy organization, and MoveOn Political Action (formerly MoveOn PAC), which is the group's PAC. Nevertheless, MoveOn in its entirety engages its members through electronic voter contact and mobilization while operating a traditional PAC that contributes money to candidates and airs independent campaign and issue ads.

By their own admission, conservatives are without an equivalent organization. There have been multiple attempts to create the "right-wing MoveOn," but most have been abandoned shortly after forming. To date, RightMarch.com is the most successful conservative Internet-based organization, but it has only a fraction of the Web presence that MoveOn has.[13]

▶ Types of Advocacy Groups

The growth in the number of PACs and the emergence of Internet-based interest groups suggest significant differences in the types of political organizations that are active in campaigns and elections. Of course, thousands of organizations choose not to get involved in campaigns at all, whereas others are active in varying degrees. The Internal Revenue Code recognizes five types of groups that can engage in political activity.[14] The first, 501(c)3 organizations, are tax-exempt nonprofit charities and private foundations. According to the tax code, they may engage in limited lobbying for legislation but may not participate in partisan campaigning. Groups in this category, such as the United Way, the American Red Cross, and Planned Parenthood, can educate voters on the issues by publishing voter guides and holding public forums, and they can organize voter registration and GOTV drives. However, all the information disseminated by these groups must remain nonpartisan, and the group cannot indicate a preference for candidates. Voter guides produced by 501(c)3 organizations, for example, cannot rate candidates; all candidates must be given equal treatment.

Three additional types of organizations—501(c)4, 501(c)5, and 501(c)6 organizations (or social-welfare groups, labor unions, and business leagues, respectively)—are allowed to lobby and engage in campaign activity, including the endorsement of candidates, as long as this is not their primary activity. Some of the most active groups in campaigns, including the NRA, the Sierra Club, various unions, and the Chamber of Commerce, are classified according to one of these three kinds of organizations. Many of these groups also establish PACs, and quite a few have formed super-PACs. This gives them maximum flexibility in accomplishing their campaign (and broader organizational) goals.

The primary purpose of the fifth type of group, 527 organizations, is to influence election outcomes. From the standpoint of the tax code, all political committees, including candidate committees, political parties, and PACs, are 527 groups. In 2000, however, the term 527s began to refer specifically to political committees that skirted campaign finance regulations; they were, in effect, PACs that did not register as such with the FEC and therefore avoided the contribution limits by which PACs must abide. Furthermore, they did not report to the FEC but instead filed periodic contribution and expenditure reports with the IRS, where the filing requirements are less demanding.

Offsetting the advantages of organizing as a 527 was the fact that these groups were limited in how they could spend their money. Because they were not PACs, they were not able to contribute to candidates' campaigns nor could they expressly advocate the election or defeat of a candidate. Theoretically, they were limited to issue advocacy. This is why, when independent expenditure-only committees (or "super-PACs") were established after the *SpeechNow* decision, 527s ceased to be used as vehicles for campaign spending. As we will soon see, super-PACs are subject to far fewer restrictions with respect to how they can spend money.

We can classify PACs, all of which must report their receipts and expenditures to the FEC, according to three types—those that are "connected," those that are "non-connected," and independent expenditure-only committees. Connected PACs, or separate segregated funds, are affiliated with another organization such as a corporation, labor union, or membership/trade association. These PACs can solicit contributions only from individuals associated with the affiliated (or "sponsoring") organization. The most rapid growth in connected PACs since the 1970s has been among those sponsored by corporations. In 1974, there were eighty-nine corporate PACs; by 2016, there were 1,621.[15] Some of the leading contributors to candidates among corporate PACs are those of AT&T, United Parcel Service, and General Electric.

Labor PACs have grown at a much slower rate. The number of PACs affiliated with unions increased from 201 in 1974 to only 278 in 2016. Some of the highest-spending labor PACs are those for the American Federation of State, County, and Municipal Employees, the United Auto Workers, the Service Employees International Union, the International Brotherhood of Electrical Workers, and the Teamsters. Finally, trade and membership PACs have risen in number from 318 to 926 since 1974. The PACs of the National Association of Realtors, the Association of Trial Lawyers of America, and the National Beer Wholesalers Association are among the most active trade organizations in the United States.

Non-connected PACs are unaffiliated with any other organization and are usually ideologically inspired or concerned with a single area of public policy (for example, the environment or abortion). These organizations can solicit contributions from anyone in the general public. Examples of leading non-connected PACs include ActBlue and EMILY's List, an organization that supports pro-choice Democratic women, on the left and the NRA and Club for Growth on the right.

A subcategory of nonconnected PACs called leadership PACs are established by candidates and elected officials. The purpose of such organizations is to further the goals of the individual who sets up the PAC. Congressional leaders might establish these PACs, for instance, to maintain or build a majority in the House and Senate. The congressional leadership PAC provides resources for traveling around the country to campaign for candidates in key races and for contributing to those candidates. A recent example of such a committee is Eye of the Tiger PAC, established by House Majority Whip Steve Scalise (who graduated from Louisiana State University, home of the Tigers). Through such activity, the individual leaders gain the support of rank-and-file members of Congress.

Virtually all presidential candidates create leadership PACs as a way of raising (and spending) money before they announce their candidacy. (Once they officially announce that they're running, presidential candidates can no longer associate with the leadership PAC and must establish a candidate committee for raising and spending money.) Like congressional leaders, they also contribute to important elected officials in key states, hoping that such support will be remembered when the presidential candidate seeks endorsements for the party's nomination. Examples of the leadership PACs of 2016 presidential contenders included Chris Christie's Leadership Matters for America, Ted Cruz's Jobs, Growth and Freedom Fund, Rand Paul's Reinventing a New Direction, and Martin O'Malley's O'Say Can You See PAC. In 2008, Barack Obama's leadership PAC was called Hopefund. Notice how the names of most of these PACs convey either a patriotic tone or reinforce a positive image of the candidate.

Finally, independent expenditure-only committees, or super-PACs, can raise money in unlimited amounts from any source and can spend that money expressly advocating the election or defeat of a candidate. The only restrictions on super-PAC spending are that they cannot contribute to candidates and cannot coordinate their efforts with candidates. As noted in Chapter 3, these committees have become significant players in campaigns in the short amount of time since the FEC issued advisory opinions, in the summer of 2010, allowing such groups to be formed. There were 504 such committees by the summer of 2012 and 1,148 by July of 2016.

Depending on their legal status, organizations campaign on behalf of their preferred candidates—or against their least preferred—at different levels. Obviously, 501(c)3 organizations are less active than 501(c)4, (c)5, or (c)6 groups, whereas PACs and super-PACs are heavily involved in campaigns. It would be a mistake, however, to treat the different organizational classifications as entirely separate entities. In a working paper several years ago, the Campaign Finance Institute concluded that many interest groups create organizations in different legal classifications but manage these entities in common. "They work *together*," write the authors, "to accomplish the group's overarching objectives."[16] The Sierra Club, for instance, is organized as a 501(c)4 but also has a PAC and a super-PAC (Sierra Club Independent Action). The next section of this chapter details the many ways in which these various organizations are active in campaigns.

▶ *Interest Group Campaign Activity*

Most of what interest groups do in campaigns will mirror the activity of political parties. In fact, party and interest group activity will often be synchronized. Recall from Chapter 5 that interest groups are part of what have come to be known as "party networks," the informal relationships between parties, candidates, political professionals, and other organizations seeking to achieve similar goals. Whether their actions are deliberately coordinated, parties and the groups allied with them can be expected to campaign in tandem. This is not to say that tension never occurs between parties and interest groups. Occasionally, for example, disagreements arise over which candidate to support for the party's nomination. An interest group may prefer an ideologically pure candidate while the party may be willing to accept an unorthodox candidate if it means greater electability. Such tension notwithstanding, parties and interest groups will often campaign hand in hand. And as we will see in this section, much of what they do overlaps.

Candidate Preparation

Like parties, interest groups often get involved early in the campaign process. They may, for example, help recruit candidates for office who would be favorable to their agenda. In general, interest groups are not as involved in recruitment as parties, but some do have extensive recruitment operations. For instance, EMILY's List seeks out candidates under its Political Opportunity Program. Among other things, the program makes available a pamphlet entitled "Thinking of Running for Office: A Guide for Democratic Women Candidates" for those contemplating a bid.[17] Conservative Christian organizations are often active in recruiting candidates, especially at the local level for offices such as school board. Other groups are less sophisticated about recruitment; they may mention the names of promising candidates to party leaders or encourage individuals they know to consider running for office, but they will not actively try to identify potential candidates they do not know.

When organizations are involved in recruitment, it is typically as part of an overall candidate preparation strategy. Another key element of such an effort is candidate training programs. Once an organization has identified a pool of potential candidates, it is likely to offer guidance on how to get elected. Candidate training may take the form of a manual, perhaps complete with a multimedia presentation, that candidates can use on their own. In addition to specific advice on how to run a campaign, a training manual from an interest group is also likely to include information on the issues relevant to the sponsoring organization. A more thorough training program, however, would be the campaign seminars offered by some interest groups. These seminars may be held with one candidate and staff, or they may be joint sessions with multiple campaigns at one location such as the organization's national or state headquarters.

GOPAC, an organization devoted to building a "farm team" of Republican candidates who can eventually run for higher offices, has one of the most sophisticated training programs available. This organization "works with experienced political professionals to determine and teach effective campaign strategies through online presentations, training manuals, and audio CDs." GOPAC calls these training programs "GOPAC University."[18] Another organization known for its training program is the National Women's Political Caucus (NWPC), a nonpartisan, pro-choice group that helps women candidates get elected. In addition to training sessions, NWPC publishes a comprehensive manual called *The Complete Training Manual for Women Candidates*.[19]

Endorsing Candidates

Even if they do not recruit or train candidates, interest groups (with the exception of 501[c]3 organizations) may choose to get involved relatively early in the electoral process by endorsing candidates in the primaries. Endorsements by key interest groups in each party can be extremely valuable to a candidate. Democratic presidential candidates, for example, compete mightily for the backing of the National Education Association, the AFL-CIO, and other unions, not to mention a variety of women's groups and civil rights organizations. On the Republican side, the NRA, the Christian Coalition, and a number of business organizations hold a great deal of sway. A group's endorsement is a signal to its members not only about which candidate to vote for but about whose campaign to contribute to or volunteer one's time for. Though it would be an overstatement to say that any group can "deliver" its members' votes, money, and time, an endorsement will influence the actions of many of them.

Though interest groups certainly want their preferred candidates to win in the general election, it is just as important to them (if not, at times, more important) to field candidates who support their agendas, but what constitutes support is not always easy to determine. A candidate who has never held elected office, for instance, will have little record to examine. When a candidate does have a voting record to evaluate, how much support is required? How many of a group's issue positions must a candidate embrace to gain an endorsement? Agreement on a bare majority certainly would not be enough to inspire an organization to give its seal of approval. Though there is not likely to be a magic threshold of agreement—would it have to be 95 percent, or would 90 percent or 80 percent or 75 percent do?—some vague sense of how often the candidate is going to be "with" them on most policy matters will be considered. The organization may also insist that candidates agree with them on certain key issues to gain endorsement. This is certainly true for single-issue groups or those that focus on a narrow policy area. The NRA, for example, simply would not endorse a candidate who supported significant, or perhaps any, gun-control legislation. Groups with a wider range of policy interests may have to weigh general agreement on the issues against disagreement on key issues.

If interest groups are too rigid in applying a litmus test to candidates during the endorsement process, they may help nominate candidates who pass such a test with flying colors only to be too outside the mainstream to win a general election. In 2010, the newly emerging Tea Party movement got involved in Republican nomination contests around the country. Local Tea Party groups worked to help very conservative Republican candidates defeat other Republican candidates whom Tea Partiers thought were not faithful enough to conservative principles. National Tea Party organizations, such as Tea Party Express, endorsed several candidates who met a certain ideological profile but were not particularly strong candidates. One such candidate was Christine O'Donnell, a conservative activist who ran against nine-term congressman Mike Castle for the Republican Party's US Senate nomination from Delaware. With the support of Tea Party (and other conservative) groups, O'Donnell beat the more moderate Castle who, had he won the nomination, would have been the over-whelming favorite to win the general election. However, O'Donnell's general-election campaign faltered almost immediately when stories about her financial troubles and a series of bizarre public statements made by her in the past garnered widespread attention. The situation was so bad that Republican operative and former George W. Bush adviser Karl Rove publicly criticized O'Donnell several weeks before the election. "One thing that O'Donnell is now going to have to answer in the general election that she didn't in the primary is her own checkered background," said Rove. "There were a lot of nutty things she has been saying that don't add up."[20]

As the O'Donnell example suggests, groups ought to take electoral viability into account when considering an endorsement. Of course, interest groups do not want to risk losing the good will of their members by asking them to support a candidate who does not appear to fully embrace the group's agenda or its positions, nor do they want to lose credibility by backing candidates with no shot at winning. Endorsing candidates who both support their agenda and are electorally viable isn't always an option, and it's not clear which way it's better to err if striking a perfect balance isn't possible. However, politically sophisticated interest groups know that to advance their agendas, they must back candidates who will have broad appeal in a general election.

The Tea Party's endorsements in 2010 and 2012 also illustrate how interest group involvement in the nomination process can lead to conflict with the party establishment. After losses by Tea Party-endorsed candidates in what were winnable Senate races in three states in 2010 (Delaware, Nevada, and Colorado) and two more in 2012 (Indiana and Missouri), many Republican leaders argued that the Party had to begin nominating better candidates. The GOP had, according to Steven Law, president of the Rove-directed super-PAC American Crossroads, "blown a significant number of races because the wrong candidates were selected." In response, Rove and his associates formed a new super-PAC in early 2013 called Conservative Victory Project (a spin-off, essentially, from American Crossroads). The new organization's goal, as Law noted at the time, is to "pick the most conservative candidate who can win,"[21] but many saw Rove's latest initiative as a way for the GOP establishment to reassert its control over the nomination process. Needless to say, conservative grassroots activists (and some Republican leaders) were not happy.[22] One Tea Party organization even sent a fund-raising email to its members that displayed a picture of Rove's face superimposed on an old photo of a Nazi SS officer (an outrage for which the group later apologized).[23]

As one might expect, organizations differ with respect to how they make their endorsement decisions. Larger organizations will often delegate the decision to a committee. For instance, WISH List, an organization that supports pro-choice Republican women, has a candidate review committee that examines the records of the candidates and decides on endorsements.[24] The General Board of the AFL-CIO, which includes its executive council members and leaders from its affiliated unions, determines its presidential endorsement after a series of events where candidates and union members meet to discuss salient issues in the election.[25]

Some groups allow their members to determine whom the organization will endorse, which has become quite easy to do via the Internet. MoveOn, for example, allows members to vote in "online primaries." In their 2003 presidential primary, Howard Dean led all balloting with 43.87 percent of the vote but fell short of the 50 percent then needed for an endorsement.[26] In early 2016, Bernie Sanders received MoveOn's endorsement when he garnered 78.6 percent of the online vote.[27]

BOX 6.1   *The MoveOn.org Political Action 2016 Presidential Endorsement Process*

Rules:

1.   Voting is open to anyone who has been a MoveOn member prior to the start of the voting period. While any person may cast a ballot, only the votes of MoveOn members prior to the start of the vote will be counted.
2.   You may change your vote as many times as you like, but only your final vote will be counted.
3.   Members will be asked to choose between endorsing Hillary Clinton, Martin O'Malley, Bernie Sanders, and making no endorsement.
4.   Voting opens Thursday, January 7 at noon ET / 9 A.M. PT and closes at 2:59 A.M. ET Monday, January 11 / 11:59 P.M. PT Sunday, January 10.
5.   This is a big decision, and one thing we've heard loud and clear from MoveOn members is that it's important for us to stand together. To win the 2016 presidential endorsement of MoveOn members, a candidate must earn a supermajority—67%, or, technically, 66.67%—of votes cast. If no candidate hits that threshold, we won't endorse in the Democratic presidential primary.
6.   If an endorsement is made, we'll run a 100% positive campaign for that candidate.
7.   No matter who's endorsed in the primary, if members choose to make an endorsement, we've heard loud and clear that MoveOn members of all stripes want us to work to support the Democratic nominee in keeping a Republican out of the White House—and we'll do that.
8.   We'll announce the results on Tuesday, January 12 after a secure confirmation of the ballots cast.

Source: MoveOn.org Political Action, http://front.moveon.org/presidentialendorsement-vote/#.WIzLAxArKCS (accessed December 12, 2016).

Regardless of who makes the actual decision, interest groups use a variety of information sources to determine whether a candidate merits endorsement. Obviously, if a candidate has a voting record, that record will be examined closely. Candidate questionnaires are also widely used and are especially valuable for candidates without a public record. As the sample questions from the National Association of Realtors below illustrate, groups expect candidates to take positions on fairly complex policy matters. Some organizations will also interview candidates face to face. Decision-makers can glean intangible information from such meetings, such as the candidate's comfort level when discussing the group's issues. Finally, groups will examine any available evidence of the candidates' viability. Expert opinions about the candidates' chances are useful, as are existing polls. Indeed, candidates may share their private polling with groups if the results indicate that they are competitive.

BOX 6.2   *Selected Questions from RPAC's 2016 Candidate Questionnaire*

National Association of Realtors® (NAR) RPAC Congressional Candidate Screening Questionnaire

It is the policy of NAR's RPAC Trustees that a candidate questionnaire must be completed for all open seat and challenger candidates for the House and Senate. A candidate interview is highly encouraged to obtain the answers to the questionnaire in person. The candidate questionnaire should be used during the interview and must be faxed to RPAC following completion of an online request for RPAC funds for the request to be considered ....

Section IV. Organizational

1. What previous relationship has this candidate had with the REALTOR® association?
2. Please name REALTORS® supportive of your candidacy and if they hold any official roles.
3. ...
4. What is your campaign's plan/strategy to win?
5. Are you using pollsters or other consultants? Please name them and provide office address and phone number.
6. Please provide most recent polling information (results, when poll was taken, who conducted poll):

Section V. NAR Legislative Concerns

I.   **Taxes**

A) REALTORS® share the concerns of many Americans that something must be done to solve our nation's fiscal crisis. However, REALTORS® also recognize that the housing market is one of the largest engines of economic growth and represents the long-term savings of millions of American families. While the Mortgage Interest Deduction (MID) remains very popular with American households, there have been suggestions to make changes such as reducing the cap on deductible interest, eliminating the deduction for second homes, converting the deduction to a credit, or eliminating the deduction entirely.

What is your position on tax reforms that would reduce or eliminate the mortgage interest deduction?

___ Support   ___ Oppose   ___ Don't Know

Please explain:

II.   **Housing & Mortgage Finance**

...

A) Currently, there is discussion about the role that government should play in the secondary mortgage market, and how the nation's

---

(continued)

Government-Sponsored Enterprises (GSEs), Fannie Mae and Freddie Mac, should be handled. The Obama Administration's 2011 white paper, "Reforming America's Housing Finance Market," provides three options for the role of government in the secondary market and the handling of the GSEs. These options range from near total privatization of the secondary mortgage market, save for the Federal Housing Administration (FHA), to the government only entering the market space during a catastrophic event, to the government providing a level of re-insurance on certain mortgage-backed securities (MBS). While many arguments regarding these approaches exist, the current problems with liquidity in the housing mortgage markets have illustrated the importance of some degree of public involvement when private lending activity is constrained.

Do you support some level of government participation in the secondary mortgage market to ensure liquidity?

___ Support   ___ Oppose   ___ Don't Know

Please explain:

B) With the collapse of the private secondary market in recent years, the FHA mortgage insurance program, which historically has operated without cost to taxpayers, has functioned as it was intended, by ensuring that American families have access to affordable mortgage financing. There are some today who, in response to the problems that have plagued the real estate and mortgage markets, propose ending all government involvement in the mortgage process—even for first time homebuyers, and others who are underserved by the private market.

Do you support continuing government programs—like FHA, that assist American families with obtaining safe, affordable mortgage financing?

___ Support   ___ Oppose   ___ Don't Know

Please explain:

...

Source: National Association of Realtors PAC (RPAC), http://www.realtoractioncenter.com/docs/rpac/2015/unprotected/candidate-questionnaire.pdf (accessed January 16, 2017).

Endorsements in a general election are a bit more straightforward but can still create controversy. Because so many groups are allied with one of the two parties, an organization's preferred general election candidate is usually obvious, but that candidate might simply be the "lesser of two evils." Or the candidate may be inexperienced, with no real chance of winning. The key decision, therefore, may be whether to endorse at all.

An organization's decision not to endorse can send as strong a message as an endorsement would have sent. In the Virginia governor's race in 2001, the NRA failed to endorse a candidate even though it had given the Republican candidate (Mark Earley) a significantly higher "grade" than the Democratic candidate (Mark Warner). The Warner campaign had worked hard to convince the NRA that it would do nothing to harm the group's interests, and the NRA's "non-endorsement" was seen as a victory for Warner. As one Earley advisor put it, "What they did was denied us the endorsement. … There was no way the NRA was going to endorse a Democrat. [But] the typical NRA grassroots apparatus that gets unleashed during an endorsement did not happen for us. That spoke volumes to single-issue voters."[28] Sometimes a group will decide not to endorse to preserve access to the eventual winner. At other times, the interest group may realize that it is unpopular in a particular district and, therefore, its endorsement would be the kiss of death to a candidate in that district. Whatever the reason, the decision not to endorse a candidate is often as significant as an endorsement.

Some groups face one other consideration when deciding on endorsements, because some want to maintain the ability to claim bipartisanship. To do so, they need to endorse at least one candidate from each party. So a group may seek the most tolerable candidate of the party they rarely support and endorse that person. In the 1998 US Senate race in New York, the gay rights organization Human Rights Campaign (HRC) provoked a backlash among its members when it endorsed Republican incumbent Alfonse D'Amato rather than his challenger, Democratic Representative Charles Schumer. In justifying that decision, the group's executive director argued, "We'll never achieve gay and lesbian civil rights without both parties engaged in that process. … And we have preserved our credibility for being consistent and true to bipartisan principles."[29]

Part of the HRC's decision was based on the incumbent status of D'Amato. Many groups' default position when two candidates are relatively equal in their support for the group's cause is to endorse the incumbent. This practice is intended, in part, to preserve access, given that the odds of winning almost always favor the incumbent, but it is also a way of rewarding officeholders who have been friendly to the group. In 2006, NARAL Pro-Choice America endorsed Republican Senator Lincoln Chafee in Rhode Island. Though Chafee had a pro-choice voting record, many pro-choice activists reacted angrily to NARAL's decision because a Democratic takeover of Congress was viewed as crucial to pro-choice interests. As the NARAL president explained the group's endorsement, not only do incumbents get the benefit of the doubt, but "we stand by our friends."[30]

Scorecards, Hit Lists, and Voter Guides

Scorecards, hit lists, and voter guides offer related ways in which interest groups can indicate their candidate preferences (see Figure 6.2). A group creates a scorecard by identifying an important set of bills in Congress (or the state legislature) and indicating the group's preferred vote on each of those bills. They then list all the individual legislators and their votes on the same bills. The percentage of each legislator's preferred votes is then calculated and listed as well. For example, John McCain voted with the HRC 0 percent of the time in the 110th Congress, whereas Barack Obama supported their position 94 percent of the time.

An interest group may also issue a so-called hit list, or a list of incumbents who are targeted for defeat by the organization because of a voting record that

FIGURE 6.2 *Pages from Human Rights Campaign's 2008 Congressional Scorecard*

KEY

- **A** HC AMDT
- **B** SO UTHWICK
- **C** PEPFAR
- **D** ETHA
- **E** HCPA
- **F** UAFA
- **G** DP TAX

● Supported HRC's position
○ Did not support HRC's position
⊗ Did not vote

SENATOR (Party)	110th SCORE	109th SCORE	108th SCORE	A	B	C	D	E	F	G
ALABAMA										
Sessions, Jeff (R)	0	0	0	○	○	○	○	○	○	○
Shelby, Richard (R)	20	0	0	○	○	●	○	○	○	○
ALASKA										
Murkowski, Lisa (R)	20	0	13	○	○	●	○	○	○	○
Stevens, Ted (R)	20	0	13	○	○	●	○	○	○	○
ARIZONA										
Kyl, Jon (R)	0	0	0	○	○	○	○	○	○	○
McCain, John (R)	0	33	25	⊗	○	⊗	○	○	○	○
ARKANSAS										
Lincoln, Blanche (D)	70	89	63	●	○	●	●	●	○	○
Pryor, Mark (D)	60	89	63	●	○	●	○	○	○	○
CALIFORNIA										
Boxer, Barbara (D)	100	100	88	●	⊗	●	●	●	●	●
Feinstein, Dianne (D)	75	88	75	●	○	●	●	●	○	●
COLORADO										
Allard, Wayne (R)	0	0	0	○	○	○	○	○	○	○
Salazar, Ken (D)	85	67	NA	●	●	●	●	●	○	○
CONNECTICUT										
Dodd, Christopher (D)	100	100	75	●	⊗	●	●	●	●	●
Lieberman, Joseph (ID)	75	89	88	●	○	●	●	●	○	●
DELAWARE										
Biden Jr., Joseph (D)	95	78	63	●	●	●	●	●	○	●
Carper, Thomas (D)	80	67	63	●	●	●	○	○	○	○
FLORIDA										
Martinez, Mel (R)	20	0	NA	○	○	●	○	○	○	○
Nelson, Bill (D)	90	89	75	●	●	●	●	●	○	○

SENATOR (Party)	110th SCORE	109th SCORE	108th SCORE	A	B	C	D	E	F	G
GEORGIA										
Chambliss, Saxby (R)	20	0	0	○	○	●	○	○	○	○
Isakson, Johnny (R)	20	0	0^	○	○	●	○	○	○	○
HAWAII										
Akaka, Daniel (D)	75	100	75	●	○	●	○	●	●	●
Inouye, Daniel (D)	95	78	88	●	●	●	●	●	●	○
IDAHO										
Craig, Larry (R)	0	0	0	○	○	○	○	○	○	○
Crapo, Mike (R)	0	0	0	○	○	○	○	○	○	○
ILLINOIS										
Durbin, Richard (D)	95	89	100	●	●	●	●	●	○	●
Obama, Barack (D)	94	89	NA	●	●	⊗	●	●	○	●
INDIANA										
Bayh, Evan (D)	90	89	75	●	●	●	●	●	○	●
Lugar, Richard (R)	60	0	13	●	○	●	○	○	○	○
IOWA										
Grassley, Chuck (R)	20	0	0	○	○	●	○	○	○	○
Harkin, Tom (D)	90	78	75	●	●	●	●	●	○	○
KANSAS										
Brownback, Sam (R)	20	0	0	○	○	●	○	○	○	○
Roberts, Pat (R)	20	0	0	○	○	●	○	○	○	○
KENTUCKY										
Bunning, Jim (R)	0	0	0	○	○	○	○	○	○	○
McConnell, Mitch (R)	20	0	0	○	○	○	○	○	○	○
LOUISIANA										
Landrieu, Mary (D)	90	89	88	●	●	●	●	●	○	○
Vitter, David (R)	0	0	0^	○	○	○	○	○	○	○

KEY

- **A** HC AMDT
- **B** SO UTHWICK
- **C** PEPFAR
- **D** ETHA
- **E** HCPA
- **F** UAFA
- **G** DP TAX

● Supported HRC's position
○ Did not support HRC's position
⊗ Did not vote

^ Indicates House Score

Source: Human Rights Campaign, "Congressional Scorecard," www.hrc.org/files/documents/Congress_Scorecard-110th.pdf (accessed May 20, 2013).

is particularly negative from the organization's perspective. Perhaps the most famous hit list is the League of Conservation Voters (LCV) Action Fund's "Dirty Dozen" list. The organization describes it this way: "Through the Dirty Dozen, LCV identifies those currently holding federal office—Democrats, Republicans and Independents alike—who consistently vote against the environment, as part of its ongoing effort to educate voters about voting records. LCV targets selected members of this list for independent campaigns in competitive races."[31]

Finally, an interest group might produce a voter guide. The issue positions of the candidates in such guides are derived from some combination of public records, candidate questionnaires, and interviews. It is usually fairly easy to determine which candidate the group prefers because the selection of issues stacks the deck against one candidate. When the group is permitted to endorse candidates, preferential treatment is to be expected, but when 501(c)3 organizations release such guides, they are supposed to remain neutral. Nevertheless, a close reading of the guides will typically reveal a preference for one candidate over another. The Christian Coalition, in particular, has come in for criticism—and a lawsuit brought by the FEC—for an alleged partisan tilt to their guides (see Figure 6.3). Nevertheless, a federal judge ruled in their favor, and they continue to distribute millions of voter guides in churches throughout the country.[32]

Contributions to Candidates

Once the campaign is in full swing, interest groups engage in activity that, as noted earlier, mirrors and indeed reinforces what parties do. Among the most important interest group activities in campaigns is the role played by PACs in helping to fund candidates. As explained in Chapter 3, PACs may contribute $5,000 to a candidate per election; they can also contribute $15,000 to national party committees per calendar year. Their financial assistance to candidates is often even greater than the contribution limits suggest because PACs can circumvent the limits by "bundling" contributions from individuals. When PACs bundle contributions, they put together checks from a number of individuals, usually members of the organization, and present the bundled contributions to the candidate. In the 2016 general election campaign, if a PAC bundled maximum donations of $2,700 from fifty individuals, it would be "contributing" $135,000. Though disclosure requirements were implemented in 2007 for registered lobbyists who bundle contributions, there is still no way to measure the amount of bundled money contributed by PACs. Some of them—such as EMILY's List (whose name is an acronym for "Early Money Is Like Yeast [it helps raise the dough]") and the conservative Club for Growth—are known for employing this tactic to a considerable degree.[33]

The total amount of PAC contributions, as one might have guessed, has increased steadily over the years. In the 1990 midterm elections, PACs gave a combined $159 million to all federal candidates; by 2002, that total had

FIGURE 6.3 *2016 Christian Coalition Voter Guide for Wisconsin*

★ *2016* Christian Coalition ★
V O T E R 🌑 G U I D E

Presidential Election

Donald Trump (R)	ISSUES	Hillary Clinton (D)
Supports	Education Vouchers that Allow Parents to Choose Public or Private School for their Children	Opposes
Supports	Voluntary Prayer in Public Schools and Facilities	Opposes
Opposes	Increase Federal Income Taxes or Income Tax Rates	Supports
Supports	Permanent Elimination of the "Death Tax"	Opposes
Unknown	Passage of a Balanced Budget Amendment to the U.S. Constitution	Opposes
Supports	Appointing Judges Who Will Adhere to a Strict Interpretation of the Constitution	Opposes
Opposes	Further Restrictions on the Right to Keep and Bear Arms	Supports
Opposes	Public Funding of Abortions (Such as Govt. Health Benefits and Planned Parenthood)	Supports
Supports	Parental Notification for Abortions by Minors	Opposes
Supports	Increase Border Security Including Additional Infrastructures	Opposes
Supports	Repealing the Nationalized Health Care System that Forces Citizens to Buy Insurance or Pay Fines	Opposes
Supports	Removing Campaign Free Speech Restrictions that are Placed on Some Organizations but Not Others	Opposes
Supports	Federal Tuition Tax Credits for Parents who Home School or Send their Child to a Private School	Opposes
Unknown	Enacting an Energy Independence Plan in First 100 Days of New Congress	Unknown
Supports	The US Should Continue to Support and Stand with the Nation of Israel Against her Enemies	Supports

donaldjtrump.com   hillaryclinton.com

★ ★ ★ *Vote on November 8th!* ★ ★ ★

FIGURE 6.3 Continued

Wisconsin
US Senate
Election

Ron Johnson (R)	ISSUES	Russ Feingold (D)
Opposes	Increase Federal Income Taxes or Income Tax Rates	Supports
Supports	Permanent Elimination of "Death Tax"	Opposes
Supports	Passage of a Balanced Budget Amendment to the U.S. Constitution	Opposes
Supports	Appointing Judges Who Will Adhere to a Strict Interpretation of the Constitution	Opposes
Opposes	Further Restrictions on the Right to Keep and Bear Arms	Supports
Opposes	Public Funding of Abortions (Such as Govt. Health Benefits and Planned Parenthood)	Supports
Supports	Parental Notification for Abortions by Minors	Opposes
Unknown	Increase Border Security Including Additional Infrastructures	Opposes
Supports	Repealing the Nationalized Health Care System that Forces Citizens to Buy Insurance or Pay Fines	Opposes
Supports	The U.S. Should Continue to Support and Stand with the Nation of Israel Against her Enemies	Supports

ronjohnsonforsenate.com   russfeingold.com

Dear friend,

You are holding one of the most powerful tools Americans have had to impact our society during elections – the Christian Coalition voter guide.

I encourage you to help spread this important information to others by making additional copies for distribution. You can visit our website at www. cc.org/voterguides to download and print voter guides, as well as forward them to others via email, Facebook and Twitter.

This is a crucial election and too much is at stake for God's people to sit on the sidelines. Be sure to make your vote count by going to the polls this coming Election Day!

Sincerely,
Roberta Combs
President, Christian Coalition

Share Christian Coalition
Voter Guides with Others!

★ ★ ★   **www.cc.org/voterguides**   ★ ★ ★

Source: Christian Coalition, "2016 Election Voter Guides," www.cc.org/sites/default/files/3/2016VGWISenate.pdf (accessed January 29, 2017).

climbed to $282 million and, in 2014, it was just under $436 million.[34] Though PACs consider party, incumbency, and competitiveness when deciding where to send their money, they generally have a preference for incumbents. Usually, the bulk of their money goes to safe incumbents. However, in some years, PACs will send more money to incumbents who are facing electoral danger. That was true of PAC giving to Democrats in 2010. After incumbents, competitive open-seat candidates receive the most PAC money, followed typically by other open-seat candidates and then competitive challengers. Finally, it should be noted that the majority party gets more PAC money—with the exception of labor money, which always goes overwhelmingly to Democrats—than the minority party.[35] This happens, in part, simply because the majority party has more members to give to, but it is also the result of money following power. The patterns of PAC giving reflect the mixed strategy of giving to reward friends and maintain access and to increase the number of legislators favorable to interest groups' causes.

In addition to monetary contributions, PACs can give "in-kind" contributions of "services, staff, and products—rather than money—to campaigns."[36] In-kind contributions are subject to the $5,000 per election limit, which means that the value of the service or product given to a candidate must be determined and is then counted toward the contribution limit. PACs may, for example, provide poll results to a campaign, but the campaign must report the value of the poll as a contribution. The amount is determined on the basis of fair-market value, which can be discounted as time passes. Thus, a poll conducted a month earlier is worth less than one done yesterday. Still, as Mark J. Rozell, Clyde Wilcox, and David Madland point out, early in a campaign, poll results are not as time-sensitive as they are late in a campaign. Thus, an interest group can provide candidates with a service of enormous value early in a campaign while the candidate gets to claim it at reduced cost.[37] Of course, interest groups, like parties, often pay for polling in bulk, so their cost is lower to begin with.

Interest groups also provide candidates with valuable information. It may take the form of policy briefings so that the candidate is up to speed on the intricacies of important issues, but it may also be strategic advice. PACs usually work closely with political consultants who can provide the organization and, in turn, candidates with message advice, voter targeting plans, and other strategic considerations. Interest groups may even provide such information to the parties. In 1994, conservative interest groups produced research and polling data for congressional Republicans that were used to develop the party's campaign manifesto, the Contract with America.[38]

Last, interest groups may provide staff members to candidates. Because the salary of a staff member would likely exceed the PAC contribution limit, complicated bookkeeping is required to keep the arrangement legal. Interest groups can also encourage their members to volunteer on certain campaigns. Though the interest group may train the individuals, volunteer efforts are not considered an in-kind contribution, so this resource can be quite valuable.

Independent Expenditures

Perhaps more important than direct financial assistance is the spending interest groups do in support of their preferred candidates—or against those they oppose. Because it is raised according to "hard dollar" contribution limits, any money spent by federal PACs can be used to advocate the election or defeat of specific candidates (as long as there is no coordination with the campaigns). Thus, PACs may choose to campaign on behalf of their favored candidates by running ads in support of their candidacies. In the past, one benefit of spending hard dollars for ads was that groups could be explicit in their support. The problem with this approach was that it is difficult to raise enough hard money—which for PACs comes in no more than $5,000 increments from individuals—to pay for extensive advertising.

This explains why 527 organizations became so popular in the early 2000s. By ostensibly engaging in "issue advocacy" and not express advocacy of candidates, groups seeking to influence elections could raise money in unlimited amounts from any source. However, 527s did have to be careful about what they said in their campaign communications. Ads that could be interpreted as nothing other than an appeal to vote for or against a candidate were forbidden.

In the wake of the *Citizens United* and *SpeechNow* rulings, however, interest groups do not have to choose between PACs, which are constrained in their fund-raising but can say whatever they want in campaign ads, and 527s, which can accept contributions in unlimited amounts but are not allowed to expressly advocate for or against candidates. By forming a super-PAC, an interest group can raise money in unlimited amounts and can communicate explicitly its support or opposition to candidates. Of course, many interest groups will still want the ability to contribute campaign funds to candidates (see the previous section). To do that, they must use a PAC, but groups that want to run campaign ads are likely, from this point forward, to establish super-PACs.

The financial activity of interest groups in campaigns, in terms of both contributions to candidates and independent expenditures, is staggering. PACs, super-PACs, and 501(c) organizations spent an enormous amount of money in the 2016 election cycle (see Table 6.1). In total, PAC contributions to candidates amounted to more than $400 million, but the independent expenditures of outside groups reached nearly $1.5 billion.[39] Indeed, the real growth in outside spending is in independent expenditures. As Jeff Smith and David Kimball report, independent expenditures by non-party groups in 2008 had been a mere $286 million.[40] The dramatic increase in independent expenditures since 2008 is due, unquestionably, to the appearance of super-PACs in elections.[41]

TABLE 6.1 *The Top 20 Super-PACs, PACs, and 501(c) Organizations, by Total Amount Spent, 2015–2016*

Organization	Type of group	Viewpoint	Amount Spent
Priorities USA/Priorities USA Action	Super-PAC	Clinton	$133,407,972
Senate Leadership Fund	Super-PAC	Senate Republicans	$87,325,140
Right to Rise USA	Super-PAC	Bush	$86,817,138
Senate Majority PAC	Super-PAC	Senate Democrats	$75,389,818
Conservative Solutions PAC	Super-PAC	Rubio	$55,443,483
National Rifle Association	501(c)	Conservative	$52,536,555
Get Our Jobs Back	Super-PAC	Trump	$50,010,166
House Majority PAC	Super-PAC	House Democrats	$47,482,381
Congressional Leadership Fund	Super-PAC	House Republicans	$40,125,691
EMILY's List	Super-PAC	Liberal	$33,167,285
Freedom Partners Action Fund	Super-PAC	Conservative	$29,728,798
US Chamber of Commerce	501(c)	Conservative	$29,106,034
AFSCME	501(c)	Liberal	$23,537,220
Granite State Solutions	Super-PAC	Ayotte (Senate)	$24,267,135
Future45	Super-PAC	Trump	$24,264,009
Club for Growth	Super-PAC/501(c)	Conservative	$23,172,639
NextGen Climate Action	Super-PAC	Liberal	$23,000,116
League of Conservation Voters	Super-PAC/501(c)	Liberal	$22,735,194
SEIU	Super-PAC/501(c)	Liberal	$22,214,768
Great America PAC	Super-PAC	Trump	$22,592,130

Source: Center for Responsive Politics, "2016 Outside Spending, by Group," https://www.open-secrets.org/outsidespending/summ.php?disp=O (accessed January 29, 2017).

Note: Where "viewpoint" lists a candidate's name, or a group of candidates (e.g., Senate Democrats), the organization is a super-PAC set up specifically to support that candidate or group of candidates.

Though the amount of money spent is truly breathtaking, the effectiveness of the spending is uncertain. One study of the "return on investment" for outside groups active in the 2012 campaign found that some of the biggest spenders were largely unsuccessful at helping their preferred candidate win. Only 1.29 percent of American Crossroads' spending, for example, had the desired effect (that is, it was money spent supporting a candidate who eventually won or opposing a candidate who lost).[42] Of course, there are any number of reasons why candidates win or lose, and outside spending can't be assessed in isolation. Furthermore, outside spending might help a candidate remain competitive who, without such support, would languish (or it might make winning more difficult for a candidate who would otherwise win easily). Many believe, for example, that Newt Gingrich and Rick Santorum would have dropped out of the 2012 Republican nomination race far earlier had it not been for the support of the super-PACs established on each candidate's behalf.[43] Still, with huge amounts of money being spent on both sides in competitive races, it seems unlikely that outside spending could be the determining factor in many of those races.

There is one effect of spending by interest groups, however, that seems quite clear. More of the campaign ads by groups are negative than are those sponsored by candidates or political parties. Through their work on the Wesleyan Media Project, Erika Franklin Fowler and Travis N. Ridout have found that 85.2 percent of ads aired by outside groups in the 2012 presidential general election were negative, compared to 51.1 percent of party ads and 54.3 percent of candidate ads.[44] This echoes findings from an early study of advertising in the 2000 election by the Brennan Center for Justice. In that study, what used to be called "electioneering ads" (or "sham issue ads" due to the fact that they masqueraded as issue ads to avoid contribution limits) were found to be far more likely to attack a candidate than were party or candidate ads.[45]

Though outside groups have, for some time now, had a tendency to be more negative in their advertising than parties or candidates, the level of negativity seems to be increasing. That is certainly the trend in campaign advertising, taken as a whole (that is, from all sources combined), in congressional elections.[46] It is not unreasonable to speculate, then, that this increase in negativity is the result of the corresponding increase in independent expenditures by outside groups.

Voter Contact and Mobilization

Of course, not all of an organization's independent expenditures will be spent on advertising, or what is sometimes referred to as the "air war." Some groups also engage extensively in the "ground war," or voter contact and mobilization. A portion of this activity involves "internal communication" or communication between the group and its members. These contacts take the form of e-mails, newsletters, magazines, and other direct mail and telephone communication. When groups communicate internally, they are reminding their members of the records of various candidates by, for example, highlighting endorsements or reporting scorecard results. Of course, they also communicate "member to member" to mobilize their associates on Election Day.

It used to be the case that labor unions could engage only in member-to-member mobilization. Thousands of union volunteers would knock on tens of thousands of doors in key races to remind members to get to the polls. Because of the *Citizens United* decision, however, unions are now able to contact all voters. According to the AFL-CIO's president, Richard Trumka, unions planned to knock on 5.5 million doors and make 5.2 million phone calls in the final four days leading up to the 2012 election.[47] Thus, though unions have always been critical to the Democratic Party's GOTV efforts, they are even more valuable today.

Liberal organizations have traditionally had very active voter mobilization operations. In 2004 and again in 2008, liberal interest groups were particularly active on the GOTV front in an attempt to counteract the Republican Party's 72-Hour Task Force. The most notable was America Votes, a coalition of more than forty left-leaning groups, including a number of high-profile 527 organizations. MoveOn has also offered assistance to Democrats with massive GOTV campaigns.

It's also worth mentioning the efforts of African-American churches. In early voting states, particularly those that allow voting on Sundays, Black churches often develop GOTV programs such as the "Souls to the Polls" weekend in Florida.[48] These initiatives (which are often referred to generically as "pews to the polls" events) coordinate rides from churches to polling places, with buses departing right after Sunday services. Given churches' tax-exempt status as 501(c)3 organizations, these initiatives are, in theory, nonpartisan events. However, because African-American voters are overwhelmingly Democratic in their party affiliation, in practice, pews to the polls operations are a huge boon to the Democratic Party.

Just as liberal groups have traditionally emphasized GOTV, conservative groups have typically paid less attention to voter mobilization. This is due, in part, to the fact that conservative organizations tend to have far fewer members, and thus fewer volunteers, than many liberal groups. Many of the leading groups on the right have simply been vehicles for big donors to spend money on television ads. That began to change in 2010 and 2012. Tea Party organizations had not only members but a tremendous amount of energy. Groups such as FreedomWorks had particularly active GOTV operations in the 2010 and 2012 election cycles. Americans for Prosperity allocated roughly half of its spending to GOTV in 2012.[49] And in 2016, conservative groups with well-developed networks in non-metro areas of the country worked to elect Republicans, including Donald Trump.[50]

In recent years, as it has become increasingly difficult to cut through the din on the airwaves, the ground war has become at least as important in campaigns as the air war, and interest groups have been eager to join battle on this front. Campaign finance rules have also changed in ways that allow certain groups to more fully engage in voter mobilization. There is no doubt that GOTV will continue to be a vital part of interest groups' campaign activity in election cycles far into the future.

The Effectiveness—and Consequences—of Interest Group Activity

In the halls of Congress and state legislatures around the country, some organizations have a great deal of influence, and others have less. Political scientists have identified many of the factors that contribute to an interest group's success in achieving its policy goals, but it is not clear that these same factors indicate influence in elections.[51] It should be noted at the outset that interest groups are involved in campaigns over ballot measures in addition to candidate campaigns. With respect to candidate campaigns, however, there are various ways to define "electoral influence." We may, for instance, think an organization influential if it can alter the agenda of a campaign. Do the campaigns address the issues that an organization emphasizes? Alternatively, by influence we may mean only electoral success. That is, of the campaigns in which a group is involved, how many are victorious? Regardless of the definition, electoral influence is a difficult concept to measure. Nevertheless, it is safe to assume that some groups have more of an impact on election outcomes than others. This section begins by examining a few of the factors that are likely to contribute to an organization's influence in elections. It will then turn to a discussion of the normative consequences of interest group activity in electoral politics.

BOX 6.3 *Interest Groups and Ballot Measures*

Interest groups not only campaign for candidates, they are active in initiatives and referenda, or "ballot measures." Though any individual can start the initiative process, few are successful without the help of interest groups. It takes money and organization to gather the thousands (and sometimes hundreds of thousands) of petition signatures required to get a measure on the ballot. Interest groups, of course, have both. Thus, with the exception of the occasional wealthy individual, interest groups are the primary actors in ballot measure campaigns.

Some critics of the initiative and referenda process fear that wealthy groups are able to utilize ballot measures to serve their own interests at the expense of the general welfare. The vast amounts of money spent by these interest groups, first to qualify a measure for the ballot and then to advertise in support of it, is thought to give them enormous advantages at the polls. That, in turn, gives them an inordinate effect on public policy. Empirical evidence, however, suggests that the critics' fear may be unfounded.

Political scientist Elisabeth Gerber has shown that spending in support of ballot measures by economic groups (which consist of representatives of organizations such as corporations and which advocate for the economic interests of those organizations) has a negative effect on both the vote margin and the probability of success of those measures.[1] To illustrate, a 2006 Rhode Island measure that would have authorized the development of a resort casino failed by a vote of 63 to 27 percent despite the fact that proponents spent roughly $9.4 million while opponents spent $3.8 million.[2]

Gerber also found that supportive spending by citizens groups (which seek public goods on behalf of autonomous individuals who constitute their membership) has no significant effect, either positive or negative, on vote margins or probability of success.[3] Thus, in Missouri in 2006, a measure to legalize stem-cell research passed only narrowly (51 percent to 49 percent) even though proponents outspent opponents by over $30 million (with the opponents spending less than $1 million).[4]

(continued)

BOX 6.3 *Interest Groups and Ballot Measures* (continued)

It may be the case that interest groups use their money not so much to "buy" favorable legislation as to thwart citizen initiatives that they dislike. Indeed, the one circumstance in which Gerber found spending by interest groups to have a significant effect is when economic groups spend in opposition to ballot measures. Of course, the "no" vote on ballot measures is generally more likely to prevail—regardless of spending levels—because voters typically prefer the status quo to the unknown consequences of a change in public policy.

So is the initiative and referendum process stacked in favor of economic interests? Not according to Gerber's research. In fact, the opposite may be the case. As Gerber concluded, "initiatives and referendums in the subject areas most often pursued by citizen interests passed at a higher rate than those in areas most often pursued by economic interests."[5]

1   Elisabeth R. Gerber, *The Populist Paradox: Interest Group Influence and the Promise of Direct Legislation*, Princeton, NJ: Princeton University Press, pp. 108 and 109.
2   Ballot Initiative Strategy Center, "2006 Initiative & Referenda Election Results," November 2006, http://bisc.3cdn.net/5052cbd4bc3c5a8d9b_v6m6bwdj5.pdf, 7 and 5 (accessed May 20, 2013).
3   Gerber, *The Populist Paradox*, pp. 108 and 109.
4   Ballot Initiative Strategy Center, "2006 Initiative," pp. 7 and 5.
5   Gerber, *The Populist Paradox*, p. 120.

Electoral Influence

When it comes to lobbying, the size of the organization does not always translate into effectiveness, but it certainly helps. This is true in elections as well. The more members an interest group has, the more volunteers it may be able to activate, and the more voters it has the potential to influence. However, groups have to be able to convert numbers into action. Many are unable to do so because of their organizational structure. Those that are established as 501(c)3 organizations have very little influence on elections, regardless of how big they may be. Some 501(c)4s limit their electoral activity and, therefore, their influence. The AARP, for example, has the largest membership of any organization in the country but has limited—or at least indirect—influence in elections because it does not endorse candidates and has no PAC.

An important factor related to size is an organization's fund-raising capacity. Obviously, the more members an organization has, the deeper the pool from which it can solicit funds, but of even greater importance may be the ability of a group's members to contribute funds. A group with a large number of middle-to low-income individuals may raise less money than a smaller organization made up of wealthy members. For instance, with just 56,000 members, the American

Association for Justice (formerly the Association of Trial Lawyers of America) PAC raised $6.8 million in 2016; by contrast, the more than 300,000-member-strong International Association of Fire Fighters raised $5.6 million.[52]

Quite apart from the wealth of an organization's members, their social profile may determine the group's clout. An organization that represents individuals of high status and prestige—doctors, for example—will typically have a great deal of credibility with lawmakers, particularly in the group's area of expertise. It is not clear, however, that status and prestige produce electoral influence. Though the American Medical Association is thought to be very effective at lobbying on health-related matters, its impact in elections is not as great. The respect that doctors command when they lobby simply does not guarantee influence in a campaign.

The geographical distribution of a group's membership also affects its influence. In lobbying the federal government, it is better for a group's members to be evenly distributed throughout the country than to be concentrated in some parts of it. However, there are no national campaigns in the United States. Even a presidential contest is determined by the outcome in several states' elections. As a result, national distribution of members is less useful to groups in campaigning than in lobbying. Indeed, a regionally based organization can be quite influential in particular districts or states. Unions, for instance, tend to be concentrated in the Northeast and the Midwest. Their impact on races is therefore greater in New Jersey, Michigan, and Illinois than in South Carolina or Mississippi.

The aforementioned factors combine in complex ways to produce electoral influence. Some organizations derive influence from their financial strength, whereas others exert it through the ability or willingness of their members to volunteer their time. EMILY's List and the NRA are two groups that are widely recognized as effective in achieving their electoral goals, but they are very different organizations. The then roughly 400,000 members of EMILY's List gave more than $19 million to that organization's PAC in the 2010 cycle and $6.5 million more to the group's super-PAC (Women Vote!). That money was spent assisting candidates both directly, through contributions, and indirectly, through independent expenditures. In contrast, the NRA's nearly 4 million members gave nearly $15.5 million to its PAC.[53] EMILY's List may have raised more money, but the NRA could have a greater presence in the election by mobilizing just a fraction of its members to volunteer in campaigns and, ultimately, to vote. Furthermore, the NRA is a single-issue group, so its potential to affect the policy debate in particular races is greater than that of EMILY's List.

Negative Effects of Interest Group Activity

Beyond the influence that groups exert in elections, we might ask what the consequences of their activity are for democracy. The most common criticism of interest group activity in elections is that it "buys" elected officials; that is, when groups contribute to candidates, those candidates are thought to repay the group with favorable votes on key legislation. The evidence for such a claim, it must be said, is mixed.[54] The problem is of the chicken-or-egg variety. Do legislators vote in agreement with groups because they have given money, or do groups give money because certain legislators are already in agreement with them? Despite disagreement over the ability of interest groups to influence votes with campaign contributions, political scientists tend to accept the proposition that money buys access to legislators. This may be enough to raise serious questions about fairness, but it is less troubling than the more sinister allegation of vote-buying.

Others worry that at least some interest groups are largely unaccountable actors in elections. This is a particular concern with respect to the activity of 501(c) organizations in campaigns. These organizations can take unlimited contributions from individuals, corporations, and unions and don't have to report those contributions to the FEC (prompting critics to refer to such financial activity as "dark money"). Though there are limitations to how much campaigning 501(c) organizations can do, some of these groups regularly bump up against those limitations and, frankly, a few completely cross the line. In addition, some 501(c) organizations funnel money to super-PACs. Because super-PACs must disclose their donors, anyone wanting to contribute to a super-PAC secretly can do so through a 501(c) organization (yet another manifestation of "dark money"). Thus, it is often difficult to know which interests are helping which candidates and, in turn, whether particular interests are receiving special treatment from lawmakers.

It is not even clear how PACs and super-PACs, who do report their financial activity to the FEC, are to be held accountable for their actions in campaigns. If, for example, some previously unknown organization ran a particularly odious campaign ad or engaged in some kind of dirty trick, who should be punished (politically speaking) for such an act? Punishing the candidate the group supports wouldn't be fair because, by law, the candidate can have nothing to do with the group's activities. In fact, it would likely take a considerable amount of investigating just to find out who was behind the group in the first place. The names of super-PACs—such as Restore Our Future (Romney 2012) or Priorities USA (Obama 2012 and Clinton 2016)—certainly don't help the average voter make sense of the motives of these groups. To a large extent, then, outside groups can act in campaigns with impunity.

Perhaps because of this lack of accountability, interest groups feel emboldened to run highly negative campaigns. As we saw earlier in this chapter, the campaign ads of outside groups are far more likely to be negative than are the ads of candidates or parties. Indeed, a high percentage of those ads rely on anger and fear to motivate the electorate.[55] This, in turn, coarsens campaign discourse and makes campaigns even nastier than they might otherwise be.

Finally, some worry about the enormous amounts of money being spent by outside groups. One fear is that well-funded groups might be able to exert outsized influence on election outcomes. As noted earlier, there is good reason to doubt that any single group would be able to work its will in an election, but there is also reason to be concerned about the potential for disproportionate influence. One way that influence could manifest itself is in a distorted campaign agenda. That is, wealthy outside groups may dictate the terms of debate in a campaign, ensuring that their interests get more attention than those of less well-funded groups. Furthermore, though outside groups aren't likely to determine the outcome of high-profile races, such as presidential elections, they could very well dominate smaller races. Exorbitant amounts of spending also lead to a campaign finance arms race between candidates, parties, and interest groups. If nothing else, this is thought to be unseemly by many citizens but may, more importantly, contribute to the perception of corruption in the system.

The Value of Interest Groups

Criticism notwithstanding, plenty may be said in defense of interest groups. First, a distinction can and should be drawn between types of interest groups. Non-connected PACs, for example, are very different from those connected to 501(c) organizations. Furthermore, relatively few groups exist exclusively in super-PAC form, though those that do get a disproportionate amount of attention from the media. Thus, to characterize the behavior of all interest groups on the basis of the activity of some high-profile organizations is misleading.

According to a classic theory of American politics called pluralism, interest groups are an important counterbalance to elites in the policy-making process. Elected officials, as Robert Dahl argued in *Who Governs?*, are actually quite responsive to a broad array of interests.[56] As it turns out, no single group dominates the process; different groups will be successful depending on the issue. The outcome is a much more democratic process than one in which an elite cadre gets its way on all matters. Though as an empirical theory pluralism has been criticized in recent years, it remains a powerful normative argument.[57]

Not only are a wide variety of interests represented by interest groups, but many groups enjoy a relatively broad base of support. Only a few are little more than front organizations for the narrow agendas of a handful of individuals. Even ideological PACs speak for millions of Americans who share their viewpoints. Still, interest groups have well-defined missions. Whereas political parties in the United States function as "big tents" and are forced to accommodate multiple constituencies, interest groups can concentrate on the needs of their members. Of course, interest groups cannot protect all their members' interests because individuals have multiple concerns. Thus, parties and interest groups complement one another nicely: The former provide general representation while the latter satisfy specific demands.

Indeed, interest groups are a crucial element in the party networks discussed at the end of Chapter 5. They play an important role in party politics from both within the party apparatus and outside it. Inside the parties, interest groups encourage open, wide-ranging debate and have introduced previously underrepresented constituencies into those debates. This is true, for example, of gays and lesbians in the Democratic Party and evangelical Christians in the Republican Party. Operating from outside the formal party structure, interest groups often act as auxiliary committees. Their activity complements and reinforces what the parties do. One of the most important aspects of this supporting role is its participatory nature. When interest groups undertake GOTV efforts, for example, they bring tens of thousands of people into the process, both as volunteers and as voters. Thus, interest groups can be said to raise the level of participation in politics.

We might note one last consequence of interest group activity in the American political process that may be considered neither positive nor negative but rather a simple fact of contemporary political life: interest groups have clearly contributed to the rise of the permanent campaign, that is, the use of campaign techniques in the process of governing. One of the earliest forays into the permanent campaign by groups was the insurance industry's effort to defeat the Clinton administration's proposed health care program in 1993. The Health Insurance Association of America (HIAA) aired campaign-like commercials featuring a fictional couple, named "Harry and Louise," who raised critical questions about the Clinton plan. The ads were later credited with having turned public opinion against the plan.[58] With the HIAA's success, other interest groups engaged in similar tactics drawn from election campaigns to advance their agendas. It should be said that this development may simply be the result of changes in the communication environment, including ubiquitous news coverage and more aggressive efforts to shape public opinion by politicians and political parties. Thus, for better or worse, interest groups have simply responded to the demands of a new context they had little to do with creating.

▶ Conclusion

Interest groups, like parties, are political organizations that are extremely active in campaigns and elections. As this chapter has shown, much of what they do is similar to what parties do, and the two often complement one another nicely. Of course, interest groups differ from parties in that only parties nominate candidates for office. And whereas interest groups' primary purpose is to advance the interests of the people they represent, parties are designed to win control of government. To advance their agendas, however, interest groups have to be concerned with who controls government, so they often get involved in campaigns.

Though they don't recruit candidates quite as actively as parties, some interest groups do encourage individuals to run for office and some provide training for first-time candidates. Many also endorse candidates, educate citizens about issues and candidates, and mobilize voters on Election Day. Of course, many also contribute money to candidates or spend independently on candidates' behalf. As the growth of PACs and the emergence of super-PACs make clear, campaign spending has become an integral part of interest groups' attempts to exert influence in politics.

That spending is not without its negative implications. It raises the spec-ter, for example, that elected officials will owe favors to those interest groups who helped them get elected. Because a significant portion of campaign spend-ing by interest groups involves "dark money," critics are also concerned about a lack of accountability. Outside groups may also add to the nasty tone of campaigns by running attack ads while hiding behind patriotic-sounding, but unfamiliar, names.

Though they are often viewed as polarizing organizations that care more about their own self-interest than the common good, interest groups are also vehicles through which many Americans engage with the political process. They mobilize millions of citizens not only to vote, but to share their con-cerns and opinions with elected officials and candidates for office. Even those citizens who do not become members of interest groups benefit from their presence in the political system. All citizens have interests affected by the gov-ernment and everyone, whether they realize it or not, is represented by groups working to protect their interests. Whether ultimately viewed as positive or negative influences, interest groups undeniably play a central role in American politics today.

► *Pedagogical Tools*

Role-Play Scenario

You are the executive director of an organization that has given you the respon-sibility of choosing the candidates your group will endorse. In a race for state representative, there is a primary for the nomination of the party with which your group is allied. The party favors Ms. Smith, who has served as a city council member in the largest city in the district for ten years but agrees with your group about 70 percent of the time. Another candidate, Ms. Jones, agrees with your group on almost every issue but has never run for office before. Write a brief memo for your executive board explaining whom you have chosen to endorse and why.

Discussion Questions

1. Why might Internet-based conservative groups not have been as successful in electoral politics as online liberal organizations?
2. How concerned should we be about the rise of super-PACs? What about the use of 501(c) organizations in campaigns?
3. Overall, do interest groups have a positive or negative impact on American politics?

Online Resources

The Center for Public Integrity, "Consider the Source" (information on particular super-PACs and nonprofit organizations involved in campaigns), www.publicintegrity.org/politics/consider-source.

The Center for Responsive Politics (a good source for tracking campaign spending by outside groups), www.opensecrets.org.

Liberal Groups

ActBlue, www.actblue.com.
Democracy for America, www.democracyforamerica.com.
MoveOn, www.moveon.org.
Priorities USA Action, http://prioritiesusaaction.org.

Conservative Groups

Americans for Prosperity, http://americansforprosperity.org.
Club for Growth, www.clubforgrowth.org.
FreedomWorks, www.freedomworks.org.
GOPAC, www.gopac.org.

Suggested Reading

Paul S. Herrnson, Christopher J. Deering, and Clyde Wilcox (eds.) (2013) *Interest Groups Unleashed*, Washington, DC: CQ Press.
David B. Magleby, J. Quin Monson, and Kelly D. Patterson (eds.) (2007) *Dancing without Partners: How Candidates, Parties, and Interest Groups Interact in the Presidential Campaign*, Lanham, MD: Rowman & Littlefield.
Mark J. Rozell, Clyde Wilcox, and Michael M. Franz (2011) *Interest Groups in American Campaigns: The New Face of Electioneering*, Oxford: Oxford University Press.

▶ Notes

1 James Madison (1787) "The Federalist Papers: No. 10," The Avalon Project, Yale Law School, http://avalon.law.yale.edu/18th_century/fed10.asp (accessed October 13, 2016).
2 Jeffrey M. Berry and Clyde Wilcox (2007) *The Interest Group Society*, 4th edn, New York: Longman, pp. 6–8.
3 See David B. Truman (1951) *The Governmental Process*, New York: Knopf.

4 See Robert H. Salisbury (1969) "An Exchange Theory of Interest Groups," *Midwest Journal of Political Science*, 13: 1–32; and Mancur Olson, Jr. (1968) *The Logic of Collective Action*, New York: Schocken.

5 Berry and Wilcox, *The Interest Group Society*, p. 39.

6 Berry and Wilcox, *The Interest Group Society*, pp. 41–44.

7 Brian Anderson and Burdett A. Loomis (1998) "Taking Organization Seriously: The Structure of Interest Group Influence," in Allan Cigler and Burdett Loomis (eds.), *Interest Group Politics*, 5th edn, Washington, DC: CQ Press, pp. 84, 96.

8 Mark P. Petracca (1992) "The Rediscovery of Interest Group Politics," in Mark P. Petracca (ed.), *The Politics of Interests: Interest Groups Transformed*, Boulder, CO: Westview Press, p. 13.

9 Federal Election Commission (2016) "PAC Count, 1974–Present," www.fec.gov/press/resources/paccount.shtml (accessed January 2, 2017).

10 Larry J. Sabato (1985) *PAC Power: Inside the World of Political Action Committees*, New York: W. W. Norton, p. 9.

11 Theda Skocpol (2003) *Diminished Democracy: From Membership to Management in American Civic Life*, Norman, OK: University of Oklahoma Press, p. 163.

12 Sourcewatch (2013) "MoveOn," www.sourcewatch.org/index.php?title=MoveOn (accessed October 13, 2016).

13 For an examination of the difficulty conservative groups have had at building a successful Internet-based advocacy organization, see Dave Karpf (2009) "Don't Think of an Online Elephant: Explaining the Dearth of Conservative Political Infrastructure Online in America," presented at the Society for Social Studies of Science Annual Meeting, Washington, DC, http://davekarpf.files.wordpress.com/2009/03/dont-think-of-an-online-elephant.pdf (accessed October 13, 2016).

14 See Erika Lunder (2006) "Tax-Exempt Organizations: Political Activity Restrictions and Disclosure Requirements," April 20. Washington, DC: Congressional Research Service.

15 All PAC figures cited in this section are taken from Federal Election Commission, "PAC Count, 1974–Present."

16 Stephen R. Weissman and Kara D. Ryan (2006) "Nonprofit Interest Groups' Election Activities and Federal Campaign Finance Policy: A Working Paper," The Campaign Finance Institute, www.cfinst.org/books_reports/pdf/NonprofitsWorkingPaper.pdf (accessed October 13, 2016).

17 The pamphlet is available at http://emilyslist.org/sites/default/files/TORFO.pdf (accessed October 13, 2016).

18 GOPAC (n.d.) "Mission," www.gopac.org/about/mission (accessed October 13, 2016). See the variety of training tools GOPAC offers at GOPAC University, www.gopac.org/university (accessed October 13, 2016).

19 See National Women's Political Caucus, www.nwpc.org/education-training (accessed April 15, 2017).

20 Andy Barr (2010) "Karl Rove: Christine O'Donnell Said 'Nutty Things,'" *Politico*, September 15, www.politico.com/news/stories/0910/42205.html (accessed October 13, 2016).

21 Jeff Zeleny (2013) "Top Donors to Republicans Seek More Say in Senate Races," *The New York Times*, February 2, www.nytimes.com/2013/02/03/us/politics/top-gop-donors-seek-greater-say-in-senate-races.html?partner=rss&emc=rss&_r=3& (accessed October 13, 2016).

22 Jeff Zeleny (2013a) "New Rove Effort Has GOP Aflame," *The New York Times*, February 6, www.nytimes.com/2013/02/07/us/politics/new-rove-effort-has-gop-aflame.html (accessed October 13, 2016); and Kenneth P. Vogel, Alexander Burns, and Tarini Parti (2013) "Karl Rove vs. Tea Party in Big Money Fight for GOP's Future," *Politico*, February 7, www.politico.com//story/2013/02/rove-vs-tea-party-for-gops-future-87296.html (accessed October 13, 2016).

23 Kenneth P. Vogel (2013) "Tea Party Group Pictures Rove in Nazi Uniform," *Politico*, February 19, www.politico.com/story/2013/02/tea-party-group-pictures-karl-rove-in-nazi-uniform-87793.html (accessed October 13, 2016).

24 Mark J. Rozell, Clyde Wilcox, and David Madland (2006) *Interest Groups in American Campaigns: The New Face of Electioneering*, Washington, DC: CQ Press, p. 120.

25 AFL-CIO (2007) "AFL-CIO Presidential Endorsement Process," March 7, www.aflcio.org/About/Exec-Council/EC-Statements/AFL-CIO-Presidential-Endorsement-Process (accessed October 13, 2016). See also, Rozell et al., *Interest Groups in American Campaigns*, p. 121.
26 MoveOn.org (n.d.) "Report on the 2003 MoveOn.org Political Action Primary," www.moveon.org/pac/primary/report.html (accessed May 18, 2013).
27 Nick Gass (2016) "MoveOn Endorses Bernie Sanders," *Politico*, January 12, www.politico.com/story/2016/01/movon-endorses-bernie-sanders-217614 (accessed January 16, 2017).
28 As quoted in Scott Bass (2005) "Chasing Bubba," *Style Weekly*, October 12, www.style-weekly.com/richmond/chasing-bubba/Content?oid=1390697 (accessed October 13, 2016).
29 As quoted in David Kirby (1998) "A Painful Coming-of-Age: Human Rights Campaign Angers Gay Voters in New York," *The Advocate*, December 8, www.thefreelibrary.com/A+painful+coming-of-age.-a053356345 (accessed October 13, 2016).
30 As quoted in John E. Mulligan (2005) "Abortion-Rights Group Endorses Chafee," *Providence Journal*, May 20, www.projo.com/news/content/projo_20050520_ naral20.255208c.html (accessed May 4, 2013).
31 League of Conservation Voters Action Fund, "LCV Action Fund's Dirty Dozen," www.lcv.org/elections/dirty-dozen (accessed October 13, 2016).
32 Bill Miller and Susan B. Glasser (1999) "A Victory for Christian Coalition," *Washington Post*, August 3, www.washingtonpost.com/wp-srv/politics/daily/aug99/fec3.htm (accessed October 13, 2016).
33 Paul S. Herrnson (2012) *Congressional Elections: Campaigning at Home and in Washington*, 6th edn, Washington, DC: CQ Press, pp. 162–163.
34 Federal Election Commission, "Summary of PAC Activity, 1990–2010," www.fec.gov/press/bkgnd/cf_summary_info/2010pac_fullsum/4sumhistory2010.pdf (accessed May 20, 2013); Federal Election Commission (2015) "Table 2: PAC Contributions to Candidates," www.fec.gov/press/summaries/2014/tables/pac/PAC2_2014_24m.pdf (January 29, 2017).
35 Evidence for the discussion in this paragraph comes from Herrnson, *Congressional Elections*, pp. 159 and 160, Tables 5.2 and 5.3.
36 Rozell et al., *Interest Groups in American Campaigns*, p. 109.
37 Rozell et al., *Interest Groups in American Campaigns*, pp. 109–110.
38 Rozell et al., *Interest Groups in American Campaigns*, p. 110.
39 For PAC contributions, see Federal Election Commission (2017) "Table 2: PAC Contributions to Candidates," www.fec.gov/press/summaries/2016/tables/pac/PAC2_2016_21m.pdf (January 29, 2017); independent expenditure figure taken from Center for Responsive Politics. "Outside Spending," www.opensecrets.org/outsidespending/fes_summ.php (January 29, 2017).
40 Jeff Smith and David C. Kimball (2012) "Barking Louder: Interest Groups in the 2012 Election," *The Forum*, 10.
41 On the rise of super-PACs generally, see Raymond J. La Raja (2012) "Why Super PACs: How the American Party System Outgrew the Campaign Finance System," *The Forum*, 10: 91–104.
42 Lindsay Young (2012) "Final Look at Outside Spenders' 2012 Return on Investment," *Sunlight Foundation Reporting Group*, December 17, http://reporting.sunlightfoundation.com/2012/return_on_investment (accessed October 13, 2016).
43 See Smith and Kimball, "Barking Louder," pp. 83–84.
44 Erika Franklin Fowler and Travis N. Ridout (2012) "Negative, Angry, and Ubiquitous: Political Advertising in 2012," *The Forum*, 10, p. 59.
45 The Brennan Center for Justice (2001) *Buying Time 2000: Television Advertising in the 2000 Federal Elections*, New York: Brennan Center for Justice at the New York University School of Law, pp. 31–33.
46 Erika Franklin Fowler, Michael M. Franz, and Travis N. Ridout (2016) *Political Advertising in the United States*, Boulder, CO: Westview Press.
47 Steven Greenhouse (2012) "Unions Recruit New Allies for Obama in Battleground States," *New York Times*, November 4, www.nytimes.com/2012/11/05/us/politics/unions-recruit-allies-on-obamas-behalf.html?_r=0 (accessed October 13, 2016).

48 See Greg Allen (2012) "Obama Campaign Looks to Black Churches in Fla," *National Public Radio*, October 29, www.npr.org/2012/10/29/163845744/obama-campaign-looks-to-black-churches-in-fla (accessed October 13, 2016).

49 Peter Wallsten and Tom Hamburger (2012) "Conservative Groups Reaching New Levels of Sophistication in Mobilizing Voters," *Washington Post*, September 20, www.washington-post.com/politics/decision2012/conservative-groups-reaching-new-levels-of-sophistica-tion-in-mobilizing-voters/2012/09/20/3c3cd8e8–026c-11e2–91e7–2962c74e7738_story.html (accessed October 13, 2016).

50 Josh Marshall (2016) "Theda Skocpol Responds to Judis," *Talking Points Memo Edblog*, November 11, http://talkingpointsmemo.com/edblog/theda-skocpol-responds-to-judis (January 29, 2017).

51 For a discussion of these factors, see Ronald J. Hrebenar (1997) *Interest Group Politics in America*, 3rd edn, Armonk, NY: M. E. Sharpe, pp. 40–45.

52 PAC receipts are taken from Center for Responsive Politics, "American Assn for Justice," www.opensecrets.org/pacs/lookup2.php?strID=C00024521&cycle=2016 (accessed January 29, 2017); and "International Assn of Fire Fighters," www.opensecrets.org/pacs/lookup2.php?strID=C00029447 (January 29, 2017). Membership figures are at the Center for Responsive Politics (n.d.) "American Assn for Justice," www.opensecrets.org/orgs/sum-mary.php?id=D000000065 (accessed January 29, 2017), and the International Association of Fire Fighters (2013) "About Us," http://client.prod.iaff.org/#page=AboutUs (accessed January 29, 2017).

53 PACs receipts are from Federal Election Commission, "Top 50 PACs, By Receipts, January 1, 2009–December 31, 2010," *Receipts for Women Vote!* are from the Center for Responsive Politics (n.d.) "Super PACs (2010 cycle)," www.opensecrets.org/pacs/super-pacs.php?cycle=2010 (accessed October 13, 2016). Membership figures for EMILY's List in 2010 are taken from EMILY's List (2012) "EMILY's List Announces New Website—and 1.5 Million Members!" June 5, http://emilyslist.org/news/releases/emily%E2%80%99s-list-announces-new-website-%E2%80%93-and-15-million-members-major-milestone-reached-ad (accessed October 13, 2016). National Rifle Association membership numbers are from National Rifle Association–Institute for Legislative Action (2012) "About NRA-ILA," www.nraila.org/about-nra-ila.aspx (accessed October 13, 2016).

54 For a recent review of much of this research, see Douglas D. Roscoe and Shannon Jenkins (2005) "A Meta-analysis of Campaign Contributions' Impact on Roll Call Voting," *Social Science Quarterly*, 86: 52–68.

55 See Fowler and Ridout, "Negative, Angry, and Ubiquitous," p. 59.

56 Robert A. Dahl (1961) *Who Governs?* New Haven, CT: Yale University Press.

57 See Jeffrey M. Berry (1997) *The Interest Group Society*, 3rd edn, New York: Longman, pp. 13–15.

58 Raymond L. Goldsteen, Karen Goldsteen, James H. Swan, and Wendy Clemeña (2001) "Harry and Louise and Health Care Reform: Romancing Public Opinion," *Journal of Health Politics, Policy and Law*, 26: 1325–1352.

7

The Media

FOR NEARLY 200 YEARS, political observers have recognized the power of the media. In nineteenth-century Europe, it was said that the press functioned as a "fourth estate"—In France, it stood alongside the church, the nobility and the people; in Britain, it rivaled the Lords Spiritual and the Lords Temporal (in the House of Lords) and the House of Commons. In the United States today, the media are often referred to as the fourth branch of American government.

The media's influence in American politics is probably best displayed in its coverage of campaigns and elections. The stories the media deem newsworthy are not always the stories that help voters make informed decisions at election time. Nevertheless, they do affect the way campaigns are run. So a crucial question becomes—when covering political campaigns, how can the media in the United States equip voters to make the choices democracy asks them to make?

Unlike the media in many democracies, media outlets in the United States are privately owned, for-profit organizations. Though the Public Broadcasting Service (PBS) and National Public Radio (NPR) are technically public entities, only a small portion of their funding actually comes from the government, and their audiences are but a fraction of the commercial media in the United States. The British Broadcasting Corporation (BBC), in comparison, is almost entirely funded by taxpayers (through a television license fee). There are endless debates about which model of media control—private or public—is better for democracy, but it is undeniable that market pressures affect the way America's commercial media cover the news. This is an important point to keep in mind as we explore the media at some length.

This chapter examines the news media in their role as an actor in campaigns and elections. After a brief look at the development of the media throughout US history, we will describe the various organizational characteristics of today's media. From there, we turn our attention to the ways in which the media actually cover campaigns and elections. That, of course, leads to an exploration of media effects, or the ways in which the media influence their audience. After a discussion of Election Night coverage, we close the chapter with a normative evaluation of the media's activity.

▶ *The Contemporary Media Environment*

The history of the media in the United States is often broken down into three periods. According to Jan Leighley, the first period was "the era of the party press," which lasted from the founding of the Republic until the mid-nineteenth century. In this era, newspapers offered openly partisan perspectives on current events. The partisan press gave way, gradually, to a more commercial approach in "the era of the penny press," named after the newspapers that sold for one cent during much of this time. In this period, which developed in the 1830s and lasted until the turn of the twentieth century, newspapers sought to make large profits by attracting a mass audience with interesting, often salacious, and occasionally embellished news (including the sensationalist reporting known as "yellow journalism").[1]

The current era of the "modern press" appeared around the turn of the twentieth century.[2] Of course, there have been great transformations in the 100 years since the end of the penny press and yellow journalism. Darrell West, in fact, recognizes three stages of media evolution since 1900, the most recent being the "fragmented media." Important technological changes occurred throughout the twentieth century. The advent of radio, beginning in 1920, brought news to a much wider audience than previously possible. (Incidentally, the first broadcast from a licensed radio station—KDKA in Pittsburgh, Pennsylvania—reported the results of the 1920 presidential election.) The ubiquity of television by the late 1950s changed the way we experienced the news and fundamentally altered the nature of politics in the United States, but two technological innovations in the late twentieth century changed the media in equally dramatic ways.

Beginning in the 1980s, the widespread availability of cable television, and twenty-four-hour news networks in particular, scattered audiences among many sources of information and created a continuous news cycle. The development of the Internet in the 1990s further splintered audiences and began to wrestle control of information away from elites. News can now be made by countless sources at any moment. As West argues, "The line between trained reporters and others in a position to communicate with the general public has disappeared, making nearly anyone with access to a Web site a virtual journalist."[3] That fact has enormous implications for the media, American politics, and campaigns and elections in the United States.

Media Organizations

Given the fragmented news environment, it would be useful to closely examine the various media organizations in operation today. Before doing so, however, it is necessary to define what is meant by the term "media." As Paul Starr has written, there are two senses in which the word is used: "first, as the various modern channels of communication created from the early seventeenth to the mid-twentieth centuries …; second, as a set of powerful institutions ('the media') that, to the despair of grammarians, people generally speak of as singular rather than plural."[4]

That set of institutions includes both entertainment and news media, and though we might like to distinguish clearly between the two, it has become increasingly difficult to do so. However, a line still exists between pure entertainment and serious news; thus, when referring to the media in this chapter, we generally mean the *news* media.

Of course, the set of institutions we call the news media consists of a diverse group of organizations. There are considerable differences, for example, between national and local news outlets. Local news is relatively inexpensive to produce, whereas national news is quite costly, even if profitable. Local media place a heavy emphasis on "news you can use": segments such as weather and traffic reports receive far more attention on local newscasts than on national ones. Furthermore, local news has been found to focus disproportionately on stories such as crime, fires, and accidents that typically command attention from a larger portion of the public than do public affairs stories.

Broadcast and print differences are as significant as the differences between national and local media. Broadcast news, whether on television or radio, must fit into a limited amount of time; print media, both newspapers and news magazines, have space for considerably more material. (The Internet allows for a combination of the two and will be discussed below.) Whereas print is a static medium, broadcasting is dynamic. This affects the content that can be provided to the audience. Complex material is better conveyed through print, but broadcasts can be more emotive.

One characteristic that distinguishes types of media outlets are the deadlines according to which they operate. Some media, such as cable news channels and newspaper websites, report the news on an ongoing basis. There is no deadline, per se, because information can be conveyed instantly. Newspapers and the network nightly news programs report once a day and, as a result, have daily deadlines by which stories must be finalized. Deadlines at news magazines such as *Time* occur weekly, though when news breaks near the deadline, weekly reporting is not unlike daily reporting.

Deadlines contribute to a tension in journalism between speed of reporting and accuracy of information. Cable news, for instance, is able to provide "breaking news" continuously, but the information reported may not always be correct. With a bit more time, journalists can get the story right; however, once a deadline approaches, they will not be able to add up-to-the-second information to those stories. A weekly deadline gives journalists time to fill in details of a story and to be a bit reflective about its implications. Thus, news organizations offer different advantages, depending, in part, upon the time pressures under which they operate.

The presence of twenty-four-hour news coverage on cable television and the Internet—or the "new media"—is affecting the way all media organizations report the news and the way campaigns attempt to make the news. In their study of this phenomenon, Richard Davis and Diana Owen point to at least two defining characteristics of the new media. The first is what we might call *interactivity*. The new media allow for, and even encourage, participation by the audience and interaction between public officials and citizens. As Davis and Owen put it: "The new media enhance the public's ability to become actors, rather than merely spectators, in the realm of media politics."[5]

An example of the political consequences of interactivity is an incident that occurred during the 2006 US Senate race in Virginia between Republican Senator George Allen and his Democratic challenger, Jim Webb. At a campaign stop in the southwestern part of the state, Allen referred to a Webb volunteer who had been trailing him with a video camera and is of Indian descent, as "macaca."[6] Video of the senator making what was interpreted as an ethnic slur was immediately uploaded to YouTube and quickly went "viral." The video prompted days of discussion on cable news networks and was thought to have contributed to Allen's eventual defeat.

In addition to interactivity, the new media also "place a high premium on entertainment."[7] This can take a number of forms. Talk shows, such as MSNBC's *Hardball with Chris Matthews* or *Hannity* on Fox News, often include blustery debates that are engaging but not particularly informative. Programming on cable television now offers a number of comedic treatments of public affairs (see Figure 7.1), including the *The Daily Show with Trevor Noah* (Comedy Central), *Full Frontal with Samantha Bee* (TBS), and *Last Week Tonight with John Oliver* (HBO). In fact, a 2004 poll by the Pew Research Center found that whereas 23 percent of eighteen-to-twenty-nine-year-olds got campaign news from the nightly network news programs, 21 percent relied on shows such as *The Daily Show* (then with host Jon Stewart).[8] In 2010, another Pew poll showed that almost as many eighteen-to-twenty-nine-year-olds sometimes or regularly watch *The Daily Show* (43 percent) as watch CNN (46 percent).[9] Satirical news shows even occasionally make real news, as when Senator John Edwards announced his 2004 candidacy for president on *The Daily Show*.

To say that entertainment is an important part of the new media's repertoire is not to say that information is not, but many observers now refer to the new media's coverage of public affairs as "infotainment." That is, the new media blend information and entertainment such that the line between them is increasingly difficult to locate. This is a cause for concern among many media analysts. Not only is it difficult to maintain a balance between information and entertainment, but the mainstream media have begun to feel pressure to produce infotainment as well.

We might add to interactivity and entertainment another prominent aspect of the new media, namely, continuous communication. The Internet and cable-news channels are viewed around the clock and can be updated with breaking news at any moment. Twitter is particularly noteworthy in this regard. Not only do Twitter users (including reporters) tweet at all hours of the day, but followers add comments continually. From a campaign perspective, this steady stream

FIGURE 7.1   *Samantha Bee Offers a Satirical Take on the News*

Source: Sthanlee B. Mirador/SIPPL Sipa USA, via AP Images.

of communication requires constant monitoring by staff members who are pre-pared for a rapid response to unflattering information. In addition, candidates themselves have begun tweeting. Donald Trump famously used Twitter during his 2016 presidential campaign to bypass traditional channels of communication. While his tweets were often controversial, the tactic also allowed him to remain at the center of campaign discussions throughout the race.

One final characteristic of the new media worth mentioning is the opinion-ated nature of so much of what it produces. Analysis and commentary dominate most of the content on talk radio, cable television chat shows, blogs and social media sites. For example, journalists tend to utilize Twitter not as venue for orig-inal reporting but as a place to comment on the news (or to provide links to new articles). Of course, the 140-character limit on tweets makes it difficult to offer anything other than pithy commentary. A number of blogs connected to main-stream news organizations and written by individuals with experience as tradi-tional journalists have emerged in recent years to cover elections. Some, such as Chris Cillizza's "The Fix" for the *Washington Post*, track virtually every move made during campaigns. However, it is rare for such a blog to do more than offer either the author's perspective on an event they have witnessed at first hand (for example, debates) or their reaction to stories being reported elsewhere.

It should be noted that there are an increasing number of news sites that exist entirely (or primarily, as in the case of *Politico*) online. There is no hard copy version of outlets like *Huffington Post, BuzzFeed,* and *The Daily Beast,* and even venerable old media publications like *Newsweek* have eliminated their print versions and now appear only online. While these venues do produce original reporting, a large proportion of the content at online-only news outlets is opinion and commentary. However, a new form of online media devoted to systematic analysis and explanation of current events has emerged in recent years. *FiveThir-tyEight,* for example, provides statistical analyses of topics in the news, and *Vox* offers in-depth "explainers" for trending news stories. The sophisticated examination of the news has found a place at traditional media sites as well. The *New York Times'* The Upshot and the *Washington Post's* The Monkey Cage offer far more analysis, including the graphic display of data, than can be found in typical news reports. Much of that analysis (or all of it, in the case of The Monkey Cage) is provided by academics.

The wide array of media sources covering campaigns and elections means that there is a tremendous amount of information about candidates for voters to sift through. There is also great variety in the types of information available, ranging from opinion and analysis to factual reporting. Finally, the many sources covering elections differ in terms of their level of credibility. Thus, today's fragmented media environment is complicated for voters to navigate, frustrating for candidates and parties who are trying to get a message to the voters, and challenging for media organizations seeking larger audiences and more profit.

Media Effects

In such a media environment, what impact does media coverage have on news users? In the 1940s and 1950s, scholars believed that the media had enormous power to influence individuals' attitudes. That was the lesson learned from witnessing the Nazi propaganda machine in Germany and the panic over the 1938 broadcast of H. G. Wells' *War of the Worlds* in the United States. The effect of the media was thought to be so direct and so powerful that the theory postulating it was called the "hypodermic needle" (or "magic bullet") model.

Empirical research allayed fears of the near-brainwashing capability of the media. In fact, by the 1970s, conventional academic wisdom held that the media had little, if any, impact on individuals' attitudes or behaviors. This "minimal consequences" school of thought posited that deeply held predispositions such as party identification, or ingrained patterns of behavior such as infrequent media use, limited the media's influence.

Today, scholars have settled on a middle ground. The media are thought to significantly influence their audience in particular ways, but their effects are not nearly as powerful as the hypodermic needle theory had suggested. There are basically four types of media effects: learning, agenda setting, priming, and framing.

Despite the fact that there are now seemingly countless sources of information about politics, the American public does not possess a wealth of political knowledge. Nevertheless, considerable evidence suggests that people do learn about politics through the media. Of course, those with more interest in politics seek out more information and, consequently, learn more. These individuals tend to rely on newspapers for their information, where policy differences between the parties are emphasized. Those with less interest in politics still pick up some information, but they tend to do so from television news, where the coverage is likely to focus on candidates.[10]

In addition to teaching the public about politics, the media have also been shown to set the public's agenda.[11] That is, "by covering some issues and ignoring others, the media influence which issues people view as important and which they view as unimportant."[12] This is not to say that the media influence the positions people take on those issues. They simply determine the issues people consider salient. Thus, for example, if the media were to devote significant coverage to global warming, that issue would rise to the top of the public's list of important issues facing the nation.

A related phenomenon is the priming effect, whereby the media influence the factors voters use to evaluate candidates.[13] As Shanto Iyengar and Jennifer McGrady explain, "The more prominent an issue becomes in the public consciousness, the more it will influence people's assessments of politicians."[14] Thus, if a person not only comes to believe that global warming is an important issue but uses it in assessing those running for office, they have been primed. Voters can be primed on both character traits and issues. If, for instance, government corruption has garnered considerable media attention, voters may seek to judge candidates according to how trustworthy they are.

Though parties, interest groups, and candidates deliberately seek to set the public's agenda and prime voters (see Chapter 9), agenda setting and priming are simply by-products of news coverage. In other words, the media are not intentionally trying to make particular issues more salient than others. Agenda setting and priming simply happen as a result of covering some issues and not others. The process that determines which issues get covered and which do not is a complex one involving a number of institutional norms and organizational incentives within newsrooms. Unfortunately, that process is beyond the scope of this book.[15]

Having said that the agenda setting and priming effects are unintentional, it is worth recognizing that because the parties and their candidates "own" different sets of issues (see Chapter 5), prominent coverage of certain issues is likely to give one party an advantage in a given election. In 2004, for example, the media covered terrorism extensively, and it was one of the most important issues—if not *the* most important—facing the nation. As a result of Republican ownership of national security issues, George W. Bush was the beneficiary of this focus on terrorism. Thus, the process of highlighting some issues rather than others has a noticeable impact on elections.

The way the media frame issues also influences the response individuals have to news stories. Shanto Iyengar distinguishes between "episodic" and "thematic" framing. The former "takes the form of a case study or event-oriented report and depicts public issues in terms of concrete instances." Thematic framing, in contrast, "places public issues in some more general or abstract context and takes the form of a 'takeout,' or 'backgrounder,' report directed at general outcomes or conditions."[16]

Iyengar's experiments have shown that individuals respond to thematic coverage by seeking political or societal solutions to problems, whereas episodic framing causes individuals to attribute responsibility to individuals. Thus, homelessness could be viewed as a social and political problem requiring a policy response or as the result of the individual failings of the homeless themselves, depending on whether a report was framed thematically or episodically. The point is simply that changing the frame changes the response to the story. Once again, however, framing is inevitable, and the media frame stories not with any particular political end in mind but to produce compelling news stories and, ultimately, to gain readers and viewers. Candidates, conversely, routinely frame issues in ways that will work to their electoral advantage. Thus, what the media do to further their institutional goals, candidates do in pursuit of their political goals.

There are those who believe that agenda setting, priming, and framing are not merely the by-products of covering the news but are the means by which the media pursue a set of political goals. The argument is that journalists have ideological or partisan biases that are revealed in the choices they make with respect to the stories they cover and the way those stories are reported. Whether intentionally or not, journalists are said to give one side of the political spectrum a distinct advantage.

Since the mid-1960s, it has primarily been conservatives who have made this claim. Journalists, they point out, tend to be more liberal (particularly on social issues) than the average American, and the percentage of journalists who consider themselves Democrats is larger than the percentage of Democratic identifiers in the electorate. Thus, conservatives argue that journalists will inevitably treat Democratic candidates more favorably than Republican ones.

Conversely, some evidence suggests that journalists are more economically conservative than the typical voter. In addition, many on the left find it hard to believe that the enormous corporate conglomerates that own the vast majority of media outlets would allow patently liberal viewpoints to dominate their news product. Thus, both liberals and conservatives complain that the media are biased against them, a tendency referred to as the "hostile media phenomenon."[17] In the end, media bias likely exists in the minds of the news audience to a far greater degree than can be demonstrated objectively.[18]

▶ Reporting Campaign News

There is no agreed-upon standard for what constitutes "news," but even a cursory look at the headlines will suggest certain elements that make a story newsworthy. One such element, obvious though it may be, is timeliness. Something that just happened is more likely to be covered than something that happened yesterday or last week. This is particularly true in an environment seemingly designed for breaking news.

News is also that which is unique. The adage that "dog bites man" is not news but "man bites dog" is, vividly illustrates the logic of the newsroom. However, the requirement that news be unique puts campaigns in a difficult spot. For example, the standard stump speech that candidates give time and again, at every campaign stop, quickly becomes tiresome to journalists. It is, literally, old news. Thus, to ensure maximum coverage of their campaigns, candidates feel pressure to change what they say regularly on the stump. However, one cardinal rule of campaigning is to stay "on message," meaning that the basic rationale for one's candidacy has to be repeated over and over for it to sink in to voters' minds. And so a fundamental tension exists between candidates trying to reach voters via the media and journalists trying to find something new to report. Of course, Donald Trump brazenly violated this cardinal rule during the 2016 presidential campaign with tweets and statements at rallies that seemed to ricochet from subject to subject and often stirred controversy. While he could have been expected to pay an electoral price for doing so, he also benefited from a media that endlessly covered his campaign speeches in the hopes that some new outrage would occur on live television.[19]

In addition to being timely and unique, newsworthy stories are those that involve concrete events. Debates or speeches, for example, will typically garner more coverage than abstract matters such as problems and their proposed solutions. Barack Obama's overseas trip in the summer of 2008 was a massive campaign event that received considerable media coverage. According to the Project for Excellence in Journalism, that story consumed more of the "newshole" in the week it occurred than any other story during the campaign, save the Pennsylvania Democratic primary.[20] The attraction of events explains why candidates give speeches or hold press conferences to announce policy proposals; events get covered, ideas in and of themselves do not.

Once a story has been deemed newsworthy, reporters have to determine how it will be covered. In doing so, they are deciding how to frame the story. Framing, according to W. Lance Bennett, "involves choosing a broad organizing theme for selecting, emphasizing, and linking the elements of a story such as the scenes, the characters, their actions, and supporting documentation."[21] For instance, reporters covering Hurricane Katrina could have focused, on the one hand, on tales of survival or loss or on eyewitness accounts; on the other hand, they could have explored the government's emergency management responsibilities, its emergency preparedness, or the nation's urban infrastructure. Taken as a whole, the coverage of a given story may utilize multiple frames but, occasionally, one frame comes to dominate, and that has consequences, as Iyengar has shown, for how individuals respond to the story. As a result, campaigns work diligently to influence the frames that reporters apply to the stories they cover.

In addition to recognizing the significance of framing, scholars have identified several general tendencies in the way stories are reported. Bennett, for
example, argues that four "information biases" influence media coverage, three
of which are relevant to campaign reporting.[22] The first bias he describes is personalization, "the overwhelming tendency to downplay the big social, economic,
or political picture in favor of the human trials, tragedies, and triumphs that sit
at the surface of events."[23] Stories with a human interest angle are easy to understand and are more appealing to the average person than stories about public
policy. The former also provoke emotion, whereas stories that require viewers or
readers to think in systemic terms can seem boring.

A related tendency is the dramatization of the news. Crises, natural or
human-made, are inherently dramatic and, therefore, newsworthy. However,
even non-crisis stories are now reported in a sensationalist manner. In 2008,
Ben Smith of *Politico* reported that John Edwards's haircuts cost $400 apiece.
The story struck a journalistic nerve and was repeated multiple times in many
outlets.[24] This sort of dramatized news with little or no public policy component
is often referred to as "soft news."[25] Describing news as soft may make it sound
harmless, but dramatic, sensationalized news tends to be negative, reflecting the
cynical "gotcha" mentality of so many of today's journalists. In addition, there is
evidence that people are more interested in negative news than in positive stories. As a result, news organizations are likely to be attracted to stories that make
individuals, and in particular politicians, look bad.

Bennett also identifies fragmentation as a tendency in reporting. Though
it may be related to the fragmented media landscape generally, fragmentation of
reporting is "the isolation of stories from each other and from their larger contexts so that information in the news becomes ... hard to assemble into a big picture."[26] In other words, stories are reported as discrete pieces of information with
little connection to one another or to broader themes. This tendency is the result
of personalization and dramatization and the limitations placed on the length
of stories in print or in broadcast reports. When stories are offered in bite-sized
pieces, there is no room for drawing connections to related stories or establishing
a broader context.

Recall Iyengar's distinction between episodic and thematic news frames.
The characteristics of news coverage identified by Bennett—and event-based
reporting—help form "episodic" news frames. Though Iyengar acknowledges
that few stories are exclusively episodic or thematic, he also notes that one format is used predominantly in most stories, and that format, at least for television
news, is likely to be episodic.[27]

Of all the familiar campaign stories, staff shake-ups may best illustrate each
of the elements identified by Bennett and Iyengar. When a candidate fires staffers
or when key staff members resign, it is always a newsworthy event. Realistically,
however, a change in staff is a discrete event with little relevance to problems
facing the nation or to the general debate between campaigns. Staff shake-ups

are personalized insofar as they are about specific individuals who have been fired or who have quit. And the reason for the shake-up, which is typically cited as "disagreements" within the campaign, provides for a dramatic story about the inner workings of a campaign. When Donald Trump fired his campaign manager Corey Lewandowski, it was reported that "Lewandowski clashed internally with Paul Manafort, the campaign's chairman and senior strategist" and that Trump's adult children had argued for Lewandowski's ouster.[28] Just two months later, Manafort would resign from the campaign because he "had lost the confidence of Jared Kushner, Trump's son-in-law and one of his closest advisers, and other members of Trump's family."[29] Eventual campaign manager Kellyanne Conway also helped to force Manafort out by "subtly undermining his strategists."[30]

Given the nature of the subject, campaign stories often become what Larry Sabato has called "feeding frenzies." A feeding frenzy is "the press coverage attending any political event or circumstance where a critical mass of journalists leap to cover the same embarrassing or scandalous subject and pursue it intensely, often excessively, and sometimes uncontrollably." Sabato notes that it is hard to say when, exactly, a critical mass of journalists is reached, but "in the video age, we truly know it when we see it; the forest of cameras, lights, microphones, and adrenaline-choked reporters" gathered around the politician under scrutiny is a tell-tale sign.[31]

Typically, feeding frenzies are triggered by behavior or an event that initially took place outside the campaign context. In the midst of a campaign, however, sensational stories are particularly attractive to the media. Of course, they are also likely to influence an election, so journalistic responsibility is critical in the reporting of such stories.

There are numerous examples of feeding frenzies during campaigns. In 1992, allegations by Gennifer Flowers of an affair with Governor Bill Clinton created a whirlwind of reporting that eventually led to a press conference at which Flowers played what she claimed were tapes of conversations between her and Clinton. Clinton responded by appearing on *60 Minutes* with his wife, Hillary, to acknowledge past problems in their marriage. Clinton survived the media's scrutiny but only with the help of a determined and aggressive campaign team. Just days before the 2000 election it was reported that Governor George W. Bush had been arrested twenty-four years earlier for driving under the influence of alcohol. The story forced Bush to hold a press conference at which he acknowledged the arrest. Some, including members of his campaign staff, believe this story cost Bush the popular vote that year.

The Game Schema and "Horserace Coverage"

Unlike coverage of any other process in American politics, campaign coverage has its own metaphor to describe how it functions. It is often said that reporters focus on the "horserace" in their coverage of campaigns. In its most literal sense, the horserace is about who is winning and who is losing an election. More generally, however, horserace coverage is interested in the competitive aspects of campaigns and elections, such as the strategic maneuvering of the candidates. This type of coverage is aired or printed at the expense of more substantive news about candidate ideologies, issue positions, or public records.

According to political scientist Thomas Patterson, reporters engage in the more general type of horserace coverage because the media have adopted a "game schema" rather than a "governing schema" in covering politics. According to the game schema, "politics is a strategic game" wherein "candidates compete for advantage" and "play the game well or poorly." Just as one might analyze a chess match, reporters chart a candidate's every move. And much like a football game, there is plenty of color commentary about the campaign. However, voters have a different framework for understanding campaigns. Voters "view politics primarily as a means for choosing leaders and solving their problems." This, according to Patterson, is a "governing schema."[32]

It is easy to exaggerate the amount of horserace coverage that takes place in campaign reporting. The authors of *Crosstalk: Citizens, Candidates, and the Media in a Presidential Campaign* found that stories about the campaign process outnumbered those about issues, particularly on local television news, but not by as much as one might have guessed. In fact, on network news, process and issues are covered just about equally and, in newspapers, issues get more coverage in the early fall until process stories become more of a focus as the election nears. Of course, the authors also found a significant number of stories about candidate personalities; that is, stories that were neither process-oriented nor issue-based.[33]

Others have found a bit more horserace coverage. Stephen Farnsworth and Robert Lichter, for example, report that 71 percent of campaign stories on network news in 2000 contained elements of the horserace, whereas only 40 percent discussed issues positions. The amount of horserace coverage in 2008 fell dramatically, according to Farnsworth and Lichter, to 41 percent of all network news stories. Unfortunately, the percentage of stories covering policy also fell, to just 35 percent (the lowest amount of policy coverage since 1992).[34] The Pew Research Center's Project for Excellence in Journalism found that 53 percent of the 2008 coverage by all sources—including cable television, radio, and prominent news websites—was framed around the horserace, but that figure dropped to just 38 percent in 2012. Policy positions were covered in less than a fourth (22 percent) of news stories.[35]

If there is good news in these results, it is that horserace coverage seems to have declined in recent years. Unfortunately, the amount of policy coverage also seems to be decreasing. The bad news is that there is still more, and perhaps considerably more, horserace coverage than policy coverage of campaigns.

It is worth noting that some news outlets, such as PBS, cover policy to a much greater degree than the networks. Farnsworth and Lichter found that 68 percent of stories on PBS's *NewsHour* in 2000 discussed policies, whereas only 30 percent had horserace content.[36] Many also point to NPR as a source that provides far more substantive coverage than horserace coverage.

Polls as News

To the extent that horserace coverage occurs, it places a heavy emphasis on public opinion polling. Poll results are useful to the media for a number of reasons. First, they meet the criteria of newsworthiness quite nicely, as the release of a new poll is a timely, unique, and concrete event. Furthermore, dozens of organizations, from the campaigns and private polling firms to colleges and universities, conduct polls. This provides an almost endless supply of news for the media during the course of a campaign. Finally, polls offer quantifiable evidence for speculation about which campaign is performing well and which is not.

Indeed, polls are so valuable to campaign coverage that media outlets began conducting their own polls long ago. One of the primary motivators for the media in developing their polling operations was election coverage. As Everett Carll Ladd and John Benson note, CBS News was the first media organization to conduct its own polling. It did so in 1967, during the Kentucky gubernatorial election and then again for the 1968 presidential primaries.[37] In 1975, CBS formed a partnership with the *New York Times* to produce poll results. The two would collaborate on polling and analysis and would share the costs of the polls. Other media outlets soon followed that model and, today, in addition to the almost forty-year-old New York Times/CBS News partnership, NBC and the *Wall Street Journal* and ABC and the *Washington Post* have polling relationships. Other media organizations have exclusive partnerships with private polling firms, such as CNN's agreement with Opinion Research Corp., Bloomberg's relationship with Selzer & Company, *USA Today's* affiliation with Suffolk University's Political Research Center, and Fox News's partnership with Anderson Robbins Research and Shaw & Company Research.

The benefit media organizations receive from producing their own poll results is that the data are from an independent source rather than from candidates or interest groups with an agenda. By conducting their own polls, media outlets can also design questions that meet their needs instead of relying on questions written by other parties with different purposes in mind. When media organizations form partnerships to produce polls, there is the additional benefit of cost sharing, which allows for more polls to be conducted. Furthermore, both organizations will receive greater prominence for their results and wider exposure for their news product.[38]

For critics of campaign coverage, however, media polls simply encourage a focus on the horserace. Indeed, the widespread use of election polls by the media raises some critical questions. For example, how newsworthy should poll results be considered? Essentially, poll results are manufactured news. This is particularly true of those that are media-sponsored. News outlets that produce polls, release the results, and then report on the implications of those results have literally made news.

Admittedly, by the standards of newsworthiness set by the contemporary media, polls merit extensive reporting. However, missing from those standards is the usefulness of potential news stories in fostering informed citizens. Media polls rarely explain why it is that a candidate is winning or losing. So if they do little, if anything, to help voters make rational choices, why are polls reported in the first place?

When poll results are released by campaigns, parties, or interest groups, there is even less reason to report them. The release of a poll by those engaged in a campaign is always self-serving. This is not to say that the results are not to be trusted. It simply means that if the news from a poll were bad for those sponsoring the poll, they would not likely release the results. When they do offer the results to the media, it is inevitably because there is some advantage in doing so. The media must, therefore, guard against being used by candidates and their supporters to further a partisan agenda.

Critics also argue that journalists often fail to provide adequate information when reporting poll results. The methodology of a particular poll must be described if readers (or viewers) are to ascertain its quality. Too often, essential methodological elements of polls are left unreported. As a result, the American Association for Public Opinion Research has created a set of questions that journalists should ask when reporting on polls.[39] Among the most important pieces of information are the sponsor of the poll, the number of respondents, the margin of error, the dates the poll was conducted, and the question wording.

BOX 7.1 *Questions to Ask When Writing about Polls*

1. Who paid for the poll and why was it done?
2. Who did the poll?
3. How was the poll conducted?
4. How many people were interviewed and what's the margin of sampling error?
5. How were those people chosen? (Probability or nonprobability sample? Random sampling? Nonrandom method?)
6. What area or what group were people chosen from? (That is, what was the population being represented?)
7. When were the interviews conducted?
8. How were the interviews conducted?
9. What questions were asked? Were they clearly worded, balanced and unbiased?
10. What order were the questions asked in? Could an earlier question influence the answer of a later question that is central to your story or the conclusions drawn?
11. Are the results based on the answers of all the people interviewed, or only a subset? If a subset, how many?
12. Were the data weighted, and if so, to what?

Source: American Association of Public Opinion Research, "Questions to Ask When Writing about Polls," http://www.aapor.org/Questions_to_Ask_When_Writing_About_Polls2.htm (accessed May 18, 2013).

Election polls differ from other public opinion polls in one very important way. Polls that attempt to capture the public's views about current affairs usually draw respondents from the entire population, but election polls are most interested in the views of those who are likely to vote on Election Day (i.e. "likely voters"). Determining who is and who is not a likely voter is a rather difficult and somewhat mysterious process. To identify likely voters, pollsters ask a series of screening questions at the beginning of the poll. These questions might ask how interested the respondent is in the upcoming election or how much attention they have been paying to the campaign, how certain the respondent is that they will vote in the upcoming election, or whether the person knows where their polling place is located. Often, more than one screening question is used, and a cumulative score is calculated to estimate the degree to which a respondent is likely to vote. Because each polling organization utilizes a different approach to identifying likely voters, the results of their pre-election polls can differ significantly. Many polling organizations treat their likely voter screens as proprietary, but Mark Blumenthal, who writes the "Pollster" blog on the *Huffington Post*, has argued that pollsters should disclose this information so that journalists and the public can better understand the results of pre-election polls.[40]

In recent election cycles, polls have also been used to forecast election winners prior to Election Day. In 2016, these forecasts were universally wrong. The *Huffington Post*'s forecast, for instance, gave Hillary Clinton a 98 percent chance of winning the presidency. *The New York Times*' The Upshot put Clinton's chances at 85 percent, but they were quick to note that "A victory by Mr. Trump remains possible: Mrs. Clinton's chance of losing is about the same as the probability that an NFL kicker misses a 37-yard field goal."[41] Nate Silver, at *FiveThirtyEight*, gave Trump the best odds, but that was still only a 28.6 percent change of winning.[42] It is important to recognize that these forecasts are simply probabilities that one candidate will win. According to the forecasts, a Trump win was unlikely, but not impossible.

Though the polls used to derive the forecasts may appear, at first blush, to have been wrong, in truth the national polls were not far off the mark. The final RealClearPolitics average of the polls had Clinton ahead by 3.3 percentage points; in fact, she won the popular vote by 2.1 points.[43] Polls in several battleground states, however, were less accurate. Indeed, polls in Pennsylvania, Michigan, and Wisconsin had Clinton ahead going into Election Day (by an average of 1.9, 3.4, and 6.5 points, respectively).[44] Of course, Trump won those states (by 0.7, 0.3, and 0.7 points, respectively) and, as a result, won the Electoral College.

Campaign Strategy as News

In addition to polling, the media's game schema consists largely of discussions about campaign strategy. These discussions are either devoid of issue content or mention issues only insofar as they are used to further a candidate's goals. Stories about the strategic imperatives faced by candidates can readily be found in news accounts on any given day. Even stories in which campaign strategy and tactics are not the primary focus will identify the electoral ramifications of a candidate's statements or actions. This is particularly true as Election Day approaches. Consider the following example from the *New York Times* on October 9, 2012:

> Continuing to embrace a more moderate political persona, Mitt Romney offered assurances on Tuesday that he would protect tax deductions for the middle class on home mortgages and charitable donations. And he also said he had no plans to pursue new laws limiting abortion. ... With new polling suggesting that he was closing the gap with President Obama in the crucial battleground of Ohio, Mr. Romney subtly distanced himself from earlier divisive statements as he sought to broaden his appeal, especially with women. ... Candidates in general election campaigns often try to appeal to a broader base of voters as the election nears ... [45]

On the same day, CNN.com reported on President Obama's creation of a national monument to honor the Latino labor and civil-rights leader Cesar Chavez. In their story, which is mostly about Chavez and the new monument to him, the CNN reporters noted, "It's no coincidence the move comes less than a month before Election Day, as the president maintains a strong lead among Latinos. A big turnout among Latino supporters in states where the race is close could help Obama win reelection against GOP challenger Mitt Romney."

Because the creation of the Chavez monument includes the preservation of 120 acres of land, the CNN reporters also felt compelled to point out that "Obama's decision to set aside the land as a national monument also sends a political message to environmentalists—a key group of voters, as many strongly supported him in 2008."[46] In the context of a campaign, everything a candidate does is portrayed as having been done, at least in part, for electoral advantage.

Even *potential* candidates, years before a campaign, are treated as if every decision they make is based on an electoral calculation. When New Jersey Governor Chris Christie announced in the spring of 2013 that he had undergone lap-band stomach surgery to control his weight, speculation immediately swirled. Wasn't this a clear sign, pundits asked, that he's planning to run for president in 2016?[47]

Perhaps not surprisingly, campaign ads garner quite a bit of attention from reporters. This was not always so. Darrell West has shown that the coverage of campaign ads increased rather dramatically in the late 1980s and 1990s. Prior to that, there was only moderate interest by the media in ads (and in the 1950s, there was virtually no interest).[48] As the subject of news stories, campaign ads are almost always viewed in terms of the strategies candidates employ. Evaluations of campaign ads are often more concerned with the effectiveness of spots in achieving their purported electoral goals than with the accuracy of the claims (though see the discussion of "ad watches" in the next section). Though campaign ads can be quite substantive, reporters rarely discuss the substance of an ad and, instead, attempt to expose the motivation behind the spot. At the same time, journalists tend to cover negative ads more than positive ads.[49] This gives the impression that campaign advertising is more negative than it may actually be.

Another popular topic within the game schema is fund-raising. Like polling, fund-raising provides journalists with a measurable, and seemingly objective, way to discuss "who's ahead and who's behind." Rather than relying on punditry and speculation, fund-raising totals are quantifiable evidence that a campaign is doing well (or is not). Of course, money is essential to any successful bid for office. However, it does not always translate into victory, particularly at the presidential level. Still, fund-raising is reported as a barometer of campaign success and, as an element of the horserace, it usually takes precedence over policy discussions. Thus, when Hillary Clinton's presidential campaign announced its 2007 third-quarter fund-raising totals on the same day in October that Barack Obama gave a major speech on foreign policy, her announcement made the front page of both the *New York Times* and the *Washington Post*; Obama's speech was covered on pages A20 and A8, respectively. Furthermore, though Obama's speech included a significant statement on nuclear nonproliferation, it was covered as an attempt to differentiate himself from Clinton on the war in Iraq.[50] A writer for the *Post* commented:

> Seeking to recharge his campaign for the autumn stretch run, Sen. Barack Obama (D-Ill.) on Tuesday used the fifth anniversary of his 2002 speech against going to war in Iraq to issue some of his strongest criticism yet of the war votes cast by Sen. Hillary Rodham Clinton (D-NY) and other Democratic presidential candidates.[51]

From the perspective of a game, every move a candidate makes has a political purpose. Undoubtedly, most are designed to achieve some electoral goal. Thus, when reporters tell us that a candidate's appearance with a group of schoolchildren was intended to help soften the candidate's image or that a speech on abortion was given to court evangelicals, voters have some context with which to understand the candidate's actions. Yet, the constant unveiling—and even questioning—of a candidate's motives surely leads to a certain level of cynicism.[52]

We might ask why reporters place so much emphasis on the horserace in the first place. It could be that this is what campaigns themselves emphasize, but we know that candidates provide a significant amount of substantive information. According to the authors of one study of campaign media,

> the national media provides a particularly hostile environment for candidates who want to talk about the issues. … It is clear from this study that candidates do provide substantive, issue-based discussions from the earliest stages of the campaign. Consequently, candidate complaints that the media are not willing to provide coverage of substantive discussions appear to be well founded.[53]

Conversely, campaigns do tout poll numbers, at least when they are favorable to the campaign, and place a great deal of emphasis on fund-raising totals. In addition, campaign operatives are often quite willing to discuss campaign strategy with journalists, even if only off the record. Thus, though they may not initiate the game schema, campaigns certainly play along.

Informing Voters

The media rely on horserace coverage and the game schema for two reasons. First, horserace coverage is interesting to news audiences. The authors of another study on media coverage of elections concluded that many news users actively seek information about who is winning an election. Far fewer, however, will seek accounts of campaign strategy; in fact, interest in campaign strategy is about half that of pure horserace coverage. "Voters are interested in the question of who will win," write the authors, "but they are much less curious about the fund-raising, advertising, and other elements of campaign tactics." Having said that, the authors are quick to note that "voters find news reports on *any* aspect of campaign strategy more interesting than news coverage of the issues."[54]

The other reason the media cover campaigns and elections as games is that doing so provides good material to fill the enormous "news hole" that now exists. Today, the media must fill air time twenty-four hours a day on cable television, and Internet sites need to be updated frequently to remain competitive. As a result, news outlets are constantly on the lookout for something to report. Over the course of a long campaign season, media outlets need a considerable amount of material: Discussions of the horserace and campaign strategy serve as unlimited fodder for journalists.

Though horserace coverage and the game schema accurately describe much of what passes for campaign reporting, there are elements of that reporting that help to inform the voters. To begin with, not all campaign coverage is devoid of policy discussion. Issues grids or matrices are a common feature of media outlets' Web pages. Thus, interested voters can compare candidates' issue positions with minimal effort.

Major media outlets also produce "ad watches" to help voters make sense of the claims made in campaign commercials. Ad watches are newspaper articles or television segments that analyze campaign spots for accuracy. They provide, as Kathleen Hall Jamieson has said, a "grammar of evaluation."[55] The point is not to offer a movie critic's review of the ads on aesthetic grounds but to issue a judgment about whether the statements in ads are factual or are not.

Ad watches were first used during the 1988 presidential campaign. Originally, spots were simply rebroadcast in full screen during the segment and reporters would evaluate the ads' claims. Because the ads appeared just as they would when aired by the candidate, the viewers were influenced by the ads themselves more than the reporter's critique.[56] In today's ad watches on television, campaign spots are shown at an angle, on less than a full screen, and inside a simulated television; the reporter interrupts the ad under examination to render a judgment on its assertions. Often, the words "true," "false" or "misleading" will be stamped onto the screen after a particular claim is made, followed by the reporter's explanation of the judgment. In newspaper ad watches, a still shot from the ad is shown along with a description of the visuals in the ad and the full text of the ad's script. The journalist writing the ad watch then evaluates the accuracy of the spot. Ad watches on media web pages are similar to those in newspapers, with the exception that Internet ad watches are able to provide a video link to the full ad.

There is some debate over the effectiveness of ad watches.[57] Nevertheless, when done well, they do provide voters with information about the claims being made by candidates. Ad watches also seem to have had an effect on those who make campaign ads. In at least one survey, a majority of political consultants agreed that ad watches have made campaigns more careful about what they say in their spots.[58] Campaigns realize that the media may scrutinize every claim made in candidates' advertisements. As a result, they are now more likely to document allegations about an opponent and must at least hesitate before blatantly stretching the truth.

One additional aspect of the media's role in elections deserves attention. Newspapers not only report on campaigns, their editorial boards also issue endorsements of candidates. Theoretically, there is a "wall of separation" between the editorial pages of a newspaper and the rest of the paper. Whereas reporters are supposed to remain neutral in their coverage, the purpose of the editorial pages is to offer opinions. At election time, editorial boards often express their views about which candidates most deserve to hold office and why. Typically, endorsements are made for races at all levels over the course of several days or weeks; some papers, however, choose to endorse only in high-profile races.

Daily newspapers in the United States used to endorse Republican presidential candidates to a greater extent than Democratic candidates. In the 1940s and 1950s, the ratio of Republican to Democratic endorsements was two to one. By the 1970s, the Republican advantage had disappeared, and in recent years, Democratic presidential candidates have had a slight edge in newspaper endorsements.[59]

We might ask whether candidate endorsements have any effect on the outcome of an election. At the presidential level, such endorsements are not likely to influence the choices voters make.[60] People typically have enough information about presidential candidates to make an independent decision. In nonpresidential elections, however, endorsements may have a bit more impact, particularly in races where voters know little or nothing about the candidates. Thus, we should expect endorsements to matter more in local races than in congressional or statewide races. Even in elections for the US House of Representatives, however, there is evidence of a significant impact of endorsements on a candidate's share of the vote.[61]

Endorsements most likely influence voters in indirect ways. For example, candidates often mention key endorsements in their campaign ads. The endorsements give the candidate credibility, and the ads ensure that the voters are aware of who is backing whom. Another way that endorsements matter is in the potential they have for influencing the campaign coverage of their newspapers. Though the aforementioned wall supposedly exists between the editorial and the news pages of a paper, Kim Fridkin Kahn and Patrick Kenney have shown that endorsements influence the tone of the coverage candidates get, at least for incumbents. This coverage—and hence the endorsements—in turn influences voters' attitudes toward the candidates.[62]

► *Election Night Coverage*

Having covered the campaign for months, if not years, the media finally turn their attention to the outcome on Election Night. In reporting election results, the tension noted earlier in this chapter between accuracy and speed is exacerbated. No media outlet wants to mistakenly report the outcome of closely watched races; however, all of them want to be the *first* to announce the winner in those races. Accuracy and speed collided, rather infamously, on Election Night 2000, resulting in a number of changes that may, or may not, have made future collisions less likely.

Much of Election Night coverage is based on exit polling conducted on behalf of the major media outlets. Exit polls consist of surveys that are given to randomly selected voters as they leave polling sites in pre-selected precincts.[63] Voters are asked a number of questions about themselves (including their party identification, ideology, religion, occupation, race, age, income, and the like) and their positions on certain issues. They are also asked what they think about the candidates and, ultimately, for whom they voted.

Exit poll results allow the media to do two things. First, when combined with other data, such as turnout figures and historical voting patterns in particular areas, exit polls help networks project winners in key races before all the ballots are counted. Second, they enable the media to explain which groups supported which candidates and that, in turn, provides an explanation for the outcome of the election. As we will see, the media's projections are not always correct, and their analyses of results are sometimes subject to criticism.

In 1990, CNN and the network news organizations formed Voter Research and Surveys (VRS) to conduct exit polls that each member organization could use. Prior to that, individual news outlets had conducted limited exit polling on their own, but the bulk of Election Night coverage consisted of reporting actual voting results collected by an entity called News Election Service (NES). With the creation of VRS, media outlets would have exit poll data that could be used with the election returns gathered by the NES to project eventual winners in key races. Though the outlets shared data, they did their own projections. In

1993, VRS and the NES were merged to form Voter News Service (VNS). This new entity conducted exit polls and gathered election returns, but it also analyzed these data and provided member organizations (including the Associated Press, which had been a member of NES, and Fox News beginning in 1996) with projections.

The arrangement under VNS worked well for a few election cycles. Occasionally, exit poll results in a given race overestimated or underestimated the margin of victory, but the projections based on VNS analyses almost always identified the correct winner. That is, until the election of 2000. The details of that Election Night debacle are too complex to fully elucidate in this text, but a brief summary is worthwhile.[64]

The drama of the evening began at 7:48 p.m. EST, when NBC projected that Al Gore would win the state of Florida. This was a significant development because the electoral math suggested that the winner of two of the three states of Florida, Pennsylvania, and Ohio would win the presidency. Roughly an hour after the announcement that Gore had won Florida, he was projected as the winner in Pennsylvania, and the election appeared virtually over.

Within an hour of the Pennsylvania projection, however, VNS reported to the members of its consortium that some of the exit poll data in Florida were flawed, and its decision to declare Gore the winner was being retracted. Four hours later, with VNS data showing a commanding lead for George W. Bush in Florida, Fox News declared Bush the winner of that state and, thus, the presidency. Other media outlets (with the exception of the Associated Press and VNS itself) followed suit and began using graphics describing Bush as the next president of the United States. Gore had even called Bush to concede at around 3:00 a.m.

However, VNS found further flaws in its data that exaggerated Bush's lead in Florida, and it quickly apprised its members of the situation. In fact, Florida was "too close to call" and would likely be headed for a recount. For the second time in a matter of hours, the major media outlets had retracted their projections in Florida. It took thirty-six days—and numerous recounts, lawsuits, and "pregnant chads"—to determine the winner of the presidency.[65]

The problems with Election Night projections in Florida in 2000 were caused by a number of factors. To begin with, exit polling employs a complicated methodology with multiple sources of potential error. Sophisticated techniques are required to select the precincts at which exit polling will be conducted and the individual voters who will be asked to take part in the survey. Inevitably, some voters will be excluded from the poll either because they refuse to participate or because pollsters could not reach them. Increasing numbers of voters are unavailable for exit polling because they vote early or by absentee ballot and are, therefore, not present at polling places on Election Day. Indeed, the Associated Press estimated that nearly 40 percent of the electorate cast ballots before Election Day in 2016.[66] If early voters are different in some systematic way from those who vote in person on Election Day, there will be error in the exit poll results.

Assuming the exit polls are accurate, the media must still create reliable formulas from which to derive projections. These complex formulas take into account prior voting behavior in given areas, but they are also based on certain assumptions made by the analysts about comparable elections. In Florida in 2000, VNS assumed that the 1998 Florida gubernatorial race would be most comparable when, in fact, the 1998 Senate race or the 1996 presidential election in Florida would have been more appropriate.[67] Obviously, faulty assumptions will hamper the media's ability to successfully project winners even if the exit polling is accurate.

Ultimately, too little *and* too much competition within the media is to blame for the fiasco of 2000. Too little competition for data existed between media outlets; they each used exactly the same (flawed) exit poll results. Thus, they all sank or swam together. At the same time, too much competition to be the first to report the winner of key races led to hasty analyses and announcements.[68]

Early Election Night projections have been controversial for some time. The main concern is that by announcing a winner before all the polls have closed, the media may inadvertently keep people who vote in the final hours of an election from going out to vote at all. It was argued in 1980, for example, that media pronouncements of Ronald Reagan's victory led to a decrease in turnout on the West Coast, where it was 5:15 p.m. when the networks began to make their official projections. Most thought that this adversely affected Democrats, who allegedly became dejected at the news of President Carter's defeat. Indeed, there is evidence that the early projections depressed turnout among Democrats in several US House races in California, resulting in several losses for the Democratic candidates.[69] Other evidence suggests that it was Republicans, not Democrats, who were more likely to stay home once they heard that their presidential nominee had won.[70] Either way, it seems at least plausible that by being so quick to declare an election over, the media are discouraging citizens from participating in democracy.

After the mistakes that occurred in 2000, VNS began revamping its computer system and its software for making projections. Nevertheless, during the midterm elections of 2002, significant problems occurred both in the exit poll and vote-counting systems. All VNS data was rendered useless, including the exit poll results that help analysts explain voting behavior. The result was the dissolution of VNS in early 2003.

To replace VNS, the consortium consisting of the Associated Press, CNN, Fox News, NBC, CBS, and ABC created the National Election Pool (NEP) to conduct exit polling. The Associated Press, which had always maintained its own vote-tabulating operation, would provide vote counts to the other consortium members and its subscribers. For the NEP, two veteran pollsters with extensive experience were hired to handle the exit polls.

Despite the new arrangement, there was more controversy concerning the exit polls in 2004. NEP released exit poll results to its members at various points throughout Election Day, just as the VNS had done in earlier years. Such information is supposed to be embargoed, but it was leaked to a number of Internet sites, including Slate.com and "The Drudge Report." Those sites, in turn, published the early results, most of which showed Democratic presidential challenger John Kerry ahead of President Bush in key battleground states. This built momentum for the idea that Kerry was on the way to victory.

Though exit poll results throughout the day had Kerry in the lead by a statistically significant margin, the networks were cautious in projecting winners in key states and never incorrectly projected a Kerry victory. Regardless of whether the media made mistakes in declaring a winner, the exit polls do appear to have been inaccurate. A report by the NEP pollsters indicates that "the exit poll estimates in the 2004 general election overstated John Kerry's share of the vote nationally and in many states."[71] The report lists a number of methodological reasons for the error but finds that it was "most likely due to Kerry voters participating in the exit polls at a higher rate than Bush voters."[72] It should be noted that before the final 2004 exit poll data were released publicly, they were adjusted to comport with the actual vote. Though this is, in fact, standard procedure, it nonetheless raises some questions about the validity of using exit polls to explain the vote.

In 2016, for example, exit polls suggested that 29 percent of Latinos voted for Donald Trump. That is a better result than Mitt Romney's 27 percent in 2012 and it is surprising given Trump's rhetoric about Hispanics during the campaign. In fact, Latino Decisions, a Latino public opinion research firm run by political scientists Gary Segura and Matt Barreto, found that Latino support for Trump was closer to 18 percent.[73] Part of the problem is that exit polls are "not designed to yield very reliable estimates of the characteristics of small, geographically clustered demographic groups."[74]

In each election since 2004, exit poll data have been guarded very closely. Analysts representing each of the consortium members are locked in a "quarantine room," with no access to the Internet or phones, and data are not released to the member organizations until 5:00 p.m. EST. Once they have the data, media outlets can report on general trends but cannot indicate how an election is likely to turn out in a given state until all of the polls are closed in that state. In recent election cycles, exit poll results have been handled cautiously, and the media have avoided making incorrect projections.

▶ *Pursuing the Common Good?*

The media are the target of a great deal of criticism. The charges are endless and many have been addressed in this chapter: they cover too much "soft news"; they emphasize conflict over consensus; they obsess about the horserace and slight policy discussions; they have partisan (or any host of other) biases. Regardless of the accuracy of these criticisms, we benefit by understanding the reasons for the media's behavior. They are actors in the electoral process not unlike political parties, interest groups, and voters; while pursuing their own self-interests, they affect the way campaigns are run and, perhaps, influence the outcome of elections.

More than parties, interest groups, or voters, however, the media are expected to protect the common good. That is why they are afforded unique recognition in the First Amendment. An inevitable tension exists between the media's pursuit of their self-interested goals and their attempts to fulfill their democratic obligations.

Media outlets, of course, are mostly commercial entities that belong to a multinational industry. Though the journalists who work for various media companies are professionals, with norms that govern their roles, the ultimate concern of their employers is to turn a profit. They do this by selling their product and, more important, by selling advertising space within their product. It is not impossible to do this while serving the public's interest; indeed, many in the media would argue that they maximize profits only when they produce quality journalism. However, the assumption within most news organizations is that readers and viewers do not want detailed discussions of policy; if they did, the audiences for NPR and PBS's *Newshour* would be far larger than they are.

So we are left with a chicken-and-egg situation. The media will not provide in-depth coverage of issues because the people do not seem to want it, but the people may not want such coverage because they have never really been exposed to it. Perhaps the solution rests with developing "media literacy" in children and establishing better habits of media consumption in young adults. Until then, the media are likely to produce only what they think will generate the highest profits.

► Conclusion

The current media environment in the United States has rightly been described as "fragmented." In recent decades, technological change has led to a proliferation of media outlets. The newest arrivals to the media landscape allow for audience interaction, are concerned with entertaining as much as informing the audience, provide round-the-clock communication, and are heavily opinion oriented. The result is not only a vast amount of information, but a great deal of "infotainment" as well. As a result, critics worry about the quality of the information available to the average voter.

In what ways, and to what extent, does the media affect voters? Clearly voters learn about candidates from the media, even if it is not always a great deal of information and the information is often not very substantive. The media also influences the issues that voters think are most important (i.e. agenda setting) and the ones they use to evaluate candidates (i.e. priming). Finally, the media have a tendency to frame stories episodically, rather than thematically, which means voters will often lack context for understanding issues and events that occur during a campaign.

The aspects of campaigns the media chooses to emphasize may fail to give voters what they need to make informed decisions. A great deal of election coverage, for example, focuses on the "horserace" and presents an election as a game, rather than a choice between governing visions. This means that polls and campaign strategy garner more attention than the candidates' policy proposals. Nevertheless, the media do try to hold candidates accountable for what they say on the campaign trail, including the claims made in their campaign ads.

On election night, media outlets race to "call" elections before their competitors do so. They are constrained, of course, by wanting to make accurate projections. Burned by the fiasco of the 2000 presidential election in Florida, news organizations have become more cautious in their use of early exit poll results to calculate likely winners.

Though there is plenty to criticize about the way the media currently operate, they are an essential piece of the American political system. Without a free media, it would be difficult to get objective information about candidates and it would be impossible to hold elected officials accountable. Still, there is no denying that media coverage of campaigns, and of politics generally, leaves a lot to be desired. Exactly how that coverage could be improved in the current media (and political) landscape is difficult to imagine. However, given that the profit motive is critical to our largely commercial media, the supply of good quality news is unlikely to increase until the demand for it does.

▶ Pedagogical Tools

Role-Play Scenario

You are a journalist for the largest newspaper in your state and have been assigned to cover the race for US Senate. In addition to the obligatory articles on fund-raising totals and poll results, your editors have asked you to propose a series of nine weekly reports (to be run from Labor Day to Election Day) on anything you want. Write a one-page memo describing the nine reports you'd like to produce.

Discussion Questions

1. Would there be any advantage to returning to a partisan media? Should the United States adopt a BBC-style, publicly subsidized media outlet? Explain your answers.
2. Where should the media draw the line in reporting about candidates' private lives?
3. How might the media balance informative coverage of elections with reporting that is entertaining enough to attract and maintain a sizable audience?

Online Resources

Axios, www.axios.com.
Columbia Journalism Review, www.cjr.org.
Nate Silver's *FiveThirtyEight*, http://fivethirtyeight.com.
Politico, www.politico.com.

Suggested Reading

Stephen J. Farnsworth and S. Robert Lichter (2011) *The Nightly News Nightmare: Television's Coverage of US Presidential Elections, 1988–2008*, Lanham, MD: Rowman & Littlefield.
David A. Jones (2016) *US Media and Elections in Flux: Dynamics and Strategies*, London and New York: Routledge.
Thomas E. Patterson (1994) *Out of Order*, New York: Vintage Books.
Markus Prior (2007) *Post-Broadcast Democracy: How Media Choice Increases Inequality in Political Involvement and Polarizes Elections*, Cambridge: Cambridge University Press.

▶ *Notes*

1 Jan E. Leighley (2004) *Mass Media and Politics: A Social Science Perspective*, Boston, MA: Houghton Mifflin, 23.
2 Leighley, *Mass Media and Politics*, p. 24.
3 Darrell M. West (2001) *The Rise and Fall of the Media Establishment*, Boston, MA: Bedford/ St. Martin's, p. 105.
4 Paul Starr (2004) *The Creation of the Media: Political Origins of Modern Communications*, New York: Basic Books, p. xi.
5 Richard Davis and Diana Owen (1998) *New Media and American Politics*, Oxford: Oxford University Press, p. 7.
6 Tim Craig and Michael D. Shear (2006) "Allen Quip Provokes Outrage, Apology," *Washington Post*, August 15, www.washingtonpost.com/wp-dyn/content/article/2006/08/14/AR2006081400589.html (accessed January 31, 2017).
7 Davis and Owen, *New Media and American Politics*, p. 7.
8 The Pew Research Center for the People and the Press (2004) "Cable and Internet Loom Large in Fragmented Political News Universe," January 11, www.people-press.org/2004/01/11/cable-and-internet-loom-large-in-fragmented-political-news-universe (accessed January 31, 2017).
9 The Pew Research Center for the People and the Press (2010) "Ideological News Sources: Who Watches and Why," September 12, www.people-press.org/2010/09/12/americans-spending-more-time-following-the-news (accessed January 31, 2017).
10 Steven Chaffee and Stacey Frank (1996) "How Americans Get Political Information: Print versus Broadcast News," *Annals of the American Academy of Political and Social Science*, 546: 48–58.
11 Shanto Iyengar and Donald R. Kinder (1987) *News That Matters: Television and American Opinion*, Chicago, IL: University of Chicago Press, pp. 16–62.
12 Shanto Iyengar and Jennifer A. McGrady (2007) *Media Politics: A Citizen's Guide*, New York: W. W. Norton, p. 210.
13 Iyengar and Kinder, *News That Matters*, pp. 63–111.

14 Iyengar and McGrady, *Media Politics*, p. 210.
15 For the classic work on this topic, see Herbert Gans (1979) *Deciding What's News: A Study of CBS Evening News, NBC Nightly News, Newsweek, and Time*, New York: Random House.
16 Shanto Iyengar (1992) *Is Anyone Responsible? How Television Frames Political Issues*, Chicago, IL: University of Chicago Press, p. 14.
17 Lauren Feldman (2014) "The Hostile Media Effect," in Kate Kenski and Kathleen Hall Jamieson (eds.), *The Oxford Handbook of Political Communication*, Oxford: Oxford University Press. First published in Oxford Handbooks Online, www.oxfordhandbooks.com/view/10.1093/oxfordhb/9780199793471.001.0001/oxfordhb-9780199793471-e-011 (accessed March 11, 2017).
18 Michael Ray Smith (2007) "Ideology," in William. David Sloan and Jenn Burleson Mackay (eds.), *Media Bias: Finding It, Fixing It*, Jefferson, NC: McFarland.
19 On media coverage of Trump's campaign for the Republican nomination, see Julia R. Azari (2016) "How the News Media Helped to Nominate Trump," *Political Communication*, 33: 677–680; and Chris Wells, Dhavan V. Shah, Jon C. Pevehouse, JungHwan Yang, Ayellet Pelled, Frederick Boehm, Josephine Lukito, Shreenita Ghosh, and Jessica L. Schmidt (2016) "How Trump Drove Coverage to the Nomination: Hybrid Media Campaigning," *Political Communication*, 33: 669–676.
20 Project for Excellence in Journalism (2008) "Amid Charges of Bias, The Media Swarm on Obama Overseas," PEJ Campaign Coverage Index: July 21–27, www.journalism.org/node/12097 (accessed January 31, 2017).
21 W. Lance Bennett (2003) *News: The Politics of Illusion*, 5th edn, New York: Longman, p. 42.
22 The fourth, the "authority-disorder bias," pertains more to the coverage of government than of campaigns. See Bennett, *News*, pp. 48–50.
23 Bennett, *News*, p. 45.
24 Ben Smith (2007) "The Hair's Still Perfect," Democrats '08 Blog, April 16, www.politico.com/blogs/bensmith/0407/The_Hairs_Still_Perfect.html (accessed January 31, 2017). For criticism of the amount of coverage this story received, see Jamison Foser (2007) "The Same Old Story, Same Old Act," *Media Matters*, July 13, http://mediamatters.org/items/200707140001 (accessed January 31, 2017).
25 See Matthew A. Buam (2003) *Soft News Goes to War: Public Opinion and American Foreign Policy in the New Media Age*, Princeton, NJ: Princeton University Press, p. 6.
26 Bennett, *News*, p. 48.
27 Iyengar, *Is Anyone Responsible?* p. 14.
28 Philip Rucker, Jose A. DelReal, and Sean Sullivan (2016) "Donald Trump Fires Embattled Campaign Manager Corey Lewandowski," *Washington Post*, June 20, www.washingtonpost.com/news/post-politics/wp/2016/06/20/trump-parts-ways-with-campaign-manager/?utm_term=.998a9ba9ad99 (accessed February 7, 2017).
29 Nolan D. McCaskill, Alex Isenstadt, and Shane Goldmacher (2016) "Paul Manafort Resigns from Trump Campaign," *Politico*, August 19, www.politico.com/story/2016/08/paul-manafort-resigns-from-trump-campaign-227197 (accessed February 7, 2017).
30 Ryan Lizza (2016) "Kellyanne Conway's Political Machinations," *New Yorker*, October 17, www.newyorker.com/magazine/2016/10/17/kellyanne-conways-political-machinations (accessed February 7, 2017).
31 Larry J. Sabato (1993) *Feeding Frenzy: How Attack Journalism Has Transformed American Politics*, New York: The Free Press, p. 6.
32 Thomas E. Patterson (1994) *Out of Order*, New York: Vintage Books, pp. 57, 59.
33 Marion R. Just, Ann N. Crigler, Dean E. Alger, Timothy E. Cook, Montague Kern, and Darrell M. West (1996) *Crosstalk: Citizens, Candidates, and the Media in a Presidential Campaign*, Chicago, IL: University of Chicago Press, pp. 99–104.
34 Stephen J. Farnsworth and S. Robert Lichter (2011) *The Nightly News Nightmare: Network Television's Coverage of US Presidential Elections, 1988–2008*, 3rd edn, Lanham, MD: Rowman & Littlefield, p. 45.

35 Pew Research Center's Project for Excellence in Journalism (2012) "Winning the Media Campaign 2012," November 2, www.journalism.org/node/31438 (accessed January 31, 2017).

36 Farnsworth and Lichter, *The Nightly News Nightmare*, p. 148. Farnsworth and Lichter have not examined PBS in subsequent studies.

37 Everett Carll Ladd and John Benson (1992) "The Growth of News Polls in American Politics," in Thomas E. Mann and Gary R. Orren (eds.), *Media Polls in American Politics*, Washington, DC: Brookings Institution Press, p. 19.

38 Thomas E. Mann and Gary R. Orren (1992) "To Poll or Not to Poll … and Other Questions," in Thomas E. Mann and Gary R. Orren (eds.), *Media Polls in American Politics*, Washington, DC: Brookings Institution Press, p. 2.

39 See also Sheldon R. Gawiser and G. Evans Witt (n.d.) "20 Questions a Journalist Should Ask about Poll Results," 3rd edn, *National Council on Public Polls*, www.ncpp.org/?q=node/4 (accessed January 31, 2017).

40 Mark Blumenthal (2007) "The Pollster.com Disclosure Project," *Pollster.com*, September 24, www.pollster.com/blogs/the_pollstercom_disclosure_pro.php (accessed January 31, 2017).

41 Josh Katz (2016) "Who Will Be President?" *New York Times*, The Upshot, November 8, www.nytimes.com/interactive/2016/upshot/presidential-polls-forecast.html (accessed February 7, 2017).

42 Nate Silver (2016) "Who Will Win the Presidency?" *FiveThirtyEight.com*, November 8, https://projects.fivethirtyeight.com/2016-election-forecast (February 7, 2017).

43 RealClearPolitics (2016) "General Election: Trump vs. Clinton vs. Johnson vs. Stein," www.realclearpolitics.com/epolls/2016/president/us/general_election_trump_vs_clinton_vs_johnson_vs_stein-5952.html (accessed February 7, 2017).

44 Final battleground state averages can be found by selecting a particular state at RealClearPolitics.com.

45 Trip Gabriel and Helene Cooper (2012) "Romney Refines Message on Taxes and Abortion," *New York Times*, October 9, www.nytimes.com/2012/10/10/us/politics/romney-pledges-to-keep-tax-deductions-for-mortgages.html (accessed January 31, 2017).

46 Josh Levs and Thom Patterson (2012) "Obama Creates Monument to Cesar Chavez: 'He Cared,'" *CNN.com*, October 9, www.cnn.com/2012/10/08/us/obama-chavez-monument (accessed January 31, 2017).

47 Alexandra Petri (2013) "Chris Christie's Lap Band Weight Loss Surgery: So He Can Run with Kids, or So He Can Run in 2016?" ComPost blog, *Washington Post*, May 7, www.washingtonpost.com/blogs/compost/wp/2013/05/07/chris-christies-lap-band-weight-loss-surgery-so-he-can-run-with-kids-or-so-he-can-run-in-2016/?utm_term=.eb02711057ba (accessed April 15, 2017).

48 Darrell M. West (2001) *Air Wars: Television Advertising in Election Campaigns, 1952–2000*, 3rd edn, Washington, DC: CQ Press, pp. 75–78.

49 West, *Air Wars*, p. 80.

50 The *Times* did, however, cover the nonproliferation aspect of the speech on p. A22 the previous day. See Jeff Zeleny (2007) "Obama to Urge Elimination of Nuclear Weapons," *New York Times*, October 2, www.nytimes.com/2007/10/02/us/politics/02obama.html (accessed January 31, 2017).

51 Alec MacGillis (2007) "Obama Revisits Key Antiwar Speech," *Washington Post*, October 3, www.washingtonpost.com/wp-dyn/content/article/2007/10/02/AR2007100202036.html (accessed January 31, 2017).

52 Joseph Cappella and Kathleen Hall Jamieson (1997) *Spiral of Cynicism: The Press and the Public Good*, Oxford: Oxford University Press.

53 Julianne F. Flowers, Audrey A. Haynes, and Michael H. Crespin (2003) "The Media, the Campaign, and the Message," *American Journal of Political Science*, 47, p. 272.

54 Shanto Iyengar, Helmut Norpoth, and Kyu S. Hahn (2004) "Consumer Demand for Election News: The Horserace Sells," *Journal of Politics*, 66: 173–174.

55 As quoted in West, *Air Wars*, p. 85.

56 West, *Air Wars*, pp. 85–86.

57 Joseph N. Cappella and Kathleen Hall Jamieson (1994) "Broadcast Adwatch Effects: A Field Experiment," *Communication Research*, 21: 342–365; and Stephen Ansolabehere and Shanto Iyengar (1996) "Can the Press Monitor Campaign Advertising? An Experimental Study," *Harvard International Journal of Press/Politics*, 1: 72–86.

58 James A. Thurber, Candice J. Nelson, and David A. Dulio (2000) "Portrait of Campaign Consultants," in James A. Thurber and Candice J. Nelson (eds.), *Campaign Warriors: Political Consultants in Elections*, Washington, DC: Brookings Institution Press, p. 23.

59 Stephen Ansolabehere, Rebecca Lessem, and James M. Snyder, Jr. (2006) "The Orientation of Newspaper Endorsements in US Elections, 1940–2002," *Quarterly Journal of Political Science*, 1: 393–404.

60 See Kathleen Hall Jamieson (2000) *Everything You Think You Know about Politics ... and Why You're Wrong*, New York: Basic Books, p. 156.

61 Paul S. Herrnson (2004) *Congressional Elections: Campaigning at Home and in Washington*, 4th edn, Washington, DC: CQ Press, p. 244.

62 Kim Fridkin Kahn and Patrick J. Kenney (2002) "The Slant of the News: How Editorial Endorsements Influence Campaign Coverage and Citizens' Views of Candidates," *The American Political Science Review*, 96: 381–394.

63 For a review of exit polling methodology, see Daniel M. Merkle and Murray Edelman (2000) "A Review of the 1996 Voter News Service Exit Polls from a Total Survey Error Perspective," in Paul J. Lavrakas and Michael W. Traugott (eds.), *Election Polls, the News Media, and Democracy*, New York: Chatham House.

64 For a detailed examination of Election Night 2000, see Stephen K. Medvic and David A. Dulio (2003) "The Media and Public Opinion," in Mark J. Rozell (ed.), *Media Power, Media Politics*, Lanham, MD: Rowman & Littlefield.

65 The Staff of the *New York Times* (2001) *36 Days: The Complete Chronicle of the 2000 Presidential Election Crisis*, New York: Times Books.

66 Hope Yen (2016) "Early Voting: Record Levels in 2016 May Give Clinton Edge," *Associated Press*, November 7, http://elections.ap.org/content/early-voting-record-levels-2016-may-give-clinton-edge (February 7, 2017).

67 Joan Konner, James Risser, and Ben Wattenberg (2001) "Television's Performance on Election Night 2000: A Report for CNN," http://edition.cnn.com/2001/ALLPOLITICS/stories/02/02/cnn.report/cnn.pdf (accessed January 31, 2017), 11.

68 Medvic and Dulio, "The Media and Public Opinion," pp. 223–225.

69 Michael X. Delli Carpini (1984) "Scooping the Voters? The Consequences of the Networks' Early Call of the 1980 Presidential Race," *Journal of Politics*, 46: 866–885.

70 John E. Jackson (1983) "Election Night Reporting and Voter Turnout," *American Journal of Political Science*, 27: 615–635.

71 Edison Media Research and Mitofsky International (2005) "Evaluation of Edison/Mitofsky Election System 2004," *National Election Pool*, January 19, http://abcnews.go.com/images/Politics/EvaluationofEdisonMitofskyElectionSystem.pdf (accessed February 7, 2017), p. 3.

72 Edison Media Research and Mitofsky International, "Evaluation of Edison/Mitofsky Election System 2004."

73 Latino Decisions (2016) "2016 Latino Election Analysis," November 9, www.latinodecisions.com/files/6514/7880/5462/PostElection2016.pdf (accessed February 7, 2017).

74 Edison Media Research and Mitofsky International, "Evaluation of Edison/Mitofsky Election System 2004," p. 62.

8 Voters

E ACH OF THE ACTORS discussed to this point—candidates, political parties, interest groups, and the media—are vital to democracy, but there is a widely held assumption that the most essential actors in the electoral process are the voters. The voters, after all, decide who wins and who loses elections. As a result, pundits speculate on their inclinations, pollsters collect their opinions, candidates respond to their demands, and political scientists study their behavior. In fact, voters are the subject of more academic research than any of the other participants in elections.

This chapter explores at least two dimensions of voting. First, it addresses voter turnout from both an aggregate and individual perspective. It identifies the factors that lead to higher (or lower) turnout levels in an election and those that explain why individuals do or do not go to the polls. Second, this chapter describes how individuals make their voting decisions. In doing so, it examines short-term and long-term influences on the vote.

Voting has come to be seen as a duty, not just a right, of all citizens. As we will see, some Americans do not fulfill their obligation to help determine the leadership of the country. When they do, they may vote for candidates on grounds that are less than ideal. The aim of this chapter is to better understand the complicated act of voting and, ultimately, to evaluate the performance of perhaps the most important actors in our democracy.

▶ Voter Turnout

The first step in the process of voting is deciding whether to cast a ballot. Voters may not consciously weigh the costs and benefits of going to the polls, but there are identifiable factors that influence the decision to vote. In the aggregate, certain conditions encourage voting, whereas others make it less likely. At the individual level, some characteristics are closely associated with voting, and others are linked to nonvoting. This section situates voter turnout in the United States within a comparative context and also looks at turnout levels over time. In addition, it examines both the aggregate and individual level factors that influence turnout.

Comparing Aggregate Turnout Levels

Many people judge the health of a democracy according to the percentage of individuals who vote. Though some find nothing inherently wrong with low voter turnout, many others believe that low turnout is an indication of problems within a political system. This debate will be discussed at the end of the chapter. For now, it must be acknowledged that turnout in the United States is notoriously low when compared to voter participation in other countries.

To make valid comparisons across differing political systems, political scientists typically measure voter turnout as the percentage of the voting age population (VAP) that casts a ballot. According to figures compiled by the Pew Research Center, the United States ranks 28th among the thirty-five countries in the Organisation for Economic Co-operation and Development (OECD) in terms of turnout percentage in the most recent national election (see Table 8.1). Whereas 87.2 percent of Belgians voted in 2014, only 54.7 percent of Americans voted in the 2016 election.[1]

TABLE 8.1   *Voter Turnout in OECD Countries' Most Recent National Elections*

Rank	Country	Year	VAP Turnout %
1	Belgium	2014	87.2
2	Turkey	2015	84.3
3	Sweden	2014	82.6
4	South Korea	2012	80.4
5	Denmark	2015	80.3
6	Iceland	2013	80.0
7	Australia	2016	79.0
8	Norway	2013	77.9
9	Israel	2015	76.1
10	New Zealand	2014	73.2
11	Finland	2015	73.1
12	France	2012	71.2
13	Netherlands	2012	71.0
14	Austria	2013	69.3
15	Italy	2013	68.5
16	Germany	2013	66.0
17	Mexico	2012	64.6
18	Hungary	2014	63.4

19	Canada	2015	62.1
19	Greece	2015	62.1
21	Portugal	2015	61.8
22	United Kingdom	2015	61.1
23	Spain	2016	60.9
24	Czech Republic	2013	60.0
25	Slovakia	2016	59.4
26	Ireland	2016	58.0
27	Luxembourg	2013	55.1
28	United States	2016	54.7
28	Estonia	2015	54.7
30	Slovenia	2014	54.1
31	Poland	2015	53.8
32	Japan	2014	52.0
33	Latvia	2014	51.7
34	Chile	2013	45.7
35	Switzerland	2015	38.6

Source: Drew Desilver (2016) "U.S. Voter Turnout Trails Most Developed Countries," Pew Research Center, August 2, http://www.pewresearch.org/fact-tank/2016/08/02/u-s-voter-turnout-trails-most-developed-countries/ (accessed February 7, 2017).

Generally speaking, the factors that explain variation in turnout levels between countries are either cultural or institutional in nature. Cultural explanations include socioeconomic considerations, such as the level of development in a country, but also political attitudes, such as the level of party identification and strength of political efficacy. Institutional factors that help determine a country's level of voter turnout include the size of electoral districts (the smaller the district, the higher the turnout); the frequency of elections (the more frequent the election, the lower the turnout); and the level of competition between parties (the more competition, the higher the turnout).[2] Other factors that correlate positively with higher turnout levels include compulsory voting, vote-by-mail, and weekend voting. Of particular interest is the fact, as noted in Chapter 2, that proportional electoral systems have significantly higher turnout than plurality or majoritarian systems.[3]

Within the United States, there are significant differences between states and regions in terms of turnout levels. Perhaps the most noticeable difference is between turnout rates in the South and the non-South. In recent years, turnout has been between 2.5 and 6.5 percentage points lower in southern states than in those outside the South.[4] This pattern reflects the checkered past of the South in terms of vote suppression and the region's traditional political culture that viewed politics as the concern of elites only,[5] but it is most often attributed to a historical lack of competition in the South. States in which the two parties have comparable electoral strength are expected to have higher turnout than those with one-party dominance.

Indeed, this is the pattern we see in most states. Table 8.2 lists the top ten and bottom ten states by turnout as a percentage of VAP in 2016. Along with the turnout rates for each of these states, the table includes the margin of victory for the presidential candidate who won the state. If we consider competitive states to be those with a margin of victory of less than ten percentage points, seven of the top ten states according to turnout were those in which the presidential race was competitive; of the bottom ten states, only three states were competitive. Clearly, competition helps to drive turnout levels.

TABLE 8.2   *States with Highest and Lowest Voter Turnout, 2016*

Rank	State	Turnout Rate (VAP)	Presidential Margin of Victory
1	Minnesota	69.4%	1.5
1	Maine	69.4%	2.9
3	New Hampshire	69.1%	0.3
4	Wisconsin	66.2%	0.7
5	Iowa	65.1%	9.4
6	Colorado	64.6%	4.9
7	Vermont	62.3%	26.4
8	Michigan	62.0%	0.3
9	Oregon	61.7%	11.0
10	Massachusetts	61.1%	27.2
42	New York	49.6%	22.5
43	Nevada	49.4%	2.4
43	Arkansas	49.4%	26.9
45	Arizona	49.2%	3.5
46	West Virginia	49.1%	41.7
47	Oklahoma	49.0%	36.4
48	Tennessee	48.6%	26.0
49	California	47.0%	30.0
50	Texas	43.4%	9.0
51	Hawaii	38.3%	32.2

Source: Voter turnout figures are from Michael P. McDonald, "2016 November General Election Turnout Rates," http://www.electproject.org/2016g (accessed February 7, 2017). Presidential margins of victory are calculated from results reported by the New York Times, "Presidential Election Results: Donald J. Trump Wins," last updated February 10, 2017, http://www.nytimes.com/elections/results/president (accessed February 12, 2017).

Of course, some states with robust voter participation are not particularly competitive, whereas a few competitive states have low turnout levels. Vermont, for example, had a turnout rate of over 62 percent, even though Hillary Clinton won the state by more than 26 points. Conversely, the battleground states of Nevada and Arizona had turnout of just over 49 percent. Thus, though electoral competition in a state does influence voter participation, it is not the sole determinate of turnout.

Other factors also affect state turnout levels. States with smaller population sizes, for example, tend to have higher turnout rates, though the effect is not overwhelming. More significant is the influence of social capital on turnout. The more civic and social organizations a state has per capita, the higher its turnout is likely to be. In addition, states with more educated populations have higher turnout than those with lower educational levels. Finally, turnout is considerably higher in states with later registration deadlines than it is in states where voters must register twenty or more days before the election. Indeed, states allowing voters to register on Election Day have the highest turnout of all (see Chapter 3).[6]

Turnout in the United States can also be examined over time. Over the last half-century or so, turnout levels are generally thought to have declined. In fact, as Figure 8.1 indicates, a fairly dramatic drop in turnout for presidential elections occurred after 1968. This was due almost entirely to the ratification of the Twenty-sixth Amendment in 1971, which allowed citizens eighteen years old and older to vote. Because eighteen-to-twenty-year-olds vote at far lower levels than those twenty-one and older, the decrease in turnout was precipitous. Since 1972, however, turnout has not declined noticeably. In the six presidential elections from 1972 to 1992, turnout as a percentage of VAP averaged 53.25 percent; from 1996 through 2016, that average was 53.12 percent. Having said that, as Figure 8.1 indicates, turnout has been quite erratic in recent elections. In the six elections from 1996 to 2016, turnout as a percentage of VAP was 48.1 percent, 50 percent and 55.4 percent, 56.9 percent, 53.6 percent, and 54.7 for a range of 8.8 percentage points; from 1972 to 1992, the range was 4.8 percentage points.[7]

Notice in Figure 8.1 that the turnout rate among the voting-eligible population (VEP) is higher than the VAP rate. Political scientist Michael McDonald has argued that using VEP produces a more accurate measure of voter turnout because it does not include those segments of the population that are ineligible to vote such as noncitizens and those in prison. The VAP, conversely, includes everyone in the country who is eighteen years of age or older.

Not only is VEP turnout higher than the VAP rate, but the gap between the two has also been increasing. As McDonald has found, the percentage of the population that is ineligible to vote has increased in recent years.[8] For example, 3.53 percent of the public were noncitizens in 1980, a number that grew to 8.51 percent by 2012.[9] The felon and ex-felon population has grown as well. Thus, when VAP is used as the denominator to calculate turnout rates, it counts millions of people who are not eligible to vote and, therefore, artificially depresses the turnout figure. Indeed, turnout as a percent of VAP was 4.6

FIGURE 8.1 *Voter Turnout in Presidential Election Years, as a Percentage of Voting Age Population (VAP) and Voting Eligible Population (VEP), 1948–2016*

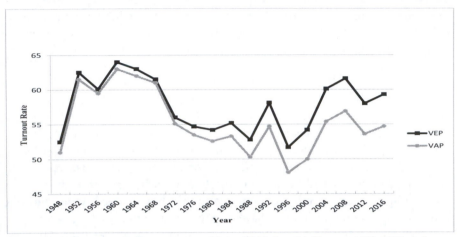

Source: Based on voter turnout figures from Michael P. McDonald, "Turnout 1980–2012.xls," http://elections.gmu.edu/Turnout 1980–2012.xls and "2016 November General Election Turnout Rates," www.electproject.org/2016g.

percentage points lower in 2016 than turnout as a percent of VEP. And the 2016 VEP turnout rate was higher than in any election since 1968, with the exception of 2004 and 2008.

Explaining Aggregate Turnout Levels

Why do aggregate turnout rates fluctuate so much, and what determines how high (or low) those rates will be in a given election year? The most obvious explanation is that the level of interest in a particular election drives turnout rates; the greater the interest, the higher turnout will be. For example, there is more interest in presidential elections than in any other elections in the United States. Thus, when presidential candidates are on the ballot, turnout will be higher than when they are not. As seen in Figure 8.2, turnout in presidential election years has been considerably higher than in nonpresidential (or midterm) election years. In fact, from 1972 through 2016, the average VEP turnout in midterm election years was 39.35 percent, compared to 56.35 percent in presidential years. To put the difference in perspective, though turnout in the presidential year of 2008 reached a thirty-two-year high of 61.6 percent (of VEP), turnout in the historic 2010 midterm elections mustered only 41 percent.[10]

Typically, higher-level races will garner more attention and produce more interest than lower-level races. The phenomenon of "ballot roll-off" illustrates

FIGURE 8.2   *Voter Turnout in Presidential and Midterm Election Years, 1932–2016*

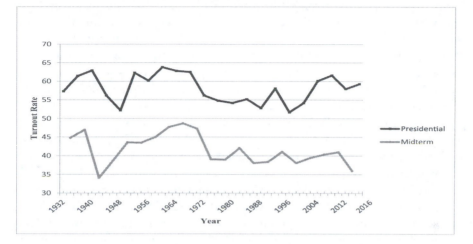

Source: Based on data from Stanley and Niemi, 2011: Figure 1–1 and McDonald, "Voter Turnout."

TABLE 8.3   *2004 Vote Totals, Lancaster County, Pennsylvania*

Office	Vote Total
President	221,278
US Senate	213,566
PA Attorney General	211,588
PA Auditor General	208,091
PA State Treasurer	212,412

Source: Pennsylvania Department of State, "2004 General Election, Official Returns, Lancaster County," http://www.electionreturns.state.pa.us/Default.aspx?EID=13&ESTID=2&CID=2325&OID=0&CDID=0&PID=0&DISTID=0&IsSpecial=0 (accessed May 27, 2013).

the point. Roll-off occurs when voters cast votes for high-profile offices at the top of the ballot but skip at least some lower-level races. Roll-off appears in aggregate turnout levels when vote totals are higher at the top of the ballot than they are down ballot. In 2004, for example, 221,278 votes were cast for president in Lancaster County, Pennsylvania. As the vote totals in Table 8.3 indicate, roughly 7,700 fewer votes were cast in Lancaster County in the race for US Senate, arguably the highest-profile office after the presidency. Vote totals fell further, by nearly 2,000, in the race for attorney general, a statewide office, and by another 3,500 in the auditor general contest, an office that is just below attorney general on the ballot.

If voters simply stopped voting at some point as they moved down the ballot, we could attribute roll-off to voter fatigue. Undoubtedly, many voters are overwhelmed by the myriad choices they face on any given ballot. Thus, voter fatigue likely explains part of the roll-off phenomenon. However, if that were the only explanation, we would see successively fewer votes cast per office as we looked down the ballot. As it turns out, that is not always the case. Thus, to return to the 2004 Lancaster County vote totals in Table 8.3, more than 4,000 more votes were cast in the race for state treasurer than for auditor general, despite the fact that the treasurer's race appears below the auditor general's race on the ballot. The most likely reason for this deviation from ballot roll-off is that a well-known figure in Pennsylvania state politics, Robert Casey, Jr. (now a US senator), was running for treasurer.

Voters are more likely to cast a vote in a race about which they know something. Martin Wattenberg has concluded that "voters skip items on the ballot … because they do not have enough information upon which to cast a vote."[11] Simply recognizing a candidate's name on the ballot is more information than voters often have about candidates. Regardless of what they know about the candidates, the more information voters have about a particular race, the more likely they are to cast a vote in it.

Races that are competitive are also likely to generate higher turnout than those that are not competitive. Indeed, Wattenberg demonstrates that the higher the margin of victory in US House races, the higher the ballot roll-off is for those races.[12] In the 2010 race for Michigan's Seventh Congressional District, for example, the margin of victory was under 5 percentage points (50.2 to 45.4), and turnout was 44.2 percent; the margin in the neighboring, and demographically similar, Sixth Congressional District was more than 28 percentage points (62.0 to 33.6), and turnout was 38.8 percent.[13] The degree of competition in these races is not the only factor that explains the different turnout levels. Even relatively slight demographic differences can influence the level of electoral participation in two districts. However, it is not unreasonable to conclude that the closeness of the race in the Seventh Congressional District explains much of its higher turnout rate.

There are two reasons that the closeness of a race leads to higher turnout. The first is that the media is likely to pay more attention to competitive races than to those that are not. This increased coverage, in turn, gives voters more information about the candidates and issues at stake in close races. The second and perhaps more significant reason that close races produce higher turnout is that close races are hotly contested by the political parties. As parties narrow the field of competitive races late in a campaign, they target resources to those races. This means an increase not only in campaign advertising but in mobilization efforts.

Parties mobilize voters by contacting them and urging them to participate. Steven Rosenstone and John Mark Hansen have shown that individuals are 7.8 percent more likely to vote in a presidential election if they have been contacted by a political party than if they have not been contacted and 10.4 percent more likely to do so in a midterm election.[14] People are also more likely to engage in other forms of participation, such as persuading others about how to vote, when a party contacts them. As Rosenstone and Hansen conclude, "Party mobilization is a powerful inducement to participation in electoral politics. By subsidizing information and by creating social connections, political campaigns lower the cost and increase the benefits of voting, persuading, volunteering, and contributing."[15]

Ultimately, aggregate-level turnout is higher in elections that can be classified as "high-stimulus." As Angus Campbell explained, "The essential difference between a low-stimulus and a high-stimulus election lies in the importance the electorate attaches to the choice between the various party-candidate alternatives which it is offered."[16] When an election is viewed as particularly salient—because the stakes are high or the choices are clear—more voters will go to the polls than when an election is thought to be unimportant.

▶ Explaining Individual Voter Turnout

Sociological Factors

Of course, many people will stay home on Election Day even in a high-stimulus election, just as some will go to the polls during a low-stimulus election. This section examines the individual-level explanations for why some people vote and others do not. Obviously, the factors that stimulate aggregate turnout also influence individuals, but they do not affect all people similarly. Thus, it is important to identify the individual characteristics of voters and nonvoters.

There are, essentially, two sets of factors that influence the likelihood that an individual will vote. The first set is what we might call sociological (or demographic) factors and include, among other things, income, education, age, race, and marital status. The second set of factors is psychological in nature: partisanship, interest in campaigns, and political efficacy are examples of psychological factors that influence voting.

The most significant of the sociological factors is education; the more years of schooling an individual has had, the more likely they are to vote. Specifically, those with some college education or with a college degree vote at higher than average levels. On the other end of the spectrum, those with less than a high school diploma are highly unlikely to vote. Finally, whereas high school graduates used to vote at higher than average levels, they have now become likely nonvoters.[17]

Education is thought to influence voting because it provides individuals with the capacity to navigate the cumbersome process of registering to vote, learning something about the candidates, locating one's polling place, and casting a ballot. To habitual voters, that process is not complicated, but to a first-time voter or to someone who votes only occasionally it is a daunting and perhaps confusing process that can be quite intimidating. Educated citizens are equipped with cognitive skills that reduce the confusion and stress of voting.[18]

Education is also likely to instill in individuals a commitment to the idea that voting is a civic duty. At virtually every level of their formal education, Americans are told that democracy requires active participation by citizens and that the most fundamental way to participate is voting. From mock elections in elementary school to discussions about campaigns in high-school civics classes, the message is sent—indirectly if not directly—that voting is an essential part of being a good citizen.

In the last half-century, education levels in the United States have increased dramatically. This has led to what Wattenberg calls an "education-turnout puzzle."[19] If education is strongly linked to voting and education levels have gone up significantly, why has there not been a corresponding rise in turnout levels? The answer is that the less-well-educated are voting at far lower rates than they had in the past. Table 8.4 lists the self-reported turnout for individuals at four different levels of education. Turnout among those with at least a college degree has remained virtually unchanged since 1952, and the rate for those with some college education has dropped by just more than 7 percentage points. However, among those with a high-school education or less, turnout has fallen by more than 13 percentage points. The gap between those with a college degree and those with no more than a high-school degree has grown from 13.2 percentage points in 1952 to 26 percentage points in 2004. Thus, though there may be fewer individuals with low levels of education today, they are voting at significantly lower rates than they were fifty years ago. Furthermore, though the better-educated have always voted at higher rates than the less-well-educated, the gap in turnout between the former and the latter has grown considerably.

Education is a key component of socioeconomic status (SES). Another major aspect of SES is income and, like education, it is significantly and positively related to voting. Quite simply, the wealthier an individual, the more likely they are to vote. However, in their classic study *Who Votes?* Raymond Wolfinger and Steven Rosenstone found that income had less of an impact on voting than we might expect. Once other variables, particularly education, are controlled for, the effect of income is reduced. "We conclude," Wolfinger and Rosenstone wrote, "that income affects turnout only to the point where a modestly comfortable

TABLE 8.4 *Turnout by Education Level, 1952 and 2004*

Education Level	1952	2004
College degree or more	93.3	92.8
Some college	86.6	79.5
High school diploma or less	80.1	66.8
Grade school or less (0–8 grades)	62.1	51.1

Source: American National Election Studies, Cumulative Datafile 1948–2004; SDA: Survey Documentation & Analysis, University of California, Berkeley, http://sda.berkeley.edu/cgi-bin32/hsda?harcsda+nes2004c (accessed May 25, 2013).

standard of living has been attained. Once this threshold has been reached, more money has no effect on the likelihood of voting."[20]

Another demographic factor that influences voting is age. The younger voters are, the less likely they are to vote. Though the eighteen-to-twenty-year-old category votes at the lowest levels of any age group, they occasionally vote at rates similar to twenty-one-to-twenty-four-year-olds. Thus, a significant threshold between higher and lower rates of voting is the age of twenty-five, with noticeable increases in turnout occurring at thirty-five and again at forty-five years of age. In virtually every election year, however, those fifty-five to sixty-four are the most likely age group to vote. Turnout drops only slightly, if at all, among those sixty-five years old and older.[21]

There are two prominent ways to explain the fact that people are more likely to vote as they get older. The first, according to Rosenstone and Hansen, is called the "life-cycle" hypothesis. It states that as people age, they become more deeply concerned with, and involved in, their communities, which leads to a greater likelihood of participating in a variety of ways. The "life-experience" hypothesis, conversely, argues that over time, people tend to "accumulate information, skills, and attachments that help them overcome the costs of political involvement."[22] The costs of participating in politics include the time and effort required to learn about candidates and issues and to understand the processes involved in voting and other forms of participation. Rosenstone and Hansen find more evidence for the "life-experience" hypothesis than for the "life-cycle" explanation.

Though gender probably does not directly influence a potential voter's likelihood to vote, there have been historical differences in turnout levels between the sexes. Prior to 1980, men voted at higher levels than women, a fact that probably extends back to 1920, when women were first given the right to vote (though we have data to confirm this only since 1964). In 1980, however, the percentage of women claiming to have voted surpassed the percentage of men who reported voting. In every election since then, women have voted at higher rates than men. In 2012, for instance, 63.7 percent of women claimed to have gone to the polls, whereas 59.8 percent of men did the same. That equates to almost 10 million more female than male voters nationally.[23]

Race and ethnicity are also variables that are often mentioned as relevant to voter participation. This is largely the result of a heightened awareness of the difficulties minorities faced in going to the polls prior to the civil rights movement. Indeed, turnout among African Americans lagged significantly behind White turnout in the 1960s because of the barriers Black voters faced in many places. Today, the gap has narrowed considerably. In fact, the Census Bureau found that in 2012, for the first time on record, the turnout rate among Blacks (66.2 percent) surpassed that of non-Hispanic Whites (64.1 percent).[24]

When Barack Obama hasn't been on the ballot, however, Whites have clearly voted at higher rates than non-Whites. One explanation for this disparity could be that minority groups are disproportionately of lower SES than

Whites. As we've already established, those who are better educated and have higher incomes vote at higher rates. Thus, because disproportionate numbers of non-Whites have lower levels of education and income, turnout rates are skewed when looking only at race.

Though this is undoubtedly true, a more complicated picture emerges when we control for education and income levels. As Table 8.5 indicates, at lower levels of income and education, Blacks voted at higher rates than Whites in 2004. It was at the higher levels of income and education that Whites outpaced Blacks. These results suggest that race interacts with non-demographic factors to influence one's likelihood to vote. For instance, perhaps GOTV efforts targeted at low-income, minority communities are relatively successful in mobilizing that group of voters (at least among Blacks). Conversely, because Blacks with higher SES won't be affected by such efforts, they are left to their own devices to get to the polls. If, in turn, they have lower levels of "social capital" in the communities

TABLE 8.5 *Self-Reported Turnout Rates, by Race (and Hispanic Origin), According to Education and Income Levels (2004)*

	White	Black	Asian	Hispanic
Education				
Less than 9th grade	37.4	38.5	12.5	11.9
9th–12th grade, no diploma	40.0	43.1	16.0	16.3
High-school graduate	57.2	52.4	29.5	27.8
Some college or associated degree	70.6	63.6	31.5	45.0
Bachelor's degree	78.5	68.7	33.0	48.1
Advanced degree	83.7	72.6	33.7	60.3
Income				
Less than $10,000	37.8	49.4	21.3	18.8
$10,000–$14,999	48.7	52.0	22.5	15.1
$15,000–$19,999	55.3	56.1	34.4	21.0
$20,000–$29,999	59.4	55.2	24.3	21.8
$30,000–$39,999	63.4	62.7	19.4	24.5
$40,000–$49,999	70.9	61.0	25.2	29.4
$50,000–$74,999	73.3	69.4	30.3	44.4
$75,000–$99,999	78.8	73.7	32.0	51.7
$100,000–$149,999	82.0	74.4	45.4	55.0
$150,000 and over	82.0	72.8	47.0	53.5

Source: US Census Bureau, "Voting and Registration in the Election of November 2004—Detailed Tables," Tables 6 and 9, http://www.census.gov/hhes/www/socdemo/voting/publications/p20/2004/tables.html (accessed May 26, 2013).

in which they live, their likelihood of voting would naturally lag behind those of their White neighbors, who can rely on greater levels of social connectedness.[25] This is all speculation, of course, and more research needs to be done to understand how race functions with respect to voter turnout.[26]

A number of additional variables are related to social connectedness and correlate highly with voting. For instance, married people vote at far higher rates than do single people, and homeowners tend to vote more than those who do not own homes. Furthermore, the longer one has lived in a given community, the more likely they are to vote, just as those who regularly attend religious services are more likely to vote than those who never attend (or even occasionally attend) religious services. Finally, union members are more likely to vote than nonunion members. The conclusion we can draw from each of these variables is that people with a connection to their community are far more likely to go to the polls than people with weak ties to their community.[27]

Psychological Factors

Recall that there are two sets of factors that explain individual-level turnout. The second includes psychological or attitudinal factors that make some people more likely to vote than others. Understanding these factors may seem like common sense, but it is important to identify them and the way they operate to influence individual voting patterns.

Interest in campaigns, and particularly interest in the outcome of a given election, is highly correlated with voting. In 2012, 89.7 percent of those who said they were "very much interested" in the campaign went to the polls, as did 76.8 percent of those who said they were "somewhat interested." Among those who said they were "not much interested," however, turnout was only 50.5 percent.[28] Thus, having an interest in an election is a fairly good indicator of whether a person is likely to vote in that election. Few of those who are uninterested in an election will cast ballots.

Partisanship is another indicator of the likelihood that someone will vote. As the authors of the classic text *The American Voter* put it, partisanship is a psychological attachment to a political party that is not reliant on "a formal membership or an active connection with a party apparatus." It can even exist "without a consistent record of party support" at the polls.[29] Party identification does, however, make one more likely to be politically engaged than someone without a party attachment.

In 2008, 86.3 percent of those who identified themselves as Democrats and 89.7 percent of Republicans claim to have gone to the polls.[30] In fact, the stronger one's partisanship, the more likely they were to vote. "Strong" Democrats and Republicans voted more than "weak" Democrats and Republicans, who in turn voted more than those who merely lean toward one of the two parties: that is, those who initially claimed to be Independents but when pressed admitted to being "closer" to the Democrats or Republicans. Conversely, fewer than half (45.3 percent) of "pure Independents"—or those who refused to say that they even lean toward one of the parties—claim to have voted.[31] The authors of *The American Voter* concluded, "Far from being more attentive, interested, and informed, Independents tend as a group to be somewhat less involved in politics."[32] Thus, identifying with one of the two major parties makes a person far more likely to vote than if they do not identify with a party.

A final psychological factor relevant to voting is political efficacy. There are, in fact, two types of efficacy: external and internal political efficacy. External political efficacy is "the extent to which citizens believe that their government is working the way it should."[33] People have high levels of external political efficacy if they believe that the government is responsive to the people. Internal political efficacy "refers to the degree to which individuals see themselves as capable of influencing the political process because of their own abilities and competence."[34] To the extent that people believe they understand politics well enough to participate and have the skills necessary to have an effect on the system, they display internal political efficacy. Having high levels of efficacy increases the probability of voting. Rosenstone and Hansen have shown that though both forms of efficacy influence the likelihood that a person will vote, external efficacy is a better predictor of voting than internal efficacy.[35]

One final explanation of voter participation—or, more precisely, of nonparticipation—draws from both sociological and psychological factors. When asked to give the reason they did not vote in a given election, registered voters most often claim to have been too busy to make it to the polls. In 2012, for example, 18.9 percent said they were too busy to vote or had a scheduling conflict. That compares to 15.7 percent who were simply not interested in the election; 14 percent who said they were sick, disabled, or kept away by a family emergency; and 12.7 percent who did not like the candidates.[36]

Interestingly, 25.5 percent of those twenty-five to forty-four years old claimed they were too busy to vote in 2012, as did more than 20.9 percent of those with at least some college education. Conversely, only 11.4 percent of those with less than a high school diploma claimed to be too busy; for them, illness, disability, or a family emergency was the prevailing excuse (25.5 percent of them offered one of these excuses).[37] Of course, individuals' claims that they were too busy to vote may be a rationalization. However, to the extent that it accurately explains behavior, this information could be valuable for reform efforts. Specifically, it suggests that treating Election Day as a national holiday would boost voter turnout.

▶ Vote Choice

Individuals who go to the polls on Election Day must decide which candidate will get their vote. For many, the choice is easy. They may, for instance, simply vote for the candidates of the party with which they identify, or they may have a clear preference for one candidate over another on the basis of character traits or issue positions. For others, this decision is a complicated one. They may find themselves "cross-pressured": That is, some factors will point in one direction (for example, party identification) though others point a different way (for example, candidates' positions on key issues).

This section of the chapter seeks to explain why people vote as they do. It first examines aggregate voting patterns. In doing so, it will describe the electoral preferences of various groups in society. (The factors that influence the outcome of elections will be covered in Chapter 10.) After the discussion of aggregate voting patterns, this section will identify the determinants of individuals' votes.

Aggregate Voting Patterns

Given the secretive nature of the ballot, the only way to explore people's voting behavior is to ask them how they voted in exit polls and other post-election surveys. Such polls and surveys provide quite a bit of data about which groups of voters tend to support which parties and candidates. For example, exit polls have consistently shown that voters who identify with a political party typically vote for the presidential nominee of that party. As Table 8.6 indicates, 89 percent of Democrats voted for Hillary Clinton in 2016, while 88 percent of Republicans voted for Donald Trump (and this in a year in which many voters were dissatisfied with their own party's nominee). Obviously, not all those with a party identification vote accordingly, but roughly nine in ten typically do, a fact we will revisit later when we discuss the influences on individual voting behavior.

This pattern of partisan loyalty should not obscure some less obvious deviations from it. For instance, William Flanigan and Nancy Zingale point out that voters who are weakly attached to their parties are more likely to "defect" from that party's nominee than those who have strong party identification.[38] Furthermore, with the exception of such years as 1964 and 1992, Democrats have historically defected from their presidential nominees at a greater rate than Republicans.[39] In congressional elections prior to 1994, however, Democrats defected at lower rates than Republicans. Since 1994, when the GOP took control of Congress for the first time in forty years, Democrats have defected slightly more than have Republicans.[40]

Voting patterns differ in congressional elections in other ways as well. The differences in party loyalty between weak and strong partisans, for instance, are usually less pronounced in congressional elections than in presidential elections, and the defection rate is more stable in the former than the latter.[41] Indeed, the defection rate can fluctuate rather dramatically in presidential elections and serves as a post hoc indicator of which party was disadvantaged in a given year: Democratic defections were numerous in 1972, for example, a year in which Richard Nixon won a landslide reelection contest.

TABLE 8.6 *Vote for Clinton and Trump by Demographic Group, 2016*

	Clinton	Trump
National Results	48.5	46.4
Democrat (36)	89	8
Independent (31)	42	46
Republican (33)	8	88
White (71)	37	57
Black (12)	89	8
Latino (11)	66	28
Asian (4)	65	27
Other (3)	56	36
Men (47)	41	52
Women (53)	55	41
18–24 years old (10)	56	34
25–29 years old (9)	54	38
30–39 years old (17)	51	39
40–49 years old (19)	46	49
50–64 years old (30)	44	52
65 and older (16)	45	52
Less than $30,000 (17)	53	40
$30–49,999 (19)	52	41
$50–99,999 (30)	46	49
$100–199,999 (24)	47	48
$200–249,999 (4)	49	47
$250,000 or more (6)	46	46
Less than $50,000 (36)	53	41
$50,000–100,000 (30)	46	49
More than $100,000 (34)	47	47
High School or less (18)	46	51
Some College (32)	43	51
College Degree (32)	49	44
Postgraduate Study (18)	58	37
Protestant (52)	39	56
Catholic (23)	46	50
Jewish (3)	71	23
Other (8)	62	29

None (15)	67	25
Urban area (34)	60	34
Suburban area (49)	45	49
Rural area (17)	34	61

Source: CNN, "Exit Polls—National President," http://www.cnn.com/election/results/exit-polls/national/president (accessed February 17, 2017).

Note: Numbers in parentheses are the percentage of all voters who are in each category. Shaded cell indicates the candidate with the advantage in that category.

Even a cursory glance at exit poll results will reveal a number of groups that overwhelming support one party or the other. Perhaps the most loyal group of voters are African Americans, roughly 90 percent of whom routinely support the Democratic presidential nominee. As one can see in Table 8.6, 89 percent of Black voters backed Clinton in 2016, while 57 percent of Whites voted for Trump. Latino voters typically vote Democratic but at a much lower rate than Black voters; 66 percent of Latino voters supported Clinton in 2016 (though some argue, based on different data, that such support was much higher).[42]

Women also tend to throw their support behind Democrats. According to the Center for American Women and Politics, in every election since 1980, there has been a "gender gap" in voting. A gender gap is defined as the "difference between the percentage of women and the percentage of men voting for a given candidate, generally the winning candidate." From 1980 to 2016, the gender gap was as small as 4 percentage points (1992) and as high as 11 percentage points (1996 and 2016), averaging 8.1 points. In four of the last six presidential elections, the gender gap was 10 points or more.[43]

It is often said that the Republican Party is the party of the wealthy and the Democratic Party the party of the poor and working classes. Though that is a gross oversimplification, exit poll results suggest that there is some truth to the stereotype. Among those earning less than $50,000 a year, 53 percent voted for Clinton in 2016. Conversely, 47 percent of those making more than $100,000 voted for her (which happened to be the same percentage that supported Trump, making 2016 an unusual year in this regard). A closer examination of the various income levels in Table 8.6 shows that the poorest group of voters, those making less than $30,000 a year, were the most Democratic, followed by those making $30,000 to $49,999. In the $50,000 to $99,999 category, in which fell the 2015 median household income ($55,775[44]), voters backed Trump, 49 percent to 46 percent. Typically, we would expect the Republican nominee to do much better among the top income groups. In 2016, however, Clinton did as well or better among these groups of voters.

As part of any measure of socioeconomic status, education can be expected to play an important role in voting behavior. That role, however, is peculiar. Typically, those with the lowest and the highest levels of education vote for

Democratic candidates. 2016, however, was not true to form. Trump won voters with less than a college degree while Clinton won among those with a college degree or a postgraduate education.

Various aspects of religion also distinguish Democratic voters from Republicans. According to data provided by the American National Election Studies (ANES), for example, a majority of Jewish voters supported the Democratic nominee in every election since 1948.[45] Exit poll results from 2016 suggest that 71 percent of Jewish voters backed Clinton.

Catholic voters were once thought to be a reliable part of the Democratic Party's New Deal coalition, but their support has not, in fact, been consistent. According to ANES data, 66 percent voted for Harry Truman in 1948, and a slim majority supported Democrat Adlai Stevenson in 1952. In 1956, however, a majority of Catholics voted to reelect President Eisenhower. They would vote for a Republican only one more time before 1980, and that was in 1972, when just more than 60 percent backed Richard Nixon. Most Catholics supported Ronald Reagan in 1980 and 1984 and a bare majority voted for Trump in 2016. In 2004, a majority of Catholics in the ANES survey said they voted for John Kerry, but exit poll results suggest that Bush won the Catholic vote.[46] Though at least a plurality of Catholics have voted Democratic in the rest of the recent presidential elections, Catholic support for Democrats can no longer be safely assumed (if indeed it ever could have been).

Though there is considerable variation between Protestant denominations, Protestants as a group have consistently backed Republicans through the years. ANES data indicate that since 1948, a majority of Protestants supported a Democratic presidential candidate only once, in 1964, though in 1992 and 1996, a plurality of Protestants voted for Bill Clinton.[47] In 2016, according to the exit polls, 56 percent of Protestants supported Donald Trump.

Of course, there are other aspects of religious belief and practice that may be relevant to voting. For instance, 26 percent of the electorate consisted of White born-again Christians in 2016; of those, 80 percent voted for Trump. Among those who attended religious services at least weekly, support for Trump was 55 percent; among those who worshiped monthly, 49 percent voted for Trump (compared to 47 percent for Clinton). However, Clinton received a plurality of the vote among Americans who said they attended religious services only a few times a year (48 percent) and a majority among those who never attend religious services (62 percent).[48]

There are a few other groups of voters for whom noticeable patterns of partisan support can be found. Union members, for instance, supported the Democratic presidential nominees in 2004, 2008, and 2012 at rates of or near 60 percent; in 2016, however, just 51 percent backed Clinton. Married voters backed the Republican candidate in the last four presidential elections, with 57, 52, 56, and 52 percent of the vote from 2004 to 2016, respectively. Urban voters tend to vote Democratic; in 2016, those living in big cities voted for Clinton over Trump by 60 percent to 34 percent. In suburbs, Trump garnered a plurality of the vote, though in rural areas he won handily. It should be noted that suburban voters are often treated as an important swing group, and they make up almost half of all voters. In 2008, Obama won this group with 50 percent of the vote to McCain's 48 percent. Finally, young voters have been supportive of Democratic candidates in recent years, though older voters are more likely to vote Republican. In 2016, Clinton got 55 percent of the vote from those eighteen to twenty-nine years old and 51 percent from those thirty to thirty-nine years old. Trump won among voters forty and older.[49]

Though the aforementioned demographic groups tend to support one party or the other in the aggregate, many people within those groups deviate from the norm. Furthermore, membership in the groups listed earlier (with the exception of party identification) does not consciously influence individual voting decisions. One does not vote for Democrats because she is Black or for Republicans because he attends church more than once a week. Demographic characteristics may indirectly affect how one makes a voting decision by structuring the way an individual perceives the political world; however, other factors determine the choices a person makes in the voting booth more directly. It is to the rather complicated process of reaching an individual voting decision that we now turn our attention.

► Individual Voting Behavior

The Role of Partisanship

Early models of voting behavior did, in fact, treat demographic characteristics as having a direct influence on the vote. This work is often called the "social determinism" or "sociological" school of voting behavior due to the heavy emphasis it placed on sociological factors. Because scholars at Columbia University conducted most of this research, it is also sometimes referred to as the "Columbia model."

In *The People's Choice*, the Columbia researchers argued, "A person thinks, politically, as he [sic] is, socially. Social characteristics determine political preference."[50] The authors found that three demographic variables could successfully predict most individuals' votes in the 1940 presidential election. Those variables, which the authors combined into an "Index of Political Predisposition," were SES, religious affiliation, and place of residence. Voters who were of high SES, were Protestant, and lived in rural areas were most likely to vote Republican, though those of low SES, Catholics, and urban-dwellers supported Democrats.[51]

What would happen, however, if a voter was a high SES Catholic? Such a voter, like the low SES Protestant, was "cross-pressured" according to the Columbia researchers. Cross-pressuring occurs when voters are pulled in different directions by their various social identities.[52] This typically results in voting decisions that are made late in the campaign. Some cross-pressured voters simply fail to resolve the conflict and do not vote. Others rely on those around them for guidance about how to vote.

In 1960, a competing model of voting behavior, often referred to as the social-psychological approach, appeared with the publication of *The American Voter*. The authors of that book were political scientists at the University of Michigan; hence their model was also dubbed the "Michigan model." This model "represented a shift in emphasis from explanation in sociological terms to the exploration of political attitudes that orient the individual voter's behavior in an immediate sense."[53] In particular, the Michigan model placed a great deal of emphasis on the influence of the party identification of the voter. The Columbia model, conversely, treated partisanship as virtually synonymous with, rather than an independent cause of, an individual's vote.

The Michigan model viewed the development of political attitudes, and ultimately the vote decision, as the product of a range of factors. Some of these were sociological, including SES and religion, though others were explicitly political, such as party identification and a personal reaction to events in the world. To explain how all of the factors interact with one another to produce a vote decision, the Michigan scholars used the metaphor of a funnel. The "funnel of causality," as they called it, suggested that (at the mouth of the funnel) many factors entered the process of forming political attitudes and that they influenced additional factors over time. As the process moved toward the vote decision (at the narrow end of the funnel), the number of factors that directly influenced a person's vote choice would have been reduced to only a few. As the authors put it, "Each cross section [of the funnel] contains all the elements that will successfully predict the next, and so on, until we have arrived at the final political act."[54]

In the Michigan model, sociological characteristics are significant for their effect on party identification. Though most people identified with the party of their parents, demographic factors were central in parental party identification. And where individuals deviated from their parents' party affiliations, sociological factors were particularly significant. However, once a person associated with a party, in whatever manner that association came about, their party identification became the most powerful predictor of the person's voting behavior. In addition, party identification was understood to be a stable, long-term psychological attachment.

Having said that, the Michigan scholars acknowledged that partisanship could not be the sole determinant of the vote. For instance, in 1952, Democrats held a three to two advantage over Republicans in party identification. And, yet, the Republicans' nominee for president, Dwight Eisenhower, handily won the election that year. Thus, other factors, most notably "evaluations of current political objects," must also influence people's votes.[55]

Today, students of voting behavior have come to believe that a person's vote is determined by some combination of three primary factors. The first is party identification, which is viewed (following *The American Voter*) as a long-term force that shapes both political attitudes and voting behavior. The remaining factors are short-term forces: One of these is the voter's own issue orientations or policy preferences; the other is the evaluation of candidates, particularly with respect to personal or character traits.[56] Each of these factors deserves a closer examination.

We have already established the strong link between party identification and the vote. Recall that in 2016, nearly 90 percent of exit poll respondents claimed to have voted for the presidential nominee of their party. Having said that, the number of people calling themselves a Democrat or Republican began to fall dramatically in the late 1960s. As Table 8.7 indicates, more than one-third of all survey respondents considered themselves Independents by 1972. The percentage of Independents bounced around in the 30s until 2000, when it reached 40.5 percent. That number reached its apex in 2012, at 43.8 percent. The number of people calling themselves Independents has grown so much in the last several decades that Independents made up a plurality of respondents in ten of the thirteen election years between 1988 and 2012.

TABLE 8.7 *Party Identification, 1952–2012 (with "Leaners" Included as Independents)*

Year	Strong/Weak Democrats (D)	Independents (and those leaning D or R)	Strong/Weak Republicans (R)
1952	47.1	22.5	27.2
1954	47.4	21.9	27.0
1956	43.6	23.4	29.1
1958	48.9	19.4	27.8
1960	45.3	22.9	29.4
1962	46.4	21.2	28.5
1964	51.7	22.8	24.6
1966	45.7	28.3	24.8
1968	45.4	29.0	24.1
1970	43.6	31.1	24.5
1972	40.4	34.7	23.5
1974	38.6	36.4	22.1
1976	39.7	36.1	23.3
1978	39.3	37.5	20.6
1980	40.8	34.6	22.5
1982	44.2	30.0	23.9
1984	37.0	34.2	27.1
1986	40.1	32.8	25.0
1988	35.1	35.7	27.6

1990	39.2	34.7	24.5
1992	35.5	38.2	25.2
1994	33.6	35.5	29.8
1996	37.8	34.7	26.4
1998	37.5	34.6	26.2
2000	34.4	40.5	23.9
2002	33.4	35.8	30.1
2004	32.0	38.8	28.9
2006	33.1	39.0	27.8
2008	36.0	38.4	25.7
2010	32.7	42.0	25.2
2012	31.8	43.8	24.4

Source: Figures for 1952–2004 from Survey Documentation & Analysis, University of California, Berkeley, "Cumulative American National Election Study, 1948–2004," http://sda.berkeley.edu/cgi-bin32/hsda?harcsda+nes2004c (accessed May 26, 2013). Figures for 2006–2012 from Pew Research Center, "2012 Values Survey—Topline Questionnaire," http://www.people-press.org/files/legacy-questionnaires/Values%20topline%20for%20release.pdf (accessed May 26, 2013).

Those looking for more evidence of a growing independence in the electorate would have found some in the rise of split-ticket voting that took place between the 1950s and the 1980s. Whereas 13 percent of voters cast ballots for candidates of different parties for president and the House of Representatives in 1952, 30 percent did so in 1972. Furthermore, at least one-fourth of voters split their tickets in every presidential election year between 1972 and 1988.[57] When combined with the rise in Independent voters, this fact seemed to suggest a weakening of party loyalties. That, in turn, could have meant that party identification was influencing voting behavior less than it once had.

However, many of today's self-proclaimed Independents actually feel an affinity toward one of the two major parties and, as some research has shown, actually vote in ways not unlike partisans.[58] Thus, to truly chart the growth in the number of Independents, it is useful to look at what might be called "pure Independents," or those who refuse to say that they lean toward one of the two major parties. In 1952, as Table 8.8 indicates, 5.8 percent of the respondents were pure Independents, a number that more than doubled (12.3 percent) by 1966. After reaching a high point of 14.7 percent in 1974, the number of pure Independents dropped to 9.1 percent in 1996 and reached a thirty-eight-year low of 7.9 percent in 2002.

It is true that the percentage of pure Independents has climbed to 1970s levels in recent years. However, split-ticket voting has declined since the 1980s and reached its lowest level (at 14 percent) since 1964 in 2012.[59]

We can conclude, therefore, that though many people like to think of themselves as Independents, most of them act like partisans. It is true that there are more

TABLE 8.8 *Party Identification, 1952–2012 (with Pure Independents)*

Year	Democrats	Pure Independents	Republicans
1952	56.8	5.8	34.3
1954	56.0	7.3	33.0
1956	49.9	8.8	37.5
1958	55.9	7.2	33.0
1960	51.6	9.8	36.1
1962	53.6	7.8	34.7
1964	61.0	7.8	30.3
1966	54.7	12.3	31.8
1968	55.2	10.5	32.8
1970	54.0	12.9	32.3
1972	51.5	13.1	33.9
1974	51.8	14.7	30.7
1976	51.5	14.6	33.0
1978	53.7	13.7	30.1
1980	52.2	12.9	32.7
1982	55.1	11.1	31.8
1984	47.9	11.0	39.5
1986	50.5	11.5	35.8
1988	46.9	10.6	40.8
1990	51.6	10.4	36.4
1992	49.8	11.6	37.5
1994	47.0	10.6	41.4
1996	51.8	9.1	38.1
1998	51.1	10.5	36.8
2000	49.8	12.3	36.8
2002	49.1	7.9	43.1
2004	49.5	9.7	40.6
2006	48.2	13.4	38.3
2008	51.2	12.6	36.3
2010	46.8	13.4	39.7
2012	47.6	13.6	39.4

Source: Figures for 1952–2004 from Survey Documentation & Analysis, University of California, Berkeley, "Cumulative American National Election Study, 1948–2004," http://sda.berkeley.edu/cgi-bin32/hsda?harcsda+nes2004c (accessed May 26, 2013). Figures for 2006–2012 from Pew Research Center, "2012 Values Survey—Topline Questionnaire," http://www.people-press.org/files/legacy-questionnaires/Values%20topline%20for%20release.pdf (accessed May 26, 2013).

pure Independents today than there have been since 1970s, but there is also less split-ticket voting than there has been since the 1960s. There is no doubt but that partisanship continues to be the key driver of voting behavior in the twenty-first century.

The Role of Issues

Though partisanship remains an essential variable in any explanation of voting behavior, scholars also recognize the importance of the short-term factors. Norman Luttbeg and Michael Gant note that a "revisionist perspective" on *The American Voter* emerged in the 1970s and placed far greater emphasis on the role of issues, both as influences on voters' choices and as determinants of one's party identification.[60] Though few issues seemed to clearly divide the American public in the 1950s (the time period of the original Michigan studies), highly controversial issues emerged in the 1960s, including civil rights and the war in Vietnam. Not surprisingly, as salient issues began to emerge, scholars found that voters placed more weight on policy considerations as they made voting decisions.

The theoretical foundations for this revisionist school are found in the work of Anthony Downs. In his classic book, *An Economic Theory of Democracy*, Downs argues that voters are rational actors who "are able and willing to employ a voting calculus by which they weigh each party's promises for future policy initiatives against the record of past performance, relative to their own needs, for maximization of utility."[61] The "rational choice" scholars who adopted Downs's perspective imagined voters and candidates arrayed on an ideological spectrum from left (or liberal) to right (or conservative). Voting, then, was conceived of in spatial terms. Individuals simply voted for the candidate nearest them on the spectrum.

There is considerable evidence for this "proximity" model of voting, but there is also empirical support for an alternate spatial model called "directional" voting. Here, voters cast their ballots for the candidate on their side of the spectrum but not necessarily the candidate closest to them on the spectrum. According to the directional model, voters are concerned with the policy direction of the country and seek candidates who will move policy in the direction they prefer. Of course, some combination of the two models is also possible.[62]

Spatial models of voting tend to treat voters as future-oriented but, as Downs had suggested, voters may consider not only parties' and candidates' claims about future policy activity but their prior records in office as well. That is, individuals can vote either prospectively or retrospectively. When voters do the former, they compare their own issue positions to "statements made by the parties or candidates about what they are going to do in the future." Conversely, retrospective voting occurs when voters examine "what the parties or candidates have done in the past."[63] Research has found that voters are more likely to vote retrospectively than prospectively, though some evidence suggests that this applies to incumbents more than challengers and that in open-seat races prospective voting predominates.[64]

When voters do take issues into consideration as they vote, there are a few policy areas on which they are likely to focus. The most obvious is the economy. There is a considerable body of research indicating that economic conditions have a significant influence on voting decisions. Voters may respond to the state of the national economy. When they cast ballots on the basis of the strength (or weakness) of the economy as a whole, it is called "sociotropic" voting. Of course, they may also vote on the basis of their own economic circumstances. This is typically referred to as "pocketbook" voting. At the aggregate level, national economic conditions have clearly been shown to have an impact on the incumbent party's share of the vote. At the individual level, both sociotropic and pocketbook voting have been found to influence voters.[65]

It is more difficult to demonstrate the impact of noneconomic issues on voting choices. Nevertheless, other issues may become salient to voters given the right conditions. For example, when foreign affairs are pressing and when candidates campaign on foreign policy, these issues become more accessible to the voters. If, however, there are no noticeable differences between the candidates on foreign policy, it is unlikely that voters will rely on it to make voting decisions. Yet, when circumstances are ripe—that is, when foreign affairs are accessible to voters and candidate differences are clear—foreign policy has been found to influence the vote.[66] Indeed, national security and foreign policy have been significant factors in each of the elections since the 9/11 terrorist attacks in 2001.

As Edward Carmines and James Stimson have pointed out, not all issues are the same. Some are what Carmines and Stimson call "hard" issues, whereas others are "easy." Hard issues are those that are complicated to understand and require some technical knowledge before a voter can come to judgment on them. They often entail debates over detailed means rather than broad goals or ends. Easy issues, conversely, are largely symbolic and stimulate arguments about ends rather than means. They typically provoke "gut reactions" instead of the sort of rational analysis in which voters would ideally be engaged. Social issues such as abortion, gay rights, and gun control tend to be easy issues. In addition to producing some of the most contentious politics in the United States, easy issues are also more likely than hard issues to trigger issue voting, according to Carmines and Stimson.[67] Thus, like economics and foreign policy, social issues can affect voting decisions.

Just as all issues are not the same, voters differ in significant ways. It is important to keep this in mind so as to avoid blanket statements about how voters behave. Some Americans are more informed about or more interested in politics, and their cognitive abilities vary as well. These factors influence the level of issue voting and the types of issues that voters consider. The key contribution of the revisionist school has been to point out that issues matter—or at least that some issues matter to some voters in some circumstances.

If issues affect the way people vote, they might also influence party identification. At some point in their lives, people consciously decide whether to affiliate with a given party. In addition, they are likely to periodically reevaluate that affiliation. Thus, partisanship can be viewed as a "running tally of retrospective evaluations."[68] This suggests at least the possibility that short-term partisan change is possible. Indeed, aggregate party identification has shifted over time (see Table 8.7 and Table 8.8), and some research has shown partisanship to be relatively erratic even at the individual level.[69] Thus, though party identification remains an essential element of voting behavior, it is no longer viewed as the long-term, stable, and unrivaled determinant of the vote that *The American Voter* suggested it was.

The Role of Candidate Evaluations

To be fair, the Michigan model did recognize the impact on voting decisions of something other than partisanship. In particular, candidate evaluations were thought to influence the voters of the 1950s. Recall that Democratic voters outnumbered Republicans by three to two in the 1952 presidential election, yet Eisenhower, a Republican, garnered more than 55 percent of the vote. The authors of *The American Voter* concluded that voters' judgments about candidate characteristics accounted for most of the divergence.

It has thus been long established that voters include candidate traits in their voting calculus. A number of characteristics have been found to influence vote choice, including competence, leadership, integrity (or trustworthiness), and empathy.[70] Though these characteristics may exhibit an independent effect, there is also a partisan element to trait assessment. Many voters are likely to perceive candidate traits through the filter of their own party identification. That is, Republicans will see Republican candidates as stronger leaders and as being more competent, trustworthy, and empathetic than Democratic candidates, and vice versa. Furthermore, even those who are not particularly partisan may assign traits to candidates on the basis of party stereotypes. Republican candidates are often perceived to be stronger leaders, and Democrats are generally viewed as more empathetic.[71]

Though competence, leadership, integrity, and empathy are valuable—even essential—qualities for elected officials to possess, superficial characteristics such as appearance also have an impact on the vote.[72] Given the subjective nature of trait assessment, it is difficult to identify all the candidate characteristics that influence voters. Ultimately, however, voters may be most affected by a candidate's "likeability."[73] In popular political analysis, likeability is measured by the question (sometimes actually posed in public opinion polls), "Which candidate would you rather have a beer (or coffee) with?" Whether that person is also the best man or woman for the job is a separate matter.

Finally, it has to be acknowledged that many voters choose many candidates on the basis of very little information. People are unlikely to vote for a candidate about whom they know nothing. Thus, when voters have no information about a candidate, they are likely to abstain. However, if a voter knows something about a candidate, even if it is just a name they recognize, the voter is likely to be positively inclined toward that candidate. This is part of the reason why incumbents have such an advantage in congressional elections (as will be explained in more detail in Chapter 10). Incumbents are known; challengers, for the most part, are not. Of course, with the exception of nonpartisan races, the most valuable piece of information remains the candidates' party affiliations. If a voter knows nothing more than the party of a given candidate, they know enough to make a choice.

► *Normative Considerations*

Voter turnout and voting behavior raise a number of normative issues that strike at the heart of democracy. Is low voter turnout a problem? Are voters irrational? This section addresses the debate over those questions. It does not provide definitive answers but simply offers a variety of perspectives on the questions.

Is Low Turnout a Problem?

It is a widely held assumption that citizens should vote. Evidence of this assumption is abundant. Schoolchildren are taught from the earliest ages that voting is a civic duty, and countless nonpartisan voter registration and mobilization organizations, particularly focused on young people and minorities, exist in the United States. So widespread is the belief that citizens ought to vote that these organizations rarely make an argument for the proposition.

The corollary of this assumption is that failing to vote is bad and that low voter turnout is a problem for democracy. Again, an explanation for why this might be the case is rarely offered. Nevertheless, there are a number of arguments that can be made. One is that citizens have an ethical obligation to vote. If at least some people must vote to sustain democracy, all voters have a responsibility to participate. Otherwise, nonvoters are "free-riding" or enjoying the benefits of democracy without having to endure the costs. This is essentially a sophisticated version of the civic duty assertion made in classrooms across the nation.

Another argument is that low voter turnout weakens the civic bonds that are necessary in a democracy. Voting may, of course, be more a consequence of such bonds than a cause of them, but Robert Putnam, citing recent research, concludes "that the act of voting itself encourages volunteering and other forms of good citizenship."[74] Low turnout is also said to be symbolically problematic. When a country such as the United States promotes democracy around the world, it is more than a bit embarrassing—and perhaps is even hypocritical—to have some of the lowest rates of participation in the most basic act of democratic citizenship.

However, the most often cited reason that low turnout is a problem is that it leads to an unrepresentative electorate. We know, for example, that the voting population has a higher proportion of older, White, wealthy, and well-educated individuals than the voting eligible population. To the extent that the political attitudes and preferences of voters and nonvoters also differ, elected officials will be representative of voters rather than entire constituencies. And if elected officials are more responsive to voters than to nonvoters, as seems reasonable to assume, public policy will be biased in favor of the interests of older, White, wealthy, and well-educated individuals.

Whether election outcomes, not to mention public policy, would differ if everyone voted is a matter of some dispute. Most political scientists who have studied the question conclude that full turnout would have no effect on elections because the policy preferences of voters and nonvoters do not, in fact, differ. However, Wattenberg provides evidence to the contrary. On a number of issues, the percentage of nonvoters supporting or opposing specific policies differs significantly from voters. On health care, for instance, a plurality of voters (45 percent) supports private insurance plans, whereas a plurality of registered nonvoters (41 percent) and a near majority of nonregistered individuals (49 percent) favor a government plan.[75] Wattenberg also shows partisan differences between voters and nonvoters. For example, in the Republican landslide election of 1994, voters identified themselves as Republican (49 percent) far more than registered nonvoters (35 percent) did.[76]

Do candidate preferences differ between voters and nonvoters? This is far more difficult to demonstrate. Some argue that if today's nonvoters began going to the polls, their vote choices would mirror those of current voters. This is because nonvoters have little political information and would be susceptible to bandwagon effects, meaning they might easily be swayed by whichever campaign was doing well (if not by the polls themselves).

Indeed, this raises the primary argument of those who see no particular problem with low voter turnout. The people who currently do not vote have little interest in, or knowledge about, politics. If they were to vote, they could be expected to make wholly uninformed decisions. In addition, they would be quite vulnerable to appeals by demagogues. In the best-case scenario, then, their presence at the polls would have no effect, but an influx of uninformed individuals into the voting booths could also be dangerous. And though those who would like to increase turnout would also provide for better voter education programs, it seems unlikely that individuals without an interest in politics would take advantage of such programs. Thus, some view low turnout as not only unproblematic but as potentially beneficial for democracy.

In a related argument, some claim that low turnout is a sign of a well-functioning government, if not a healthy democracy. Advocates of this perspective point out that turnout typically goes up when there is discontent within the electorate. Low turnout, therefore, must be an indication of a satisfied citizenry.

Though not a defense of low turnout, others would point out that citizens are every bit as free to abstain from voting as they are to exercise their right to vote. Contrary to what we are often told, this perspective maintains that there is no obligation to vote and that adults can decide for themselves whether they should vote. Low turnout, in other words, is not good or bad; it simply reflects the choices made by free individuals.

Besides, many believe it is irrational to vote in the first place. A single vote has rarely, if ever, decided the outcome of an election. This is particularly true in high-profile races such as a presidential election. Even in the razor-thin 2000 election in Florida, George Bush beat Al Gore by 537 votes. If one nonvoter had decided instead to show up at the polls, the outcome would have been precisely the same regardless of how they would have voted. Thus, if voters think that by going to the polls they are helping their candidate win, they are naïve. As evidence of the irrationality of voting, turnout is highest in those elections (i.e. presidential) in which voters are least likely to affect the outcome and lowest in those (i.e. local races) in which the odds of having an effect are greatest.

As an aside, it should be noted that the rationality of voting has been ingeniously defended. Political scientists John Ferejohn and Morris Fiorina have argued that voters go to the polls using the "minimax regret" principle. Rather than seek to maximize their expected utility (that is, to help elect their preferred candidate), a rational voter would seek to minimize their maximum regret. That would occur if their preferred candidate were to lose by one vote while they failed to vote. Thus, though voting may not be able to secure one's ideal outcome, it completely eliminates the voter's worst-case scenario.[77]

One can certainly question whether minimax regret really motivates people to vote. There are, however, multiple reasons for voting. People vote out of a sense of duty or patriotism or because those with whom they associate are likely to vote or because they enjoy the social aspects of going to their polling places and seeing neighbors. These may not be strictly rational reasons, but they are good enough to get many, many people to the polls on Election Day.

Can We Trust the Voters?

The rationality—or lack thereof—of voting raises another normative issue: just how reliable are the decisions made by voters? Assuming they are rational in going to the polls, are voters rational in the voting booth? Traditionally, many political scientists have felt that issue-based voting was the ideal. Voters should arrive at their own positions on issues, should learn the candidates' positions, and then vote for the candidate with whom they agree the most. When *The American Voter* found that voters relied heavily on their partisan attachments or, failing that, on candidate characteristics, some concluded that the electorate was behaving irresponsibly.

This view is still widely held today. In a recent book entitled *The Myth of the Rational Voter*, economist Bryan Caplan declares that voters are "worse than ignorant; they are, in a word, irrational—and vote accordingly." Furthermore, when rational politicians seek irrational voters' approval, "it is a recipe for mendacity."[78] For Caplan, much of the problem stems from the fact that voters have little information, particularly about the economy, and that their policy preferences differ from experts, who know much more and, it is assumed, are likely to make better policy judgments. For example, though economists believe free trade is a better economic policy than protectionism, the public is stubbornly protectionist.[79]

Whether the opinions of experts are worthy of deference is a matter of some debate. At least in some contexts, expert judgment has been shown to be unreliable.[80] And the "wisdom of crowds" has recently been lauded.[81] However, the fact that voters have so little information about politics and policy does give one pause. In 1995, the Program on International Policy Attitudes at the University of Maryland conducted a poll of American attitudes about foreign aid. Nearly two-thirds (64 percent) of the respondents favored reducing the amount spent on foreign aid. When asked what percentage of the US budget was allocated for this purpose, the median response was 15 percent; when asked what percentage should be spent, the median response was 5 percent.[82] In actuality, US foreign aid spending at the time was less than 1 percent of the federal budget, an amount only 18 percent said was too much. So what are we to conclude about the public's position on foreign aid? Does the public really want to cut foreign aid or, as they appear comfortable with spending 5 percent of the budget on aid, do they actually support spending five times more than we currently spend? Clearly, part of the public's opposition to foreign aid is based on inaccurate information.

A lack of specific information, however, does not necessarily mean that voters' judgments are irrational. The public's desire to reduce foreign aid is based, at least in part, on a certain set of values, as is their support for protectionist measures. Values, in turn, have more to do with ends than with means. Though voters may not be good at grasping the details of public policy, their collective judgment about ends have been shown to be stable, coherent, and ultimately rational.[83]

A large body of research has also demonstrated that people are capable of making rational decisions without storing the information upon which those decisions were made. In *The Reasoning Voter*, Samuel Popkin argues that voters engage in "low-information rationality." That is, "voters use shortcuts to obtain and evaluate information," which means "they are able to store far more data about politics than measurements of their textbook knowledge would suggest."[84] This view is in keeping with conclusions from psychology that people are "cognitive misers" who try to make the best (or most accurate) decisions they can make with the least amount of cognitive effort.[85] Specifically, voters have been shown to engage in "online" (or "impression-driven") information processing rather than "memory-based processing."[86] In online processing, a voter keeps a running tally of judgments about politicians and parties but discards specific bits of information once the tally has been updated. Memory-based information processing requires voters to access specific pieces of information to make a judgment at any point in time. By processing information online, voters are able to arrive at rational decisions even if they cannot justify those decisions later.

It could also be argued that any irrationality found on the part of voters is caused in large measure by the behavior of other political actors. In *An Economic Theory of Democracy*, for example, Downs had argued that it is rational for parties and candidates to be ambiguous about issue positions so as to alienate as few voters as possible (see Chapter 9 for more on "strategic ambiguity").[87] In addition, as was discussed in Chapter 7, the media are obsessed with the game schema and, in particular, the horserace. Thus, if voters rely disproportionately on candidates' personal traits or on partisanship, it may only be because candidates and the media have given them little else to use.

The legendary political scientist V. O. Key claimed that "voters are not fools."[88] There is no denying, however, that they possess very little information about politics. Given this, how good are the decisions they make on Election Day? The answer to this question will determine just how much faith we can have in democracy. Perhaps it helps to keep in mind that elections are blunt instruments for influencing public policy and that voters are called upon to determine the direction of policy, not the details of it. Surely they are capable of doing that.

▶ Conclusion

In many ways, voters are the central actors in the election drama. It is they, after all, who decide who will control the reins of government. This chapter explores the two most important (and obvious) aspects of voters' behavior, namely voter turnout and vote choice.

Voter turnout can be examined at the aggregate and individual levels. At the aggregate level, turnout in the United States lags far behind turnout in most other industrialized democracies. There are several reasons for this poor showing, including the electoral system in use in the United States and the fact that voters are asked to go to the polls with extreme frequency. Aggregate turnout also varies between the states. In general, the more competitive elections are between the two major parties, the higher turnout will be in a state. Finally, turnout can be traced over time. Though many assume that turnout has declined in recent years, it has not declined noticeably since 1972, the first election following ratification of the Twenty-sixth Amendment, which lowered the voting age to 18. In fact, turnout in several recent presidential elections has been as high as turnout in some pre-1972 races.

A number of factors have been found to affect individuals' propensity to vote. Some of these, like income, age, race and marital status, are sociological (or demographic) factors. The most significant of these factors is education level. The higher the education level, the more likely someone is to vote. There are also psychological factors that influence the likelihood of voting. These include interest in campaigns, political efficacy and, most importantly, strength of partisanship.

Once they've decided to go to the polls, voters need to decide how to cast their ballots. More than any other factor, a person's partisanship determines how they will vote. In a typical presidential election, around 90 percent of Democrats will vote for the Democratic nominee and 90 percent of Republicans will vote for the Republican candidate. Party identification is a powerful psychological attachment, which is part of many citizens' self-identity. It acts as a perceptual screen through which voters see the world. As a result, they are quite likely to view their own party's candidate positively and the candidate of the other party negatively.

But not everyone votes for their party's candidates in every election. Even at the presidential level, roughly one in ten voters will "defect" and vote for the other party's nominee. What causes them to do so? Often, it's the candidates' positions on key issues or their (or their party's) performance in certain policy areas that make the difference. The state of the economy is certainly the most important issue or policy area to most voters. When the state of the economy is strong, some voters will vote for the incumbent (or the incumbent party) regardless of party; when it's weak, voters may gravitate to the challenger even if they are of the other party. Other issues can matter depending on circumstances (e.g., national security in a time of high external threat) and on individual voters' interests.

Finally, candidate characteristics and traits can matter. As noted, most partisans will find the candidates of their own party more attractive than the other party's candidates on an array of characteristics. However, when differences between the candidates on a particular trait (e.g., trustworthiness) are stark, and when the candidate of one's own party is inferior on that trait, voters may be open to crossing party lines.

Normative questions about voting abound. Does low voter turnout matter? Presumably, if voter turnout sank to very low levels, everyone would recognize it as a problem. But how low is too low? Some argue that low turnout is likely to mean certain kinds of voters have been discouraged from going to the polls and that, in turn, means the election results will not represent the entire citizenry.

There are those who wonder how much faith we should have in voters in the first place. Some voters can appear fickle and many voters are not particularly well informed. Of course, voters use cues, like party affiliation, to make judgments, but whether the use of such cues is rational is a matter of debate. Ultimately, democracy requires "the people" to determine the direction of the country. If we can't trust voters to make sound decisions, democracy itself might be infeasible.

▶ *Pedagogical Tools*

Role-Play Scenario

Your town is holding an election with only one item on the ballot—a referendum to decide whether the town will sell bonds to pay for renovations to the local high school. Even though the issue has been contentious, you haven't been following the debate that closely. However, you do have a child who will be entering high school just as the proposed renovations are done. The election is tomorrow, and you have an important meeting at work in the morning. Will you vote?

Discussion Questions

1. How problematic is low voter turnout in the United States? Explain your answer.
2. Is it rational to vote? Justify your position.
3. Can voters be trusted to make sound decisions in the voting booth? Explain your answer.
4. Is there anything wrong with voting a straight ticket, that is, voting for candidates of only one party? Explain your answer.

Online Resources

American National Election Study Data, Survey Documentation and Analysis Data Archive, University of California, Berkeley (includes "Cumulative American National Election Study, 1948–2004"), http://sda.berkeley.edu/archive.htm.

Professor Michael McDonald's United States Election Project, Voter Turnout Web Page, www.electproject.org.

Project Vote Smart, www.votesmart.org.

Suggested Reading

Michael S. Lewis-Beck, William G. Jacoby, Helmut Norpoth, and Herbert F. Weisberg (2008) *The American Voter Revisited*, Ann Arbor, MI: University of Michigan Press.

Samuel L. Popkin (1991) *The Reasoning Voter: Communication and Persuasion in Presidential Campaigns*, Chicago:, IL University of Chicago Press.

Meredith Rolfe (2012) *Voter Turnout: A Social Theory of Political Participation*, Cambridge: Cambridge University Press.

Paul M. Sniderman and Edward H. Stiglitz (2012) *The Reputational Premium: A Theory of Party Identification and Policy Reasoning*, Princeton, NJ: Princeton University Press.

Martin P. Wattenberg (2015) *Is Voting for Young People?* 4th edn, London and New York: Routledge.

▶ *Notes*

1 Drew Desilver (2016) "US Voter Turnout Trails Most Developed Countries," Pew Research Center, August 2, www.pewresearch.org/fact-tank/2016/08/02/u-s-voter-turnout-trails-most-developed-countries (accessed February 7, 2017). Note: Figures for the United States and Australia were updated by the author.

2 Pippa Norris (2004) *Electoral Engineering: Voting Rules and Political Behavior*, Cambridge: Cambridge University Press, p. 157.

3 Mark N. Franklin (2002) "The Dynamics of Electoral Participation," in Lawrence LeDuc, Richard G. Niemi, and Pippa Norris (eds.), *Comparing Democracies 2: New Challenges in the*

Study of Elections and Voting, Thousand Oaks, CA: Sage Publications, p. 159; and Richard S. Katz (1997) *Democracy and Elections*, Oxford: Oxford University Press, pp. 241–243.

4 Turnout differentials calculated for author by Anne Hazlett. Data from Michael P. McDonald (n.d.) "Turnout 1980–2012.xls," http://elections.gmu.edu/Turnout 1980–2012.xls (accessed May 24, 2013).

5 Daniel J. Elazar (1966) *American Federalism: A View from the States*, New York: Thomas Y. Crowell.

6 Martin P. Wattenberg (2002) *Where Have All the Voters Gone?* Cambridge, MA: Harvard University Press, Table 2.1, p. 39.

7 Voter turnout figures from 1980 to 2012 are from McDonald, "Turnout 1980–2012.xls" and "2016 November General Election Turnout Rates."

8 Michael P. McDonald and Samuel L. Popkin (2001) "The Myth of the Vanishing Voter," *American Political Science Review*, p. 95.

9 McDonald, "Turnout 1980–2012.xls."

10 Turnout rates used for the calculation of averages for can be found in Harold W. Stanley and Richard G. Niemi (eds.) (2011) "Table 1.1, Voter Turnout Rates: United States, South, and Non-South, 1789–2010 (percent)," *Vital Statistics on American Politics, 2011–2012*, Online Edition. Washington, DC: CQ Press, http://library.cqpress.com/vsap/vsap11_tab1-1 (accessed May 25, 2013); and Michael McDonald, "Voter Turnout," United States Election Project, www.electproject.org/home/voter-turnout/voter-turnout-data (accessed February 12, 2017).

11 Wattenberg, *Where Have All the Voters Gone?* p. 144.

12 Wattenberg, *Where Have All the Voters Gone?* Table 6.3, p. 132.

13 Author's calculations using VAP figures from the Public Mapping Project (n.d.) "Michigan 2010 Census Selected Statistics," www.publicmapping.org/resources/state-resources/michigan/michigan-2010-census-statistics (accessed January 31, 2017).

14 Steven J. Rosenstone and John Mark Hansen (2003) *Mobilization, Participation, and Democracy in America*, New York: Longman, Tables 5.1 and 5.2, p. 130 and 132.

15 Rosenstone and Hansen (2003) *Mobilization*, p. 177.

16 Angus Campbell, Philip E. Converse, Warren E. Miller, and Donald E. Stokes (1966) *Elections and the Political Order*, New York: John Wiley & Sons, p. 41.

17 Wattenberg, *Where Have All the Voters Gone?* Table 3.3, p. 69.

18 Raymond E. Wolfinger and Steven J. Rosenstone (1980) *Who Votes? New Haven*, CT: Yale University Press, pp. 35–36.

19 Wattenberg, *Where Have All the Voters Gone?* pp. 74–80.

20 Wolfinger and Rosenstone, *Who Votes?* p. 25.

21 Martin P. Wattenberg (2007) *Is Voting for Young People?* New York: Pearson Longman, Table 4.1, p. 99.

22 Rosenstone and Hansen, *Mobilization*, p. 137.

23 Center for American Women and Politics (2011) "Gender Differences in Voter Turnout," www.cawp.rutgers.edu/sites/default/files/resources/genderdiff.pdf (accessed February 17, 2017).

24 US Department of Commerce; US Census Bureau (2013) "The Diversifying Electorate—Voting Rates by Race and Hispanic Origin in 2012 (and Other Recent Elections)," Figure 1, www.census.gov/prod/2013pubs/p20-568.pdf (accessed January 31, 2017).

25 For a critique of this social capital explanation, see Rodney E. Hero (2003) "Social Capital and Racial Inequality in America," *Perspectives on Politics*, 1: 113–122.

26 But see Jan E. Leighly and Arnold Vedlitz (1999) "Race, Ethnicity, and Political Participation: Competing Models and Contrasting Explanations," *Journal of Politics*, 61: 1092–1114.

27 Wattenberg, *Where Have All the Voters Gone?*, p. 69, Table 3.3; and Rosenstone and Hansen, *Mobilization*, pp. 130–131, Table 5.1.

28 Data provided on the Survey Documentation and Analysis website of the University of California, Berkeley, http://sda.berkeley.edu/sdaweb/analysis/?dataset=nes2012 (accessed February 17, 2017).

29 Angus Campbell, Philip E. Converse, Warren E. Miller, and Donald E. Stokes (1960) *The American Voter*, New York: John Wiley & Sons, p. 121.

30 Data provided on the Survey Documentation and Analysis website of the University of California, Berkeley, http://sda.berkeley.edu/cgi-bin/hsda?harcsda+nes08new (accessed January 31, 2017). Variables used were v085036a (whether or not R voted) and v083097 (party identification).

31 Data provided on the Survey Documentation and Analysis website of the University of California, Berkeley. Strength of party-identification variable is v083098a; the variable for those who are closer to one of the parties, or are "pure Independents," is v083098b.

32 Campbell et al., *The American Voter*, p. 143.

33 William H. Flanigan and Nancy H. Zingale (2006) *Political Behavior of the American Electorate*, 11th edn, Washington, DC: CQ Press, p. 22.

34 Flanigan and Zingale, *Political Behavior of the American Electorate*.

35 Rosenstone and Hansen, *Mobilization*, pp. 130 and 141–145, Table 5.1.

36 US Department of Commerce; US Census Bureau (n.d.) "Voting and Registration in the Election of November 2012–Detailed Tables," Table 10, www.census.gov/hhes/www/socdemo/voting/publications/p20/2012/tables.html (accessed May 26, 2013).

37 US Census Bureau, "Voting and Registration in the Election of November 2012."

38 Flanigan and Zingale, *Political Behavior of the American Electorate*, p. 81.

39 Flanigan and Zingale, *Political Behavior of the American Electorate*, p. 83.

40 Flanigan and Zingale, *Political Behavior of the American Electorate*, p. 85.

41 Flanigan and Zingale, *Political Behavior of the American Electorate*, p. 83.

42 See Gabriel Sanchez and Matt A. Barreto (2016) "In Record Numbers, Latinos Voted Overwhelmingly Against Trump. We Did the Research," Monkey Cage, *Washington Post*, November 11, www.washingtonpost.com/news/monkey-cage/wp/2016/11/11/in-record-numbers-latinos-voted-overwhelmingly-against-trump-we-did-the-research/?utm_term=.634df5e24d6b (accessed February 17, 2017). However, see also Harry Enten (2016) "Trump Probably Did Better With Latino Voters Than Romney Did," FiveThirtyEight.com, November 18, https://fivethirtyeight.com/features/trump-probably-did-better-with-latino-voters-than-romney-did (accessed February 17, 2017).

43 Center for American Women and Politics (2017) "The Gender Gap: Voting Choices in Presidential Elections," Eagleton Institute of Politics, Rutgers University, www.cawp.rutgers.edu/sites/default/files/resources/ggpresvote.pdf (accessed February 17, 2017).

44 US Department of Commerce; US Census Bureau (2016) "Household Income: 2015," www.census.gov/content/dam/Census/library/publications/2016/demo/acsbr15-02.pdf (accessed February 17, 2017).

45 Data for 1948–2004 available at the Survey Documentation and Analysis website of the University of California, Berkeley, http://sda.berkeley.edu/cgi-bin/hsda?harcsda+nes2004c; 2008 data at http://sda.berkeley.edu/cgi-bin/hsda?harcsda+nes08new (accessed January 31, 2017).

46 ANES data from 1948 to 2004 at the Survey Documentation and Analysis website of the University of California, Berkeley, http://sda.berkeley.edu/cgi-bin/hsda?harcsda+nes2004c (accessed January 31, 2017). Two thousand and four exit-poll results from "America Votes 2004–Election Results: US President/National/Exit Poll," CNN.com, www.cnn.com/ELECTION/2004/pages/results/states/US/P/00/epolls.0.html (accessed January 31, 2017).

47 See n.46 for source for ANES results.

48 Twenty sixteen exit-poll results that are not shown in Table 8.6 can be found at CNN, "Exit Polls—National President," www.cnn.com/election/results/exit-polls/national/president (accessed February 17, 2017).

49 CNN, "Exit Polls—National President." Previous years' exit polls can be found by searching the Internet for "presidential exit polls [year]."

50 Paul Lazarsfeld, Bernard Berelson, and Hazel Gaudet (1968) *The People's Choice: How the Voter Makes Up His Mind in a Presidential Campaign*, 3rd edn, New York: Columbia University Press, p. 27.

51 Lazarsfeld et al., *The People's Choice*, pp. 16–27. See also Bernard R. Berelson, Paul F. Lazarsfeld, and William N. McPhee (1954) *Voting: A Study of Opinion Formation in a Presidential Campaign*, Chicago, IL: University of Chicago Press.

52 Lazarsfeld et al., *The People's Choice*, p. 53.

53 Campbell et al., *The American Voter*, p. 16.

54 Campbell et al., *The American Voter*, p. 16.

55 Campbell et al., *The American Voter*, p. 529.

56 Norman R. Luttbeg and Michael M. Gant (1995) *American Electoral Behavior, 1952–1992*, 2nd edn, Itasca, IL: F. E. Peacock Publishers, p. 15.

57 Harold W. Stanley and Richard G. Niemi (eds.) (2015) "Table 3.10, Split-Ticket Voting, 1952–2012 (percent)," *Vital Statistics on American Politics, 2015–2016*, Washington, DC: CQ Press.

58 See Bruce Keith, David B. Magleby, Candice J. Nelson, Elizabeth Orr, Mark C. Westlye, and Raymond E. Wolfinger (1992) *The Myth of the Independent Voter*, Berkeley, CA: University of California Press; and David B. Magleby, Candice J. Nelson, and Mark C. Westlye (2011) "The Myth of the Independent Voter Revisited," in Paul M. Sniderman and Benjamin Highton (eds.), *Facing the Challenge of Democracy: Explorations in the Analysis of Public Opinion and Political Participation*, Princeton, NJ: Princeton University Press, pp. 238–263.

59 Stanley and Niemi, "Table 3.10."

60 Luttbeg and Gant, *American Electoral Behavior, 1952–1992*, pp. 24–27 and 35–38.

61 Jack Dennis (1991) "The Study of Electoral Behavior," in William Crotty (ed.), *Political Science: Looking to the Future, Volume Three: Political Behavior*, Evanston, IL: Northwestern University Press, p. 62. See also Anthony Downs (1957) *An Economic Theory of Democracy*, New York: Harper & Row.

62 See Samuel Merrill III and Bernard Grofman (1999) *A Unified Theory of Voting: Directional and Proximity Spatial Models*, Cambridge: Cambridge University Press.

63 Luttbeg and Gant, *American Electoral Behavior, 1952–1992*, p. 37.

64 Richard G. Niemi and Herbert F. Weisberg (eds.) (1993) *Controversies in Voting Behavior*, 3rd edn, Washington, DC: CQ Press, p. 140.

65 Gregory B. Markus (1988) "The Impact of Personal and National Economic Conditions on the Presidential Vote: A Pooled Cross-Sectional Analysis," *American Journal of Political Science*, 32: 137–154; and Gregory B. Markus (1992) "The Impact of Personal and National Economic Conditions on Presidential Voting, 1956–1988," *American Journal of Political Science*, 36: 829–834.

66 John H. Aldrich, John L. Sullivan, and Eugene Borgida (1989) "Foreign Affairs and Issue Voting: Do Presidential Candidates 'Waltz before a Blind Audience'?" *American Political Science Review*, 83: 123–141.

67 Edward G. Carmines and James A. Stimson (1980) "The Two Faces of Issue Voting," *American Political Science Review*, 74: 78–91.

68 Morris P. Fiorina (1993) "Explorations of a Political Theory of Party Identification," in Richard G. Niemi and Herbert F. Weisberg (eds.), *Classics in Voting Behavior*, Washington, DC: CQ Press, p. 255.

69 Niemi and Weisberg, *Controversies in Voting Behavior*, pp. 268–272.

70 Niemi and Weisberg, *Controversies in Voting Behavior*, pp. 142–146.

71 Danny Hayes (2005) "Candidate Qualities through a Partisan Lens: A Theory of Trait Ownership," *American Journal of Political Science*, 49: 908–923.

72 Shawn W. Rosenberg, Lisa Bohan, Patrick McCafferty, and Kevin Harris (1986) "The Image and the Vote: The Effect of Candidate Presentation on Voter Preference," *American Journal of Political Science*, 30: 108–127.

73 On the value of a "likability heuristic," in general, see Paul M. Sniderman, Richard A. Brody, and Philip E. Tetlock (1991) *Reasoning and Choice: Explorations in Political Psychology*, Cambridge: Cambridge University Press, Chapter 6.

74 Robert D. Putnam (2000) *Bowling Alone: The Collapse and Revival of American Community*, New York: Simon & Schuster, p. 35.

75 Wattenberg, *Where Have All the Voters Gone?* p. 117, Table 5.6.

76 Wattenberg, *Where Have All the Voters Gone?* p. 114, Table 5.4.

77 John A. Ferejohn and Morris P. Fiorina (1974) "The Paradox of Not Voting: A Decision Theoretic Analysis," *American Political Science Review*, 68: 525–536.

78 Bryan Caplan (2007) *The Myth of the Rational Voter: Why Democracies Choose Bad Policies*, Princeton, NJ: Princeton University Press, pp. 2 and 166.

79 Caplan, *The Myth of the Rational Voter*, Chapter 3.

80 See Philip Tetlock (2005) *Expert Political Judgment: How Good Is It? How Can We Know?* Princeton, NJ: Princeton University Press.

81 James Surowiecki (2004) *The Wisdom of Crowds: Why the Many Are Smarter Than the Few and How Collective Wisdom Shapes Business, Economies, Societies and Nations*, New York: Doubleday.

82 Program on International Policy Attitudes (2001) "Americans on Foreign Aid and World Hunger: A Study of US Public Attitudes," www.pipa.org/OnlineReports/ForeignAid/ForeignAid_Feb01/ForeignAid_Feb01_rpt.pdf (accessed January 31, 2017).

83 Benjamin I. Page and Robert Y. Shapiro (1992) *The Rational Public: Fifty Years of Trends in Americans' Policy Preferences*, Chicago, IL: University of Chicago Press.

84 Samuel L. Popkin (1991) *The Reasoning Voter: Communication and Persuasion in Presidential Campaigns*, Chicago, IL: University of Chicago Press, pp. 9 and 213.

85 Susan T. Fiske and Shelley E. Taylor (1991) *Social Cognition*, New York: McGraw-Hill; see also Patrick K. Stroh (1995) "Voters as Pragmatic Cognitive Misers: The Accuracy-Effort Trade-off in the Candidate Evaluation Process," in Milton Lodge and Kathleen M. McGraw (eds.), *Political Judgment: Structure and Process*, Ann Arbor, MI: University of Michigan Press, Chapter 9.

86 See Niemi and Weisberg, *Controversies in Voting Behavior*, pp. 144–145.

87 Downs, *An Economic Theory of Democracy*, pp. 135–137.

88 V. O. Key, with Milton Cummings (1966) *The Responsible Electorate: Rationality in Presidential Voting, 1936–1960*, Cambridge, MA: Belknap Press of Harvard University Press, p. 3.

9 Campaigns

POLITICAL CAMPAIGNS are indispensable in a democracy. Though they are often treated as nothing more than candidates' attempts to win elections, they are far more than that. They provide an opportunity for anyone with an interest in the direction of the country to participate in the process of shaping that direction. Furthermore, they are a time when voters can evaluate the performances and promises of the parties and their candidates. It is hard to imagine how democracy could function without campaigns.

And yet many Americans dislike campaigns. They believe them to be too negative, too drawn out, and too expensive. How can this view be reconciled with the claim that campaigns are an essential element of democracy? To acknowledge the importance of campaigns is not to say that all campaigns are equally beneficial. Some are better than others at providing voters with the kind of information they need to render judgment. Furthermore, the norms and laws that govern campaigns in a particular country—what we might call the country's campaign system—may better foster democratic deliberation than the campaign system of other countries. The obligation to debate one's opponent, for example, may exist in one place but not another. The length of campaigns, the amount and sources of campaign funds, and the limits (or lack thereof) on campaign advertising are only a few of the other aspects of campaigns that may help or hinder their ability to fulfill their democratic role.

Though much of what has been covered to this point in the book is relevant to campaigns, this chapter devotes specific attention to campaigning in the United States. It begins by describing many of the differences between campaigns at various levels of government. The bulk of the chapter, however, is spent exploring campaign strategy and tactics, because the operation of campaigns is central to understanding their role in a political system and to assessing their performance. Finally, a brief normative discussion of campaigns in the United States will conclude the chapter and will address many of the commonly heard complaints about campaigns.

► *How Campaigns Differ*

Campaigns at all levels have the same basic goal—to get more votes than the opponent at election time. Regardless of the office sought, campaigns pursue this goal in much the same way. For example, they all attempt to control the terms of debate between the candidates. In doing so, they portray their own candidate as the best choice for the office sought (and they may also suggest that the opponent is a risky, or even dangerous, choice). All campaigns also try to get as many of their supporters to the polls as possible.

Yet there are significant differences between campaigns. Many of these reflect disparities in the scope of the campaign, which is determined primarily (though not entirely) by the office sought. Presidential campaigns are conducted nationally or at least in multiple states simultaneously. US Senate, gubernatorial and other statewide offices, and a few races for US House of Representatives (in states with only one representative) are conducted throughout entire states. Most congressional and all state legislative and local elections are held in districts that constitute some fraction of a state.

The geographical area covered by campaigns leads to vastly different campaign sizes. One way to measure the size of a campaign is by the number of staff members it employs. Serious presidential campaigns will usually have hundreds of paid staffers. Campaigns at other levels have nowhere near that number.

Campaign size could also be measured by the number of campaign offices a candidate has. Presidential campaigns will have multiple offices in key states. During the 2012 campaign, Barack Obama established almost 800 field offices throughout the nation and 131 offices in Ohio alone.[1] Again, the larger the area covered by a campaign, the more offices the campaign will have. A Senate campaign may have three or four offices located in different parts of a state, whereas House campaigns rarely have more than one.

The level of spending in campaigns also differs tremendously. In 2012, according to the Center for Responsive Politics, US House candidates raised an average of $495,030 for their campaigns, US Senates candidates an average of $1,743,377, and presidential candidates an average of $56,113,797.[2] Though occasionally a House campaign will spend more than some Senate campaigns, Senate candidates can typically expect to spend many times more than a House candidate. The amount of spending in gubernatorial campaigns can be similar to that of Senate campaigns, but spending in other statewide races is likely to be far lower. Of course, state legislative and local races, with the exception of major city mayoral races, will have relatively low levels of spending.

One major difference between campaigns concerns the sources of campaign funds. The vast majority of candidates, at all levels, rely on private contributions from individuals and from PACs and political parties. Some campaigns, however, receive public funding from the government. Though a few states offer candidates full or partial public funding, at the federal level only presidential campaigns can receive public funds. Today, no serious presidential candidate accepts public funding during the primaries or the general election (see Chapter 3).

Campaigns also differ in terms of the amount of media coverage they receive. Clearly, presidential campaigns attract the most attention. To the extent that congressional races get national coverage during presidential years, it tends to be focused on the respective parties' battle for control of the House and Senate and not as much on individual races. In midterm elections, however, congressional races move up in priority and are given ample coverage. In those years, key individual contests are given considerable attention, though the national media are still interested in control of Congress. Individual races get most of their coverage, however, from regional and state media outlets. When there is a gubernatorial campaign in a state, it will receive as much coverage as, if not more than, a US Senate race would garner. Local media provide most of the reporting on House races, though particularly competitive contests will get state and even national attention. Non-gubernatorial statewide races and state legislative and local campaigns receive far less coverage. Of course, many local elections are held when higher-level races are not on the ballot (often in the spring). This allows the media to give local races more attention than they would otherwise get, but local campaigns still often struggle to get sufficient coverage.

Finally, the subject matter that campaigns discuss differs depending upon the level of office sought and, to some extent, the branch of government in question. Local races for mayor, city council, or county commissioner are often concerned with roads and other infrastructure issues, economic development, and crime. The economy and education play a large role in state-level races, as do taxes and various social services. Issues such as gay rights, abortion, and gun control are also perennial issues in state elections. At the federal level, a wide variety of issues can capture the candidates' attention, even when the issues are primarily a matter of state concern. Of course, some issues are exclusively (or primarily) the domain of the federal government, such as Social Security, federal taxes, and foreign and defense policy.

Not only does the level of office help determine the subject matter of campaigns, but the branch of government an office resides in matters as well. Obviously, campaigns for judicial seats will have a fundamentally different set of issues to address than will those for executive or legislative offices. Statewide executive branch offices other than governor will be highly focused on the policy sphere for which they are responsible. And though there is considerable overlap between the policy concerns of a chief executive (such as president or governor) and legislative offices, the emphasis in campaigns will likely diverge. Presidential candidates, for example, are far more likely to discuss foreign policy than are candidates for the US House or Senate (though in a time of war, congressional candidates will be more interested in addressing foreign policy than they otherwise would be). Governors tend to focus on economic development to a greater extent than do state legislative candidates.

Thus, there are many ways in which campaigns differ. These differences undoubtedly affect the way campaigns are run, particularly with respect to campaign strategy. Having said that, there are some remarkably similar aspects to campaigns at all levels and of all types. Many of these similarities will become apparent in the sections that follow.

▶ The Campaign Plan

Campaigns are extremely dynamic. As in a chess match, each move made by one side affects the future moves of the other side. However, campaigns are also guided by plans that they should follow regardless of the instability of day-to-day occurrences. This creates a considerable amount of tension within a campaign. As events unfold, often in unexpected ways, how will the campaign react? If the campaign's plan is based on sound principles, the answer is to follow the plan. As former deputy chairman of the DNC William Sweeney has written, "A campaign without a plan is a journey without a map."[3]

Campaign plans must take into consideration a number of elements in the campaign. These include the environment within which the campaign takes place, the candidates' backgrounds and records, the audience for the campaign, and the resources needed to mount a serious effort.[4] To account for each of these elements in the plan, a vast amount of information must be gathered. Though some of this information will be readily available, some may require research on the part of the campaign.

The Campaign Environment

The campaign environment is perhaps the most complex of the elements. There are dozens of aspects to the environment that must be taken into account by campaign planners. Much of this will be obvious but, nonetheless, is important to spell out in the plan. For instance, the plan must specify the jurisdiction in which the race will take place. Is the race a local or statewide contest? What are the physical boundaries of the district? To answer these questions, basic information must be gathered. In a presidential campaign, the plan should identify the states—whether early states in the nomination process or swing states in the general election—that will receive most of the campaign's attention. Determining which states will be battlegrounds is a strategic decision, if also a tactical one, that requires the analysis of multiple pieces of information.

Beyond a description of where the race will occur, the plan should also provide detailed information about the jurisdiction. There is a tremendous amount of demographic data, such as education and per capita income levels, the racial makeup of the area, the rural/urban split, and religious affiliations, that should be gathered. Key institutions and organizations in the area, including universities and vital businesses and industries, should also be acknowledged. Finally, major media markets in the district or state must be identified.

Of critical importance to the campaign plan are the political conditions in the jurisdiction. What is the breakdown of elected officials by party affiliation in the district? Which politicians are popular, and which out of favor with the voters? Are there local political controversies currently garnering considerable attention? It is important to also keep in mind the other races on the ballot and to determine which of those are high profile or likely to be competitive.

Because the economy is a critical factor in so many elections, it is also useful to be aware of economic conditions in the jurisdiction. What is the local (or state) unemployment rate? Are home sales robust or sluggish? What is the price of a gallon of gas? Though voters' opinions about the economy will be gathered by polls, it is valuable to have an objective measure of the health of the economy in the area in which the candidate is running.

Candidates' Backgrounds and Records

After having profiled the district, the campaign plan should do the same for the candidates. In addition to a detailed list of the candidates' experiences and a description of their backgrounds, a brief biographical sketch should be developed for each of the candidates. Voters like to know something about who candidates are as people, and the campaign will want a pithy—and positive—version of its candidate's life story to use in its literature. A campaign will also attempt to establish a (less positive) "narrative" about the opponent's biography.

In addition to basic biographical information, the strengths and weaknesses of both candidates must be clearly established. Again, some of this information, such as legislative voting records or public statements, will be readily available. Other information may be obtained only through opposition research. Typically, opposition research consists of searching publicly available, but often difficult-to-find or obscure, databases for information about a candidate's financial history, education, potential criminal record or lawsuits in which they have been involved, and real estate transactions, to name but a few. Campaigns have even been known to hire investigators to examine the private lives of their opponents. Though candidates are often reluctant to undergo intense scrutiny by their own campaigns, it is critical that the people running a campaign be aware of potentially damaging information about both their own candidate and the opponent.[5]

The Audience

The voters, of course, constitute the main audience for the campaign. To reach them, the campaign needs a thorough understanding of their attitudes and behaviors. There are two categories of information about voters that should be included in a campaign plan. One is polling data, which will provide the campaign with useful data about public opinion relevant to the campaign. Occasionally, potential candidates will commission "feasibility polls" before they decide to enter a race. These polls help determine how well known the person is, what voters think of him or her (to the extent they are known at all), and the chances they have of winning. Typically, however, the first poll conducted for a candidate is a "benchmark poll." These polls are long and comprehensive and are used to assess the candidates' standing within the electorate and the mood of the voters and to identify the issues that are most important to them. The results of a benchmark poll are also used to develop a campaign strategy.[6]

Equally important is the prior voting behavior of the district or state in which the race is taking place. Both turnout rates and patterns of voting preferences should be analyzed by the campaign. However, precinct-level voting behavior is more useful than aggregate voting behavior because the former allows the campaign to target specific areas for persuasion and mobilization.

Generally speaking, campaigns treat voters as belonging to one of three groups. There are those voters who support the candidate, those who oppose the candidate, and undecided voters.[7] Within the undecided category, campaigns have to determine which voters are potential supporters and target them for persuasion. Those who are already identified as supporters need reinforcement during the campaign but, more important, the campaign needs to mobilize these voters on Election Day. Strategies and tactics for doing so will be discussed later in this chapter.

Voters are not the only audience for the campaign. Candidates hope to influence the behavior of political parties and interest groups as well. In particular, campaigns hope to gain financial support from these organizations, but they are also interested in recruiting volunteers. In addition, the media are an especially important audience for campaigns. The campaign plan will ultimately include ways to receive "earned" or "free" media, which is the coverage campaigns get when they do something newsworthy. Candidates hope to get favorable coverage from campaign reporters and from pundits who analyze key races.

Resources

One final element of the campaign plan is a discussion of the resources needed to run a successful campaign. Clearly, the most important resource is money, and the campaign will have to estimate how much is required on the basis of the size of the jurisdiction, the cost of media in that area, and the historical levels of spending in races for the office in question. Once fund-raising goals are established, the campaign must identify potential contributors. If the candidate has run for office before, the campaign will begin with previous donors. If the candidate is a novice, they may turn first to friends and family, though fund-raising lists can be obtained from the parties or other candidates.

Additional resources are also necessary for a serious campaign. Perhaps the most precious nonmonetary resource of all is time. The campaign plan will lay out a time frame for the campaign, usually working backward from Election Day. When, for example, will the campaign begin television advertising? What is the voter registration deadline? By when should milestone fund-raising goals be met? Time, as William Sweeney has noted, is "a dwindling resource [that] separates political efforts from all other public relations or marketing efforts. A political campaign without the immediate sense of the time remaining in the election burned into its consciousness for daily performance and accountability lacks the intensity to win."[8]

An indispensable campaign resource is people. Campaigns need dozens or hundreds of volunteers, depending upon the size of the campaign, to do everything from making phone calls and stuffing envelopes to canvassing voters door to door and working at the polls on Election Day. In addition, the campaign staff is of vital importance for the operation of the campaign. The campaign plan should outline the campaign organization and identify key staff positions that need to be filled (see Chapter 4). Finally, political consultants of various types are hired if the campaign can afford them. Though some staffers may resent their presence in a campaign, a consultant's knowledge and expertise is necessary for any serious bid for office.

The plan is not complete, of course, until each of the elements discussed previously have been fused into a blueprint for victory. That blueprint will include a campaign strategy and the tactics needed to implement the strategy. Though tactics can be thought of as the tools for constructing a campaign, the strategy serves as the instructions for assembly.

▶ Campaign Strategy

Campaign strategy, according to Ron Faucheux, the former editor and publisher of *Campaigns and Elections* magazine, is simply an answer to the question, "How will we win?"[9] Developing that answer requires a considerable amount of expertise. In most serious campaigns today, professional political consultants craft strategies for candidates. Their value to a campaign lies not only in the thorough research they provide but in the experience they have gained in the dozens (if not hundreds) of campaigns on which they have worked.

The Campaign Message

Fundamentally, campaigns are communication events. That means the strategy will find its ultimate expression in a "message." The campaign's message, which is sometimes referred to as its *theme*, is the rationale for electing one's own candidate and defeating the opponent. When a candidate is asked why a person should vote for him or her, the answer given should be the campaign's message.

TABLE 9.1 *Hypothetical Message Box for Donald Trump's 2020 Presidential Campaign against Elizabeth Warren*

	What Trump will say about …	*What Warren is likely to say about …*
Trump	His business skills and unconventional approach to governing have put America back on the right track.	He is incompetent and dangerous and his policies have done nothing to improve the conditions in the country.
Warren	She is very liberal, doesn't have a record of accomplishment, and her policies will wreck the economy and won't keep us safe.	She will fight for working families against Wall Street and big business and will protect the most vulnerable among us.

In developing the message, campaigns often use a device called a *message box* not only to articulate its own message but to anticipate the opponent's message as well. Though the campaign's message is typically a positive statement about why the candidate deserves to be elected, the message box also includes a negative message about the opponent. Table 9.1 provides a message box for a hypothetical 2020 Donald Trump reelection campaign against Senator Elizabeth Warren of Massachusetts. The box includes Trump's messages about himself and Warren and the messages the Trump campaign could expect from Warren about each candidate. These messages recognize the candidates' strengths and weaknesses, which may be obvious or may be revealed only through polling. The valuable information gleaned from polls helps to explain why pollsters have become the chief strategists in so many campaigns nowadays.[10]

The content of such messages varies from campaign to campaign depending on the context. However, there are a few tried-and-true messages candidates often adopt in one form or another. For instance, when the public is unhappy with the direction of the country or when a candidate is a challenger, change is a common theme. This was the message of Bill Clinton's presidential campaign in 1992, Barack Obama's in 2008, and Donald Trump's in 2016. Conversely, in a time of crisis or when a candidate is an incumbent, experience is likely to be a campaign theme. For his reelection campaign, Bill Clinton adopted this approach in 1996. In 2008, Senator McCain contrasted his experience, both in war and in government, with Obama's inexperience and naivety.

Occasionally, a message of change will take the specific form of moral renewal. After the Watergate scandal in 1976, Jimmy Carter promised never to lie to the American people and took honesty in government as a theme. Similarly, in 2000, George Bush expressed disapproval of Presidential Clinton's behavior while in the White House and pledged to return honor and dignity to the presidency.

Campaign messages can also be built around particularly salient issues. When an issue dominates the campaign environment, at least one candidate is likely to put it at the center of their campaign message. In 2004, for instance, terrorism and national security figured prominently in most of what the Bush campaign communicated to the voters. Often the state of the economy becomes part of a candidate's message, particularly when that candidate is a challenger during bad economic times. Thus, in 1992 and 2008, a central element in both Bill Clinton's and Barack Obama's promise of change was the economy. Indeed, the now famous sign in the Clinton campaign headquarters reminded the staff, "It's the economy, stupid."

Candidate Positioning

It is often said that the goal of campaign strategies is to "position" candidates to maximize votes by situating them in an optimal spot along the ideological spectrum. Determining exactly where the optimal spot is turns out to be a rather complicated process. In a two-party electoral system such as the one in the United States, it is often thought that the vote-maximizing position is in the center of the political spectrum because that is where the bulk of the electorate is located. Thus, in a general election, candidates are likely to campaign as centrists and are expected to converge toward the median voter. This proposition is based on theoretical work by Anthony Downs, who concluded that "there are more voters in the middle than at the extremes. Therefore each party structures its policies so that its net position is moderate."[11]

To converge toward the center, candidates are expected to adopt similar positions on at least key issues. "Parties in a two-party system," Downs postulated, "deliberately change their platforms so that they resemble one another." Candidates may also make only vague policy pronouncements that blur differences between them. As Downs put it, parties and candidates will often "becloud their policies in a fog of ambiguity." Incidentally, Downs suggests that this rational activity on the part of parties and candidates leads to irrational behavior by the voters who are likely to find it difficult to make decisions based on policy positions when differences between the candidates are not clear.[12]

In reality, however, parties and candidates are often easily distinguishable. That is especially true in the present era, when partisan polarization is so rampant. Nevertheless, empirical research has cast doubt on the convergence hypothesis for some time.[13] Consider the fact that in a primary, the median voter is likely to be, or at least is perceived by the candidates to be, located toward the wings of the parties. To win a primary, therefore, candidates will be pulled away from the center. That makes it very difficult to dart back to the middle for the general election. In addition, candidates often have clearly defined positions on issues and have ideological identities that are difficult to alter. Finally, the lack of competition that exists in most legislative districts at both the state and national level makes convergence less necessary. When a candidate faces no real threat from the other party, they are free to take positions that may be to the left or right of the median voter in the district.[14]

Admittedly, when intense party competition exists in a particular race, candidates may attempt to moderate their positions. They may also make statements on high-profile but largely symbolic issues to send a signal to voters that they are not ideologically out of step with the majority. A classic example of this move was Bill Clinton's 1992 denunciation of rapper Sister Souljah, who, after the Los Angeles riots of that year, had suggested that Black people should kill White people rather than other Black people. In a speech to the civil rights organization, the Rainbow Coalition, Clinton criticized Sister Souljah and called her statement racist. So famous is that incident that the term "Sister Souljah moment" has come to describe an attempt by a candidate to distance himself from supposed allies who are viewed as ideologically extreme by publicly rebuking or disagreeing with them.[15]

There is, however, an alternative approach, and it is one that applies in all campaign settings, regardless of the level of competition. Candidates of opposing parties can, and generally do, emphasize entirely different sets of issues. Recall the concept of "issue ownership" discussed in Chapter 5. That concept suggests that the two parties generally "own," or have an advantage on, different policy areas. The typical voter is thought to trust Democrats more on issues such as health care, unemployment, and education whereas the Republicans are thought better at handling national security, moral issues, and taxes. Byron Shafer and William Claggett call the two sets of issues owned by Democrats and Republicans the "economic/welfare factor" and the "cultural/national factor," respectively.[16]

As a result of issue ownership, Democrats can be expected to emphasize those issues that they own, whereas Republicans will highlight those on which they have an advantage. By campaigning on different issues, candidates are "deliberately priming" voters to make voting decisions based on issues upon which they or their party have advantages over their opponents.[17] This sort of priming is intentional, which differentiates it from the unintentional priming that the media produces by nature of covering some issues rather than others (see Chapter 7).[18] Recent empirical research indicates that campaigns do, in fact, follow this basic strategy and that it has a significant influence on voters.[19]

Having said that, two caveats are necessary: First, candidates prime voters not only on issues but on image, or traits, as well. Indeed, the parties may own certain traits, just as they own particular issues.[20] Second, candidates in high-profile races may be forced to discuss issues for which they are at a disadvantage. In presidential races, for example, Democrats must address national security and Republicans will be asked about health care. In such instances, candidates must frame issues in the best possible light for their campaigns. Presumably, as one moves down the ballot, framing of this sort is less necessary because far less attention is paid to those races, and candidates can stick more successfully to discussing the issues they have chosen to emphasize.[21]

There are, of course, dozens of strategic decisions that have to be made in a campaign. Not only does the basic message have to be developed, but the candidate must decide which voters to target, which issues to emphasize, when to raise those issues, and how to talk about them, in addition to many other considerations. Once a basic strategy has been agreed on, the campaign then has to implement it. This is where tactics come into play.

▶ Campaign Tactics

Campaign tactics are the means by which a campaign implements its strategy. The most brilliant strategy on paper will be completely ineffective if the campaign staff does not have the tactical skills needed to carry out that strategy. In truth, the line between strategy and tactics is often blurry, but many of the tasks campaigns must perform are essentially (or purely) logistical. This section identifies the tactics that virtually all campaigns employ.

Fund-Raising

Among the most important campaign tactics is fund-raising. Though modern campaigns are essentially communication events, it is difficult to communicate with voters—or with a large number of them at any rate—without financial resources. As a result, once the campaign has determined the amount of money a successful effort requires, it must begin raising that money immediately.

There are multiple ways to raise money. Perhaps the most visible is the fund-raising event. These range in size from small coffee klatches in supporters' homes to large galas with celebrity entertainment. Some events, particularly those boasting well-known performers, are arranged by the campaigns themselves. Other events are hosted by leading contributors to the campaigns. Though these may seem like small events, they can raise considerable money. In March of 2007, for example, a supermarket magnate held a fund-raiser for Hillary Clinton at his home in Beverly Hills for which guests, including Barbra Streisand, paid $2,300 apiece to attend. The event raised $2.6 million, double the amount raised by an earlier fund-raiser for Barack Obama hosted by Steven Spielberg, David Geffen, and Jeffrey Katzenberg.[22]

Most of the fund-raising a campaign will do will not be as public as such events. Indeed, the candidates will devote a considerable amount of time, especially early in the campaign, to making personal appeals to individuals and PACs. A survey of candidates at all levels conducted by the Center for American Politics and Citizenship at the University of Maryland in 2000 found that nearly 29 percent of all candidates devoted at least a fourth of their campaign schedules to raising money; 55 percent of statewide candidates and almost 43 percent of US House candidates spent more than a quarter of their time on fund-raising.[23]

When candidates make direct solicitations to individuals, it is typically to wealthy people who can contribute hundreds, if not thousands, of dollars to the campaign. Smaller individual contributions are raised by phone, online, and by direct mail. The latter has been a staple of campaigns since the 1970s, when limits on the amount individuals could contribute were put in place. Direct mail fund-raising letters usually attempt to stir emotion in the potential donor. Often, that emotion is negative and is evoked by the mention of a bogeyman from the other side of the political spectrum. Though direct mail can be quite successful, it is a costly endeavor and can take some time to cultivate a donor base that produces significant funds.

Digital fund-raising, conversely, is relatively inexpensive and can generate considerable resources in short periods of time. For instance, long-shot Republican presidential candidate Ron Paul raised $4.2 million in one twenty-four-hour period in November 2007.[24] Internet fund-raising first appeared promising in 2000, when John McCain raised $1.4 million in the three days after his victory in the New Hampshire Republican primary.[25] It seemed to reach maturity, however, in the 2004 Howard Dean and, later, John Kerry presidential campaigns. Dean raised $20 million, or 40 percent of his total, via the Internet, and Kerry, as the Democratic presidential nominee, would eventually raise $89 million (33 percent of his total) online.[26] In 2008 and 2012, Barack Obama took digital fund-raising to an entirely new level. In 2012, his campaign raised $504 million from email, social media sites, mobile devices, and the Obama campaign website. That was a considerable increase from the astonishing $403 million he had raised in 2008.[27]

Digital solicitations can be sent to potential donors at virtually no cost, and links provided in e-mails or texts make contributing quite easy. Though they are typically much shorter than direct mail letters, fund-raising appeals via the Internet use similar techniques to activate donors. Indeed, the 2012 Obama campaign ran ongoing experiments to determine how to craft the most effective fund-raising appeals. This included testing different subject lines on e-mails and different messages, amounts asked for, and formatting. Once the campaign knew what would work best, it would blast the carefully crafted appeal to millions of supporters. Among the most successful subject lines on an email from the President was "I will be outspent" (see Figure 9.1).[28]

Television Advertising

As mentioned previously, campaign fund-raising is necessary so that the campaign can communicate to the voters. The most expensive form of communication is advertising, which is sometimes referred to as *paid media*. Though radio can play an important role in a campaign, particularly to target specific groups of voters, most of our discussion will focus on television advertising. Scholars mark 1952 as the year that television ads, or "spots," first played a significant role in a campaign. Though some ads had been run in a few previous campaigns, the 1952 presidential campaign introduced television ads as a central piece of a campaign's arsenal.[29]

There are many ways to classify campaign spots, but most can be described quite simply as positive, negative, or comparative. A variety of types exist within

FIGURE 9.1   *2012 Obama Fund-Raising Email*

From: **Barack Obama** <info@barackobama.com>
Date: Tue, Jul 10, 2012 at 8:33 AM
Subject: Re: I will be outspent
To: ███████████████████

Laura --

For the second month in a row, Romney and the Republicans outraised us -- this time by $35 million.

I wrote to you recently about this new reality and its potential consequences.

We can get outspent and still win in November. But we cannot get outspent dramatically, month after month, and expect to have a chance.

I have no doubt we can close this gap before it's too late with folks like you chipping in what you can, when you can.
But that's up to you. **Will you make a donation today?**

What's at stake is more important than my legacy as president, or even what we've accomplished together or still hope to do.

This is about whether ordinary people can still decide who wins a presidential election in this country -- even up against billionaires and outside groups trying to drown you out.

Everything we've built by knocking on doors, talking to people on the ground, and asking millions of Americans to own what happens in November is at risk.

I firmly believe we can win -- and do it the right way.

At a critical moment like this, I need you to double down.

Please donate $25 or more today:

https://donate.barackobama.com/Outraised

Thank you -- for everything you've done before and everything you're doing now. It matters.

Barack

> Paid for by Obama for America
> Contributions or gifts to Obama for America are not tax deductible
> This email was sent to: ███████████████
> Update address | Unsubscribe

each of these categories, but the basic orientation of the ad helps explain its purpose. Thus, positive ads are those that sing the praises, in one way or another, of the sponsoring candidate. The most common type is the biographical spot. These ads tell the life story of the candidate and highlight character traits that make the candidate fit for office. A good example of a purely biographical ad is one called "Heart" for John Kerry in 2004 (which, like the other ads mentioned in this section, can be viewed online at "The Living Room Candidate." Available at www.livingroomcandidate.com). The ad begins with Kerry talking about his place of birth and the commitment to public service his parents instilled in him. He then explains why he enlisted in Vietnam, and his fellow veterans talk about his valor. The ad ends on an optimistic note and describes Kerry as having had "a lifetime of service and strength." Many biographical ads also mention critical issues facing the nation and explain why candidates' backgrounds make them particularly qualified to handle those issues. The classic ad of this type is Dwight Eisenhower's "The Man from Abilene" from the 1952 campaign. It reminds the viewer of his success as a general and trumpets his ability to "deal with the Russians."

Nonbiographical positive ads review a candidate's record in office or announce a candidate's position on a key issue or issues. They are also often "feel good" spots that evoke patriotism or optimism. One of the most famous examples of the latter is Ronald Reagan's 1984 ad called "Prouder, Stronger, Better" (which is better known as the "morning in America" spot). In it, the narrator reviews the successes of Reagan's first term and announces: "It's morning again in America and under the leadership of President Reagan our country is prouder and stronger and better."

Negative ads are typically the most memorable ads from a campaign. These spots are often called *attack ads* because they criticize the opponent in some manner. In their purest form, attack ads make little or no mention of the sponsoring candidate. Among the most famous (or infamous, depending upon one's perspective) negative ads are two from the 1988 George H. W. Bush campaign titled "Tank Ride" and "Revolving Door"; a spot for the 2004 George W. Bush campaign called "Windsurfing"; a 1992 Clinton ad called "Maine"; and a classic from the John F. Kennedy campaign in 1960 titled "Nixon's Experience?"

Keep in mind that not all campaign advertising is done by candidates. The parties and interest groups also run spots intended to influence the outcome of elections. Campaign finance laws dictate what can and cannot be said, depending on how the money was raised to pay for the ads (see Chapter 3 for details). Nevertheless, noncandidate ads often play a critical role in a campaign. A recent example of the potential impact of such advertising is the effect of the Swift Boat Veterans for Truth commercials that attacked John Kerry after the 2004 Democratic National Convention. The group's first ad—titled "Any Questions?"— raised doubts about Kerry's war record claims. The ad garnered considerable media attention and, despite being "contradicted by Kerry's former crewman and by Navy records," is thought to have damaged Kerry just as the general election campaign was beginning.[30]

There are many other examples of well-known noncandidate ads that are thought to have had an impact in an election. The infamous "Willie Horton ad" from 1988 criticized Michael Dukakis for a prison furlough program that was in place in Massachusetts when he was governor. Under that program, a convict named Willie Horton was given a weekend pass from prison and, while out, raped a woman and stabbed her fiancé. The ad, paid for by a group calling themselves the National Security PAC, told Horton's story, concluding, "Weekend Prison Passes: Dukakis on Crime."[31] This ad is now widely viewed as implicitly racist because, among other things, it shows Horton's mug shot for an undue length of time.[32]

As noted in Chapter 6, noncandidate ads are more likely to be negative than either candidate or political party ads. In 2012, roughly 85 percent of ads sponsored by outside groups were attack ads whereas just more than half of candidate and party ads were negative.[33] Perhaps because they can hide behind innocuous-sounding names, groups appear to be quite comfortable leveling attacks, occasionally even vicious ones, against candidates they oppose.

Typically, negative ads are critical of the opponent's record or positions on important issues. Indeed, John Geer has shown that "negative appeals are far more issue oriented than positive appeals."[34] In presidential candidates' ads, 72 percent of negative appeals are about issues, compared to only 49 percent of the appeals in positive ads.[35] Nevertheless, negative ads do sometimes raise questions about the opponent's character and qualifications for office. Regardless of the substance of the attack, these ads often rely on visual, and occasionally aural, devices to enhance the negative feelings toward the opponent. Thus, unflattering photographs or ominous music often appear in attack ads. The result is a powerful emotional appeal and a warning against voting for the target of the attack.

Psychologists have repeatedly found that "negative information more strongly influences people's evaluations than comparably extreme positive information."[36] This explains the popularity of negative ads among media consultants. Put simply, political operatives believe attack ads work. Political scientists, conversely, have their doubts. In a quantitative meta-analysis of the research on the effects of negative advertising, Richard Lau and his colleagues found no "consistent, let alone strong, evidence that negative ads work to the advantage of their sponsors and/or the disadvantage of their targets," and concluded, "There is simply no compelling evidence that negative advertising 'works.'"[37]

The last general category of campaign ads is what is often called *comparative*, or *contrast*, ads. These are spots that compare the record or position of the ad's sponsor to that of the opponent. Often, such an ad will alternate, with corresponding change in background music, between praise for the sponsoring candidate and criticism of the opponent. Occasionally, a comparative ad will begin with an attack on the target and end with a positive view of the sponsor. The ad "Blackboard" for Michael Dukakis in 1988 is an example of a comparative spot that takes this approach. Generally speaking, these ads are quite substantive, as it is more acceptable to compare records and issue positions than to openly compare character traits.

It should be acknowledged that some campaign ads do not fit neatly into even these general categories. This is true of a number of well-known ads, including the most famous campaign spot of all time, Lyndon Johnson's "Peace Little Girl" from 1964 (better known as the "Daisy" ad). In that advertisement, a young girl counts petals on a flower as the camera moves ever closer to her face. When she reaches nine, a man's voice begins a countdown from ten as the camera moves toward the girl's eye. When the girl's pupil fills the screen and the countdown reaches zero, an atomic bomb explodes. As a mushroom cloud is released, Johnson says, "These are the stakes: To make a world in which all of God's children can live, or to go into the darkness. We must either love each other, or we must die." The ad ends with the announcer declaring, "Vote for President Johnson on November 3rd. The stakes are too high for you to stay home." The purpose of the ad is clearly to suggest that only Johnson can keep the United States safe, but it also implies that if Barry Goldwater were to win the election, the country would find itself in a potentially world-ending war. It is hard not to view this as a negative ad; negative emotions are evoked, and it is reasonable to see this as an attack on Goldwater. And, yet, Goldwater is never mentioned in the ad, and the overt message is about Johnson's ability to protect the American people.

A similar ad is Ronald Reagan's famous 1984 ad "Bear" (or "Bear in the Woods"). Over images of a grizzly bear and threatening music, the only words spoken are by an announcer who says, "There is a bear in the woods. For some people the bear is easy to see. Others don't see it at all. Some people say the bear is tame. Others say it's vicious and dangerous. Since no one can really be sure who's right, isn't it smart to be as strong as the bear? If there is a bear?" The ad is clearly about standing up to the Soviet Union, which is represented by the bear. However, the wording is strange, and the images are symbolic, making the ad rather abstract. The result is a campaign spot that is neither positive nor negative.

Reagan's "Bear" ad raises another question about campaign spots: how effective are they? Darrell West's analysis of "Bear" found that it had no effect on the public's policy agenda, most likely because it was too abstract for the public to comprehend. He found other ads, however, that did help set the public's agenda. For instance, crime rose on people's list of important issues facing the nation after they viewed George Bush's 1988 "Revolving Door" ad.[38]

Do campaign ads have the ultimate effect? That is, do candidates' ads help them gain votes and win elections? Unfortunately, there have been too few studies of this question to draw a clear conclusion. What evidence does exist is mixed at best. However, there have been demonstrated effects of ads in terms of citizen learning; that is, individuals learn about candidates from watching ads. In fact, some studies find ads to have more of an informing effect than media reports. Some scholars, however, fear another effect, one that is unique to negative advertising: that attack ads depress turnout. There is some evidence for this claim but just as much (if not more) that negative ads either boost turnout or have no effect one way or the other.[39]

Other Forms of Communication

Campaigns communicate with voters in ways other than television advertising. Indeed, there has been a noticeable shift in emphasis in recent election cycles from the "air war" (that is, television and radio advertising) to the "ground war" (or non-broadcast forms of communication and mobilization).[40] A staple tactic in the ground war is the use of direct mail. When considered as a group, candidates at all levels probably use more direct mail than television advertising because low-level campaigns often cannot afford television spots. This is particularly true for candidates in urban settings, where media costs are usually exorbitant.

Direct mail can raise issues not addressed, for whatever reason, in television advertising, or it can be used to reinforce or supplement the messages in television ads. Mail pieces can provide more information than a thirty-second spot and can refine the message for different subsets of voters. Whereas television advertising hits whoever may be viewing a particular channel at a certain time, mail can be sent directly to its intended target. Indeed, if a campaign's information and targeting lists are detailed enough, it is possible to send a mailing on abortion to a pro-life voter at one address and a piece related to gun control to the sportsman next door.

FIGURE 9.2 *A Negative Direct Mail Piece.*

Source: http://casadelogo.typepad.com/factesque/2006/10/fitzgerald_call.html.

Noncandidate groups, such as interest groups and political parties, also rely heavily on direct mail, as it allows groups to operate in a campaign without drawing attention. This "under-the-radar" aspect of direct mail use contributes to the nasty tone of so much of this form of communication. Figure 9.2 is an example of just how negative direct mail can be. In it, the National Republican Congressional Committee attacks 2004 Democratic congressional candidate Ginny Schrader for alleged anti-American behavior.

There are a variety of additional ways in which campaigns communicate with voters. For example, volunteers make telephone calls to hundreds of voters from "phone banks" set up in campaign headquarters. In the early phases of the campaign, these calls are used to identify potential supporters who will be targeted for persuasive messages later in the campaign. Those persuasive messages can be delivered in a number of ways, including additional phone calls. Increasingly, campaigns use "robo-calls" to reach voters. A robo-call is a pre-recorded message, typically from a well-known politician or celebrity.

Email and text messaging have become absolutely essential forms of campaign communication. They are not only inexpensive, but they reach recipients immediately. This makes them valuable as means for providing supporters with last-minute campaign appeals. Of course, these forms of communication are limited to use with those who sign up to receive them. That means email and text messages are not very useful for attempting to reach large numbers of voters who are persuadable but as yet unconnected to the campaign.

For reaching a mass audience, campaigns rely heavily on social networking services such as Facebook and Twitter. When friends and followers of a candidate respond to the candidate's posts, all of their friends and followers receive information about the campaign even if they aren't directly connected to the candidate. As with other aspects of their digital operation, the 2012 Obama campaign made masterful use of social networks. Rather than passively hoping that their supporters would share campaign messages with their networks of friends and family, the Obama campaign developed a Facebook app that gave the campaign access to their supporters' Facebook friends. That enabled the campaign to ask Obama supporters to share specific messages with specific friends. As *Time* magazine reported after the election, "More than 600,000 supporters followed through with more than 5 million contacts, asking their friends to register to vote, give money, vote or look at a video designed to change their mind."[41]

In 2016, Donald Trump famously made frequent use of Twitter to communicate with the public. Many observers think he did so effectively. Some argue that Twitter enabled him to bypass the conventional media to reach his supporters directly. Others thought he used strategically timed controversial tweets to distract the public and the media when he was in the midst of a negative news story. Still other observers believe his use of Twitter was not effective. Mr. Trump seemed to tweet impulsively, often causing needless controversy or making a controversial story even worse (see Figure 9.3). This view may well have been held by his own campaign staff, who reportedly prevented him from tweeting in the waning days of the campaign.[42]

A more traditional but still widely used form of voter contact is canvassing door to door. As with telephone calls, initial contact is intended to identify potential supporters. Later visits deliver "literature" that will be handed to the voter directly or "dropped" on a doorstep if the voter is not home. In local elections, and to a limited extent in larger campaigns as well, candidates themselves often walk neighborhoods to meet voters and attempt to garner support.

FIGURE 9.3 *A Controversial Donald Trump Tweet*

For decades, candidates have placed advertisements in newspapers. This is a relatively inexpensive form of advertising but, with shrinking readership, it may not reach as many voters as other methods. However, habitual newspaper readers tend to be likely voters, so newspaper ads are quite efficient for reaching part of the voting public.

Increasingly, however, campaigns are advertising on the Internet. One advantage of Web ads is that they can be produced and posted very quickly, allowing campaigns to respond to events almost instantly. More important, however, is the fact that they can be tailored to users on the basis of their online behavior (e.g., searches, purchases).[43] It is possible, for example, to target an online ad to a voter between the ages of eighteen and twenty-nine who is interested in the environment. If that person were to search the Internet for information about hybrid cars, a candidate could deliver an ad about their plans for alternative energy. According to one estimate, about $1 billion would be spent on digital advertising, about half of that on social media, in the 2016 elections. That is a 5,000 percent increase in digital ad spending from 2008.[44]

The tailoring of campaign messages for specific voters, whether through online advertising or direct mail, is often referred to as *microtargeting*, and it has become widely used in campaigns that have substantial resources. The process merges consumer behavior and demographic information with voting behavior to allow campaigns to target individuals as opposed to groups of voters by geographical area (as campaigns had done in the past).[45] Once correlations between particular characteristics and voting proclivities are established, individual voters possessing given characteristics can be identified and targeted. In one of the earliest uses of this approach, the 2002 Massachusetts gubernatorial campaign of Mitt Romney recognized that those who subscribed to premium cable television were among the most likely to consider voting for Romney. Armed with lists of premium cable subscribers, the campaign was able to target those individuals with appeals to vote for Romney.[46]

To the extent that campaigns can develop very specific profiles of different groups of voters and then find individuals who match such profiles, candidates can speak directly to the interests and concerns of each voter. Though this may sound like a positive development, many voters are uncomfortable with such narrow appeals. In an impressive study of the effectiveness of targeted campaign messages, Eitan Hersh and Brian F. Schaffner found that voters prefer to receive general appeals based on "broad principles and collective benefits" than appeals tailored to their specific interests.[47] Furthermore voters who are not the targets of narrower appeals are likely to penalize candidates who make them. Thus, microtargeting may not be worth the effort.

Free Media Coverage and Debates

Though candidates spend significant amounts of money on advertising, they also work hard to gain free, or "earned," media coverage. For candidates in high-profile races, this is not particularly difficult. Candidates for lower-level races, however, have to be creative about attracting media attention. For example, can-didates often hold press conferences when there is an urgent matter to address. The topic for a press conference must be enticing, however, or the media may not attend. Reporters are most likely to show up to events that make for good video or photographs. Thus, if a candidate wants to announce a proposal for education, they are likely to do so at a school, surrounded by children.

Of course, candidates also give speeches on the campaign trail. Many of these occur with little or no notice by the media. Again, however, high-profile candidates will often attract attention for their speeches, particularly if the speech is billed as a major policy statement or if it addresses concerns about the candi-date. Barack Obama's March 2008 speech on race, in which, among other things, he distanced himself from his former pastor Jeremiah Wright, was widely cov-ered by the media, and commentators spent days reviewing his performance.

An event sure to attract media coverage is a debate between candidates. Of course, some candidates see no reason to debate their opponent. An incumbent with a large lead in the polls has nothing to gain and much to lose from debating. As a result, a candidate may refuse to debate, despite the fact that such a decision seems to contradict basic tenets of democratic campaigning. Typically, however, the expectation that candidates confront one another at least once exerts enough pressure to force even hesitant candidates into a debate.

At the nonpresidential level, local or state chapters of the League of Women Voters or the local media will often sponsor debates. During the presidential nomination process, interest groups and the national media host debates. Corpo-rations even get in on the act occasionally. In the run-up to the 2012 Republican nomination, the Tea Party Express, the American Principles Project and the Her-itage Foundation were among the organizations cosponsoring candidate debates, as were Google and Facebook.[48]

The first modern general election debate between presidential candidates was famously held in 1960 between John F. Kennedy and Richard Nixon. This debate was also the first televised debate, and it has been the subject of something like an urban legend over the years. It is said that those who watched the debate on television found Kennedy to be the winner, whereas those who listened on the radio thought Nixon won. This is taken as an illustration of the power of image over substance. In fact, recent experiments by James Druckman do indicate that television viewers, relying more heavily on personality, were significantly more likely to conclude that Kennedy won than were radio listeners.[49]

There were no presidential debates after the 1960 debate until 1976. Since then, there have been debates in every presidential election. The Commission on Presidential Debates has produced these debates since its formation in 1987. The Commission acts as a neutral organizer of the debates and sets, among other things, the dates and venues for the debates. Nevertheless, the nominees of both parties have to agree to the terms of the debates, and this can involve a con-siderable amount of negotiation. In 2004, the Memorandum of Understanding between the Kerry and Bush campaigns ran to thirty-two pages with detailed instructions, including, "The Commission shall use best efforts to maintain an appropriate temperature according to industry standards for the entire debate."[50]

It is often thought that the post-debate analysis conducted by the media has a greater impact on voters' perceptions of the candidates' performances than those performances themselves. In 1976, for instance, President Gerald Ford answered a question about Soviet dominance in Eastern Europe by saying, "There is no Soviet domination of Eastern Europe and there never will be under a Ford administration."[51] In surveys conducted immediately after the debate, few respondents mentioned Ford's comment; within days, however, the statement was widely recognized as a gaffe.[52]

While post-debate commentary certainly has a significant impact on voters' perceptions, the debates themselves have various effects on voters. Those watching debates learn candidates' issue positions and develop impressions about the candidates' character traits. Debates can even influence vote intention, though the evidence suggests that they strengthen preexisting preferences more than they alter those preferences.[53] Candidate debates have at least the potential to affect the outcome of an election and, for this reason, they are critical moments in the life of a campaign.

Polling

In addition to the various forms of communication that candidates engage in during a campaign, they also conduct multiple polls. As noted earlier, a benchmark poll is used at the beginning of a campaign to help establish the campaign strategy. During the campaign, a number of shorter "trend" or "brushfire" polls will be used to develop, refine, and gauge the success of the campaign's strategy. Brushfire polls are particularly valuable in testing the campaign's central message.[54]

In well-funded campaigns, "tracking polls" will be conducted daily near the end of the campaign. The results of one day's poll are merged with the results of the previous two days to produce a rolling average. This allows the campaign to closely monitor the voters' reactions to its activity. In particular, tracking polls help determine which campaign ads are most successful, thereby allowing the campaign to put more money behind effective ads and to pull those that are not having the desired effect.

Finally, pollsters can offer non-quantitative information to the campaign in the form of "focus groups," which consist of ten to twelve voters who are selected by the campaign based on a particular profile they fit (for example, suburban, stay-at-home mothers). The focus group is essentially a conversation between the pollster and the members of the group. It reveals, in the voters' own words, how they are thinking about the candidates and their messages. Focus groups are also used to preview specific campaign ads by voters before the ads are placed on the air.[55]

Voter Mobilization

As Election Day approaches, a campaign's attention turns to mobilizing voters. Earlier in the campaign, voter registration would have been a priority; as the campaign wore on, supporters (or potential supporters) would have been identified. The goal as the campaign draws to a close is to get as many of those supporters to the polls as possible.

The GOTV operation begins when either early or absentee voting begins. Campaigns make sure that those who need absentee ballots get them, and they encourage people to vote early in states that allow this practice. However, the bulk of the GOTV effort occurs in the last few days of the campaign. Most of the voter contact methods mentioned previously are used to mobilize voters. Potential voters will receive direct mail, telephone calls (both pre-recorded and live), and e-mails. Volunteers from the campaign, a political party, and/or interest groups are also likely to visit supporters. Ultimately, campaigns try to reach potential voters in as many ways and as many times as possible before—not to mention on—Election Day. As one political consultant put it, "Campaigns with sufficient money are using every conceivable means to pierce that veil of indifference that the voters have put up."[56]

Unfortunately for campaigns, until recently there was no way to know what worked and what did not. However, in an extensive study of mobilization tactics, Donald Green and Alan Gerber have shown that the most effective method of getting voters to the polls is door-to-door contact, followed by live phone calls (robo-calls have no effect). The former generated one vote per fourteen contacts, and the latter produced one vote per thirty or thirty-five contacts (depending upon whether the call was made by a commercial phone bank or by volunteers). Partisan leafleting generated one voter for every sixty-six registered voters who received material; nonpartisan leafleting produced one vote per 200 contacts. Direct mail did no better (or only marginally better, depending on whether the mail was nonpartisan or partisan) than nonpartisan leafleting, and email contact had no discernible effect.[57]

The central Green and Gerber finding—that person-to-person contact is the best method for mobilizing voters—has apparently been accepted by the parties and by campaign consultants. In recent years, considerable resources and effort have been put into this aspect of the ground war. In fact, Democrats had been emphasizing grassroots campaigning for some time. They did so, in large measure, by relying on union volunteers to go door to door in key precincts. The Republicans, conversely, traditionally devoted few resources to voter mobilization and more to advertising. In fact, an old political joke maintains that Democrats think GOTV means "get-on-the-van," while Republicans think it stands for "get-on-television."

The difference in approaches was evident to Republicans after the 2000 presidential cliffhanger in Florida. In fact, George W. Bush underperformed in a number of states in 2000; that is, his final vote percentage was lower than the last-minute polls suggested it would be. After studying the discrepancies, the RNC decided that far more effort needed to be placed on voter mobilization and that it had to consist of person-to-person contact. The result was an operation called the 72-Hour Task Force. The goal of the 72-Hour Task Force was to aggressively target the Republican Party's base by putting thousands of volunteers in key districts around the country to contact those voters in person during the final seventy-two hours before the election.[58] The party tested this operation in 2001 and implemented it in the 2002 midterm elections as a dry run for the presidential election to follow. In 2004, the 72-Hour Task Force was widely credited with boosting Republican turnout and helping to secure President Bush's reelection victory.

The Democrats had their own massive GOTV operation in 2004 but, as in the past, it relied mostly on outside groups.[59] America Votes, a coalition of progressive interest groups supporting John Kerry for president, and America Coming Together (ACT), a left-wing GOTV organization, mobilized voters in battleground states and districts. Though these efforts failed to elect Kerry in 2004, the Democratic-affiliated GOTV operation did exceed its turnout goals.[60] America Votes helped Democrats win control of Congress in 2006 and complemented the Obama campaign's impressive GOTV effort in 2008, but ACT closed shop in 2005.

In 2016, the RNC handled most of the voter mobilization effort for Trump. They claimed that by Election Day they were going to have knocked on 17 million doors. This was a vast improvement over the 11.5 million households contacted in 2012. Party volunteers were also using a newly developed phone app to target potential Republican voters.[61] On the Democratic side, the Clinton campaign directed the GOTV operation, just as the Obama campaign had done in 2012. Though many observers believed Clinton had an advantage over Trump in terms of voter mobilization, some Democrats worried that Clinton's operation lagged behind Obama's 2012 effort.[62] The election results, particularly in places like Wisconsin, Michigan, and Pennsylvania, suggest they were right to be concerned.

Given a fragmented audience's expanded entertainment options and the widespread availability of digital video recording systems, television advertising is likely to become a relatively inefficient means of communication with voters. As a result, the ground game will continue to play an increasingly vital role in campaigns. For many observers, this is a positive—indeed a democratic—trend in American politics. It harkens back to a day when torchlight parades stirred the party faithful to march to the polls. Nevertheless, there are still concerns about the health of campaigns in the United States. The next section takes a brief look at the functions of campaigns and, ultimately, addresses the question of whether campaigns are beneficial to our democracy.

▶ Normative Considerations

As mentioned at the outset of this chapter, Americans tend to dislike campaigns and have for quite some time. A long list of grievances exists, but Stanley Kelley's 1960 catalog of campaign offenses could well apply today: "excessive and sentimental concern with personality, appeals to prejudice and irrationality, libelous accusations, gross distortions of fact, promises not to be fulfilled, and evasiveness and ambiguity in the presentation of a meager offering of issues."[63] Are contemporary campaigns worthy of condemnation on these or any other grounds? Before we can answer that question, it would be useful to establish the standards by which campaigns are to be judged.

Recall that in Chapter 1, the functions of campaigns were described in some detail. Campaigns were said to serve as a forum for debate, discussion, and deliberation. They also promote citizen participation and allow "outsiders" an opportunity to voice their opinions. Fundamentally, however, campaigns help citizens formulate their preferences and, ultimately, decide for whom to vote on Election Day. To do so rationally, campaigns must satisfy certain criteria. To the extent that they answer the following questions in the affirmative, according to Kelley, campaigns will have performed their most basic duty:

> Are voters exposed to the arguments of both sides? Does the discussion facilitate the identification of distortions and of false statements of fact? Are the candidates' statements of their views and intentions clear? Do candidates define their points of disagreement? Do campaigners offer evidence for their assertions and give reasons for favoring (or for having favored) particular policies? Are the sources of information clearly identified?[64]

There may be no objective way to answer these questions. Nevertheless, it is worth contemplating each of them to draw at least a preliminary conclusion about the state of campaigning in the United States today. So, are voters exposed to both candidates' arguments? Undoubtedly they are, whether by advertising and direct mail or by debates. The media may help or hinder this exposure, but campaigns expend considerable resources to get the word out about their candidates and, by and large, they are successful; there is considerable evidence that people learn from campaigns.[65]

Are misleading statements, not to mention lies, easily identified? Here the answer is not as obvious. Fact-checking efforts by the media (including the *Tampa Bay Times*' PolitiFact) and other watchdog groups (FactCheck.org of the University of Pennsylvania's Annenberg Public Policy Center, among them) can assist in pointing out distortions, but some recent research suggests that the conclusions drawn by fact-checking sites are often inconsistent.[66] Furthermore, campaigns are often tempted to stretch the truth. It is probably rare that misstatements are made willfully; instead, the nature of campaigning creates an intense us-versus-them mentality in which campaigners come to believe the worst about an opponent. Though compelling evidence contradicts the claims made by the Swift Boat Veterans for Truth about John Kerry's war record, they no doubt sincerely believed that he was lying about that record. In the middle of a campaign, it becomes very difficult to discern the truth when charges and countercharges of lying are tossed about liberally.

The next two questions ought to be treated jointly, as they are closely related to one another. Do candidates clearly state their positions and their points of disagreement? They certainly do the latter. Negative campaigning often serves to sharpen differences between candidates. Furthermore, as mentioned earlier in this chapter, comparative and attack advertisements have been shown to have considerable policy content. Of course, some negative campaigning is simply intended to raise doubts, substantive or otherwise, about the opponent and may do little more than confuse voters.

This leads us to the first part of our question: Just how clear are candidates in stating their own positions? Recall that Anthony Downs considered it rational for candidates and parties to be ambiguous in their campaign statements. In fact, candidates do often make vague pronouncements and value-based statements that are unobjectionable and, as a result, are not very useful to the voters. However, they also issue policy proposals that can be quite specific. For instance, the health care plans of most of the candidates running for president in 2008 were quite detailed, and they stimulated serious discussion between the candidates. Hillary Clinton and Barack Obama, for example, argued over the wisdom of health insurance mandates.

To complicate matters, candidates are also engaged in deliberately priming voters. When they do so, they are emphasizing different sets of issues even if they are clearly stating their own positions. This makes dialogue between the candidates—something many observers think is necessary for a properly functioning campaign—difficult, if not impossible, to achieve. More than ambiguity, then, we should be worried about candidates simply talking past one another.

Do campaigns provide evidence for their claims and justification for their policy positions? By and large, they do. In an age of intense media scrutiny, campaigns are forced to cite sources for the assertions they make. Candidates, for example, often cite independent studies to bolster their claims about the extent of a problem or the ability of a particular policy to successfully address that problem. Yet there is no good way for the voter to know whether this evidence is credible. Furthermore, complex policy debates often have conflicting pieces of evidence. Does gun control reduce gun violence or not? There are statistics and studies to bolster both sides of the argument. Finally, facts can be chosen selectively and can be taken out of context to serve as evidence of something other than what they originally meant. Thus, the better question may be, do campaigns provide *valid* evidence for their claims and how are we to know?

Candidates are also expected to justify positions they take. It is hard to image a candidate stating a position and not explaining—or being asked to explain—why they took that position. And those justifications receive considerable scrutiny. In 2004, John Kerry was asked about his vote against an $87 billion supplemental defense spending package for Iraq and Afghanistan. Kerry had voted for an earlier version of the package that repealed tax cuts for the wealthy, but he voted against the final version of the bill, which did not repeal the tax cuts. In trying to explain that he supported funding the military operations, he said, "I actually did vote for the $87 billion before I voted against it." That explanation, which sounds as though Kerry wanted to have it both ways, eventually found its way into a negative ad by the Bush campaign against Kerry.[67]

Finally, Kelley asked whether sources of information are clearly identified. He was writing at a time when anonymous campaign appeals were relatively common. Candidates must now approve the messages in their campaign ads, and campaign communications of all sorts have long been required to contain a "Paid for by ... " disclaimer. Thus, voters should know when a candidate or a party is behind an ad. Interest groups, conversely, present something of a problem. Group names are often vague and patriotic, such as FreedomWorks (a conservative organization), America's Power (a coal industry group), and Working America (a group affiliated with the AFL-CIO). Not only do the names of groups often obscure their identity, their communications routinely mimic candidate rhetoric. It is often hard to distinguish the campaign ads of candidates and independent groups, particularly when those ads are negative. To this day, for instance, many people believe that the Bush campaign produced the infamous "Willie Horton" ad in 1988 when, in fact, it was an ad by the vaguely named National Security PAC.

In the end, American campaigns are flawed but not as appalling as they are often made out to be. Of the six questions we reviewed in this section, we can answer "yes" to two of them, can provide a qualified "yes" to another, and on three there is mixed evidence. On balance, therefore, we can conclude that campaigns do more good than harm and that they enable voters to make reasonably rational choices. This is the conclusion Roderick Hart comes to after an impressive study of campaign discourse. "Campaigns are hardly perfect," writes Hart,

> but they make politicians and their constituents more interdependent, more imme-
> diately engaged, and also foster genuine give-and-take. ... I have also found that
> campaigns reinvigorate the political process, bringing regional perspectives to
> bear on national matters. ... Finally, campaigns continually help the American
> people find their center point ... There is much that is wrong with campaigns, and
> those sins have been amply documented elsewhere. But far more sinful would be
> to overlook the great good done every four years when the American people are
> confronted with their political leaders and asked to choose among them.[68]

This conclusion should not make us any less vigilant in trying to improve campaigns, but it should make us hesitate before offering knee-jerk condemnation of the current condition of those campaigns.

▶ Conclusion

Political campaigns are among the most dramatic events in American politics. As a result, they create a great deal of interest in, and excitement about, elections. However, not all campaigns are equally interesting or exciting. In general, the larger the scope of the campaign, the more attention it will receive from the media and, consequently, the voters. Beyond their scope and the attention they command, campaigns differ in a number of other ways including the amount of money spent, the issues discussed, and the office at stake (i.e. executive, legislative, or even judicial) and the expectations voters have of that office.

All campaigns, regardless of size, need a plan for success. Campaign plans are developed at the earliest stages and are based on several considerations including the campaign environment (i.e. the jurisdiction and the conditions therein), the candidates and their backgrounds, and the makeup of the electorate. The plan will also identify the resources needed for an effective operation. Those resources include money, of course, but also people, including paid staff and volunteers.

Campaigns must also develop strategies. A campaign's strategy is simply the answer to the question, "How will we win?" The most important element of the strategy is the candidate's message, or the rationale for electing the candidate (and defeating the opponent). The strategy will also determine ways in which the candidate can "position" him or herself on important issues. This is not to say that candidates simply adopt the most popular positions on issues. Instead, candidates have to decide which issues to emphasize ("deliberate priming") and how to explain (or frame) their positions on issues on which they may be out of step with the voters.

Campaign plans and strategies have to be implemented and there are a host of tactics used for that purpose. For example, candidates can raise money by holding fund-raising events or through direct solicitations (which can be done by phone, by mail, or online). Campaigns also spread their messages in a variety of ways. The most obvious, and most expensive, way is through television advertising, but candidates also communicate through direct mail, social media, door-to-door canvassing, and Internet advertising. Finally, campaigns attempt to earn media coverage (or "free media") and candidates participate in debates; campaigns make use of polling to adjust their efforts throughout the campaign; and, perhaps most important of all, they work extremely hard to get voters to the polls.

Many political observers are highly critical of the way campaigns function. The charges range from excessive negativity to blatant disregard for the truth. Upon closer inspection, however, we are likely to conclude that campaigns do more good than harm. If nothing else, they engage the electorate and motivate people to participate in elections.

▶ *Pedagogical Tools*

Role-Play Scenario

For this scenario, you will have to select a candidate in a competitive race for the US House of Representatives.[69]

A candidate for the US House of Representatives has hired you as the lead political consultant for their campaign. Write a campaign plan for the candidate that includes (1) a description of the campaign environment (i.e. national conditions, the district, the candidates, and the electorate) and (2) a campaign strategy for your candidate (including a message box).

Discussion Questions

1. What is the most likely consequence of the reliance on polls in campaigns: better manipulation of voters or better representation of their interests? Explain your answer.
2. Is negative campaigning helpful or harmful to democracy? Why?
3. Are there good reasons to be concerned about "microtargeting?" What might those reasons be?
4. On the basis of Stanley Kelley's criteria, what is your own assessment of American campaigns? Are there criteria that should have been included in Kelley's list of questions that were not? If so, what are they?

Online Resources

Campaigns and Elections, www.campaignsandelections.com.
FactCheck.org, Annenberg Public Policy Center of the University of Pennsylvania, www.factcheck.org.
The Living Room Candidate, Presidential Campaign Commercials, 1952–2004, www.livingroomcandidate.org.
PolitiFact, www.politifact.com.

Suggested Reading

Donald P. Green and Alan S. Gerber (2015) *Get Out the Vote: How to Increase Voter Turnout*, 3rd edn, Washington, DC: Brookings Institution Press.
Eitan D. Hersh (2015) *Hacking the Electorate: How Campaigns Perceive Voters*, Cambridge: Cambridge University Press.
Sasha Issenberg (2012) *The Victory Lab: The Secret Science of Winning Campaigns*, New York: Crown Publishers.
Richard J. Semiatin (2016) *Campaigns on the Cutting Edge*, 3rd edn, Washington, DC: CQ Press.
Darrell M. West (2014) *Air Wars: Television Advertising and Social Media in Election Campaigns, 1952–2012*, 6th edn, Washington, DC: CQ Press.

▶ *Notes*

1 John Sides (2012) "Mapping Romney and Obama Field Offices," *The Monkey Cage*, November 6, http://themonkeycage.org/2012/11/06/mapping-romney-and-obama-field-offices (accessed March 24, 2017).
2 *Center for Responsive Politics (n.d.) "2016 Election Overview: Stats at a Glance," www.opensecrets.org/overview/index.php?cycle=2016&type=A&display=A (accessed February 19, 2017). Averages are based on data released by the Federal Election Commission on February 18, 2017.*

3 William R. Sweeney (2004) "The Principles of Campaign Planning," in James A. Thurber and Candice J. Nelson (eds.), *Campaigns and Elections American Style*, 2nd edn, Boulder, CO: Westview Press, p. 17.

4 Sweeney, "The Principles of Campaign Planning," pp. 23–31.

5 John Bovée (1999) "Opposition Research," in David D. Perlmutter (ed.), *The Manship School Guide to Political Communication*, Baton Rouge, LA: Louisiana State University Press.

6 Stephen K. Medvic (2003) "Campaign Pollsters and Polling: Manipulating the Voter or Taking the Electorate's Pulse," in Robert Watson and Colton Campbell (eds.), *Campaigns and Elections: Issues, Concepts, and Cases*, Boulder, CO: Lynne Rienner Publishers, pp. 35–36.

7 Joel C. Bradshaw (2004) "Who Will Vote for You and Why: Designing Campaign Strategy and Message," in James A. Thurber and Candice J. Nelson (eds.), *Campaigns and Elections American Style*, 2nd edn, Boulder, CO: Westview Press, pp. 38–40.

8 Sweeney, "The Principles of Campaign Planning," p. 21.

9 Ron Faucheux (1994) "The Message," *Campaigns and Elections*, May, p. 47.

10 See Medvic, "Campaign Pollsters and Polling," pp. 39–41.

11 Anthony Downs (1957) *An Economic Theory of Democracy*, New York: Harper & Row, p. 134.

12 Downs, *An Economic Theory of Democracy*, pp. 115, 136, and 135–139.

13 Bernard Grofman (2004) "Downs and Two-Party Convergence," *Annual Review of Political Science*, 7: 25–46.

14 Barry C. Burden (2004) "Candidate Positioning in US Congressional Elections," *British Journal of Political Science*, 34: 211–227.

15 Joan Vennochi (2007) "Sister Souljah Moments," *Boston Globe*, September 16, www.boston.com/news/nation/articles/2007/09/16/sister_souljah_moments (accessed March 24, 2017).

16 Byron E. Shafer and William J. M. Claggett (1995) *The Two Majorities: The Issue Context of Modern American Politics*, Baltimore, MD: The Johns Hopkins University Press, pp. 23–24.

17 Stephen K. Medvic (2001) *Political Consultants in US Congressional Elections*, Columbus, OH: Ohio State University Press; Stephen K. Medvic (2006) "Understanding Campaign Strategy: 'Deliberate Priming' and the Role of Professional Political Consultants," *Journal of Political Marketing*, 5: 11–32.

18 Lawrence R. Jacobs and Robert Y. Shapiro (1994) "Issues, Candidate Image, and Priming: The Use of Private Polls in Kennedy's 1960 Presidential Campaign," *The American Political Science Review*, 88, p. 528.

19 See James N. Druckman (2004) "Priming the Vote: Campaign Effects in a US Senate Election," *Political Psychology*, 25: 577–594; and James N. Druckman, Lawrence R. Jacobs, and Eric Ostermeier (2004) "Candidate Strategies to Prime Issues and Image," *Journal of Politics*, 66: 1180–1202.

20 Danny Hayes (2005) "Candidate Qualities through a Partisan Lens: A Theory of Trait Ownership," *American Journal of Political Science*, 49: 908–923.

21 Stephen K. Medvic (2004) "Developing 'Paid Media' Strategies: Media Consultants and Political Advertising," in David A. Schultz (ed.), *Lights, Camera, Campaigns! Media, Politics, and Political Advertising*, New York: Peter Lang, p. 33.

22 Steve Gorman (2007) "Clinton Doubles Obama Sum in Hollywood Fund-Raiser," Reuters, March 26, www.reuters.com/article/entertainmentNews/idUSN2345209520070326 (accessed March 24, 2017).

23 Peter L. Francia and Paul S. Herrnson (2001) "Begging for Bucks," *Campaigns and Elections*, April, pp. 51–52.

24 Associated Press (2007) "Paul Sets One-Day GOP Fundraising Record," *NBC News*, November 6, www.msnbc.msn.com/id/21646939 (accessed March 24, 2017).

25 Bruce Bimber and Richard Davis (2003) *Campaigning Online: The Internet in US Elections*, Oxford: Oxford University Press, p. 39.

26 Monica Postelnicu, Justin D. Martin, and Kristen D. Landreville (2006) "The Role of Campaign Web Sites in Promoting Candidates and Attracting Campaign Resources," in Andrew Paul Williams and John C. Tedesco (eds.), *The Internet Election: Perspectives on the Web in Campaign 2004*, Lanham, MD: Rowman & Littlefield, p. 105.

27 Michael Scherer (2012a) "Exclusive: Obama's 2012 Digital Fundraising Outperformed 2008," *Time.com*, November 15, http://swampland.time.com/2012/11/15/exclusive-obamas-2012-digital-fundraising-outperformed-2008 (accessed March 24, 2017).

28 Joshua Green (2012) "The Science Behind Those Obama Campaign E-Mails," *Bloomberg Businessweek*, November 29, www.bloomberg.com/news/articles/2012-11-29/the-science-behind-those-obama-campaign-e-mails (accessed March 24, 2017).

29 See Darrell M. West (2001) *Air Wars: Television Advertising in Election Campaigns, 1952–2000*, 3rd edn, Washington, DC: CQ Press, p. 3; and Kathleen Hall Jamieson (1996) *Packaging the Presidency: A History and Criticism of Presidential Campaign Advertising*, 3rd edn, Oxford: Oxford University Press.

30 FactCheck.org (2004b) "Republican-Funded Group Attacks Kerry's War Record," updated August 22, http://dev.factcheck.org/2004/08/republican-funded-group-attacks-kerrys-war-record (accessed March 24, 2017).

31 The Willie Horton ad can be viewed at www.youtube.com/watch?v=EC9j6Wfdq3o (accessed March 24, 2017).

32 See Tali Mendelberg (2001) *The Race Card: Campaign Strategy, Implicit Messages, and the Norm of Equality*, Princeton, NJ: Princeton University Press, Chapter 5.

33 Erika Franklin Fowler and Travis N. Ridout (2012) "Negative, Angry, and Ubiquitous: Political Advertising in 2012," *The Forum*, 10, p. 59.

34 John G. Geer (2006) *In Defense of Negativity: Attack Ads in Presidential Campaigns*, Chicago, IL: University of Chicago Press, p. 60. See also Kathleen Hall Jamieson, Paul Waldman, and Susan Sherr (2000) "Eliminate the Negative? Categories of Analysis for Political Advertisements," in James A. Thurber, Candice J. Nelson, and David A. Dulio (eds.), *Crowded Airwaves: Campaign Advertising in Elections*, Washington, DC: Brookings Institution Press, pp. 57–60.

35 Geer, *In Defense of Negativity*, p. 61.

36 Tiffany A. Ito, Jeff T. Larsen, N. Kyle Smith, and John T. Cacioppo (1998) "Negative Information Weighs More Heavily on the Brain: The Negativity Bias in Evaluative Categorizations," *Journal of Personality and Social Psychology*, 75, p. 887.

37 Richard R. Lau, Lee Sigelman, Caroline Heldman, and Paul Babbitt (1999) "The Effects of Negative Political Advertisements: A Meta-Analytic Assessment," *American Political Science Review*, 93, p. 859.

38 See West, *Air Wars*, pp. 115–116.

39 For a review of the campaign advertising literature, see Kenneth Goldstein and Travis N. Ridout (2004) "Measuring the Effects of Televised Political Advertising in the United States," *Annual Review of Political Science*, 7: 205–226.

40 David B. Magleby and J. Quin Monson (eds.) (2004) *The Last Hurrah: Soft Money and Issue Advocacy in the 2002 Congressional Elections*, Washington, DC: Brookings Institution Press, pp. 7–8.

41 Michael Scherer (2012b) "Friended: How the Obama Campaign Connected with Young Voters," *Time*, November 20, http://swampland.time.com/2012/11/20/friended-how-the-obama-campaign-connected-with-young-voters (accessed March 24, 2017).

42 Marcus Gilmer (2016) "Report: Donald Trump's Campaign Won't Let Him Tweet Anymore," *Mashable*, November 6, http://mashable.com/2016/11/06/trump-cant-tweet/#c5I.MKicP5qC (accessed March 4, 2017).

43 Tanzina Vega (2012) "Online Data Helping Campaigns Customize Ads," *New York Times*, February 20, www.nytimes.com/2012/02/21/us/politics/campaigns-use-microtargeting-to-attract-supporters.html?pagewanted=all&_r=0 (accessed March 24, 2017).

44 Issie Lapowsky (2015) "Political Ad Spending Online is About to Explode," *Wired.com*, August 18, www.wired.com/2015/08/digital-politcal-ads-2016 (accessed March 4, 2017).

45 See Rasmus Kleis Nielsen (2012) *Ground Wars: Personalized Communication in Political Campaigns*, Princeton, NJ: Princeton University Press, pp. 137–146; and Eitan D. Hersh (2015) *Hacking the Electorate: How Campaigns Perceive Voters*, Cambridge: Cambridge University Press.

46 Sasha Issenberg (2012c) *The Victory Lab: The Secret Science of Winning Campaigns*, New York: Crown Publishers, p. 132.

47 Eitan D. Hersh and Brian F. Schaffner (2013) "Targeted Campaign Appeals and the Value of Ambiguity," *Journal of Politics*, 75, p. 522.

48 See the full list of Republican presidential debates at 2016 Election Central. "2012 Primary Debate Schedule," www.uspresidentialelectionnews.com/2012-debate-schedule/2011-2012-primary-debate-schedule (accessed March 24, 2017).

49 James N. Druckman (2003) "The Power of Television Images: The First Kennedy-Nixon Debate Revisited," *Journal of Politics*, 65, p. 568.

50 Bush-Cheney '04 and Kerry-Edwards '04 (2004) "Memorandum of Understanding on Debates," September 22, http://news.findlaw.com/hdocs/docs/election2004/debates-2004mou.html (accessed March 24, 2017).

51 See the discussion of this statement in "Debating Our Destiny; 1976: No Audio and No Soviet Domination," 2000. Public Broadcasting Service, www.pbs.org/newshour/debatingourdestiny/dod/1976-broadcast.html (accessed May 18, 2013).

52 Kathleen Hall Jamieson and David S. Birdsell (1988) *Presidential Debates: The Challenge of Creating an Informed Electorate*, Oxford: Oxford University Press, p. 172.

53 William L. Benoit and Glenn J. Hansen (2004) "Presidential Debate Watching, Issue Knowledge, Character Evaluation, and Vote Choice," *Human Communication Research*, 30: 121–144; and Kim L. Fridkin, Patrick J. Kenney, Sarah Allen Gershon, Karen Shafer, and Gina Serignese Woodall (2007) "Capturing the Power of a Campaign Event: The 2004 Presidential Debate in Tempe," *Journal of Politics*, 69: 770–785.

54 Medvic, "Campaign Pollsters and Polling," p. 36.

55 Medvic, "Campaign Pollsters and Polling," pp. 36–37.

56 As quoted in Larry Powell and Joseph Cowart (2003) *Political Campaign Communication: Inside and Out*. Boston, MA: Allyn & Bacon, p. 134.

57 Donald Green and Alan S. Gerber (2004) *Get Out the Vote! How to Increase Voter Turnout*, Washington, DC: Brookings Institution Press, p. 94, Table 8.1.

58 Peter Ubertaccio (2007) "Machine Politics for the Twenty-First Century? Multilevel Marketing and Party Organizations," in John C. Green and Daniel J. Coffey (eds.), *The State of the Parties: The Changing Role of Contemporary American Parties*, Lanham, MD: Rowman & Littlefield, pp. 181–185.

59 David B. Magleby, J. Quin Monson, and Kelly D. Patterson (eds.) (2007) *Dancing without Partners: How Candidates, Parties, and Interest Groups Interact in the Presidential Campaign*, Lanham, MD: Rowman & Littlefield, pp. 8–18.

60 See Mat Bai (2004) "Who Lost Ohio?" *The New York Times Magazine*, November 21, www.nytimes.com/2004/11/21/magazine/21OHIO.html?_r=0 (accessed March 24, 2017).

61 Dana Bash and Abigail Crutchfield (2016) "The Final Get-Out-the-Vote Flurry Begins," *CNN*, November 4, www.cnn.com/2016/11/04/politics/get-out-the-vote-efforts-2016-election (accessed March 4, 2017).

62 Patricia Murphy (2016) "Democrats Worry about Hillary Clinton's Ground Game," *The Daily Beast*, October 17, www.thedailybeast.com/articles/2016/10/17/democrats-worry-about-hillary-clinton-s-ground-game.html (accessed March 4, 2017).

63 Stanley Kelley, Jr. (1960) *Political Campaigning: Problems in Creating an Informed Electorate*, Washington, DC: The Brookings Institution, p. 2.

64 Kelley, *Political Campaigning*, p. 16.

65 See Shanto Iyengar and Adam F. Simon (2000) "New Perspectives and Evidence on Political Communication and Campaign Effects," *Annual Review of Psychology*, 51: 154–156.

66 Morgan Marietta, David C. Barker, and Todd Bowser (2015) "Fact-Checking Polarized Politics: Does the Fact-Check Industry Provide Consistent Guidance on Disputed Realities?" *The Forum*, 13: 577–596.

67 FactCheck.org (2004a) "Did Kerry Vote 'No' on Body Armor for Troops?" updated March 18, http://dev.factcheck.org/2004/03/did-kerry-vote-no-on-body-armor (accessed March 24, 2017).

68 Roderick Hart (2000) *Campaign Talk: Why Elections Are Good for Us*, Princeton, NJ: Princeton University Press, p. 102.

69 A current "Competitive House Race Chart" can be downloaded from the Cook Political Report at www.cookpolitical.com (accessed March 24, 2017).

10 Elections

ELECTION DAY is the culmination of months, perhaps years, of campaigning. On that day, the voters reach a collective decision about who will lead their city, state, or nation. When the principles of democracy are widely held and the norms of democratic transition are well established, those vying for power will accept the voters' verdict without a violent struggle (though all too often in the United States, legal battles may ensue). In the history of humankind, the nonviolent transfer of power is a rare occurrence.

Election results possess considerable power. They can bring about significant change in society and set the course for public policy that will affect not only the United States but the rest of the world as well. It matters, therefore, who wins elections. It is not an exaggeration to say that the course of history would have been different had, for example, Al Gore been sworn in as president on January 20, 2001, instead of George W. Bush.

Of course, not every election is as momentous as the 2000 election. After a brief discussion of the uniqueness of presidential elections, this chapter will explore the categorization of elections. It will then turn to an explanation of how election outcomes are determined. If elections are as important as has been suggested here, it is worth understanding the factors that influence them. Particular attention will be paid to the question of whether, given the predictability of elections, campaigns have any impact. Finally, the chapter will ask whether election winners can ever legitimately claim a "mandate" from their victories.

▶ The Uniqueness of Presidential Elections

Most elected offices in the United States are filled in the same way—parties nominate candidates, usually in direct primaries, who then compete for office in a general election in which the candidate with most votes wins. There are variations on this process—some states do not use direct primaries to nominate candidates, and some jurisdictions require a majority of the vote to win—but, by and large, elections from city council to the US Senate and from Maine to California are held in similar ways (which have been described in various chapters throughout this book). One glaring exception, however, is the system for electing presidents. The operation of presidential elections is unique and so complex that an explanation of the process is in order.

The "Invisible Primary"

Like other candidates, presidential hopefuls must first win their parties' nomination before they can compete in the general election. Unlike all other candidates in the United States, however, presidential candidates must compete in multiple nomination contests over a period of several months that culminate in an official nomination at the party's national convention. Complicating matters is the fact that the nomination contests in which they compete differ from state to state.

The entire nomination process starts years before the first contest is held in January or February of the presidential election year. Officially, a number of candidates will announce their 2020 candidacy for president immediately after the 2018 midterm elections. Unofficially, the serious candidates have been running for president since Donald Trump won in November 2016. The earliest stage of the presidential nomination process has come to be known as the invisible primary.[1] The invisible primary is the attempt by presidential hopefuls to garner support from politically influential individuals, including elected officials and party activists, in states that are critical to winning the party's nomination. Fundamentally, candidates are seeking two forms of support: endorsements and contributions. They are also attempting to line up campaign assistance, from both volunteers and the leading professional campaign consultants. Because so few people have ever run a presidential campaign, experienced consultants are in high demand.

The dynamic of the invisible primary is something of a self-fulfilling prophecy. Candidates perceived to be viable are able to raise money and secure endorsements, which make them more viable and better able to raise additional money and secure further endorsements. Those who are not viewed as viable at the start of the process have a difficult time raising money and getting endorsements, and they rarely manage to break into the top tier of candidates. It happens—Donald Trump being perhaps the best example—but not often.

When candidates do emerge from the shadows to become serious candidates, it makes for an interesting story, but rarely much else. Before 2016, the only dark horse candidate to have earned his party's nomination was Jimmy Carter in 1976. In fact, since 1976, only three candidates who led in national polls going into the Iowa caucuses did not eventually win their party's nomination—Gary Hart in 1988, Howard Dean in 2004, and Hillary Clinton in 2008.[2] Though the eventual winner in each of those races might not have been considered the front-runner, they were well positioned to assume the lead early in the nomination process. Michael Dukakis, for example, trailed Hart in the polls by only a small margin in 1988 and had actually raised more money than Hart had going into the Iowa caucuses.[3] In 2004, John Kerry had been considered the frontrunner by pundits early in the race and had more money than any other candidate, save Dean. And though Barack Obama was considered a long shot when he announced his candidacy in January of 2007, his presidential bid was described at the time as "accelerating his already rapid emergence in national politics and establishing him as his party's most formidable rival" to Hillary Clinton.[4] To be sure, he did trail Clinton in the national polls by roughly twenty points on the eve of the Iowa caucuses, but he also had raised just as much money as she had in 2007. Thus, the hope that a candidate could appear out of nowhere to win the first contest, as Carter had done, and then carry that momentum to the nomination is little more than fantasy.

The invisible primary is, then, instrumental in determining the parties' nominees. In fact, the authors of an important study of this phenomenon call it "the modern analog of the smoke-filled room at the old style party conventions—the venue in which the party makes up its collective mind about whom to nominate." These scholars find that a candidate's standing in the polls and their share of party insider endorsements influence success in the nomination process independently. However, "during the invisible primary, endorsements seem to affect polls more than polls affect endorsements. And in the state primaries, endorsements seem to predict the outcome better than the polls."[5] The difference between the effects of endorsements and the effects of polls is not statistically significant, but it does lead the authors to the conclusion that party insiders are at least as valuable, and probably more valuable, in the early stages of the nomination battle than public support.

This understanding of the way nominations operate has come to be known as the "party decides" theory, named after the title of the book in which it appears. The theory plausibly explains the outcome of presidential nominations from 1980 through the 2000 election. After that, the party "regulars" (sometimes referred to as the party "establishment") began to have a much harder time coalescing behind a favorite candidate. Indeed, there was no obvious establishment favorite on the Democratic side in 2004 or the Republican side in 2008, 2012 or 2016. In 2008, Democratic insiders backed Hillary Clinton early in the process but then rallied behind Obama as he showed signs of strength. Thus, in five of the last six contested nomination battles, the party regulars either couldn't decide on preferred candidate or picked one whom they later abandoned.

Many believe that the 2016 Republican nomination of Donald Trump was a final blow to the party decides theory of nominations. However, it is important to note what, exactly, the theory predicts. It posits that when party insiders select a preferred candidate, that candidate should win the nomination. The theory says nothing about what will happen when the insiders fail to unite behind a candidate. There is no doubt that Republican insiders were quite unified in their opposition to Donald Trump. However, in the absence of a consensus alternative to

Trump, the party was powerless to direct the outcome of the nomination. Thus, the real problem with the party decides theory is that it fails to account for the fact that party insiders have had such a difficult time in recent election cycles coalescing behind a candidate.

In a brief 2016 article, the authors of *The Party Decides* grappled with this inability to explain recent presidential nominations. They pointed to three factors that make it difficult for party regulars to control the nomination. Those factors are intra-party disharmony (or a lack of unity among the party's factions), "opportunities for insurgents to communicate with voters, and the availability of funding to insurgents."[6] Obviously, when party factionalism is high, it will be harder for party insiders to agree on a single candidate who should be the party's nominee. In addition, the ability of candidates to communicate directly to voters via social media outlets (think of Trump's use of Twitter) and an increase in the number of debates before and during the primaries, means that the "invisible primary" is not so invisible anymore. Indeed, the authors refer to this emerging communication environment as a "new 'media primary.'"[7] Finally, the availability of large amounts of money far earlier in the process (including support of individual candidates by super-PACs devoted to them) means that a candidate with sufficient funding can garner attention in a way they couldn't have done in past cycles.

In many ways, Donald Trump's nomination in 2016 is an anomaly; in others, it is just the latest example of a nomination process in transition. Regardless, the prevailing theories of presidential nominations are clearly in need of revision.

Nomination Contests

The actual nomination contests begin with the Iowa caucuses in January of the election year. That contest has become extremely important in the nomination process, triggering as it does both "momentum" for those candidates who win or exceed expectations and a "winnowing" of the field of candidates as those who do not finish near the top begin dropping out of the race.[8] Candidates who win in Iowa get a noticeable bounce in the New Hampshire polls, but an Iowa victory does not necessarily produce a win in New Hampshire. In 2008, the winner of the Iowa caucuses in both parties—Barack Obama (D) and Mike Huckabee (R)—lost in New Hampshire. And though Ted Cruz took first place in the 2016 Iowa caucuses, the senator from Texas finished third in New Hampshire.

The reason a win in Iowa does not automatically mean victory in New Hampshire is because Iowa and New Hampshire are not only very different states, they have very different systems for choosing convention delegates. While Iowa is a caucus, New Hampshire is a primary, and an open primary at that (see Chapter 5). Caucuses are lengthy meetings and require considerable effort on the part of voters; as a result, participants are relatively dedicated party loyalists. Voting in New Hampshire's primary is not only quick and easy, but independent voters can vote in the primary of their choice. This means that the average primary voter in New Hampshire is not likely to be as committed a partisan as is the Iowa caucus-goer. That, in turn, means that maverick candidates can sometimes win in New Hampshire, as Gary Hart (1984), Pat Buchanan (1996), John McCain (2000), and Donald Trump (2016) each did.

Candidates can secure the nomination without winning both Iowa and New Hampshire, but it is extremely difficult to do so without winning one or the other. In fact, since 1968, only two candidates in either party have gone on to get their party's nomination without winning either state—George McGovern, who lost to Edmund Muskie in both states in 1972, and Bill Clinton in 1992. Thus, winning in either Iowa or New Hampshire is almost a necessity for winning the nomination. This is because voters in later states take cues from the results in the first two contests. Winning early gives the impression that a candidate is "electable," and this idea helps build momentum. In fact, a study by two Brown University economists indicates that voters in Iowa and New Hampshire have as much as twenty times the impact on the nomination as do voters in later states.[9]

Even Bill Clinton's 1992 loss in New Hampshire (after having conceded Iowa to the state's favorite son, Senator Tom Harkin) provides some evidence for conclusion that the early states determine the outcome of the nomination. When a series of controversial stories about Clinton's past received extensive coverage prior to the February 18 primary, Clinton was written off as a damaged candidate. However, his second-place showing behind former Massachusetts Senator Paul Tsongas allowed him to declare himself the "Comeback Kid," and that kept him in the race until primaries in the South began to occur in March. After convincing wins in six southern states on "Super Tuesday" (held on March 10 that year), Clinton coasted to the nomination.

As the nomination contests proceed beyond Iowa and New Hampshire, attention turns to the delegate count. Keep in mind that the presidential nominations officially take place at the parties' national conventions in the summer of the election year. At the conventions, the candidate in each party with support from a majority of the delegates wins the party's nomination. Delegates are allocated to the candidates, with some exceptions, according to the results of the caucuses and primaries in the states. Thus, unlike a direct primary, where the winner automatically gets the party's nomination, presidential candidates must accumulate delegates by winning nomination contests in state after state.

The rules for delegate allocation differ in the two parties and from state to state. As noted in Chapter 5, Democrats typically award their delegates proportionally. Thus, if a Democratic candidate wins 40 percent of the vote in a state's primary, they will get (roughly) 40 percent of that state's delegates to the national convention. (The system is not, in reality, quite this proportional because there is a threshold of 15 percent that candidates must garner before they can be awarded delegates.) Republicans, conversely, used to use variations on the winner-take-all method. Under winner-take-all rules, a candidate who wins the most votes in a state, even if it is only 35 percent of the total vote, will be awarded all of the state's delegates. In practice, the Republican rules vary because the states have some flexibility in how they allocate delegates. Some states, for instance, award a portion of their delegates at the state level and a portion at the congressional level. Nevertheless, rules changes adopted in 2012, and more or less retained in 2016, made the Republican process somewhat more proportional.[10]

Delegate allocation rules produced a prolonged Democratic nomination process in 2008. Usually, by mid-March of an election year, it becomes clear who the nominees of the two parties will be. In 2008, however, the Democratic contest continued until June 3. Given the Democratic Party's proportional allocation rules, Barack Obama and Hillary Clinton split the pledged delegates roughly evenly in most states (or balanced a big loss in one state with a sizable victory in another). Many Democratic Party operatives worried that the extended contest would weaken the eventual nominee, though others thought they would be stronger for having survived such a grueling process. However, the best existing empirical evidence suggests that divisive primaries have little or no impact on a presidential candidate's general election prospects.[11]

When one of the candidates seeking the nomination is the president or vice president, the nomination contests are basically a formality. Presidents and sitting vice presidents are rarely denied their party's nomination if they seek it. This does not mean they will not be challenged. In 1952, Senator Estes Kefauver opposed President Harry Truman for the Democratic Party nomination and beat Truman in the New Hampshire primary, causing Truman to announce that he would not seek reelection. That same year, Truman's vice president, Alben Barkley, announced his intention to run for president, but when organized labor failed to back his candidacy, he withdrew from the race. In 1968, Senator Eugene McCarthy challenged President Lyndon Johnson. McCarthy finished a close second to Johnson in New Hampshire, prompting Senator Robert Kennedy to enter the race and, soon thereafter, forcing Johnson to drop out.

As it turns out, challenges to presidents are quite common. Over the last sixty years, there have been twelve presidential elections in which the president was eligible for reelection. In five of those, the president faced a fairly high-profile challenge. In addition to 1952 and 1968, President Gerald Ford faced a challenge from Ronald Reagan in 1976, Senator Ted Kennedy challenged President Carter in 1980, and Patrick Buchanan opposed President Bush in 1992. In 1972, President Nixon faced insignificant challenges from the right and left within the Republican Party. Despite the rebuffs in 1952 and 1968 and multiple challenges in other years, presidents seeking nomination have proven extremely resilient.

The General Election

Once the nominees have emerged, the general election campaign unofficially begins. There used to be a period of time in the spring, short though it may have been, when the parties' nominees rested and their campaigns regrouped. Today, the candidates begin the fall campaign as soon as possible. If the nominees have opted out of the primary matching fund program, the campaigns renew their fund-raising efforts by soliciting contributions from those who might have supported another candidate during the nomination process. The campaigns also begin to engage one another through earned media and advertising. It is not unusual for the two parties' standard bearers to begin their general election advertising in late spring, right after wrapping their nominations. During the summer, this back and forth begins to intensify. In addition, a candidate who is not the sitting president may announce their choice of vice presidential running mate during this period.

Officially, the general election begins when the candidates have been nominated at their national conventions. At that point, attention turns to the "swing states," or those states in which the presidential contest will be competitive. Recall that the presidential general election is not a national popular vote. Instead, it is the Electoral College that determines who becomes president. This is perhaps the most distinctive aspect of presidential elections in the United States.

Today, the Electoral College system consists of a series of popular votes in the states (see Chapter 2 for details). Presidential candidates compete state by state and in the District of Columbia for electoral votes. In virtually every state, the candidate with the most votes statewide (though not necessarily a majority) receives all of that state's electoral votes. A candidate then needs a majority of all the electoral votes, or 270, to become president.

There are multiple combinations of states that will give a candidate 270 electoral votes. In reality, however, the election always hinges on a handful of swing states. Political scientist Daron Shaw, who served as an adviser to the campaigns of George W. Bush, identified thirteen states that both Bush and Gore considered "battleground" states in 2000 and only seven that both Bush and Kerry categorized as swing states in 2004.[12] In 2016, *Politico* identified eleven battleground states.[13] The small number of battleground states is the result of so many states being safely in the Democratic or Republican column.

Though presidential elections may be a foregone conclusion in most states, there is fierce competition in the swing states. In some recent years, the Electoral College vote has been so close that the outcome of the election has come down to the result in one state—Florida in 2000 and Ohio in 2004. Before 1992, however, observers believed that Republicans had a "lock" on the Electoral College. The GOP had won five of six elections, and the number of states that were thought to be solidly Republican was growing. Since 1992, however, the notion of a Republican lock has been discarded. Presidential elections are now far more competitive, with the Democrats winning four of the seven elections between 1992 and 2016 (though they've actually won the popular vote in six of those seven elections).

Table 10.1 shows the number of times each state voted for the Republican or Democratic nominee for president between 1992 and 2016. Notice the advantage Democrats have over Republicans in terms of the number of electoral votes in the parties' "solid" columns. The number of electoral votes in solidly

TABLE 10.1 State Presidential Election Results, by Number of Victories per Party, 1992–2016

Solid Republican[a]	Leans Republican[b]	Swing States (R Edge)[c]	Toss-Up (R Edge)[d]	Toss-Up (D Edge)[e]	Swing States (D Edge)[f]	Leans Democratic[g]	Solid Democratic[h]
Alabama (9)	Arizona (11)	Arkansas (6)	Florida (29)	Colorado (9)	Nevada (6)	New Hampshire (4)	California (55)
Alaska (3)	Georgia (16)	Kentucky (8)	Virginia (13)	Ohio (18)	Iowa (6)	New Mexico (5)	Connecticut (7)
Idaho (4)	Indiana (11)	Louisiana (8)				Michigan (16)	Delaware (3)
Kansas (6)	Montana (3)	Missouri (10)				Pennsylvania (20)	DC (3)
Mississippi (6)	N. Carolina (15)	Tennessee (11)				Wisconsin (10)	Hawaii (4)
Nebraska (5)		West Virginia (5)					Illinois (20)
N. Dakota (3)							Maine (4)
Oklahoma (7)							Maryland (10)
S. Carolina (9)							Massachusetts (11)
S. Dakota (3)							Minnesota (10)
Texas (38)							New Jersey (14)
Utah (6)							New York (29)
Wyoming (3)							Oregon (7)
							Rhode Island (4)
							Vermont (3)
							Washington (12)
102	56	48	42	27	12	55	196

Source: For 1992–2008 tallies, see Harold W. Stanley and Richard B. Niemi (eds.) (2011), Vital Statistics on American Politics, 2011–2012, online edition, Washington, DC: CQ Press, Table 1.3, http://library.cqpress.com/vsap/vsap07_tab1–3 (accessed May 29, 2013). Results of the 2012 election were found at the Washington Post, "2012 Presidential Election Results," http://www.washingtonpost.com/wp-srv/special/politics/election-map-2012/president/ (accessed March 12, 2017). Results of 2016 election were found at Politico, "2016 Presidential Election Results," http://www.politico.com/2016-election/results/map/president (accessed March 12, 2017).

Note: Numbers in parentheses are the 2016 electoral votes for each state; numbers at the bottom of each column are the total number of electoral votes in that column.

a States that voted for the Republican candidate in all seven elections between 1992 and 2016.

b States that voted for the Republican candidate in six of the seven elections.

c States that voted for the Republican candidate in five of the seven elections.

d States that voted for the Republican candidate in four of the seven elections.

e States that voted for the Democratic candidate in four of the seven elections.

f States that voted for the Democratic candidate in five of the seven elections.

g States that voted for the Democratic candidate in six of the seven elections.

h States that voted for the Democratic candidate in all seven elections between 1992 and 2016.

Democratic states was even greater—242—through the 2012 election. The solidly Democratic states had been dubbed, collectively, the "blue wall" (a reference to the color used to indicate Democratic victories on electoral maps).[14] But that term had exaggerated the Democrats' advantage because a number of those states have often been quite competitive.[15]

Indeed, in 2016, three of the states in the blue wall—Michigan, Pennsylvania, and Wisconsin—cast their electoral votes for the Republican nominee. Two other states in the Democrats' solid column—Maine and Minnesota— were decided by less than three percentage points and one of the "lean Democratic" states—New Hampshire—was among the closest states in the country. Conversely, no solid Republican state has been competitive for at least four election cycles and only Arizona, Georgia, and North Carolina among the "lean Republican" states were even remotely competitive. In other words, the Republican states are much more reliably Republican than the Democratic states are Democratic. Nevertheless, the Democrats do begin with a fairly sizable cushion—251 to 158 when solid and lean states are combined—even if they have to put more effort into shoring up their states than Republicans have to put into theirs.

The foregoing discussion should have established the uniqueness of the presidential election process. It is a method of filling a national office by an indirect vote of the people as represented by the states. There is, in fact, no other system like it in the democratic world. As Matthew Shugart has noted, by continuing to use this eighteenth-century institution, the United States is resisting the trend in the rest of the world toward direct, popular election of presidents.[16] It is likely to continue to do so for the foreseeable future.

▶ *Categorizing Elections*

This chapter opened with a claim about the significance of elections. Though they are extremely important political events, not all elections are equally important. Some seem to alter the entire political landscape in the country; others appear to have little if any impact whatsoever. The eminent political scientist V. O. Key first articulated this dichotomous view of elections in 1955. Key argued that a few elections in American history could be considered "critical elections." A critical election, according to Key, is one

> in which voters are, at least from impressionistic evidence, unusually deeply concerned, in which the extent of electoral involvement is relatively quite high, and in which the decisive results of the voting reveal a sharp alteration of the preexisting cleavage within the electorate. Moreover, and perhaps this is the truly differentiating characteristic of this sort of election, the realignment made manifest in the voting in such elections seems to persist for several succeeding elections.[17]

Key's suggestion that "realignments" take place during critical elections stimulated an entire body of research into this phenomenon. Scholars who built on Key's work identified various periods of party dominance that are launched by critical elections and that last until another critical election alters partisan coalitions and creates new cleavages within the electorate (see Chapter 5).[18] Thus, 1932 is often viewed as a critical, or "realigning," election because it forged the New Deal coalition (a coalition that Key saw forming in 1928, which he thinks is the critical election for the party era that followed it). However, if 1932 brought about an era of Democratic dominance, what could be said of the 1952 or 1956 election, in which Republican Dwight Eisenhower became president? For that matter, what could be said of 1936, 1940, and all the other elections of the New Deal era in which a Democrat won the presidency without altering the party's majority status?

In addition to realigning elections, the authors of *The American Voter* recognized two other categories of presidential elections. A "deviating" election is said to be one in which "the basic division of partisan loyalties is not seriously disturbed, but the attitude forces on the vote are such as to bring about the defeat of the majority party."[19] Again, 1952 is considered a classic example of such an election; 1912, when Democrat Woodrow Wilson won the presidency in a Republican era, is another.

Campbell and his coauthors also classified some contests as "maintaining" elections. These are elections "in which the pattern of partisan attachments prevailing in the preceding period persists and is the primary influence on forces governing the vote."[20] If one accepts the notion that American electoral history can be broken into periods of party dominance punctuated by realignments, then as Campbell et al., point out, most presidential elections are maintaining elections.

Given the categories of elections described to this point, the 1896 election becomes problematic. It was one that Key considered critical, but it did not exactly change the majority party. Republicans were likely still the majority party going into the 1896 election, but the preceding era was one of fierce two-party competition. The election of 1896 solidified a Republican majority that would last for nearly four decades. In addition, 1896 is said by some to have rearranged the two parties' coalitions. The Democratic base became more rural and favored the free coinage of silver, the most contentious economic issue of the time; Republicans dominated cities and supported the gold standard.

However, if the election of 1896 did not fundamentally overturn the previous partisan alignment, into what category can it be placed? Gerald Pomper suggested that it be considered a "converting" election. A converting election is one that looks like a realigning election in many ways—including "a low linear correlation to the average vote in the four preceding elections"—except that "the majority party would retain its status."[21]

Though this view of American electoral history—known generally as the "realignments perspective"—is widely held (with variations, depending upon the scholar), it has recently come under attack by David Mayhew. In *Electoral Realignments*, Mayhew identifies fifteen empirical claims made by the realignments literature and examines the validity of those claims. He concludes that "the claims of the realignments genre do not hold up well, and … its illuminative power has not proven great."[22] In particular, the hypothesis that realignments occur at regular intervals (generally thought to be of thirty-two to thirty-six years) had no basis in the historical or statistical evidence.[23]

Discussions of critical elections and realignments place the focus of American electoral history on presidential elections. However, midterm elections deserve attention too, as many have been significant. For instance, the midterm elections of 1894, in which Republicans gained a record 120 seats in the House of Representatives, ranks among the most important in American history, as does the midterm of 1930, when Democrats gained forty-nine House seats. So influential were these two midterm elections that scholars often consider them "pre-realignment midterms," occurring as they did just before the critical elections of 1896 and 1932.[24] Even if they do not presage a partisan realignment, midterm elections can change the course of American politics as much as presidential elections.

Typically, the aggregate outcome of midterm elections is determined by local factors in individual districts throughout the nation. Increasingly, however, midterm elections have become "nationalized," meaning that national factors will influence races around the country in more or less similar ways.[25] Nationalization inevitably benefits one party over the other, and this produces what is often called a "wave election."[26] Wave elections are those in which one party, capitalizing on the national sentiment favoring it, captures an unusually large number of seats in the House, if not the Senate. Recent examples include 1974, when Watergate cost Republicans forty-eight House seats; 1994, when Republicans picked up fifty-four seats in the House and ten in the Senate, gaining control of both chambers in the process, because of general dissatisfaction with the Clinton administration and the Democratic Congress; 2006, when discontent over the war in Iraq and a series of Republican congressional scandals enabled the Democrats to regain control of both the House and the Senate; and 2010, when the Tea Party movement and anger at the Obama administration helped Republicans gain sixty-three seats and to once again become the majority in the House.

To this point, our discussion has focused on supposed patterns in election outcomes without offering insight into how those outcomes are determined. The next section proposes an explanation for election results. It does so first by examining the factors that influence individual-level races. Because the dynamics are fairly different, it will treat presidential and congressional (or executive and legislative) elections separately. It then considers aggregate, or overall, election results in Congress.

► Explaining Election Outcomes

What explains the outcome of presidential elections? Do those factors differ from the factors determining the outcome of individual congressional elections? Why does a party win or lose a particular number of congressional seats in a given election year? Political scientists have produced an enormous body of research to answer these questions. Though debates about the relative importance of certain factors continue, we nonetheless have a firm grasp of the dynamics of elections and their outcomes.

Presidential Elections

We begin by examining presidential elections because they are the most visible, and thus the most familiar, elections in the United States. Despite this fact, they pose something of a problem for political scientists. Because they occur only every fourth year and because the United States is still a relatively young country, there have been so few presidential elections that it is difficult to generalize about them. Beginning with the first truly contested election in 1800, there have been only fifty-four presidential elections. The number of elections that can be used in statistical analyses is even smaller, as data for many variables were not available until the twentieth century. In fact, many quantitative studies of presidential elections begin with 1948, the first year that the national survey called the American National Election Study was conducted. That gives us a total of seventeen presidential elections that can be systematically analyzed. This number is too low to produce truly reliable results. Some scholars have addressed this problem by studying state-by-state presidential election results.[27] Most, however, have simply proceeded tentatively, recognizing the potential problems with analyses of national presidential election results.

Before proceeding, a point of clarification is in order. Election outcomes can be studied in one of two ways. We can examine voters' individual choices, or we can analyze election results, that is, the collective decisions voters make. In the former approach, the dependent variable (or the phenomenon being explained) is the individual's vote choice (meaning a vote for the Republican or the Democratic candidate in a given race). In the latter, the dependent variable is the final vote total (the percentage of the vote for the Republican or the Democrat in a race). Though the two are obviously related, the independent variables that affect the dependent variable can differ, sometimes considerably. Individual vote choices were explained in Chapter 8. In this chapter, we are interested in the voters' aggregate decisions or the collective vote for the candidates.

So what factors matter most in explaining the outcome of presidential elections? Clearly, national conditions—both political and economic—play a prominent role. One of the most important political factors is the popularity of the sitting president. The president's approval rating in the summer before the election has been shown to be highly correlated with the vote for the incumbent party, both when the incumbent is running for reelection (.90) and when the race is an open seat (.73).[28] Table 10.2 lists the Gallup presidential approval ratings for the incumbent in midsummer of election years from 1948 through 2016 and the result of the fall election in those years. With the exception of 1960, in every year that the president's approval rating was above 46 percent, his party won the popular vote (though in 2000 and 2016 the incumbent president had an approval rating above 46 percent and the nominee of his party lost the Electoral College); conversely, in every year that the president's approval rating was below 47 percent, except 1948, his party lost.

Incumbency itself matters as well. James Campbell finds that from 1868 to 2004, incumbents seeking a second term had a median popular vote of 54.7 percent, whereas in-party nonincumbents garnered 49.9 percent.[29] Or, as David Mayhew puts it, the in-party won the White House in two-thirds of the races between 1792 and 2004 in which the incumbent president was seeking reelection but only half (or fewer than half if we include 2008) of the open-seat races.[30] In fact, since Franklin D. Roosevelt defeated Herbert Hoover in 1932, only three sitting presidents have lost reelection bids—Gerald Ford in 1976, Jimmy Carter in 1980, and George H. W. Bush in 1992—whereas eleven incumbents were reelected (including FDR three times and Barack Obama in 2012).

Of course, since the ratification of the Twenty-Second Amendment in 1951, no president has been allowed to run for more than a second term in office, but that does not stop the president's party from trying to hold onto the White

TABLE 10.2   *Midsummer Gallup Presidential Approval Ratings and Election Results, 1948–2016*

Year	President	Approval Rating	Date of Poll	In-Party Victory?
1948	Truman	39%	6/18–24	Yes
1952	Truman	29%	7/13–18	No
1956	Eisenhower	70%	7/12–17	Yes
1960	Eisenhower	49%	7/16–21	No
1964	Johnson	74%	6/25–30	Yes
1968	Johnson	40%	7/18–23	No
1972	Nixon	57%	6/23–26	Yes
1976	Ford	45%	6/11–14	No
1980	Carter	33%	7/11–14	No
1984	Reagan	55%	7/13–16	Yes
1988	Reagan	54%	7/15–18	Yes
1992	G. H. W. Bush	32%	7/24–26	No
1996	Clinton	57%	7/18–21	Yes
2000	Clinton	59%	7/14–16	No[a]
2004	G. W. Bush	47%	7/08–11	Yes
2008	G. W. Bush	31%	7/10–13	No
2012	Obama	49%	7/09–12	Yes
2016	Obama	49%	7/14–16	No[a]

Source: Roper Center, Public Opinion Archives, University of Connecticut, http://www.ropercenter.uconn.edu/data_access/data/presidential_approval.html (accessed May 29, 2013). The Obama approval rating of 2016 is taken from the Gallup daily tracking poll, found at PollingReport.com, http://www.pollingreport.com/obama_job1.htm (accessed March 18, 2017).

a The in-party won the popular vote in both 2000 and 2016.

House for more than two terms. This, it turns out, has been extremely difficult to do. Since the Democrats won their fifth straight presidential term in 1948, no party has won the presidency for more than two consecutive terms except the Republicans from 1980 to 1992. Thus, though incumbency seems to help the sitting president win reelection, attempting to extend a party's control of the White House beyond two terms appears to hurt the nominee of the incumbent's party.

Economic conditions are at least as significant as political conditions, if not more so, in their influence on election outcomes. There are a number of ways to account for the state of the economy. One of the economic variables of choice is a measure of change in the gross national product or gross domestic product for some period of time prior to the election.[31] The higher the growth rate, the better the in-party's presidential candidate is expected to do. Though it is doubtful that many voters are aware of the precise level of change in gross domestic product, this variable is thought to capture the general state of the economy well enough to stand for voters' overall perceptions of economic conditions.

Scholars have employed a variety of alternative economic variables to explain presidential election results. Some use the change in per capita income or a measure of perceptions of personal finances; others find job creation to be significant; still others rely on a measure of consumer confidence. Though some of these variables perform better at explaining election outcomes, all of them are significant. Depending on which variables they use and in what combination with the political conditions reviewed earlier, scholars are routinely able to explain more than 85 percent of the variance in election results.

In addition to political and economic variables, the candidates themselves—or, more precisely, evaluations of the candidates—have also been shown to affect election outcomes. The influence of candidate evaluations is difficult to isolate because people are likely to give high marks to those candidates for whom they intend to vote. Nevertheless, candidates who are generally better liked than their opponents have a significantly better chance of winning.[32]

One final factor deserves attention. The influence of war on election outcomes is not well understood at this point, but common sense tells us that this most serious of presidential responsibilities must have an impact on voters' decisions on Election Day. Since World War II, the United States has been at war during a presidential election six times (assuming the major US military engagement in Vietnam began in 1965 and including the war in Afghanistan in 2012 and 2016).[33] War seems to have taken an electoral toll on the in-party in at least two of those elections. In 1952, the stalemate in Korea clearly contributed to the Democrats' loss, whereas Vietnam drove President Johnson from office in 1968 and created an enormous obstacle for Hubert Humphrey, the eventual Democratic nominee. In 2008, the war in Iraq had become unpopular—roughly two-thirds of the American people had come to oppose it by October 2008[34]—but it was not the salient issue it had been in 2004. Thus, though it contributed to President Bush's low approval rating, which in turn influenced the election, the war's direct effect on the outcome in 2008 may have been minimal.

In four other elections during war, 1972, 2004, 2012, and 2016, the party in power appears not to have been harmed. In 1972, negotiations to end the war in Vietnam achieved a breakthrough about a month before the election, and President Nixon claimed that peace was at hand. Similarly, the Afghan War was seen as coming to an end in 2012 as President Obama had announced a drawdown of US troops in June of 2011. In 2016, the war in Afghanistan (as well as fighting in Iraq and Syria) was hardly mentioned, though the broader war on terrorism was certainly an issue. Finally, with respect to the war in Iraq, opposition to the war was mounting in 2004, and it may well have cost President Bush votes. However, the broader issue of terrorism certainly bolstered his reelection effort. As many voters linked the war in Iraq with the fight against terrorism, it is hard to gauge just how much of an effect the war itself had in that election.

In the end, there are simply too few wartime elections to know how major military conflict affects election outcomes. To the extent that a prolonged war hurts a president's approval ratings, it will also damage their reelection efforts or the election prospects of the in-party. Unfortunately, there is mixed evidence on the question of how war affects presidential popularity.[35] We are left, then, to speculate that war's influence on elections depends on how much support there is for a particular war at election time and on how the presidential candidates handle the issue during the campaign.

Congressional Elections: District Level

As we will see, some of the same factors that influence the outcome of presidential elections also have an impact on individual congressional races. There are, however, a number of factors that are unique to congressional elections. Before examining them, it is worth recalling that very few congressional elections are competitive. In fact, the number of US House races classified by Charlie Cook, a leading election analyst, as "toss ups" or leaning toward one party has routinely been between thirty and sixty since 1998 (with the exception of 2010).[36] As mentioned in Chapter 2, part of the explanation for this lack of competition is, arguably, that congressional districts are drawn to favor one party or the other. Thus, district composition may act to predetermine the outcome of many congressional elections.

The factor that is most often cited as determining the outcome of congressional elections, however, is the "incumbency advantage." This is the advantage incumbents have over their challengers by virtue of holding the office they happen to be seeking. When incumbents run for reelection to the House of Representatives, the odds are overwhelmingly in their favor. Table 10.3 lists the reelection rates for incumbents in the US House and Senate between 1960 and 2014. During that time, the average incumbent reelection rate in the House was 94.8 percent. In recent elections (with the exception of 2010), that rate has been even higher; in the eight elections from 1998 to 2014, not including 2010, 96.5 percent of representatives won reelection.[37] Even in years thought to be bad for incumbents, roughly nine of every ten seeking reelection are successful in their bids. For example, with fallout from Watergate widespread in 1974, 89.6 percent of incumbents still managed to win.

The incumbency advantage is not as great in the Senate. Reelection rates there have been as low as 64 percent (in 1976 and 1980) and average 85.5 percent. In 2006, though 94.5 percent of members of the House won reelection, only 79.3 percent of Senators did the same. Much of the explanation for the diminished incumbency advantage in the Senate is that the upper chamber attracts better-quality challengers than does the House.

Indeed, challenger quality has long been thought to be a significant influence in congressional elections.[38] Though there are many ways to define a "quality"

TABLE 10.3 *Incumbent Reelection Rates for the US House and Senate, 1960–2014*

Year	House	Senate
1960	93.5	96.6
1962	96.2	85.3
1964	88.4	87.5
1966	90.0	96.6
1968	98.8	83.3
1970	96.9	79.3
1972	96.6	80.0
1974	89.6	92.0
1976	96.6	64.0
1978	95.0	68.2
1980	92.1	64.0
1982	92.4	93.3
1984	96.1	89.7
1986	98.5	75.0
1988	98.5	85.2
1990	96.3	96.9
1992	93.1	85.2
1994	91.9	92.3
1996	94.5	95.0
1998	98.5	89.6
2000	98.5	79.3
2002	97.9	88.9
2004	98.3	96.2
2006	94.5	79.3
2008	95.2	83.3
2010	86.3	91.3
2012	92.9	95.5
2014	96.4	82.1

Source: Harold W. Stanley and Richard B. Niemi (eds.) (2015) "Table 1.19, Incumbent Reelection Rates: Representatives, Senators, and Governors, General Elections, 1960–2014," Vital Statistics on American Politics, 2015–2016, online edition, Washington, DC: CQ Press, http://dx.doi.org.ezproxy.fandm.edu/10.4135/9781483380292.n1 (accessed March 18, 2017).

Note: Reelection rates are based on all incumbents running in the general election. That is, the calculation does not include those incumbents who lost in primaries.

candidate, typically we mean a candidate who has held prior elected office. These candidates have a base of support acquired in previous elections and have experienced the rigors of a campaign. Most important, they have a proven ability to mount a successful effort, both in terms of fund-raising and organization.

As members of the nation's most prestigious elected body, senators are likely to attract serious challengers with considerable experience. Often, a member of the House or a former governor will attempt to defeat a senator. In the House, conversely, a much smaller percentage of challengers will have held prior elected office. Though serious House challengers often come from the state legislative ranks, the typical challenger is a novice. This is particularly true when a district overwhelmingly favors the incumbent's party. In fact, most voters cannot even recognize the name of the challenger in a list of candidate names.[39]

Another reason for incumbents' high reelection rates is that vulnerable incumbents leave office rather than facing likely defeat. Incumbents caught in scandals are especially likely to retire if they do not resign before their terms expire. Furthermore, in an election year in which one party faces certain disadvantages, many incumbents of that party may choose to retire rather than try to withstand the national tide. In advance of the 2008 election, a year that many observers thought would be a good one for Democrats, thirteen House Republicans had announced by the end of 2007 that they would not seek reelection, and another seven were reported to be considering retirement. At the same point in time, only one Democratic member of the House had announced his retirement.[40]

The advantage incumbents enjoy stems from a number of institutional arrangements in Congress. For instance, the committee system allows members to specialize in policy areas that are important to their constituents. Furthermore, congressional parties demand very little loyalty in roll call voting, allowing representatives to put their districts' interests over the interests of the party when necessary. Members of Congress also have considerable resources, including staff and travel and mail allowances, to communicate with their constituents throughout their terms in office. Among other things, staffers help representatives provide significant amounts of constituency service. In addition, members of Congress keep their names in front of voters by using the "franking privilege" to send newsletters free of charge to constituents and by attending numerous community functions in their districts. In his famous study of Congress, David Mayhew summed up the electoral benefits of the institution by suggesting, "If a group of planners sat down and tried to design a pair of American national assemblies with the goal of serving members' reelection needs year in and year out, they would be hard pressed to improve on what exists."[41]

It is often assumed that incumbents also have an advantage over challengers because of their fund-raising superiority. It is true that incumbents raise and spend a significantly larger amount of money than their challengers. In 2014, for instance, the median amount raised by Republican and Democratic House members, respectively, was $1,314,446 and $1,187,316. Republican and Democratic challengers, however, had raised median amounts of just $47,757 and $53,681, respectively.[42] To put that in perspective, for every dollar their challengers raised, incumbents raised more than $24.

Close inspection of spending patterns, however, shows that incumbent expenditures have no effect on their prospects for winning.[43] In fact, there is considerable evidence that the more incumbents spend the worse they do at the polls.[44] What could explain such a counterintuitive result? Essentially, incumbents spend reactively. That is, the closer their races, the more they spend. Conversely, incumbents who are likely to win safely do not have to spend much money. Thus, an incumbent who wins with 52 percent of the vote is likely to have spent significantly more than an incumbent who wins with 72 percent of the vote.

The spending figure that seems to matter, then, is the amount spent by the challenger. Indeed, the more a challenger spends, the better they do. To actually win, however, challengers need to spend a considerable amount of money. In the 2014 election, for instance, the Campaign Finance Institute reported that successful House challengers spent an average of $2.1 million (while their incumbent opponents spent just under $3 million in losing efforts).[45]

Other resources also help nonincumbents garner more of the vote. Hiring political consultants, for example, has been shown to boost challengers' vote totals.[46] Though consultants cannot help a challenger overcome the incumbency advantage, a professionally run campaign does apparently perform better than an amateur one.

To this point, this section has focused on races in which an incumbent is seeking reelection. In races where there is no incumbent, called open-seat races, candidate quality and spending remain significant determinants of outcomes. When comparing candidates for open congressional seats with challengers to incumbents, the former group is more likely to have held prior elected office. When both candidates in an open-seat race are quality candidates, however, the effect is obviously eliminated or diminished (depending on how "experience" is measured). That leaves money as the key determinant of competitive open-seats races. More money is spent, on average, in open-seat races than in races where an incumbent is present. In 2014, House incumbents spent an average of $1.45 million, challengers averaged spending $499,000, and open-seat candidates spent an average of $1.36 million.[47] Though the candidate who spends the most money is still more likely to win, candidates in competitive open-seat races will often spend roughly equivalent amounts of money.

The potential for open-seat candidates to be equally matched means that other factors will also be important for determining these races. As congressional election scholars Gary Jacobson and Jamie Carson put it, "Because candidates competing for open seats are normally much more closely balanced in skills and resources than are challengers and incumbents, partisan trends, both local and national, more strongly influence the outcomes."[48] Locally, the partisan composition of the district is of enormous importance. Like congressional elections generally, most open-seat races turn out to be uncompetitive due to partisan advantages for one side or the other. Incidentally, this means that the primary of the party with an advantage will be more competitive than the general election for many open seats. When a general election victory is virtually assured and when no incumbent is running, the nomination of the favored party in a district becomes extremely valuable, and many quality candidates can be expected to throw their hats in the ring.

As Jacobson notes, however, national factors will also have an impact. In fact, whether we look at incumbent reelection contests or open-seat races, national political conditions such as the president's popularity or the economy will occasionally be salient in individual races. The best way to gauge their influence is to examine these factors from an aggregate perspective, which we do below. At this point, however, it is enough to recognize that, for example, a campaign stop from a popular president or an ad linking an incumbent to an unpopular president may have an effect on the outcome of individual congressional elections.

Before moving to a discussion of aggregate congressional election outcomes, Senate elections deserve mention. As noted earlier, Senate elections are considerably more competitive than House elections, at least as measured by incumbent reelection rates. Why are senators more likely to lose than representatives? The short answer is that "they are more likely to face formidable challengers who manage to wage intense campaigns."[49] As in House races, challenger quality and spending are two of the most important factors in Senate elections. Alan Abramowitz and Jeffrey Segal found that challenger spending had the largest effect on Senate election outcomes. Challenger experience trailed only measures of state partisanship and the incumbent's primary performance in explanatory power. In open-seat races, the relative experience and relative spending of the two candidates, in that order, were the two most powerful explanatory variables.[50]

It should come as no surprise that Senate races are far more expensive than House races. Whereas the average general election House candidate spent $1.09 million (including primary spending) in 2014, the average Senate candidate spent just under $8 million.[51] It is difficult to say how much a competitive Senate challenger would need to spend because states differ tremendously in size, but a review of the amounts spent by winning challengers in 2014 will give some indication: Tom Cotton, $13.9 million in Arkansas; Cory Gardner, $12.3 million in Colorado; Thom Tillis, $11 million in North Carolina; and Dan Sullivan, $7.98 million in Alaska.[52] Thus, even in small states, Senate challengers need $8 million to $14 million to be competitive; in larger states, it can cost well past $30 million to win.

One last aspect of Senate elections is worth mentioning. As noted, Abramowitz and Segal found that state partisanship has a significant influence on Senate election outcomes. However, state boundaries cannot be gerrymandered as House districts can, and most states are large enough to have a sufficient number of both Republican and Democratic voters to make for at least potentially competitive statewide elections. State size also makes it difficult for senators to cultivate a "home style" that fits neatly with their constituencies.[53] The result is that senators fit their states, both in partisan and ideological terms, less well than House members fit their districts.

Congressional Elections: Aggregate Level

In examining aggregate congressional election outcomes, one of the most import-ant factors to consider is whether the election is a midterm or a presidential year. The dynamics of the two types of election years are quite different. Obviously, in a presidential year, the bulk of the media coverage is devoted to the presidential election. In a midterm year, a handful of high-profile, competitive races get atten-tion, but the primary focus is on how many seats one party or the other is likely to pick up on Election Day.

Midterm elections are typically bad for the party controlling the White House. Since World War II, the president's party has lost seats in the House in all but two midterm elections—1998 and 2002 (Table 10.4). In the Senate, the president's party has lost seats in all but five midterms. The average seat loss in the House during that time period was twenty-six. However, some midterm elections produce far greater losses than that for the in-party. Going back to the nineteenth century, we find losses of ninety-six House seats in 1874, eighty-five seats in 1890, 116 seats in 1894, seventy-five seats in 1922, and seventy-one seats in 1938. In more recent years, the largest losses of seats have been in 1974 (for-ty-eight seats lost for Republicans), 1994 (fifty-four seats lost for Democrats), and 2010 (sixty-three seats lost for Democrats).

The loss of seats for the president's party is thought to be particularly bad in the middle of a second term due to the so-called "six-year itch." The theory is that voters inevitably get tired of an administration after six years in office. The orig-inal conceptualization of this phenomenon treated 1938, 1958, 1966, and 1974 as sixth-year elections in multi-termed presidencies.[54] The average loss of House seats in those years was fifty-three, compared to an average loss of less than seven seats in the second year midterm elections of those presidencies. If we update the numbers by adding 1986, 1998, 2006, and 2014 to the list of sixth-year elections, the average loss drops to just fewer than thirty-two seats. This compares to an average loss of twenty seats in the second year midterm elections of multi-termed presidencies during that entire period. Obviously, the gap between second-year and sixth-year midterm election losses has narrowed, suggesting that the "six-year itch" is declining as a distinct phenomenon. Indeed, the average loss in the last four second-term midterm elections (1986, 1998, 2006, and 2014) has been just under eleven seats while the average loss in the first midterm election of those presidencies has been nearly thirty-four seats.

Some observers have criticized both the theory and the original concep-tualization of the six-year itch. First, as election analyst Stuart Rothenberg has pointed out, "the 1966 and 1974 midterm elections were not true second mid-terms in a two-term presidency, since neither Johnson nor Ford had served anything close to six years in the White House when those elections occurred." Furthermore, 1998 was a sixth-year election and, yet, the president's party gained seats. Election results are produced by circumstances, argues Rothenberg, not an "inevitable 'souring'" on the president.[55]

TABLE 10.4 *Congressional Seat Gains/Losses by President's Party, 1932–2016*

Year	House Seats Gained/Lost	Senate Seats Gained/Lost	Year	House Seats Gained/Lost	Senate Seats Gained/Lost
1932 (D)	93	12	1976 (D)	1	1
1934 (D)	9	10	1978 (D)	-15	-3
1936 (D)	11	6	1980 (R)	34	12
1938 (D)	-71	-6	1982 (R)	-26	1
1940 (D)	5	-3	1984 (R)	16	-1
1942 (D)	-45	9	1986 (R)	-5	-8
1944 (D)	21	0	1988 (R)	-3	0
1946 (D)	-55	-12	1990 (R)	-7	-1
1948 (D)	75	9	1992 (D)	-9	1
1950 (D)	-29	-6	1994 (D)	-54	-10
1952 (R)	22	1	1996 (D)	3	-2
1954 (R)	-18	-1	1998 (D)	4	0
1956 (R)	-2	0	2000 (R)	-2	-5
1958 (R)	-47	-13	2002 (R)	8	1
1960 (D)	-20	0	2004 (R)	3	4
1962 (D)	-5	3	2006 (R)	-30	-6
1964 (D)	37	1	2008 (D)	24	5
1966 (D)	-47	-4	2010 (D)	-63	-4
1968 (R)	5	6	2012 (D)	7	2
1970 (R)	-12	3	2014 (D)	-12	-9
1972 (R)	12	-2	2016 (R)	-6	-2
1974 (R)	-48	-5			

Source: Harold W. Stanley and Richard B. Niemi (eds.) (2015) "Table 1.10, House and Senate Election Results by Congress, 1788–2014," Vital Statistics on American Politics, 2015–2016, online edition, Washington, DC: CQ Press, 2015, Table 1.10, http://dx.doi.org.ezproxy.fandm.edu/10.4135/9781483380292.n1(accessed March 18, 2017).

Note: Shaded rows are presidential election years. The party of the sitting president (in midterm years) or winning presidential candidate (in presidential years), is in parentheses.

Whether there is a six-year itch, there is certainly a tendency for the party in power to lose seats during midterm elections. Why would we expect such losses to occur? A seemingly obvious explanation is that a number of congressional candidates who would not be able to win on their own ride into office on the "coattails" of their party's successful presidential nominee. In the subsequent midterm election, without their presidential candidate on the ballot, these candidates lose.

There is some evidence for a coattail effect in congressional elections. One way to track coattails is to look at seat gains during presidential elections. If successful presidential candidates were to have coattails, we might expect that their party would gain seats in Congress as a result of the presidential candidate's victory. Indeed, the party winning the presidency gained seats in the House in every presidential election year between 1932 and 1984 except twice (in 1956 and 1960; see Table 10.4). In the eight elections between 1988 and 2016, however, the party winning the White House lost seats in four. This suggests a decrease in the coattail effect in recent years.

Of course, a gain in seats by the party of the winning presidential candidate does not necessarily mean that candidate had coattails. Another measure of the potential for presidential coattails is the number of congressional districts in which the results in the presidential election and the election for the House of Representatives were split between the two parties. The larger the number of split results, the less likely the presence of coattails. From 1916 to 1952, the percentage of districts with split results averaged 13.9 percent and was never higher than 21.3 (in 1948). From 1956 to 1988, however, an average of 34 percent of congressional districts had split results for president and the House. A full 45 percent of districts had split results in 1984. In this latter period of time, it's hard to argue that presidents had long coattails but, in 1992, the percentage of districts supporting a presidential candidate of one party and a House candidate of the other began to drop, and it reached its lowest level since 1920 in 2012 (when 6 percent of districts had split results). In presidential election years since 1992 (not including 2016) an average of 17.8 percent of districts have had split results.[56] This suggests an opposite conclusion from the one in the previous paragraph; namely, that coattail effects may be increasing after a period from the mid-1950s to the late 1980s when split results were rather numerous. However, this conclusion must also be qualified. Rather than evidence of coattails, these results may simply suggest that partisanship is on the rise, and split-ticket voting is declining.

Still, Gary Jacobson and Jamie Carson provide evidence that an individual's presidential vote influences their vote for Congress. For instance, in 2004, the difference in the probability of a person's voting for the Democratic House candidate between a John Kerry voter and someone who voted for President Bush was .50 (controlling for several other factors that influence a person's vote). Since 1980, Jacobson and Carson find the influence of the presidential vote on the congressional vote to have been highest in 2012, though 1996, 2000, and 2004 also showed signs of considerable coattail influence.[57] "Plainly," they conclude, "nontrivial coattail effects have been discernible in recent elections."[58]

A theory of in-party midterm losses called "surge and decline" is related to coattails but is more sophisticated.[59] According to this view, presidential elections provide a "surge" of information that both increases turnout and favors one party over the other. As a result, the electorate during a presidential election consists of more voters with weak partisanship and low political interest than typically seen in a midterm election. In addition, more voters can be expected to defect from their basic party identification when they cast a ballot. This surge of support for the winning party's presidential candidate also helps its congressional candidates. The corresponding "decline" in information and interest in the subsequent midterm election leaves a smaller electorate that votes more in line with its partisan predispositions, resulting in a loss of seats for the president's party in midterm elections.[60]

In the years since the surge-and-decline thesis was first proposed, there has been significant criticism of it. First of all, no differences have been found between midterm and presidential electorates. Furthermore, surge and decline cannot explain variation in seat loss from midterm to midterm. Why, for example, did Democrats lose five seats in 1962 but forty-seven in 1966? Surge and decline certainly cannot explain why Democrats gained four seats in the 1998 midterm elections or Republicans gained eight in 2002.

Another theoretical explanation for why the president's party loses seats in midterm elections is that voters seek to keep the policy direction of the country in equilibrium. Because the president's policy direction will necessarily be to the left (if a Democrat) or the right (if a Republican), "balancing theory" suggests that voters are likely to attempt to pull policy back to the center by electing members of the opposition party. By examining "generic ballot" polls—that is, polls that ask respondents which party they intend to vote for in congressional elections—Joseph Bafumi, Robert Erikson, and Christopher Wlezien find evidence for balancing behavior on the part of voters. As the authors conclude,

> during the midterm election year, the electorate shifts away from the presidential party in its vote choice for reasons that have nothing to do with the electorate's attitudes toward the president. By default, this is balancing: the electorate votes against the presidential party to give more power to the other party.[61]

Importantly, balancing is not entirely at odds with surge and decline. "In presidential years," as Bafumi and colleagues explain, "the winning presidential party is advantaged in the congressional elections, due to the surge/coattails phenomenon."[62] In the midterm elections, the president's party is no doubt harmed by the loss of this advantage. But it is also likely to be the victim of the electorate's attempt not to allow the policy direction of the country drift too far left or right.

Clearly, the particular circumstances in any given election year will affect the aggregate outcome of congressional elections. Most of these circumstances are the same ones that influence presidential elections. For instance, midterm elections are widely believed to be referenda on the sitting president.[63] In fact, the president's popularity does have a significant effect on seat change in the

House, both in midterm and presidential election years.[64] The higher a president's approval, the better their party will do in congressional races. There is evidence that in midterm elections, the degree to which presidential approval has an impact varies from year to year.[65] Nevertheless, it is generally the case that the party of a popular president will gain more seats in Congress—or lose fewer, as the case may be—than will the party of an unpopular president.

As in presidential elections, the economy has been shown to have a significant effect on congressional elections, though it should be said that this conclusion is not universally accepted.[66] Again, the performance of the economy can be measured in any number of ways. Using the percentage change in per-capita real income, Jacobson demonstrates that the greater the growth in income during the election year, the better the president's party will do in congressional elections (though the effect is not statistically significant when candidate quality is controlled for).[67]

Some factors that influence the outcome of congressional elections are unique to congressional races. For instance, it has been repeatedly shown that the number of seats a party holds in Congress prior to an election will affect how many seats it gains or loses in that election. As Barbara Hinckley pointed out: "The more seats held by one of the two American parties before the election, the larger the loss will appear after the election, even if nothing else happens or is changed at all."[68] This phenomenon is sometimes referred to as *exposure*. A party holding an inordinate number of seats prior to an election will have to defend more vulnerable, or exposed, seats than usual. The result is that the more seats a party has above its average over some number of election cycles, the more seats it will lose in a given election.[69]

Similarly, when a party is forced to defend a large number of open seats, it is likely to gain fewer or lose more seats in total. And when one party is able to recruit higher-quality nonincumbents, it is likely to gain seats.[70] Of course, the number of open seats a party has and the number of quality candidates it can field vary from year to year. The explanation for this variation is the strategic behavior of politicians. Serious candidates wait until the time is right to make a bid for office. In years that are generally perceived as good for the in-party, fewer incumbents of that party will retire, and fewer out-party candidates will have prior office-holding experience. However, in years that are thought to be bad for the president's party, the opposite will be true. As Jacobson and Kernell have shown, politicians pay close attention to national political and economic conditions and respond to them accordingly. Those conditions do not, therefore, have to directly affect voters' decision-making processes to have an impact on election outcomes. The strength of the parties' candidates themselves reflect the influence of national conditions.[71]

▶ Do Campaigns Matter?

Much of the discussion of election outcomes in this book has focused on circumstantial factors or those that establish the context within which an election will take place, as opposed to those that are campaign-specific. Though the examination of individual-level congressional election outcomes indicated that candidate spending has an effect on the electoral prospects of nonincumbents, most of the predictors of election outcomes are structural; that is, they are known before the campaigns even begin. These include the state of the economy, the president's popularity, and the presence (or absence) of an incumbent. If elections are determined by these non-campaign factors, we might ask whether campaigns even matter.

At first blush, it may appear that the answer is no, campaigns do not matter. Indeed, the success of "forecasting" models of elections would implicitly confirm this conclusion. In recent years, a number of scholars have built models that predict the outcome of presidential elections (or the seat change resulting from congressional election outcomes) months before any voter casts a ballot.[72]

An economist developed one of the earliest presidential election forecasting models. Perhaps not surprisingly, that model, which has been revised in the years since its original publication, relies heavily on economic indicators.[73] Nevertheless, it can explain a large portion of the variance in the presidential popular vote.

Early attempts to forecast election outcomes by political scientists relied almost exclusively on presidential popularity to predict a sitting president's reelection chances.[74] As these political science models evolved, they began forecasting all presidential elections.[75] In addition, they combined measures of the strength of the economy with presidential approval ratings.[76] Later, additional variables, such as whether the in-party is seeking a third term, were added to the models.[77] Attempts were also made to predict the aggregate outcome of congressional elections. Today, a number of models exist, each expressing some variation on the basic economic performance/presidential popularity approach to forecasting.[78]

Despite the fact that these models can be quite effective in predicting presidential election outcomes, they are not perfect. If even 98 percent of the variance in election outcomes is explained by forecasting models (a level of accuracy no model achieves), there are factors at work that have not been captured in the models. Those factors are likely to be related to the vagaries of campaigns. Indeed, some forecasters account for this by including trial-heat poll results in their models.[79]

The room left open for campaign influence, as James Campbell (himself one of the most effective election forecasters) has suggested, means that the question is not whether campaigns matter but, instead, how much they matter. Campbell's own specific answer to that question is that they account for an average of four percentage points in presidential elections. In some years, the campaign will not have a noticeable effect; conversely, "campaign effects have frequently exceeded six percentage points and in one election the campaign made a net difference of about nine percentage points."[80]

It should be noted that Campbell treats as campaign effects some of the factors we described earlier as circumstantial. So, for example, the election-year economy is part of what he calls "systematic campaign effects" that also include incumbency and the natural tightening of a race that regularly occurs during presidential elections. These factors he differentiates from "idiosyncratic campaign effects" such as gaffes and issues that emerge unexpectedly. What we have called circumstantial factors, Campbell calls the "pre-campaign context." That context includes partisan and ideological divisions in the country, preexisting assessments of the candidates, and the pre-election-year state of the economy.[81]

Incumbency and the state of the election-year economy are elements of the campaign for Campbell because, though they may not be able to be affected by the campaigns, the candidates must make them salient to the voters. A challenger has to prime voters to incorporate a weak economy into their voting calculus; a popular incumbent has to emphasize their success in office. Since this is precisely what campaigns do—and only the most inept campaign would fail to do so—it should come as no surprise that we find significant campaign effects of this sort. As Campbell explains, "The pre-campaign factors that allow us to predict elections with some degree of accuracy do so because they help to systematically guide the course of campaigns. ... In short, elections are largely predictable because campaigns are largely predictable."[82]

In his impressive study of the effects of presidential campaign events, Daron Shaw identified 144 major campaign effects between 1952 and 1992. These include campaign messages such as prospective and retrospective policy statements and valence, or value, statements and attacks on opponents; party activities such as national conventions, presidential and vice presidential debates, and attempts at party unity; mistakes such as scandals and gaffes; and outside occurrences such as national or international events.[83] Shaw finds that many of these events moved the polls considerably, and some had long-lasting effects. In particular, national conventions, presidential debates, party unity activities, and gaffes showed significant influence, with conventions having the largest impact.[84]

More recently, Robert Erikson and Christopher Wlezien examined nearly 2,000 polls from 1952 to 2008 to determine whether presidential campaigns alter vote intentions. They find that vote intentions do change over the course of a campaign but typically very slowly. And those intentions move in predictable ways. The "fundamentals" of presidential elections (e.g., the state of the economy and presidential approval) are important, but "The campaign (gradually) brings these things to the voters."[85] It does so, in particular, at three important moments when voters are paying most attention: at the beginning of the nomination process, during the national conventions, and in the few days leading up to Election Day.

The conclusion that presidential campaigns influence voters by drawing their attention to the fundamentals, and particularly the state of the economy, is similar to the one Lynn Vavreck draws in her masterful study, *The Message Matters*. For Vavreck, presidential candidates must respond to the state of the economy by either embracing it if it works to their advantage (either because they are from the incumbent party when the economy is good or they are from the opposition party when it is bad) or emphasizing other issues if it doesn't.[86] When candidates are able to implement the appropriate strategy, Vavreck finds that their campaigns can influence election outcomes. As she puts it, "The economy matters, but candidates' discourse about the economy matters, too. Further, candidates' rhetoric about other issues can drive out the importance of the economy if they choose the right issue. The structural conditions matter, but they can be overcome."[87]

Campaign effects have not only been found in presidential elections. As noted earlier, numerous studies have shown that campaign spending has an impact on congressional election outcomes, as do other resources such as the use of professional political consultants. The experiments of Stephen Ansolabehere and Shanto Iyengar have also demonstrated the significant impact of campaign advertising on voter attitudes and behavior.[88] And a growing body of research has examined the priming, agenda setting, and learning effects of campaigns.

There is still a tremendous amount of work that needs to be done to understand how campaigns affect voters and, ultimately, election outcomes. Fortunately, political scientists are devoting an increasing amount of attention to this subject. A recent anthology titled *Capturing Campaign Effects* reviews most of this scholarship and grapples with major methodological problems in studying political campaigns.[89] New data sets are also becoming available that will allow unprecedented opportunities for gauging campaign effects. The National Annenberg Election Survey, which conducted tens of thousands of interviews both online and by telephone throughout the campaigns in 2000, 2004 and 2008, is particularly promising.[90]

In asking whether campaigns matter, we must admit that the answer for many elections is no because the outcome is clear from the beginning. It is hard to imagine how Walter Mondale could have improved his odds of beating President Reagan in 1984 regardless of how he altered his campaign, just as it is difficult to see how Robert Dole could have defeated President Clinton in 1996. Furthermore, as has been noted, in the vast majority of congressional elections, district partisanship, not to mention the incumbency advantage, serves to dash the hopes of one of the candidates before they have made the first stump speech. However, surprising upsets do occur. And a handful of congressional races in every election cycle are identified as competitive at the outset of the campaign. Three of the last five presidential races have also been decided by razor-thin margins, and one of the others (2012) was very close for most of the campaign. Thus, campaigns can matter, often do matter, and occasionally make all the difference between who wins and who loses.

▶ *Do Elections Matter?*

If there is debate over whether campaigns matter, surely there can be no disagreement that elections matter. After all, they are the mechanism for determining who shall have power in a government. When that government is the most influential in the world, the consequences of elections must be enormous. Nevertheless, it is worth asking whether elections matter and not simply because we asked the same of campaigns.

If elections simply replace one personality with another, with no corresponding change in public policy, elections would not be very consequential. This is precisely the situation in countries with one-party rule. However, even where there is competition between parties, if the policy proposals of those parties do not differ significantly, it hardly matters which one wins. For elections to matter, therefore, there must be differences between the platforms of at least two parties competing for office, the voters must be aware of those differences, and the winning party must be able to implement its policy proposals.

These are the conditions, more or less, that have been identified as necessary for a party (or candidate) to declare a "mandate" after an election victory.[91] The precise meaning of the term is difficult to define, but a mandate is thought to be something like an instruction from the voters to the winners of an election to do in office what during the campaign they said they would do. There has been considerable debate over whether mandates can ever be claimed legitimately. Skeptics argue that voters are largely unaware of the policy differences between candidates and parties. Whether this is due to a lack of interest on the part of the voters, strategic ambiguity on the part of candidates, or the media's obsession with the horserace is immaterial. If voters do not know what the parties will do in office, they cannot very well be endorsing a set of policy proposals with their votes.

In 1994, for example, Republican candidates for Congress signed the "Contract with America," which was a pledge to act immediately on ten reform proposals if they should take control of Congress. After their historic victory that year, in which they did become the majority in Congress, Republicans claimed a mandate to implement the Contract. The problem, some say, was that polls taken on the eve of the election revealed that no more than three in ten voters had even heard of the Contract with America, let alone could recite the policy proposals contained in it.[92]

Typically, mandates are invoked at the presidential level, but presidents cannot unilaterally change policy; Congress has a constitutional role to play as well. The separation of powers in the US system of government, therefore, limits a president's ability to act on, if not claim, a mandate. Furthermore, the voters' recent fondness for divided government suggests that they have rarely given a victorious presidential candidate even the pretense of a mandate. During seventeen of the last twenty-five Congresses, one party has controlled the White House while the other party had a majority in at least one branch of Congress; and eight of the last seventeen presidential elections (through 2016) produced divided results between the president and Congress. In four of the nine elections with unified results, the party winning the White House simultaneously lost seats in the House of Representatives. That leaves just five presidential elections between 1952 and 2016–1952, 1964, 1976, 2004, and 2008—in which the voters gave one party control of both the White House and Congress and in which that party gained seats in the House as they won the presidency. And yet presidents claimed mandates in at least ten of the elections since 1952.[93]

One of the biggest barriers to the claim of an electoral mandate is the fact that election results are blunt instruments for determining voters' policy preferences. Candidates run on an array of issue positions. Even though candidates emphasize far fewer issues than they take positions on, it is impossible to know whether the voters embraced the entire agenda or just parts of it and, if only parts of it, which policies they preferred. Of course, this all assumes that voters make decisions on the basis of issues in the first place. However, a raft of research, most of which was discussed in Chapter 8, suggests that partisanship and candidate personality/character traits are more central to the vote decision than are policy considerations.

Having said this, the legitimacy of mandates is largely a subjective judgment. To the extent that a president can convince Congress (and the media) that they were given a mandate by the American people, they can instigate policy change. In that way, then, mandates are real, and claims to them can have an impact on the policy agenda, provided that other political actors view the claims as legitimate.[94] As the authors of a study of electoral mandates maintain, "elections play a much larger role in a society than the traditional instrumental role of determining a winner. In our analysis, it is the electoral mandate that is the driving force behind the expressive, or communicative, role of elections and a major link between voters and politicians."[95]

To this point, it has been assumed that for elections to matter, voters must act prospectively; that is, they must treat elections as a way to determine the future direction of the government. In fact, some have suggested that voters are mostly engaged in making retrospective judgments on the performance of the party in power.[96] Do elections matter less when they function retrospectively as opposed to prospectively?

Elections as assessments of past performance may not at first appear to be the democratic ideal. In this capacity, they seem to offer only a general conclusion about voter satisfaction with how elected officials have done their jobs. Voters decide either to return a party to power or to "throw the bums out." As such, they are primarily about holding politicians accountable for their actions in office. However, accountability is essential in a democracy. Elected officials should have to answer for their actions, and elections are the primary mechanism for ensuring that they do. Theoretically, retrospective voting can even influence the future direction of government. By punishing elected officials who have not acted in satisfactory ways, voters can incentivize politicians to perform better and be more responsive.[97] Thus, whether elections are retrospective judgments on performance or prospective verdicts about public policy, they have significant consequences and play an indispensable role in democracy.

▶ Conclusion

After months, or even years, of campaigning, candidates face the voters' judgment on Election Day. Typically, that judgment is final. That is, losing an election means failing to gain the office one is seeking. Presidential elections, however, are state-by-state contests and a candidate can lose in many states but still end up victorious.

Indeed, presidential elections—both the parties' nominations and the general election—are unlike elections for any other office in the United States. The nomination process begins with an "invisible primary" years before the first nominating contest takes place. During that phase, presidential candidates are seeking the support, in the form of contributions and endorsements, of influential party leaders. The hope is that they can translate such support into votes in the early contests and beyond. Until recently, party insiders were able to steer the nomination toward their preferred candidate. The 2016 Republican Party nomination suggests that those insiders may have less influence then they once had.

The path to the presidential nomination is a long one. The goal is to accumulate a majority of the delegates to the party's national convention so as to secure the party's nomination. Those delegates are earned in nomination contests (i.e. primaries and caucuses) held throughout the winter and spring of the election year in all fifty states, Washington, DC, and the US territories. Victories in the early contests, which begin with Iowa and New Hampshire, are thought to give a candidate momentum as they move into later contests.

Once candidates are nominated by both parties at their national conventions, the general election begins in earnest. The goal here is to win a majority (270) of the Electoral College votes. Because the electoral votes of most states are virtually preordained to go to one party or the other, the candidates spend most of their campaign resources (including their time) in several "battleground" states where the outcome could go either way. Until recently, Democrats were thought to have a significant advantage in the Electoral College, but three states—Wisconsin, Michigan, and Pennsylvania—flipped by the smallest of margins toward Donald Trump, giving him the victory in 2016.

Some presidential elections seem more consequential than others. As a result, elections have been categorized by political scientists according to the extent to which they alter prevailing party divisions in the electorate. "Critical elections" are those that upset the partisan balance and lead to "realignments" in the coalitions that make up the parties. Midterm elections can also bring about major changes in the balance of power within Congress. In "wave elections," one party is swept into office, or at least gains an abnormally large number of seats, because the issues in congressional districts around the country have been "nationalized."

There are, in fact, a number of factors that help to explain general election outcomes at both the presidential and congressional levels. Presidential elections are influenced by the sitting president's approval rating, whether the incumbent president is seeking reelection, whether the party currently holding the White House is seeking a third consecutive term, and, perhaps most importantly, the state of the national economy.

Congressional elections can be explained both at the district level and in the aggregate (i.e. the total number of seats gained or lost by the parties). At the district level, incumbency matters a great deal. Incumbent members of Congress rarely lose. In addition, the amount of nonincumbent spending by a candidate matters as does the underlying partisanship of a district. In the aggregate, mid-term elections are typically bad for a sitting president's party, though exactly why this is the case is a matter of some dispute. In presidential election years, the winning presidential candidate often has "coattails." That is, congressional candidates of the party that wins the White House will get a boost from the top of the ticket (and, hence, may ride into office on the coattails of their presidential candidate). The number of seats gained or lost by a party in congressional elections is also influenced by the number of seats it held prior to the election (the more seats held, the more that are vulnerable to being lost) and, of course, by national economic conditions.

Two questions about election outcomes are important to consider. The first is whether campaigns have any impact on the outcome of elections. That is, do campaigns matter? Many political scientists have argued that the "fundamentals" of elections, like the president's approval rating, the state of the economy, or incumbency, determine the outcome of elections. Since these factors can't be altered by the candidates, campaigns might be thought to be largely ineffective. However, a considerable amount of recent research suggests that campaigns may be better or worse at taking advantage of the fundamentals. In close races, in particular, campaign decisions could make all the difference. Though it might be true that many elections are foregone conclusions, it does not follow that campaigns don't matter. Indeed, they can and often do matter, at least in certain circumstances.

The second question is whether elections matter for the future direction of the country. Do elections give the winning party a "mandate" to govern? In order for the winning party to claim a mandate, the public would have to know what the party intends to do once in office. In other words, voters would have to make "prospective" judgments about which party's agenda they prefer. Since voters' knowledge of policy proposals is rather thin, they may be incapable of issuing mandates. Nevertheless, voters are perfectly capable of making judgments about past performance. To the extent that they vote "retrospectively," voters are holding those in power accountable for their actions. Elections, then, matter as an indispensable tool for ensuring accountability, which is an essential feature of representative democracy.

▶ *Pedagogical Tools*

Role-Play Scenario

You are a political scientist applying for a grant to study campaigns and elections. Write a brief application that identifies (a) your research question, (b) a hypothesis that provides an answer to that question, and (c) a theoretical justification of your hypothesis (that is, explain why your hypothesis operates as you think it does).

Discussion Questions

1. What is the most consequential election (whether "critical" or not) since 1932? Explain your answer.
2. On balance, do you think holding the Iowa caucuses and New Hampshire primaries early in the nomination process is a good way or a bad way to nominate candidates for president? Why?
3. How problematic is the limited number of swing states in presidential elections or competitive districts in congressional elections? Defend your answer.
4. What is the use of campaigns if they have limited effect on most election outcomes?
5. Can a winning presidential candidate or political party ever claim a mandate? Why or why not?

Online Resources

Election forecasting from PollyVote, www.pollyvote.com.
An interactive Electoral College map, www.270towin.com.
Dave Leip's Atlas of US Presidential Elections, www.uselectionatlas.org.
The Green Papers (a website "dedicated to the dissemination of facts, figures, tidbits and commentary" on elections), www.thegreenpapers.com.

Suggested Reading

James E. Campbell (2008) *The American Campaign: US Presidential Campaigns and the National Vote*, 2nd edn, College Station, TX: Texas A&M University Press.
Robert S. Erikson and Christopher Wlezien (2012) *The Timeline of Presidential Elections: How Campaigns Do (and Do Not) Matter*, Chicago, IL: University of Chicago Press.
William G. Mayer and Jonathan Bernstein (eds.) (2012) *The Making of the Presidential Candidates 2012*, Lanham, MD: Rowman & Littlefield.
Lynn Vavreck (2009) *The Message Matters: The Economy and Presidential Campaigns*, Princeton, NJ: Princeton University Press.

▶ Notes

1 Arthur Hadley (1976) *The Invisible Primary*, Upper Saddle River, NJ: Prentice-Hall.
2 Rudy Giuliani led in many national polls on the eve of the 2008 Iowa caucuses, but at least one poll (Pew Research Center) had John McCain in the lead. Just before the Iowa caucuses in early January 2012, Newt Gingrich led in several national polls. However, Mitt Romney led the Republican pack in the last Gallup poll of 2011.
3 William G. Mayer (2004) "The Basic Dynamics of the Contemporary Nomination Process: An Expanded View," in William G. Mayer (ed.), *The Making of the Presidential Candidates 2004*, Lanham, MD: Rowman & Littlefield.

4 Shailagh Murray and Chris Cillizza (2007) "Obama Jumps into Presidential Fray," *Washington Post*, January 17, www.washingtonpost.com/wp-dyn/content/article/2007/01/16/AR2007011600529.html (accessed April 11, 2017).

5 Marty Cohen, David Karol, Hans Noel, and John Zaller (2008b) "The Invisible Primary in Presidential Nominations, 1980–2004," in William G. Mayer (ed.), *The Making of the Presidential Candidates 2008*, Lanham, MD: Rowman & Littlefield, pp. 2 and 23. See also Marty Cohen, David Karol, Hans Noel, and John Zaller (2008a) *The Party Decides: Presidential Nominations Before and After Reform*, Chicago, IL: University of Chicago Press.

6 Marty Cohen, David Karol, Hans Noel, and John Zaller (2016) "Party Versus Faction in the Reformed Presidential Nominating System," *PS: Political Science & Politics*, 49, p. 702.

7 Cohen et al., "Party Versus Faction," p. 704.

8 Andrew E. Busch (2008) "The Reemergence of the Iowa Caucuses: A New Trend, an Aberration, or a Useful Reminder?" in William G. Mayer (ed.), *The Making of the Presidential Candidates 2008*, Lanham, MD: Rowman & Littlefield, p. 63.

9 Brian Knight and Nathan Schiff (2007) "Momentum and Social Learning in Presidential Primaries," NBER Working Paper No. W13637, November, http://ssrn.com/abstract=1033762 (accessed April 11, 2017).

10 See interview with political scientist Josh Putnam in John Sides (2016) "Everything You Need to Know about Delegate Math in the Presidential Primary," The Monkey Cage, *Washington Post*, February 16, www.washingtonpost.com/news/monkey-cage/wp/2016/02/16/everything-you-need-to-know-about-delegate-math-in-the-presidential-primary/?utm_term=.650d1cfcf05a (accessed March 4, 2017).

11 Lonna Rae Atkeson (1998) "Divisive Primaries and General Election Outcomes: Another Look at Presidential Campaigns," *American Journal of Political Science*, 42: 256–271.

12 Daron R. Shaw (2006) *The Race to 270: The Electoral College and the Campaign Strategies of 2000 and 2004*, Chicago, IL: University of Chicago Press, pp. 64 and 66, Tables 3.7 and 3.8.

13 Charlie Mahtesian (2016) "What Are the Swing States in 2016?" *Politico*, June 15, www.politico.com/blogs/swing-states-2016-election/2016/06/what-are-the-swing-states-in-2016-list-224327 (accessed March 4, 2017).

14 Ronald Brownstein (2009) "The Blue Wall," *National Journal*, January 17, http://i.usatoday.net/news/TheOval/National-Journal-1-16-2009.pdf (accessed April 11, 2017).

15 For a list of 2004 battleground states, see Shaw, *The Race to 270*, p. 66, Table 3.8; 2008 battleground states can be found in Dan Balz and Alec Macgillis (2008) "Battleground States," *Washington Post*, June 8, www.washingtonpost.com/wp-dyn/content/graphic/2008/06/08/GR2008060800566.html (accessed April 11, 2017); and 2012 battleground states can be found at National Public Radio (2012) "Swing State Scorecard," http://apps.npr.org/swing-state-scorecard (accessed April 11, 2017); and *Politico*, "2012 Swing States," www.politico.com/2012-election/swing-state (accessed April 11, 2017).

16 Matthew Soberg Shugart (2004) "The American Process of Selecting a President: A Comparative Perspective," *Presidential Studies Quarterly*, 34: 632–655.

17 V. O. Key, Jr. (1955) "A Theory of Critical Elections," *Journal of Politics*, 17, p. 4.

18 Walter Dean Burnham (1970) *Critical Elections and the Mainsprings of American Politics*, New York: W. W. Norton, p. 1.

19 Angus Campbell, Philip E. Converse, Warren E. Miller, and Donald E. Stokes (1960) *The American Voter*, New York: John Wiley & Sons, pp. 532–533.

20 Campbell et al., *The American Voter*, p. 531.

21 Gerald M. Pomper (1968) *Elections in America: Control and Influence in Democratic Politics*, New York: Dodd, Mead & Company, p. 110.

22 David R. Mayhew (2002) *Electoral Realignments: A Critique of an American Genre*, New Haven, CT: Yale University Press, p. 141.

23 Mayhew, *Electoral Realignments*, Chapter 4.

24 Andrew E. Busch (1999) *Horses in Midstream: US Midterm Elections and Their Consequences, 1894–1998*, Pittsburgh, PA: University of Pittsburgh Press, Chapter 3.

25 David W. Brady, Robert D'Onofrio, and Morris Fiorina (2000) "The Nationalization of Electoral Forces Revisited," in David W. Brady, John F. Cogan, and Morris Fiorina (eds.), *Continuity and Change in House Elections*, Palo Alto, CA: Stanford University Press and Hoover Institution Press.

26 See William F. Connelly (2006) "Wall vs. Wave?" *The Forum*, 4, www.bepress.com/forum/vol4/iss3/art3 (accessed April 11, 2017).

27 See James E. Campbell (1992) "Forecasting the Presidential Vote in the States," *American Journal of Political Science*, 36: 386–407.

28 Thomas M. Holbrook (2012) "Incumbency, National Conditions, and the 2012 Presidential Election," *PS: Political Science and Politics*, 45, p. 640; see also James E. Campbell (2004) "The Presidential Election of 2004: The Fundamentals and the Campaign," *The Forum*, 2, www.bepress.com/forum/vol2/iss4/art1 (accessed April 11, 2017).

29 Campbell, "The Presidential Election of 2004," p. 8.

30 David R. Mayhew (2008) "Incumbency Advantage in US Presidential Elections: The Historical Record," *Political Science Quarterly*, 123, p. 212.

31 There are far too many studies to cite here; for a thorough review of this literature, see Michael S. Lewis-Beck and Mary Stegmaier (2000) "Economic Determinants of Electoral Outcomes," *Annual Review of Political Science*, 3: 183–219.

32 Stanley Kelley, Jr., and Thad W. Mirer (1974) "The Simple Act of Voting," *American Political Science Review*, 68: 572–591.

33 See Kurt Taylor Gaubatz (1999) *Elections and War: The Electoral Incentive in the Democratic Politics of War and Peace*, Palo Alto, CA: Stanford University Press, pp. 169–170.

34 Based on CNN/Opinion Research Corporation Polls reported at PollingReport.com (n.d.) "Iraq," www.pollingreport.com/iraq.htm (accessed April 11, 2017).

35 Paul Brace and Barbara Hinckley (1991) "The Structure of Presidential Approval: Constraints within and across Presidencies," *Journal of Politics*, 53, p. 994.

36 Charles E. Cook, Jr. (n.d.) "Accuracy," *The Cook Political Report*, http://cookpolitical.com/about/accuracy (accessed April 11, 2017).

37 Author's calculations based on data in Harold W. Stanley and Richard B. Niemi (eds.) (2015) "Table 1.19, Incumbent Reelection Rates: Representatives, Senators, and Governors, General Elections, 1960–2014," *Vital Statistics on American Politics, 2015–2016*. Online Edition. Washington, DC: CQ Press, http://dx.doi.org.ezproxy.fandm.edu/10.4135/9781483380292.n1 (accessed March 18, 2017).

38 Barbara Hinckley (1980) "House Re-elections and Senate Defeats: The Role of the Challenger," *British Journal of Political Science*, 10: 441–460; and Jon R. Bond, Cary Covington, and Richard Fleisher (1985) "Explaining Challenger Quality in Congressional Elections," *Journal of Politics*, 47: 510–529.

39 Barbara Hinckley (1981) *Congressional Elections*, Washington, DC: CQ Press, p. 23, Table 2.3.

40 Cook Political Report (2007) "2008 House Summary," *Cook Political Report*, December 19, www.cookpolitical.com/races/report_pdfs/2008haag_summary_dec19.pdf (accessed January 2, 2008).

41 David R. Mayhew (1974) *Congress: The Electoral Connection*, New Haven, CT: Yale University Press, pp. 81–82.

42 Federal Election Commission (2015) "Congressional Table 4: 24-Month Median Receipts of Senate and House Candidates from January 1, 2013 through December 31, 2014," www.fec.gov/press/summaries/2014/tables/congressional/ConCand4_2014_24m.pdf (accessed March 18, 2017).

43 Gary C. Jacobson (1978) "The Effects of Campaign Spending in Congressional Elections," *American Political Science Review*, 72: 469–491.

44 Stephen Ansolabehere and Alan Gerber (1994) "The Mismeasure of Campaign Spending: Evidence from the 1990 US House Elections," *Journal of Politics*, 56: 1106–1118.

45 Campaign Finance Institute (n.d.) "Table 3.3: House Campaign Expenditures: Incumbents and Challengers, Major Party General Election Candidates by Election Outcome,

1974–2014 (full cycle, mean net dollars)," www.cfinst.org/pdf/vital/VitalStats_t3.pdf (accessed March 18, 2017).

46 Stephen K. Medvic (2001) *Political Consultants in US Congressional Elections*, Columbus, OH: Ohio State University Press.

47 Campaign Finance Institute (n.d.) "Table 3.2: House Campaign Expenditures: Major Party General Election Candidates, 1974–2014 (full cycle, net dollars)," www.cfinst.org/pdf/vital/VitalStats_t2.pdf (accessed March 18, 2017).

48 Gary C. Jacobson and Jamie L. Carson (2016) *The Politics of Congressional Elections*, 9th edn, Lanham, MD: Rowman & Littlefield, p. 134.

49 Jonathan S. Krasno (1994) *Challengers, Competition, and Reelection: Comparing Senate and House Elections*, New Haven, CT: Yale University Press, p. 154.

50 Alan I. Abramowitz and Jeffrey A. Segal (1992) *Senate Elections*, Ann Arbor, MI: University of Michigan Press, pp. 109 and 115, Tables 4.2 and 4.3.

51 Campaign Finance Institute (n.d.) "Table 3.2," and Campaign Finance Institute (n.d.) "Table 3.5: Senate Campaign Expenditures, Major Party General Election Candidates, 1974–2014 (full cycle, net dollars)," www.cfinst.org/pdf/vital/VitalStats_t5.pdf (accessed March 18, 2017).

52 Figures obtained from OpenSecrets.org's summary of congressional races, (accessed March 18, 2017).

53 On home styles, see Richard Fenno (1978) *Home Style: House Members in Their Districts*, Boston, MA: Little, Brown.

54 Kevin Phillips (1984) *"Reelection Paradox: Landslide and Loss of Power,"* *Christian Science Monitor*, November 2, p. 16.

55 Stuart Rothenberg (2005) "Midterms Spell Trouble, but 'Itch' Theory Is a Real Head-Scratcher," *Rothenberg Political Report*, September 15, http://rothenbergpoliticalreport.com/news/article/midterms-spell-trouble-but-itch-theory-is-a-real-head-scratcher (accessed April 11, 2017).

56 Author's calculations based on data provided in Harold W. Stanley and Richard B. Niemi (eds.) (2015) "Table 1.14, Split Presidential and House Election Outcomes in Congressional Districts, 1900–2012," *Vital Statistics on American Politics, 2015–2016*, Online Edition, Washington, DC: CQ Press, http://dx.doi.org.ezproxy.fandm.edu/10.4135/9781483380292.n1 (accessed March 18, 2017).

57 Jacobson and Carson, *The Politics of Congressional Elections*, p. 195.

58 Jacobson and Carson, *The Politics of Congressional Elections*, p. 197.

59 Angus Campbell (1966) "Surge and Decline: A Study of Electoral Change," in Angus Campbell, Philip E. Converse, Warren E. Miller, and Donald E. Stokes (eds.), *Elections and the Political Order*, New York: John Wiley & Sons.

60 See James E. Campbell (1987) "The Revised Theory of Surge and Decline," *American Journal of Political Science*, 31: 965–979.

61 Joseph Bafumi, Robert S. Erikson, and Christopher Wlezien (2010) "Balancing, Generic Polls and Midterm Congressional Elections," *Journal of Politics*, 72, p. 718.

62 Bafumi et al., "Balancing," p. 719.

63 For a review of the midterm-as-referenda literature, see James E. Campbell (1997) *The Presidential Pulse of Congressional Elections*, 2nd edn, Lexington, KY: University of Kentucky Press, Chapter 4.

64 Jacobson and Carson, *The Politics of Congressional Elections*, pp. 186–187.

65 Alan I. Abramowitz (1985) "Economic Conditions, Presidential Popularity, and Voting Behavior in Midterm Congressional Elections," *Journal of Politics*, 47: 31–43.

66 Robert S. Erikson (1990) "Economic Conditions and the Congressional Vote: A Review of the Macrolevel Evidence," *American Journal of Political Science*, 34: 373–399.

67 Jacobson and Carson, *The Politics of Congressional Elections*, pp. 186–187.

68 Hinckley, *Congressional Elections*, p. 123.

69 Jacobson and Carson, *The Politics of Congressional Elections*, p. 186.

70 Alan Abramowitz (2006) "Using the Generic Vote to Forecast the 2006 House and Senate Elections," *The Forum*, 4, www.bepress.com/forum/vol4/iss2/art3 (accessed April 11, 2017).

71 Gary C. Jacobson and Samuel Kernell (1983) *Strategy and Choice in Congressional Elections*, 2nd edn, New Haven, CT: Yale University Press.

72 For a review, see Thomas Holbrook (2010) "Forecasting US Presidential Elections," in Jan E. Leighley (ed.), *The Oxford Handbook of American Elections and Political Behavior*, Oxford: Oxford University Press.

73 Ray C. Fair (1978) "The Effect of Economic Events on Votes for President," *Review of Economics and Statistics*, 60: 159–173; and Ray C. Fair (1996) "The Effect of Economic Events on Votes for President: 1992 Update," *Political Behavior*, 18: 119–139. See also Ray C. Fair (2012) *Predicting Presidential Elections and Other Things*, 2nd edn, Palo Alto, CA: Stanford University Press.

74 Randall J. Jones (2002) *Who Will Be in the White House? Predicting Presidential Elections*, New York: Longman, p. 30. See Lee Sigelman (1979) "Presidential Popularity and Presidential Elections," *Public Opinion Quarterly*, 43: 532–534; and Michael Lewis-Beck and Tom Rice (1982) "Presidential Popularity and Presidential Vote," *Public Opinion Quarterly*, 46: 534–537.

75 Richard Brody and Lee Sigelman (1983) "Presidential Popularity and Presidential Elections: An Update and Extension," *Public Opinion Quarterly*, 47: 325–328.

76 Michael Lewis-Beck and Tom Rice (1984) "Forecasting Presidential Elections: A Comparison of Naïve Models," *Political Behavior*, 6: 9–21; and Michael Lewis-Beck and Tom Rice (1992) *Forecasting Elections*, Washington DC: CQ Press.

77 Alan I. Abramowitz (1988) "An Improved Model for Predicting Presidential Election Outcomes," *PS: Political Science and Politics*, 21: 843–847.

78 Presidential forecasts are generally published before each presidential election in an issue of *PS: Political Science and Politics*. See the October 2016 issue for a symposium that includes a number of predictions for the 2016 presidential election and a postmortem in the April 2017 issue.

79 See James E. Campbell (2004a) "Forecasting the Presidential Vote in 2004: Placing Preference Polls in Context," *PS: Political Science and Politics*, 37: 763–767.

80 James E. Campbell (2000) *The American Campaign: US Presidential Campaigns and the National Vote*, College Station, TX: Texas A&M University Press, pp. 187 and 188.

81 Campbell, *The American Campaign*, p. 58.

82 Campbell, *The American Campaign*, p. 193.

83 Daron R. Shaw (1999) "A Study of Presidential Campaign Event Effects from 1952 to 1992," *Journal of Politics*, 61: 387–422. See also Shaw, *The Race to 270*.

84 Shaw, "A Study of Presidential Campaign Event Effects from 1952 to 1992," pp. 408–414. See also Thomas M. Holbrook (1994) "Campaigns, National Conditions, and US Presidential Elections," *American Journal of Political Science*, 38: 973–998.

85 Robert S. Erikson and Christopher Wlezien (2012) *The Timeline of Presidential Elections: How Campaigns Do (and Do Not) Matter*, Chicago, IL: University of Chicago Press, p. 178.

86 Lynn Vavreck (2009) *The Message Matters: The Economy and Presidential Campaigns*, Princeton, NJ: Princeton University Press, pp. 31–33.

87 Vavreck, *The Message Matters*, p. 159.

88 Stephen Ansolabehere and Shanto Iyengar (1995) *Going Negative: How Political Advertisements Shrink and Polarize the Electorate*, New York: Free Press.

89 Henry E. Brady and Richard Johnston (eds.) (2006) *Capturing Campaign Effects*, Ann Arbor, MI: University of Michigan Press.

90 Daniel Romer, Kate Kenski, Kenneth Winneg, Christopher Adasiewicz, and Kathleen Hall Jamieson (2006) *Capturing Campaign Dynamics, 2000 and 2004: The National Annenberg Election Survey*, Philadelphia, PA: University of Pennsylvania Press; and Kate Kenski, Bruce W. Hardy, and Kathleen Hall Jamieson (2010) *The Obama Victory: How Media, Money, and Message Shaped the 2008 Election*, Oxford: Oxford University Press.

91 See G. Bingham Powell, Jr. (2000) *Elections as Instruments of Democracy: Majoritarian and Proportional Visions*, New Haven, CT: Yale University Press, Chapter 4.

92 Gary C. Jacobson (1996) "The 1994 House Elections in Perspective," in Philip A. Klinkner (ed.), *Midterm: The Elections of 1994 in Context*, Boulder, CO: Westview Press, p. 6.

93 For claims of a mandate between 1952 and 1996, see Patricia Heidotting Conley (2001) *Presidential Mandates: How Elections Shape the National Agenda*, Chicago, IL: University of Chicago Press, p. 54, Table 4.1. The figure given in the text includes claims of a mandate by President Obama in 2012, but not 2008; by President Bush in 2004, but not in 2000; and by President Trump in 2016.

94 See Lawrence J. Grossback, David A. M. Peterson, and James A. Stimson (2006) *Mandate Politics*, Cambridge: Cambridge University Press.

95 James H. Fowler and Oleg Smirnov (2007) *Mandates, Parties, and Voters: How Elections Shape the Future*, Philadelphia, PA: Temple University Press, p. 143.

96 Morris Fiorina (1981) *Retrospective Voting in American National Elections*, New Haven, CT: Yale University Press.

97 For a recent review of the scholarly literature on retrospective voting and its consequences, see Andrew Healy and Neil Malhotra (2013) "Retrospective Voting Reconsidered," *Annual Review of Political Science*, 16: 285–306.

11 Conclusions

C AMPAIGNS and elections are among the most important events in the life of a democracy. Campaigns help the citizenry come to a collective decision about who should control the levers of power in the country, and elections make the use of those levers legitimate. At some level, these processes are familiar to nearly every American citizen, yet few have a thorough understanding of how they function. This book is an attempt to explain those processes both in terms of the structure and rules governing their operation and in terms of the behavior of the various actors who participate in campaigns and elections.

Those actors—candidates and their campaign staffs, political parties, interest groups, the media, and voters—are the focus of this book. Highlighting their individual roles is not intended to detract from the significance of the structural elements of campaigns and elections. Indeed, election laws and electoral systems establish the frameworks within which these processes occur in a country, and they constrain, or enable, the behavior of the actors who are central to this text, but it is those actors who actually conduct campaigns and decide elections. Each plays a critical role in carrying out the processes we find so important to democracy.

This chapter begins by painting a broad picture of campaigns and elections in the United States. The preceding chapters provided ample detail about how they operate; this one takes a step back to characterize the system in its entirety. The chapter then introduces a new element—campaign ethics—and revisits the phenomenon of the "permanent campaign." A discussion of campaigns and elections from an ethical standpoint provides standards for judging the health of the system. The permanent campaign allows us to explore the nexus between campaigning and governing and the future of both.

▶ Campaigns and Elections: The Big Picture

Campaigns and elections in the United States can be characterized in any number of ways, but three attributes seem to have emerged throughout this book.

First and foremost, elections and the campaigns that precede them have become central to politics and government in the country. This was not always the case. The Framers certainly recognized the importance of elections, but they did not particularly emphasize them in the Constitution. Only the House of Representatives was originally designed to be directly elected by the people. Furthermore, as noted in Chapter 2, less than one in five words in the original Constitution pertained to elections; that grew to roughly one in three words in the seventeen amendments beyond the Bill of Rights. This suggests that as the country matured and became more democratic, elections came to be viewed as having a vital role to play in the political system.

The centrality of elections today is reflected in the fact that the United States holds more elections than nearly any other advanced democracy in the world. In fact, as Mark Franklin points out, "only Switzerland and the United States call their voters to the polls more than once a year on average."[1] Citizens now choose the nominees of the parties, install elected officials at the local, state, and national level, and vote directly on issues.

Second, campaigns and elections in the United States can be said to be unique. This stems, in part, from having two relatively uncommon electoral systems in place throughout the country. Congressional and state legislative elections are held under the single member plurality system, which is used less often in other countries than some version of proportional representation. With respect to presidential elections, there are few institutions in the world like the Electoral College. Though a majority vote of electors in the Electoral College is required to win, the electors themselves are selected in plurality elections in each of the states. This state influence in a national election is extremely unusual.

The federal system in the United States, though by no means unique in and of itself, becomes quite exceptional when combined with the separation of powers that exists at all levels. The result is national and state, not to mention local, elections for both legislative and executive branches. In many jurisdictions at subnational levels, there are also judicial elections. Furthermore, the staggered terms of office among the different branches is a relatively rare element, as is the highly decentralized system of election regulation.

The way campaigns operate in the United States is also distinctive. For instance, they are longer than campaigns in virtually all other countries. They certainly cost more money and rely more heavily on private sources of funding than campaigns in most democracies. The party system tends to be weaker as well, producing campaigns that are candidate-centered. Though none of the aforementioned aspects of campaigns and elections (with the exception of the Electoral College) is literally one of a kind, the combination of elements makes the entire system unique.

Finally, the numerous proposals that exist for reform of the system indicate that campaigns and elections in the United States are flawed. Just how they are flawed and to what extent depend on one's perspective. However, the endless debates about campaign finance, the Electoral College, legislative redistricting, the presidential nominating system, and voting rights, to name only some of the points of contention, suggest that there are many aspects of the American system that could be improved.

Some of the flaws are the result, at least in part, of the behavior of the key actors in campaigns and elections. Those who believe low voter turnout is problematic attribute it to many sources, including restrictive voter registration laws and a lack of competitive elections, but it can also be blamed on the voters' lack of interest in politics. Likewise, the absence of substantive discussion of policy proposals is said to be due to the media's obsession with the horserace or candidates' unwillingness to take unambiguous issue positions.

These alleged misbehaviors raise the question of how we are to evaluate the actors involved in campaigns and elections. That, in turn, is necessary for judging the health of the American system for electing government officials. The next section briefly explores campaign ethics, with an emphasis on the standards that can be applied to the behavior of those participating in campaigns and elections in the United States.

▶ Campaign Ethics

There is tremendous disagreement over what is and what is not acceptable behavior in campaigns and elections. For example, some observers believe there is a duty to vote, whereas others argue that individuals have no such obligation. Some find horserace coverage to be a violation of the media's democratic responsibilities, whereas others think it is a perfectly acceptable reaction to market pressures. The position one takes on these and other matters depends on what one expects of campaign actors.

One of two standards can be applied to the behavior of those involved in campaigns. The first, which has been called the *civic responsibility* standard, maintains that campaign actors must put a commitment to democracy above their own self-interest. "Campaigns are public debates over how society should operate," according to this perspective. "Thus agents have a duty to elevate the quality of dialogue in the campaign, and to this end their pursuit of their own interests should be more constrained."[2]

The second conception, which we might call the *self-interest* or *laissez-faire* standard (laissez-faire is a French term meaning "leave alone"), argues that campaign actors "should be free to pursue their own interests subject to few ethical constraints beyond the universal moral rules that bind us all."[3] That is, as long as they do not lie, cheat, steal, or physically harm others, campaign actors are free to do whatever they need to do to fulfill their self-interests. Though few people would admit to holding this view, many act as though they subscribe to it.

There are two lines of defense for the laissez-faire perspective. The first is a sort of political "invisible hand" argument. The public's interest is best protected, according to this viewpoint, when each of the actors pursues their self-interest.

The campaign system, it is argued, is not unlike the US legal system. Each is an adversarial system in which the contestants put forward their best case. It is assumed that when the final decision is made, justice—or the better candidate—will have emerged.

The second line of defense could be called the realist's defense. With the stakes as high as they are in elections, we simply cannot expect the participants in a campaign to sacrifice votes for the abstract goal of enhancing democracy. And there is no point holding actors to a standard that few, if any, will ever meet in the real world.

The civic responsibility perspective responds to the first argument by pointing out that a campaign is not like a courtroom. There are, for instance, no rules of evidence in a campaign. And though the media may act like judges when there is a dispute about the accuracy or fairness of candidates' claims, the media are not disinterested actors in the process. There is also no neutral jury to hear both sides, deliberate and weigh the evidence, and render a verdict. We may assume the voters will play that role, but without the very standard the civic responsibility perspective would impose on them, voters will make judgments from behind subjective lenses of partisanship, ideology, and self-interest.

To the realist, the proponent of civic responsibility would say that our collective commitment to democracy must take priority over our self-interests; otherwise, campaign actors may well sacrifice democracy in the pursuit of votes. Furthermore, we cannot discard ethical standards simply because most, or even all, of the actors will fall short of those standards. Indeed, unless actors are held to a high standard of behavior, the conduct of campaigns will quickly spiral downward.

The question of whether citizens have a duty to vote puts into relief these divergent viewpoints. The civic responsibility perspective would clearly say they do. Without citizen participation in elections, there is no democracy; with only low levels of voter turnout, democracy is a sham. Thus, citizens are ethically obligated to vote and are guilty of unethical behavior when they do not go to the polls. From the laissez-faire point of view, however, citizens are not required to vote. If the individual decides to stay home on Election Day, they have done nothing wrong.

Even if everyone could agree on a preferable approach to campaign ethics, it is unlikely that there would be universal agreement on its application. This is best illustrated by a few hypothetical examples. Assume in the first case that we are applying the civic responsibility standard to a gubernatorial campaign. The board of directors of an interest group decides that the challenger would make a better governor than the incumbent. However, the board decides not to endorse either candidate in the race because the incumbent is likely to win, and it does not want to jeopardize access to the sitting governor. From the civic responsibility perspective, actors are obligated not to impede democratic deliberation for the sake of their own interests. In this case, has the group's decision run afoul of the standard? In other words, has the group impeded democratic deliberation by staying neutral in the race?

In the second hypothetical case, assume that we are applying the laissez-faire standard to a congressional campaign. Candidate A voted fifteen times in the state legislature to increase education funding but voted five times against educational funding bills that included elements, not related to funding, that she opposed. Candidate B runs a campaign ad stating that Candidate A "repeatedly voted against more money for our schools." From the laissez-faire perspective, a statement in an ad would have to be untrue to be unethical. In this case, the claim is technically true, but the implication is not. So has the ad crossed the line of acceptability? Has Candidate A lied about Candidate B's record?

The difficulty in reaching agreement on ethical violations in campaigns has not stopped a number of reform advocates from trying to improve campaign conduct. Most of the reform proposals intended to change the behavior of campaign actors are, in truth, little more than "best practices." One approach is to train candidates, political consultants, or journalists to become aware of the ethical implications of their behavior. For instance, campaign management programs at a number of universities now include an ethical component as part of the curriculum. In 2005, the city of Livermore, California, held a televised workshop on campaign ethics for elected officials and candidates in which "guidelines for running an ethical campaign" were discussed. Participants in the workshop were asked to sign a pledge to, among other things, "be truthful ... act with integrity ... be relevant ... [and] be approachable."[4]

Pledges such as this, which are often referred to as candidate *codes of conduct*, are another popular approach taken by those seeking to improve campaign behavior. These codes are voluntary, of course, which means that the only enforcement mechanism is public pressure on candidates to sign and abide by them. In Maine, candidates for governor, the US Senate, and the House of Representatives are given the Maine Code of Fair Campaign Practices when they file their candidacies (see Figure 11.1). Though this code is also voluntary, the official nature of the document's distribution is intended to give the code added weight.

In their study of campaign reform efforts such as these, Sandy Maisel, Darrell West, and Brett Clifton found little evidence that they achieve their goal of improving campaign conduct.[5] Part of the reason for this is that there are few incentives for campaign actors to improve their behavior or disincentives not to. Of course, we would like campaign actors to do the right thing regardless of incentives but, as the hypothetical cases presented earlier make clear, we may not even agree about what it means for candidates, the parties, interest groups, and voters to do the right thing.

▶ *The "Permanent Campaign"*

The election calendar in the United States ensures that there is literally always a campaign being waged for one office or another. Candidates are endlessly polling,

FIGURE 11.1 *Maine Code of Fair Campaign Practices*

2014 Election Year

COMMISSION ON GOVERNMENTAL ETHICS AND ELECTION PRACTICES
Mail: 135 State House Station, Augusta, Maine 04333
Office: 45 Memorial Circle, Augusta, Maine

Website: www.maine.gov/ethics
Phone: 207-287-4179
Fax: 207-287-6775

2014 MAINE CODE OF FAIR CAMPAIGN PRACTICES
(Optional under 21-A M.R.S.A. § 1101(2))

I shall conduct my campaign and, to the extent reasonably possible, insist that my supporters conduct themselves, in a manner consistent with the best Maine and American traditions, discussing the issues and presenting my record and policies with sincerity and candor.

I shall uphold the right of every qualified voter to free and equal participation in the election process.

I shall not participate in and I shall condemn defamation of and other attacks on any opposing candidate or party that I do not believe to be truthful, provable and relevant to my campaign.

I shall not use or authorize and I shall condemn material relating to my campaign that falsifies, misrepresents or distorts the facts, including, but not limited to, malicious or unfounded accusations creating or exploiting doubts as to the morality, patriotism or motivations of any party or candidate.

I shall not appeal to and I shall condemn appeals to prejudices based on race, creed, sex or national origin.

I shall not practice and I shall condemn practices that tend to corrupt or undermine the system of free election or that hamper or prevent the free expression of the will of the voters.

I shall promptly and publicly repudiate the support of any individual or group that resorts, on behalf of my candidacy or in opposition to that of an opponent, to methods in violation of the letter or spirit of this code.

I, the undersigned candidate for election to public office in the State of Maine, hereby voluntarily endorse, subscribe to and solemnly pledge to conduct my campaign in accordance with the above principles and practices.

_____   _____
Date   Candidate's Signature

_____   _____
Office Sought and District   Printed Name

Rev. 01/13

Source: www.maine.gov/ethics/pdf/062014Code_000.pdf.

fund-raising, building coalitions, seeking endorsements, introducing themselves to voters, debating, and advertising (in one form or another). In this sense, campaigning is a permanent feature of American politics.[6]

However, there is another way, as noted in Chapter 5, in which the "permanent campaign" has become part of our civic experience. In this second sense of the phrase, those in elected office engage in a "continuing political campaign" to maintain public approval.[7] This requires the use of campaign tactics—such as polling and advertising—to govern.

The permanent campaign, in the governing sense of the term, did not appear overnight. Its roots extend to early attempts to "go public" by presidents such as Theodore Roosevelt.[8] It was certainly previewed, if not launched, by the widespread use of polling in the White House during the Johnson and Nixon administrations.[9] It was introduced conceptually during Jimmy Carter's transition and implemented institutionally in the Office of Political Affairs, which was created by Ronald Reagan.[10] The permanent campaign was perfected, however, in the Clinton administration and showed no signs of abating under either George W. Bush or Barack Obama.[11]

There are numerous ways in which elected officials now use campaign tactics in the process of governing. For example, the counsel of political consultants has increasingly been sought between elections. After engineering President Bush's election victory in 2000, for instance, Karl Rove became a senior adviser to the president. Obama campaign strategists David Axelrod and, later, David Plouffe also became senior advisers to the president after the 2008 election. Indeed, the original conceptualization of the permanent campaign is found in a memo written by President-elect Carter's campaign pollster.

Polling is a significant aspect of the permanent campaign. The national committee of the president's party conducts ongoing polling for the president. This is used to gauge the salience of various issues, which in turn is used to help prioritize these issues on the president's agenda. It is also used to time policy activity (for example, the announcement of particular proposals). Finally, polls help presidents identify the most effective arguments for their policies. Though the use of polling by presidents does seem to increase as elections near, all presidents use it extensively throughout their time in the White House.[12] It is important to note that presidents are unlikely to adopt or change positions on the basis of poll results. However, when they deny relying on polls at all, as they often do, they are being disingenuous.

In addition to polling, presidents use travel to bolster support for their initiatives. George W. Bush's 2005 campaign to privatize Social Security included a "60 Stops in 60 Days" national barnstorming effort.[13] To push for gun-control legislation after the tragic shootings at Sandy Hook Elementary School in December 2012, President Obama traveled around the country calling on Congress to "demonstrate political courage" and to at least hold a vote on measures that would strengthen background checks for gun purchasers and ban assault weapons.[14] These campaign-style events almost always occur in the districts or states of wavering legislators.

Such tours utilize techniques that appear regularly during campaign stump speeches. For instance, the backdrop, or "wallpaper," behind the president will often include short phrases, repeated multiple times, in an attempt to reinforce the president's message. Alternatively, individuals or objects selected to send an

FIGURE 11.2 *President Obama, Flanked by Law Enforcement Officers, Campaigns for Gun Control Legislation*

Source: Getty Images/Craig F. Walker.

unmistakable visual message to viewers will be positioned behind the president during speeches. When President Obama stumped for gun-control legislation, he was flanked by police officers in uniform, suggesting that law enforcement backed the measures he was advocating (see Figure 11.2).

The permanent campaign of President Obama even had an organizational component outside the White House. After the 2008 election, President Obama's campaign organization, Obama for America, was transformed into Organizing for America (OFA). The first Obama administration did not rely on the OFA as much as some observers thought, and many supporters hoped, it would. However, a new version of OFA (Organizing for Action) was formed as a 501(c)4 organization, with Obama campaign manager Jim Messina as its national chairperson, after the 2012 election.[15] The new OFA was actively involved in mobilizing support for President Obama's agenda from the very beginning of his second term. In March of 2013, the OFA announced that it would hold more than 100 events around the country in support of gun-control measures backed by the President.[16]

Presidents are not the only actors engaged in permanent campaigning. Interest groups have used advertising to influence other elite actors, if not the public, during legislative battles. Among the most famous examples of this are the "Harry and Louise" ads run by the Health Insurance Association of America during the debate over the Clinton healthcare proposal in 1993–1994.[17] In 2005, AARP, the lobbying organization for older Americans, launched an advertising campaign against the Bush Social Security proposals.[18] And in March of 2013, an organization with substantial financial support from New York City Mayor Michael Bloomberg—Mayors Against Illegal Guns—began an aggressive advertising campaign in support of pending gun-control legislation in fifteen states where US Senators were thought to be persuadable.[19] (In 2014, Mayors Against Illegal Guns merged with Moms Demand Action for Gun Sense in America to form Everytown for Gun Safety.)

Members of Congress, or party caucuses in Congress, also routinely use campaign tactics to advance their legislative agendas. Polling is ubiquitous on Capitol Hill. Creative attempts to garner earned media are also commonplace. During high-profile debates, the parties often establish "war rooms" where members are able to conduct interviews with the press and respond rapidly to claims and counterclaims from the opposition. When Congress was considering a "Patients' Bill of Rights" in 2001, Senate Democrats established an "ICU," or Intensive Communication Unit, for this purpose. Republicans responded with the "Patients First Delivery Room." These war rooms often include props that generate extensive media coverage. The Democratic ICU, for instance, converted a conference room in the Capitol into a hospital room.[20]

According to Hugh Heclo, there are three consequences of "transforming politics and public affairs into a twenty-four-hour campaign cycle of pseudoevents for citizen consumption." First, the permanent campaign exaggerates differences between political actors. Second, it tends to privilege short-term, dramatic problems and ignore long-term, chronic ones. Finally, it encourages finger pointing and a politics of blame.[21]

There is irony in all of this. Though the permanent campaign is intended to enable elected officials to govern effectively by helping them maintain public support, it is more likely to undermine efforts to govern by polarizing the various actors involved in the political process. Many are also concerned that citizens become less able to differentiate campaigning and governing, and this makes it difficult for them to fulfill their proper role in either process. Perhaps more troubling is the possibility that politicians in permanent campaign mode come to be viewed as manipulative and, ultimately, untrustworthy. In an age in which cynicism is already rampant, this development threatens the legitimacy of the entire democratic system.

▶ Pedagogical Tools

Role-Play Scenario

You work for an organization dedicated to improving the conduct of campaigns. The director of the organization wants to develop a code of conduct that candidates would be asked to sign voluntarily at the beginning of a campaign. Draft a candidate code of conduct for your organization.

Discussion Questions

1. In addition to being central to American politics and being unique and flawed, how else might you describe campaigns and elections in the United States?
2. Which standard of campaign ethics do you think is preferable and why?
3. How would the process of governing look different without the permanent campaign?

Online Resources

Institute for Local Government (California), "Ethics on the Campaign Trail." Available at www.ca-ilg.org/campaigning-office.

The Markkula Center for Applied Ethics, Santa Clara University, "Campaign Ethics," https://www.scu.edu/ethics/focus-areas/government-ethics/resources/what-is-government-ethics/campaign-ethics/.

Organizing for Action, https://www.ofa.us/.

Suggested Reading

Brendan J. Doherty (2012) *The Rise of the President's Permanent Campaign*, Lawrence, KS: University Press of Kansas.

L. Sandy Maisel, Darrell M. West, and Brett M. Clifton (2007) *Evaluating Campaign Quality: Can the Electoral Process Be Improved?* Cambridge: Cambridge University Press.

Candice J. Nelson, David A. Dulio, and Stephen K. Medvic (eds.) (2002) *Shades of Gray: Perspectives on Campaign Ethics*, Washington, DC: Brookings Institution Press.

▶ *Notes*

1 Mark N. Franklin (2004) *Voter Turnout and the Dynamics of Electoral Competition in Established Democracies since 1945*, Cambridge: Cambridge University Press, p. 98.
2 Dale E. Miller and Stephen K. Medvic (2002) "Campaigns Ethics: Civic Responsibility or Self-Interest?" in Candice J. Nelson, David A. Dulio, and Stephen K. Medvic (eds.), *Shades of Gray: Perspectives on Campaign Ethics*, Washington, DC: Brookings Institution Press, p. 27. Unless otherwise noted, the discussion that follows is taken from this source.
3 Miller and Medvic, "Campaigns Ethics" p. 27.
4 The City of Livermore, California (2005) "Campaign Ethics and Voter Guidelines," Special newsletter. This document can now be found in the "Report to the Mayor and City Council, NO: 11–202," 2011. City of Sunnyvale, California, September 13, http://sunnyvale.ca.gov/Portals/0/Sunnyvale/CouncilReports/2011/11-202.pdf (accessed March 24, 2017).
5 L. Sandy Maisel, Darrell M. West, and Brett M. Clifton (2007) *Evaluating Campaign Quality: Can the Electoral Process Be Improved?* Cambridge: Cambridge University Press.
6 Anthony King (1997) *Running Scared: Why America's Politicians Campaign Too Much and Govern Too Little*, New York: Free Press.

7 The phrase is from a memo by President Carter's pollster, Pat Cadell, as quoted in Sidney Blumenthal (1982) *The Permanent Campaign*, rev. edn, New York: Simon & Schuster, p. 56.
8 Samuel Kernell (2006) *Going Public: New Strategies of Presidential Leadership*, 4th edn, Washington, DC: CQ Press.
9 Lawrence R. Jacobs and Robert Y. Shapiro (1995) "The Rise of Presidential Polling: The Nixon White House in Historical Perspective," *Public Opinion Quarterly*, 59: 163–195.
10 On the permanent campaign in the Carter Administration, see Blumenthal, *The Permanent Campaign*. On the Office of Political Affairs, see Bradley Patterson (2000) *The White House Staff: Inside the West Wing and Beyond*, Washington, DC: Brookings Institution Press, p. 206.
11 Stephen K. Medvic and David A. Dulio (2004) "The Permanent Campaign in the White House: Evidence from the Clinton Administration," *White House Studies*, 4: 301–317.
12 Kathryn Dunn Tenpas and James A. McCann (2007) "Testing the Permanence of the Permanent Campaign: An Analysis of Presidential Polling Expenditures, 1977–2002," *Public Opinion Quarterly*, 71: 349–366.
13 Jonathan Weisman (2005) "Cost of Social Security Drive Cited," *Washington Post*, April 7, www.washingtonpost.com/wp-dyn/articles/A32389-2005Apr6.html (accessed March 24, 2017).
14 Justin Sink (2013) "Obama Plans Road Trip to Prod Senate to Move on Gun-Control Legislation," *The Hill*, March 25, http://thehill.com/homenews/administration/290169-obama-to-prod-senators-takes-gun-control-message-on-the-road (accessed March 24, 2017).
15 Paul Steinhauser (2013) "'Obama for America' to Morph into 'Organizing For Action,'" CNN.com, January 18, http://politicalticker.blogs.cnn.com/2013/01/18/obama-for-america-to-morph-into-organizing-for-action (accessed March 24, 2017).
16 Sink, "Obama Plans Road Trip."
17 Darrell West, Diane Heith, and Chris Goodman (1996) "Harry and Louise Go to Washington: Political Advertising and Health Care Reform," *Journal of Health Politics, Policy, and Law*, 21: 35–68.
18 Robert Pear (2004) "In Ads, AARP Criticizes Plan on Privatizing," *New York Times*, December 30, www.nytimes.com/2004/12/30/politics/30retire.html?_r=1&oref=slogin (accessed March 24, 2017).
19 Brett LoGiurato (2013) "For the First Time, the NRA Is Up Against an Adversary with Money to Spend," *Business Insider*, March 24, www.businessinsider.com/bloomberg-gun-control-ad-campaign-michael-mayors-illegal-guns-12-million-2013-3 (accessed March 24, 2017).
20 Julie Malone (2001) "Patients' Rights Vote in View; Details Argued as PR War Rages," *Atlanta Journal and Constitution*, June 21, 3A.
21 Hugh Heclo (2000) "Campaigning and Governing: A Conspectus," in Norman Ornstein and Thomas Mann (eds.), *The Permanent Campaign and Its Future*, Washington, DC: American Enterprise Institute and The Brookings Institution, p. 30.

Appendix

Constitutional Provisions Directly Related to Elections

▶ *ARTICLE I*

Section 2

Clause 1: The House of Representatives shall be composed of Members chosen every second Year by the People of the several States, and the Electors in each State shall have the Qualifications requisite for Electors of the most numerous Branch of the State Legislature.

Clause 2: No Person shall be a Representative who shall not have attained to the Age of twenty five Years, and been seven Years a Citizen of the United States, and who shall not, when elected, be an Inhabitant of that State in which he shall be chosen. …

Clause 4: When vacancies happen in the Representation from any State, the Executive Authority thereof shall issue Writs of Election to fill such Vacancies.

Section 3

Clause 1: The Senate of the United States shall be composed of two Senators from each State, chosen by the Legislature thereof … (This Clause has been affected by Clause 1 of amendment XVII).

Clause 2: … one third may be chosen every second Year; and if Vacancies happen by Resignation, or otherwise, during the Recess of the Legislature of any State, the Executive thereof may make temporary Appointments until the next Meeting of the Legislature, which shall then fill such Vacancies (This Clause has been affected by Clause 2 of amendment XVIII).

Clause 3: No Person shall be a Senator who shall not have attained to the Age of thirty Years, and been nine Years a Citizen of the United States, and who shall not, when elected, be an Inhabitant of that State for which he shall be chosen.

Section 4

Clause 1: The Times, Places and Manner of holding Elections for Senators and Representatives, shall be prescribed in each State by the Legislature thereof; but the Congress may at any time by Law make or alter such Regulations, except as to the Places of choosing Senators.

Section 5

Clause 1: Each House shall be the Judge of the Elections, Returns and Qualifications of its own Members. …

▶ *ARTICLE II*

Section 1

Clause 1: The executive Power shall be vested in a President of the United States of America. He shall hold his Office during the Term of four Years, and, together with the Vice President, chosen for the same Term, be elected, as follows

Clause 2: Each State shall appoint, in such Manner as the Legislature thereof may direct, a Number of Electors, equal to the whole Number of Senators and Representatives to which the State may be entitled in the Congress: but no Senator or Representative, or Person holding an Office of Trust or Profit under the United States, shall be appointed an Elector.

Clause 3: The Electors shall meet in their respective States, and vote by Ballot for two Persons, of whom one at least shall not be an Inhabitant of the same State with themselves. And they shall make a List of all the Persons voted for, and of the Number of Votes for each; which List they shall sign and certify, and transmit sealed to the Seat of the Government of the United States, directed to the President of the Senate. The President of the Senate shall, in the Presence of the Senate and House of Representatives, open all the Certificates, and the Votes shall then be counted. The Person having the greatest Number of Votes shall be the President, if such Number be a Majority of the whole Number of Electors appointed; and if there be more than one who have such Majority, and have an equal Number of Votes, then the House of Representatives shall immediately choose by Ballot one of them for President; and if no Person have a Majority, then from the five highest on the List the said House shall in like Manner choose the President. But in choosing the President, the Votes shall be taken by States, the Representation from each State having one Vote; A quorum for this Purpose shall consist of a Member or Members from two thirds of the States, and a Majority of all the States shall be necessary to a Choice. In every Case, after the Choice of the

President, the Person having the greatest Number of Votes of the Electors shall be the Vice President. But if there should remain two or more who have equal Votes, the Senate shall choose from them by Ballot the Vice President (This Clause has been superseded by amendment XII).

Clause 4: The Congress may determine the Time of choosing the Electors, and the Day on which they shall give their Votes; which Day shall be the same throughout the United States.

Clause 5: No Person except a natural born Citizen, or a Citizen of the United States, at the time of the Adoption of this Constitution, shall be eligible to the Office of President; neither shall any Person be eligible to that Office who shall not have attained to the Age of thirty five Years, and been fourteen Years a Resident within the United States.

▶ *ARTICLE IV*

Section 4

The United States shall guarantee to every State in this Union a Republican Form of Government. ...

▶ *ARTICLE VI*

Clause 3: ... no religious Test shall ever be required as a Qualification to any Office or public Trust under the United States.

▶ *AMENDMENT XII*

The Electors shall meet in their respective states, and vote by ballot for President and Vice-President, one of whom, at least, shall not be an inhabitant of the same state with themselves; they shall name in their ballots the person voted for as President, and in distinct ballots the person voted for as Vice-President, and they shall make distinct lists of all persons voted for as President, and of all persons voted for as Vice-President, and of the number of votes for each, which lists they shall sign and certify, and transmit sealed to the seat of the government of the United States, directed to the President of the Senate;—The President of the Senate shall, in the presence of the Senate and House of Representatives, open all the certificates and the votes shall then be counted;—The person having the greatest number of votes for President, shall be the President, if such number be a majority of the whole number of Electors appointed; and if no person have such majority, then from the persons having the highest numbers not exceeding three on the list of those voted for as President, the House of Representatives shall choose immediately, by ballot, the President. But in choosing the President, the votes shall be taken by states, the representation from each state having one vote; a quorum for this purpose shall consist of a member or members from two-thirds of the states, and a majority of all the states shall be necessary to a choice. And if the House of Representatives shall not choose a President whenever the right of choice shall devolve upon them, before the fourth day of March next following, then the Vice-President shall act as President, as in the case of the death or other constitutional disability of the President (This sentence has been superseded by section 3 of amendment XX).—The person having the greatest number of votes as Vice-President, shall be the Vice-President, if such number be a majority of the whole number of Electors appointed, and if no person have a majority, then from the two highest numbers on the list, the Senate shall choose the Vice-President; a quorum for the purpose shall consist of two-thirds of the whole number of Senators, and a majority of the whole number shall be necessary to a choice. But no person constitutionally ineligible to the office of President shall be eligible to that of Vice-President of the United States.

▶ *AMENDMENT XV*

Section 1

The right of citizens of the United States to vote shall not be denied or abridged by the United States or by any State on account of race, color, or previous condition of servitude.

▶ *AMENDMENT XVII*

The Senate of the United States shall be composed of two Senators from each State, elected by the people thereof, for six years; and each Senator shall have one vote. The electors in each State shall have the qualifications requisite for electors of the most numerous branch of the State legislatures.

When vacancies happen in the representation of any State in the Senate, the executive authority of such State shall issue writs of election to fill such vacancies: Provided, That the legislature of any State may empower the executive thereof to make temporary appointments until the people fill the vacancies by election as the legislature may direct. ...

▶ *AMENDMENT XIX*

The right of citizens of the United States to vote shall not be denied or abridged by the United States or by any State on account of sex.

▶ *AMENDMENT XXII*

Section 1

No person shall be elected to the office of the President more than twice, and no person who has held the office of President, or acted as President, for more than two years of a term to which some other person was elected President shall be elected to the office of the President more than once. …

▶ *AMENDMENT XXIII*

Section 1

The District constituting the seat of government of the United States shall appoint in such manner as the Congress may direct:

A number of electors of President and Vice President equal to the whole number of Senators and Representatives in Congress to which the District would be entitled if it were a state, but in no event more than the least populous state; they shall be in addition to those appointed by the states, but they shall be considered, for the purposes of the election of President and Vice President, to be electors appointed by a state; and they shall meet in the District and perform such duties as provided by the twelfth article of amendment.

▶ *AMENDMENT XXIV*

Section 1

The right of citizens of the United States to vote in any primary or other election for President or Vice President, for electors for President or Vice President, or for Senator or Representative in Congress, shall not be denied or abridged by the United States or any state by reason of failure to pay any poll tax or other tax.

▶ *AMENDMENT XXVI*

Section 1

The right of citizens of the United States, who are 18 years of age or older, to vote, shall not be denied or abridged by the United States or any state on account of age.
Source: http://uscode.house.gov/pdf/Organic%20Laws/const.pdf

Bibliography

1936 Constitution of the USSR. Chapter XI, Articles 139, 134. Available at www.departments. bucknell.edu/russian/const/36cons04.html#chap11 (accessed August 7, 2012).

2016 Election Central, "2012 Primary Debate Schedule." Available at www.uspresidentialelectionnews.com/2012-debate-schedule/2011-12-primary-debate-schedule (accessed May 29, 2013).

Abramowitz, Alan I. (1985) "Economic Conditions, Presidential Popularity, and Voting Behavior in Midterm Congressional Elections," *Journal of Politics*, 47: 31–43.

—— (1988) "An Improved Model for Predicting Presidential Election Outcomes," *PS: Political Science and Politics*, 21: 843–847.

—— (2006) "Using the Generic Vote to Forecast the 2006 House and Senate Elections," *The Forum*, 4. Available at www.bepress.com/forum/vol4/iss2/art3 (accessed June 1, 2013).

Abramowitz, Alan I. and Jeffrey A. Segal (1992) *Senate Elections*, Ann Arbor, MI: University of Michigan Press.

Abramowitz, Alan I. and Steven Webster (2016) "The Rise of Negative Partisanship and the Nationalization of US Elections in the 21st Century," *Electoral Studies*, 41: 12–22.

Abramowitz, Alan, Brad Alexander, and Matthew Gunning (2006) "Don't Blame Redistricting for Uncompetitive Elections," *PS: Political Science and Politics*, 39: 87–90.

—— (2006) "Incumbency, Redistricting, and the Decline of Competition in US House Elections," *Journal of Politics*, 68: 75–88.

ACE Project (n.d.) "Self-Initiated versus State-Initiated Registration," *ACE Encylopaedia of the Administration and Cost of Elections*. Available at http://aceproject.org/ace-en/topics/vr/vra/vra10 (accessed September 6, 2012).

Ackerman, Bruce and Ian Ayres (2002) *Voting with Dollars: A New Paradigm for Campaign Finance*, New Haven, CT: Yale University Press.

AFL-CIO (2007) "AFL-CIO Presidential Endorsement Process," March 7. Available at www.afl-cio.org/About/Exec-Council/EC-Statements/AFL-CIO-Presidential-Endorsement-Process (accessed May 22, 2013).

Aldrich, John H. (1995) *Why Parties? The Origin and Transformation of Political Parties in America*, Chicago, IL: University of Chicago Press.

Aldrich, John H., John L. Sullivan, and Eugene Borgida (1989) "Foreign Affairs and Issue Voting: Do Presidential Candidates 'Waltz before a Blind Audience'?" *American Political Science Review*, 83: 123–141.

Alexander, Herbert E. (1984) *Financing Politics: Money, Elections, and Political Reform*, Washington, DC: CQ Press.

Allen, Greg (2012) "Obama Campaign Looks to Black Churches in Fla," *NPR*, October 29. Available at www.npr.org/2012/10/29/163845744/obama-campaign-looks-to-black-churches-in-fla (accessed May 22, 2013).

Allen, Mike and James Carney (2006) "Campaign 2006: The Republicans' Secret Weapon," *Time*, October 1. Available at www.time.com/time/printout/0,8816,1541295,00.html (accessed May 3, 2013).

Alt, James E. (1994) "The Impact of the Voting Rights Act on Black and White Voter Registration in the South," in Chandler Davidson and Bernard Grofman (eds.), *Quiet Revolution in the South: The Impact of the Voting Rights Act, 1965–90*, Princeton, NJ: Princeton University Press.

Alvarez, R. Michael and Garrett Glasgow (1997) "Do Voters Learn from Presidential Election Campaigns?" California Institute of Technology (unpublished manuscript).

Anderson, Brian and Burdett A. Loomis (1998) "Taking Organization Seriously: The Structure of Interest Group Influence," in Allan Cigler and Burdett Loomis (eds.), *Interest Group Politics*, 5th edn, Washington, DC: CQ Press.

Annenberg Public Policy Center of the University of Pennsylvania (2004) "Large Majority of Democrats Still Bitter Over 2000, National Annenberg Election Survey Shows," March 19. Available at http://editor.annenbergpublicpolicycenter.org/wp-content/uploads/2004_03_floridarecount_3-19_pr1.pdf (accessed June 3, 2013).

Ansolabehere, Stephen and Alan Gerber (1994) "The Mismeasure of Campaign Spending: Evidence from the 1990 US House Elections," *Journal of Politics*, 56: 1106–1118.

Ansolabehere, Stephen and Shanto Iyengar (1995) *Going Negative: How Political Advertisements Shrink and Polarize the Electorate*, New York: The Free Press.

—— (1996) "Can the Press Monitor Campaign Advertising? An Experimental Study," *Harvard International Journal of Press/Politics*, 1: 72–86.

Ansolabehere, Stephen, John M. de Figueiredo, and James M. Snyder Jr. (2003) "Why Is There So Little Money in US Politics?" *Journal of Economic Perspectives*, 17: 105–130.

Ansolabehere, Stephen, Rebecca Lessem, and James M. Snyder, Jr. (2006) "The Orientation of Newspaper Endorsements in US Elections, 1940–2002," *Quarterly Journal of Political Science*, 1: 393–404.

Ari Berman (2016) "Voting Rights in the Age of Trump," *The New York Times*, November 19, www.nytimes.com/2016/11/22/opinion/voting-rights-in-the-age-of-trump.html (accessed December 30, 2016).

Associated Press (2007) "Paul Sets One-Day GOP Fundraising Record," *NBC News*, November 6. Available at www.msnbc.msn.com/id/21646939 (accessed May 18, 2013).

Atkeson, Lonna Rae (1998) "Divisive Primaries and General Election Outcomes: Another Look at Presidential Campaigns," *American Journal of Political Science*, 42: 256–271.

Axline, Keith (2006) "Election '08: Vote by TiVo," *Wired.com*, November 14. Available at www.wired.com/news/technology/1,72113-0.html (accessed September 6, 2012).

Aylsworth, Leon E. (1931) "The Passing of Alien Suffrage," *American Political Science Review*, 25: 114–116.

Azari, Julia R. (2016) "How the News Media Helped to Nominate Trump," *Political Communication*, 33: 677–680.

Bafumi, Joseph, Robert S. Erikson, and Christopher Wlezien (2010) "Balancing, Generic Polls and Midterm Congressional Elections," *Journal of Politics*, 72: 705–719.

Bai, Mat (2004) "Who Lost Ohio?" *New York Times Magazine*, November 21. Available at www.nytimes.com/2004/11/21/magazine/21OHIO.html?_r=0 (accessed May 30, 2013).

Balz, Dan and Alec Macgillis (2008) "Battleground States," *Washington Post*, June 8. Available at www.washingtonpost.com/wp-dyn/content/graphic/2008/06/08/GR2008060800566.html (accessed May 30, 2013).

Banks, Jeffrey S. and D. Roderick Kiewiet (1989) "Explaining Patterns of Candidate Competition in Congressional Elections," *American Journal of Political Science*, 33: 997–1015.

Banzhaf, John F. III (1968) "One Man, 3,312 Votes: A Mathematical Analysis of the Electoral College," *Villanova Law Review*, 13: 304–346.

Barabas, Jason and Jennifer Jerit (2004) "Redistricting Principles and Racial Representation," *State Politics and Policy Quarterly*, 4: 415–435.

Barr, Andy (2010) "Karl Rove: Christine O'Donnell Said 'Nutty Things.'" *Politico*, September 15. Available at www.politico.com/news/stories/0910/42205.html (accessed May 19, 2013).

Bash, Dana and Abigail Crutchfield (2016) "The Final Get-Out-the-Vote Flurry Begins," *CNN*, November 4. Available at www.cnn.com/2016/11/04/politics/get-out-the-vote-efforts-2016-election (accessed March 4, 2017).

Bass, Scott (2005) "Chasing Bubba," *Style Weekly*, October 12. Available at www.styleweekly.com/richmond/chasing-bubba/Content?oid=1390697 (accessed May 22, 2013).

Bazelon Center for Mental Health Law, "Voting," www.bazelon.org/Where-We-Stand/Self-Determination/Voting.aspx (accessed April 15, 2017).

Becker, Amanda (2012) "The Phantom Commission: Agency Formed to Restore Confidence in Elections Is in Disarray," *Roll Call*, November 1. Available at www.rollcall.com/issues/58_33/Agency-Formed-to-Restore-Confidence-in-Elections-Is-in-Disarray-218616-1.html (accessed May 9, 2013).

Bennett, W. Lance (2003) *News: The Politics of Illusion*, 5th edn, New York: Longman.

Benoit, William L. and Glenn J. Hansen (2004) "Presidential Debate Watching, Issue Knowledge, Character Evaluation, and Vote Choice," *Human Communication Research*, 30: 121–144.

Berelson, Bernard, Paul Lazarsfeld, and William H. McPhee (1954) *Voting: A Study of Opinion Formation in a Presidential Campaign*, Chicago, IL: University of Chicago Press.

Berg-Andersson, Richard E. (2006) "The Green Papers: Off Year Election 2005," *The Green Papers*, June 13. Available at www.thegreenpapers.com/G05/GovernorsByElectionCycle.phtml (accessed August 14, 2012).

—— (2008) "2008 Chronological Cumulative Allocation of Delegates," *The Green Papers*, April 13. Available at www.thegreenpapers.com/P08/ccad.phtml (accessed May 18, 2013).

—— (2013a) "The Green Papers: Indiana 2012 General Election," *The Green Papers*, February 20. Available at www.thegreenpapers.com/G12/IN (accessed May 7, 2013).

—— (2013b) "The Green Papers: Washington 2012 General Election," *The Green Papers*, April 2. Available at www.thegreenpapers.com/G12/WA (accessed May 7, 2013).

—— (n.d.) "The Green Papers: 2010 Midterm Election," *The Green Papers*. Available at www.thegreenpapers.com/G10 (accessed May 7, 2013).

Berns, Walter (2001) "Outputs: The Electoral College Produces Presidents," in Gary L. Gregg III (ed.) *Securing Democracy: Why We Have an Electoral College*, Wilmington, DE: ISI Books.

Berry, Jeffrey M. (1997) *The Interest Group Society*, 3rd edn, New York: Longman.

Berry, Jeffrey M. and Clyde Wilcox (2007) *The Interest Group Society*, 4th edn, New York: Longman.

Bianco, William T. (1984) "Strategic Decisions on Candidacy in US Congressional Districts," *Legislative Studies Quarterly*, 9: 351–364.

Bibby, John F. (1999) "Party Networks: National-State Integration, Allied Groups, and Issue Activists," in John C. Green and Daniel M. Shea (eds.), *The State of the Parties: The Changing Role of Contemporary American Parties*, 3rd edn, Lanham, MD: Rowman & Littlefield.

Bimber, Bruce and Richard Davis (2003) *Campaigning Online: The Internet in US Elections*, Oxford: Oxford University Press.

Blumenthal, Mark (2007) "The Pollster.com Disclosure Project," *Pollster.com*, September 24. Available at www.pollster.com/blogs/the_pollstercom_disclosure_pro.php (accessed May 16, 2013).

Blumenthal, Sidney (1982) *The Permanent Campaign*, rev. edn, New York: Simon & Schuster.

Bond, Jon R., Cary Covington, and Richard Fleisher (1985) "Explaining Challenger Quality in Congressional Elections," *Journal of Politics*, 47: 510–529.

Bond, Jon R., Richard Fleisher, and Jeffery C. Talbert (1997) "Partisan Differences in Candidate Quality in Open Seat House Races, 1876–1994," *Political Research Quarterly*, 50: 281–299.

Bonneau, Chris W. and Melinda Gann Hall (2009) *In Defense of Judicial Elections*, London and New York: Routledge.

Bovée, John (1999) "Opposition Research," in David D. Perlmutter (ed.), *The Manship School Guide to Political Communication*, Baton Rouge, LA: Louisiana State University Press.

Brace, Paul and Barbara Hinckley (1991) "The Structure of Presidential Approval: Constraints within and across Presidencies," *Journal of Politics*, 53: 993–1017.

Bradshaw, Joel C. (2004) "Who Will Vote for You and Why: Designing Campaign Strategy and Message," in James A. Thurber and Candice J. Nelson (eds.), *Campaigns and Elections American Style*, 2nd edn, Boulder, CO: Westview Press.

Brady, David W., Robert D'Onofrio, and Morris Fiorina (2000) "The Nationalization of Electoral Forces Revisited," in David W. Brady, John F. Cogan, and Morris Fiorina (eds.), *Continuity and Change in House Elections*, Palo Alto, CA; Stanford University Press and Hoover Institution Press.

Brady, Henry E., and Richard Johnston (eds.) (2006) *Capturing Campaign Effects*, Ann Arbor, MI: University of Michigan Press.

Brennan Center for Justice (2001) *Buying Time 2000: Television Advertising in the 2000 Federal Elections*, New York: The Brennan Center for Justice at the New York University School of Law.

—— (2006) "The Machinery of Democracy," October 10. Available at www.brennancenter. org/publication/machinery-democracy (accessed May 11, 2013).

Brians, Craig Leonard and Bernard Grofman (2001) "Election Day Registration's Effect on US Voter Turnout," *Social Science Quarterly*, 82: 170–183.

Broder, David S. (1972) *The Party's Over: The Failure of Politics in America*, New York: Harper & Row.

Brody, Richard and Lee Sigelman (1983) "Presidential Popularity and Presidential Elections: An Update and Extension," *Public Opinion Quarterly*, 47: 325–328.

Brown, Robert D. and Justin Wedeking (2006) "People Who Have Their Tickets But Do Not Use Them: 'Motor Vehicle,' Registration, and Turnout Revisited," *American Politics Research*, 34: 479–504.

Brownstein, Ronald (2009) "The Blue Wall," *National Journal*, January 17. Available at http://i.usatoday.net/news/TheOval/National-Journal-1-16-2009.pdf (accessed May 30, 2013).

Brunell, Thomas L. (2008) *Redistricting and Representation: Why Competitive Elections Are Bad for America*, London and New York: Routledge.

Bryce, James (1921) *Modern Democracies*, vol. I, New York: Macmillan.

Buam, Matthew A. (2003) *Soft News Goes to War: Public Opinion and American Foreign Policy in the New Media Age*, Princeton, NJ: Princeton University Press.

Buchanan, Patrick J. (1992) "1992 Republican National Convention Speech," August 17. Available at http://buchanan.org/blog/1992-republican-national-convention-speech-148 (accessed May 18, 2013).

Bullock, Charles S. III (2005) "Redistricting: Racial and Partisan Considerations," in Matthew J. Streb (ed.), *Law and Election Politics: The Rules of the Game*, Boulder, CO: Lynne Rienner Publishers.

Bullock, Charles S. III, Ronald Keith Gaddie, and Anders Ferrington (2002) "System Structure, Campaign Stimuli, and Voter Falloff in Runoff Primaries," *Journal of Politics*, 64: 1210–1224.

Burden, Barry C. (2004) "Candidate Positioning in US Congressional Elections," *British Journal of Political Science*, 34: 211–227.

Burke, Thomas F. (1997) "The Concept of Corruption in Campaign Finance Law," *Constitutional Commentary*, 14: 127–149.

Burnett, Kristin D. (2011) "Congressional Apportionment," Washington, DC: US Department of Commerce. Available at www.census.gov/prod/cen2010/briefs/c2010br-08.pdf (accessed May 8, 2013).

Burnham, Walter Dean (1970) *Critical Elections and the Mainsprings of American Politics*, New York: W. W. Norton.

Burns, John F. (2002) "Threats and Responses: Baghdad; 11 Million Voters Say the Iraqi President Is Perfect," *New York Times*, October 17. http://www.nytimes.com/2002/10/17/world/threats-responses-baghdad-11-million-voters-say-iraqi-president-perfect.html (accessed February 14, 2005).

Burris, Arthur L. and Eric A. Fischer (2016) "The Help America Vote Act and Election Administration: Overview and Selected Issues for the 2016 Election," *Congressional Research Service*, October 18. Available at https://fas.org/sgp/crs/misc/RS20898.pdf (accessed June 29, 2016).

Busch, Andrew E. (1999) *Horses in Midstream: US Midterm Elections and Their Consequences, 1894–1998*, Pittsburgh, PA: University of Pittsburgh Press.

—— (2008) "The Reemergence of the Iowa Caucuses: A New Trend, an Aberration, or a Useful Reminder?" in William G. Mayer (ed.), *The Making of the Presidential Candidates 2008*, Lanham, MD: Rowman & Littlefield.

Bush-Cheney '04 and Kerry-Edwards '04 (2004) "Memorandum of Understanding on Debates," September 22. Available at http://news.findlaw.com/hdocs/docs/election2004/debates2004mou.html (accessed May 30, 2013).

Cain, Bruce E., Karin MacDonald, and Michael McDonald (2005) "From Equality to Fairness: The Path to Political Reform since Baker v. Carr," in Thomas E. Mann and Bruce E. Cain (eds.), *Party Lines: Competition, Partisanship, and Congressional Redistricting*, Washington, DC: Brookings Institution Press.

Campaign Finance Institute (2012) "President Obama Is Ahead of 2007 Pace, Romney Even; Corporations Supplied a Quarter of the Romney Super PAC Funds," Table 1. February 2. Available at www.cfinst.org/Press/PReleases/12-02-02/President_Obama_is_Ahead_of_2007_Pace_Romney_Even_Corporations_Supplied_a_Quarter_of_the_Romney_Super_PAC_Funds.aspx (accessed May 28, 2013).

—— (n.d.) "Campaign Finance eGuide: Bipartisan Campaign Reform Act." Available at www.cfinst.org/legacy/eguide/shays.html (accessed September 6, 2012).

—— (n.d.) "eGuide Update Page." Available at www.cfinst.org/legacy/eguide/update/bcra.html (accessed September 6, 2012).

—— (n.d.) "Table 3.2: House Campaign Expenditures: Major Party General Election Candidates, 1974–2014 (full cycle, net dollars)." http://www.cfinst.org/pdf/vital/VitalStats_t2.pdf (March 18, 2017).

—— (n.d.) "Table 3.3: House Campaign Expenditures: Incumbents and Challengers, Major Party General Election Candidates by Election Outcome, 1974–2014 (full cycle, mean net dollars)." http://www.cfinst.org/pdf/vital/VitalStats_t3.pdf (March 18, 2017).

—— (n.d.) "Table 3.5: Senate Campaign Expenditures, Major Party General Election Candidates, 1974–2014 (full cycle, net dollars)." Available at www.cfinst.org/pdf/vital/VitalStats_t5.pdf (accessed March 18, 2017).

Campbell, Angus (1966) "Surge and Decline: A Study of Electoral Change," in Angus Campbell, Philip E. Converse, Warren E. Miller, and Donald E. Stokes (eds.), *Elections and the Political Order*, New York: John Wiley & Sons.

Campbell, Angus, Philip E. Converse, Warren E. Miller, and Donald E. Stokes (1960) *The American Voter*, New York: John Wiley & Sons.

—— (1966) *Elections and the Political Order*. New York: John Wiley & Sons.

Campbell, James E. (1987) "The Revised Theory of Surge and Decline," *American Journal of Political Science*, 31: 965–979.

—— (1992) "Forecasting the Presidential Vote in the States," *American Journal of Political Science*, 36: 386–407.

—— (1997) *The Presidential Pulse of Congressional Elections*, 2nd edn, Lexington, KY: University of Kentucky Press.

—— (2000) *The American Campaign: US Presidential Campaigns and the National Vote*, College Station, TX: Texas A&M University Press.

—— (2004a) "Forecasting the Presidential Vote in 2004: Placing Preference Polls in Context," *PS: Political Science and Politics*, 37: 763–767.

—— (2004b) "The Presidential Election of 2004: The Fundamentals and the Campaign." *The Forum*, 2. http://www.bepress.com/forum/vol2/iss4/art1 (May 30, 2013).

Canon, David T. (1990) *Actors, Athletes, and Astronauts: Political Amateurs in the United States Congress*, Chicago, IL: University of Chicago Press.

Caplan, Bryan (2007) *The Myth of the Rational Voter: Why Democracies Choose Bad Policies*, Princeton, NJ: Princeton University Press.

Cappella, Joseph N. and Kathleen Hall Jamieson (1994) "Broadcast Adwatch Effects: A Field Experiment," *Communication Research*, 21: 342–365.

—— (1997) *Spiral of Cynicism: The Press and the Public Good*, Oxford: Oxford University Press.

Carmines, Edward G. and James A. Stimson (1980) "The Two Faces of Issue Voting," *American Political Science Review*, 74: 78–91.

Carney, Eliza Newlin (2013) "Rules of the Game: Lame-Duck FEC Invites Scofflaws," *Roll Call*, April 5. Available at www.rollcall.com/news/rules_of_the_game_lame_duck_fec_invites_scofflaws-223626-1.html?pg=1 (accessed May 14, 2013).

Carpini, Michael X. Delli (1984) "Scooping the Voters? The Consequences of the Networks' Early Call of the 1980 Presidential Race," *Journal of Politics*, 46: 866–885.

Carrette, George J. (2003) "US Constitution: How Fast to Amend?" November 27. Available at http://people.delphiforums.com/gjc/amend-howfast.html (accessed August 14, 2012).

Carter, Elisabeth and David M. Farrell (2010) "Electoral Systems and Election Management," in Lawrence LeDuc, Richard G. Niemi, and Pippa Norris (eds.), *Comparing Democracies 3: Elections and Voting in the 21st Century*, Thousand Oaks, CA: Sage Publications.

Carter, Jimmy, Gerald R. Ford, Lloyd N. Cutler, and Robert H. Michel (eds.) (2002) *To Assure Pride and Confidence in the Electoral Process: Report of the National Commission on Federal Election Reform*, Washington, DC: Brookings Institution Press.

Casey, Linda, Nadeanne Haftl, Kevin McNellis, Robin Parkinson, Peter Quist, and Denise Roth Barber (2012) "An Overview of Campaign Finances, 2009–10 Election," *National Institute on Money in State Politics*. Available at www.followthemoney.org/press/ReportView. phtml?r=487 (accessed May 16, 2013).

CBS DC (2012) "Obama Sets All-Time Fundraising Record, Crushes Final Romney Totals," *CBS DC*, December 7. Available at http://washington.cbslocal.com/2012/12/07/obama-sets-all-time-fundraising-record-crushed-final-romney-totals (accessed May 28, 2013).

Center for American Women and Politics (2011) "Gender Differences in Voter Turnout," Eagleton Institute of Politics, Rutgers University. Available at www.cawp.rutgers.edu/fast_facts/voters/documents/genderdiff.pdf (accessed May 25, 2013).

—— (2013) "State by State Information," Eagleton Institute of Politics, Rutgers University. Available at www.cawp.rutgers.edu/fast_facts/resources/state_ fact_sheet.php#states (accessed May 16, 2013).

—— (2016) "Current Numbers," www.cawp.rutgers.edu/current-numbers (accessed January 3, 2017).

—— (2017) "The Gender Gap: Voting Choices in Presidential Elections," Eagleton Institute of Politics, Rutgers University. Available at www.cawp.rutgers.edu/sites/default/files/resources/ggpresvote.pdf (accessed February 17, 2017).

Center for Governmental Studies at the University of Virginia (2001) "The Report of the National Symposium on Presidential Selection," University of Virginia Center for Governmental Studies. Available at www.centerforpolitics.org/downloads/rnsps.pdf (accessed May 18, 2013).

Center for Responsive Politics. (n.d.) "2012 Overview: Stats at a Glance." Available at www.opensecrets.org/overview/index.php?cycle=2012&type=A&display=A (accessed May 28, 2013).

—— (n.d.) "American Assn for Justice." Available at www.opensecrets.org/orgs/summary.php?id=D000000065 (accessed May 20, 2013).

—— (n.d.) "Super PACs (2010 cycle)." Available at www.opensecrets.org/pacs/superpacs.php?cycle=2010 (accessed May 20, 2013).

—— (n.d.) "Super PACs." Available at www.opensecrets.org/pacs/superpacs.php (accessed May 14, 2013).

Center for Responsive Politics (2017) "Super PACs," January 2, www.opensecrets.org/pacs/superpacs.php (accessed January 2, 2017).

Center for Voting and Democracy. (n.d.) "Instant Runoff Voting." Available at www.fairvote.org/instant-runoff-voting#.Ua0KN-s1Yxe (accessed May 9, 2013).

Chaffee, Steven and Stacey Frank (1996) "How Americans Get Political Information: Print versus Broadcast News," *Annals of the American Academy of Political and Social Science*, 546: 48–58.

Chaturvedi, Ashish and Arnab Mukherji (2004) "Do Elections Incite Violent Crime?" Department of Economics, University of California, Irvine and RAND Graduate School (unpublished manuscript).

Cillizza, Chris (2005) "Party Chairmen Say Yes to Paychecks," *Washington Post*, December 20. Available at www.washingtonpost.com/wp-dyn/content/article/2005/12/19/AR2005121901931.html (accessed May 18, 2013).

City of Sunnyvale, California (2011) "Report to the Mayor and City Council, NO: 11–202," September 13. Available at http://sunnyvale.ca.gov/Portals/0/Sunnyvale/CouncilReports/2011/11-202.pdf (accessed June 2, 2013).

CNN.com (2004) "America Votes 2004—Election Results: US President/National/Exit Poll." Available at www.cnn.com/ELECTION/2004/pages/results/states/US/P/00/epolls.0.html (accessed May 27, 2013).

—— (2008) "Election Center 2008: Exit Polls." Available at www.cnn.com/ELECTION/2008/results/polls/#USP00p1 (accessed May 27, 2013).

—— (2012) "America's Choice 2012—President: Full Results." Available at www.cnn.com/election/2012/results/race/president (accessed May 26, 2013).

Coates, Ta-Nehisi Paul (2007) "Is Obama Black Enough?" *Time*, February 1. Available at www.time.com/time/nation/article/0,8599,1584736,00.html (accessed November 23, 2012).

Cohen, Marty, David Karol, Hans Noel, and John Zaller (2008a) *The Party Decides: Presidential Nominations Before and After Reform*, Chicago, IL University of Chicago Press.

—— (2008b) "The Invisible Primary in Presidential Nominations, 1980–2004," in William G. Mayer (ed.), *The Making of the Presidential Candidates 2008*, Lanham, MD: Rowman & Littlefield.

Collier, David and Robert Adcock (1999) "Democracy and Dichotomies: A Pragmatic Approach to Choices about Concepts," *Annual Review of Political Science*, 2: 537–565.

Conley, Patricia Heidotting (2001) *Presidential Mandates: How Elections Shape the National Agenda*, Chicago, IL: University of Chicago Press.

Connelly, William F. (2006) "Wall vs. Wave?" *The Forum*, 4. Available at www.bepress.com/forum/vol4/iss3/art3 (accessed June 1, 2013).

Cook Political Report (2007) "2008 House Summary," December 19. Available at www.cookpolitical.com/races/report_pdfs/2008 haag_summary_dec19.pdf (accessed January 2, 2008).

Cook, Charles E. Jr.. (n.d.) "Accuracy," *The Cook Political Report*. Available at http://cookpolitical.com/about/accuracy (accessed June 1, 2013).

Corrado, Anthony (1999) "On the Issue of Issue Advocacy: A Comment," *Virginia Law Review*, 85: 1803–1812.

—— (2005a) "Money and Politics: A History of Federal Campaign Finance Law," in Anthony Corrado, Thomas E. Mann, Daniel Ortiz, and Trevor Potter (eds.), *The New Campaign Finance Sourcebook*, Washington, DC: Brookings Institution Press.

—— (2005b) "Public Funding of Presidential Campaigns," in Anthony Corrado, Thomas E. Mann, Daniel R. Ortiz, and Trevor Potter (eds.), *The New Campaign Finance Sourcebook*, Washington, DC: Brookings Institution Press.

Cox, Gary W. and Jonathan N. Katz (2002) *Elbridge Gerry's Salamander: The Electoral Consequences of the Reapportionment Revolution*, Cambridge: Cambridge University Press.

Cox, Gary W. and Michael C. Munger (1989) "Closeness, Expenditures, and Turnout in the 1982 US House Elections," *American Political Science Review*, 83: 217–231.

Craig, Tim and Michael D. Shear (2006) "Allen Quip Provokes Outrage, Apology," *Washington Post*, August 15. Available at www.washingtonpost.com/wp-dyn/content/article/2006/08/14/AR2006081400589.html (accessed May 16, 2013).

Cunningham, Frank (2002) *Theories of Democracy: A Critical Introduction*, London and New York: Routledge.

Dahl, Robert A. (1961) *Who Governs?* New Haven, CT: Yale University Press.

—— (1989) *Democracy and Its Critics*, New Haven, CT: Yale University Press.

—— (1990) "Myth of the Presidential Mandate," *Political Science Quarterly*, 105: 355–372.

—— (1998) *On Democracy*, New Haven, CT: Yale University Press.

—— (2001) *How Democratic Is the American Constitution?* New Haven, CT: Yale University Press.

Davidson, Chandler and Bernard Grofman (eds.) (1994) *Quiet Revolution in the South: The Impact of the Voting Rights Act, 1965–90*, Princeton, NJ: Princeton University Press.

David Weigel (2016) "Democrats Vote to Bind Most Superdelegates to State Primary Results," *Washington Post*, July 23, www.washingtonpost.com/news/post-politics/wp/2016/07/23/democrats-vote-to-bind-most-superdelegates-to-state-primary-results/?utm_term=.8a910033de21 (accessed January 7, 2017).

Davis, Richard and Diana Owen (1998) *New Media and American Politics*, Oxford: Oxford University Press.

Dennis, Jack (1991) "The Study of Electoral Behavior," in William Crotty (ed.), *Political Science: Looking to the Future*, vol. III: *Political Behavior*, Evanston, IL: Northwestern University Press.

Dennis W. Johnson (2001) *No Place for Amateurs: How Political Consultants Are Reshaping American Democracy*, London and New York: Routledge, p. 7.

Desilver, Drew (2016) "US Voter Turnout Trails Most Developed Countries," Pew Research Center, August 2. Available at www.pewresearch.org/fact-tank/2016/08/02/u-s-voter-turnout-trails-most-developed-countries (accessed February 7, 2017).

Diamond, Martin (1977) *The Electoral College and the American Idea of Democracy*, Washington, DC: American Enterprise Institute.

Dionne, E. J. and William Kristol (eds.) (2001) *Bush v. Gore: The Court Cases and the Commentary*, Washington, DC: Brookings Institution Press.

Don Gonyea (2016) "Here's Why the Republican National Committee Says It Won Tuesday," *National Public Radio*, November 14, www.npr.org/2016/11/14/502045531/heres-why-the-republican-national-committee-says-it-won-tuesday (accessed January 16, 2017).

Downs, Anthony (1957) *An Economic Theory of Democracy*, New York: Harper & Row.

Druckman, James N. (2003) "The Power of Television Images: The First Kennedy-Nixon Debate Revisited," *Journal of Politics*, 65: 559–571.

—— (2004) "Priming the Vote: Campaign Effects in a US Senate Election," *Political Psychology*, 25: 577–594.

Druckman, James N., Lawrence R. Jacobs, and Eric Ostermeier (2004) "Candidates' Strategies to Prime Issues and Image," *Journal of Politics*, 66: 1180–1202.

Dudley, Robert L. and Alan R. Gitelson (2002) *American Elections: The Rules Matter*, New York: Longman.

Dulio, David A. (2004) *For Better or Worse: How Political Consultants Are Changing Elections in the United States*, Albany, NY: State University of New York Press.

Dulio, David A. and Candice J. Nelson (2006) *Vital Signs: Perspectives on the Health of American Campaigning*, Washington, DC: Brookings Institution Press.

Early Voting Information Center at Reed College (n.d.) "Early Voting Calendar, 2012." Available at http://reed.edu/earlyvoting/calendar (accessed May 11, 2013).

Edison Media Research and Mitofsky International (2005) "Evaluation of Edison/Mitofsky Election System 2004," *National Election Pool*, January 19. Available at http://abcnews.go.com/images/Politics/EvaluationofEdisonMitofskyElectionSystem.pdf (accessed February 7, 2017).

Edwards, George C. III (2004) *Why the Electoral College Is Bad for America*, New Haven, CT: Yale University Press.

Elazar, Daniel J. (1966) *American Federalism: A View from the States*, New York: Thomas Y. Crowell.

Eldersveld, Samuel J. and Hanes Walton, Jr. (2000) *Political Parties in American Society*, 2nd edn, Boston, MA: Bedford/St. Martin's.

Election Data Services (2004) "New Study Shows 50 Million Voters Will Use Electronic Voting Systems, 32 Million Still with Punch Cards in 2004," February 12. Available at www.subdudesite.com/WebPages_Local/RefInfo/GovmtCitizen/VotingMachines/images_voting/VoteMethodsStudy2004_wMap_andGraph.pdf (accessed May 30, 2013).

—— (2008) "Nation Sees Drop in Use of Electronic Voting Equipment for 2008 Election—A First," October 17. Available at www.electiondataservices.com/images/File/NR_VoteEquip_Nov-2008wAppendix2.pdf (accessed May 13, 2013).

Elkins, Stanley and Eric McKitrick (1993) *The Age of Federalism*, Oxford: Oxford University Press.

EMILY's List (2003) "Thinking of Running for Office: A Guide for Democratic Women Candidates." Available at http://emilyslist.org/sites/default/files/TORFO.pdf (accessed May 22, 2013).

—— (2012) "EMILY's List Announces New Website—and 1.5 Million Members!" June 5. Available at http://emilyslist.org/news/releases/emily%E2%80%99s-list-announces-new-website-%E2%80%93-and-15-million-members-major-milestone-reached-ad (accessed May 2013).

Enten, Harry (2016) "Trump Probably Did Better with Latino Voters Than Romney Did," *FiveThirtyEight.com*, November 18. Available at https://fivethirtyeight.com/features/trump-probably-did-better-with-latino-voters-than-romney-did (accessed February 17, 2017).

Epstein, David, Rodolfo O. de la Garza, Sharyn O'Halloran, and Richard H. Pildes (eds.) (2006) *The Future of the Voting Rights Act*, New York: Russell Sage Foundation.

Erikson, Robert S. (1990) "Economic Conditions and the Congressional Vote: A Review of the Macrolevel Evidence," *American Journal of Political Science*, 34: 373–399.

Erikson, Robert S. and Christopher Wlezien (2012) *The Timeline of Presidential Elections: How Campaigns Do (and Do Not) Matter*, Chicago, IL: University of Chicago Press.

Ezra, Marni (2005) "Nomination Politics: Primary Laws and Party Rules," in Paul S. Herrnson, Colton Campbell, Marni Ezra, and Stephen K. Medvic (eds.), *Guide to Political Campaigns in America*, Washington, DC: CQ Press.

FactCheck.org (2004a) "Did Kerry Vote 'No' on Body Armor for Troops?" updated March 18. Available at www.factcheck.org/did_kerry_vote_no_on_body_armor.html (accessed May 18, 2013).

—— (2004b) "Republican-Funded Group Attacks Kerry's War Record," updated August 22. Available at www.factcheck.org/republican-funded_group_attacks_kerrys_war_record.html (accessed May 30, 2013).

Fair, Ray C. (1978) "The Effect of Economic Events on Votes for President," *Review of Economics and Statistics*, 60: 159–173.

—— (1996) "The Effect of Economic Events on Votes for President: 1992 Update," *Political Behavior*, 18: 119–139.

—— (2012) *Predicting Presidential Elections and Other Things*, 2nd edn, Palo Alto, CA: Stanford University Press.

FairVote (n.d.) "Instant Runoff Voting." Available at www.fairvote.org/instant-runoff-voting#. UYrG5isjpv1 (accessed May 8, 2013).

—— (n.d.) "The American Plan." Available at www.fairvote.org/?page=965 (accessed May 3, 2013).

Farber, David (1994) *Chicago '68*, Chicago, IL: University of Chicago Press.

Farnsworth, Stephen J. and S. Robert Lichter (2011) *The Nightly News Nightmare: Network Television's Coverage of US Presidential Elections, 1988–2008*, 3rd edn, Lanham, MD: Rowman & Littlefield.

Farrell, David M. (2011) *Electoral Systems: A Comparative Introduction*, 2nd edn, New York: Palgrave Macmillan.

Faucheux, Ron (1994) "The Message," *Campaigns and Elections*, May: 46–49.

Federal Commission on Election Reform (2005) *Building Confidence in US Elections*, Washington, DC: American University.

Federal Election Commission (2011) "Both Major Parties to Receive Public Funding for 2012 Conventions," November 8. Available at www.fec.gov/press/20111108convtfunding.shtml (accessed May 28, 2013).

—— (2015) "Congressional Table 4: 24-Month Median Receipts of Senate and House Candidates from January 1, 2013 through December 31, 2014." Available at www.fec.gov/press/summaries/2014/tables/congressional/ConCand4_2014_24m.pdf (accessed March 18, 2017).

—— (2016) "PAC Count, 1974–Present." Available at www.fec.gov/press/resources/paccount.shtml (accessed January 2, 2017).

—— (2016) "Presidential Election Campaign Fund." Available at www.fec.gov/press/bkgnd/fund.shtml (accessed January 2, 2017).

—— (n.d.) "2012 Reporting Dates." Available at www.fec.gov/info/report_dates_2012.shtml#ie (accessed May 15, 2013).

—— (n.d.) "2016 Coordinated Party Expenditure Limits." Available at www.fec.gov/info/charts_cpe_2016.shtml (accessed January 16, 2017).

—— (n.d.) "House Non Incumbent Winners and Their Opponents: Median Disbursements." Available at www.fec.gov/press/bkgnd/cf_summary_info/2010can_fullsum/3houseclose2010.pdf (accessed May 16, 2013).

—— (n.d.) "Presidential Campaign Receipts through December 31, 2012." Available at www.fec.gov/press/summaries/2012/ElectionCycle/file/presidential_summaries/Pres1_2012_24m.pdf (accessed May 15, 2013).

—— (n.d.) "Presidential Spending Limits for 2012." Available at www.fec.gov/pages/brochures/pubfund_limits_2012.shtml (accessed May 15, 2013).

—— (n.d.) "Summary of PAC Activity, 1990–2010." Available at www.fec.gov/press/bkgnd/cf_summary_info/2010pac_fullsum/4sumhistory2010.pdf (accessed May 20, 2013).

—— (n.d.) "Summary Reports Search." Available at www.fec.gov/finance/disclosure/srssea.shtml (accessed May 31, 2013).

—— (n.d.) "Top 50 PACs, by Receipts, January 1, 2009–December 31, 2010." Available at www.fec.gov/press/bkgnd/cf_summary_info/2010pac_fullsum/8top50pacreceipts2010.pdf (accessed May 20, 2013).

Feldman, Ariel J., J. Alex Halderman, and Edward W. Felten (2006) "Security Analysis of the Diebold AccuVote-TS Voting Machine" (unpublished manuscript). Center for Information Technology Policy, Princeton University. Available at http://citpsite.s3-website-useast-1.amazonaws.com/oldsite-htdocs/pub/ts06full.pdf (accessed May 13, 2013).

Feldman, Lauren (2014) "The Hostile Media Effect," in Kate Kenski and Kathleen Hall Jamieson (eds.), *The Oxford Handbook of Political Communication*, Oxford: Oxford University Press. First published in Oxford Handbooks Online, http://www.oxfordhandbooks.com/view/10.1093/oxfordhb/9780199793471.001.0001/oxfordhb-9780199793471-e-011 (accessed March 11, 2017).

Fenno, Richard (1978) *Home Style: House Members in Their Districts*, Boston, MA: Little, Brown.

Ferejohn, John A. and Morris P. Fiorina (1974) "The Paradox of Not Voting: A Decision Theoretic Analysis," *American Political Science Review*, 68: 525–536.

Ferling, John (2004) *Adams vs. Jefferson: The Tumultuous Election of 1800*. Oxford: Oxford University Press.

Fiorina, Morris (1981) *Retrospective Voting in American National Elections*, New Haven, CT: Yale University Press.

—— (1993) "Explorations of a Political Theory of Party Identification," in Richard G. Niemi and Herbert F. Weisberg (eds.), *Classics in Voting Behavior*, Washington, DC: CQ Press.

Fiske, Susan T. and Shelley E. Taylor (1991) *Social Cognition*, New York: McGraw-Hill.

Flanigan, William H. and Nancy H. Zingale (2006) *Political Behavior of the American Electorate*, 11th edn, Washington, DC: CQ Press.

Florida Division of Elections (2016) "2016 Qualifying Fees," Florida Department of State. Available at http://dos.myflorida.com/media/695241/qualifying-fees.pdf (accessed January 4, 2017).

Flowers, Julianne F., Audrey A. Haynes, and Michael H. Crespin (2003) "The Media, the Campaign, and the Message," *American Journal of Political Science*, 47: 259–273.

Foley, Edward B. (1994) "Equal-Dollars-per-Voter: A Constitutional Principle of Campaign Finance," *Columbia Law Review*, 94: 1209–1210.

—— (2005) "Is There a Middle Ground in the Voter ID Debate?" *Election Law @ Moritz*, September 6. Available at http://moritzlaw.osu.edu/electionlaw/comments/2005/050906. php (accessed September 6, 2012).

Fortier, John C. (ed.) (2004) *After the People Vote: A Guide to the Electoral College*, 3rd edn, Washington, DC: AEI Press.

Foser, Jamison (2007) "The Same Old Story, Same Old Act," *Media Matters*, July 13. Available at http://mediamatters.org/items/200707140001 (accessed May 16, 2013).

Fowler, Erika Franklin and Travis N. Ridout (2012) "Negative, Angry, and Ubiquitous: Political Advertising in 2012," *The Forum*, 10: 51–61.

Fowler, Erika Franklin, Michael M. Franz, and Travis N. Ridout (2016) *Political Advertising in the United States*, Boulder, CO: Westview Press.

Fowler, James H. and Oleg Smirnov (2007) *Mandates, Parties, and Voters: How Elections Shape the Future*, Philadelphia, PA: Temple University Press.

Fowler, Linda L. (1993) *Candidates, Congress, and the American Democracy*, Ann Arbor, MI: University of Michigan Press.

Fowler, Linda L. and Robert D. McClure (1989) *Political Ambition: Who Decides to Run for Congress*, New Haven, CT: Yale University Press.

Fox, Richard L. and Jennifer L. Lawless (2005) "Black and White Differences in Nascent Political Ambition: Race and the Decision Dynamics of the Initial Run for Elective Office." Presented at the Annual Meeting of the American Political Science Association, Washington, DC.

Francia, Peter L. and Paul S. Herrnson (2001) "Begging for Bucks," *Campaigns and Elections*, April: 51–52.

Francis Wilkinson (2016) "Voter Fraud Myths and Realities: Q&A [with Richard Hasen]," *Bloomberg View*, December 19, www.bloomberg.com/view/articles/2016-12-19/voter-fraud-myths-and-realities-q-a (accessed December 30, 2016).

Franklin, Mark N. (2002) "The Dynamics of Electoral Participation," in Lawrence LeDuc, Richard G. Niemi, and Pippa Norris (eds.), *Comparing Democracies*, vol. II: *New Challenges in the Study of Elections and Voting*, Thousand Oaks, CA: Sage.

—— (2004) *Voter Turnout and the Dynamics of Electoral Competition in Established Democracies since 1945*, Cambridge: Cambridge University Press.

Fridkin, Kim L., Patrick J. Kenney, Sarah Allen Gershon, Karen Shafer, and Gina Serignese Woodall (2007) "Capturing the Power of a Campaign Event: The 2004 Presidential Debate in Tempe," *Journal of Politics*, 69: 770–785.

Gabriel, Trip and Helene Cooper (2012) "Romney Refines Message on Taxes and Abortion," *New York Times*, October 9. Available at www.nytimes.com/2012/10/10/us/politics/romney-pledges-to-keep-tax-deductions-for-mortgages.html (accessed May 23, 2013).

Gangale, Thomas (2004) "The California Plan: A 21st Century Method for Nominating Presidential Candidates," *PS: Political Science and Politics*, 37: 81–87.

Gans, Herbert (1979) *Deciding What's News: A Study of CBS Evening News, NBC Nightly News, Newsweek, and Time*, New York: Random House.

Garamone, Jim (2004) "Pentagon Decides against Internet Voting This Year," US Department of Defense, American Forces Press Service, February 6. Available at www.defense.gov/news/newsarticle.aspx?id=27362 (accessed May 13, 2013).

Garrett, R. Sam and Shawn Reese (2016) "Funding of Presidential Nominating Conventions: An Overview," Congressional Research Service, https://fas.org/sgp/crs/misc/R43976.pdf (accessed January 2, 2017).

Gaskins, Keesha and Sundeep Iyer (2012) "The Challenge of Obtaining Voter Identification," Brennan Center for Justice. July 18. Available at www.brennancenter.org/publication/challeng e-obtaining-voter-identification (accessed May 8, 2013).

Gaubatz, Kurt Taylor (1999) *Elections and War: The Electoral Incentive in the Democratic Politics of War and Peace*, Palo Alto, CA: Stanford University Press.

Gawiser, Sheldon R. and G. Evans Witt (n.d.) *20 Questions a Journalist Should Ask about Poll Results*, 3rd edn, National Council on Public Polls. Available at www.ncpp.org/?q=node/4 (accessed May 16, 2013).

Geer, John G. (2006) *In Defense of Negativity: Attack Ads in Presidential Campaigns*, Chicago, IL: University of Chicago Press.

Gelman, Andrew and Gary King (1994) "Enhancing Democracy through Legislative Redistricting," *American Political Science Review*, 88: 541–559.

Gerber, Alan and Donald Green (1999) "Misperceptions about Perceptual Bias," *Annual Review of Political Science*, 2: 189–210.

Gerber, Alan S., Donald P. Green, and Ron Shachar (2003) "Voting May Be Habit-Forming: Evidence from a Randomized Field Experiment," *American Journal of Political Science*, 47: 540–550.

Gibson, Rachel (2001–2002) "Elections Online: Assessing Internet Voting in Light of the Arizona Democratic Primary," *Political Science Quarterly*, 116: 561–583.

Gilmer, Marcus (2016) "Report: Donald Trump's Campaign Won't Let Him Tweet Anymore," *Mashable*, November 6. Available at http://mashable.com/2016/11/06/trump-cant-tweet/#c5I.MKicP5qC (accessed March 4, 2017).

Giroux, Gregory (2013) "Crossroads GPS to FEC: No Means No," *Bloomberg.com*, April 10. Available at http://go.bloomberg.com/political-capital/2013-04-10/crossroads-gps-to-fec-nomeans-no (accessed May 15, 2013).

Goidel, Robert K., Donald A. Gross and Todd G. Shields (1999) *Money Matters: Consequences of Campaign Finance Reform in US House Elections*, Lanham, MD: Rowman & Littlefield.

Golder, Matt (2005) "Democratic Electoral Systems around the World, 1946–2000," *Electoral Studies*, 24: 103–121.

Goldsteen, Raymond L., Karen Goldsteen, James H. Swan, and Wendy Clemeña (2001) "Harry and Louise and Health Care Reform: Romancing Public Opinion," *Journal of Health Politics, Policy and Law*, 26: 1325–1352.

Goldstein, Kenneth and Travis N. Ridout (2004) "Measuring the Effects of Televised Political Advertising in the United States," *Annual Review of Political Science*, 7: 205–226.

Goodman, Josh (2009) "Why Turnout in Virginia Wasn't Quite as Bad as You Think," *Governing*, November 6. Available at www.governing.com/blogs/politics/Why-Turnout-in-Virginia.html (accessed May 28, 2013).

GOPAC (n.d.) "GOPAC University." Available at www.gopac.org/university (accessed May 22, 2013).

—— (n.d.) "Mission." Available at www.gopac.org/about/mission (accessed May 22, 2013).

Gora, Joel M. (2003) "The Legacy of *Buckley* v. *Valeo*," *Election Law Journal*, 2: 55–67.

Gorman, Steve (2007) "Clinton Doubles Obama Sum in Hollywood Fund-Raiser," *Reuters*, March 26. Available at www.reuters.com/article/entertainmentNews/idUSN2345209520070326 (accessed May 18, 2013).

Green, Donald and Alan S. Gerber (2004) *Get Out the Vote! How to Increase Voter Turnout*, Washington, DC: Brookings Institution Press.

Green, Joshua (2012) "The Science Behind Those Obama Campaign E-Mails," *Bloomberg Businessweek*, November 29. Available at www.businessweek.com/articles/2012-11-29/thescience-behind-those-obama-campaign-e-mails (accessed May 29, 2013).

Greenhouse, Steven (2012) "Unions Recruit New Allies for Obama in Battleground States," *New York Times*, November 4. Available at www.nytimes.com/2012/11/05/us/politics/unionsrecruit-allies-on-obamas-behalf.html?_r=0 (accessed May 22, 2013).

Gregg, Gary L. III (2001) *Securing Democracy: Why We Have an Electoral College*, Wilmington, DE: ISI Books.

Grofman, Bernard (2004) "Downs and Two-Party Convergence," *Annual Review of Political Science*, 7: 25–46.

Gronke, Paul (2005) "Ballot Integrity and Voting by Mail: The Oregon Experiment," A Report for the Commission on Federal Election Reform. Portland, OR: The Early Voting Information Center at Reed College. Available at http://people.reed.edu/~gronkep/docs/Carter%20Baker%20Report-publicrelease.pdf (accessed May 13, 2013).

Gross, Donald A. and Robert K. Goidel (2003) *The States of Campaign Finance Reform*, Columbus, OH: Ohio State University Press.

Gross, Kenneth A. (2002) "Constitutional Restrictions on Federal and State Regulations of the Election Process," in Jimmy Carter, Gerald R. Ford, Lloyd N. Cutler, and Robert H. Michel (eds.), *To Assure Pride and Confidence in the Electoral Process*, Washington, DC: Brookings Institution Press.

Grossback, Lawrence J., David A. M. Peterson, and James A. Stimson (2006) *Mandate Politics*, Cambridge: Cambridge University Press.

Gunlicks, Arthur B. (1993) *Campaign and Party Finance in North America and Western Europe*, Boulder, CO: Westview Press.

Hadley, Arthur (1976) *The Invisible Primary*, Upper Saddle River, NJ: Prentice Hall.

Hart, Roderick P. (1994) *Seducing America: How Television Charms the Modern Voter*, Oxford: Oxford University Press.

Hart, Roderick P. (2000) *Campaign Talk: Why Elections Are Good for Us*, Princeton, NJ: Princeton University Press.

Hasen, Richard L. (2003) *The Supreme Court and Election Law: Judging Equality from Baker v. Carr to Bush v. Gore*, New York: New York University Press.

—— (2008) "Initial Thoughts on *FEC* v. *Davis*: The Court Primes the Pump for Striking Down Corporate and Union Campaign Spending Limits and Blows a Hole in Effective Public Financing Plans," *Election Law Blog*, June 26. Available at http://electionlawblog.org/archives/011095.html (accessed May 10, 2013).

—— (2010) "Citizens United and the Orphaned Antidistortion Rationale," *Georgia State University Law Review*, 27 (4), Article 18. Available at http://digitalarchive.gsu.edu/gsulr/vol27/iss4/18 (accessed May 12, 2013).

—— (2011) "Citizens United and the Illusion of Coherence," *Michigan Law Review*, 109: 581–623.

—— (2012) "Of Super PACs and Corruption," *Politico*, March 22. Available at www.politico.com/news/stories/0312/74336.html (accessed May 13, 2013).

—— (2013) "Is Voting Rights Act Section 2 in Constitutional Danger from the Supreme Court?" *Election Law Blog*, July 17, http://electionlawblog.org/?p=53071 (accessed June 21, 2016).

Hayduk, Ron (2006) *Democracy for All: Restoring Immigrant Voting Rights in the United States*, London and New York: Routledge.

Hayes, Danny (2005) "Candidate Qualities through a Partisan Lens: A Theory of Trait Ownership," *American Journal of Political Science*, 49: 908–923.

Hayes, Danny and Jennifer L. Lawless (2016) *Women on the Run: Gender, Media, and Political Campaigns in a Polarized Era*, Cambridge: Cambridge University Press.

Healy, Andrew and Neil Malhotra (2013) "Retrospective Voting Reconsidered," *Annual Review of Political Science*, 16: 285–306.

Heclo, Hugh (2000) "Campaigning and Governing: A Conspectus," in Norman Ornstein and Thomas Mann (eds.), *The Permanent Campaign and Its Future*, Washington, DC: American Enterprise Institute and The Brookings Institution.

Held, David (1987) *Models of Democracy*, Stanford, CA: Stanford University Press.

Help America Vote Act (2002) Pub.L (107-252). Available at www.eac.gov/assets/1/workflow_staging/Page/41.PDF (accessed May 9, 2013).

Hero, Rodney E. (2003) "Social Capital and Racial Inequality in America," *Perspectives on Politics*, 1: 113–122.

Herrnson, Paul S. (1988) *Party Campaigning in the 1980s*, Cambridge, MA: Harvard University Press.

—— (1997) "United States," in Pippa Norris (ed.), *Passages to Power: Legislative Recruitment in Advanced Democracies*, Cambridge: Cambridge University Press.

—— (2002) "National Party Organizations at the Dawn of the Twenty-First Century," in L. Sandy Maisel (ed.), *The Parties Respond: Changes in American Parties and Campaigns*, 4th edn, Boulder, CO: Westview Press.

—— (2004) *Congressional Elections: Campaigning at Home and in Washington*, 4th edn, Washington, DC: CQ Press.

—— (2012) *Congressional Elections: Campaigning at Home and in Washington*, 6th edn, Washington, DC: CQ Press.

—— (2016) *Congressional Elections: Campaigning at Home and in Washington*, 7th edn, Washington, DC: CQ Press.

Hersh, Eitan D. (2015) *Hacking the Electorate: How Campaigns Perceive Voters*, Cambridge: Cambridge University Press.

Hersh, Eitan D. and Brian F. Schaffner (2013) "Targeted Campaign Appeals and the Value of Ambiguity," *Journal of Politics*, 75: 520–534.

Hershey, Marjorie Randon (2013) *Party Politics in America*, 15th edn, Upper Saddle River, NJ: Pearson.

Hetherington, Marc (2015) "Why Polarized Trust Matters," *The Forum*, 13: 445–458.

Hetherington, Marc J., Meri T. Long, and Thomas J. Rudolph (2016) "Revisiting the Myth: New Evidence of a Polarized Electorate," *Public Opinion Quarterly*, 80: 321–350.

Highton, Benjamin (2004) "Voter Registration and Turnout in the United States," *Perspectives on Politics*, 2: 507–515.

Hillygus, Sunshine D. (2005) "Campaign Effects and the Dynamics of Turnout Intention in Election 2000," *Journal of Politics*, 67: 50–68.

Hillygus, Sunshine D. and Simon Jackman (2003) "Voter Decision Making in Election 2000: Campaign Effects, Partisan Activation, and the Clinton Legacy," *American Journal of Political Science*, 47: 583–596.

Hinckley, Barbara (1980) "House Re-elections and Senate Defeats: The Role of the Challenger," *British Journal of Political Science*, 10: 441–460.

—— (1981) *Congressional Elections*, Washington, DC: CQ Press.

Holbrook, Thomas M. (1994) "Campaigns, National Conditions, and US Presidential Elections," *American Journal of Political Science*, 38: 973–998.

—— (2010) "Forecasting US Presidential Elections," in Jan E. Leighley (ed.), *The Oxford Handbook of American Elections and Political Behavior*, Oxford: Oxford University Press.

—— (2012) "Incumbency, National Conditions, and the 2012 Presidential Election," *PS: Political Science and Politics*, 45: 640–643.

Hrebenar, Ronald J. (1997) *Interest Group Politics in America*, 3rd edn, Armonk, NY: M. E. Sharpe.

International Association of Fire Fighters (2013) "About the IAFF." Available at www.iaff.org/about/default.asp (accessed May 20, 2013).

International Institute for Democracy and Electoral Assistance (2002) *Voter Turnout since 1945: A Global Report*. Available at www.idea.int/publications/vt/upload/VT_screenopt_2002.pdf (accessed May 9, 2013).

Inter-Parliamentary Union (1994) "Declaration on Criteria for Free and Fair Elections," Geneva, Switzerland: Inter-Parliamentary Council. Available at www.ipu.org/cnl-e/154-free.htm (accessed May 7, 2013).

Issacharoff, Samuel, Pamela S. Kaplan, and Richard H. Pildes (2012) *The Law of Democracy: Legal Structure of the Political Process*, 4th edn, Westbury, NY: Foundation Press.

Issenberg, Sasha (2012a) "Man Microtargets for Food, But Sometimes There Must Be a Beverage," *Slate*, September 28. Available at www.slate.com/blogs/victory_lab/2012/09/28/microtargeting_beer_you_are_not_what_you_drink_html (accessed May 18, 2013).

—— (2012b) "Why Obama Is Better at Getting Out the Vote," *Slate*, November 5. Available at www.slate.com/articles/news_and_politics/victory_lab/2012/11/obama_s_get_out_the_vote_effort_why_it_s_better_than_romney_s.html (accessed May 18, 2013).

—— (2012c) *The Victory Lab: The Secret Science of Winning Campaigns*, New York: Crown.

Ito, Tiffany A., Jeff T. Larsen, N. Kyle Smith, and John T. Cacioppo (1998) "Negative Information Weighs More Heavily on the Brain: The Negativity Bias in Evaluative Categorizations," *Journal of Personality and Social Psychology*, 75: 887–900.

Iyengar, Shanto (1992) *Is Anyone Responsible? How Television Frames Political Issues*, Chicago, IL: University of Chicago Press.

Iyengar, Shanto and Donald R. Kinder (1987) *News That Matters: Television and American Opinion*, Chicago, IL: University of Chicago Press.

Iyengar, Shanto and Jennifer A. McGrady (2007) *Media Politics: A Citizen's Guide*, New York: W. W. Norton.

Iyengar, Shanto, Helmut Norpoth, and Kyu S. Hahn (2004) "Consumer Demand for Election News: The Horserace Sells," *Journal of Politics*, 66: 157–175.

Iyengar, Shanto and Adam F. Simon (2000) "New Perspectives and Evidence on Political Communication and Campaign Effects," *Annual Review of Psychology*, 51: 149–169.

Jackie Calmes (2015) "Senate Report Cites IRS Mismanagement in Targeting of Tea Party Groups," *The New York Times*, August 5, www.nytimes.com/2015/08/06/us/politics/senate-report-cites-irs-mismanagement-in-targeting-of-tea-party-groups.html (accessed January 2, 2017).

Jackson, Brooks (1990) *Broken Promise: Why the Federal Election Commission Failed*, New York: Twentieth Century Fund.

Jackson, John E. (1983) "Election Night Reporting and Voter Turnout," *American Journal of Political Science*, 27: 615–635.

Jacobs, Lawrence R. and Robert Y. Shapiro (1994) "Issues, Candidate Image, and Priming: The Use of Private Polls in Kennedy's 1960 Presidential Campaign," *American Political Science Review*, 88: 527–540.

—— (1995) "The Rise of Presidential Polling: The Nixon White House in Historical Perspective," *Public Opinion Quarterly*, 59: 163–195.

—— (2000) *Politicians Don't Pander: Political Manipulation and the Loss of Democratic Responsiveness*, Chicago, IL: University of Chicago Press.

Jacobson, Gary C. (1978) "The Effects of Campaign Spending in Congressional Elections," *American Political Science Review*, 72: 469–491.

—— (1996) "The 1994 House Elections in Perspective," in Philip A. Klinkner (ed.), *Midterm: The Elections of 1994 in Context*, Boulder, CO: Westview Press.

—— (2006) "Competition in US Congressional Elections," in Michael P. McDonald and John Samples (eds.), *The Marketplace of Democracy: Electoral Competition and American Politics*, Washington, DC: Brookings Institution Press.

Jacobson, Gary C. and Samuel Kernell (1983) *Strategy and Choice in Congressional Elections*, New Haven, CT: Yale University Press.

Jacobson, Gary C. and Jamie L. Carson (2016) *The Politics of Congressional Elections*, 9th edn, Lanham, MD: Rowman & Littlefield.

Jamieson, Kathleen Hall (1996) *Packaging the Presidency: A History and Criticism of Presidential Campaign Advertising*, 3rd edn, Oxford: Oxford University Press.

—— (2000) *Everything You Think You Know about Politics … and Why You're Wrong*, New York: Basic Books.

Jamieson, Kathleen Hall and David S. Birdsell (1988) *Presidential Debates: The Challenge of Creating an Informed Electorate*, Oxford: Oxford University Press.

Jamieson, Kathleen Hall, Paul Waldman and Susan Sherr (2000) "Eliminate the Negative? Categories of Analysis for Political Advertisements," in James A. Thurber, Candice J. Nelson, and David A. Dulio (eds.), *Crowded Airwaves: Campaign Advertising in Elections*, Washington, DC: Brookings Institution Press.

Jarding, Steve and Dave Saunders (2006) *Foxes in the Henhouse*, New York: Touchstone.

Jean Chung (2016) "Felony Disenfranchisement: A Primer," The Sentencing Project, www.sentencingproject.org/publications/felony-disenfranchisement-a-primer (accessed December 30, 2016).

Johnson, Dennis W. (2000) "The Business of Political Consulting," in James A. Thurber and Candice J. Nelson (eds.), *Campaign Warriors: Political Consultants in Elections*, Washington, DC: Brookings Institution Press.

Johnson-Cartee, Karen S. and Gary A. Copeland (1997) *Manipulation of the American Voter: Political Campaign Commercials*, Westport, CT: Praeger.

—— (2001) *No Place for Amateurs: How Political Consultants Are Reshaping American Democracy*, London and New York: Routledge.

Johnston, Michael (1979) "Patrons and Clients, Jobs and Machines: A Case Study in the Uses of Patronage," *American Political Science Review*, 73: 385–398.

Jones, Randall J. (2002) *Who Will Be in the White House? Predicting Presidential Elections*, New York: Longman.

Judd, Nick (2013) "Republican Party's Technology Revival Hopes to Hinge on Data and Data Analysis," *Techpresident.com*, February 7. Available at http://techpresident.com/news/23479/republican-partys-technology-revival-hopes-hinge-more-just-skype (accessed May 18, 2013).

Just, Marion R., Ann N. Crigler, Dean E. Alger, Timothy E. Cook, Montague Kern, and Darrell M. West (1996) *Crosstalk: Citizens, Candidates, and the Media in a Presidential Campaign*, Chicago, IL: University of Chicago Press.

Kahn, Kim Fridkin and Patrick J. Kenney (2002) "The Slant of the News: How Editorial Endorsements Influence Campaign Coverage and Citizens' Views of Candidates," *American Political Science Review*, 96: 381–394.

Kamarck, Elaine C. (2006) "Assessing Howard Dean's Fifty State Strategy and the 2006 Midterm Elections," *The Forum*, 4: Article 5.

Karlawish, Jason H., Richard J. Bonnie, Paul S. Appelbaum, Constantine Lyketsos, Bryan James, David Knopman, Christopher Patusky, Rosalie Kane, and Pamela S. Karlan (2004) "Addressing the Ethical, Legal, and Social Issues Raised by Voting by Persons with Dementia," *Journal of the American Medical Association*, 292: 1345–1350.

Karpf, Dave (2009) "Don't Think of an Online Elephant: Explaining the Dearth of Conservative Political Infrastructure Online in America." Presented at the Society for Social Studies of Science Annual Meeting, Washington, DC. Available at http://davekarpf.files.wordpress.com/2009/03/dont-think-of-an-online-elephant.pdf (accessed May 19, 2013).

Katrina vanden Heuvel (2016) "The Most Progressive Democratic Platform Ever," *Washington Post*, July 12, www.washingtonpost.com/opinions/the-most-progressive-democratic-platform-ever/2016/07/12/82525ab0-479b-11e6-bdb9-701687974517_story.html?utm_term=.24e197c1387c (accessed January 16, 2017).

Katz, Josh (2016) "Who Will Be President?" *New York Times*, The Upshot, November 8. Available at https://www.nytimes.com/interactive/2016/upshot/presidential-polls-forecast.html (accessed February 7, 2017).

Katz, Richard (1997) *Democracy and Elections*, Oxford: Oxford University Press.

Kazee, Thomas A. (ed.) (1994) *Who Runs for Congress? Ambition, Context, and Candidate Emergence*, Washington, DC: Congressional Quarterly.

Keith, Bruce, David B. Magleby, Candice J. Nelson, Elizabeth Orr, Mark C. Westlye, and Raymond E. Wolfinger (1992) *The Myth of the Independent Voter*, Berkeley, CA: University of California Press.

Kelley, Stanley, Jr. (1960) *Political Campaigning: Problems in Creating an Informed Electorate*, Washington, DC: The Brookings Institution.

—— (1966) *Professional Public Relations and Political Power*, Baltimore, MD: Johns Hopkins University Press.

Kelley, Stanley, Jr.. and Thad W. Mirer (1974) "The Simple Act of Voting," *American Political Science Review*, 68: 572–591.

Kenski, Kate, Bruce W. Hardy, and Kathleen Hall Jamieson (2010) *The Obama Victory: How Media, Money, and Message Shaped the 2008 Election*, Oxford: Oxford University Press.

Kernell, Samuel (2006) *Going Public: New Strategies of Presidential Leadership*, 4th ed. Washington, DC: CQ Press.

Key, V. O., Jr. (1949) *Southern Politics in the State and Nation*, New York: Alfred A. Knopf.

—— (1955) "A Theory of Critical Elections," *Journal of Politics*, 17: 3–18.

—— (1964) *Politics, Parties and Pressure Groups*, 5th edn, New York: Crowell.

Key, V. O. Jr.. and Milton Cummings (1966) *The Responsible Electorate: Rationality in Presidential Voting, 1936–60*, Cambridge, MA: Belknap Press of Harvard University Press.

Keyssar, Alexander (2000) *The Right to Vote: The Contested History of Democracy in the United States*, New York: Basic Books.

—— (2003) "Shoring Up the Right to Vote for President: A Modest Proposal," *Political Science Quarterly*, 118: 181–190.

Kimberling, William C. (n.d.) "The Electoral College," Washington, DC: Federal Election Commission. Available at www.fec.gov/pdf/eleccoll.pdf (accessed August 14, 2012).

Kim Fridkin Kahn and Patrick J. Kenney (2002) "The Slant of the News: How Editorial Endorsements Influence Campaign Coverage and Citizens' Views of Candidates," *The American Political Science Review*, 96: 381–394.

King, Anthony (1997) *Running Scared: Why America's Politicians Campaign Too Much and Govern Too Little*, New York: Free Press.

Kirby, David (1998) "A Painful Coming-of-Age: Human Rights Campaign Angers Gay Voters in New York," *The Advocate*, December 8. Available at www.thefreelibrary.com/A+painful+coming-of-age.-a053356345 (accessed May 22, 2013).

Kirshner, Alexander (2003) *The International Status of the Right to Vote*, Washington, DC: Democracy Coalition Project.

Klein, Joe (2006) *Politics Lost: How American Democracy Was Trivialized by People Who Think You're Stupid*, New York: Doubleday.

Klinkner, Philip A. (1996) "Court and Country in American Politics: The Democratic Party and the 1994 Election," in Philip A. Klinkner (ed.), *Midterm: Election of 1994 in Context*, Boulder, CO: Westview Press.

Knack, Stephen (1999) "Drivers Wanted: Motor Voter and the Election of 1996," *PS: Political Science and Politics*, 32: 237–243.

—— (2001) "Election-Day Registration: The Second Wave," *American Politics Research*, 29: 69–74.

Knight, Brian and Nathan Schiff (2007) "Momentum and Social Learning in Presidential Primaries," NBER Working Paper No. W13637, November. Available at http://ssrn.com/abstract=1033762 (accessed June 1, 2013).

Kolodny, Robin (1998) *Pursuing Majorities: Congressional Campaign Committees in American Politics*, Norman, OK: University of Oklahoma Press.

—— (2000) "Electoral Partnerships: Political Consultants and Political Parties," in James A. Thurber and Candice J. Nelson (eds.), *Campaign Warriors: Political Consultants in Elections*, Washington, DC: Brookings Institution Press.

Konner, Joan, James Risser, and Ben Wattenberg (2001) "Television's Performance on Election Night 2000: A Report for CNN." Available online at http://election2000.stanford.edu/cnnelectionreport.pdf (accessed May 16, 2013).

Krasno, Jonathan S. (1994) *Challengers, Competition, and Reelection: Comparing Senate and House Elections*, New Haven, CT: Yale University Press.

Krasno, Jonathan S. and Donald Philip Green (1988) "Preempting Quality Challengers in House Elections," *Journal of Politics*, 50: 920–936.

Kreiss, Daniel (2012) *Taking Our Country Back: The Crafting of Networked Politics from Howard Dean to Barack Obama*, Oxford: Oxford University Press.

Krosnick, Jon A., Joanne M. Miller, and Michael P. Tichy (2004) "An Unrecognized Need for Ballot Reform: The Effects of Candidate Name Order on Election Outcomes," in Marion R. Just, Edward J. McCaffrey, and Ann N. Craiger (eds.), *Rethinking the Vote: The Politics and Prospects of American Election Reform*, Oxford: Oxford University Press.

Kurtz, Karl (2012) "Changes in Legislatures Using Multimember Districts after Redistricting," *The Thicket at State Legislatures*. Available at http://ncsl.typepad.com/the_thicket/2012/09/a-slight-decline-in-legislatures-using-multimember-districts-after-redistricting.html (accessed April 15, 2017).

La Raja, Raymond J. (2012) "Why Super PACs: How the American Party System Outgrew the Campaign Finance System," *The Forum*, 10: 91–104.

Ladd, Everett Carll and John Benson (1992) "The Growth of News Polls in American Politics," in Thomas E. Mann and Gary R. Orren (eds.), *Media Polls in American Politics*, Washington, DC: Brookings Institution Press.

Lapowsky, Issie (2015) "Political Ad Spending Online Is About to Explode," *Wired.com*, August 18. Available at https://www.wired.com/2015/08/digital-politcal-ads-2016 (accessed March 4, 2017).

Latino Decisions (2016) "2016 Latino Election Analysis," November 9. Available at www.latinodecisions.com/files/6514/7880/5462/PostElection2016.pdf (accessed February 7, 2017).

Lau, Richard R., Lee Sigelman, Caroline Heldman, and Paul Babbitt (1999) "The Effects of Negative Political Advertisements: A Meta-Analytic Assessment," *American Political Science Review*, 93: 851–875.

Lausen, Marcia (2007) *Design for Democracy: Ballot + Election Design*, Chicago, IL: University of Chicago Press.

Lawless, Jennifer L. and Richard L. Fox (2010) *It Still Takes a Candidate: Why Women Don't Run for Office*, rev. edn, Cambridge: Cambridge University Press.

Lawson, Steven F. (1976) *Black Ballots: Voting Rights in the South, 1944–69*, New York: Columbia University Press.

Lazarsfeld, Paul, Bernard Berelson, and Hazel Guadet (1944) *The People's Choice*, New York: Columbia University Press.

—— (1968) *The People's Choice: How the Voter Makes Up His Mind in a Presidential Campaign*, 3rd edn, New York: Columbia University Press.

League of Conservation Voters Action Fund, "LCV Action Fund's Dirty Dozen." Available at www.lcv.org/elections/dirty-dozen (accessed June 3, 2013).

Leighley, Jan E. (2004) *Mass Media and Politics: A Social Science Perspective*, Boston, MA: Houghton Mifflin.

Leighley, Jan E. and Arnold Vedlitz (1999) "Race, Ethnicity, and Political Participation: Competing Models and Contrasting Explanations," *Journal of Politics*, 61: 1092–1114.

Lessig, Lawrence (2011) *Republic, Lost: How Money Corrupts Congress—and a Plan to Stop It*, New York: Twelve.

Levs, Josh and Thom Patterson (2012) "Obama Creates Monument to Cesar Chavez: 'He Cared.'" *CNN.com*, October 9. Available at www.cnn.com/2012/10/08/us/obama-chavez-monument (accessed May 23, 2013).

Lewis-Beck, Michael and Tom Rice (1982) "Presidential Popularity and Presidential Vote," *Public Opinion Quarterly*, 46: 534–537.

—— (1984) "Forecasting Presidential Elections: A Comparison of Naïve Models," *Political Behavior*, 6: 9–21.

—— (1992) *Forecasting Elections*, Washington DC: CQ Press.

Lijphart, Arend (1999) *Patterns of Democracy: Government Forms and Performance in Thirty-Six Countries*, New Haven, CT: Yale University Press.

Lewis-Beck, Michael and Mary Stegmaier (2000) "Economic Determinants of Electoral Outcomes," *Annual Review of Political Science*, 3: 183–219.

Livingston, Mark (2003) "Banzhaf Power Index," April 14. Available at www.cs.unc.edu/~livingst/Banzhaf (accessed August 14 2012).

Lizza, Ryan (2016) "Kellyanne Conway's Political Machinations," *New Yorker*, October 17. Available at www.newyorker.com/magazine/2016/10/17/kellyanne-conways-political-machinations (accessed February 7, 2017).

Lilliana Mason (2015) " 'I Disrespectfully Agree': The Differential Effects of Partisan Sorting on Social and Issue Polarization," *American Journal of Political Science*, 59, p. 142.

LoGiurato, Brett (2013) "For the First Time, the Nra Is Up Against an Adversary with Money to Spend," *Business Insider*, March 24. Available at www.businessinsider.com/ bloomberg-guncontrol-ad-campaign-michael-mayors-illegal-guns-12-million-2013-3 (accessed June 2, 2013).

Longley, Lawrence D. and Neal R. Peirce (1999) *The Electoral College Primer 2000*, New Haven, CT: Yale University Press.

López Pintor, Rafael and Maria Gratschew (2002) "Voter Turnout since 1945: A Global Report," International Institute for Democracy and Electoral Assistance, www.idea. int/ publications/vt/upload/VT_screenopt_2002.pdf, (accessed June 29, 2016).

Lowenstein, Daniel Hays, Richard L. Hasen, and Daniel P. Tokaji (2012) *Election Law: Cases and Materials*, 5th edn, Durham, NC: Carolina Academic Press.

Lunder, Erika (2006) "Tax-Exempt Organizations: Political Activity Restrictions and Disclosure Requirements," April 20, Washington, DC: Congressional Research Service.

Luttbeg, Norman R. and Michael M. Gant (1995) *American Electoral Behavior, 1952–92*, 2nd edn, Itasca, IL: F. E. Peacock Publishers.

McCann, James A., Ronald B. Rapoport, and Walter J. Stone (1999) "Heeding the Call: An Assessment of Mobilization into H. Ross Perot's 1992 Presidential Campaign," *American Journal of Political Science*, 43: 1–28.

McCaskill, Nolan D., Alex Isenstadt, and Shane Goldmacher (2016) "Paul Manafort resigns from Trump campaign," *Politico*, August 19. Available at www.politico.com/story/2016/08/ paul-manafort-resigns-from-trump-campaign-227197 (accessed February 7, 2017).

McDonald, Laughlin (2003) *A Voting Rights Odyssey: Black Enfranchisement in Georgia*, Cambridge: Cambridge University Press.

McDonald, Michael P. (2004) "A Comparative Analysis of Redistricting Institutions in the United States, 2001–2," *State Politics and Policy Quarterly*, 4: 371–395.

—— (2012) "2012 Early Voting Statistics," United States Elections Project. Available at http:// elections.gmu.edu/early_vote_2012.html (accessed May 12, 2013).

McDonald, Michael P. and Samuel L. Popkin (2001) "The Myth of the Vanishing Voter," *American Political Science Review*, 95: 963–974.

—— (2006a) "Drawing the Line on District Competition," *PS: Political Science and Politics*, 39: 91–94.

—— (2006b) "Redistricting and Competitive Districts," in Michael P. McDonald and John Samples (eds.), *The Marketplace of Democracy: Electoral Competition and American Politics*, Washington, DC: Brookings Institution Press.

McDonald, Michael P. (n.d.) "Turnout 1980–2012.xls," http://elections.gmu.edu/Turnout 1980-2012.xls (accessed May 24, 2013).

McDonald, Michael (2016) "2016 November General Election Early Voting," United States Elections Project, www.electproject.org/early_2016 (accessed January 2, 2017).

MacGillis, Alec (2007) "Obama Revisits Key Antiwar Speech," *Washington Post*, October 3. Available at www.washingtonpost.com/wp-dyn/content/article/2007/10/02/ AR2007100202036.html (accessed May 16, 2013).

Macpherson, C. B. (1977) *The Life and Time of Liberal Democracy*, Oxford: Oxford University Press.

Madison, James (2008) "The Federalist Papers: No. 10," *The Avalon Project*, Yale Law School. Available at http://avalon.law.yale.edu/18th_century/fed10.asp (accessed May 18, 2013).

Maestas and Rugeley, "The Candidates," p. 145.

Magleby, David B. and J. Quin Monson (eds.) (2004) *The Last Hurrah: Soft Money and Issue Advocacy in the 2002 Congressional Elections*, Washington, DC: Brookings Institution Press.

Magleby, David B., Candice J. Nelson, and Mark C. Westlye (2011) "The Myth of the Independent Voter Revisited," in Paul M. Sniderman and Benjamin Highton (eds.), *Facing the Challenge of Democracy: Explorations in the Analysis of Public Opinion and Political Participation*, Princeton, NJ: Princeton University Press.

Magleby, David B., J. Quin Monson, and Kelly D. Patterson (eds.) (2007) *Dancing without Partners: How Candidates, Parties, and Interest Groups Interact in the Presidential Campaign*, Lanham, MD: Rowman & Littlefield.

Mahtesian, Charlie (2016) "What Are the Swing States in 2016?" *Politico*, June 15. Available at www.politico.com/blogs/swing-states-2016-election/2016/06/what-are-the-swing-states-in-2016-list-224327 (accessed March 4, 2017).

Maisel, L. Sandy (2002) *Parties and Elections in America: The Electoral Process*, 3rd edn, *Post-Election Update*. Lanham, MD: Rowman & Littlefield.

Maisel, L. Sandy, Cherie Maestas, and Walter J. Stone (2002) "The Party Role in Congressional Competition," in L. Sandy Maisel (ed.), *The Parties Respond: Changes in American Parties and Campaigns*, 4th edn, Boulder, CO: Westview Press.

Maisel, L. Sandy, Darrell M. West, and Brett M. Clifton (2007) *Evaluating Campaign Quality: Can the Electoral Process Be Improved?* Cambridge: Cambridge University Press.

Malone, Julie (2001) "Patients' Rights Vote in View; Details Argued as PR War Rages," *Atlanta Journal and Constitution*, June 21, 3A.

Mann, Thomas E. (2005) "The FEC: Administering and Enforcing Campaign Finance Law," in Anthony Corrado, Thomas E. Mann, Daniel R. Ortiz, and Trevor Potter (eds.), *The New Campaign Finance Sourcebook*, Washington, DC: Brookings Institution Press.

Mann, Thomas E. and Gary R. Orren (1992) "To Poll or Not to Poll … and Other Questions," in Thomas E. Mann and Gary R. Orren (eds.), *Media Polls in American Politics*, Washington, DC: Brookings Institution Press.

Manza, Jeff and Christopher Uggen (2006) *Locked Out: Felon Disenfranchisement and American Democracy*, Oxford: Oxford University Press.

Manza, Jeff, Clem Brooks, and Christopher Uggen (2004) "Public Attitudes toward Felon Disenfranchisement in the United States," *Public Opinion Quarterly*, 68: 280–281.

Marietta, Morgan, David C. Barker, and Todd Bowser (2015) "Fact-Checking Polarized Politics: Does the Fact-Check Industry Provide Consistent Guidance on Disputed Realities?" *The Forum*, 13: 577–596.

Mark Walsh (2016) "Appeals Courts Are Dismantling Stricter Voter ID Laws," *ABA Journal*, November 1, www.abajournal.com/magazine/article/voter_id_laws (accessed December 30, 2016).

Markus, Gregory B. (1988) "The Impact of Personal and National Economic Conditions on the Presidential Vote: A Pooled Cross-Sectional Analysis," *American Journal of Political Science*, 32: 137–154.

—— (1992) "The Impact of Personal and National Economic Conditions on Presidential Voting, 1956–88," *American Journal of Political Science*, 36: 829–834.

Marshall, Josh (2016) "Theda Skocpol Responds to Judis," *Talking Points Memo Edblog*, November 11. Available at http://talkingpointsmemo.com/edblog/theda-skocpol-responds-to-judis (accessed January 29, 2017).

Martinez, Michael D. and David Hill (1999) "Did Motor Voter Work?" *American Politics Quarterly*, 27: 296–315.

Marty Cohen, David Karol, Hans Noel, and John Zaller (2016) "Party Versus Faction in the Reformed Presidential Nominating System," *PS: Political Science & Politics*, 49, p. 702.

Massachusetts Elections Division (2016) "How to Run for Office in Massachusetts," *Secretary of the Commonwealth of Massachusetts*. Available at www.sec.state.ma.us/ELE/elepdf/Candidates-Guide-generic.pdf (accessed January 4, 2017).

Mauer, Marc (2004) "Felon Disenfranchisement: A Policy Whose Time Has Passed?" *Human Rights*, 31: 1, http://www.americanbar.org/publications/human_rights_magazine_home/human_rights_vol31_2004/winter2004/irr_hr_winter04_felon.html (accessed May 9, 2013).

Mayer, William G. (2004) "The Basic Dynamics of the Contemporary Nomination Process: An Expanded View," in William G. Mayer (ed.), *The Making of the Presidential Candidates*, Lanham, MD: Rowman & Littlefield.

Mayer, William G., Emmett H. Buell, Jr.., James E. Campbell, and Mark Joslyn (2002) "The Electoral College and Campaign Strategy," in Paul D. Schumaker and Burdett A. Loomis (eds.), *Choosing a President: The Electoral College and Beyond*, New York: Chatham House Publishers/Seven Bridges Press.

Mayhew, David R. (1974) *Congress: The Electoral Connection*, New Haven, CT: Yale University Press.

—— (2002) *Electoral Realignments: A Critique of an American Genre*, New Haven, CT: Yale University Press.

—— (2008) "Incumbency Advantage in US Presidential Elections: The Historical Record," *Political Science Quarterly*, 123: 201–228.

Medvic, Stephen K. (2001) *Political Consultants in US Congressional Elections*, Columbus, OH: Ohio State University Press.

—— (2003) "Campaign Pollsters and Polling: Manipulating the Voter or Taking the Electorate's Pulse," in Robert Watson and Colton Campbell (eds.), *Campaigns and Elections: Issues, Concepts, and Cases*, Boulder, CO: Lynne Rienner Publishers.

—— (2004) "Developing 'Paid Media' Strategies: Media Consultants and Political Advertising," in David A. Schultz (ed.), *Lights, Camera, Campaigns! Media, Politics, and Political Advertising*, New York: Peter Lang.

—— (2005) "Campaign Organization and Political Consultants," in Paul S. Herrnson (ed.), *Guide to Political Campaigns in America*, Washington, DC: CQ Press.

—— (2006) "Understanding Campaign Strategy: 'Deliberate Priming' and the Role of Professional Political Consultants," *Journal of Political Marketing*, 5: 11–32.

—— (2013) *In Defense of Politicians: The Expectations Trap and Its Threat to Democracy*, London and New York: Routledge.

Medvic, Stephen K. and David A. Dulio (2003) "The Media and Public Opinion," in Mark J. Rozell (ed.), *Media Power, Media Politics*, Lanham, MD: Rowman & Littlefield.

—— (2004) "The Permanent Campaign in the White House: Evidence from the Clinton Administration," *White House Studies*, 4: 301–317.

Mendelberg, Tali (2001) *The Race Card: Campaign Strategy, Implicit Messages, and the Norm of Equality*, Princeton, NJ: Princeton University Press.

Merkle, Daniel M. and Murray Edelman (2000) "A Review of the 1996 Voter News Service Exit Polls from a Total Survey Error Perspective," in Paul J. Lavrakas and Michael W. Traugott (eds.), *Election Polls, the News Media, and Democracy*, New York: Chatham House.

Merrill, Samuel III and Bernard Grofman (1999) *A Unified Theory of Voting: Directional and Proximity Spatial Models*, Cambridge: Cambridge University Press.

Miller, Arthur H. and Martin P. Wattenberg (1985) "Throwing the Rascals Out: Policy and Performance Evaluation of Presidential Candidates, 1952–80," *American Political Science Review*, 79: 359–372.

Miller, Bill and Susan B. Glasser (1999) "A Victory for Christian Coalition," *Washington Post*, August 3. Available at www.washingtonpost.com/wp-srv/politics/daily/aug99/fec3.htm (accessed May 4, 2013).

Miller, Dale E. and Stephen K. Medvic (2002) "Campaigns Ethics: Civic Responsibility or Self-Interest?" in Candice J. Nelson, David A. Dulio, and Stephen K. Medvic (eds.), *Shades of Gray: Perspectives on Campaign Ethics*, Washington, DC: Brookings Institution Press.

Miller, Joanne M. and Jon A. Krosnick (1998) "The Impact of Candidate Name Order on Election Outcomes," *Public Opinion Quarterly*, 62: 291–330.

Mohen, Joe and Julia Glidden (2001) "The Case for Internet Voting," *Communications of the ACM*, 44: 72–85.

Monmonier, Mark (2001) *Bushmanders and Bullwinkles: How Politicians Manipulate Electronic Maps and Census Data to Win Elections*, Chicago, IL: University of Chicago Press.

MoveOn.org (2008) "MoveOn Endorsement Throws Progressive Weight Behind Barack Obama," February 1. Available at http://moveon.org/press/pr/obamaendorsementrelease. html (accessed May 18, 2013).

—— (n.d.) "Report on the 2003 MoveOn.org Political Action Primary." Available at www. moveon.org/pac/primary/report.html (accessed May 18, 2013).

Mulligan, John E. (2005) "Abortion-Rights Group Endorses Chafee," *Providence Journal*, May 20. Available at www.projo.com/news/content/projo_20050520_naral20.255208c. html (accessed May 4, 2013).

Murphy, Patricia (2016) "Democrats Worry About Hillary Clinton's Ground Game," *The Daily Beast*, October 17. Available at www.thedailybeast.com/articles/2016/10/17/democrats-worry-about-hillary-clinton-s-ground-game.html (accessed March 4, 2017).

Murray, Shailagh and Chris Cillizza (2007) "Obama Jumps into Presidential Fray," *Washington Post*, January 17. Available at www.washingtonpost.com/wp-dyn/content/article/2007/01/16/AR2007011600529.html (accessed June 1, 2013).

Nate Silver (2016) "Who Will Win the Presidency?" *FiveThirtyEight.com*, November 8, https://projects.fivethirtyeight.com/2016-election-forecast (February 7, 2017).

National Association of Secretaries of State (2005) "Administering Elections in a Nonpartisan Manner," February 6. Available at http://nass.org/index.php?option=com_docman&task=doc_download&gid=89 (accessed May 13, 2013).

——(2008) *"The Case for Regional Presidential Primaries in 2012 and Beyond: Report of the NASS Subcommittee on Presidential Primaries."* Available at www.nass.org/index.php?option=com_docman&task=doc_download&gid=144 (accessed May 18, 2013).

—— (2010) "Voter Registration Deadlines and Polling Place hours for the 2012 General Election." Available at www.nass.org/index.php?option=com_content&view=article&id=330: voter-registration-deadlines-and-polling-place-hours-forthe-2010-general-election&catid=33: elections-a-voting&Itemid=391 (accessed May 10, 2013).

—— (2016) "2016 General Election: Voter Registration Deadlines and Polling Place Hours," www. nass.org/elections-voting/voter-registration-deadlines-polling-place-hrs-2016-general (accessed January 2, 2017).

National Conference of State Legislatures (2008) "Redistricting Commissions: Legislative Plans." Available at www.ncsl.org/legislatures-elections/redist/2009-redistricting-commissions-table.aspx (accessed May 9, 2013).

—— (2011) "Limits on Campaign Contributions During the Legislative Session," December 6. Available at www.ncsl.org/legislatures-elections/elections/limits-on-contributions-during-session.aspx (accessed May 14, 2013).

—— (2012a) "2012 State and Presidential Primary and Caucus Dates," May 29. Available at www.ncsl.org/legislatures-elections/elections/2012-primary-dates-in-state-order.aspx (accessed May 17, 2013).

—— (2012b) "Recall of State Officials," June 6. Available at www.ncsl.org/legislatureselections/elections/recall-of-state-officials.aspx (accessed May 7, 2013).

—— (2012c) "State Limits on Contributions to Candidates, 2011–12 Election Cycle," June 1. Available at www.ncsl.org/Portals/1/documents/legismgt/Limits_to_Candidates_2011-12v2.pdf (accessed May 13, 2013).

—— (2013a) "Initiative, Referendum and Recall." Available at www.ncsl.org/legislatures-elections/elections/initiative-referendum-and-recall-overview.aspx (accessed May 7, 2013).

—— (2013b) "Pennsylvania Voter Identification Requirements." Available at www.ncsl.org/legislatures-elections/elections/voter-id.aspx#PA (accessed May 8, 2013).

—— (2013d) "Public Financing of Campaigns: An Overview," January 23. Available at www.ncsl.org/legislatures-elections/elections/publicfinancing-of-campaigns-overview.aspx (accessed May 13, 2013).

—— (2013e) "Voter Identification Requirements." Available at www.ncsl.org/legislatures-elections/elections/voter-id.aspx#Legislation (accessed May 8, 2013).

—— (n.d.) "Absentee and Early Voting." Available at www.ncsl.org/legislatures-elections/elections/absentee-and-early-voting.aspx (accessed May 11, 2013).

—— (n.d.) "Voter Identification Requirements." Available at www.ncsl.org/legislatures-elections/elections/voter-id.aspx (accessed May 13, 2013).

—— (2013) "The Term Limited States." Available at www.ncsl.org/legislatures-elections/legisdata/chart-of-term-limits-states.aspx (accessed May 9, 2013).

National Conference of States Legislatures (2015) "Legislator Demographics," www.ncsl.org/research/about-state-legislatures/who-we-elect-an-interactive-graphic.aspx# (accessed January 6, 2017).

National Conference of State Legislatures (2015) "State Public Financing Options: 2015–2016 Election Cycle," July 17, www.ncsl.org/Portals/1/documents/legismgt/elect/StatePublic-FinancingOptionsChart2015.pdf (accessed January 2, 2017).

National Conference of State Legislatures (2015) "State Limits on Contributions to Candidates, 2015–2016 Election Cycle," www.ncsl.org/Portals/1/documents/legismgt/elect/ContributionLimitstoCandidates2015-2016.pdf (accessed January 2, 2017).

National Conference of State Legislatures (2015) "Initiative and Referendum States," www.ncsl.org/research/elections-and-campaigns/chart-of-the-initiative-states.aspx (accessed December 30, 2016).

National Conference of State Legislatures (2015) "Redistricting Commissions: State Legislative Plans," www.ncsl.org/research/redistricting/2009-redistricting-commissions-table.aspx (accessed December 30, 2016).

National Conference of State Legislatures (2016) "State Primary Election Types," www.ncsl.org/research/elections-and-campaigns/primary-types.aspx (accessed January 7, 2017).

National Conference of State Legislatures (2016) "Electronic Transmission of Ballots," www.ncsl.org/research/elections-and-campaigns/internet-voting.aspx (accessed January 2, 2017).

National Conference of State Legislatures (2016) "2016 Primary Dates," February 9, www.ncsl.org/research/elections-and-campaigns/2016-state-primary-dates.aspx (accessed January 7, 2017).

National Labor Relations Board (1997) "*The National Labor Relations Board and YOU*, Washington, DC: National Labor Relations Board." Available at http://nlrb.lettercarriernetwork.info/NLRB5.PDF (accessed May 7, 2013).

National Public Radio (2012) "Swing State Scorecard." Available at http://apps.npr.org/swing-state-scorecard (accessed May 9, 2013).

National Rifle Association/Institute for Legislative Action (2012) "About NRA-ILA." Available at www.nraila.org/about-nra-ila.aspx (accessed May 20, 2013).

National Women's Political Caucus (2010) "Campaign Training Manuals." Available at www.nwpc.org/trainingmanuals (accessed May 22, 2013).

News21 (2012) "Election Fraud in America," August 12. Available at http://votingrights.news21.com/interactive/election-fraud-database (accessed May 8, 2013).

New York Times (2001) *36 Days: The Complete Chronicle of the 2000 Presidential Election Crisis*, New York: Times Books.

New York Times/CBS News Poll (2008) "2008 Republican National Delegate Survey," July 23–August 26. Available at http://graphics8.nytimes.com/packages/pdf/politics/20080901-poll.pdf (accessed May 3, 2013).

Nick Gass (2016) "MoveOn Endorses Bernie Sanders," *Politico*, January 12, www.politico.com/story/2016/01/movon-endorses-bernie-sanders-217614 (accessed January 16, 2017).

Nielsen, Rasmus Kleis (2012) *Ground Wars: Personalized Communication in Political Campaigns*, Princeton, NJ: Princeton University Press.

Niemi, Richard G. and Herbert F. Weisberg (eds.) (1993) *Controversies in Voting Behavior*, 3rd edn, Washington, DC: CQ Press.

Nimmo, Dan (1970) *The Political Persuaders: The Techniques of Modern Election Campaigns*, Englewood Cliffs, NJ: Prentice Hall.

Norris, Pippa (2004) *Electoral Engineering: Voting Rules and Political Behavior*, Cambridge: Cambridge University Press.

Office for Democratic Institutions and Human Rights (2005) "2 November 2004 Elections: OSCE/ODIHR Election Observation Mission Final Report," Warsaw: Organization for Security and Co-operation in Europe. Available at www.osce.org/odihr/elections/usa/14028 (accessed May 7, 2013).

Ohlemacher, Stephen (2007) "Census Shows Early Primary States Are Far from 'Average,'" *Boston Globe*, May 17. Available at www.boston.com/news/nation/washington/articles/2007/05/17/census_shows_early_primary_states_are_far_from_average (accessed May 18, 2013).

Olson, Mancur, Jr. (1968) *The Logic of Collective Action*, New York: Schocken.

Oregon Secretary of State (2012) "Frequently Asked Questions." Available at www.oregonvotes.gov/pages/faq/index.html (accessed May 12, 2013).

Oregon Secretary of State (2016) "Voting in Oregon," http://sos.oregon.gov/voting/Pages/voteinor.aspx (accessed January 2, 2017).

Ortiz, Daniel R. (1997) "The First Amendment at Work: Constitutional Restrictions on Campaign Finance Regulation," in Anthony Corrado, Thomas E. Mann, Daniel R. Ortiz, Trevor Potter, and Frank J. Sorauf (eds.), *Campaign Finance Reform: A Sourcebook*, Washington, DC: Brookings Institution Press.

P2012.org (2013a) "Democratic National Committee—2012." Available at www.p2012.org/parties/committees/dnc12.html (accessed May 16, 2013).

—— (2013b) "Republican National Committee–2012." Available at www.p2012.org/parties/committees/rnc12.html (accessed May 16, 2013).

Page, Benjamin I. and Robert Y. Shapiro (1992) *The Rational Public: Fifty Years of Trends in Americans' Policy Preferences*, Chicago, IL: University of Chicago Press.

Panagopoulos, Costas (2004) "The Polls-Trends: Electoral Reform," *Public Opinion Quarterly*, 68: 623–640.

Parker, Suzi (2012) "Women Make Historic Gains in the US Senate," *Washington Post*, November 7. Available at www.washingtonpost.com/blogs/she-the-people/wp/2012/11/07/women-make-historic-gains-in-the-u-s-senate (accessed May 16, 2013).

Pateman, Carole (1970) *Participation and Democratic Theory*, Cambridge: Cambridge University Press.

Patterson, Bradley (2000) *The White House Staff: Inside the West Wing and Beyond*, Washington, DC: Brookings Institution Press.

Patterson, Thomas E. (1994) *Out of Order*, New York: Vintage Books.

Pear, Robert (2004) "In Ads, AARP Criticizes Plan on Privatizing," *New York Times*, December 30. Available at www.nytimes.com/2004/12/30/politics/30retire.html?_r=1&oref=slogin (accessed May 27, 2013).

Pennsylvania Department of State (n.d.) "2016 General Elections: Official Returns." Available at www.electionreturns.pa.gov/ENR_New/General/OfficeResults?OfficeID=13&ElectionID=undefined&ElectionType=undefined&IsActive=undefined (accessed December 30, 2016).

Perry, James M. (1968) *The New Politics: The Expanding Technology of Political Manipulation*, New York: Clarkson N. Potter.

Persily, Nathaniel (2005) "Forty Years in the Political Thicket: Judicial Review of the Redistricting Process since *Reynolds* v. *Sims*," in Thomas E. Mann and Bruce E. Cain (eds.), *Party Lines: Competition, Partisanship, and Congressional Redistricting*, Washington, DC: Brookings Institution Press.

Peterson, Geoff and Mark Wrighton (1998) "Expressions of Distrust: Third-Party Voting and Cynicism in Government," *Political Behavior*, 20: 17–34.

Petracca, Mark P. (1992) "The Rediscovery of Interest Group Politics," in Mark P. Petracca (ed.), *The Politics of Interests: Interest Groups Transformed*, Boulder, CO: Westview Press.

Petri, Alexandra (2013) "Chris Christie's Lap Band Weight Loss Surgery: So He Can Run with Kids, or So He Can Run in 2016?" ComPost blog, *Washington Post*, May 7. Available at www.washingtonpost.com/blogs/compost/wp/2013/05/07/chris-christies-lap-band-weight-loss-surgery-so-he-can-run-with-kids-or-so-he-can-run-in-2016 (accessed May 24, 2013).

Petrocik, John R. (1996) "Issue Ownership in Presidential Elections, with a 1980 Case Study," *American Journal of Political Science*, 40: 825–850.

Petrocik, John R., William L. Benoit, and Glenn J. Hansen (2003–4) "Issue Ownership and Presidential Campaigning, 1952–2000," *Political Science Quarterly*, 118: 599–626.

Pew Research Center for the People and the Press (2000) "Voters Side with Bush for Now," November 14. Available at www.people-press.org/reports/display.php3?ReportID=24 (accessed May 15, 2013).

—— (2004) "Cable and Internet Loom Large in Fragmented Political News Universe," January 11. Available at www.people-press.org/2004/01/11/cable-and-internet-loom-large-in-fragmented-political-news-universe (accessed May 22, 2013).

—— (2010) "Ideological News Sources: Who Watches and Why," September 12. Available at www.people-press.org/files/legacy-pdf/652.pdf (accessed May 22, 2012).

—— (2012) "Question Search, The Pew Research Center for the People and the Press Poll Database," June 28–July 9. Available at www.peoplepress.org/question-search/?qid=1814098&pid=51&ccid=51#top (accessed May 17, 2013).

Pew Research Center's Project for Excellence in Journalism (2012) "Winning the Media Campaign 2012," November 2. Available at www.journalism.org/node/31438 (accessed May 24, 2013).

Pew Research Center (2016) "Party Identification Trends, 1992–2016," September 13, www.people-press.org/2016/09/13/party-identification-trends-1992-2016 (accessed January 5, 2017).

Phillips, Kevin (1984) "Reelection Paradox: Landslide and Loss of Power," *Christian Science Monitor*, November 2. Available at www.csmonitor.com/1984/1102/110212.html (accessed July 22, 2017).

Pitkin, Hannah F. (1967) *The Concept of Representation*, Berkeley, CA: University of California Press.

Plasser, Fritz and Gunda Plasser (2002) *Global Political Campaigning: A Worldwide Analysis of Campaign Professionals and Their Practices*, Westport, CT: Praeger.

Politico (2012) "2012 Swing States." Available at www.politico.com/2012-election/swing-state (accessed May 9, 2013).

PollingReport.com. (n.d.) "Iraq." Available at www.pollingreport.com/iraq.htm (accessed May 27, 2013).

Pomper, Gerald (1968) *Elections in America: Control and Influence in Democratic Politics*, New York: Dodd, Mead, & Company.

Popkin, Samuel L. (1991) *The Reasoning Voter: Communication and Persuasion in Presidential Campaigns*, Chicago, IL: University of Chicago Press.

Posner, Richard A. (2001) *Breaking the Deadlock: The 2000 Election, the Constitution, and the Courts*, Princeton, NJ: Princeton University Press.

Postelnicu, Monica, Justin D. Martin, and Kristen D. Landreville (2006) "The Role of Campaign Web Sites in Promoting Candidates and Attracting Campaign Resources," in Andrew Paul Williams and John C. Tedesco (eds.), *The Internet Election: Perspectives on the Web in Campaign 2004*, Lanham, MD: Rowman & Littlefield.

Potter, Chris (2016) "Judge Eases Ballot Requirements for Third-Party Candidates," *Pittsburgh Post-Gazette*, July 2. Available at www.post-gazette.com/early-returns/erstate/2016/07/01/Federal-judge-gives-third-parties-a-helping-hand-on-PA-ballot/stories/201607010174 (accessed January 4, 2017).

Powell, G. Bingham Jr. (2000) *Elections as Instruments of Democracy: Majoritarian and Proportional Visions*, New Haven, CT: Yale University Press.

Powell, Larry and Joseph Cowart (2003) *Political Campaign Communication: Inside and Out*, Boston, MA: Allyn & Bacon.

Program on International Policy Attitudes (2001) "Americans on Foreign Aid and World Hunger: A Study of US Public Attitudes." Available at www.pipa.org/OnlineReports/ForeignAid/ForeignAid_Feb01/ForeignAid_Feb01_rpt.pdf (accessed May 28, 2013).

Project for Excellence in Journalism (2008) "Amid Charges of Bias, the Media Swarm on Obama Overseas," *PEJ Campaign Coverage Index*, July 21–27. Available at www.journalism.org/node/12097 (accessed May 18, 2013).

Public Broadcasting Service (2000) "Debating Our Destiny; 1976: No Audio and No Soviet Domination." Available at www.pbs.org/newshour/debatingourdestiny/dod/1976-broadcast.html (accessed May 18, 2013).

Public Mapping Project (n.d.) "Michigan 2010 Census Selected Statistics." Available at www.publicmapping.org/resources/state-resources/michigan/michigan-2010-censusstatistics (accessed May 25, 2013).

Putnam, Josh (2011) "Republican Delegate Allocation Rules: 2012 vs (2008)," *FrontloadingHQ*, December 24. Available at http://frontloading.blogspot.com/2011/12/republican-delegate-allocation-rules.html (accessed May 17, 2013).

Putnam, Robert D. (2000) *Bowling Alone: The Collapse and Revival of American Community*, New York: Simon & Schuster.

Rahn, Wendy M. (1993) "The Role of Partisan Stereotypes in Information Processing about Political Candidates," *American Journal of Political Science*, 37: 472–496.

Raskin, Jamin B. (1993) "Legal Aliens, Local Citizens: The Historical, Constitutional, and Theoretical Meanings of Alien Suffrage," *University of Pennsylvania Law Review*, 141: 1391–1470.

—— (2004) "A Right-to-Vote Amendment for the US Constitution: Confronting America's Structural Democracy Deficit," *Election Law Journal*, 3: 559–573.

Raskin, Jamin B. and John Bonifaz (1994) *The Wealth Primary: Campaign Fundraising and the Constitution*, Washington, DC: Center for Responsive Politics.

Raskin, Jamin and Matthew Spalding (2005) "Should Non-citizens Be Permitted to Vote?" *Legal Affairs*, May 10–13, 2005. Available at http://legalaffairs.org/webexclusive/debate-club_ncv0505.msp (accessed August 14, 2012).

Republican National Committee (2016) "RNC Launches Data Center 2016," Press release, August 3. Available at https://www.gop.com/rnc-launches-data-center-2016 (accessed January 16, 2017).

RealClearPolitics (2016) "General Election: Trump vs. Clinton vs. Johnson vs. Stein," www.realclearpolitics.com/epolls/2016/president/us/general_election_trump_vs_clinton_vs_johnson_vs_stein-5952.html (accessed February 7, 2017).

Richard Winger (ed.) (2016) *Ballot Access News*, March 1, 31, http://ballot-access.org/2016/03/27/march-2016-ballot-access-news-print-edition (accessed January 5, 2017).

Richard E. Berg-Andersson (n.d.) "Democratic Convention" and "Republican Convention," *The Green Papers*, www.thegreenpapers.com/P16/D and www.thegreenpapers.com/P16/R (accessed January 7, 2017).

Richard E. Berg-Andersson (n.d.) "2008 Chronological Cumulative Allocation of Delegates" and "2016 Chronological Cumulative Allocation of Delegates," *The Green Papers*, www.thegreenpapers.com/P16/ccad.phtml and www.thegreenpapers.com/P08/ccad.phtml (accessed January 7, 2017). For prior years, see Thomas Gangale (2004) "The California Plan: A 21st Century Method for Nominating Presidential Candidates," *PS: Political Science and Politics*, 37: 81–87.

Riker, William H. (1982) "The Two-Party System and Duverger's Law: An Essay on the History of Political Science," *American Political Science Review*, 76: 753–766.

Riley, Michael and Jordan Robertson (2017) "Russian Cyber Hacks on US Electoral System Far Wider Than Previously Known," *Bloomberg.com*, June 13. Available at https://www.bloomberg.com/politics/articles/2017-06-13/russian-breach-of-39-states-threatens-future-u-s-elections (accessed June 13, 2017).

Robert Farley (2016) "Trump Sticks with Bogus Voter Fraud Claims," FactCheck.org, November 28, www.factcheck.org/2016/11/trump-sticks-with-bogus-voter-fraud-claims (accessed December 30, 2016); and Michael Wines (2016) "All This Talk of Voter Fraud? Across US, Officials Found Next to None," *The New York Times*, December 18, www.nytimes.com/2016/12/18/us/voter-fraud.html (accessed December 30, 2016).

Romer, Daniel, Kate Kenski, Kenneth Winneg, Christopher Adasiewicz, and Kathleen Hall Jamieson (2006) *Capturing Campaign Dynamics, 2000 and 2004: The National Annenberg Election Survey*, Philadelphia, PA: University of Pennsylvania Press.

Roscoe, Douglas D. and Shannon Jenkins (2005) "A Meta-Analysis of Campaign Contributions' Impact on Roll Call Voting," *Social Science Quarterly*, 86: 52–68.

Rose, Richard and Harve Mossawir (1967) "Voting and Elections: A Functional Analysis," *Political Studies*, 15: 173–201.

Rosenberg, Shawn W., Lisa Bohan, Patrick McCafferty, and Kevin Harris (1986) "The Image and the Vote: The Effect of Candidate Presentation on Voter Preference," *American Journal of Political Science*, 30: 108–127.

Rosenkranz, E. Joshua (ed.) (1999) *If Buckley Fell: A First Amendment Blueprint for Regulating Money in Politics*, New York: The Century Foundation Press.

Rosenstone, Steven J. and John Mark Hansen (2003) *Mobilization, Participation, and Democracy in America*, New York: Longman.

Rosenstone, Steven J., Roy L. Behr, and Edward H. Lazarus (1996) *Third Parties in America*, 2nd edn, Princeton, NJ: Princeton University Press.

Ross, Tara (2004) *Enlightened Democracy: The Case for the Electoral College*, Los Angeles, CA: World Ahead Publishing, Inc.

Rothenberg, Stuart (2005) "Midterms Spell Trouble, but 'Itch' Theory Is a Real Head-Scratcher," *Rothenberg Political Report*, September 15. Available at http://rothenbergpoliticalreport.com/news/article/midterms-spell-trouble-but-itch-theory-is-a-real-head-scratcher (accessed June 1, 2013).

Rozell, Mark J., Clyde Wilcox, and David Madland (2006) *Interest Groups in American Campaigns: The New Face of Electioneering*, Washington, DC: CQ Press.

Rucker, Philip, Jose A. DelReal, and Sean Sullivan (2016) "Donald Trump Fires Embattled Campaign Manager Corey Lewandowski," *Washington Post*, June 20. Available at https://www.washingtonpost.com/news/post-politics/wp/2016/06/20/trump-parts-ways-with-campaign-manager/?utm_term=.998a9ba9ad99 (accessed February 7, 2017).

Rusk, Jerrold G. (2001) *A Statistical History of the American Electorate*, Washington, DC: CQ Press.

Sabato, Larry J. (1981) *The Rise of Political Consultants: New Ways of Winning Elections*, New York: Basic Books.

—— (1985) *PAC Power: Inside the World of Political Action Committees*, New York: Norton.

—— (1993) *Feeding Frenzy: How Attack Journalism Has Transformed American Politics*, New York: The Free Press.

Safire, William (1993) *Safire's New Political Dictionary*, New York: Random House.

Salisbury, Robert H. (1969) "An Exchange Theory of Interest Groups," *Midwest Journal of Political Science*, 13: 1–32.

Samples, John (2006) *The Fallacy of Campaign Finance Reform*, Chicago, IL: University of Chicago Press.

Sanchez, Gabriel and Matt A. Barreto (2016) "In Record Numbers, Latinos Voted Overwhelmingly Against Trump. We Did the Research," Monkey Cage, *Washington Post*, November 11. Available at https://www.washingtonpost.com/news/monkey-cage/wp/2016/11/11/in-record-numbers-latinos-voted-overwhelmingly-against-trump-we-did-the-research/?utm_term=.634df5e24d6b (accessed February 17, 2017).

Savage, Charlie (2012) "Holder, at NAACP Event, Criticizes Voter ID Laws," The Caucus, *New York Times*, July 10. Available at http://thecaucus.blogs.nytimes.com/2012/07/10/holder-at-na-a-c-p-event-criticizes-voter-id-laws (accessed May 8, 2013).

Schattschneider, E. E. (1942) *Party Government*, New York: Rinehart.

Scherer, Michael (2012a) "Exclusive: Obama's 2012 Digital Fundraising Outperformed 2008," *Time.com*, November 15. Available at http://swampland.time.com/2012/11/15/exclusive-obamas-2012-digital-fundraising-outperformed-2008 (accessed May 29, 2013).

—— (2012b) "Friended: How the Obama Campaign Connected with Young Voters," *Time*, November 20. Available at http://swampland.time.com/2012/11/20/

friended-how-the-obama-campaign-connected-with-young-voters (accessed May 29, 2013).

Schlesinger, Joseph A. (1966) *Ambition and Politics: Political Careers in the United States*, Chicago, IL: Rand McNally.

Schotland, Roy A. (2005) "Judicial Elections," in Paul S. Herrnson (ed.), *Guide to Political Campaigns in America*, Washington, DC: CQ Press.

Schultz, David (ed.) (2002) *Money, Politics, and Campaign Finance Reform Law in the States*, Durham, NC: Carolina Academic Press.

Schumaker, Paul D. and Burdett A. Loomis (2002) "Reaching a Collective Judgment," in Paul D. Schumaker and Burdett A. Loomis (eds.), *Choosing a President: The Electoral College and Beyond*, New York: Chatham House Publishers/Seven Bridges Press.

Schumer, Chuck (2007) "2008 Senate Recruiting," *Daily Kos*, March 21. Available at www.dailykos.com/story/2007/3/21/141618/799 (accessed November 23, 2012).

Schumpeter, Joseph (1976) *Capitalism, Socialism and Democracy*, London: Allen & Unwin.

Sentencing Project (2012) "Felony Disenfranchisement Laws in the United States," Washington, DC. Available at http://sentencingproject.org/doc/publications/fd_bs_fdlawsinus_Nov20 12.pdf (accessed May 8, 2013).

Shafer, Byron E. (1983) *Quiet Revolution: The Struggle for the Democratic Party and the Shaping of Post-Reform Politics*, New York: Russell Sage Foundation.

Shafer, Byron E. and William J. M. Claggett (1995) *The Two Majorities: The Issue Context of Modern American Politics*, Baltimore, MD: Johns Hopkins University Press.

Shah, Paru (2014) "It Takes a Black Candidate: A Supply-Side Theory of Minority Representation," *Political Research Quarterly*, 67: 266–279.

Shanto Iyengar, Gaurav Sood, and Yphtach Lelkes (2012) "Affect, Not Ideology: A Social Identity Perspective on Polarization," *Public Opinion Quarterly*, 76: 405–431.

Shanto Iyengar and Sean J. Westwood (2015) "Fear and Loathing across Party Lines: New Evidence on Group Polarization," *American Journal of Political Science*, 59: 690–707.

Shaw, Daron R. (1999) "A Study of Presidential Campaign Event Effects from 1952 to 1992," *Journal of Politics*, 61: 387–422.

—— (2006) *The Race to 270: The Electoral College and the Campaign Strategies of 2000 and 2004*, Chicago, IL: University of Chicago Press.

Shugart, Matthew Soberg (2004) "The American Process of Selecting a President: A Comparative Perspective," *Presidential Studies Quarterly*, 34: 632–655.

Sides, John (2012) "Mapping Romney and Obama Field Offices," *The Monkey Cage*, November 6. Available at http://themonkeycage.org/2012/11/06/mapping-romney-and-obama-field-offices (accessed May 28, 2013).

—— (2016) "Everything You Need to Know About Delegate Math in the Presidential Primary," Monkey Cage, *Washington Post*, February 16. Available at https://www.washingtonpost.com/news/monkey-cage/wp/2016/02/16/everything-you-need-to-know-about-delegate-math-in-the-presidential-primary/?utm_term=.650d1cfcf05a (accessed March 4, 2017).

Sigelman, Lee (1979) "Presidential Popularity and Presidential Elections," *Public Opinion Quarterly*, 43: 532–534.

Sink, Justin (2013) "Obama Plans Road Trip to Prod Senate to Move on Gun-Control Legislation," *The Hill*, March 25. Available at http://thehill.com/homenews/administration/290169-obama-toprod-senators-takes-gun-control-message-on-the-road (accessed June 2, 2013).

Skocpol, Theda (2003) *Diminished Democracy: From Membership to Management in American Civic Life*, Norman, OK: University of Oklahoma Press.

Sloan, Melanie (2013) "No Vote of Confidence for FEC," *Politico*, April 30. Available at www.politico.com/story/2013/04/no-vote-of-confidence-for-fec-90783.html (accessed May 14, 2013).

Smith, Ben (2007) "The Hair's Still Perfect," Democrats '08 Blog, April 16. Available at www.politico.com/blogs/bensmith/0407/The_Hairs_Still_Perfect.html (accessed May 16, 2013).

Smith, Bradley A. (2001) *Unfree Speech: The Folly of Campaign Finance Reform*, Princeton, NJ: Princeton University Press.

Smith, Jeff and David C. Kimball (2012) "Barking Louder: Interest Groups in the 2012 Election," *The Forum*, 10: 80–90.

Smith, Michael Ray (2007) "Ideology," in William David Sloan and Jenn Burleson Mackay (eds.), *Media Bias: Finding It, Fixing It*, Jefferson, NC: McFarland.

Smith, Pamela, Michelle Mulder, and Susannah Goodman (2012) "Counting Votes 2012: A State by State Look at Voting Technology Preparedness," Verified Voting Foundation. Available at www.verifiedvotingfoundation.org/wp-content/uploads/2012/09/Counting-Votes2012_Final_August2012.pdf (accessed May 13, 2013).

Smithsonian National Museum of American History (2004) "Vote: The Machinery of Democracy." Available at http://americanhistory.si.edu/vote/index.html (accessed September 6, 2012).

Sniderman, Paul M., Richard A. Brody, and Philip E. Tetlock (1991) *Reasoning and Choice: Explorations in Political Psychology*, Cambridge: Cambridge University Press.

Solop, Frederic I. (2001) "Digital Democracy Comes of Age: Internet Voting and the 2000 Arizona Democratic Primary Elections," *PS: Political Science and Politics*, 34: 289–293.

Sorauf, Frank J. (1992) *Inside Campaign Finance: Myths and Realities*, New Haven, CT: Yale University Press.

Sourcewatch. (n.d.) "MoveOn." Available at www.sourcewatch.org/index.php?title=MoveOn (accessed May 19, 2013).

Southwell, Priscilla L. (2005) "Five Years Later: A Re-assessment of Oregon's Vote by Mail Electoral Process," *PS: Political Science and Politics*, 37: 89–93.

—— (2011) *Vital Statistics on American Politics, 2011–2012*, Washington, DC: CQ Press.

Stanley, Harold W. and Richard B. Niemi (eds.) (2015) *Vital Statistics on American Politics, 2015–16*, Washington, DC: CQ Press.

—— (2011) *Vital Statistics on American Politics, 2011–2012.*, Washington, DC: CQ Press.

Starr, Paul (2004) *The Creation of the Media: Political Origins of Modern Communications*, New York: Basic Books.

Steinhauser, Paul (2013) "'Obama for America' to Morph into 'Organizing for Action.'" *CNN.com*, January 18. Available at http://politicalticker.blogs.cnn.com/2013/01/18/obama-for-america-to-morph-into-organizing-for-action (accessed June 2, 2013).

Stephen D. Ansolabehere (2014) "Declaration of Stephen D. Ansolabehere," *Veasey* v. *Perry*, US District Court for the Southern District of Texas, Corpus Christi Division (No. 2: 13-cv-00193), 2; 42, http://moritzlaw.osu.edu/electionlaw/litigation/documents/Veasey6552.pdf (accessed December 30, 2016).

Stepleton, J. T. (2015) "2014 Candidate Elections Overview," *National Institute on Money in State Politics*, http://followthemoney.org/research/institute-reports/2014-candidate-elections-overview (accessed January 3, 2017).

Stevenson, Randolph R. and Lynn Vavreck (2000) "Does Campaign Length Matter? Testing for Cross-National Effects," *British Journal of Political Science*, 30: 217–235.

Stoner, James R. Jr. (2001) "Federalism, the State, and the Electoral College," in Gary L. Gregg II (ed.), *Securing Democracy: Why We Have an Electoral College*, Wilmington, DE: ISI Books.

Stratmann, Thomas (2005) "Some Talk: Money in Politics; A (Partial) Review of the Literature," *Public Choice*, 124: 135–156.

Strauss, David A. (1994) "Corruption, Equality, and Campaign Finance Reform," *Columbia Law Review*, 94: 1369–1389.

Stroh, Patrick K. (1995) "Voters as Pragmatic Cognitive Misers: The Accuracy-Effort Trade-Off in the Candidate Evaluation Process," in Milton Lodge and Kathleen M. McGraw (eds.), *Political Judgment: Structure and Process*, Ann Arbor, MI: University of Michigan Press.

Stromer-Galley, Jennifer (2003) "Voting and the Public Sphere: Conversations on Internet Voting," *PS: Political Science and Politics*, 36: 727–731.

Surowiecki, James (2004) *The Wisdom of Crowds: Why the Many Are Smarter Than the Few and How Collective Wisdom Shapes Business, Economies, Societies and Nations*, New York: Doubleday.

Sweeney, William R. (2004) "The Principles of Campaign Planning," in James A. Thurber and Candice J. Nelson (eds.), *Campaigns and Elections American Style*, 2nd edn. Boulder, CO: Westview Press.

Tenpas, Kathryn Dunn and James A. McCann (2007) "Testing the Permanence of the Permanent Campaign: An Analysis of Presidential Polling Expenditures, 1977–2002," *Public Opinion Quarterly*, 71: 349–366.

Terrence McCoy (2014) "Not One Vote Cast Against Kim Jong Un in His First Election," *Washington Post*, March 10, www.washingtonpost.com/news/morning-mix/wp/2014/03/10/not-one-vote-cast-against-kim-jong-un-in-his-first-election/?utm_term=.130ef2a4241e (accessed December 30, 2016).

Tetlock, Philip (2005) *Expert Political Judgment: How Good Is It? How Can We Know?* Princeton, NJ: Princeton University Press.

Thompson, Dennis F. (2002) *Just Elections: Creating a Fair Electoral Process in the United States*, Chicago, IL: University of Chicago Press.

Thurber, James A. and Candice J. Nelson (eds.) (2000) *Campaign Warriors: Political Consultants in Elections*, Washington, DC: Brookings Institution Press.

Thurber, James A., Candice J. Nelson, and David A. Dulio (2000) "Portrait of Campaign Consultants," in James A. Thurber and Candice J. Nelson (eds.), *Campaign Warriors: Political Consultants in Elections*, Washington, DC: Brookings Institution Press.

Toner, Robin (2006) "Ad Seen as Playing to Racial Fears," *New York Times*, October 26. Available at www.nytimes.com/2006/10/26/us/politics/26tennessee.html?pagewanted=all (accessed May 18, 2013).

Tonn, Mari Boor and Valerie A. Endress (2001) "Looking Under the Hood and Tinkering with Voter Cynicism: Ross Perot and 'Perspective Incongruity,'" *Rhetoric and Public Affairs*, 4: 281–308.

Toobin, Jeffrey (2001) *Too Close to Call: The Thirty-Six Day Battle to Decide the 2000 Election*, New York: Random House.

Truman, David B. (1951) *The Governmental Process*, New York: Knopf.

Ubertaccio, Peter (2007) "Machine Politics for the Twenty-First Century? Multilevel Marketing and Party Organizations," in John C. Green and Daniel J. Coffey (eds.), *The State of the Parties: The Changing Role of Contemporary American Parties*, Lanham, MD: Rowman & Littlefield.

United Kingdom Parliament (n.d.) "Current State of the Parties." Available at www.parliament.uk/mps-lords-and-offices/mps/current-state-of-the-parties (accessed January 5, 2017).

United States General Accounting Office (2001) *Elections: The Scope of Congressional Authority in Election Administration*, Washington, DC: General Accounting Office. Available at www.gao.gov/new.items/d01470.pdf (accessed August 14, 2012).

US Census Bureau (2013) *The Diversifying Electorate: Voting Rates by Race and Hispanic Origin in 2012 (and Other Recent Elections)*. Available at www.census.gov/prod/2013pubs/p20-568.pdf (accessed May 26, 2013).

—— (2016) "Household Income: 2015." Available at https://www.census.gov/content/dam/Census/library/publications/2016/demo/acsbr15-02.pdf (accessed February 17, 2017).

—— (n.d.) Voting and Registration in the Election of November 2012: Detailed Tables. "Table 10—Reasons for Not Voting, by Selected Characteristics: November 2012." Available at www.census.gov/hhes/www/socdemo/voting/publications/p20/2012/tables.html (accessed May 26, 2013).

US Department of Justice (n.d.) *About the National Voter Registration Act*, Washington, DC: Department of Justice. Available at www.justice.gov/crt/about/vot/nvra/activ_nvra.php (accessed May 13, 2013).

US Department of State, Bureau of International Information Programs, InfoUSA (n.d.) *The Administrative Structure of State Election Offices*, Washington, DC: Department of State. Available at http://usinfo.org/enus/government/elections/tech3.html (accessed May 13, 2013).

US Election Assistance Commission (2009) *2008 Election Administration and Voting Survey: A Summary of Key Findings*, Washington, DC: EAC. Available at www.eac.gov/assets/1/Documents/2008%20Election%20Administration%20and%20Voting%20Survey%20EAVS%20Report.pdf (accessed May 11, 2013).

US Election Assistance Commission, Voting System Testing and Certification Division (2011) *A Survey of Internet Voting*, Washington, DC: EAC. Available at www.eac.gov/assets/1/Documents/SIV-FINAL.pdf (accessed May 12, 2013).

US Election Assistance Commission (2013) "2012 Election Administration and Voting Survey: A Summary of Key Findings," September, www.eac.gov/assets/1/Page/990-050%20EAC%20VoterSurvey_508Compliant.pdf (accessed January 2, 2017).

Valentino, Nicholas A., Vincent L. Hutchings, and Ismail K. White (2002) "Cues that Matter: How Political Ads Prime Racial Attitudes during Campaigns," *American Political Science Review*, 96: 75–90.

Vavreck, Lynn (2009) *The Message Matters: The Economy and Presidential Campaigns*, Princeton, NJ: Princeton University Press.

Vega, Tanzina (2012) "Online Data Helping Campaigns Customize Ads," *New York Times*, February 20. Available at www.nytimes.com/2012/02/21/us/politics/campaigns-use-microtargeting-to-attract-supporters.html?pagewanted=all&_r=0 (accessed May 29, 2013).

Vennochi, Joan (2007) "Sister Souljah Moments," *Boston Globe*, September 16. Available at www.boston.com/news/nation/articles/2007/09/16/sister_souljah_moments (accessed May 18, 2013).

VerifiedVoting.org (2012) "Counting Votes 2012: A State by State Look at Voting Technology Preparedness," www.verifiedvotingfoundation.org/wp-content/uploads/2012/09/CountingVotes2012_Final_August2012.pdf, pp. 24 and 5 (accessed June 29, 2016).

Virginia State Board of Elections (2013) "Candidate Campaign Committees," revised January 1. Available at www.sbe.virginia.gov/Files/CandidatesAndPACs/LawsAndPolicies/Candidates-Summary.pdf, 12 (accessed June 3, 2013).

Vogel, Kenneth P. (2011) "Supreme Court Issues Limited Campaign Finance Ruling," *Politico*, June 27. Available at www.politico.com/news/stories/0611/57851.html (accessed May 14, 2013).

—— (2013) "Tea Party Group Pictures Rove in Nazi Uniform," *Politico*, February 19. Available at www.politico.com/story/2013/02/tea-party-group-pictures-karl-rove-in-nazi-uniform-87793.html (accessed May 19, 2013).

Vogel, Kenneth P., Alexander Burns, and Tarini Parti (2013) "Karl Rove vs. Tea Party in Big Money Fight for GOP's Future," *Politico*, February 7. Available at www.politico.com//story/2013/02/rove-vs-tea-party-for-gops-future-87296.html (accessed May 19, 2013).

Wallsten, Peter and Tom Hamburger (2012) "Conservative Groups Reaching New Levels of Sophistication in Mobilizing Voters," *Washington Post*, September 20. Available at www.washingtonpost.com/politics/decision2012/conservative-groups-reaching-new-levels-of-sophistication-in-mobilizing-voters/2012/09/20/3c3cd8e8-026c-11e2-91e7-2962c74e7738_story.html (accessed May 22, 2013).

Wand, Jonathan N., Kenneth W. Shotts, Jasjeet S. Sekhon, Walter R. Mebane, Jr., Michael C. Herron, and Henry E. Brady (2001) "The Butterfly Did It: The Aberrant Vote for Buchanan in Palm Beach County, Florida," *American Political Science Review*, 95: 793–810.

Washington, George (2008) "Washington's Farewell Address, 1796," *The Avalon Project*, Yale Law School. Available at http://avalon.law.yale.edu/18th_century/washing.asp (accessed May 18, 2013).

Washington Post (2016) "Money Raised as of Nov. 28," www.washingtonpost.com/graphics/politics/2016-election/campaign-finance (accessed January 2, 2017).

Wattenberg, Martin P. (1986) *The Decline of American Political Parties, 1952–84*, Cambridge, MA: Harvard University Press.

—— (2002) *Where Have All the Voters Gone?* Cambridge, MA: Harvard University Press.

—— (2007) *Is Voting for Young People?* New York: Pearson Longman.

Wattenberg, Martin P. and Craig Leonard Brians (1999) "Negative Campaign Advertising: Demobilizer or Mobilizer?" *American Political Science Review*, 93: 891–899.

Wawro, Gregory (2001) "A Panel Probit Analysis of Campaign Contributions and Roll-Call Votes," *American Journal of Political Science*, 45: 563–579.

Weisman, Jonathan (2005) "Cost of Social Security Drive Cited," *Washington Post*, April 7. Available at www.washingtonpost.com/wp-dyn/articles/A32389-2005Apr6.html (accessed May 27, 2013).

Weissman, Stephen R. and Kara D. Ryan (2006) "Nonprofit Interest Groups' Election Activities and Federal Campaign Finance Policy: A Working Paper," The Campaign Finance Institute. Available at www.cfinst.org/books_reports/pdf/NonprofitsWorkingPaper.pdf (accessed May 18, 2013).

Wells, Chris, Dhavan V. Shah, Jon C. Pevehouse, JungHwan Yang, Ayellet Pelled, Frederick Boehm, Josephine Lukito, Shreenita Ghosh, and Jessica L. Schmidt (2016) "How Trump Drove Coverage to the Nomination: Hybrid Media Campaigning," *Political Communication*, 33: 669–676.

West, Darrell M. (2001) *Air Wars: Television Advertising in Election Campaigns, 1952–2000*, 3rd edn, Washington, DC: CQ Press.

—— (2001) *The Rise and Fall of the Media Establishment*, Boston, MA: Bedford/St. Martin's.

West, Darrell M. and John Orman (2003) *Celebrity Politics*, Upper Saddle River, NJ: Prentice Hall.

West, Darrell, Diane Heith, and Chris Goodman (1996) "Harry and Louise Go to Washington: Political Advertising and Health Care Reform," *Journal of Health Politics, Policy, and Law*, 21: 35–68.

Whitaker, Paige L. and Thomas H. Neale (2001) *The Electoral College: An Overview and Analysis of Reform Proposals*, Washington, DC: Congressional Research Service.

Winger, Richard (ed.) (2012) *Ballot Access News*, 28: 7. Available at www.ballotaccess.org/2013/01/04/December-2012-ballot-access-news-print-edition (accessed May 17, 2013).

Wolfinger, Raymond E. and Jonathan Hoffman (2001) "Registering and Voting with Motor Voter," *PS: Political Science and Politics*, 33: 85–92.

Wolfinger, Raymond E. and Steven J. Rosenstone (1980) *Who Votes?* New Haven, CT: Yale University Press.

Wright, Stephen G. (1989) "Voter Turnout in Runoff Elections," *Journal of Politics*, 51: 385–396.

Yen, Hope (2016) "Early Voting: Record Levels in 2016 May Give Clinton Edge," *Associated Press*, November 7. Available at http://elections.ap.org/content/early-voting-record-levels-2016-may-give-clinton-edge (accessed February 7, 2017).

Young, Lindsay (2012) "Final Look at Outside Spenders' 2012 Return on Investment," Sunlight Foundation Reporting Group, December 17. Available at http://reporting.sunlightfoundation.com/2012/return_on_investment (accessed May 21, 2013).

Zakaria, Fareed (2004) *The Future of Freedom: Illiberal Democracy at Home and Abroad*, Cambridge: Cambridge University Press.

Zaller, John R. (1992) *The Nature and Origins of Mass Opinion*, Cambridge: Cambridge University Press.

Zeleny, Jeff (2007) "Obama to Urge Elimination of Nuclear Weapons," *New York Times*, October 2. Available at www.nytimes.com/2007/10/02/us/politics/02obama.html (accessed May 23, 2013).

Zeleny, Jeff (2013a) "New Rove Effort Has GOP Aflame," *New York Times*, February 6. Available at www.nytimes.com/2013/02/07/us/politics/new-rove-effort-has-gop-aflame.html (accessed May 19, 2013).

—— (2013b) "Top Donors to Republicans Seek More Say in Senate Races," *New York Times*, February 2. Available at www.nytimes.com/2013/02/03/us/politics/top-gop-donors-seek-greater-say-in-senate-races.html?partner=rss&emc=rss&_r=3& (accessed May 19, 2013).

Legal Cases

Buckley v. Valeo (1976) 424 US 1.

California Democratic Party v. Jones (2000) 530 US 567.

Citizens United v. Federal Election Commission (2010) 558 US 310.

Davis v. Federal Election Commission (2008) 554 US 724.

FEC v. Wisconsin Right to Life (2007) 551 US 449.

Gray v. Sanders (1963) 372 US 368.

Harper v. Virginia State Board of Elections (1966) 393 US 145.

Lane v. Wilson (1962) 307 US 268.

Shaw v. Reno (1993) 509 US 630.

Shelby County v. Holder 2013. 570 US 2.

Smith v. Allwright (1944) 321 US 649.

Washington State Grange v. Washington State Republican Party (2008) 552 US 442.

Index

Page numbers in *italics* denote figures, those in **bold** denote tables.